For Larry,

Saw this book and thought of you! Hope you will enjoy each and every page!

Love,
Irish

"Tell my father I died with my face to the enemy."

COLONEL ISAAC E. AVERY, 6TH NORTH CAROLINA

An Illustrated History of Courage Under Fire

Great Battles of the Civil War

Edited by Neil Kagan, Harris J. Andrews, and Paula York-Soderlund
Introduction by Brian C. Pohanka

OXMOOR HOUSE – BIRMINGHAM, ALABAMA

HOMAGE TO THE UNKNOWN SOLDIER

No relic or memento of the Civil War was more treasured by the citizen soldiers of both sides than a photograph of themselves in uniform. The ambrotypes and tintypes that appear on pages 1-5 have survived long after the vicissitudes of time caused the identities of the men in the pictures to be lost.

In 1900, an old Confederate reflecting on the forgotten thousands of his generation, who, like these men, had gone off to war, nostalgically wrote: "No herald ever blew his trumpet in the marketplace or on the housetops and told the story of their deeds to an assembled people, their statues do not stand in any national Valhalla, crowned with laurel—they were born, they lived, they fought, they died—that was all."

Turning the pages of Great Battles of the Civil War *you will find the story of these courageous soldiers and the drama of a great nation locked in mortal combat with itself.*

Oxmoor House®

© 2002 by Oxmoor House, Inc.
Book Division of Southern Progress Corporation
P.O. Box 2463, Birmingham, Alabama 35201

This book is a compilation of material previously published by Time Life Inc. © 1977, 1983, 1984, 1985, 1986, 1987, 1990, 1991, 1995, 1996, 1997, 1998, 2000, Time Life Inc.

FIRST EDITION

Library of Congress Control Number: 2002105574
ISBN 0-8487-2704-5

PRINTED IN THE UNITED STATES OF AMERICA

Great Battles of the Civil War
was prepared by:

Kagan & Associates, Inc.
Falls Church, Virginia 22314

President / Editor-in-Chief: NEIL KAGAN
Editors: HARRIS J. ANDREWS, PAULA YORK-SODERLUND
Designers: ANTONIO ALCALÁ, MARY DUNNINGTON
 Studio A, Alexandria, Virginia
Text Editor: PAUL MATHLESS
Associate Editor / Proofreader: CELIA BEATTIE
Photo Coordinator: ANNE WHITTLE

Special Contributors: SHARYN KAGAN (administration), BARBARA L. KLEIN (index), SUSAN FINKEN (rights and permissions)

Contents

Introduction

At Fredericksburg, Virginia, on a chill December day in 1862, General Orlando Poe watched spellbound as rank upon rank of fellow Union soldiers charged to their doom. Though the ground was strewn with blue-clad bodies, the survivors marched as if on parade, flags flying, and bayonets glistening in the sunlight.

"Their devotion transcended anything I ever saw or even dreamed of," Poe wrote; "men walked right up to their death as though it were to a feast." Awed by the pageantry, and shocked by the slaughter, Confederate commander Robert E. Lee turned to his staff and said, "It is well war is so frightful, else we should grow too fond of it."

The carnage at Fredericksburg added 18,000 casualties to a conflict that in four years claimed the lives of more than 620,000 Americans. Nearly half a million men were wounded, many permanently maimed, while others were afflicted with chronic illness. One hundred forty years later we still grapple with the repercussions of that tragic era and those epic battles that were the fiery crucible that redefined a nation.

While the institution of slavery was the conflict's most important cause, the average soldier was neither an abolitionist nor a slaveholder. Most Northerners fought to preserve the Union, and most Southerners fought to preserve the political integrity of their respective states. Both sides fought to maintain what they saw as the most fundamental ideals of the nation's Founding Fathers. The volunteers who marched to war in the spring of 1861 were utterly convinced of the righteousness of their cause and filled with martial enthusiasm. As Texan John Stevens put it, "Our patriotism was just bubbling up and boiling over and frying and fizzing."

The volunteer regiments were instructed in rigidly choreographed, close-order tactics that had changed little since Napoleon's time. The 83d Pennsylvania's Oliver Willcox Norton informed his parents that "the first thing in the morning is drill, then drill, then drill again. Then drill, drill, a little more drill. Then drill, and lastly, drill. Between drills we drill, and sometimes stop to eat a little and have a roll call." Private Norton was inevitably evolving into the disciplined, unquestioning member of the team that a soldier was expected to be.

Civil War tactics were predicated on a doctrine that emphasized massed firepower rather than marksmanship. Each soldier was expected to maintain elbow contact with the man on either side, while a scant 13

Bayonets fixed and musket barrels polished, the 96th Pennsylvania Infantry parades in their winter encampment near Washington in the spring of 1862. By the end of the war the 96th had participated in every major battle fought by the Army of the Potomac.

Men of Company M, 3d Rhode Island Heavy Artillery, put two 100-pounder Parrott rifles into action, firing on Fort Sumter from Battery Rosecrans on Morris Island, in the autumn of 1863. An empty gun carriage at right in this photograph by Haas and Peale had held a third 100-pounder, until it burst.

inches separated the front and rear ranks of a regimental line of battle. In theory, Civil War engagements consisted of blocks of men endeavoring to smash away through their foe with volleys of musketry, then exploiting their success at the point of the bayonet.

The quality of leadership was crucial to the outcome of the battles and campaigns of 1861 to 1865. From the lieutenants to the generals, the men who led troops in the Civil War came in every variety: the brilliant and the dull-witted, the reckless and the cautious, the pious and the profane.

"No great mental powers are needed to maneuver a brigade of infantry," claimed Federal brigadier general Francis Barlow. "The difficulty of the problem increases as the numbers increase, and therefore it happens that many a man can handle a brigade admirably, who can do nothing with a corps or even a division." Perhaps the most common cause of mistakes on the battlefield was poor staff work. A general's staff could vary in number from six to eight officers for a brigade commander up to as many as two dozen or more for an army commander. But in battles in which the fronts of the opposing armies often measured more than five miles, generals habitually found their overworked staffs inadequate to oversee the execution of important orders.

Despite the flaws found in both Northern and Southern armies, one of the irrefutable facts of the Civil War was the superiority of Confederate military leadership in the first two years of the conflict. Although a majority of West Point graduates stood by the Union, many of the military academy's most distinguished alumni cast their lot with the Confederacy, and Confederate president Jefferson Davis was himself a graduate of West Point. The South had an established military tradition that made the pursuit of an army career far more attractive than in the North. Schools such as the Virginia Military Institute and the South Carolina Military Academy provided Confederate forces with some two dozen generals and scores of talented regimental officers. The fledgling Confederate States of America faced an immediate threat to its survival that made the recognition of military talent of vital importance.

The Federal army was saddled with the existing military structure, a hierarchy founded upon seniority rather than ability. Political patronage was a fact of life for the Lincoln administration, and the price for the cooperation of the Northern governors was often the promotion of a political crony to the rank he was not qualified to hold. At the beginning of the war Federal commanders often worked at cross-purposes, and coordination seemed an unattainable goal. In 1862 General Thomas J. "Stonewall" Jackson defeated four separate Federal contingents in Virginia's Shenandoah Valley despite odds that were 4 to 1 in his opponents' favor.

Repeated failures spurred Abraham Lincoln's frustrating quest for generals who would vigorously prosecute the war and make full use of the North's superior resources of industry, transport, and manpower. Nowhere was this more evident than in the case of the Army of the Potomac. Organized in the wake of the humiliating Federal defeat at Bull Run on July 21, 1861, the army was brought to a superb state of drill and discipline by General George B. McClellan. But McClellan's measured and cautious approach to war was outmatched by the audacity of his Confederate counterpart, General Robert E. Lee. The commander of the Army of Northern Virginia was invariably willing to risk defeat to attain victory. Lee's hard-hitting attacks pushed McClellan's army away from the Confederate capital at Richmond in the summer of 1862, and the calculated gamble of dividing his forces in the face of a numerically superior foe enabled Lee to outflank and vanquish Federal armies at Second Manassas and Chancellorsville. Twice Lee led his proud and devoted soldiers into Northern territory, but the costly engagements of Antietam and Gettysburg revealed a salient fact of that war: For all their bravery and skill the Confederates were too few in number to effect the destruction of an entire Federal army.

While Lee's military brilliance thwarted a succession of opponents in Virginia, it was fortunate for the Union cause that for a crucial year and a half the Confederacy's most important western force—the Army of Tennessee —was entrusted to General Braxton Bragg. Bragg was a good organizer and had served with distinction in the April 1862 Battle of Shiloh. But Bragg was also dour, irascible, and quirky. Unlike the gentlemanly and tactful Lee, he was unable to mollify his quarrelsome subordinates, many of whom bore an ill-concealed contempt for their commander. "He loved to crush the spirit of his men," lamented Tennessee private Sam Watkins. "Not a single soldier in the whole army ever loved or respected him."

In September 1863 Bragg failed to pursue General William Rosecrans' shattered Federal army from the battlefield of Chickamauga. In November his humiliating defeat at Chattanooga brought about his transfer and coincided with the emergence of General Ulysses S. Grant as the preeminent Federal leader. Grant was singularly colorless by 19th-century standards of martial bearing, but he had the aggressive instinct so many Federal commanders lacked. His early victories had secured the Tennessee River for the Union, and he had demonstrated a remarkable capacity for tactical skill during the campaign that culminated in the July 4, 1863, surrender of the Confederate stronghold of Vicksburg, Mississippi.

By early 1864 the Confederacy had lost more than 100,000 square miles of territory, had relinquished vital river and rail transportation arteries, and was slowly starving from the effects of the Federal naval blockade of coastal ports. With his elevation to command of all Federal armies, Grant dispatched his most trusted subordinate, General William Tecumseh Sherman, on a three-army drive aimed at the heart of the Confederacy. Sherman's dogged campaign against Confederate commanders Joseph Johnston and John Bell Hood succeeded in capturing the vital rail hub of Atlanta, Georgia, and was followed by an epic march to Savannah and the sea. The swath of destruction gouged through the Southern heartland inflicted a mortal wound to Confederate hopes.

When Grant came east in the spring of 1864, the war in Virginia entered its last and deadliest phase. Resolved not to repeat the failures of earlier commanders, Grant pushed Lee's army back on Richmond. Forced to go on the defensive, Lee's troops fought from the cover of earthen-and-log breastworks and inflicted terrible losses on the more numerous Federals, who were frequently compelled to entrench in turn. While many Federal officers despaired at the casualty rates, Grant knew that a war of attrition would inevitably work to the North's advantage. By the summer of 1864 Lee was confined to the defenses of Richmond and Petersburg, and the stage was set for the final campaign that ended in Confederate surrender at Appomattox.

The soldiers of the Civil War were sustained by bonds of comradeship forged in fire and blood. Beyond the dry casualty statistics published in the newspapers lay nightmare scenes of agony and desolation. "The air is putrid with decaying bodies of men and horses," a Georgia infantryman wrote after one engagement. "My God, my God, what a scourge is war." That those men in blue and gray fought on, through hardship and frustration, suffering and defeat, was testimony to their inherent idealism and belief in something greater than self—something beyond patriotism and duty.

Perhaps Union general Joshua Lawrence Chamberlain put it best when he reflected, "The muster rolls on which the name and oath were written were pledges of honor,—redeemable at the gates of death. And they who went up to them, knowing this, are on the list of heroes." The history of the great battles recounted in this volume is the story of those selfless heroes.

Brian C. Pohanka
Alexandria, Virginia

Federal cavalry horses wait along a rail fence (below) amid the ruins of Richmond, across the street from the Confederate treasury building (far right). "As the sun rose on Richmond, such a spectacle was presented as can never be forgotten," recalled resident Sallie Putnam. "Above all this scene of terror, hung a black shroud of smoke through which the sun shone with a lurid angry glare . . . as if loath to shine over a scene so appalling."

Shiloh
Early Battles in the West

YANKEES ON THE MOVE—It took only two days after arriving at his new headquarters in Nashville, Tennessee, in September 1861 for General Albert Sidney Johnston to conclude that the situation for the Confederacy in the western theater of war was desperate. He fired off a telegram to his friend Jefferson Davis, president

of the Confederacy, pleading for help. "We have not over half the *armed* forces that are now likely to be required," Johnston lamented. What was worse, there were no rifles or muskets to give to the recruits who were straggling in, no uniforms or other equipment of any sort.

Gloomy as it was, Johnston's telegram was an understatement. He had been given the most daunting task assigned to any general in this first year of the Civil War—to take command of the entire western two-thirds of the Confederacy and protect it from Union invasion. This meant trying to defend a line more than 300 miles long from the Cumberland Mountains in the east all the way to the Mississippi River. In addition, Johnston was to make sure the Federals did not control the Mississippi itself or play havoc beyond the river in Missouri and Arkansas.

To guard the huge area, Johnston found that he had fewer than 20,000 men, most of them untrained and untested and armed with old shotguns and flintlocks brought from home, if anything. As one of Johnston's aides bluntly put it, "He had no army."

Johnston had been assigned the job because it was agreed throughout the South—this before Robert E. Lee had fought a battle—that he was by all odds the best officer in the Confederate army. A handsome, courtly 58-year-old West Point graduate, Johnston had had a somewhat checkered career that included resigning from the U.S. Army twice to become a farmer and then a cotton planter. But by the time the Civil War began he had been promoted to brigadier general and named the army's top commander on the West Coast. He then had led a company of fellow Southern sympathizers, bent on joining the Confederate army, on a hair-raising trek across 800 miles of mountains and desert from San Francisco to Texas.

Finally reaching the Confederate capital of Richmond by railroad, Johnston had been given a hero's welcome—

Above: The "Shiloh" citation, as shown on the 1st Florida Battalion's flag, was a hard-won honor. The commander of the brigade in which the 1st Florida served reported, "The desperation with which the troops fought brings new luster to the arms of the state they represented."

Opposite: Private W. J. Coker of the Confederate 3d Tennessee was captured at Fort Donelson in February 1862. He spent several grueling months as a prisoner before being exchanged after the Shiloh campaign. In the photograph Coker holds a Model 1822 smoothbore musket converted from flintlock to percussion.

*Albert Sidney John-
ston, portrayed in
1860 wearing his
U.S. Army uniform,
became the Confeder-
acy's oldest active gen-
eral at the age of 58.
He was a man of
heroic physique and
high reputation. But
his opponent, Ulysses
S. Grant, called him
"vacillating and unde-
cided in his action."*

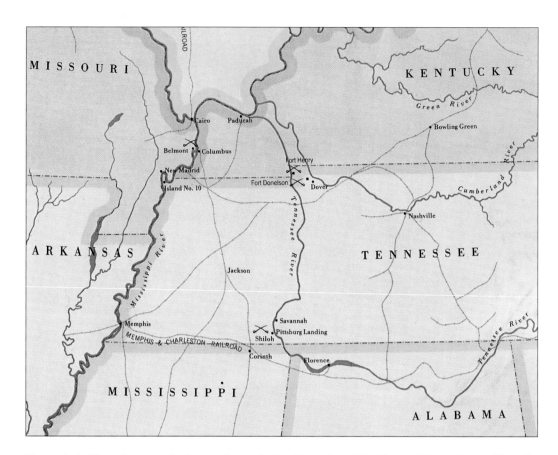

The war in the West—that vast region between the Appalachian Mountains and the Mississippi River—began with small-scale clashes between local forces in Missouri. But by November of 1861, the lines were drawn for a greater war between major armies, with Kentucky and Tennessee as the battle ground. Most of the battles would be fought for Confederate-held rail-hub towns and forts on the Mississippi, Cumberland, and Tennessee Rivers, which served as avenues of invasion for Federal forces spearheaded by flotillas of gunboats. In the first year of the war, the Federal campaign to take the strategic town of Corinth, Mississippi, would bring Yankee and Rebel armies to battle at Shiloh on the banks of the Tennessee.

and almost immediately was sent to Nashville to save the western Confederacy from the Union threat. "I hoped and expected that I had others who would prove generals," President Davis said, "but I knew I had one, and that was Sidney Johnston."

The threats were not as menacing as the Confederate leaders in Richmond thought, at least for the moment. In the fall of 1861 the Federal forces scattered about Kentucky, Illinois, and Missouri numbered about twice as many men as Johnston had, but they, too, were mostly raw recruits lacking arms and other gear. And the western forces on both sides would remain ill equipped for some time, getting leftovers and hand-me-downs after the armies in the East were supplied.

But the perils Johnston faced in the long run were very real, in large measure because of geography. The western Confederacy was divided by long, wide rivers navigable for hundreds of miles by gunboats and transports. Unlike the smaller streams in the East, which generally flowed west to east across the paths of the

marching armies, the western rivers flowed north to south for much of their length—huge daggers pointing deep into the southern heartland.

Greatest of the rivers, of course, was the Mississippi, which figured prominently in the Union's overall strategy, the so-called Anaconda Plan devised by the U.S. Army's savvy commanding general, Winfield Scott. According to Scott's master plan, Federal forces would conquer the length of the Mississippi and, combining this with a naval blockade of the South's seaports, slowly squeeze the Confederacy to death as if in the coils of a giant snake.

Nearly as critical for Johnston were two other big rivers, the Tennessee and the Cumberland, which, flowing out of the southern highlands, emptied into the Ohio before that river met the Mississippi. The Cumberland, hooking through the Confederate state of Tennessee, flowed right through Nashville, an exceedingly important city that was busily manufacturing guns, ammunition, and other war matériel

The Tennessee River flows placidly through heavily wooded country near Knoxville in this 1861 painting by the noted Southern landscape artist James Cameron. Eastern Tennessee's mountains and primeval forests made that region ideal for guerrilla operations and difficult territory for any army to control.

for the Confederate armies.

Just as crucial was the northward-flowing Tennessee, a ready-made 200-mile-long invasion route stretching all the way into Alabama. In a few months, in the spring of 1862, a Federal army would plunge south on the Tennessee almost to the Alabama border. There, in a forlorn backwoods region marked only by a tiny Methodist meeting house called Shiloh Church, the invading Federals and Johnston's army would hammer each other in the first huge and crucially important battle of the Civil War, a ferocious and bloody two-day clash in which more men would be killed and wounded than in all the battles of all the nation's previous wars, and one that would have lasting effects on the course of the entire conflict.

For the time being, though, Johnston tried mightily to stretch his tiny force in a defensive line clear across southern Kentucky. His first aim was to hang on to at least parts of the key border state, hoping—though Kentucky had declared itself

> *"I hoped and expected that I had others who would prove generals but I knew I had one, and that was Sidney Johnston."*

JEFFERSON DAVIS, PRESIDENT OF THE CONFEDERACY

The Louisville Citizen Guards, photographed in their bivouac at the Louisville Fair Grounds in August 1860, were part of the 5,000-man Kentucky State Guard, commanded by General Simon Bolivar Buckner. When Kentucky proclaimed neutrality, the governor ordered the state guard to repel incursions from either side.

officially neutral—that the Southern partisans there might still swing the state over to the Confederate side. He also desperately needed to shield Nashville and prevent the Federals from rampaging south on the rivers.

Anchoring the line's western end were about 11,000 men under Major General Leonidas Polk at the Mississippi River town of Columbus, Kentucky. The 55-year-old Polk, a dignified, silver-haired West Pointer, had early abandoned a military career to take religious orders, eventually becoming the Episcopal bishop of Louisiana. He had been persuaded by President Davis, however, to put on a uniform again and help organize Confederate forces in Tennessee.

Not known as an aggressive officer, Polk had nonetheless moved quickly to seize the strategic high bluffs at Columbus in early September 1861, before Johnston arrived. Placing scores of guns on the heights overlooking the river, Polk was ready to blast anything afloat and block any Federal thrust down the Mississippi.

To protect Nashville, Johnston sent Brigadier General Simon Bolivar Buckner, a capable West Pointer from Kentucky, along with a column of troops, to the town of Bowling Green, 60 miles north of Nashville. There two rivers, the Green and the Barren, formed a barrier against any southward Federal attack. As the winter of 1861-1862 progressed, Johnston added troops to this main force until it numbered about 22,000 men, and he put Major General William J. Hardee, the old army's expert on drill and tactics, in overall command.

Having covered what he thought were the likeliest points of attack, General Johnston sent a Nashville politician and newspaper editor by the name of Felix Zollicoffer far to the east to command a tiny army of 4,000 men guarding the Cumberland Gap. Finally Johnston dispatched a few troops and some military engineers to hurry the construction of two heavily armed bastions already being built on bends in the Tennessee and Cumberland Rivers just south of the Tennessee line. If

made as formidable as Johnston fervently hoped, Fort Henry and Fort Donelson would block any Federal attempts to steam up the rivers with gunboats and smash the center of his line.

Facing the Confederates were two Federal armies totaling more than 37,000 men when Johnston arrived and growing rapidly as new regiments flowed in from the various midwestern states. Union forces in the West were split between two commands, the Department of the Ohio, with a forward headquarters in Louisville, Kentucky, and the Department of the Missouri, headquartered in St. Louis.

The officer in charge in St. Louis during the summer and early fall of 1861 was the dashing, handsome Major General John Charles Frémont. Known as the Pathfinder, Frémont had gained fame before the Civil War by exploring and mapping—sometimes incorrectly it turned out—several of the passes through the Rocky Mountains.

Frémont made his share of mistakes in St. Louis as well. He occasioned much ridicule by strutting about with a sort of personal royal guard, a company of Unionist Kentuckians all six feet or so tall. He also cluttered his staff with European fortune hunters—footloose officers from a half-dozen European armies eager to associate with the famous Frémont, who wore flashy uniforms draped with gold and silver bangles that contemptuous Missourians called "chicken guts."

In the fall of 1861 Frémont did something far more foolish, and dangerous. Alarmed by the number of Confederate guerrilla bands spreading havoc in Missouri—like Kentucky it was a border state with many Southern sympathizers—Frémont issued a proclamation declaring martial law and decreed that any citizen caught with a gun in Federally controlled areas would be court-martialed and shot. In doing so, General Frémont invited the wholesale killing of Unionists in reprisal by the Confederates and a wild escalation of internecine bloodshed in Missouri and

BOLIVAR BUCKNER'S LEGACY

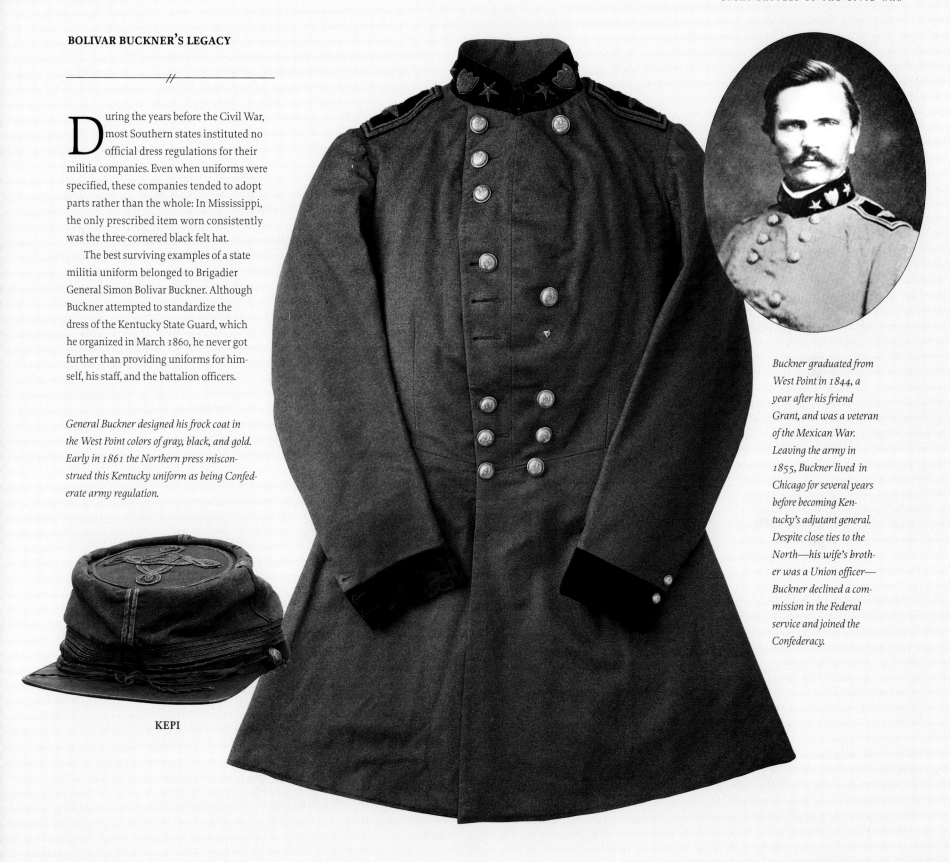

During the years before the Civil War, most Southern states instituted no official dress regulations for their militia companies. Even when uniforms were specified, these companies tended to adopt parts rather than the whole: In Mississippi, the only prescribed item worn consistently was the three-cornered black felt hat.

The best surviving examples of a state militia uniform belonged to Brigadier General Simon Bolivar Buckner. Although Buckner attempted to standardize the dress of the Kentucky State Guard, which he organized in March 1860, he never got further than providing uniforms for himself, his staff, and the battalion officers.

General Buckner designed his frock coat in the West Point colors of gray, black, and gold. Early in 1861 the Northern press misconstrued this Kentucky uniform as being Confederate army regulation.

KEPI

Buckner graduated from West Point in 1844, a year after his friend Grant, and was a veteran of the Mexican War. Leaving the army in 1855, Buckner lived in Chicago for several years before becoming Kentucky's adjutant general. Despite close ties to the North—his wife's brother was a Union officer—Buckner declined a commission in the Federal service and joined the Confederacy.

This photograph, taken in October 1861—one of Ulysses Grant's earliest wartime portraits—shows the recently appointed brigadier general sporting a dress uniform and a long, square-cut beard. This image of Grant is unusual: Later in the war he was known for the simplicity of his dress, and he generally wore his beard cropped close.

> ## "Find out where your enemy is, get at him as soon as you can and strike him as hard as you can, and keep moving on."

elsewhere. In addition, Frémont's proclamation declared that the slaves of Southern sympathizers would be set free, a move that would have alienated millions in Missouri, Kentucky, and parts of the North who favored the Union cause but still opposed any idea of emancipation.

The inflammatory proclamation alarmed President Abraham Lincoln, who quickly annulled it and two months later relieved Frémont of his job. But while still in St. Louis Frémont unwittingly performed an invaluable service for the Union. Needing a commander for the Federal force forming at Cairo, Illinois—the strategic spot where the Ohio River met the Mississippi—he chose a seemingly unlikely candidate, a rather scruffy-looking brigadier general named Ulysses S. Grant. He had been strongly impressed, Frémont said, by Grant's "dogged persistence" and "iron will."

The Ohio-born Grant was a man under a cloud, as he remained for some time. A West Point graduate, he had fought with bravery and dash in the Mexican War of 1846-1848, escaping his dull behind-the-lines job as a regimental quartermaster to take part in two of the war's bloodier battles.

After the war, however, Grant was assigned to a remote, forlorn post in California. Separated from his wife and family, whom he could not afford to bring along,

serving under a martinet, and feeling a failure, he took to the bottle—or so the story went. Whether Grant drank enough to interfere with his duties is not known, but he got the reputation in the old tight-knit officer corps of being a drunk. In 1854 he was in effect forced to resign from the Regular Army.

In the following years Grant tried farming and failed at it, then drifted from one ill-paying job to another, ending up at age 39 as a lowly clerk in a Galena, Illinois, leather goods store run by his brother. But with the coming of war Grant saw his opportunity. Pulling a few strings, he gained command of a new regiment, the 21st Illinois Infantry, which had mutinied against its incompetent colonel. "In a very few days," one soldier wrote, Grant quietly "reduced matters in camp to perfect order."

His efficiency noticed, Grant was promoted to brigadier general in July 1861, taking over in Cairo in early September. There he again got things running smoothly by imposing organization and discipline on the Federal troops massing there, despite the fact that the old, low-lying river town was a nightmarish spot. Cold and damp, Cairo was infested with gambling halls, bordellos, and bars that kept drunken soldiers circulating through the guardhouse.

Grant was a born general with a genius for military organization—and a taste for fighting. The purpose of war, he said simply, was to "find out where your enemy is, get at him as soon as you can and strike him as hard as you can, and keep moving on." Grant's troops, who dubbed him "the quiet man," trusted him because, without any of the posturing common among generals of the time, he looked out for their welfare and got things done fast and against all odds. "He habitually wears an expression," one soldier said, "as if he had determined to drive his head through a brick wall and was about to do it."

Once in command at Cairo, Grant showed his penchant for fast action by immediately moving 50 miles up the Ohio with part of his force to occupy Paducah, Kentucky, which controlled access to the mouths of the Cumberland and Tennessee Rivers. General Polk had intended to capture the strategically vital town, but Grant forestalled him, sending in infantry and artillery before Polk's troops arrived. It was not the last time Grant would get to a place faster than Bishop Polk.

Grant also proved his willingness to fight by loading about 3,000 men on river transports to assault Belmont, Missouri, a one-horse hamlet on the west bank of the Mississippi across from General Polk's main position at Columbus. The attack failed when Polk sent reinforcements across the river and then blasted the Federals with his artillery. But Grant extricated his men with aplomb, showing a coolness in crisis that would become his hallmark.

By no means as prone to action was Grant's new superior in St. Louis, Major General Henry W. Halleck, who succeeded Frémont in November 1861. The ultimate desk general, the 47-year-old Halleck had spent most of his time in the army doing staff work—and carefully cultivating his own career. He was by universal agreement a master at covering his own flanks through caution and never doing anything rash.

Commandeered for wartime service, the steamboat Aleck Scott unloads newly recruited Federal soldiers at Cairo, Illinois. Strategically situated at the confluence of the Ohio and Mississippi Rivers, the ramshackle community of Cairo became a Yankee stronghold and the principal staging area for General Grant's advance against the Confederate armies in Kentucky and Tennessee.

But Halleck also had a reputation for being highly intelligent—his army nickname was Old Brains—and for having an acute sense of strategy. Ultimately Halleck would give Grant the green light to smash at A. S. Johnston's line in the campaign that would culminate at the Battle of Shiloh—but not without imposing delays that caused Grant fits of frustration.

The other Federal force facing Johnston, the army of the Department of the Ohio, was commanded through the late fall and early winter of 1861-1862 by a fellow Ohioan and near classmate of Grant's at West Point, Brigadier General William Tecumseh Sherman. Red-headed, rail thin, intense, and as voluble as Grant was silent, Sherman talked so incessantly when ideas flashed through his mind that his aides complained the chatter made them dizzy. But Sherman became, like Grant, a past master at military movement, a daring tactician, and—as he would prove at Shiloh—an imperturbable leader in battle.

Sherman's high-strung nature caused him a reversal, however. While Sherman was in charge at Louisville, Johnston proceeded to do what any smart general would when facing a larger enemy—stage an elaborate bluff to trick the enemy into inaction while building up his own force. Urged on by Johnston, General Buckner sent his infantry regiments marching and countermarching around Bowling Green making shows of force. At the same time Confederate cavalry patrols—some led by a future terror to the Federals named Nathan Bedford Forrest—ranged through central and southern Kentucky, smashing a small, isolated Union camp at Barboursville and occupying briefly the towns of Albany and Hopkinsville.

Mistaking bluff for reality, Sherman became highly alarmed, sending messages to Washington demanding to be reinforced with a fantastic number—200,000 men—to meet an imagined Confederate offensive all across Kentucky. Soon he was

Brigadier General William Tecumseh Sherman, portrayed in this rare photograph about the time of Shiloh, was praised as "a gallant and able officer" in Grant's official battle report to General Halleck. Halleck commended Sherman to Washington and got him promoted to major general of volunteers, retroactive to the first day of the battle.

in the throes of something like a nervous breakdown and was briefly relieved of duty. By early 1862, however, he was commanding a new division at Paducah and would shortly find himself in the vanguard of Grant's army.

Taking Sherman's place in Louisville was Brigadier General Don Carlos Buell, an exceedingly methodical 44-year-old West Pointer who believed he must have his troops thoroughly equipped and trained before doing anything whatever. Buell was not much concerned by Buckner's saber rattling—but he made no move to attack the Confederates at Bowling Green either, even when his army had grown to an impressive 45,000 men. In fact, when Halleck unleashed Grant to attack, he was forced to threaten and cajole Buell before the latter agreed to join the Federal move southward.

While Buckner's troops at Bowling Green were making feints toward Louisville, Felix Zollicoffer, the politician-general guarding eastern Kentucky, actually advanced toward the enemy, moving his 4,000 men to the northwest from near the Cumberland Gap to Mill Springs, Kentucky. Sadly for Zollicoffer, he maneuvered himself into an untenable position on the north bank of the rain-swollen Cumberland River—and then found that a Federal force commanded by a capable West Pointer, Brigadier General George H. Thomas, was bearing down on him.

The Confederates' only option was to attack first and hope for the best. This they did on the morning of January 19, 1862, with a couple of regiments, bone-weary from slogging through winter mud, lunging at the Federal line. General Thomas struck back hard, crushing in the Rebel flanks. Zollicoffer himself was shot dead when he nearsightedly blundered into a Federal unit, and the demoralized remnants of his force only escaped across the Cumberland River by scrambling aboard some barges and an old river steamer.

With the disastrous little Battle of Mill Springs, Johnston's right flank was destroyed, but the terrain in eastern Kentucky was so rough that Thomas could not press his pursuit. Still, the war was closing in on Johnston's main forces. Spring was coming and with it, surely, a Federal attack. To his despair, Johnston found that Forts Henry and Donelson, guarding the Cumberland and the Tennessee, were by no means as strong as he had hoped.

Fort Henry had been poorly sited to begin with, standing on such low ground that its lower works flooded whenever the Tennessee River rose. While loudly bemoaning "its wretched military position," the post commander, a Kentucky-born West Pointer and brigadier general named Lloyd Tilghman, had inexplicably delayed construction of works on the strategic heights directly across the river from Fort Henry. Nor had he done much to bolster the far better situated Fort Donelson, 12 miles away across a stretch of rugged, hilly land separating the Tennessee from the Cumberland.

General Johnston tried to spur Tilghman to action, but it was essentially too late. Federal scouts had reported that Fort Henry was vulnerable, and Grant was chafing to attack—as was an equally feisty U.S. Navy man, Flag Officer Andrew Hull Foote, recently sent west to command a freshwater fleet of gunboats that had grown

> "The General commanding has the gratification of announcing the achievement of an important victory … by the troops under General Thomas, over the rebel forces, some twelve thousand strong, …"

BRIGADIER GENERAL DON CARLOS BUELL

In a congratulatory general order, Brigadier General Don Carlos Buell praised Brigadier General George Thomas for his victory over Brigadier General Felix Zollicoffer's 4,000-man Confederate force at Mill Springs, Kentucky, on January 19, 1862. The Federal success wrecked the eastern end of the Confederate defensive line in the western theater.

Federal colonel Speed S. Fry shoots and kills Confederate brigadier general Felix Zollicoffer in an imaginative engraving of the close-range fighting at Mill Springs, Kentucky. One of Zollicoffer's officers, at right, warns him too late, "It's the enemy, General!"

The Federal river fleet lies at anchor on the Ohio River near the Mound City naval station, five miles north of Cairo, Illinois. The St. Louis (center) was the first of Eads' seven nearly identical iron-clads. To distinguish the boats, different-colored bands were painted on their smokestacks.

In a patriotic lithograph of 1862, Flag Officer Andrew H. Foote plants his feet firmly on the deck of a gunboat. A devout Presbyterian, Foote often gathered his crews on deck and preached fire-and-brim-stone sermons.

steadily in the past few months. A passionate evangelical Christian, Foote preached hellfire sermons to his crews—and cut their grog ration—but like Grant he thought the way to wage war was to hit the enemy with implacable fury and get it over with.

The builder of Foote's strange fleet was a single-minded civilian named James B. Eads, a St. Louis riverman and expert at salvaging hulks wrecked on Mississippi sand bars. The first gunboats were three ordinary river steamers, their sides armored with thick oak beams. They immediately proved useful on reconnaissance runs, their wooden sides easily deflecting small arms fire. But everyone knew they would be shot to splinters by heavy guns like the ones Leonidas Polk had at Columbus, or the ones that poked through embrasures at Forts Henry and Donelson.

So Eads developed on the spot an entirely new sort of vessel armored with heavy iron plating, each boat 175 feet long and carrying 13 heavy cannon. Eads' gunboats were appallingly ugly and scowlike—they resembled enormous turtles, one observer said—but they had powerful steam engines and shallow draft and were ideal for river warfare.

Eads' shipyards, working with furious haste, produced seven of these gunboats, all named for western river ports: *Cairo, Louisville, Pittsburgh, Carondelet, Mound City, Cincinnati,* and *St. Louis*. To them Eads added a pair of older boats he had fitted with iron sides, the *Essex* and the *Benton*.

With these fearsome vessels wharved at Cairo, Grant and Foote impatiently

wired General Halleck, pleading for permission to steam up the Tennessee and smash Fort Henry. The arrogant Halleck abruptly put them off. But soon he felt heavy pressure from President Lincoln and others in Washington to do something to hit the Confederates. Mindful of his reputation as always, Halleck grudgingly gave the go-ahead, wiring Grant to "make your preparations to take and hold" the fort.

Grant immediately got the vanguard of a 17,000-man force aboard a fleet of transports. On February 2, 1862, the entire flotilla, Foote's gunboats in the lead, churned up the Ohio giving off dense clouds of Stygian smoke and then turned to the right, splashing their way southward into the mouth of the Tennessee toward Fort Henry. It was the first leg of an offensive that would take them up the Tennessee to Pittsburg Landing and the fateful collision with the Confederate army at Shiloh Church.

STRUGGLE FOR THE REBEL RIVER FORTS

By January 1862 some 20,000 Federal troops under the command of General U. S. Grant had gathered near Cairo, Illinois, at the confluence of the Ohio and Mississippi Rivers. From his base of operations, Grant was ready and eager to strike at the northernmost outposts of General Johnston's Confederate forces. Fort Henry, the earthen bastion guarding the Tennessee River, seemed particularly vulnerable to assault.

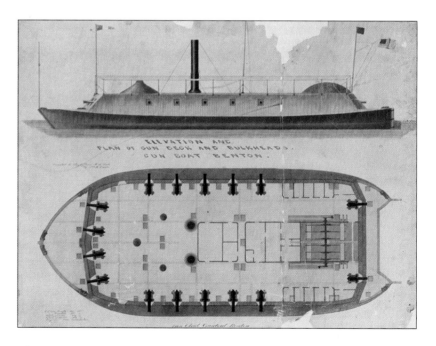

The U.S.S. Benton was the largest and most powerful vessel of the Federal river fleet. This drawing was made for her conversion from a snag boat to an ironclad mounting 16 cannon.

Grant believed that if Henry capitulated to the Union the 5,000-man garrison at Fort Donelson, on the Cumberland River, would soon follow suit.

Having earlier rejected the plan, Grant's superior, Major General Henry Halleck, changed his mind and on January 30 authorized a Federal offensive against the two forts. On February 2 Grant began shuttling his soldiers by transport up the Ohio, then south up the Tennessee to the vicinity of Fort Henry. The Yankee troopships were escorted by a fleet of three timbered and four ironclad gunboats under the command of Flag Officer Andrew Foote. When the advance of the troops was delayed by a lack of transports and the heavy current of the rain-swollen rivers,

Grant decided on February 5 to allow Foote to launch a naval assault on Fort Henry before the Rebel garrison could be reinforced.

Conditions at the fort could not have been worse. High river waters had flooded several batteries with two feet of water. Henry's commander, General Tilghman, decided to evacuate. Retaining his gun crews, he dispatched all but 150 of his 2,500-man garrison to Fort Donelson, a dozen miles to the east. On February 6 Foote's flotilla steamed to within 300 yards of the Southern earthwork, raking the defenders with deadly salvoes. Despite the lopsided odds, Tilghman's gunners acquitted themselves well, damaging Foote's flagship, the *Cincinnati*, and putting the *Essex*

A 6-inch gun in Fort Henry bursts during the Federal gunboat attack, killing a sergeant and wounding the rest of the crew. After 70 minutes of bombardment, only four of the fort's 17 guns were still in action.

"Fort Henry is ours."

The Federal gunboat flotilla attacks Fort Henry four abreast on February 6, 1862. As the flagship Cincinnati (left), the Carondelet and the St. Louis shell the fort, the Essex is hit in the boiler and put out of action.

Born to an aristocratic Maryland family, Brigadier General Lloyd Tilghman graduated from West Point in 1836 but left the army to pursue a career as a railroad engineer in Paducah, Kentucky. Exchanged six months after his surrender at Fort Henry, Tilghman assumed command of a brigade in the defense of Vicksburg. On May 16, 1863, he was killed by a Federal shell at the Battle of Champion's Hill, Mississippi.

out of action with an exploded boiler. But the outcome was a foregone conclusion; after 70 minutes of shelling, only four of Tilghman's 17 artillery pieces were still serviceable, and the Confederate commander surrendered to his naval counterpart. Without losing a single infantryman, Grant was able to telegraph the good news to Washington: "Fort Henry is ours."

Grant had hoped to be in position to invest Fort Donelson by February 8, but his plans were hindered by continued heavy rain that turned the roads to quagmires. It was February 12 before the Federal commander dispatched two divisions, marching on parallel roads, to cut off the Rebel bastion on the Tennessee River.

As Grant was closing in, Johnston was debating whether to unite his forces for a climactic battle at Donelson or to abandon the post altogether. In the end he settled for a compromise, opting to reinforce the garrison with 12,000 troops under the overall command of Brigadier General John B. Floyd, former U.S. secretary of war. With little hope that Donelson could sustain a protracted siege, Johnston hoped that Floyd would buy time for the remainder of the Southern

army to withdraw from their precarious bases of operation at Columbus and Bowling Green and move southward.

Although he was now outnumbered by Fort Donelson's defenders, Grant on February 13 closed in on the outermost Rebel trenches with the divisions of Brigadier Generals Charles F. Smith and John A. McClernand. Hoping to match the success he had had at Fort Henry, Grant counseled his subordinates not to bring on a general engagement until Flag Officer Foote arrived with the gunboats. But despite their superior's orders, both Smith and McClernand permitted a series of disjointed assaults that were thrown back with heavy loss. That night both sides shivered in subfreezing temperatures as the icy rains became a blizzard.

On February 14 Grant was reinforced by 5,000 fresh troops, who were organized into a third division under the command of Brigadier General Lew Wallace. Foote was also now on hand with four ironclad and two wooden gunboats, and at 2:00 p.m., with cannons blazing, the flotilla steamed toward the river face of Fort Donelson. But Donelson was not to be so easily overcome; nearly half the Rebel shells

"The air was full of objects that flew like birds, and seemed to whisper softly as they went."

SERGEANT HENRY O. DWIGHT

20th Ohio Infantry, Whittlesey's Brigade

Marching at a double-quick to shore up the faltering line of McClernand's division, Sergeant Dwight and his comrades came upon the stragglers and walking wounded of Colonel Richard Oglesby's brigade, which had borne the brunt of the Confederate assault on Fort Donelson. Oglesby's line was broken, and more than 800 of his men killed, wounded, or captured, but even so the Confederates failed to exploit their success.

Finally we came out into an open woods on a hill where a number of Regiments were lying at rest. Farther down the road seemed to be a deep valley shrouded in thick forest, whence came the most deafening sound of musketry. My lips began to be very dry and [I] knew that I was considerably frightened at this sudden entrance upon the skirts of the battlefield. It is the unknown that terrifies and our feeling our way into this battle in the way that we did was to all of us one of the most trying experiences of the whole war. Where we were, what we were going to do, what the bearing upon our army or the rebels of the tremendous roar of sound in our front—all these problems were constantly coming before our minds and as constantly being referred to the future for an answer.

Then came an order for us to lay aside our heavy knapsacks and pile them under care of a guard. Next we discovered that as we moved on, the air was full of objects that flew like birds, and seemed to whisper softly as they went. When once or twice we heard these flying objects hit trees with a sharp crack, it occurred to us that they were bullets from rebel guns. Wounded men were pouring toward us in streams from all directions, some with a bleeding arm or shoulder, some with a finger gone, some carried on stretchers by four or five men. With them were numbers of stragglers, who with pretence of caring for the wounded were getting off the field as fast as possible.

found a target, and the battered ironclads were forced to withdraw. More than 50 sailors were dead or dying, and Foote himself was among the dozens of wounded.

Despite their success in repelling the naval assault, both Floyd and his second in command, Brigadier General Gideon J. Pillow, had little hope of sustaining a drawn-out siege. That night they settled upon a daring strategy. At dawn Pillow would lead a breakout through enemy lines nearest the river, and as the troops of General Buckner covered the rear, the Rebel garrison would cut its way through to Nashville, 75 miles to the south.

At first the gambit seemed to pay off. At 6:00 a.m., screaming the Rebel yell, Pillow's troops took the Yankees by surprise, pierced the line of McClernand's division, and gained the planned escape route on the Forge road. After repeated calls for assistance, Lew Wallace dispatched a portion of his division to McClernand's aid, but by 8:00 a.m. the Union right flank had been bent back at nearly a right angle to its initial position. Grant, who had been conferring with Flag Officer Foote when the unexpected blow struck, hurried to the scene of combat.

As the firing subsided, Grant determined to regain the initiative. Assuming that the enemy must have weakened their defenses in order to bolster their strike force, he ordered C. F. Smith, commanding the left, to launch an all-out assault on the trenches to his front. Smith personally led a bayonet charge that overran the outermost Confederate works, while Wallace and McClernand counterattacked and Foote's gunboats renewed their bombardment.

The advantage was lost for the Southern forces when General Pillow inexplicably brought his troops to a halt even as their breakout was succeeding. Floyd concurred with Pillow's decision, and by early afternoon the Confederates were pulling back into their fortifications. Floyd and Pillow then determined to avoid becoming prisoners of the Federals; they steamed south on transports with a handful of their command, leaving it to Buckner to open negotiations with the Federal commander for the surrender of Fort Donelson.

Grant's demand for "unconditional and immediate surrender" sealed the fate of the Confederate garrison. Nathan Bedford Forrest, the fiery cavalry colonel, managed to cut his way out with some 700 troopers, but nearly 15,000 Southern soldiers and 65 cannon fell into Yankee hands in the North's first great victory of the Civil War.

Many of the Rebel soldiers fighting at Fort Donelson were armed with antiquated flintlock smoothbore muskets like the D. Nippes Model 1840 shown here.

General Ulysses S. Grant, on horseback (center), watches his troops advance on Fort Donelson, atop the distant ridge. Two black servants carry a wounded Federal officer (right) to an impromptu field hospital on the battlefield. The white-bearded horseman is Colonel Joseph D. Webster, Grant's chief of staff.

CIVILIAN---Extra.

(BY TELEGRAPH.)

Glorious News!

Fort Donelson Captured!

15,000 Rebel Prisoners!

Generals Buckner, Johnston, Floyd and Pillow among those Captured.

The following dispatch has just been received from the West:

CINCINNATI, Ohio,
February 17th, 11.30 A. M.

Fort Donelson fell yesterday. Federal forces captured 15,000 prisoners, including Generals Buckner, Pillow, Johnston and Floyd.

The hastily printed Northern broadside (above) exaggerates the extent of the Federal victory at Fort Donelson. Of the four generals said to have been captured, only Buckner was actually taken prisoner. This 128-pound spherical solid shot (below), 10 inches in diameter, was recovered from the Fort Donelson battlefield. The Confederate batteries defending the fort mounted several 10-inch Columbiad cannon.

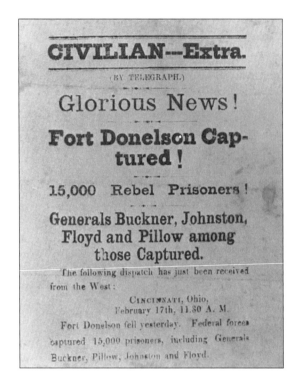

With defiance in their eyes, captured Confederates pose for a Northern photographer soon after their arrival at Camp Douglas, Illinois, the prison for most of Fort Donelson's former garrison. The Rebels wear prisoner of war identity tags about their necks and are clad in Federal overcoats, which were issued to them following the surrender.

Brigadier General Gideon J. Pillow (left), second in command of the Confederate garrison at Fort Donelson, proposed that the defenders cut their way through the besieging Yankees. But when the decision to surrender was made, Pillow chose to avoid capture by taking a steamboat to Nashville with his commander, General John B. Floyd (right). Their escape was criticized by many in the South as cowardice in the face of the enemy. General Buckner's stoic decision to remain with his troops stood in marked contrast to his superiors' abandonment of Fort Donelson's doomed garrison. In an unseemly display of favoritism, General Floyd—a former Virginia governor and U.S. secretary of war—permitted only his Virginia brigade to leave with him. The following month President Davis removed Floyd from command.

THE PUSH TO PITTSBURG LANDING

The capture of Forts Henry and Donelson by Grant's Federal army broke the back of the Confederate defensive line in northern Tennessee and Kentucky. As the Yankees prepared to continue their advance southward, Confederate commander A. S. Johnston was shocked by the magnitude of the disaster, lamenting, "We lost all."

With the victorious Federal troops poised on the Cumberland and Tennessee Rivers, threatening to sever the rail link between Memphis and Nashville, Johnston realized that he must quickly pull back the widely separated elements of his army lest they be cut off and destroyed in detail. He would have to abandon his northern outpost at Bowling Green, yielding the crucial border state of Kentucky to the enemy. Even worse, the Southern commander knew that Nashville—a vital transportation and supply center—must also soon be given up. Johnston saw no choice but to regroup, concentrate, and reinforce his scattered contingents. Only then could he give battle to his powerful enemy.

Some 14,000 Rebel soldiers under Johnston's personal command withdrew from Bowling Green to Nashville, with General Buell's 50,000-man Army of the Ohio in slow but relentless pursuit. Nearly a third of Johnston's army had fallen sick campaigning in the frigid rains, and with the odds more than 3 to 1 against him, the Southern commander dared not risk a battle for the Tennessee capital. On February 18 Johnston began to evacuate Nashville, continuing his retreat southeastward toward Murfreesboro. As Buell closed in on the city, its inhabitants were seized with panic, and hundreds of civilian refugees followed in the wake of the bedraggled and dispirited Rebel columns.

Nashville surrendered to Buell's army on February 25, and that same day, some 150 miles to the northwest, General Polk began withdrawing his Confederate troops from their base at Columbus, Kentucky. Polk had been effectively blocking a Federal advance down the Mississippi. But as his men fell back across the state of Tennessee, a vital stretch of the great river was opened to the enemy; Major General John Pope led 25,000 Federal troops to capture the outnumbered Southern garrisons at New Madrid, Missouri, and Island No. 10, on the Mississippi.

General Johnston was under bitter attack in the Confederate press, his abilities now questioned by the Southern public as well as by many of his most trusted subordinates. But President Davis stood by his western commander, and the retreat continued. Murfreesboro was abandoned on February 28, and Johnston led his men south into Alabama, his troops reaching the town of Decatur on March 15. Along with Kentucky, most of central Tennessee was now under Federal control. Johnston knew he had to somehow reverse the deteriorating situation.

General Pierre Gustave Toutant Beauregard, the ambitious Louisianan whose victories at Fort Sumter and Manassas had made him a Confederate hero, had been dispatched to the western theater early in February. Johnston assigned Beauregard the task of marshaling reinforcements from garrisons throughout the lower South. Their rendezvous point would be the strategic rail hub of Corinth, Mississippi—just

HOW A SOLDIER SAVED HIS COLORS

When Fort Donelson fell to Federal forces on February 16, 1862, Andrew S. Payne, colorbearer of the 14th Mississippi Infantry Regiment, vowed that he would never give up his unit's battle flag to the Yankees. It was a beautiful hand-painted flag, presented by a group of patriotic ladies to the Shubuta Rifles, one of the regiment's companies. More important, the regiment fought hard and well under the flag before being forced to surrender: Seventeen men were killed and 85 were wounded in a futile effort to retake a portion of the entrenchments of the fort. Payne refused to dishonor his comrades by giving up the flag.

Before the prisoners were shipped off to Camp Douglas, near Chicago, Payne cut out the center of the flag and sewed it into the lining of his coat; thus he carefully preserved the emblems on both sides of the flag: Lady Liberty dressed in a toga, holding a picture of Jefferson Davis in one hand and a beribboned sword in the other; and on the reverse, an eagle with its claws about a snake that had invaded its nest of eaglets in a magnolia tree. The flag was still concealed in Payne's coat when, on October 16, 1862, he and most of his comrades were sent back to Mississippi in an exchange of prisoners. There, at last, Payne returned the flag to his regiment.

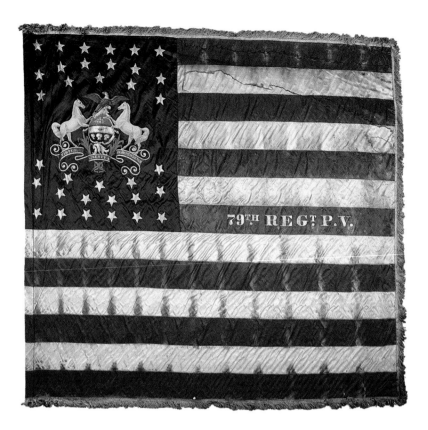

The 79th Pennsylvania Infantry, part of Brigadier General James S. Negley's brigade, carried the national colors (above) when the regiment marched from Bowling Green, Kentucky, to occupy Nashville on March 3, 1862. The silk flag bears the Pennsylvania coat of arms in the center of the field of stars.

south of the Tennessee border, 25 miles west of the Alabama line. Johnston, Polk, and the other retreating columns would join them there.

Though nursing a severe bronchial infection, Beauregard energetically carried out his orders. Brigadier General Daniel Ruggles arrived at Corinth with 5,000 troops from the defenses of New Orleans, and Major General Braxton Bragg brought 10,000 men from Mobile. By March 24 both Polk and Johnston had the last of their regiments encamped in the environs of the town, bringing the concentrated strength of the Army of the Mississippi to 40,000 soldiers. Determined to hold Corinth, Johnston assessed the dispositions of his enemy and began to consider the possibility of launching a counteroffensive.

Despite Federal triumphs at Henry and Donelson, Johnston's principal opponent—newly promoted Major General U. S. Grant—had been experiencing his share of trouble in the month following his victory. Relations between Grant and his superior officer, General Halleck, had become strained, with Halleck charac-

terizing Grant's administration as one of "neglect and inefficiency." Envious of his subordinate's newfound fame, and believing allegations that Grant had resumed the heavy drinking that so marred his prewar military career, Halleck removed Grant from field command on March 4 and placed General C. F. Smith in charge of active operations.

Halleck ordered Smith to continue up the Tennessee to the vicinity of Savannah, a town on the river's east bank. There Smith would link up with a division newly arrived from Paducah, Kentucky, led by General Sherman. Halleck wanted Smith to establish a base of operations and launch a series of raids on enemy lines of communication, but not to attempt a major engagement. "It would be better to retreat," Halleck advised, "than to risk a general battle."

Smith arrived at Savannah on March 11 but injured his leg in a fall the following day. What had at first seemed a minor cut and abrasion turned life threatening with the onset of tetanus, and Smith would die of the infection five weeks later. With Smith out of action, Halleck—newly designated commander of the Department of the Mississippi—turned again to Grant. Two weeks after being shelved, the hero of Fort Donelson was back in charge of active operations on the Tennessee.

Following Halleck's instructions, Grant gathered Federal forces along the banks of the Tennessee in the vicinity of Savannah, where the river made a sweeping loop to the west. On March 16, the day before Grant arrived at Savannah, the last of Sherman's division had moved 10 miles downstream to Pittsburg Landing, a rustic moorings on the Tennessee's west bank. Only 22 miles northeast of the Rebel stronghold at Corinth, Pittsburg Landing seemed an obvious point of concentration from which to resume the offensive against Johnston's army. Though he continued to maintain his headquarters at Savannah, over the following days Grant deployed five divisions at Pittsburg Landing, with a sixth—commanded by Lew Wallace—at Crump's Landing, six miles to the north.

With nearly 40,000 troops on hand, the Yankee camps sprawled across the rugged, wooded countryside west and south of Pittsburg Landing, some near a one-room log meeting house called Shiloh Church. Freed from the confines of the river transports, the Federal soldiers enjoyed their respite from active campaigning, and despite the nearby presence of an enemy army, evidently no one considered erecting defensive earthworks and rifle pits. As Sherman later admitted, digging in was thought to be "evidence of weakness."

Opposite: Federal troops of the 51st Ohio Infantry, Army of the Ohio, form for a dress parade in the shadow of the Tennessee state capitol building in Nashville on March 4, 1862. A correspondent for the New York Times reported that "at present an air of gloom hangs heavily over the whole city. The stores are closed almost without exception, and the inhabitants gather in sullen knots to talk over the new order of things." After its capture, Nashville became a major supply base and headquarters for Federal operations in the western theater.

"At present an air of gloom hangs heavily over the whole city. The stores are closed . . . and the inhabitants gather in sullen knots to talk over the new order of things."

"God keep the Rebel soldiers for the Lincolnites will not."

PRIVATE GEORGE S. RICHARDSON

6th Iowa Infantry, McDowell's Brigade

Private Richardson's regiment reached Pittsburg Landing in late March after an uncomfortable voyage in poor weather on the steamer Crescent City. The only noteworthy occurrence on board was the issue of new Springfield rifles. In a letter to his parents, Richardson described the situation and morale of the Federal army.

Pittsburg Landing
March 29th, 1862
Dear Father and Mother,

Here we are in Dixie Land looking forward with great anxiety to what we expect will prove to be a successful victory in favor of the Federal forces who are now in Tennessee. We were on the boat 10 days and when we received orders to march out and camp, we did it cheerfully. The boys are all well and in fine spirits.

You would be surprised to see the different camps which now line the woods in southern Dixie. There are about 80,000 troops in the vicinity and more coming all the time. What the movements will be in the future is more than I can say, for there is no one allowed to know anything about what is going on except as the movements are executed.

There are a great many deserters from the Rebel Army coming to seek protection from the Union troops and according to their stories there are about 40,000 rebels 18 miles from here on the R.R. that runs from Memphis to Charleston. The roads are so bad at present that it will be impossible to get artillery over the roads until they are fixed, but the roads will be ready to move over in a few days and then God keep the Rebel soldiers for the Lincolnites will not.

While his troops relaxed, Grant was eager to make a move against Johnston's growing force to the west. Believing enemy morale to be low, the Federal commander thought the time right for a decisive strike. But Halleck insisted that Grant await the arrival of substantial reinforcements before risking battle. On March 16 Buell's army had started from Nashville on the 120-mile march to Savannah. Once Buell linked up with Grant, the Yankees would have better than 2-to-1 odds in their favor, and Halleck would be confident of a Union victory.

But the methodical Buell was moving with characteristic caution, his column hampered by bad weather, muddy roads, and the destruction the retreating Confederates had left in their wake. When Buell's vanguard reached Columbia, 35 miles southwest of Nashville, the Federals found the bridge that spanned the rain-swollen Duck River in ruins. Buell himself did not leave Nashville until March 25, a week after his lead division had arrived at Columbia. His troops had neither the skill nor the tools necessary to quickly rebuild the

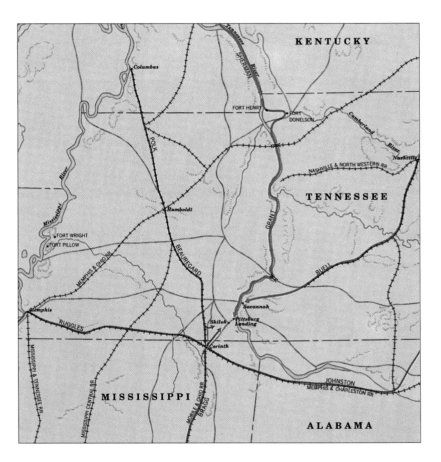

After capturing Forts Henry and Donelson in February 1862, Grant moved his army south on the Tennessee River to Pittsburg Landing, where he and Sherman waited for Buell's force to arrive from recently captured Nashville. The Confederate commander, A. S. Johnston, reinforced by Ruggles and Bragg, marched out from Corinth, hoping to strike Grant and Sherman before Buell could join them.

Two days before the battle, A. E. Mathews of the 31st Ohio Infantry sketched the humble log meeting house known as Shiloh Church. Following the engagement, Mathews' drawing was published in the form of a lithograph (above)—one of the few contemporary illustrations of the battlefield.

bridge, and it was April 2 before subsiding water allowed the Army of the Ohio to cross the Duck and continue their march for Savannah. Three days later the first of Buell's divisions arrived at Savannah, only to find that no transports were on hand to ferry them upriver across the Tennessee to Pittsburg Landing. The division commander, Brigadier General William "Bull" Nelson, was told it would be April 8 before the move could be undertaken.

Realizing that Federal strength was increasing by the day, Johnston decided that his army would have to strike before Buell's forces linked up with Grant. Not all the desired reinforcements had arrived, but for the time being the Confederate troops at Corinth were nearly equal in number to their opponents at Shiloh Church and Pittsburg Landing. Functioning as Johnston's second in command, Beauregard had organized the army into four corps led by Generals Bragg, Polk, Hardee, and Brigadier General John C. Breckinridge. And it was Beauregard who devised the daring strategy that his superior now embraced.

Johnston accepted Beauregard's plan on April 2 and the following day began shifting his troops to their staging area at Monterey, Tennessee, a point halfway

between Corinth and Shiloh Church. The Southern leaders hoped to launch their assault at dawn on April 5. But heavy rains and the inevitable confusion of marching large numbers of troops from widely scattered locations over rugged terrain made it necessary to delay the attack until the following day, April 6. After two months of retreat and humiliation, Johnston intended to drive the complacent Yankees into the Tennessee River and turn the tide of war in the West.

SURPRISE ATTACK AT SHILOH CHURCH

In spite of the mud, disorder, and nagging delays, by the evening of April 5 most of A. S. Johnston's 40,000-man Confederate army was in position to attack the Yankee camps at Shiloh Church. On the very eve of the offensive, however, Johnston's second in command, General Beauregard, expressed grave doubts about the wisdom of carrying out the attack. The troops were exhausted by the confused marching and countermarching that had brought them to their jumping-off point. Most of the soldiers were nearly out of food, and the men of Braxton Bragg's division had

"'Perhaps the Yanks won't shoot me if they see me wearing such flowers, for they are a sign of peace.'"

PRIVATE HENRY M. STANLEY

6th Arkansas Infantry, Hindman's Brigade

Later famed as a journalist and African explorer, Stanley fought at Shiloh as a teenage volunteer in the Dixie Grays—Company E of the 6th Arkansas. The illegitimate son of a Welsh farmer and a butcher's daughter, he had immigrated to the United States three years before the outbreak of the war.

Next to me, on my right, was a boy of seventeen, Henry Parker. I remember it because, while we stood-at-ease, he drew my attention to some violets at his feet, and said, "It would be a good idea to put a few into my cap. Perhaps the Yanks won't shoot me if they see me wearing such flowers, for they are a sign of peace." "Capital," said I, "I will do the same." We plucked a bunch, and arranged the violets in our caps. The men in the ranks laughed at our proceedings, and had not the enemy been so near, their merry mood might have been communicated to the army.

We loaded our muskets, and arranged our cartridge-pouches ready for use. Our weapons were the obsolete flintlocks, and the ammunition was rolled in cartridge-paper, which contained powder, a round ball, and three buckshot. When we loaded we had to tear the paper with our teeth, empty a little powder into the pan, lock it, empty the rest of the powder into the barrel, press paper and ball into the muzzle, and ram home. Then the Orderly-sergeant called the roll, and we knew that the Dixie Greys were present to a man. Soon after, there was a commotion, and we dressed up smartly. A young Aide galloped along our front, gave some instructions to the Brigadier Hindman, who confided the same to his Colonels, and presently we swayed forward in line, with shouldered arms. Newton Story, big, broad, and straight, bore our company-banner of gay silk, at which the ladies of our neighbourhood had laboured.

As we tramped solemnly and silently through the thin forest, and over its grass, still in its withered and wintry hue, I noticed that the sun was not far from appearing, that our regiment was keeping its formation admirably, that the woods would have been a grand place for a picnic; and I thought it strange that a Sunday should have been chosen to disturb the holy calm of those woods.

Before we had gone five hundred paces, our serenity was disturbed by some desultory firing in front. It was then a quarter-past five. "They are at it already," we whispered to each other. "Stand by, gentlemen,"—for we were all gentlemen volunteers at this time,—said our Captain, L. G. Smith. Our steps became unconsciously brisker, and alertness was noticeable in everybody. The firing continued at intervals, deliberate and scattered, as at target-practice. We drew nearer to the firing, and soon a sharper rattling of musketry was heard. "This is the enemy waking up," we said. Within a few minutes, there was another explosive burst of musketry, the air was pierced by many missiles, which hummed and pinged sharply by our ears, pattered through the tree-tops, and brought twigs and leaves down on us. "Those are bullets," Henry whispered with awe.

A sketch by Confederate soldier-artist William L. Sheppard depicts the charge of Braxton Bragg's Confederates into a camp of Benjamin Prentiss' startled Federals at dawn on April 6, 1862.

consumed their five-day allotment of rations two days earlier than planned. Worst of all, Beauregard feared the Yankees were well aware of the Southern soldiers to their front. For two days Hardee's division—the first of Johnston's units to take position—had been skirmishing with Federal pickets and scouting patrols. The enemy, Beauregard thought, must be "entrenched to the eyes," ready and waiting for the impending assault. But Johnston was adamant: The attack would proceed as planned.

The Confederate commander had initially intended to carry out an assault *en echelon*—a series of carefully timed blows that would commence with Polk's division on the left, followed at intervals by Bragg in the center and Hardee on the right. Brigadier General John C. Breckinridge's division would be held in reserve, to be used as needed. In the final hours before the attack, Johnston apparently agreed to Beauregard's suggestion that the assault be made in three successive waves, rather than en echelon. The change in tactics would prove to be an unfortunate decision. But Johnston was correct in his belief that the Federal high command was unaware of the Confederate army massed just south of Shiloh Church. "The main force of the enemy is at Corinth," Grant informed General Halleck.

"I have scarcely the faintest idea of an attack being made upon us."

One Yankee officer was convinced that something was up, however. At 3:00 a.m. on the morning of April 6, Colonel Everett Peabody—a brigade commander in Benjamin Prentiss' division—took it upon himself to dispatch five companies drawn from the 25th Missouri and the 12th Michigan on a reconnaissance beyond Shiloh Church. Shortly after 5:00 a.m. the Federal patrol ran into the advance pickets of Hardee's Confederate division. Their exchange of fire marked the beginning of the great battle, which quickly escalated as Hardee sent forward the brigades of Thomas C. Hindman and Sterling A. M. Wood, and Peabody brought his brigade into line to defend their threatened encampment.

At 6:30 a.m. Johnston gave the order for a general advance and 10 minutes later rode to the front with his staff to take personal charge of the attack. Beauregard was left behind at headquarters to shuttle troops forward as needed. Any doubts Johnston may have entertained about his subordinate's ability to oversee the operation were swept aside in the enthusiasm of the moment. "Tonight," Johnston remarked to a staff officer, "we will water our horses in the Tennessee River."

With the brigade of Patrick R. Cleburne in the vanguard, Hardee's and Polk's

CORPORAL LEANDER STILLWELL

61st Illinois Infantry, Miller's Brigade

Stillwell remembered the surprise that swept through the camps of the Federal soldiers, who had no inkling of an impending attack. A member of Prentiss' division, Stillwell was destined to be in the thick of the action.

//

We had "turned out" about sunup, answered to roll-call, and had cooked and eaten our breakfast. We had then gone to work, preparing for the regular Sunday morning inspection, which would take place at nine o'clock. The boys were scattered around the company streets and in front of the company parade grounds, engaged in polishing and brightening their muskets, and brushing up and cleaning their shoes, jackets, trousers, and clothing generally. It was a most beautiful morning. The sun was shining brightly through the trees, and there was not a cloud in the sky. It really seemed like Sunday in the country at home.... The wagons were silent, the mules were peacefully munching their hay, and the army teamsters were giving us a rest. I listened with delight to the plaintive, mournful tones of a turtle-dove in the woods close by, while on the dead limb of a tall tree right in the camp a woodpecker was sounding his "long roll" just as I had heard it beaten by his Northern brothers a thousand times on the trees in the Otter Creek bottom at home.

Suddenly, away off on the right, in the direction of Shiloh church, came a dull, heavy "Pum!" then another, and still another. Every man sprung to his feet as if struck by an electric shock, and we looked inquiringly into one another's faces. "What is that?" asked every one, but no one answered. Those heavy booms then came thicker and faster, and just a few seconds after we heard that first dull, ominous growl off to the southwest, came a low, sullen, continuous roar. There was no mistaking that sound. That was not a squad of pickets emptying their guns on being relieved from duty; it was the continuous roll of thousands of muskets, and told us that a battle was on.

What I have been describing just now occurred during a few seconds only, and with the roar of musketry the long roll began to beat in our camp. Then ensued a scene of desperate haste, the like of which I certainly had never seen before, nor ever saw again.

divisions slammed into the Yankee right flank, held by Sherman's division. For several days Sherman had blithely dismissed warnings of a Rebel presence just beyond his camps as the false alarms of jumpy volunteers. "Oh, tut, tut!" he scoffed at one subordinate. "You militia officers get scared too easily." But now the magnitude of the threat was all too clear, as Sherman galloped through a hail of bullets in a desperate attempt to steady his wavering lines.

Cleburne's initial attack was stymied by Colonel Ralph Buckland's brigade of Sherman's division. But when Bragg's division swept forward in the second wave of the Confederate onslaught, Colonel Jesse Hildebrand's brigade on Sherman's left was hit in front and flank, and gave way. For a time, elements of Sherman's division made a determined stand near the crossroads at Shiloh Church, but soon even the most stalwart soldiers were forced to take to their heels lest they be killed or captured.

While Sherman's line unraveled, the Confederate juggernaut was forcing back the troops of Prentiss' division in the Federal center. Colonel Madison Miller's brigade was hit in the front and flank, and Peabody's brigade was virtually destroyed

"Oh, tut, tut! You militia officers get scared too easily."

in a vain endeavor to defend their campground against Hardee's assault. Colonel Peabody was shot dead from his horse, and his surviving soldiers joined the chaotic retreat northward. By 8:45 a.m. the entire Federal front had given way, and the Union reserves were beset with throngs of fugitives, stragglers, and walking wounded making their way toward Pittsburg Landing and the river.

But not all the Federal troops were stampeded. Prentiss succeeded in rallying about a thousand of his men along a wooded crest edged by a sunken road that seemed a promising defensive position. At 9:00 a.m. Prentiss drove back a Rebel charge, and his men regained a measure of confidence. As the Federals caught their breath, they were bolstered by reinforcements from the divisions in the rear that had yet to be engaged. Bolstered by a brigade from John McClernand's division, and another from Stephen Hurlbut's, Sherman was able to patch together a line along the road that led east to Pittsburg Landing. Sherman held out on Prentiss' right until 10:00 a.m., when the attack of Polk's division compelled the Yankees to continue their fighting retreat north of the Corinth-Pittsburg road.

While McClernand covered the withdrawal of Sherman's battered division, other units moved forward to assist Prentiss. Two of Hurlbut's brigades and three from the division of General C. F. Smith—now lead by Brigadier General William H. L. Wallace—came into position alongside Prentiss' troops in the sunken road.

The British general who called America's Civil War armies "armed mobs" might have seen the men of the 21st Missouri Volunteers. Displaying a variety of uniforms and arms, the Federals were apparently as poorly disciplined as they were equipped. Grant considered them a rough bunch: While cruising upriver on a transport, the men kept up "a constant fire all the way" at objects on the riverbank. Even "the citizens on shore were fired at," wrote Grant.

Batteries unlimbered their guns in support, and the Federals prepared to breast the coming storm.

While his army tottered on the brink of disaster, General Grant was making his way to the sound of the guns from his headquarters in Savannah. Nursing a severely sprained ankle from a recent riding accident, Grant stopped briefly at Crump's Landing, where Lew Wallace was ordered to hold his division in readiness to march to the battlefield. Disembarking at Pittsburg Landing, Grant and his staff rode to the front, through crowds of stragglers whose demoralization showed all too clearly the extent of the crisis that gripped the embattled Union army. Grant realized that unless his lines held and Buell's Army of the Ohio could be hastened to the field, defeat was all but inevitable.

HORNET'S NEST

Notwithstanding their stunning success, by late morning the advancing Confederate forces had become nearly as disorganized as the retreating Federals. Many Rebel soldiers stopped to pillage the captured Yankee camps, stuffing empty haversacks with their enemy's abandoned rations and hunting for souvenirs. Because Johnston rode forward with the assault, overall direction of the attack fell to Beauregard, who had established his headquarters in Sherman's old camp near Shiloh Church. Beauregard was committing troops piecemeal, ordering commanders to lead their troops to the sound of the heaviest firing. The inevitable result was a chaotic intermingling of regiments and brigades, scattered across a five-mile front in rugged terrain and in many cases separated from their respective divisions. The Confederate high command had clearly lost control of the battle.

Though reeling from the shock of the surprise attack, many Federal units rallied around their officers and regimental colors and fell into line alongside General Prentiss' survivors and the as yet unbloodied brigades of Hurlbut's and W. H. L. Wallace's divisions. By 10:30 a.m. nearly 5,000 Union soldiers and a half-dozen artillery batteries were in position along the sunken road, with its fringe of tangled thickets and scattering of timber that provided the Yankees a natural stronghold from which to breast the Rebel tide. In order to get to Pittsburg Landing the Confederates would first have to cross a bullet-swept open field and seize the Yankee position—soon to be dubbed the Hornet's Nest.

Johnston inadvertently granted the Federals a crucial hour to establish their new line when he diverted two fresh Confederate brigades advancing toward Prentiss, sending them to the Rebel right flank to ward off a suspected counterattack there. The supposed threat turned out to be one of Sherman's brigades—a mere

Captain Andrew Hickenlooper, mounted on his horse, Gray Eagle, directs his famous 5th Ohio Battery in the Hornet's Nest, a defensive position the Federals held through most of the first day's fighting at Shiloh. Hickenlooper's gun crews, though shorthanded, managed to fire withering blasts every 30 seconds.

While the defenders of the Hornet's Nest continued to hold their embattled position, the troops on their right—elements of Sherman's and McClernand's divisions—were coming under heavy pressure from Polk's Confederate division, aided by scattered units of Hardee's and Breckinridge's commands. By midafternoon the Union right was beginning to give way, exposing the western flank of W. H. L. Wallace's division, which began to bend back toward Prentiss.

The Confederates were also gaining ground on the Yankee left, where Stuart's isolated brigade was retreating before the assault of Brigadier General James R. Chalmers' brigade. Meanwhile General Johnston took personal charge of a renewed effort to smash the Hornet's Nest salient. By 2:00 p.m. Brigadier General John McArthur's brigade on the eastern end of the Union line had given way and was falling back on Pittsburg Landing. Shouting "I will lead you!" Johnston spurred his horse, Fire Eater, along the battle line, exhorting his troops to charge with the bayonet.

Two of Breckinridge's brigades, led by Brigadier General John S. Bowen and Colonel Winfield Scott Statham, swept through a 10-acre peach orchard just to the east

In this hand-colored tintype, Private Thomas Holman of Company C, 13th Tennessee, wears a trimmed battle shirt typical of early-war Confederate uniforms. Wounded on April 6, Holman was among the regiment's 137 casualties.

three regiments commanded by Colonel David Stuart—that had become separated from their division. At 11:00 a.m. one of Brigadier General Benjamin F. Cheatham's brigades charged the Hornet's Nest, but it lacked support and was easily repulsed.

Profiting from the Confederates' lack of tactical coordination, the Union line threw back several more assaults over the next hour. Then, at 12:30 p.m., General Bragg ordered Colonel Randall Lee Gibson to hurl the four regiments of his brigade against the center of Prentiss' line. Three times Gibson's Arkansas and Louisiana troops charged into an onslaught of musketry and canister, only to be hurled back with staggering loss. At one point the Southerners actually got among the guns of Captain Andrew Hickenlooper's Ohio battery before being driven out by the counterattacking 8th Iowa Infantry. By 2:30 p.m. Gibson's brigade had been virtually annihilated, with little to show for its sacrifice.

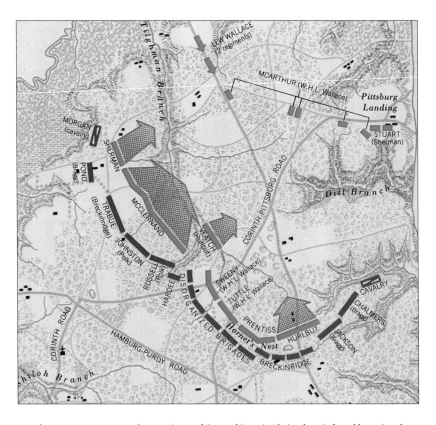

At about 10:30 a.m. on April 6, survivors of General Prentiss' brigade, reinforced by units of W. H. L. Wallace's division, formed a line in a sunken road connecting the Corinth-Pittsburg and Hamburg-Savannah roads. The strong position, dubbed the Hornet's Nest, was the scene of fierce fighting through the day.

General A. S. Johnston lies dying on the battlefield at Shiloh in this sketch by an unknown artist. While leading an attack against Federal positions in the peach orchard, Johnston was fatally wounded by a Minié ball that severed an artery in his right leg.

of the Hornet's Nest. The assault crushed back the left flank of Hurlbut's position, bending the Federal line into the shape of a horseshoe and raking the defenders of the Hornet's Nest with a deadly cross fire. Caught up in the enthusiasm of the moment, Johnston either failed to notice or chose to ignore a wound in the calf of his right leg. At about 2:30 p.m. Johnston's staff officers were shocked to see the general suddenly reel in the saddle. They helped him to the ground, and before they could determine the extent of his injuries, Johnston bled to death. Command of the Confederate forces on the field now fell to General Beauregard, though it was some time before word of Johnston's mortal wounding reached him.

Meanwhile, Breckinridge's troops continued their attack, shoving Hurlbut's division back up the Hamburg-Savannah road and pushing on toward Pittsburg Landing. As the noose continued to tighten around the Hornet's Nest, Brigadier General Daniel Ruggles paved the way for a climactic Confederate assault by massing 62 cannon that unleashed a torrent of iron on the wavering Union defenders. By 5:00 p.m. the Hornet's Nest was virtually surrounded, and the Rebel ranks closed in for the kill.

Many of W. H. L. Wallace's men managed to cut their way out to the north, though Wallace himself was shot from his horse with a fatal wound. At 5:30 p.m. General Prentiss surrendered what was left of his division, and within half an hour the last resistance had collapsed. Some 2,300 Union soldiers were marched to the rear as prisoners, while hundreds more lay dead or wounded in the blood-soaked thickets.

"General Johnston was such a lovable man that his staff as well as his soldiers worshipped him; and his staff seemed stupefied with grief at the great calamity."

LIEUTENANT GEORGE W. BAYLOR

Staff, General Albert S. Johnston

Born on the Texas frontier in 1832, George Baylor was a well-known Indian fighter by the time of the Civil War. As a lieutenant in the Regular Army he served in Arizona in 1861 before accepting the post of aide to General Johnston. After Shiloh, Baylor was given command of the 2d Texas and fought in Louisiana. In April 1865 he shot and killed his commanding officer, Major General John A. Wharton, in a duel in Houston, Texas.

—//—

Major O'Hara then told me that General Johnston was seriously if not fatally wounded, and his staff were looking for a surgeon. Seeing me in the uniform of one, he had come after me. He said the General was in an awfully hot place, but I said I was going to him, and he replied, "We will go together."

We soon joined as sad a group as ever assembled on a battle field or around a dying bed. General Johnston was such a lovable man that his staff as well as his soldiers worshipped him; and his staff seemed stupefied with grief at the great calamity. He was not seriously wounded—a six-shooter navy ball or buckshot had severed an artery just below the right knee, and he had slowly bled to death. There was a little stream of dark blood that had run along on the ground and formed a little puddle six feet from where he was lying. A simple torque made with a stick and a handkerchief would have stopped the flow of blood until medical aid could have been had. Unfortunately, Dr. Yandall had been ordered by the General to stop and attend to a lot of wounded Confederate and Union soldiers. No doubt his kind heart was moved when he saw the old familiar blue uniform and recalled his brother officers and the scenes they had passed through together.

This battle flag was carried at Shiloh by a hard-fighting Confederate outfit. Company A of New Orleans' Crescent Regiment was among the units that accepted the surrender of Federal remnants surrounded in the Hornet's Nest.

The stand at the Hornet's Nest, though ultimately futile, had bought precious time for the Federal army to regain its equilibrium. Sherman and McClernand had been able to retreat with their units more or less intact, and as stragglers were rounded up and brought forward into line, Grant was able to throw together a formidable new defensive position to confront the Rebel onslaught.

FINAL LINE

Following the capture of the Hornet's Nest, an hour of daylight remained for the Confederates to follow up their costly success. But heavy casualties, the intermingling of units from dozens of different brigades, and the death of General Johnston made a coordinated advance impossible. Having battled for 12 straight hours, hundreds of exhausted Rebels simply stopped where they were and began cooking their evening meal, while others wandered off to loot the captured Yankee camps. Far in the rear of his disorganized forces, General Beauregard was out of touch with the situation at the front, and the job of carrying on the fight fell to his subordinates, most of whom had no clear idea of what was expected of them.

While Southern officers attempted to sort out the confusion, Grant continued to strengthen his new line of defense. On the right of the line, he posted the remnants of Sherman's and McClernand's divisions along the Hamburg-Savannah road to screen the long-awaited approach of Lew Wallace's troops down that route. Exasperated by Wallace's dilatory advance from Crump's Landing, Grant was relieved to learn that the 6,000 fresh soldiers were finally nearing the scene of battle.

The lead elements of Buell's Army of the Ohio were also arriving on the field. Buell himself had come ashore at Pittsburg Landing early in the afternoon, and by 5:30 p.m. Colonel Jacob Ammen's brigade had been ferried across the Tennessee. Ammen was accompanied by his division commander—huge, hot-tempered Brigadier General William "Bull" Nelson—who ordered his troops to force their way at bayonet point through the throng of fugitives that obstructed his route of march to the bluffs overlooking the landing. With the remainder of Nelson's division beginning to cross the river, Ammen's brigade filed into line and prepared to meet whatever the enemy would throw against them.

Braxton Bragg, the dour and irascible commander of Beauregard's Second Corps, was one of the few Southern leaders who recognized the importance of pressing the attack before night fell. Seeing that the Yankees were strengthening their defenses opposite the Confederate right, at 6:00 p.m. Bragg instructed two of his brigade commanders to form their ranks for an assault. "Sweep everything forward," the general ordered. "Drive the enemy into the river."

Obeying Bragg's command, Brigadier Generals James R. Chalmers and John K. Jackson led their troops toward the far left of the Federal line. Both brigades had seen heavy fighting earlier in the day, and although Chalmers' soldiers had replenished their cartridge boxes from captured ordnance supplies, Jackson's men were almost out of ammunition and would have to rely on the bayonet alone.

A stream known as Dill's Branch flowed through a steep and brush-filled ravine directly in front of the Yankee line, and this natural moat slowed and disorganized the advancing Southern brigades. Suspecting that the Confederates might attempt to cut him off from the river, Grant had deployed more than 60 artillery pieces along a half-mile front opposite the Rebel right flank, including a battery of siege guns.

Ill tempered and authoritarian by nature, General Braxton Bragg, the Confederacy's eighth-ranking general officer, constantly complained of the poor discipline of his troops. When at his order Colonel Randall Gibson's small Louisiana brigade failed to break the Hornet's Nest line after four bloody repulses, Bragg unjustly accused Gibson of being an "arrant coward."

In a photograph taken shortly after the battle, Federal soldiers stand near the 24-pounder siege guns of Captain Relly Madison's Battery B, 2d Illinois Light Artillery. Intended to besiege Corinth and strengthen Grant's final line of defense, the guns were dragged into line facing south along the road to Pittsburg Landing.

These five huge cannon, originally intended to be used against the defenses of Corinth, hurled their heavy-caliber shells into the oncoming ranks, while on the Tennessee the gunboats *Tyler* and *Lexington* added their salvos to the barrage. The roar and shriek of 53-pound naval shells—exploding overhead and blasting entire trees to splinters—had a demoralizing effect on the Confederate attackers, and when the Yankee infantry opened fire, the Rebel brigades recoiled.

At 6:30 p.m., with the sun going down, General Beauregard decided to call off the assault. He would rest his exhausted troops and resume the offensive on the following morning, April 7. In the meantime Beauregard dispatched news to the Confederate government in Richmond announcing "a complete victory." But as events would soon show, victory was far from won.

All through the hours of darkness, as a chill rain added to the suffering of the wounded and the misery of the men hunkered down in line of battle, the Federal reinforcements continued to arrive. Lew Wallace had finally made his appearance and deployed his fresh division on the Union right, extending the Federal line to the banks of Owl Creek. By midnight four brigades of the Army of the Ohio had dis-

"I propose to attack at daylight, and whip them."

embarked at Pittsburg Landing and taken a position above the Dill's Branch ravine. With more troops arriving by the hour, General Buell hoped to have three divisions on hand by daybreak.

Buell was scornful of the fighting abilities of Grant's soldiers and considered himself independent of Grant's authority. Without consulting his fellow army commander, Buell told his officers to prepare to launch a dawn counterattack.

But Grant was equally determined to seize the initiative from the Confederates, remarking to one of his staff officers, "I propose to attack at daylight, and whip them."

FEDERAL RESURGENCE

General Beauregard's Confederate army was in no condition to resume the offensive on April 7. "Our force was disorganized, demoralized, and exhausted," corps commander Braxton Bragg recalled. Despite the fact that many regiments were nearly out of ammunition, and some entirely so, Bragg observed angrily that officers had failed to provide for their troops: "Although millions of cartridges were around them, not one officer in ten supplied his men, relying on the enemy's retreat." To the rear, however, Beauregard was more sanguine. Unaware that Lew Wallace's division and half of Buell's Army of the Ohio had arrived on the field, Beauregard was confident that all he had to do was hold his ground while Grant retreated across the Tennessee. To Beauregard it seemed highly unlikely that the Federals would attempt to counterattack, and he chose to rest his men rather than have them dig in overnight. But with some 45,000 troops on the field—more than twice what the Rebels had on hand—Grant was determined to strike back and regain the ground that had been lost the previous day.

The lead elements of Buell's army advanced at sunrise, and Nelson's division quickly routed the startled Southern pickets to their front. At 7:00 a.m. Brigadier General Thomas L. Crittenden's division extended Nelson's line to the west, followed an hour later by Brigadier General Lovell Rousseau's brigade of Brigadier General Alexander M. McCook's division. By 8:00 a.m. Buell had 15,000 soldiers in position across a mile-wide front, ready to launch a full-scale assault.

This bugle was shot from the hands of Private Frederick Barnhart of Company B, 15th Indiana Infantry, during the action on April 7. After the battle, Barnhart recovered the battered horn as a memento.

> *"Although millions of cartridges were around them, not one officer in ten supplied his men, relying on the enemy's retreat."*

The flag of the 6th Arkansas Infantry of General Thomas Hindman's brigade bears the so-called silver moon insignia, which was distinctive to units serving in General William Hardee's division.

Shocked at the sudden appearance of the Yankee formations deploying in his front, General Hardee dispatched several brigades at 10:00 a.m. to blunt the vanguard of Nelson's division as it advanced near the peach orchard where so much heavy fighting had taken place the day before. At first the Federals wavered, but Colonel William B. Hazen's brigade shored up the line and pushed on to take part of a Rebel battery. In a desperate effort to maintain the Confederate right flank, brigades led by General Chalmers and Colonels Preston Smith and George Maney again lashed out at Nelson's division. The counterattack gained ground in heavy fighting but was brought to a halt by point-blank canister fire from Captain William Terrill's battery of the 5th U.S. Artillery.

While Nelson was fighting to the east, Crittenden's and McCook's troops—advancing in the Federal center—were slowed by heavy underbrush and faced with stout resistance from a line Bragg had patched together with scattered Confederate units. But on the western edge of the battlefield, Lew Wallace's 6,000-man division had been steadily gaining ground since going on the offensive at 6:30 a.m. Wallace

The 1st Ohio and a battalion of the 15th U.S. Regulars overrun two guns of Captain Robert Cobb's Kentucky battery in the area used as a review field for the Federal camps. William R. McComas, who sketched the action for Leslie's Illustrated, depicted Federal soldiers manning the captured guns. In fact, the artillery pieces had been rendered useless when the Confederate gunners spiked their vents.

was supported by some 7,000 troops formed from the battered remnants of Sherman's and McClernand's divisions, anxious to recapture the camps that had been overrun the previous day. Spirited counterattacks by Daniel Ruggles and Sterling Wood slowed but could not halt the Federal onslaught, and by 11:00 a.m. the Union advance was nearing the intersection of the Corinth and Purdy roads, a half-mile north of Shiloh Church.

Believing there was an opportunity to split the Federal line at the junction of Wallace's and Buell's forces, Braxton Bragg ordered Patrick Cleburne to launch an attack with his brigade. With only 800 fighting men left, Cleburne questioned the wisdom of such a move, but Bragg was adamant and the attack proceeded. Caught in a lethal cross fire, Cleburne's brigade collapsed before the advance of Sherman's and McClernand's men. Benjamin Cheatham led his brigade to Cleburne's support and fiercely assailed the pursuing Federals. Their nerves frayed from the battle on April 6, numbers of Sherman's and McClernand's troops broke for the rear. But when

Rousseau's brigade swung down on Cheatham's flank, the Rebels gave way. With the line restored, the Union juggernaut lumbered on toward Shiloh Church.

At 2:30 p.m. Beauregard issued orders for a general withdrawal toward the defenses of Corinth, and over the next hour he committed his last reserves in an attempt to stem the tide of blue-clad soldiers. Realizing too late that Buell's Army of the Ohio had joined Grant on the field, Beauregard took personal charge of the last-ditch defense, riding among his demoralized troops and exhorting them to a final effort. For a time the remnants of Ruggles' division and Wood's brigade held near Shiloh Church, but soon they too were streaming from the field in retreat. In obedience to orders the Southern soldiers set fire to the tents and equipment in the captured Yankee camps before trudging down the muddy road to Corinth.

With more than two hours of daylight remaining, the Federals might well have pressed on with little effective resistance from their beaten foe. But both Grant and Buell were content to have driven the enemy from the field, while regaining all the

A Federal army sanitation crew burns the carcasses of horses killed in action near the peach orchard at Shiloh. In the battle's grisly aftermath, about 500 horses were found dead on the field.

ground that had been lost the day before. The Union armies had lost more than 13,000 men—11,000 of them in Grant's Army of the Tennessee. And with a quarter of his original force killed, wounded, or missing, Grant considered his troops "too much fatigued to pursue."

The Confederate loss was equally horrific—some 10,700 men—but the blow to Southern morale cut much deeper. Having come so close to victory, to abandon the bloody field where so many comrades lay was enough to shake even the stoutest resolve and raise grave doubts as to the future of the Southern Confederacy in the war's western theater.

DISMAL RETREAT TO CORINTH

As General Beauregard's exhausted Confederate troops stumbled back toward Corinth on April 8, the day after the battle, Nathan Bedford Forrest and 350 of his cavalrymen rode as a rear guard. Right on Forrest's tail came four Federal infantry brigades commanded by Sherman, who intended to make sure that the enemy had in fact cleared out.

Forrest, spoiling for a fight, soon spotted Sherman's skirmishers threading their way through a belt of downed trees—the place became known as Fallen Timbers—and immediately decided to attack. Yelling "Charge! Charge!" he led his troopers forward, bugles blaring and sabers slashing, straight for the spot where Sherman and his aides were observing the action. "We ingloriously fled pell mell through the mud," Sherman recalled, adding that "if Forrest had not already emptied his pistols as he passed the skirmish line, my career would have ended right there."

But Forrest himself careened on too far, outdistancing his men and riding straight into the Federal main line. Finally realizing that he was alone, he whirled his horse and tried to cut his way out. Then, though wounded by a Federal bullet, he reached down, snatched up a Union soldier by the collar, and flung him onto his horse's rump. With a human shield guarding him from further fire, Forrest galloped away, throwing the frightened soldier to the ground when out of range.

The fierce little skirmish at Fallen Timbers proved to be the only notable fight on April 8. General Grant, although he was eager to follow and destroy the Confederate army, feared that neither his exhausted men nor General Buell's troops were up to the demanding task. As Grant wrote, he "had not the heart to order the men who had fought desperately for two days, lying in the mud and rain whenever not fighting," and "did not feel disposed to positively order Buell, or any part of his command, to pursue."

Though unharried by the Federals, the Confederate retreat to Corinth was still a gruesome ordeal, especially for the wounded, who were often piled two deep in crude wagons that lurched and plunged and slithered along the muddy, rutted road. It was all made worse when about nightfall another violent storm hit with driving sleet and hailstones, some of which were, a Confederate officer recalled, "as large as partridge eggs."

Finally Beauregard's half-frozen, bone-weary survivors straggled into Corinth—which itself became a scene of horror as more than 5,000 wounded men were laid out on floors and porches and sidewalks, and surgeons worked around the clock cutting off bullet-shattered limbs. At most 30,000 men remained ready for duty, and 10,000 of those would soon be ill with typhoid and dysentery when Corinth's water supply turned foul.

Grant's and Buell's armies, 70,000 strong, could well have smashed into Corinth after a few days' rest and destroyed Beauregard's crippled force. But Grant, failing to move immediately, had thrown away his chance. By April 11 General Halleck had arrived from St. Louis on a gunboat to take personal command in the field.

Halleck's first move was to rudely shove Grant, whom he still distrusted, into a powerless subordinate position so humiliating that Grant almost resigned from the army on the spot. Halleck then spent three weeks reorganizing his force, dividing it into what amounted to three corps under Generals Buell, Thomas, and Pope. Now leading a huge army of at least 110,000 men, Halleck nevertheless exhibited caution in the extreme, taking almost a month to move the 20 miles from Pittsburg Landing to the outskirts of Corinth. After each short forward move the troops were ordered to lay networks of corduroyed roads. At every stop they dug elaborate entrenchments—just in case, as Halleck constantly imagined, the Confederates counterattacked.

Halleck's extraordinary caution was hardly necessary. Beauregard had in fact received some reinforcements—about 12,000 men led by Major Generals Sterling Price and Earl Van Dorn. But the battered Confederates, at most 55,000 strong, were in no condition to hold off Halleck's juggernaut.

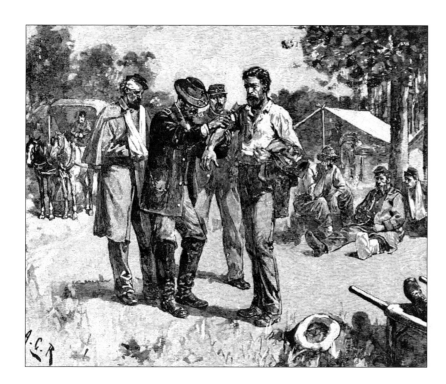

Working hastily during the Shiloh battle, a Federal surgeon examines a soldier's wounded arm while other casualties await their turn for treatment. The tent facility, set up on the second day of fighting, was the first American hospital ever established on a battlefield.

"*The screams from the operating table resounded through the woods.*"

LIEUTENANT WILLIAM C. THOMPSON
6th Mississippi Infantry, Cleburne's Brigade

Lieutenant Thompson joined Company B of the 6th Mississippi—known as the Simpson Fencibles—in July 1861. After the Battle of Shiloh he served with his regiment in most of the battles fought by the Army of Tennessee, until his capture in December 1864 at the Battle of Franklin. Exchanged in March 1865, Thompson was on a medical furlough when the war ended.

T he heart-rending scene at the hospital is one I would like to forget. Piles of dead soldiers were all around, and lying in rows were others who were dying. Doctors and their assistants were moving among the wounded, examining and aiding those who were not beyond help. The screams from the operating table resounded through the woods, for the surgeons were taking off arms and legs of a succession of men carried to them. Teams drawing ambulances were being urged to hasten, hauling the wounded from the field and back to a safer place. Other wagons were collecting and bringing in more wounded. They were being unloaded like so many butchered hogs, and the wagon beds were streaming blood. Once unloaded, the wagons were off to the front again, to collect more unfortunates. Many were dead when unloaded, others died soon afterwards.

The beaten Confederate army evacuates Corinth, Mississippi, as Federal forces under General Halleck advance on the town. When the victors entered Corinth, General Lew Wallace found "not a sick prisoner, not a rusty bayonet, not a bite of bacon—nothing but an empty town."

Opposite: Typical of the Confederates called upon to defend Tennessee, members of the Clinch Rifles, Company A, 5th Georgia Volunteers, lounge before a wall tent with their black servant. In April 1862 they helped guard the Cumberland Gap before participating in the siege of Corinth.

Beauregard's only option was to get his army out of Corinth before it was smashed to bits. To mask the retreat he contrived an ingenious deception. On his orders, dozens of railroad trains were shunted into Corinth, each one greeted with rousing cheers as though they were bringing in a constant stream of reinforcements. The trains clattering into Corinth were in fact empties while those going out were loaded with equipment and supplies Beauregard was trying to save.

The ploy was good enough to fool Halleck, who remained convinced his army was in mortal danger. Finally on May 30, when Buell's and Pope's advance units were poised at last to smash into Corinth, a large explosion rocked the town, plainly indicating that the Confederates were destroying some last bits of ammunition. Rushing in, the Federals found no enemy soldiers, virtually no equipment, and hardly a morsel of food. Corinth had been stripped—except for mocking signs reading, "These premises to let; inquire of G. T. Beauregard," painted here and there by departing Confederates.

Proclaiming his retreat "equivalent to a brilliant victory," Beauregard hustled his army 50 miles south to the area of Tupelo, Mississippi. Once there he was abruptly fired from command by President Jefferson Davis, who was furious that Corinth had been lost without a fight and alarmed that a huge Federal army was ready to rampage throughout the Deep South almost unopposed.

But Davis need not have worried so much. Halleck, satisfied with taking Corinth, was not about to rampage anywhere. Sending General Pope on a brief and half-hearted pursuit of the Confederates, Halleck busied himself sending telegrams to Washington trumpeting his great victory in the battle that never was.

Then, in one of the Civil War's most bizarre moves, he split up his own powerful army, sending Buell off to the northeast on what proved a futile campaign to take Chattanooga, sending Grant to Memphis, and leaving Pope to sit protecting Corinth. In doing so, Halleck all but negated the victory at Shiloh and frittered away a chance, as Grant later wrote, to prosecute a "great campaign for the suppression of the rebellion" that might well have ended the war.

SHILOH CASUALTIES

FEDERAL		CONFEDERATE	
Killed	*1,754*	*Killed*	*1,723*
Wounded	*8,408*	*Wounded*	*8,012*
Missing	*2,885*	*Missing*	*959*
Total	*13,047*	*Total*	*10,694*

OUTFITTING THE RANK AND FILE

T he Civil War soldier carried on his back nearly everything he would need to fight the enemy and survive the elements. Because of shortages of cloth, dye, and leather in the Confederacy, however, Federal troops were generally better equipped than their foes.

The assorted gear of a fully equipped infantryman—shown here and on the following pages—might weigh as much as 50 pounds. To lighten their load, soldiers on campaign often discarded what they viewed as excess items, particularly overcoats and other articles of clothing. One Federal general declared that an "army half the size of ours could be supplied with what we waste."

At the very least, the pared-down veteran had to tote a rifle with bayonet, a cartridge box, a haversack, blankets, and a canteen, all held in place by canvas or leather straps crisscrossing the torso. This burdensome arrangement led one private to complain, "I can appreciate the feeling of an animal in harness now."

Fresh-faced militiamen of the 1st Virginia Infantry, wearing uniforms typical of the early days of the war, exuded confidence and pride. Observed a foreigner visiting the Confederacy in 1861: "Every private feels a determination, not only to carry his regiment through the fight, but to see his country through the War."

SHELL JACKET

Because it was easily manufactured and required less cloth than the frock coat, the shell jacket was authorized by the Confederate Quartermaster's Department as the standard upper garment for enlisted men. The left sleeve of Private John Blair Royal's jacket (right) bears the marks of the Federal shell that wounded him at Chancellorsville.

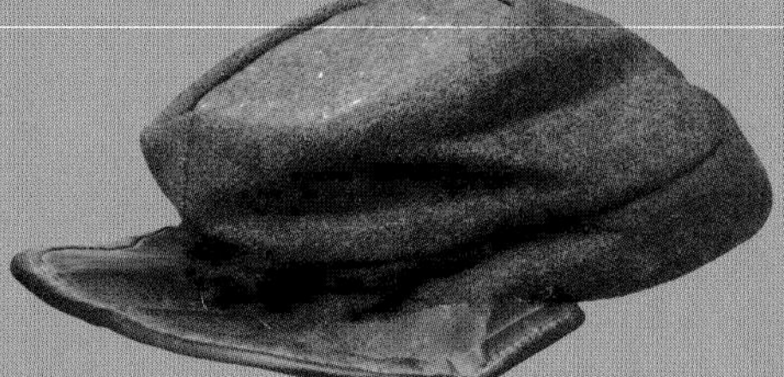

ENLISTED MAN'S KEPI

Despite some difficulty in obtaining materials, Confederate quartermasters supplied kepis, the regulation headgear, throughout the war. This wool jean kepi, with an oilcloth brim, was probably issued by the Richmond clothing depot.

STANDARD ARMY SHOES

Although standard army shoes were made of sturdy leather, they often wore out in 20 to 30 days.

HOMEMADE SOCKS

Soldiers greatly preferred socks knitted at home to the coarse military issue. Mattie Mayo, a nurse's aide in a Richmond hospital, never finished the socks that she was knitting for a Confederate soldier.

SLOUCH HAT

Felt slouch hats were popular among Rebels. Claimed one Virginian, "A man who has never been a soldier does not know the amount of comfort there is in a good soft hat."

RICHMOND DEPOT TROUSERS

Lined with light brown cotton and unbleached osnaburg, these blue wool trousers were probably issued to either Sergeant Major Allen C. Redwood or Private Henry Redwood by the Richmond depot. The buttons are of japanned tin.

SOUTH CAROLINA STATE BUTTON

A HOMESPUN COTTON SHIRT

Confederate infantrymen wore a wide variety of shirts from drab army issue to fancy shirts made from any available fabric including bed-spreads and wildly patterned tablecloths.

HORTER, MAGEE & GEORGE INFANTRY BELT AND PLATE

GEORGIA STATE BUTTON

REBEL WEAPONS AND ACCOUTERMENTS

Confederate infantryman Hugh Lawson Duncan of the 39th Georgia proudly displays a British Enfield rifle musket in this photo, most likely taken at the time of his enlistment in March 1862.

COMB

CANVAS HAVERSACK

.58-CAL. GARDNER CARTRIDGE AND
AMMUNITION PACK, CONFEDERATE-MADE

CAP POUCH AND
PERCUSSION CAPS

MILITIA BOX
KNAPSACK

CHANGE PURSE
AND BANK NOTES

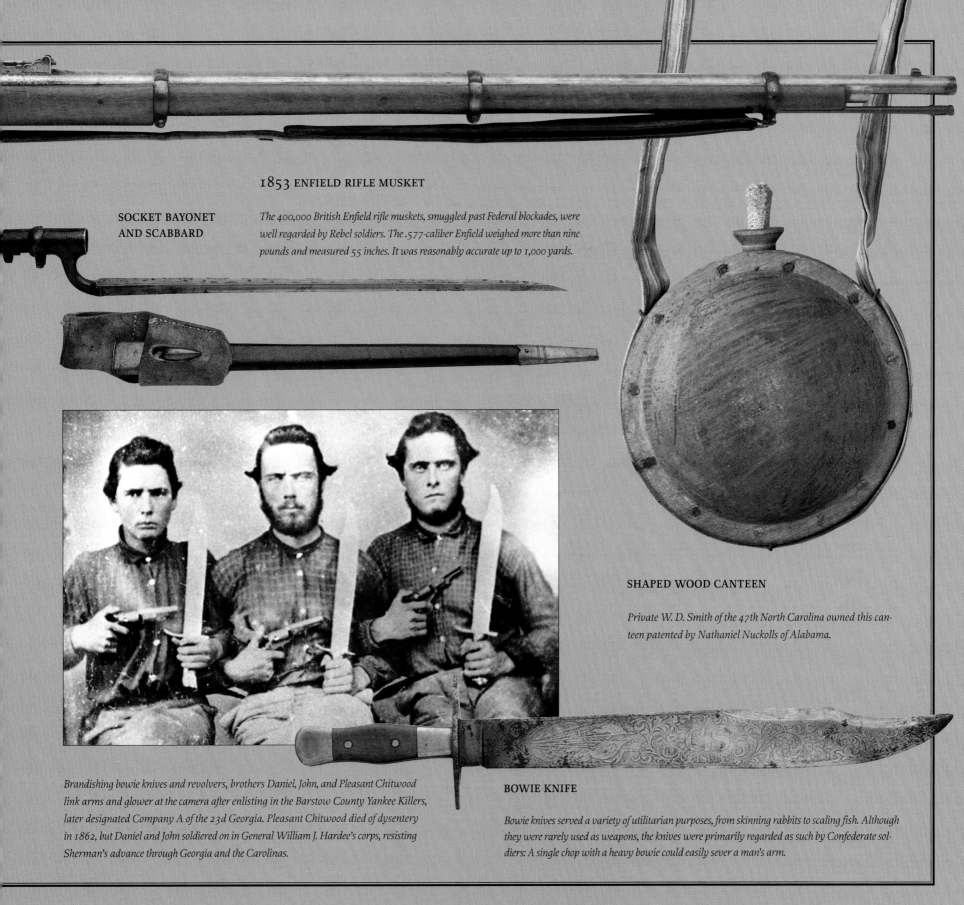

1853 ENFIELD RIFLE MUSKET

The 400,000 British Enfield rifle muskets, smuggled past Federal blockades, were well regarded by Rebel soldiers. The .577-caliber Enfield weighed more than nine pounds and measured 55 inches. It was reasonably accurate up to 1,000 yards.

SOCKET BAYONET AND SCABBARD

SHAPED WOOD CANTEEN

Private W. D. Smith of the 47th North Carolina owned this canteen patented by Nathaniel Nuckolls of Alabama.

Brandishing bowie knives and revolvers, brothers Daniel, John, and Pleasant Chitwood link arms and glower at the camera after enlisting in the Barstow County Yankee Killers, later designated Company A of the 23d Georgia. Pleasant Chitwood died of dysentery in 1862, but Daniel and John soldiered on in General William J. Hardee's corps, resisting Sherman's advance through Georgia and the Carolinas.

BOWIE KNIFE

Bowie knives served a variety of utilitarian purposes, from skinning rabbits to scaling fish. Although they were rarely used as weapons, the knives were primarily regarded as such by Confederate soldiers: A single chop with a heavy bowie could easily sever a man's arm.

UNION INFANTRYMEN DRESSED FOR WAR

FORAGE CAP

This forage cap belonged to Private Jacob Muschbach and bears his company letter atop its red star-shaped XII Corps badge, as well as his regimental numbers denoting the 128th Pennsylvania.

Members of the 8th Kansas Infantry strike a warlike pose in this 1862 photograph. The 8th Kansas saw heavy fighting at the Battle of Chickamauga.

FATIGUE JACKET

After Gettysburg, Sergeant Henry H. Stone's family asked him to send home his jacket (above) as a souvenir. But Stone refused to part with the garment in which he had survived action in five battles, including a gunshot wound at Gettysburg. In May 1864, during fierce fighting at Spotsylvania Court House, Stone was captured and interned at Andersonville, Georgia.

U.S. ARMY CORPS BADGES

The popular corps badges reflected soldiers' pride in their outfits. The shape of the badge denoted the corps and provided a means by which commanders could identify their units in the field.

5TH NEW YORK INFANTRY, V CORPS

132D PENNSYLVANIA INFANTRY, II CORPS

1ST DIVISION VI CORPS

5TH OHIO INFANTRY XII CORPS

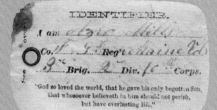

SLOUCH HAT

Soldiers often modified their issue hats by poking them in or creasing them to achieve the effect they desired. Private John M. Mitchell of the 79th Illinois Volunteer Infantry folded in the crown of his Federal-issue Hardee hat (above) in order to lower the crown. The hat was pierced by a bullet at Liberty Gap, Tennessee, in June 1863, but Mitchell was not seriously harmed.

U.S. ARMY IDENTIFICATION TAG

As war casualties mounted, men purchased nametags, which they wore so that their bodies could be easily identified if they were killed in battle. Distributed by the civilian Christian Commission, which provided aid to soldiers, parchment tags like the one belonging to Private Azra Mills of the 9th Maine Infantry (above) were water-resistant.

FEDERAL TROUSERS

Sergeant Charles A. Hunter, whose trousers are pictured here, won the Medal of Honor for his valor during the Federal assault on Fort Gregg outside Petersburg in March 1865.

ENLISTED MAN'S OVERCOAT

Made of jean cloth, this state contract overcoat is typical of the garments produced by private contractors in the first years of the war. A shortage of the regulation sky-blue kersey in 1861 and 1862 resulted in thousands of dark blue, black, and even brown coats.

U.S. ARMY SHOES

Squaretoed brogans, variously called mudscows and gunboats by Federal soldiers, were issued for $1.96 a pair in 1861.

U.S. ARMY ENLISTED MAN'S SHIRT AND NECK STOCK

Generally distributed at the rate of three a year, Federal-issue shirts were often made of heavy, coarsely woven wool that soldiers found uncomfortable next to their skin.

BATTLEFIELD ESSENTIALS

This ambrotype portrait shows an anonymous Federal infantry-man armed with a musket and wearing a knapsack containing blankets, tent basics, and personal items. Ambrotypes were mirror images, thus it should be noted that the Union soldier's haversack, canteen, and bayonet actually would have been worn on the left side and his cap pouch and cartridge box on the right.

CANTEEN

The owner of this 1858 canteen, a member of the 9th Massachusetts Infantry, painted his regimental designation over a I Corps badge.

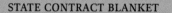

STATE CONTRACT BLANKET

Because woolen mills were unable to supply sufficient cloth to fill the army's demands for blankets, the Quartermaster's Department adopted expedients such as this lightweight brown blanket made of a mixture of wool and cotton.

BROOKS' PATENT TOILET AND WRITING KIT

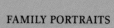

FAMILY PORTRAITS

HAVERSACK

The haversack belonged to Private Edgar S. Yergason during his service with the 22d Connecticut, a nine-month regiment serving in the defenses of Washington, D.C., and at the siege of Suffolk, Virginia.

LEATHER BELT, CARTRIDGE BOX, AND BAYONET SCABBARD

The leather belt, 1855 cartridge box, and bayonet scabbard shown here were captured by the Rebels from a member of General Truman Seymour's division, X Corps, at the Battle of Olustee, Florida, in February 1864.

WALLET AND BANK NOTES

ALMANAC

.58-CAL. CARTRIDGE AND AMMUNITION PACK

HANDKERCHIEF

U.S. MODEL 1861 SPRINGFIELD RIFLE MUSKET

The rugged Model 1861 Springfield saw more action from 1862 through 1865 than any other Federal arm. More than 700,000 of the .58-caliber Springfields—favored over their Model 1855 predecessors for their simple construction and reliability—were manufactured during the war.

SOCKET BAYONET

BIBLE

Antietam
The Bloodiest Day

ACROSS THE POTOMAC—On Wednesday, September 3, 1862, some 40,000 Confederate troops were bivouacked in the fields surrounding the tiny hamlet of Dranesville, Virginia. They were lean and sun-browned, their uniforms soiled and tattered; some were barefoot, and many wore shoes that were in the last stages of dilapidation. But despite their motley appearance, and the exhaustion that followed weeks of strenuous marching, the Rebel soldiers were flushed with confidence. Four days earlier they had achieved the crowning glory of an epic campaign by inflicting a crushing defeat on Major General John Pope's Yankee forces —a victory to be savored all the more because it had occurred at Bull Run, the same battlefield where another Federal army had been put to flight in July 1861.

Then, as now, the vanquished Union troops had pulled back into the defenses of Washington, D.C., leaving a Confederate army poised at the doorstep of the Federal capital. The Southern leaders had failed to follow up their success the preceding year, but now the troops were veterans and their commander a man whose genius for waging war was unexcelled—General Robert E. Lee.

In less than three months the revered commander, known to his admiring soldiers as Marse Robert, had managed to shift the field of operations from the very outskirts of the Confederate capital of Richmond to the environs of Washington. "His army had acquired that magnificent morale which made them equal to twice their numbers," recalled Lieutenant Colonel E. Porter Alexander, "and his confidence in them, & theirs in him, were so equal that no man can yet say which was greatest." Like their leader, the fighting men of the Army of Northern Virginia sensed that the scales of war had begun to tip in favor of the Confederacy.

Never one to rest on his laurels, Lee was determined to exploit the signal victory of Second Manassas—not by assaulting the formidable earthworks ringing Washington but by crossing the Potomac River—and for the first time carrying the war onto Northern soil.

As he outlined his plans in a communication to Confederate president Jefferson Davis, Lee was nursing a painful injury he had sustained the day following the engagement at Manassas. The general had dismounted

Above: The drum shown here was cut down to size so it could be carried by Thomas Floyd, a drummer boy with the 125th Pennsylvania, of Crawford's brigade.

Opposite: From the Maryland shore of the Potomac a Federal scout takes aim at Robert E. Lee's Rebels as they wade across the river from Virginia at White's Ford on September 4, 1862. One of James Ewell Brown "Jeb" Stuart's staff officers commented about the crossing that "there were few moments . . . of excitement more intense, of exhilaration more delightful."

from his favorite horse, Traveller, and was about to examine a map held by one of his staff officers when a gust of wind sent the parchment flapping in the animal's face. The horse shied, and when Lee grabbed for its bridle, he stumbled and fell heavily on his hands. He severely sprained both arms; for the next several weeks they would be splinted and bandaged, with the right arm confined to a sling. Though compelled to ride in an ambulance for several days, Lee shrugged off the inconvenience as he embarked on his daring new strategy.

Although he realized that his troops were undersupplied and numerically inferior to his Federal opponents, Lee felt that his army could "not afford to be idle." With the enemy seemingly in "a very demoralized and chaotic condition," Lee judged the time right to cross the Potomac into Maryland and, if all went well, to continue on across the Mason-Dixon line into Pennsylvania. Lee hoped the invasion would provide a temporary respite to war-ravaged Virginia, allow him to replenish his army's supplies in the verdant farmland of central Maryland and rally pro-Southern Marylanders to the Confederate cause. If and when the Federals sallied out of the Washington defenses, a Southern victory on Northern soil might well force President Abraham Lincoln to the negotiating table.

President Davis acceded to the general's proposal, and Lee's offensive quickly got under way. " 'On to Maryland!' is now the cry," wrote Confederate artillerist

This 1862 photograph of Robert E. Lee was the first picture of him taken after the Civil War began. Lee had recently grown his wiry white beard, which, he told his daughter, "is much admired."

efforts to take Richmond two months earlier, Lee assessed his opponent as "an able general but a very cautious one." If McClellan was true to form, Lee had every reason to expect that several weeks would pass before the reorganized enemy army marched forth to give battle.

The 35-year-old George McClellan possessed a sharp mind and charismatic presence; no officer was more proficient at organizing, training, and inspiring his soldiers. It was McClellan who had raised a magnificent fighting machine from the shambles of the defeat at First Manassas. And yet a year and a half of war had shown McClellan to be so deliberate in his strategy that time and again he had yielded the initiative to his Southern foes. Moreover, his disdain for civilian authority had made him a most contentious subordinate. McClellan seemed to view the Army of the Potomac as his personal property and to have taken a perverse delight in General Pope's misfortunes. Secretary of the Navy Gideon Welles noted that President Lincoln, in tendering command to McClellan, "was greatly distressed," but confessed that McClellan "had beyond any officer the confidence of the army."

"It is an army of which General Lee may well be proud, a better never shouted under a Roman Eagle."

William M. Owen, "and the heads of columns are directed toward the Potomac." On September 4 the lead elements of the Southern force began crossing the river at White's Ford near Leesburg. "Just now it does appear as if God were truly with us," exulted Major Walter Taylor of Lee's staff. "All along our lines the movement is onward." As the regimental bands played "Maryland! My Maryland," the jubilant gray-clad columns emerged on the northern bank of the Potomac and continued toward the prosperous town of Frederick, 11 miles away. "A dirtier, more ragged, exhausted set would be hard to find the world over," Lieutenant John H. Chamberlayne confessed in a letter to his sister; but, he noted, "it is an army of which General Lee may well be proud, a better never shouted under a Roman Eagle." Chamberlayne added: "Whatever Lee's plans are, they will be good, and his army can carry them out."

As his proud fighters pushed on through a pristine countryside as yet untouched by war, Lee learned that the enemy forces at Washington had been placed under the command of Major General George B. McClellan. Having thwarted McClellan's

When an anti-Union riot broke out in his hometown in April 1861, Baltimore native James Ryder Randall, an English professor teaching at a Louisiana college, was moved to write the secessionist poem "Maryland! My Maryland." Set to the music of "Tannenbaum, O Tannenbaum," the song became a favorite among Southerners, who were outraged by the Federal dominance of the state.

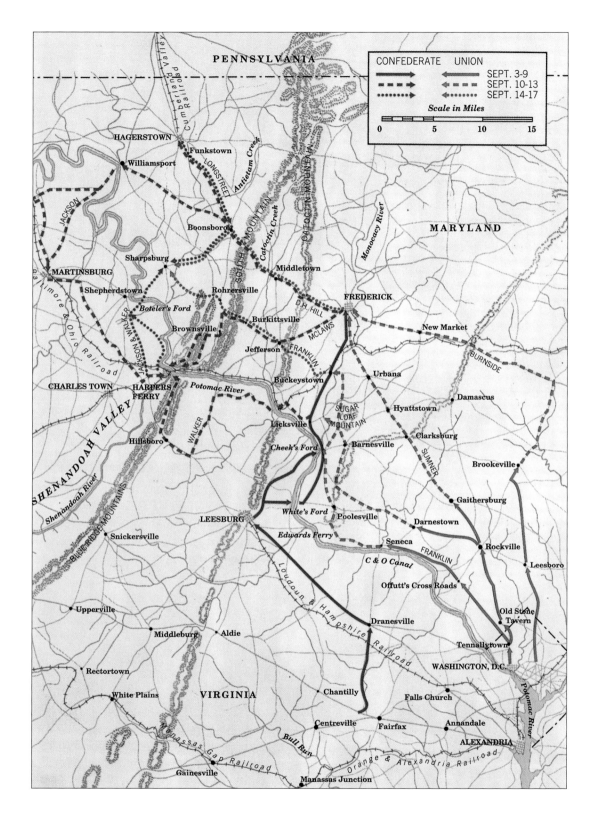

1862

August 28-30	Battle of Second Manassas Pope's defeated Federals fall back to Washington defenses
September 1	Battle of Chantilly
September 3	Confederates move northward
September 4-7	Lee crosses Potomac River
September 5	Federal Army of Virginia and Army of the Potomac consolidate under McClellan's command; Federals begin march into Maryland
September 6	Confederates enter Frederick
September 10	Lee divides his army and moves west
September 12	McClellan reaches Frederick
September 12-15	Confederates besiege and capture Harpers Ferry
September 14	Battles at South Mountain (Turner's Gap, Fox's Gap, Crampton's Gap)
September 15-16	Lee falls back on Sharpsburg; Federals follow up
September 17	Battle of Antietam
September 18-19	Lee recrosses the Potomac
September 20	Battle of Shepherdstown
September 22	Emancipation Proclamation issued
October 1-4	Lincoln visits Antietam battlefield
October 26	Federals begin crossing the Potomac into Virginia
November 7	McClellan relieved of command

Fired by his stunning victory over John Pope's Federals at Second Manassas, Lee wasted little time carrying the war north. After shifting to Leesburg, the Rebel army swiftly crossed the Potomac and reached Frederick, Maryland, on September 6. Pausing there for a few days, Lee then ordered a bold four-way split of his army. Longstreet and D. H. Hill headed north toward Boonsboro and Hagerstown; the rest of the army, divided into three columns under Stonewall Jackson's command, converged on Harpers Ferry. The Federals, now reunited under McClellan, took up the pursuit on September 5. A week later they clashed with the Confederate rear guard at Frederick. All day on September 14 the Federals hammered at the screen of Rebel defenders holding the South Mountain passes, eventually forcing them to fall back that night. The next day, as the Federals ponderously resumed the chase, the garrison at Harpers Ferry surrendered, and Lee ordered his scattered army to recombine with all haste in the vicinity of Sharpsburg.

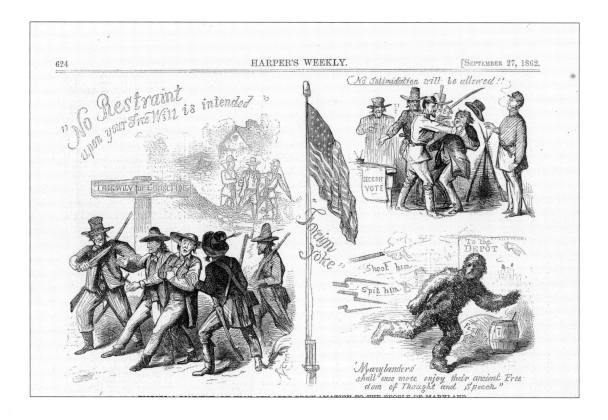

624   HARPER'S WEEKLY.   [September 27, 1862.

Despite the cordiality shown the Army of Northern Virginia by many citizens of western Maryland, Unionist sympathies still prevailed in the region. Farther north, the reaction to Lee's Maryland proclamation was more pronounced, as seen in the September 27 issue of Harper's Weekly (left), featuring cartoons lampooning Lee's purported intent to liberate Maryland from the yoke of Union oppression.

The soldiers' adoration of McClellan was made strikingly evident when "Little Mac" rode forth to greet the disheartened survivors of Pope's debacle at Manassas. "Up went caps in the air and a cheer broke out which, as the news travelled, was taken up and carried to the rear of the column," Brigadier General John Gibbon recalled. "Such cheers I never heard before," noted Lieutenant Stephen Minot Weld

"*The people of the South have long wished to aid you in throwing off this foreign yoke, …*"

Jr.; "Every one felt happy and jolly." Edmund R. Brown of the 27th Indiana thought "every one who was the least discouraged or doubtful before, was now buoyant and full of confidence." Within hours of McClellan's assumption of command, a measure of order began to return to the army as the war-weary troops pitched camp and stragglers made their way back to their units. Major Thomas Hyde of the 7th Maine expressed the prevailing opinion when he wrote to his mother, "McClellan is the only man who can save the country."

In a remarkable display of alacrity for the habitually deliberate commander, McClellan by September 7 had established his headquarters at Rockville, Maryland, 15 miles northwest of Washington. Rather than wait to complete his reorganization in the capital's defenses, McClellan was determined to confront Lee's invasion. Leaving two corps to safeguard the capital, he began shifting his force of some 70,000 men—a tenth of whom were new recruits—in three parallel columns across a 25-mile front. It was far from a lightning advance but much swifter than Lee had expected from the cautious leader of the Army of the Potomac.

As McClellan got his pursuit under way, Lee's forces were converging on the prosperous central Maryland town of Frederick. On September 8, the Confederate commander issued an appeal to the citizens of Maryland, stating: "The people of the South have long wished to aid you in throwing off this foreign yoke, to again enjoy the inalienable rights of freedom, and restore freedom and sovereignty to your state." Unfortunately for Southern hopes, the response to Lee's proclamation was lukewarm at best. Central Maryland proved to be predominantly Union in sentiment, and no groundswell of support was forthcoming.

A subordinate once wrote of Lee that the general was "audacity personified"; and at Frederick the Southern commander devised a plan fully in keeping with his reputation as a military gambler. He would divide his army into four columns, three of which—led by his ablest corps commander, Thomas J. "Stonewall" Jackson—would advance on the town of Harpers Ferry, the strategic Federal stronghold located

Severely devalued by fall 1862, these Virginia bank notes were used by Confederate soldiers to pay for goods as they were passing through Boonsboro, Maryland. Worthless by war's end, the notes were kept by the recipients as mementos of the time Lee's army came to town.

Confederates marching through Frederick call a halt on Market Street in this rare photograph taken from an upper window of J. Rosenstock's store. "They were the dirtiest men I ever saw," a local woman noted, "a most ragged, lean and hungry set of wolves. Yet there was a dash about them that the northern men lacked."

"He was overwhelmed by the ladies, they kissed his clothes, threw their arms about his horse's neck, and committed all sorts of extravagances."

Dubbed the Young Napoleon early in the war, General George McClellan, a brilliant military organizer and administrator, held the unflagging respect and loyalty of those he commanded, sentiments not shared by official Washington. By the summer of 1862 the 35-year-old soldier's career had been blemished by his lackluster performance in the Peninsula campaign, and it was with grave doubts that President Lincoln reconfirmed McClellan as the commander of the Army of the Potomac, saying, "If he can't fight himself, he excels in making others ready to fight."

General McClellan reaches for the hand of a child thrust up to greet him as he rides through Frederick on Dan Webster, his powerful dark bay. "The whole population turned out, wild with joy," a Federal officer wrote. "When McClellan appeared, the crowd became so demonstrative that we were forcibly brought to a halt."

at the convergence of the Shenandoah and Potomac Rivers. By capturing Harpers Ferry, Lee would free the vital corridor of Virginia's Shenandoah Valley from a potential enemy movement to his rear. Jackson would then march to Boonsboro, 20 miles north of Harpers Ferry, and reunite with the remainder of Lee's forces, under the command of General James Longstreet. If all went according to plan, the rendezvous of Jackson and Longstreet would occur on September 12, leaving Lee time to confront McClellan on ground of the Confederate commander's choosing.

With McClellan on the move, haste was vital. And with the issuing of Special Orders No. 191, the Army of Northern Virginia resumed its march, trudging through Frederick on September 10. The Rebels received a decidedly cool reception. "I have never seen a mass of such filthy, strong-smelling men," one local youth recalled. "They are the roughest set of creatures I ever saw: their features, hair, and clothing matted with dirt and filth, and the scratching they kept up gave warrant of vermin in abundance." Some citizens flaunted the Stars and Stripes at the passing columns; John E. Crow of the 12th Virginia remembered a local woman sporting the U.S. flag on her apron. "You are a nice specimen," she snapped, "you miserable ragamuffin rebel!"

McClellan reached the outskirts of Frederick on September 12 and prepared for the next phase of his move against Lee. General in Chief Henry W. Halleck had rejected McClellan's request that the vulnerable garrison at Harpers Ferry be evacuated, and the army commander feared that Lee was indeed moving against the isolated outpost. As so often in the past, Little Mac believed his force to be at a significant numerical disadvantage; he reported to Washington that Lee had "not less than 120,000 men"—far more than the Southern commander actually possessed north of the Potomac.

But McClellan's concerns gave way to jubilation on September 13 when soldiers of the 27th Indiana stumbled on a copy of Lee's Special Orders No. 191, wrapped around three cigars and lying in a field formerly occupied by Southern troops. Apparently a Confederate courier or staff officer had accidentally dropped the document. The discovery provided the Federal commander with a detailed timetable and routes of march for the dispersed Southern columns. If the garrison at Harpers Ferry could continue to hold out, thus frustrating Lee's effort to reunite his forces, the Army of the Potomac would be able to divide and defeat the Rebels in detail. In possession of Lee's plans, McClellan felt that he now held a potentially decisive advantage over his foe, even if the enemy reunited at Boonsboro or Hagerstown. "I think Lee has made a gross mistake," McClellan wired President Lincoln, "and that he will be severely punished for it."

Portions of the Army of the Potomac got under way later that same day, although not with the "forced marches" that McClellan had promised General in Chief Halleck. It would be September 14 before the vast blue columns began wending their way over the Catoctin Mountain range, across the Middletown Valley, and on toward the ridge of South Mountain. McClellan directed his forces in the direction of the two principal gaps in South Mountain. The corps of Major Generals Joseph Hooker

Grateful citizens of Frederick, Maryland, offer food and drink to troops in the vanguard of McClellan's army on September 17, 1862. Only hours earlier, the last of Lee's Confederates had evacuated the pro-Union town.

and Jesse L. Reno were to secure Turner's Gap and push on to Boonsboro. Major General William B. Franklin's VI Corps was given the crucial assignment of advancing through Crampton's Gap—seven miles farther south—and marching to relieve the beleaguered garrison at Harpers Ferry.

As the Federals passed through Frederick, they received a much warmer reception than the Confederates had experienced three days earlier. "The stars and stripes floated from every building and hung from every window," wrote Major Rufus Dawes of the 6th Wisconsin Infantry. "Little children stood at nearly every door, freely offering cool water, cakes, pies and dainties." When McClellan rode past, General Gibbon noted, "he was overwhelmed by the ladies, they kissed his clothes, threw their arms about his horse's neck, and committed all sorts of extravagances."

As McClellan made his triumphant passage through Frederick, Stonewall Jackson was tightening the noose on the Yankee defenders of Harpers Ferry—some 14,000 troops commanded by Colonel Dixon S. Miles. On the afternoon of September 13, two Confederate divisions led by Major General Lafayette McLaws seized the commanding elevation of Maryland Heights, overlooking the town. Meanwhile, Brigadier General John G. Walker's 2,000-man division had occupied Loudoun Heights, which commanded the Shenandoah River flank of Harpers Ferry. Having

Nestled in a spectacular setting, Harpers Ferry could also boast of its strategic location. Situated at the convergence of the Potomac and Shenandoah Rivers and at the site of a Baltimore & Ohio Railroad bridge, it was a vital link in the North's east-west communications. At the same time, Confederates bent on invasion had to have Harpers Ferry to secure a supply line back into Virginia. In this 1862 image taken before the siege, the Potomac flows past Harpers Ferry (right) to its confluence with the Shenandoah River just beyond the town. Crossing the Potomac are the railroad bridge and a half-finished pontoon bridge that would be used by the Federals who abandoned Maryland Heights (left). The promontory to the right, Loudoun Heights, was left undefended by the Federals and became an artillery platform during the siege for John Walker's Confederates.

pushed his hard-marching "foot cavalry" on a wide-ranging arc across the Potomac and south through Martinsburg, Virginia, Stonewall Jackson and the remainder of his force were closing in on the western approaches to Harpers Ferry. On the afternoon of September 14, Jackson's artillery opened a heavy bombardment on Colonel Miles' garrison, now entirely surrounded and unable to offer effective resistance.

Frustrated that his risky plan was two days behind schedule, Robert E. Lee had left the division of Major General D. H. Hill to hold the gaps of South Mountain while he continued on to Hagerstown with Longstreet's corps. Early on September 14, when Lee received word that McClellan was approaching South Mountain in great strength, the Confederate commander ordered Longstreet back to Hill's support. If the Southern troops were unable to delay the Federal columns at South Mountain, Lee risked disaster.

There had been nothing in the lost orders about a Confederate defense of South Mountain; and when the vanguard of McClellan's army encountered stiff resistance there, the Federal commander was caught off guard. For much of September 14, the fighting raged along the National Road as Hooker's troops slowly battled their way up the approaches to Turner's Gap. A mile farther south at Fox's Gap, General Reno's IX Corps reinforced Brigadier General Jacob D. Cox's Kanawha Division in an effort to flank Hill's position. The vanguard of Longstreet's column arrived to shore up Hill's embattled defenders, and as night fell the combat raged on. Eventually Federal numbers told, and both Turner's Gap and Fox's Gap were secured. McClellan judged his success "a glorious victory," but in fact the stubborn Rebel defense had purchased crucial time for Lee's scattered forces.

To Lee, however, time seemed to be running out, and the general reluctantly prepared to call off his invasion of Maryland. Fearing that McLaws' 8,000 men would be ensnared by the southernmost Federal column, Lee ordered that general to evac-

---

"Through God's blessing, Harpers Ferry and its garrison are to be surrendered."

---

uate his position on Maryland Heights. "The day has gone against us," Lee wrote, "this army will go by Sharpsburg and cross the river."

Entrusted with the crucial mission of relieving the garrison at Harpers Ferry, General Franklin's VI Corps managed to disperse the outnumbered Confederate defenders of Crampton's Gap, the southernmost pass in the South Mountain range. Had Franklin pressed on across Pleasant Valley, he might well have broken the siege and surrounded McLaws' force in the process. But believing he faced a superior and well-entrenched foe, the cautious Franklin decided to halt for the night, only six miles from Harpers Ferry.

One of the units that broke out from Harpers Ferry, the 8th New York Cavalry, carried this flag during their harrowing ride north to Pennsylvania, and safety.

Fate again smiled on the Southern cause. On the morning of September 15, Lee received a dispatch from Stonewall Jackson, stating: "Through God's blessing, Harpers Ferry and its garrison are to be surrendered." Nearly 12,500 troops and 73 Yankee artillery pieces fell into Rebel hands. Granted yet another reprieve, Lee reconsidered his decision to abandon Maryland without a fight. Shifting Longstreet's and D. H. Hill's columns toward the little town of Sharpsburg, Lee ordered Jackson to march north immediately and rejoin the rest of the Confederate force. Major General A. P. Hill's division would finish the task of paroling the Federal prisoners at Harpers Ferry, then likewise veer north for Sharpsburg. It was a remarkable turn of events for the Southern leader, whose daring strategy had now paid off. "That Lee was the man for the hour cannot be gainsaid," one Federal soldier admitted, "for, like the successful gambler, he was ever ready to take great chances at desperate odds."

Jackson's three divisions crossed the Potomac near Shepherdstown on the afternoon of September 16 and pushed on to Sharpsburg. His men straggled badly; many had not slept for 48 hours or more. Even with their arrival Lee was still greatly outnumbered by McClellan's forces, who were beginning to concentrate opposite him. McLaws' troops would not arrive at Sharpsburg until the morning of September 17, and A. P. Hill's division even later. Many of Lee's most trusted subordinates doubted the wisdom of giving battle against such odds. But with the future of the Confederacy at stake, the Southern commander was determined to fight before retreating from Northern soil.

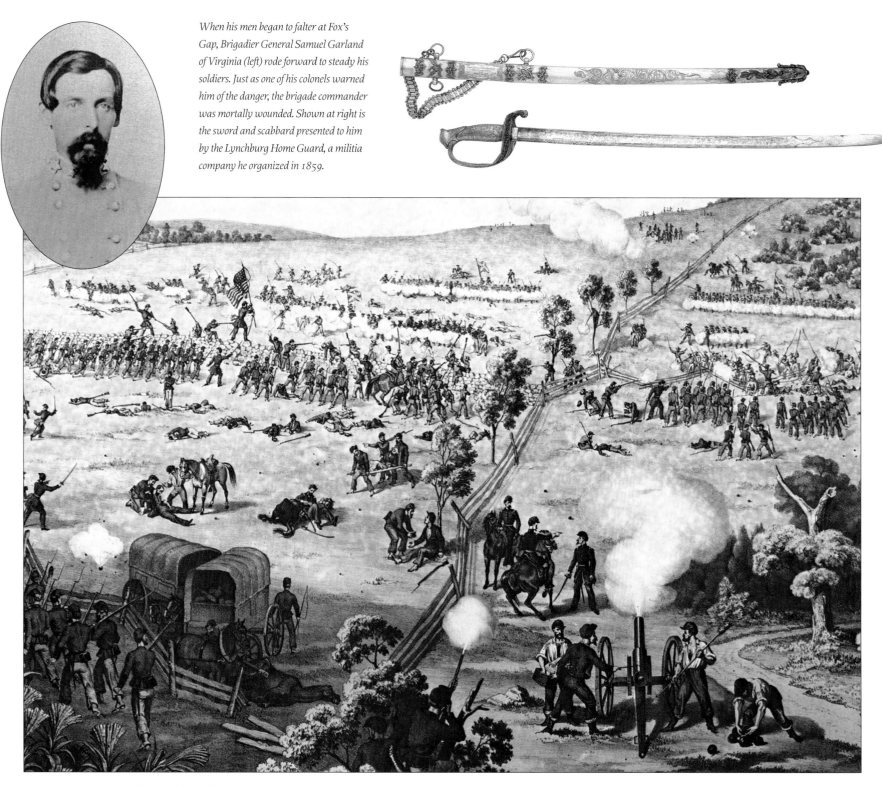

When his men began to falter at Fox's Gap, Brigadier General Samuel Garland of Virginia (left) rode forward to steady his soldiers. Just as one of his colonels warned him of the danger, the brigade commander was mortally wounded. Shown at right is the sword and scabbard presented to him by the Lynchburg Home Guard, a militia company he organized in 1859.

Ohio regiments storm uphill against the 23d and 12th North Carolina Infantry at Fox's Gap. In the left foreground, two soldiers attend to Lieutenant Colonel Rutherford B. Hayes, knocked from his horse by a bullet. Far up the slope, beside the rail fence, Confederate general Samuel Garland falls mortally wounded behind the line of battle.

Throughout September 16 the opposing forces exchanged intermittent shellfire, as McClellan methodically positioned his forces for an assault. The valley of Antietam Creek provided a natural barrier between the two armies, and the Union commander wanted to establish a bridgehead on the western bank of the stream before committing his troops to the offensive. By nightfall of the 16th, Hooker had crossed the stream at a ford north of Lee's position and stood poised with three divisions facing the Confederate left flank. Following a brief but savage skirmish, both sides waited for the dawn and the great bloodletting all knew would come with the rising sun.

SOUTH MOUNTAIN

The first crisis of General Robert E. Lee's daring invasion of Maryland came on September 14, when advance elements of three of General George McClellan's Federal corps arrived at South Mountain, an extension of the Blue Ridge Mountains stretching roughly 50 miles from the Potomac River northward into Pennsylvania. Lee, counting on McClellan to move slowly, had divided his army since crossing the Potomac a week before, leaving only a single division, commanded by D. H. Hill, to hold the passes snaking through South Mountain. Six divisions under Stonewall Jackson were 15 miles to the southwest, laying siege to Union-held Harpers Ferry; the remaining two Confederate divisions under Longstreet were strung out to the northwest between Boonsboro and Hagerstown.

The usually dilatory McClellan, however, had moved westward from Washington to meet the Confederate invasion faster than Lee had anticipated. By the morning of Sunday, September 14, lead elements of three Federal corps were advancing on the roads leading to South Mountain. A swift breakthrough would give McClellan a chance, as he said, "to whip Bobbie Lee," smashing first one part and then another of the Confederate army.

Alerted to his danger, Lee fired off messages instructing Longstreet to hurry back southward and urging Jackson to capture Harpers Ferry with all possible speed and also join up. To the small force he had nearby—some of Jeb Stuart's cavalry and D. H. Hill's brigades—Lee issued a do-or-die order: Turner's Gap, the main pass through South Mountain, "must be held at all hazards."

The battle got under way in earnest about 9:00 a.m. when Union general Jacob Cox, deciding to outflank the Confederates holding Turner's Gap, sent his 3,000-man division from Jesse Reno's IX Corps onto the Old Sharpsburg Road leading to Fox's Gap just to the south. After a bitter, bloody two-hour fight, the Federals managed to rout the Confederate blocking force—General Samuel Garland's 1,000-man brigade—from its defensive positions, killing Garland in the process. The North Carolinians, demoralized by the loss of their leader, fell back toward Fox's Gap.

Now in command of the situation, Cox's Federals moved north along a ridge road toward their main objective, Turner's Gap. But with success in sight, the

"I could see dimly through the dense sulphurous battle smoke and the line from Shakespeare's Tempest flitted across my brain: Hell is empty and all the devils are here."

PRIVATE FREDERICK C. FOARD
20th North Carolina Infantry, Garland's Brigade

After Garland's men finally broke and ran, Colonel Duncan McRae, Garland's successor, tried to stem the rout, but the battered brigade had seen enough fighting for the day. Foard had just returned to the ranks after recovering from a wound received in June. In late 1863 Foard transferred to the cavalry; he was captured the following summer but escaped and served until the war's end.

———————————————— // ————————————————

At last the enemy charged us three lines of battle deep. We resisted stubbornly retarding their progress in our front but being unopposed in the intervals between the regiments they advanced more rapidly and got around both of our flanks and were about to completely surround us which compelled a hasty and precipate retreat with the sure alternative of death or capture.

As I pulled my trigger with careful aim throwing a musket ball and three buck shot into them at not more than twenty yards distant I could see dimly through the dense sulphurous battle smoke and the line from Shakespeare's Tempest flitted across my brain: Hell is empty and all the devils are here. Before I could reload our line broke on both sides of me and it was a sharp run until we had extracted ourselves from the flanking columns. Just as our line broke, Jimmie Gibson from Concord, one of General Hill's old Davidson students was shot down. Texas Dan Coleman . . . had been detailed to the ambulance corps, . . . Jimmie exclaimed, "Great God, Dan don't leave me." Dan ran back in face of the enemy's fire, took Jimmie on his shoulder the enemy's line being not 10 yards distant and ran out with him. . . .

The youngest officer on Stonewall Jackson's staff, 23-year-old Lieutenant Henry Kyd Douglas (left) was a native of nearby Shepherdstown whose familiarity with the area proved immensely valuable to his commander. During the march from Harpers Ferry to Sharpsburg, Douglas scribbled this short note (below) to his father.

Federals were slowed by a makeshift defensive line cobbled together around a couple of guns by a desperate D. H. Hill. Then they were stopped entirely by fresh Rebel brigades that had just arrived from the rear. Suddenly pressed by the Confederates, Cox pulled back before Fox's Gap and waited for reinforcements.

It was not until midafternoon that the first of the remaining three divisions of the IX Corps arrived to support Cox. Meanwhile D. H. Hill's line had been bolstered by his three remaining brigades and, shortly afterward, by two more from Longstreet. Wasting little time, the Confederate commander hurled his troops at the stalled Federals. Badly managed, the counterattack failed; but two more brigades from Longstreet's corps arrived to prevent any decisive breakthrough by the Federals.

More Federal attacks followed. By 4:00 p.m. Hooker's I Corps had finally come up and started to advance, intending to approach Turner's Gap by a sweep around the Confederate left. After a bitter fight, the divisions of Generals John Hatch and George Meade eventually outflanked the lone Rebel brigade under Robert Rodes defending the northerly ridges, then also pushed back some of Longstreet's men who moved up to help.

The commander of the IX Corps, General Reno, had no sooner come on the scene to direct the renewed assault of Rodman's and Sturgis' divisions than a bullet cut him down not far from the spot where General Garland had been killed. Carried off down the mountain, Reno died within the hour. He was the highest-ranking Federal officer to fall during the campaign.

As a diversion for the attacks on the Rebel flanks, General John Gibbon's brigade was ordered to march straight up the National Road into Turner's Gap. Gibbon, fighting hard, neared the crest but was stopped there by Alfred Colquitt's brigade, which was securely positioned behind boulders and stone walls.

At this point, just as Meade and Hatch seemed about to rout the still badly outnumbered Confederate defenders at the northern end of the line, darkness descended and put an end to the fighting. Lee had lost more than 2,000 men, but his force remained intact behind the South Mountain barrier.

While this daylong battle was going on, another Union force, the VI Corps under General William Franklin, attacked Crampton's Gap seven miles to the south—but only after wasting most of the day in reconnaissance and deployment. Finally, around 4:00 p.m., the Federals launched a mass head-on charge that quickly broke Colonel William Parham's Virginia brigade and two cavalry regiments under Colonel Thomas Munford, who were holding the gap. Confederate reinforcements—General Howell Cobb's brigade—climbed the western slope, only to be swept up in the rush to the rear. But Franklin failed to follow up his victory. He told his men to make camp instead of pushing forward six miles farther, as ordered by

Laundry dries on the line behind a farmhouse near the middle bridge spanning Antietam Creek. The quiet countryside around Sharpsburg, settled mainly by hardworking farmers of German and Dutch descent, was untouched by the war until Lee's invasion.

With the two armies massing around their town, residents of Sharpsburg flee westward toward the Potomac River, where bluffs along its banks offer protection from the shells that will soon fill the air. Some residents left for distant towns within the first week or so of the Confederate invasion, but by Sunday, September 14, when the first Rebel cavalry showed up, the roads out of town were fast filling up with troops, making flight from the area a much more difficult proposition. The remaining townspeople found what shelter they could. Some escaped to the river, while others sought refuge in the nearest stone cellar.

McClellan, to help the embattled garrison at Harpers Ferry.

Without Franklin's aid, badly led by the seemingly befuddled Colonel Dixon Miles, and staring down the barrels of Jackson's guns that virtually ringed the town, the defenders of Harpers Ferry shortly gave up, surrendering on the next day, September 15. Into Confederate hands fell 73 artillery pieces, 13,000 small arms, and 12,500 men, the largest capitulation of Federal forces during the war. The surrender also allowed Jackson to start northward along the Charles Town Turnpike to join up with Lee.

For his part, Lee decided to abandon South Mountain and retreat westward, reuniting his army near the small Maryland town of Sharpsburg. There he drew up his divisions on an undulating ridge behind a lazy watercourse called Antietam Creek. McClellan followed, but slowly; his first divisions only reached the east side of the creek on the afternoon of the 15th. Then McClellan paused again, spending an entire day deploying his army—allowing Lee, now reinforced by Jackson, to prepare for what one Wisconsin officer foresaw would be "a great enormous battle, a great tumbling together of all heaven and earth."

"A great enormous battle, a great tumbling together of all heaven and earth."

THE BLOODIEST DAY

The Army of the Potomac began its massive onslaught against Lee's outnumbered forces at dawn on September 17. McClellan intended to launch a series of blows, beginning on the north and extending southward along the front of the Confederate line. As fog hugged the valley of Antietam Creek, the three divisions of Joseph Hooker's I Corps—which had crossed to the west bank of the stream the day before—swept south against the Confederate left, where Stonewall Jackson's men waited near the little church of a pacifist sect called the Dunkers. Behind Hooker, Joseph Mansfield's XII Corps crossed the stream

Major General Joseph Hooker, commander of the Federal I Corps, chafed mightily at the constraints of higher authority. "I don't think Hooker ever liked any man under whom he was serving," a subordinate remarked. "He always thought that full credit was not given him for his fighting qualities."

Confederate brigadier general John Bell Hood, a Kentucky-born West Pointer, was given command of Texas troops when his native state rejected secession. An implacable warrior, Hood possessed, in the words of a contemporary, "a sad Quixote face, the face of an old crusader who believed in his cause, his cross, his crown."

Launching the initial assault of the battle, Federal troops from I Corps charge with fixed bayonets through the Cornfield, on the northern section of the battlefield. They carry their guns at right shoulder shift to avoid entangling the long weapons in the corn or accidentally stabbing their comrades in the ranks ahead.

and prepared to advance in the second wave.

As hundreds of shells from the opposing batteries shrieked and roared over-head, Hooker's troops encountered stiff resistance from Jackson's line. George Meade's and James Ricketts' divisions emerged from the cover of the woods that ringed farmer David Miller's Cornfield, only to be savaged by the volleys of Alexander Lawton's Confederate division, which anchored Jackson's right.

At 7:00 a.m., an hour and a half into the fight, the wavering Rebel line at the Cornfield's southern edge was shored up by Harry T. Hays' Louisiana brigade, nick-named the Tigers, who were in turn brought to a standstill near the East Woods by the last reserves of Ricketts' Federal division. In 15 minutes of combat the Louisianans lost 323 of 500 men; Yankee losses were equally horrific. North and west of the Cornfield, Abner Doubleday's division was gaining ground against Jackson's left, where the fence-lined Hagerstown pike led past the Cornfield's western edge. With the hard-fighting midwesterners of John Gibbon's Iron Brigade in the vanguard, the Yankees cleared the ravaged Cornfield and pushed into the open field beyond, headed for the center of Jackson's line at the Dunker Church.

At the moment that Gibbon's spearhead began to falter, the Federals were hit on the right by a daring counterattack from William E. Starke, who had assumed command of two brigades when division commander John R. Jones was wounded. Emerging from the cover of the West Woods, Starke was shot dead in the forefront of the charge. But his soldiers gained the rail fence along the Hagerstown pike and poured round after round into the Yankee formations. The Federals stood their ground. The Rebels recoiled into the West Woods and again Hooker's corps rolled forward, toward the Dunker Church.

With the Confederate left threatening to collapse, Jackson committed his last reserves—John Bell Hood's division. Battling with characteristic ferocity, Hood's men, including the Texas Brigade, shoved the Federals back across the Cornfield. The Rebels' success cost them dearly, however, with the 1st Texas sustaining the highest casualty rate—more than 82 percent—of any unit of the entire war. Hood had brought Hooker's offensive to a halt, but he was unable to do more. Now Mansfield's 7,200-man XII Corps moved through the East Woods to the battlefield, and the Southerners had to rally to confront this new threat.

Though a veteran with decades of service, Mansfield had never led troops in battle, and most of his men were raw recruits. Consequently, the regiments of the XII Corps failed to form a proper line of battle and advanced in a chaotic jumble. The unwieldy column was caught in a cross fire between Jackson's troops and several brigades of D. H. Hill's division. Mansfield was mortally wounded, and the leading elements of his corps were brought to a standstill at the Cornfield's eastern edge. Lashing out from amid the chaos, George S. Greene led XII Corps brigades in a charge that routed two of Hill's brigades. He drove westward almost to the Dunker Church before the Confederates rallied and repulsed the charge.

By 9:00 a.m. the Federal assaults had ground to a halt. Hooker was wounded, Mansfield dying, and thousands of men had fallen without any appreciable gain.

Captain Houston B. Lowrie of Company C, known as the Orange Grays, of the 6th North Carolina Infantry, was killed during Colonel Evander Law's charge through the Cornfield.

The flag of the 1st Texas, now partially restored, was badly tattered when Private Samuel Johnson of the 9th Pennsylvania Reserves picked it up in the Cornfield.

"The batteries on each side ceased firing until the little party was disposed of."

CAPTAIN WILLIAM W. BLACKFORD

Staff, Major General J. E. B. Stuart

The engineer officer on Stuart's staff, Captain Blackford spent most of the day on the far left of the Confederate line along with two-thirds of the Rebel cavalry. Although Stuart's three cavalry brigades saw little action, his horse artillery under Major John Pelham wrought havoc on the Federals all through the battle from its positions atop Nicodemus Hill and Hauser's Ridge.

Between our cavalry lines and the enemy stood a handsome country house in which, it seems, all the women and children in the neighborhood had assembled for mutual protection, not thinking that part of the country would be the scene of conflict. Between us and the house was a roughly ploughed field. When the cannonade began, the house happened to be right in the line between Pelham's battery and that of the enemy occupying the opposite hills, the batteries firing clear over the top of the house at each other. When the crossing shells began screaming over the house, its occupants thought their time had come, and like a flock of birds they came streaming out in "Mother Hubbards," and even less, hair streaming in the wind and children of all ages stretched out behind, and tumbling at every step over the clods of the ploughed field. Every time one would fall, the rest thought it was the result of a cannon shot and ran the faster. It was impossible to keep from laughing at this sudden eruption and impossible to persuade them to return. I galloped out to meet them and represented to them that they were safe, probably, where they had been, but it was no use; so swinging up before and behind as many children as my horse could carry, I escorted them to our lines and quieted the fears of the party, assuring them that they were not in danger of immediate death. Seeing what was going on, the batteries on each side ceased firing until the little party was disposed of.

Watching from his headquarters at the Philip Pry house on the eastern bluff of Antietam Creek, McClellan was now relying on Edwin V. Sumner's II Corps to break the impasse. With McClellan holding back one division as a reserve, Sumner had led two divisions across the stream in preparation for an assault on the now-depleted center of the Confederate line. But rather than coordinate the movements of his subordinates, Sumner impetuously joined John Sedgwick's division in a charge on the West Woods. The rest of his force veered off to the left toward a sunken farm lane that was being defended by elements of Longstreet's corps.

Pushing past the Dunker Church and into the West Woods, Sumner and Sedgwick at first met light resistance from the Rebel batteries atop a ridge called Nicodemus Hill. Fixated on the guns, Sumner was unaware of the crisis looming on his left until it was too late. Seizing the opportunity to flank the advancing Yankees, Jubal A. Early (who had taken over for the wounded Lawton) and Lafayette McLaws hurled their divisions on the naked left of Sedgwick's division. Unable to deploy their three brigades into an effective front, the Yankees were sent reeling from the West Woods with heavy losses.

While Sedgwick's division was meeting with disaster, French launched the first of three successive assaults on the Confederate center, where the Sunken Road provided a natural trench for the Rebel defenders. Wave after wave of Union troops charged forward, only to be mowed down by their hidden enemy. Hill's and Longstreet's men mounted several counterattacks but were unable to drive back French's soldiers. It was noon before Sumner's remaining division, led by Israel B. Richardson, arrived and swept the Rebels from the Sunken Road, now a corpse-strewn "bloody lane." Though stretched to the breaking point, Lee's center managed to hold along the Hagerstown pike.

Shaken by the carnage and loath to renew the assault in the northern portion of the field, McClellan yet hoped that his left wing, the IX Corps, now under Ambrose E. Burnside, would fulfill his directive to cross Antietam Creek and strike Lee's understrength southern flank. But throughout the morning Burnside had been stymied in his efforts to charge across the southernmost of the three bridges spanning the creek. Despite his vast superiority in numbers, Burnside did not get his troops across the bridge until nearly 1:00 p.m. Once they gained the west bank, however, his divisions rolled forward, fighting their way up the bluffs to the outskirts of Sharpsburg. Once again, disaster loomed for Lee's army. But the Federals were stymied. Burnside's delays had given A. P. Hill time to march his division north from Harpers Ferry, where it had been occupied in paroling captured Yankees. Covering 17 miles in eight hours of forced marching, Hill arrived in the nick of time. By 4:00 p.m. his troops had succeeded in halting Burnside's advance.

Lee's embattled line had held, though at great cost. McClellan, unwilling to risk his last reserves in another attack, was content to maintain his bridgehead on the west bank of Antietam Creek. By late afternoon the fighting was all but over, as both armies, bloodied and dazed by the terrible slaughter, prepared for what many thought would be a resumption of the battle on the morning of September 18.

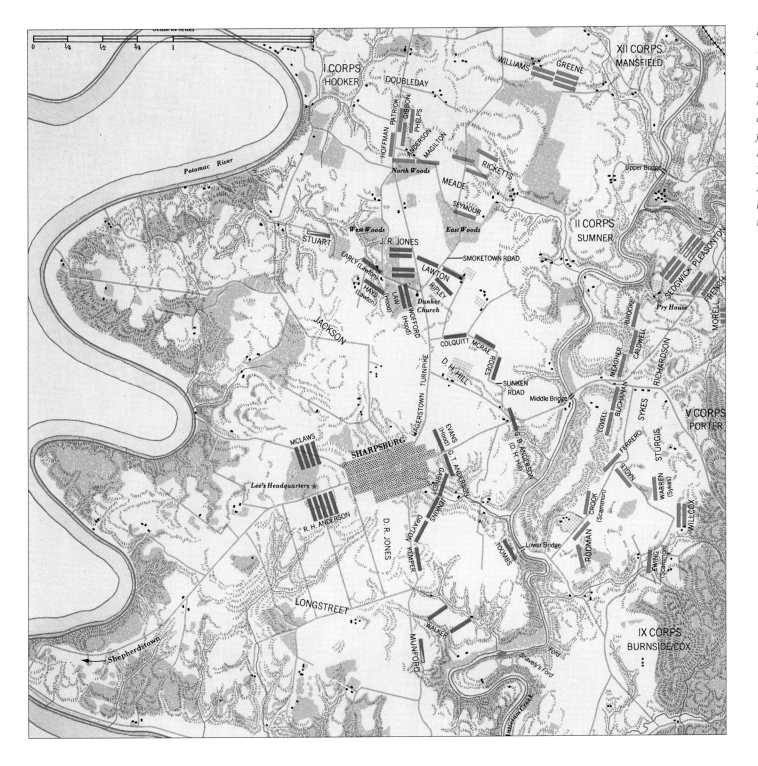

*By dawn on September
17, Lee's army was
arrayed north and east
of Sharpsburg, with two
Rebel divisions in reserve
and another on its way
from Harpers Ferry. Two
Federal corps, the I and
XII, had crossed over
Antietam Creek the night
before and had taken position to open the battle.*

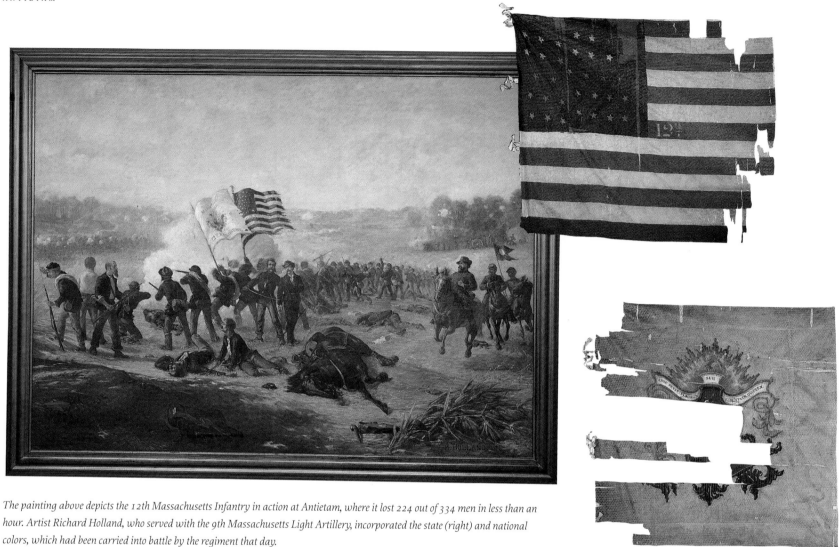

The painting above depicts the 12th Massachusetts Infantry in action at Antietam, where it lost 224 out of 334 men in less than an hour. Artist Richard Holland, who served with the 9th Massachusetts Light Artillery, incorporated the state (right) and national colors, which had been carried into battle by the regiment that day.

EAST WOODS AND CORNFIELD

While Lee was completing his deployments on the afternoon of September 16—placing Jackson on the Confederate left, north of Sharpsburg, and Longstreet in the center—McClellan moved at last. The Federal commander ordered Hooker's I Corps to cross Antietam Creek still farther to the north; he then sent Mansfield's XII Corps across the creek's upper bridge to support Hooker. The Federal attack, with Hooker leading, would hit Jackson's flank at dawn the next morning.

Precisely as ordered, Hooker sent his corps forward at 6:00 a.m. Abner Double-day's division marched south through the morning mist on the Federal right, with Ricketts' division on the left and Meade's troops in the center. Almost immediately, however, as Doubleday's columns emerged from a stand of trees later dubbed the North Woods, more than a dozen Rebel guns under Major John Pelham atop Nicode-mus Hill opened a furious and deadly fire on the advancing Federals. These guns

were joined by Stephen D. Lee's four batteries positioned in front of the Dunker Church. Hooker's guns blasted back, his massed batteries firing from a ridge behind the North Woods and four batteries of big 20-pounders shooting from across Antietam Creek. "Each discharge was at first discernable," a Union colonel later recalled, "but after a little grew so rapid from all the guns brought into play from both sides that it became one prolonged roar."

Under this cannonade, the Federals continued forward. Truman Seymour's brigade of Meade's division on the Union left drove to the southern edge of the East Woods, where it ran into the far right of the Confederate line held by Trimble's brigade, led that day by Colonel James A. Walker. After a deadly exchange of fire, the Federals were forced to take cover back in the woods.

At almost the same moment, Ricketts' lead brigade under Abram Duryée

This Alexander Gardner photograph, taken two days after the battle, looks north from a position just south of the Smoketown road and encompasses much of the open, gently rolling Miller farm property. Barely visible as a white streak at the base of the distant North Woods lies the blood-soaked Cornfield. The guns and men arrayed in the foreground were part of Captain Joseph Knap's Pennsylvania battery, which provided artillery support during the XII Corps attack.

pushed forward to the northern edge of the soon-to-be-infamous Cornfield. After two Federal batteries brought up in support sent a few rounds of canister into the Cornfield, Duryée's men advanced into the head-high corn. They emerged from the south side of the field only to be raked by volleys from a brigade of Georgians commanded by Marcellus Douglass.

The fight continued as the two brigades, less than 200 yards apart, hammered each other; then the skirmish intensified as Seymour's troops rushed to aid Duryée's men and Walker's already bloodied brigade moved west to reinforce the Georgians. "They stood and shot each other," said New York soldier Isaac Hall, "till the lines melted away like wax." Still more Union troops entered the cauldron, William Hartsuff's brigade arriving to back up Duryée and Seymour.

At 6:45 a.m. Walker's Confederate brigade pulled back, having lost 228 of its

"They stood and shot each other till the lines melted away like wax."

nearly 700 men. But Douglass' troops held on—and were reinforced at the last minute by the Louisiana Tigers. The Tigers charged straight ahead, driving the Federals back across the Cornfield with what one Union officer later called "the most deadly fire of the war." Then it was the Tigers' turn as the Federals rolled a battery right into the Cornfield and pounded the Louisianans at point-blank range. As the Tigers staggered back, the last of Ricketts' brigades, under William Christian,

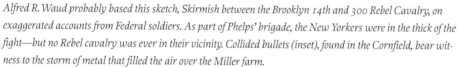

Alfred R. Waud probably based this sketch, Skirmish between the Brooklyn 14th and 300 Rebel Cavalry, on exaggerated accounts from Federal soldiers. As part of Phelps' brigade, the New Yorkers were in the thick of the fight—but no Rebel cavalry was ever in their vicinity. Collided bullets (inset), found in the Cornfield, bear witness to the storm of metal that filled the air over the Miller farm.

Colonel Hugh W. McNeil, commander of the 13th Pennsylvania Reserves, nicknamed the Bucktails for their distinctive cap ornament, was shot down at dusk on September 16 during a firefight between Seymour's brigade and Rebel skirmishers in the East Woods.

came up and charged into the body-strewn field. By 7:00 a.m. the bloodletting had finally forced a stalemate. Both Ricketts' Federal and Lawton's Rebel divisions had been reduced to human wreckage, and neither would see more action that day.

While the slaughter in the East Woods and the Cornfield was going on, Doubleday's division on the Federal right was fighting its way down both sides of the Hagerstown Turnpike. Gibbon's brigade, despite heavy flanking fire from John R. Jones' Confederates, gained a foothold in the West Woods and then advanced farther down the pike, forcing back two Virginia brigades led by Colonel Andrew Grigsby. Quickly, however, another threat appeared as the two remaining brigades from Jones' division, led by General William Starke, rushed from the woods and took cover behind a rail fence bordering the west side of the pike. From there they emptied a murderous fire into the Federal vanguard only 30 yards away. The Federals swiftly wheeled to meet the threat; and shortly two regiments of Gibbon's Iron Brigade were firing on the flank and rear of the Rebel troops, killing Starke and making a grim scene of grotesquely tangled corpses along the rail fence.

With the Confederates now falling back on both sides of the turnpike, Gibbon's men, followed by the brigades of Marsena Patrick and Walter Phelps, surged toward the small white building called the Dunker Church. At this desperate moment, Jackson's main reserve, John Bell Hood's division, stormed past the church and then fanned out. William Wofford's Texas brigade rushed toward the southern edge of the Cornfield, and Evander Law's brigade headed for the East Woods. At the same time D. H. Hill's division marched at a double-quick past the Roulette and Mumma farms to support Hood's counterattack. The Federals, reeling backward, were saved by one of Meade's brigades.

Posted behind a fence at the northern edge of the Cornfield, Meade's men loosed point-blank volleys at Wofford's oncoming troops. The Rebels were also greeted by a hail of canister from guns Gibbon had brought into play, and they were taken in the flank by Federal infantry along the pike. By 7:30 Hood's assault had come to a halt, some of his regiments all but annihilated. Back in the cover of the West Woods, a fellow officer asked Hood, "Where is your division?" "Dead on the field," Hood replied.

Two days after the battle, dead Confederates, probably from Starke's brigade, remain where they fell along a fence line on the west side of the Hagerstown pike. After rushing forward to stem Doubleday's advance, the Rebels were caught in a cross fire that took a heavy toll.

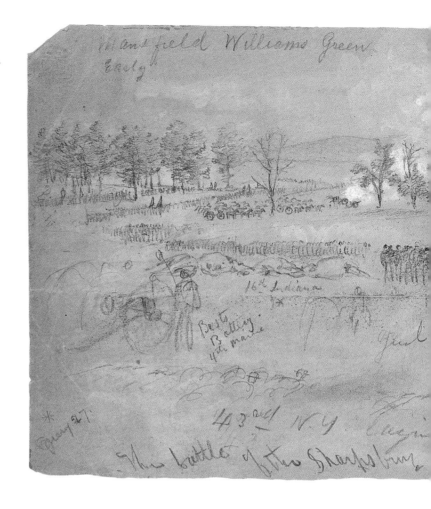

Major General Joseph Mansfield (left), a 40-year Regular Army veteran, had lobbied tirelessly for a field command. When it finally came, it lasted only two days. In this sketch showing the deployment of Williams' division, Alfred Waud indicated Mansfield's position—just left of the two mounted officers—though the general had already been mortally wounded and carried off by the time the battle line had fully deployed as shown.

EAST WOODS TO DUNKER CHURCH

Held in reserve during Hooker's assaults, the 7,200 men of General Joseph Mansfield's XII Corps advanced about 7:30 a.m. to renew the attack on the Confederate left. The corps contained many raw units, however, and getting them ready proved to be a painfully slow operation. Moreover, Mansfield was himself new to battle, in his first field command at the age of 58. Fearing that his untested units might panic and run, he bunched his troops in tight, unwieldy columns, ideal targets for enemy fire. While trying to untangle the confusion, Mansfield was shot in the chest and mortally wounded. Immediately Brigadier General Alpheus S. Williams, the leader of one of the XII Corps' two divisions, took command and managed with surprising speed to get the Federal brigades in line of battle and moving forward.

First to hit the Confederates was Samuel Crawford's brigade from Williams' division, which advanced toward the dreaded Cornfield—only to be savaged by the remnants of Hood's troops in the East Woods and then turned back by Roswell Ripley's brigade, which had moved up from the Mumma farm into the Cornfield. The battle lines in fact had hardly changed since Hooker's initial attacks had begun two

hours before. Confederates still clung to the Cornfield and the nearby East Woods. The West Woods were occupied by remnants of Lawton's and Jones' Confederate divisions. The Cornfield especially was a ghastly charnel house, with hundreds of shattered corpses sprawled amid the stubble. Hundreds more wounded men writhed in agony as the fighting once more raged around them.

Stopped at first, General Williams countered by pushing George Gordon's brigade on the Union right into the pasture north of the Cornfield, where it was quickly caught up in a vicious firefight with Ripley's Confederates. D. H. Hill, meanwhile, rushed his last two brigades into action, sending Alfred Colquitt's men to bolster Ripley's and Garland's brigades—now under Duncan McRae—into the East Woods. At the same time General George Greene launched his Union division into the East Woods, where the brigades led by Hector Tyndale and Henry Stainrook shifted the weight of numbers back in favor of the Federals.

The Confederates held firm at first, peppering the ranks of the oncoming Federals with fire; but then disaster struck. McRae's North Carolinians, many of them

3rd Wisconsin
Col. Ruger Wounded

still shaken by the death of their original leader, Samuel Garland, at South Mountain three days before, overheard one of their officers yelling in alarm, "They are flanking us! See, yonder's a whole brigade!" Shortly one of McRae's regiments panicked, then the entire brigade. "In a moment the most unutterable stampede occurred," recalled McRae, who watched in astonishment as his line melted away and vanished from the field.

The sudden retreat created a dangerous gap in the Confederate defense, and into it charged Greene's Federals. A descendant of Nathanael Greene, a distinguished general of the American Revolution, George Greene spurred his men forward, driving the Rebels from the East Woods and, supported by Gordon's brigade, forcing them to fall back from the Cornfield. With the Confederate flank broken wide open, the Federals advanced along both sides of the Smoketown road, driving fast toward the Dunker Church.

The lead regiment, the 102d New York, moved so fast, in fact, that Greene had to ride forward and order the troops to pause while he brought up supporting

artillery. "You are bully boys," he cried, "but don't go any farther!" Then, with the guns firing, the Federals charged once more. S. D. Lee's Confederate batteries were driven from the strategic high ground to the east of the church, a main objective of the Union attacks all morning.

The Federals, now in control of the narrow battlefield east of the Hagerstown Turnpike, seemed to have cracked Jackson's defenses. Some Union troops had even gotten into the West Woods—although largely by mistake. These were Pennsylvanians from Crawford's brigade who got separated from Williams' division and found themselves in the woods almost at the Dunker Church's front door.

The situation looked so promising for the Federals that General Hooker, riding forward to get parts of his I Corps moving again, was convinced that the Union troops were about "to drive the rebel army into the Potomac or destroy it." Hooker's efforts were frustrated when he was hit in the foot by a Confederate sharpshooter's bullet and, faint from pain and loss of blood, had to be carried to the rear.

In fact this second Federal assault, for all of Greene's efforts, was running out of steam. Hooker's I Corps was badly scattered. The XII Corps had also become disorganized after the hard fighting and swift advance; it had suffered 25 percent casualties. Worse, Greene's regiments were running out of ammunition and faced increasingly heavy fire from Confederates hidden in the West Woods.

Realizing he had to regroup, Greene halted his advance on the eastern edge of the high ground 200 yards from the church and sent men back to round up more ammunition. Soon the firing on both sides subsided and a partial lull descended on the field—where more than 8,000 Americans, about half Union and half Confederate, had already been wounded or killed in the three hours since 6:00. But the fighting was far from over as another massive assault, this time by the Federal II Corps, was about to begin.

Above: After serving for barely a month, Private John Young Shitle of the 48th North Carolina, Manning's brigade, was mortally wounded on September 17 and died three days later in captivity. He may have been hit during Manning's costly assaults on Greene's division, but family tradition holds that he was struck while reading a letter informing him of the death of his young daughter, Esther.

Opposite: Braving a deadly storm of shot and shell, Federal troops from Hooker's I Corps charge toward the Dunker Church (top right) during the early-morning fighting.

Colorbearers of the 34th New York display the regimental and the national flags that they carried into battle at Antietam. In the morning fighting in the West Woods, the regiment, whose ranks had already been badly depleted during McClellan's Peninsula campaign, suffered 154 casualties—nearly half of its strength.

WEST WOODS AND SUNKEN ROAD

After the brief lull about 9:00 a.m., the Federals launched a third attack on Lee's troops. John Sedgwick's division of Edwin Sumner's II Corps forded Antietam Creek and marched straight toward the West Woods. Sumner's objective—like Hooker's and Mansfield's before him—was to smash the enemy's left flank and wheel south for Sharpsburg.

Once near the woods, Sedgwick's men were shelled by Rebel artillery and peppered with musket fire from Jubal Early's brigade, Jackson's last reserve, and from the survivors of the early-morning carnage. But the Federals kept on until, suddenly, a torrent of fire blasted Sedgwick's exposed left flank. The barrage came from reinforcements that Lee, sensing a crisis, had detached from Longstreet's corps and sent hurrying north.

First to hit the Federals were Kershaw's, Barksdale's, and Semmes' brigades from Lafayette McLaws' division. These troops were backed by a brigade led by Colonel George T. Anderson. Soon sheets of fire from the Rebels in the West Woods were blasting Sedgwick's men.

Sedgwick and the 65-year-old Sumner, who rode through the lines frantically waving his hat, tried to turn their brigades to meet the attack, but it was too late. In minutes hundreds of men from Gorman's and Dana's brigades had been cut

Confederate dead, most likely from Captain W. W. Parker's Virginia battery of S. D. Lee's battalion, lie near the scarred Dunker Church. The church suffered extensive damage from all types of rounds. The church's Bible (inset) was taken by a New York soldier as a souvenir and was not returned until after his death years later.

down, while hundreds more were fleeing from the woods and across the Hagerstown pike. By the time Oliver Howard's brigade, bringing up the Union rear, had joined the retreat, Sedgwick had lost almost half of his division—2,255 men killed, wounded, or missing.

Flushed with victory, the Confederates dashed after the Federals, chasing them into the open ground near the pike. Once in the open, however, they were hurled back in turn by devastating fire from I Corps and XII Corps guns positioned to cover the II Corps retreat. McLaws' division lost a third of its men before the lead brigades regained the cover of the woods.

The murderous seesaw fighting continued as George Gordon's brigade from XII Corps, urged on by the now-desperate Sumner, rushed across the Cornfield toward the northern end of the West Woods. But Gordon's men were assailed by Rebels sheltered behind a low ridge in front of the West Woods.

More successful were the XII Corps brigades led by the combative George Greene. Now resupplied with ammunition, they hurled back an assault by Kershaw's brigade, then drove the troops of Manning's brigade 200 yards into the woods behind Dunker Church. No reinforcements arrived to support Greene's near breakthrough, however, and his weary men were eventually forced to retreat by pressure from troops of the brigades of Ransom, McRae, and two regiments under John R. Cooke.

The nearest fresh Federal units were in fact only about a half mile to the southeast—William French's division of Sumner's II Corps, which had followed Sedgwick across Antietam Creek. But French, instead of moving straight ahead, had inexplicably veered south toward the farm of William Roulette—and the center of the Confederate line.

That line was dangerously thin, Longstreet having sent much of his corps north to reinforce Jackson. All that remained were brigades from D. H. Hill's division, three of them badly torn up in the earlier fighting. Fortunately for the Confederates, the two strongest brigades, led by Robert Rodes and George B. Anderson, were in the center. They occupied a superb defensive position—an old, worn-down country lane called the Sunken Road that made an excellent rifle trench. Before the day was over, it would have a new name: Bloody Lane.

French's three brigades moved smartly ahead, pushing back lines of enemy skirmishers, then climbing a ridge and starting down the other side toward the Sunken Road. Rodes' and Anderson's men, almost invisible in their ready-made trench, held their fire until the Federals were so close, recalled the 6th Alabama's John Gordon, "we might have seen the eagles on their buttons."

Finally the Confederates fired a shattering volley at almost point-blank range,

Braving Confederate artillery fire, the three brigades of Sedgwick's division, advancing in a broad front formation, push across open ground toward the West Woods. The artist, James Hope of the 2d Vermont Infantry, condensed some of the action. In reality, the Confederate guns, intended to represent S. D. Lee's batteries, had been driven off before Sedgwick's advance.

Only minutes after he replaced the wounded General Anderson as brigade commander, Colonel Charles C. Tew (above) of the 2d North Carolina was cut down by enemy fire. At right, lying strewn across the Sunken Road are the dead of the 2d North Carolina; the body leaning against the bank at lower right is probably that of Tew.

virtually wiping out the first rank of the Union brigade, led by Max Weber and made up mostly of German immigrants. Another volley felled most of the second rank. Weber's survivors stood bravely for a moment, then fell back behind the crest of the ridge. As they retreated, a second brigade commanded by Colonel Dwight Morris was also shot to pieces, as was a third led by Nathan Kimball.

As the slaughter continued, four more Rebel brigades—Pryor's, Posey's, Cumming's, and Wright's—moved past the Piper farm to support D. H. Hill's position in the Sunken Road, and Israel Richardson's Union division arrived to reinforce French.

The first of Richardson's units to attack, the tough Irish Brigade from New York, led by Thomas Meagher, was cut to shreds like those before. But the next, Caldwell's brigade, urged forward by Richardson himself, managed to get around the Confederate right flank. There Colonel Francis Barlow with two New York regiments

gained a knoll that looked straight down the Sunken Road. Firing madly, Barlow's men turned the road into a slaughter pen of piled and twisted corpses. Anderson's and Rodes' brigades began to crumble and then—partly because of a confusion in orders—fled for the rear.

The Confederate line now broken, the Federals clambered across the bodies in the Sunken Road, then moved toward the Hagerstown pike. In a desperate attempt to hold, D. H. Hill assembled a ragtag band of survivors and attacked, allowing Longstreet enough time to collect 20 cannon near the Piper farm. Their furious fire halted the Federal advance, and French and Richardson pulled their men back to reorganize. Another thrust by William Franklin's VI Corps, poised less than two miles to the northeast, might have crushed the Confederate center and destroyed Lee's army. But the cautious McClellan refused to order Franklin to attack, dooming the battle to continue its murderous course on another front.

"This sunken road, named by some writers 'The Bloody Lane,' was a good many rods long, and, for most of the way, there were enough dead and badly wounded to touch one another as they lay side by side."

SERGEANT CHARLES A. FULLER

61st New York Infantry, Caldwell's Brigade

Sergeant Fuller gave full credit for driving the Rebels from the Sunken Road to Colonel Francis Barlow of the 61st New York, who took over for Brigadier John Caldwell when the general was reported to be hiding behind a haystack in the rear. Promoted to lieutenant in January 1863, Fuller was wounded at Gettysburg and discharged.

As we got a view of the situation it was seen that the rebels were in a sunken road, having sides about four feet in height; this formed for them a natural barricade. Barlow, with the eye of a military genius (which he was) at once solved the problem. Instead of halting his men where Meagher had, he rushed forward half the distance to the rebel line, halted and at once opened fire. We were so near to the enemy, that, when they showed their heads to fire, they were liable to be knocked over. It did not take them long to discover this, and for the most part, they hugged the hither bank of this sunken road. Barlow discovered that by moving his men to the left and a little forward he could rake the position of the Confederates. This he did, and our firing was resumed with vigor. The result was terrible to the enemy. They could do us little harm, and we were shooting them like sheep in a pen. If a bullet missed the mark at the first it was liable to strike the further bank, and angle back, and take them secondarily, so to speak. In a few minutes white rags were hoisted along the rebel line. The officers ordered "cease firing," but the men were slow of hearing, and it was necessary for the officers to get in front of the men and throw up their guns.

Finally the firing ceased, then Barlow ordered the men forward. They advanced on a run, and when they came to the bank of the sunken road, they jumped the rebels to the rear. Those able to move were glad to get out of this pit of destruction. Over three hundred were taken, who were able to march to the rear.

The dead and wounded were a horrible sight to behold. This sunken road, named by some writers "The Bloody Lane," was a good many rods long, and, for most of the way, there were enough dead and badly wounded to touch one another as they lay side by side. As we found them in some cases, they were two and three deep. Perhaps a wounded man at the bottom, and a corpse or two piled over him. We at once took hold and straightened out matters the best we could, and made our foes as comfortable as the means at hand afforded—that is, we laid them so that they were only one deep, and we gave them drink from our canteens.

BURNSIDE BRIDGE

Still feeding his army into the battle piecemeal, McClellan about 10:00 a.m. belatedly ordered Major General Ambrose Burnside's IX Corps to cross Antietam Creek and attack the Confederate right flank. Burnside, thinking he faced a large enemy force, moved cautiously as well. But finally he ordered Brigadier General George Crook's brigade to march toward the handsome stone span crossing the creek below Sharpsburg—known ever after as the Burnside Bridge—and also dispatched Brigadier General Isaac Rodman's division to ford the creek a couple of miles downstream.

The Confederate right was, in fact, held by only five brigades of Brigadier General David R. Jones' division, four of them deployed on ridges south and east of Sharpsburg. Guarding the bridge and its vicinity were three regiments of Georgians and a company of South Carolinians—perhaps 550 men in all—led by Brigadier General Robert A. Toombs.

The Georgians, however, occupied ideal terrain—a steep wooded bluff 100 feet high that loomed over the bridge and the road leading to it on the creek's east bank. The slope was crossed by a stone wall and strewn with boulders that

In the third attempt to take Burnside Bridge, the 51st New York and the 51st Pennsylvania cross the span at last, under fire from Toombs' Georgians along the far bluff. In a change of strategy, the two 51sts charged straight down the hill in front of the bridge rather than approach by the road along the creek. Though stymied at first by Rebel volleys, the Federals ultimately outlasted the Confederates' dwindling ammunition supply.

Considered one of the most promising members of the West Point class of May 1861, 25-year-old Colonel Henry W. Kingsbury was hit four times and mortally wounded while leading the 11th Connecticut in the doomed first charge at Burnside Bridge. The regiment carried the bullet-torn flag at right in the attack and in every fight up to the war's end.

provided Toombs' men with near-perfect rifle pits from which to pick off the enemy attackers.

The initial Federal assaults were fiascos. The men of the 11th Connecticut, deployed as skirmishers for Crook, tried first to gain a foothold on the 125-foot-long bridge. The regiment was quickly thrown back by Rebel fire, losing 139 men—a third of the unit. Then Crook, who had unaccountably failed to scout the terrain, led his brigade of three Ohio regiments blundering into a wood. The troops ended up a quarter mile north of the bridge. Next came James Nagle's brigade from Brigadier General Samuel Sturgis' division. Nagle's attack fell apart when two of his regiments, marching along the road paralleling the creek, were shot to pieces by Toombs' riflemen.

Finally, well past noon, Burnside ordered still another attack by Sturgis' other brigades led by Brigadier General Edward Ferrero. Nearing the bridge, the men of the 51st New York and 51st Pennsylvania ran into such withering fire that they ducked for what cover they could find. At last a handful of Pennsylvanians dashed onto the narrow span—and in a rush the men of both regiments followed.

Firing a few final volleys, Toombs' Georgians ran for the rear—as they had been ordered to do. They were almost out of ammunition and Toombs also knew that Rodman's Federal division, crossing at Snavely's Ford downstream, would soon fall

Federal soldiers pose on the hotly contested Burnside Bridge in this postbattle photograph taken from the wooded bluff on the west bank of Antietam Creek. From this position, General Toombs' Georgians held the bridge for hours, picking off Federals emerging from the tree line beyond the field on the far bank.

CLARA BARTON

Union Nurse

When war broke out, Barton left her job at the U.S. Patent Office to head her own relief agency, which in 1881 would become the American Red Cross. Having followed the Union army to Antietam, Barton was a great help to the surgeons on the field and an invaluable comfort to the wounded Union soldiers. When one surgeon laid eyes on her, he exclaimed, "God has indeed remembered us."

Just outside the door lay a man wounded in the face—the ball having entered the lower maxillary on the left side, and lodged among the bones of the right cheek—his imploring look drew me to him—when placing his fingers upon the sharp protrubrance, he said Lady will you tell me what this is that burns so—I replied that it must be the ball which had been too far spent to cut its way entirely through—

It is terribly painful he said won't you take it out? I said I would go to the tables for a surgeon "No! No!" he said, catching my dress—"they cannot come to me, I must wait my turn for this is a little wound." You can get the ball, there is a knife in my pocket—please take the ball out for me.

This was a new call—I had never severed the nerves and fibers of human flesh—and I said I could not hurt him so much—he looked up, with as nearly a smile as such a mangled face could assume saying—"You cannot hurt me dear lady—I can endure any pain that your hands can create—please do it,—t'will relieve me so much."

I could not withstand his entreaty—and opening the best blade of my pocket knife—prepared for the operation...

I do not think a surgeon would have pronounced it a scientific operation, but that it was successful I dared to hope from the gratitude of the patient.

I assisted the sergeant to lie down again—brave and cheerful as he had risen, and passed on to others.

Returning in half an hour I found him weeping—the great tears rolling silently down his manly cheeks—I thought his effort had been too great for his strength—and expressed my fears—"Oh! No! No! Madam," he replied—"It is not for myself I am very well—but—pointing to another just brought in, he said, "This is my comrade and he tells me that our regiment is all cut to pieces—that my captain was the last officer left—and he is dead."

Oh! God—what a costly war—This man could laugh at pain, face death without a tremor, and yet weep like a child over the loss of his comrades and his captain.

"Oh! God—what a costly war ..."

CLARA BARTON

Federal soldiers, part of a burial detail, stand among Confederate dead on the Miller farm in this Alexander Gardner photograph. Owing to the September heat, most of the dead were quickly buried in mass graves, only to be disinterred later and moved to family plots or other cemeteries.

Several days after the battle, Federal soldiers relax by a dead tree on the Mumma farm. At the foot of the tree is the new grave of Private John Marshall of the 28th Pennsylvania Infantry.

on his flank and rear. Skedaddling fast, the Georgians retreated to positions on another rise a half-mile back. They had done their job, stalling the Federals for three hours.

The bridge secured, the rest of Sturgis' battered division rushed across and soon linked up on the left with Rodman's division and on the right with General Crook's troops, who had discovered a ford 250 yards above the bridge. One strong, swift push, it seemed, would sweep away the Confederate right and possibly destroy Lee's entire army.

But trouble soon developed as General Sturgis, complaining that his troops were low on ammunition and too weary to go on, pulled his division back. As a replacement, Brigadier General Orlando B. Willcox's brigades headed for the front. But with Willcox in reserve a mile east of the creek, more time was lost as his men struggled across the traffic-clogged bridge.

"I have heard of the dead lying in heaps but never saw it till this battle. Whole ranks fell together."

At long last, about 3:00 p.m., the Federals lurched forward, 8,000 men backed by 22 cannon for close support on a front three-quarters of a mile wide. As they came on, one Confederate officer wrote, "the earth seemed to tremble beneath their tread."

Willcox's brigades on the Union right advanced astride the road leading to Sharpsburg. Although harassed by Confederate skirmishers hidden behind haystacks and fences, and hit by blasts from batteries Lee had gathered during the Federal delay, the Federals pushed Joseph Walker's South Carolina brigade back to the outskirts of the town. On the Federal left, Rodman's division, with Colonel Harrison Fairchild's brigade in the lead, charged over a series of ridges and, despite heavy losses from more Confederate batteries, drove back James Kemper's and Thomas Drayton's brigades after a vicious exchange of volleys.

But as the Federals neared Sharpsburg and tried to cut Lee's line of retreat, they were attacked suddenly on the left flank by brigades from the veteran division of Major General A. P. Hill that had just arrived from Harpers Ferry. Hill, alerted by Lee at 6:30 that morning, had marched his men northward at a furious pace, covering 17 miles in less than eight hours. Almost without pausing he threw his 3,000 men into the battle.

Brigadier General Maxcy Gregg's brigade attacked first, hitting Colonel Edward Harland's troops on the Federal far left and throwing back two green Federal regiments with heavy losses. Soon two more of Hill's brigades attacked, punching another hole in the Union line.

With the Federal left broken in a matter of minutes, Brigadier General Jacob Cox—commanding for Burnside on the battlefield—ordered a general withdrawal to the west bank of Antietam Creek. By 5:30 the battle had ended, McClellan refusing to commit reserves that, Longstreet later said, could have "taken Lee's army and everything in it."

The next day, September 18, McClellan failed to attack again or even press his foe, although he could have called on two more fresh divisions just arrived from the rear. Lee for his part called for a truce to bury the dead, then gathered his battered army and retreated to safety across the Potomac at the nearest ford. What might have been a crushing Union triumph—and was certainly the bloodiest one-day clash in American history, with total casualties of 22,717—ended inconclusively in a draw. But Lee's great invasion of the North had been stopped.

RETURN TO VIRGINIA

Dawn of September 18 revealed a scene of unparalleled carnage. More than 22,000 Union and Confederate soldiers had been killed, wounded, or captured. Nearly 4,000 corpses were strewn over the rolling countryside surrounding the shell-torn town of Sharpsburg. The battle along Antietam Creek would stand as the bloodiest single day in American history, and it was a sight no survivor would ever forget.

"I have heard of the dead lying in heaps," Union artillery officer Emory Upton wrote his sister, "but never saw it till this battle. Whole ranks fell together." Stonewall Jackson's aide, Henry Kyd Douglas, recalled: "It was a dreadful scene, a veritable field of blood. My horse trembled under me in terror, looking down at the ground, sniffing falteringly as a horse will over or by the side of human flesh; afraid to stand still, hesitating to go on, his animal instinct shuddering at this cruel human misery."

Both armies were exhausted, and except for a few brief skirmishes and an occasional exchange of artillery fire the day passed without significant fighting. Content with having checked Lee's invasion, McClellan trumpeted the grim stalemate as a great victory, writing his wife, Nellie, "Those in whose judgement I rely tell me that I fought the battle splendidly & that it was a masterpiece of art." With 14 Rebel guns and nearly 40 flags as trophies, the Federal commander informed General in Chief Halleck that "victory was complete." But in reality the victory was far from total.

Despite his army's staggering losses, two of McClellan's corps—the V and VI—had been only partially engaged. Given the Federals' numerical advantage, a renewed offensive on September 18 might well have succeeded in destroying all or part of Lee's forces. But Little Mac was content to rest on his laurels. "Everybody looks pleased," noted McClellan's staff officer David Hunter Strother, "but I feel as if an indecisive victory was in our circumstances equivalent to a defeat."

Confederate officers likewise recognized that McClellan had missed a golden opportunity. "Not twice in a life time does such a chance come to any general," noted Lieutenant Colonel E. Porter Alexander. "The Confederate army was worn & fought to a perfect frazzle."

Although Lee held his ground on the 18th, he realized that to remain north of the Potomac was to court disaster. That night the Army of Northern Virginia pulled back and headed toward a new base of operations at Winchester, Virginia. "We do not boast a victory," admitted Lee's adjutant, Walter Taylor. Some of Lee's officers expressed deep regret at the outcome and questioned the wisdom of Lee's having given battle at Sharpsburg in the first place. But all had nothing but praise for their soldiers, many of whom had paid the ultimate sacrifice for the Confederacy. "The fight of the 17th has taught us the value of our men," Taylor wrote, "who can even when weary with constant marching & fighting & when on short rations, contend with and resist three times their own number."

McClellan's tentative efforts to pursue Lee's column met with near disaster for the Federals on September 20, when troops of the V Corps forded the Potomac south of Shepherdstown. The Confederates counterattacked. While most of the Federals managed to make their escape, the 118th Pennsylvania regiment was cut off and driven over a precipitous bluff, whereupon, as Marylander Jonathan T. Scharf recalled, "our men shot them like dogs in the river." Before risking another crossing, McClellan decided to rest and resupply his war-weary soldiers, many of whom had been lacking proper clothing, footwear, and accouterments since the end of the

---

"The fight of the 17th has taught us the value of our men who can even … resist three times their own number."

Peninsula campaign three months earlier. "I have *hundreds* of men in my command without shoes," General George Meade wrote his wife. "Our artillery horses and train animals have been literally starving." But Lee's ragged and depleted units were in even worse shape; and by failing to press on, McClellan fell into increasing disfavor with President Lincoln and his senior advisers.

But if the great bloodletting at Antietam failed to achieve the decisive victory Lincoln desired, Lee's retreat was at least perceived as a strategic success for the Union. And the president was determined to take moral and political advantage of Lee's withdrawal. On September 22 Lincoln gathered his cabinet and announced his intention to issue the Emancipation Proclamation he had drawn up two months earlier, decreeing freedom for the Confederacy's 3.5 million slaves. The proclamation was decried in the South and hotly debated in the North. Some abolitionists felt the president had not gone far enough. "I can't see what *practical* good it can do now," wrote Massachusetts officer Robert G. Shaw. "Wherever our army has been, there remain no slaves, and the Proclamation will not free them where we don't

go." But Lincoln well knew that by linking the Northern war effort to the abolition of slavery, he was effectively denying the Confederacy any hope of foreign recognition. Because of Antietam and the Emancipation Proclamation, the Confederacy would have to continue fighting alone.

In early October Lincoln visited the Army of the Potomac, ostensibly to learn the details of the recent battle, but in reality to try to get McClellan moving again. The general demurred, as he did again 10 days later in response to the president's written appeal. "Are you not over-cautious when you assume that you can not do what the enemy is constantly doing?" Lincoln asked. "If we never try, we shall never succeed." It was October 26 before McClellan finally got under way, crossing the Potomac and moving southward toward the town of Warrenton, Virginia. But Lincoln had had enough of his cautious army commander. At 11:30 on the night of November 6, McClellan received orders to relinquish command of the Army of the Potomac to Major General Ambrose E. Burnside.

Urging his subordinates to give unqualified loyalty to his successor, McClellan bade an emotional farewell on November 10 to the soldiers who had never ceased to admire and trust the Young Napoleon. Ohioan Thomas Galwey described the "half-shout and half-sob" that swept through the ranks as the general rode past in a last review of the troops, some of whom yelled out: "Send him back! Send him back!" Galwey thought, "A very mutinous feeling is apparent everywhere."

But McClellan departed, and the grumbling gave way to grim determination. "The Army are not satisfied with the change," Brigadier General Winfield Scott Hancock wrote his wife, Almira, "and consider the treatment of McClellan most ungracious and inopportune. Yet I do not sympathize with the movement going on to resist the order. 'It is useless,' I tell the gentlemen around me. 'We are serving no one man; we are serving our country.' "

BATTLE OF ANTIETAM CASUALTIES

FEDERAL		CONFEDERATE	
Killed	*2,108*	*Killed*	*1,546*
Wounded	*9,540*	*Wounded*	*7,752*
Missing	*753*	*Missing*	*1,018*
Total	*12,401*	*Total*	*10,316*

MARYLAND CAMPAIGN CASUALTIES

FEDERAL		CONFEDERATE	
Total	*27,000*	*Total*	*14,000*

Eager to capitalize on the Confederate retreat and the moral impact of the Emancipation Proclamation, Lincoln yearned to pursue the Rebels into Virginia. In a continuing effort to spur McClellan into action, the frustrated president traveled to the battlefield on October 1. Here he is shown conferring privately with his reluctant general on October 4, the last day of his visit. Content with having captured dozens of Confederate flags, one of which is seen in the lower left corner, the Young Napoleon cited numerous excuses for remaining in camp. Lincoln later lamented, "He has got the slows."

REPORTING THE WAR

To meet the public's hunger for war news, a host of reporters, artists, and photographers swarmed over both armies, feeding stories and pictures to local papers and national periodicals such as those below. Although the press was fiercely patriotic, that did not keep an Illinois paper from labeling Lincoln "a worse traitor than Jefferson Davis," while a South Carolina publication described Davis as "this little head of a great country."

The Lincoln administration tried to clamp down on the press in response to what it saw as treasonous abuses of the First Amendment, but eventually it relaxed its restraints. The president, who sometimes did not hesitate to place war needs ahead of constitutional niceties, cautioned one of his generals: "You will only suppress newspapers when they may be working palpable injury to the military in your charge. In this you have a discretion to exercise with great caution, calmness, and forbearance."

The Confederacy was as eager as the Union to censor news about military operations, and met with just as little success. The Southern press, however, did try to maintain public morale, running commentaries and humorous vignettes to boost Southern spirits. But extreme shortages of newsprint and ink, an uncertain postal service, and a populace with little spare money to buy publications forced many Southern papers out of business.

NEW YORK ILLUSTRATED NEWS

HARPER'S WEEKLY
A JOURNAL OF
CIVILIZATION

FRANK LESLIE'S
ILLUSTRATED
NEWSPAPER

THE SOUTHERN
ILLUSTRATED NEWS

As stocks of newsprint dwindled, many Southern editors were reduced to putting out sporadic editions—such as Vicksburg's Daily Citizen—on any paper they could find, including the back of wallpaper.

Correspondents for the New York Herald gather around their paper's ever-moving field headquarters in August 1863; the men had probably covered the Battle of Gettysburg. Like the armies they followed, war correspondents endured extreme weather, poor food, forced marches, even enemy fire. But their dispatches helped readers at home better understand the course of the conflict.

Horace Greeley was owner and editor of the New York Tribune, which had more than a million readers during the war. Solidly behind Lincoln, the paper functioned almost as a government mouthpiece.

In 1861 most of the country's newspapers were printed on hand-fed single-sheet presses (left). As demand for news increased, higher-capacity power presses became more common in the North, but the South, with manpower and paper shortages, had to rely on the simpler machines.

THE NEW SCIENCE OF PHOTOGRAPHY

Introduced in 1839, photography had, by the beginning of the war, developed into a full-fledged industry capable of mass production. Among its most popular products were family groupings, battlefield views, and the *carte de visite*—an inexpensive paper print, often of a soldier proudly posing in his new uniform while looking soulful or brandishing weapons in a warlike manner. Newspapers and magazines, although not yet able to print photographs, reproduced painstakingly hand-engraved versions of them.

The best-known wartime photographer was Mathew Brady, a pioneer in the field who increasingly employed assistants to do the actual work in his studios and at battle sites. Brady was credited with many war photographs he never took; his main accomplishments were to run his business, oversee the work, and use advertising and promotion to make his enterprise famous.

Civil War-era photography was complicated, the equipment bulky and fragile. Working in a horse-drawn wagon fitted out as a mobile darkroom, a photographer began the process by preparing a wet plate-glass negative, using two chemical baths. He then had about 15 minutes in which to slide the plate into a camera set on a tripod, expose it to the view he wished to record, and develop it before it dried. Dust, water, unwanted light, and breakage could ruin the plate. The need for long exposure times—up to 30 seconds even on the sunniest days—limited photography to still subjects. Photographers often staged battlefield scenes, arranging live soldiers or the bodies of dead ones to give the feel of immediacy and drama.

It became common for soldiers to have photographs, such as this one by Mathew Brady, taken with their families and to carry the photographs with them on campaigns and into battle.

In 1861 Mathew Brady was a noted and successful portraitist with thriving studios in Washington, D.C., and New York—and failing eyesight. As the war went on and his vision worsened, he took fewer and fewer images himself, limiting his work to setting up the shots and poses. He so infuriated his staff photographers by taking credit for their work that many eventually left his employ and struck out on their own.

The Civil War-era camera consisted of a set of bulky wooden boxes and a lens. The inner box, loaded with an 8-by-10-inch glass negative, slid forward and back to sharpen the image; the knob on the front moved the lens for finer focus.

This 1864 Brady photograph taken at the Federal supply base at Port Royal, Virginia, shows a mobile darkroom (lower right). Soldiers dubbed the darkroom on wheels a "whatsit" because of its strange appearance. It was simply a delivery wagon made lightproof. Inside the darkroom, the photographer coated glass plates with a light-sensitive colloidal emulsion before exposing them in the camera. After exposure, the negatives were brought back to the darkroom and bathed in a solution to "fix" the image for later printing.

One of the Civil War's most accomplished photographers, Alexander Gardner headed west after the war to record the construction of the railroads. The 1867 image above shows him seated beside his portable darkroom and conferring with an assistant near Fort Riley, Kansas.

This 1864 profile of Abraham Lincoln by Mathew Brady was the model used decades later by sculptor Victor D. Brenner to create the Lincoln penny. The image is shown as it appears on Brady's glass negative and then as a positive print made by direct contact with that negative.

FIELD PHOTOGRAPHERS

Photographing war was a revolutionary idea in 1861. Equally revolutionary was its effect: For the first time in history, a shocked and shaken public saw close-up views of violent death on a massive scale.

Mathew Brady was the leader of this revolution. His genius lay in organizing the biggest and best corps of photographers he could find to go out and capture images of the war, which he sold to newspapers, periodicals, and individuals. Among his most talented lensmen were Alexander Gardner and Timothy O'Sullivan.

Brady's men were soon joined by countless others. More than 300 photographers covered the Army of the Potomac alone. One of them, Captain Andrew J. Russell of the 141st New York Volunteers, was assigned to document the building of military railroads. He seized the chance to photograph Yankee troops preparing for battle and even some of the waiting enemy.

Photographic coverage on the Confederate side was limited. The Union blockade curtailed the importation of photographic equipment and supplies. As more and more Southern newspapers were forced to cease publication, Southern photographers chose not to follow the armies, but to remain in their portrait studios, where they could have at least some income.

TIMOTHY O'SULLIVAN

Cobbler John Burns, who offered his services to the 150th Pennsylvania Volunteers, was the only known civilian to have fought at Gettysburg.

ANDREW J. RUSSELL

A Federal locomotive derailed by Confederate raiders near Brandy Station, Virginia, in 1864.

**UNKNOWN PHOTOGRAPHER,
WORKING FOR MATHEW BRADY**

*Sailors and marines of the U.S. gunboat Mendota on
picket duty at the mouth of the James River.*

ALEXANDER GARDNER

*Officers of the 3d Pennsylvania pose near
Harrison's Landing, Virginia, on the banks
of the James River.*

COMBAT ARTISTS

Nearly as dangerous as being a participant!"—that's how Edwin Forbes, an artist for *Frank Leslie's Illustrated Newspaper*, described the experience of portraying Civil War battles.

Since the technology of the time did not permit combat photography, it fell to sketch artists to create a visual record of the actual fighting. Newspapers and magazines commissioned artists such as Forbes, Alfred R. Waud, Theodore Davis, and Winslow Homer to depict the battles, as well as soldier life.

Accompanying the armies on their campaigns, these artists were in the field and frequently under fire. "To really see a battle," Theodore Davis wrote, "one must accept the most dangerous situations. It is only by going over the actual ground during the battle that one can decide what were its most interesting features."

As the bullets and shells flew and men fell, the artists would make hasty, rough sketches augmented with notes. Later they would expand their sketches into detailed pen-and-ink drawings or watercolors. Rushed to publishers, these pictures would then be rendered into engravings, eventually rolling off the presses to give eager readers a view of the drama of war, often at its most ferocious.

Left: Drummer boys, according to Forbes, were "the most picturesque little figures in the Union army." He added that their pranks and high spirits gave "much life to camp or march."

Below: Forbes marveled at the multitude of mule-drawn supply wagons, such as the one shown here, that traveled with the army and "filled the roads on the march."

EDWIN FORBES

Above: An easel stands ready in Forbes' tent-studio, where he refined his field sketches.

ALFRED R. WAUD

Waud (left) poses for Mathew Brady with his sketch pad and other tools of his trade. The artist accompanied the Army of the Potomac throughout the war, submitting his work to Harper's Weekly. In the Waud sketch below, soldiers of General Winfield Scott Hancock's corps cross the Rapidan River in Virginia on a pontoon bridge at Ely's Ford. In the foreground, a supply wagon splashes across the ford, while cavalrymen patrol the river's banks. All day long on May 4, 1863, seemingly endless columns of the Army of the Potomac crossed the river, heading south toward a fateful meeting with the Rebels at the town of Chancellorsville.

WINSLOW HOMER

Harper's Weekly hired Homer (above) to record the life of soldiers at the front. He often accompanied the 61st New York, using the regiment's men as his subjects. In addition to his work for Harper's, Homer produced a collection of studies he eventually made into oil paintings.

STUDY OF AN INFANTRYMAN

PRISONERS FROM THE FRONT

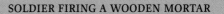

THEODORE DAVIS

A 23-year-old artist for Harper's Weekly, Davis took extraordinary risks to achieve authenticity in his work. Though wounded twice during the war, he managed to publish more than 250 drawings.

SOLDIER FIRING A WOODEN MORTAR

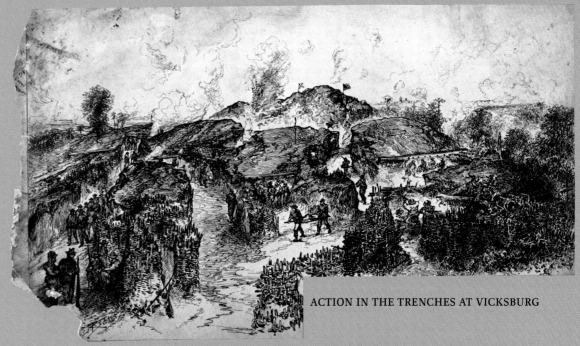

ACTION IN THE TRENCHES AT VICKSBURG

Two Union officers standing just beyond enemy musket range survey Rebel positions southwest of Fredericksburg while their infantrymen take cover in captured rifle pits. On May 3 these troops of William T. H. Brooks' division would advance toward Chancellorsville and suffer a bloody repulse at nearby Salem Church.

Chancellorsville
Rebels Resurgent

INTO THE WILDERNESS—Major General Joseph Hooker, the new commander of the Army of the Potomac who would direct Federal operations at Chancellorsville, got his celebrated nickname, it is said, because of a typographical error. Someone at a New York newspaper, about to print a report of a battle that had

taken place during the abortive 1862 Federal campaign on the Virginia Peninsula, provisionally tagged the story "Fighting—Joe Hooker." The tag was not for publication, but it was printed by mistake and without the dash, so the headline appeared as "Fighting Joe Hooker." The nickname stuck and the general was known ever after as Fighting Joe. Hooker himself professed to loathe the sobriquet. It caused him "incalculable injury," he claimed, by making the public think he was "a hot-headed, furious young fellow, accustomed to making furious and needless dashes at the enemy."

Much of the Northern public seemed delighted, however, when President Abraham Lincoln appointed someone called Fighting Joe to command the army in January 1863. Maybe here was a bold warrior able to smash General Robert E. Lee's stubborn Army of Northern Virginia and send it reeling back toward Richmond. In any case, certainly Hooker could do no worse than his predecessor, Major General Ambrose E. Burnside, author of the catastrophic Federal defeat in December 1862 at the Battle of Fredericksburg.

Lincoln had put Burnside in command the previous November when Burnside's predecessor, Major General George B. McClellan, failed dismally to pursue the Confederates after the Battle of Antietam, giving the masterful Lee two months to reorganize his battered forces—and place them squarely in the Federal army's path near Culpeper, Virginia. Finally losing patience with McClellan's "slows," Lincoln fired him and turned to Burnside in the desperate hope that a change in command would produce some results.

At first Burnside moved swiftly and decisively. Choosing not to attack Lee at Culpeper, he marched the entire Federal army 40 miles southeast around the Confederate flank to the banks of the Rappahannock River across from Fredericksburg.

Burnside's plan called for crossing the river at Fredericksburg and attacking the town head-on, but he stalled,

General A. P. Hill and his nine-man escort came under friendly fire that wounded or unhorsed all except the general himself. Captain James Boswell—Jackson's topographical engineer—was shot from the saddle and killed as he rode beside Hill. One bullet pierced the sketchbook (above) that Boswell carried in his breast pocket.

Hooker assembled his personal staff for a group portrait by photographer Timothy O'Sullivan. The senior officers, seated in front, are (from left) Colonel Henry F. Clarke (chief commissary), General Henry J. Hunt (chief of artillery), Colonel Rufus Ingalls (chief quartermaster), Hooker, and General Daniel Butterfield (chief of staff).

waiting for the pontoon bridges he would need. When the bridging gear finally arrived, Burnside stalled again—giving Lee time to catch up. Within days Lieutenant General James Longstreet had rushed southeast from Culpeper to Fredericksburg with his First Corps and had begun fortifying the heights behind the town. Racing after Longstreet came Lieutenant General Thomas J. "Stonewall" Jackson with his fast-marching "foot cavalry."

Dithering and unable to improvise a better plan, on December 12 Burnside at last moved most of his 120,000-man army across the river and, after another day's delay, ordered a series of suicidal assaults on the dug-in Confederates. The result was a dreadful butchery, with dozens of Union regiments torn to bits by massed Confederate fire as the Federals struggled to cross open fields toward the heights. "We might as well have tried to take Hell," one Union soldier said. The attacks, Longstreet coolly summed up, were "desperate and bloody, but utterly hopeless."

Having sacrificed more than 12,000 men for no gain whatever, on December 15 Burnside pulled his entire force back across the Rappahannock and into the camps around Falmouth. There things went from bad to worse. Appalled by the senseless

"I have seen a whole regiment so drunk that they were hard put to find 15 sober men for picket duty."

killing, troops began to desert at a rate of more than 200 per day. Thousands more fell ill with scurvy and dysentery. Angry and dejected soldiers took to the bottle en masse. "I have seen a whole regiment so drunk," a Pennsylvania soldier wrote, "that they were hard put to find 15 sober men for picket duty."

Burnside made the situation worse by trying to launch another attack, sending his troops trudging westward up the Rappahannock on January 20 toward a pair of fords. There, in theory, they would cross the river and sweep in behind the Confederates. But then rain began to fall in torrents. "The bottom literally dropped out of

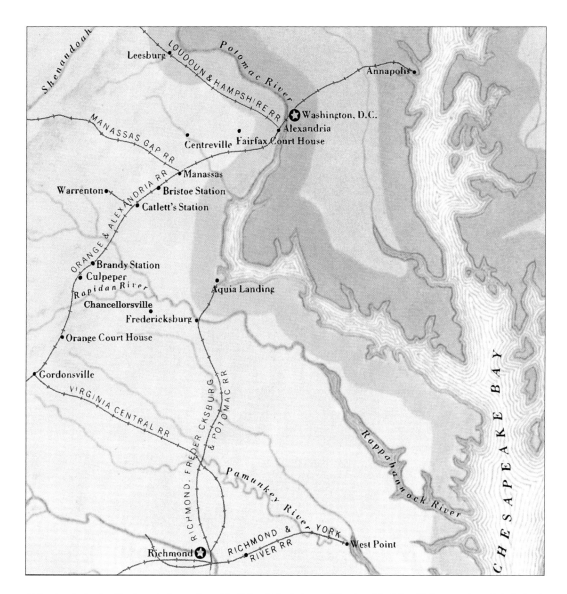

CHRONOLOGY

1862

| December 13 | Battle of Fredericksburg |

1863

January 26	Hooker assumes command of the Army of the Potomac
March 17	Battle of Kelly's Ford
April 5-10	Lincoln visits Hooker; Grand Review of Federal army
April 27	Army of the Potomac begins to move
April 28-29	Federals cross Rappahannock at upper fords and south of Fredericksburg
April 30	Hooker's main force converges on Chancellorsville; Confederates move west to meet the threat
May 1-4	Battle of Chancellorsville
May 1	Hooker pushes east, then orders a recall
May 2	Jackson flanks the Federals and rolls up their right
May 3	Stuart renews attack; Hooker falls back north; Federals take Marye's Heights; Sedgwick repulsed at Salem Church
May 4	Lee turns on Sedgwick; Hooker decides to withdraw
May 5-6	Federals recross the Rappahannock
May 10	Death of Jackson

Following the Battle of Antietam in September 1862, Robert E. Lee's Army of Northern Virginia withdrew southward, deploying in two separate wings near Winchester and Culpeper. In November the new commander of the Union's Army of the Potomac, Major General Ambrose Burnside, shifted his forces east from Warrenton, intending to seize Fredericksburg and descend on a direct route south to capture Richmond. Lee matched the Federal movements in time to turn Burnside back in the first Battle of Fredericksburg in December. Both armies then went into winter camp on opposite sides of the Rappahannock River to await the return of warmer weather and a renewal of the fight.

the whole immediate country," one veteran wrote. Wagons sank up to their axles in mud, and cannon became so mired that in one case 150 men straining on ropes could not dislodge a single gun. After four days of agony, Burnside called off the thwarted attack.

The infamous Mud March sealed Burnside's fate, his officers complaining loudly to the White House and the War Department about his incompetence. Soon after, Lincoln relieved Burnside of command—and named Fighting Joe Hooker to take over.

To many in the army, Hooker was a dubious choice. A West Pointer, he had been brevetted three times for bravery during the Mexican War of 1846-1848, and he had proved a tough, reliable brigade and corps commander on the Peninsula and at Antietam, where he led the first furious attack on the Confederate left. But Hooker was also known for being inordinately ambitious and abrasive, and for singing his own praises to the press. He was, one critic said, "a veritable Bombastes Furioso." He was also said to be fond of the bottle, and he most certainly had a penchant for making blustery, unguarded remarks. Recently he had publicly condemned

Lincoln's handling of the war and called for a dictator to take over.

Lincoln knew well all the negatives, but he had decided to gamble on Hooker's driving energy, his apparent eagerness to fight, and his proven flair as a combat leader. In a forthright letter to Hooker, Lincoln chided him for his outspoken opinions—and then urged him on. "Only those generals who gain successes can set up dictators," the president pointedly wrote. "What I now ask of you is military success, and I will risk the dictatorship." Lincoln then added, "Beware of rashness, but with energy, and sleepless vigilance, go forward, and give us victories." Hooker carried the letter in his pocket and showed it to friends. "He talks to me like a father,"

Hooker ordered each of the seven corps in his army to adopt distinctive insignia to be worn on the soldiers' caps as a ready means of identification. Designed by General Butterfield, the badges proved both utilitarian and a boost to morale. The three insignia above represent (from left) II Corps, I Corps, and V Corps.

"Never was the magic influence of a single man more clearly shown."

he said. "I shall not answer this letter until I have won him a great victory."

But victories would have to wait, Hooker knew, until he had reorganized the demoralized army at Falmouth. To everyone's astonishment, Fighting Joe quickly proved himself an excellent administrator. He mandated new sanitary rules, requiring the use of proper latrines and making the troops clean up and air out their fetid huts. He cut desertions by setting up a liberal system of furloughs. He vastly improved the hospital services.

Hooker also won the men's hearts by forcing the army's vast but laggard supply corps to provide fresh vegetables, mostly onions and potatoes, twice a week. Most surprising of all, he ordered that fresh, chewable bread be delivered at least four times a week, to supplant the usual issue of maggot-infested, tooth-breaking hardtack.

Hooker also insisted that the men exercise. He called for long sessions of close-order drill, and he livened the drill with frequent parades, which he reviewed sitting ramrod straight on a large white horse. Within weeks of Fighting Joe's arrival, a Wisconsin officer wrote home that "the army is in excellent condition as far as the health and spirit of the men are concerned." A Maine captain recalled that "never was the magic influence of a single man more clearly shown."

Hooker also reorganized the army's command structure, dismantling the huge, unwieldy "grand divisions" invented by General Burnside and cutting them up into seven more-maneuverable corps, their commanders all reporting directly to him. To distinguish the corps, Hooker's able chief of staff, Brigadier General Daniel Butterfield, devised a system of badges—various geometric shapes cut from colored cloth—for the men and officers to wear on their caps or hats. The shapes indicated the corps, and the color designated the division within it. A red diamond, for example, was worn by soldiers of the 1st Division of the III Corps, a white diamond by those of the corps' 2d Division.

A black felt hat, belonging to Lieutenant Henry Brewster of the 57th New York, bears the badge of the 1st Division, II Corps.

The emblems did wonders for morale, the men wearing them "like badges of honor." More vitally, the varicolored lozenges and stars and crosses would allow officers to immediately tell even in the heat of battle which units soldiers belonged to.

Even more important for the future, Hooker created a separate cavalry corps modeled on the wide-ranging Confederate legions headed by the famous Major General James Ewell Brown "Jeb" Stuart. Previously, the Union horsemen had been dispersed among the various infantry corps and divisions. Now all Federal troopers would be grouped in an independent three-division corps ready and able to act on its own.

To command the new Federal cavalry, Hooker named Brigadier General George Stoneman, a West Point classmate of Stonewall Jackson's. Stoneman shared some of Jackson's intensity if not his furious combativeness. And if less dashing than Stuart, he would soon be ready to throw a division of his horsemen against the enemy in the first full-scale all-cavalry battle in the East.

The huts of a Federal winter encampment sprawl across a hillside near Stoneman's Switch, a mile from Fredericksburg. The group gathered in the foreground of Andrew J. Russell's photograph includes portly Chaplain Jeremiah Shindel of the 110th Pennsylvania, whose hat bears the white diamond insignia of the III Corps.

Regiments of Confederates relieve the tedium of their winter bivouac near Fredericksburg with a huge snowball fight that ultimately involved 9,000 officers and men. The good-humored battle was touched off on January 29, 1863, by spirited Texas and Georgia troops, many of whom had never seen snow before.

As the armies massed for battle along the Rappahannock, Confederate and Union soldiers engaged in a lively if illicit commerce across the river. On the north bank of the Rappahannock, Union pickets (right) launch a shingle fitted with a paper sail and laden with a cargo of coffee. Confederates across the river wait to return the vessel with tobacco. A Confederate's scrawled message (above, right), shipped aboard a small boat at Fredericksburg, requests coffee and stamps in trade. Officers on both sides generally overlooked such illegal bartering by the troops.

Contemplating his reforms, Hooker was immensely pleased with himself and the situation. He had "the finest army on the planet," he told Lincoln, boasting to the president that it was not a question of whether he would take Richmond, but only when.

Lee's Confederates, camped about three miles away on the other side of the Rappahannock, were in far less happy shape. Fiercely proud of their victory at Fredericksburg, the troops were still freezing and half starved. An officer of a Louisiana brigade reported that of his 1,500 men 400 had no shoes and a great many were also bereft of shirts, socks, and blankets. As for overcoats, they were so rare as to be "objects of curiosity."

Food was desperately scarce, in part because a drought the previous summer had stunted crops. Also at fault were the Southern rail lines that, badly overstrained by the war, struggled to deliver what supplies there were. Shipments were so sporadic that Lee's commissary officers were forced to cut the meat ration to a miserable four ounces of bacon per man per day, and to reduce the sugar ration as well. Vegetables were so scarce that to avoid scurvy Lee ordered each regiment "to send a daily detail to gather sassafras buds, wild onions, lamb's quarter and poke sprouts." Some of Lee's less squeamish troops began to shoot and cook rats—which one of them optimistically claimed "tasted like young squirrel."

Almost as bad from a military point of view, the army's draft horses were in deplorable shape for lack of fodder, long since exhausted in northern Virginia. The animals would have perished by the thousands if forced to pull wagons and guns along muddy roads. This would have left the Confederate army, as Lee said, "destitute of the means of transportation." In short, Lee could not for the moment move his army anywhere, to attack or even shift defensive positions.

Still more critical was a shortage of manpower. At full strength Lee's army was a scant two-thirds the size of Hooker's, and in February he was forced to send Longstreet marching off to southern Virginia with the 13,000 men of John Bell Hood's and George E. Pickett's divisions. A Union corps, it was reported, was moving down the Potomac, which might mean an attack on Richmond. Even after this danger proved illusory, Longstreet stayed south to collect supplies for the army.

These thronging problems made the tightly self-controlled Lee unusually ill tempered and snappish. When his daughter Agnes suggested she come for a visit, Lee wrote back saying, "The only place I am to be found is in camp, and I am so cross now that I am not worth seeing anywhere."

Lee did make one brilliant move, however, during the long winter. His artillery, especially with Longstreet gone, was badly outgunned by the Federals. Hooker had more than 410 cannon, Lee only about 220—and many of the Confederate pieces were old smoothbores. To try to make up for the shortfall, Lee consolidated his field pieces in independent battalions of about 16 guns each, or four batteries. This way he could order scores of guns massed quickly at any crucial spot to blast away at the enemy. In the great battle to come, Lee would use his ability to concentrate artillery fire with devastating effect.

"The suffering from cold, hunger, and nakedness was intense and widespread."

CAPTAIN ALEXANDER C. HASKELL
Staff, Brigadier General Samuel McGowan

While Hooker's Yankees enjoyed their plentiful rations, Lee's Army of Northern Virginia was forced to get by on far less. Haskell, assistant adjutant general for McGowan's South Carolina brigade, was one of seven brothers who fought for the South. He served until the end of the war despite four wounds, one of which cost him his left eye.

That winter was probably the most dreary and miserable we had. It was the first picture the world had of the magnitude and the horrors of our strife, and took our people and our government unprepared. The suffering from cold, hunger, and nakedness was intense and widespread. There were thousands on duty in the perpetual snow and mud, without shoes, often no blanket, hardly any overcoats, and many without coats, nothing often but a ragged homespun shirt. Many received aid from home, but much of this was lost by defective transportation, and for the poor fellows from across the Mississippi nothing could come....

It was at this date the Confederate Congress law was in force, taking away from officers the right to buy from the Commissary rations for their servants, allowing a ration for the officers alone. I went, one day, quite a distance to General Lee's Head Quarters on business. He chanced to come out just as I was taking my leave, and as it was the hour for dinner he politely insisted on my sharing the meal. Of course I could not decline. Entering the tent, there was before us a crude board table with camp stools around it; on it a beautiful glass dish of "Virginia Pickles" sent by some hospitable Virginia lady; the balance of the dinner was a plate of corn bread, or "pones," and a very small piece of boiled bacon. The grand old General said Grace, and as we took our seats he raised the knife saying, "Mike (that was the name of his faithful Irish attendant) has harder work than we have in Quarters, and must be fed," he cut off a thick slice for Mike and, having laid it on the side of the dish, proceeded to help the rest of us and, finally, himself to each a slice but a fraction of Mike's.

ROBERT E. LEE
THE GRAND OLD GENERAL

Though related to the first families of Virginia, Robert E. Lee grew up in genteel poverty. His father, Henry "Light-Horse Harry" Lee, had lost the family fortune before abandoning his family. Robert later claimed he owed everything, including his deep sense of honor, to his mother, Ann. Lee entered West Point in 1825, graduating second in his class, and won a spot in the elite Corps of Engineers. He distinguished himself during the Mexican War and there learned the skills most vital to his future career as a tactician and leader of men. Appointed Superintendent of West Point in 1852, he tightened discipline and raised academic standards. At the onset of the Civil War, Lee was offered command of the Union forces. A Virginian first and foremost, he tendered his resignation from the U.S. Army. "I could take no part," Lee wrote, " in an invasion of the southern States."

Lee wed Mary Custis (left), grand-daughter of Martha Washington, in 1831. They made their home (below) in Arlington, Virginia. A devoted husband and father, Lee greatly missed his wife and seven children during his frequent absences from home.

Robert E. Lee poses with his 8-year-old son Rooney (William Henry Fitzhugh Lee) around 1845. Following in their father's footsteps, Rooney and his older brother Custis became Confederate generals.

Astride his gray mount Traveller, General Robert E. Lee pauses beneath an oak tree with his senior officers to reconnoiter an enemy position. The aggressive strategy Lee embraced after taking command of the Army of Northern Virginia in the spring of 1862 reversed for a time the tide of the Civil War in the eastern theater.

A powerful man, nearly six feet tall, Robert E. Lee was soft spoken, polite and even diffident. On the field of battle, his manner changed. "No man who saw his flashing eyes and sternly set lips," said an observer, "is ever likely to forget them."

On the table at right are Lee's sword belt, field glasses, Colt navy revolver, hat and gauntlets. Below the table are his riding boots. The camp table itself was carved for Lee by his mess boy: the removable top was a checkerboard on the reverse side.

Confederate cavalry general Fitzhugh Lee (left) helped bring about the battle at Kelly's Ford by issuing a challenge to his old friend William Averell (seated, far left), commander of a Union cavalry division. The two men had been classmates at West Point. Averell secured a victory of sorts, and many considered the battle a turning point in the fortunes of the Federal cavalry in the East. Whatever advantage that was gained, however, was largely tossed aside several weeks later when the bulk of Hooker's cavalry arm went off on Stoneman's ill-fated raid.

Major John Pelham became one of the finest artillery commanders in the Confederacy—known throughout Lee's army as the Gallant Pelham. The death of the young major at Kelly's Ford, at the age of 25, occasioned widespread grief. General Jeb Stuart issued an order stating that Pelham's "noble nature and purity of character are enshrined as a sacred legacy in the hearts of all who knew him."

The two armies, both engrossed in solving their various problems, had little contact through the late winter except for an occasional skirmish. Until, that is, the cavalry battle near Kelly's Ford.

The raid was the brainchild of Brigadier General William W. Averell, a division commander in General Stoneman's new Federal cavalry corps. In mid-March, with the roads firming up, Averell thought it would be a fine idea to test out his troopers by riding westward up the Rappahannock, crossing at Kelly's Ford, and driving away some Confederate horsemen known to be in the area.

Averell was also responding to a Confederate challenge. The leader of the Rebel cavalry regiments near Kelly's Ford was Brigadier General Fitzhugh Lee, a nephew of Robert E. Lee, whom Averell had known at West Point. A rival then—both were

---

"The gallant Pelham will be mourned by the nation."

---

superb horsemen—Fitz Lee had recently led a sharp little raid across the river and taken 150 Federal cavalrymen prisoner. He had also left a note daring Averell to "return my visit." If he did, Averell was to bring along a sack of coffee, a rare luxury for the Confederates though plentiful in Union commissaries.

Averell mustered six regiments of Union horsemen and parts of two others, about 3,000 men in all, plus a battery of horse artillery. With the 4th New York Cavalry in the lead, the Federal force reached Kelly's Ford early on the morning of March 17.

At first the raid did not go well. Scanning the far bank, the New Yorkers spotted a spiked wooden barrier blocking the road. To help smash the obstacle, 20 dismounted troopers from the 16th Pennsylvania came up armed with axes and waded into the frigid river water. They were immediately driven back, however, by heavy fire from the Confederate defenders.

With that, Averell brought up two guns, which began blasting away at the Rebels. Under cover of the artillery fire, Lieutenant Simeon Brown and a detachment of 18 Rhode Island troopers rode into the ford, followed by the ax-wielding Pennsylvanians. Only three of Brown's brave Rhode Islanders made it to the far shore, but they and the Pennsylvanians somehow managed to reach the barrier and hack it apart. In minutes, more men of the 1st Rhode Island had made it across and scattered the enemy pickets.

Fitz Lee, hearing of the fracas, swiftly rode forward from his headquarters at Culpeper, deploying his 800 troopers between Kelly's Ford and Brandy Station, a small town on the Orange & Alexandria Railroad that Lee assumed was Averell's target. As his skirmishers rode forward, however, Lee found to his surprise that Averell's men were mostly in defensive positions a mere mile and a half from the ford. Averell

had decided not to charge blindly ahead into an all-out fight with Lee and his seasoned horsemen.

Averell also faced—though he did not know it—Stuart himself and the star artillerist Major John Pelham, the hero of a half-dozen previous battles, including Antietam and Fredericksburg, for his daring use of his guns.

Stuart and Pelham, who by chance had both been nearby on separate errands, arrived just as Fitz Lee ordered one squadron of the 3d Virginia Cavalry to dismount and fire at some Federals positioned behind a stone wall. The rest of the regiment, backed by the 5th Virginia, made a mounted charge.

Pelham, dashing up on his borrowed mount, joined in the charge of the 5th as the troopers were pouring through a gap in the stone wall. Just then a Federal shell exploded with a huge roar just above Pelham's head, hurling him from his horse. He lay on the ground apparently unhurt, his eyes open and his heart beating. But a fragment from the shell had pierced the back of his head. Carried to Culpeper, the much loved and admired Pelham died only moments after surgeons located the tiny wound. His body, taken to Richmond, lay in state in the capitol before being returned to his native Alabama. "The gallant Pelham," Jeb Stuart said, "will be mourned by the nation."

At Kelly's Ford on March 17, the 1st Rhode Island and 6th Ohio ride headlong into the 4th Virginia (far left) in one of the war's first large-scale cavalry charges.

Edwin Forbes, an artist working for Frank Leslie's Illustrated Newspaper, sketched Sergeant Major William J. Jackson in a Federal camp near Fredericksburg. Jackson's unit, the 12th New York, was among dozens of "two-year" regiments whose terms of service were due to expire in early May. The loss of these veteran soldiers was a matter of grave concern to Northern leaders.

Moments after Pelham was wounded, the Federals countercharged and retook the stone wall. At the same time Colonel Alfred N. Duffié, Averell's boldest subordinate, made a charge of his own, his troopers hurling back the Confederates and killing or capturing a good number of Lee's Virginians.

These successes, though, did not tempt Averell to pursue very far, and when he heard from a prisoner that he faced Jeb Stuart as well as Fitz Lee he "deemed it proper

to withdraw." Bugles sounded recall and the Federals made their way back across the Rappahannock. Behind him Averell left a sack of coffee and a brief note: "Dear Fitz. Here's your coffee. Here's your visit. How do you like it?"

This rousing set-to took place on Saint Patrick's Day. Less than three weeks later, on the Easter weekend, President Lincoln sailed down the Potomac to visit Hooker and spur him on. The president was beset by criticism of his handling of the war, the roads were drying out, and Hooker had boasted that his force was ready.

To impress and entertain his guest, Hooker staged a pair of soul-stirring shows. First, 15,000 men of General Stoneman's Cavalry Corps paraded out on a large field

---

"Dear Fitz. Here's your coffee. Here's your visit. How do you like it?"

---

for Lincoln to review. A couple of days later Hooker mustered two-thirds of his entire force for what was known ever after as the Grand Review—85,000 infantrymen marching past the smiling president in massed formations two companies wide, battle-torn flags whipping in the breeze. The huge parade was, one officer said, "the most magnificent military pageant ever witnessed on this continent."

Hooker also had welcome news for the president. In a matter of days he would launch his great campaign. First to move would be General Stoneman with 10,000 of his troopers. They would ride well up the Rappahannock, cross that river, then ford the Rapidan and fall on the rear of Robert E. Lee's army, cutting its supply routes and communications.

This initial move was thwarted when torrential rains once again pelted down, swelling the rivers and making the upstream fords impassable for almost two weeks. But by April 25 Hooker had elaborated a new and still bolder plan. Three of his infantry corps would follow the cavalry upstream, cross at several fords, and double back toward a country crossroads called Chancellorsville, thus enveloping Lee's far left. At the same time other corps would remain around Fredericksburg to threaten Lee's right flank or move where they were needed most.

The plan, Hooker wrote the president, could hardly fail. His main fear, he said, was that Robert E. Lee and his army would at the first show of force retreat so fast as to "escape being seriously crippled." It was a curious notion to have about an enemy general who never before had panicked, or fled, or done anything but fight tooth and nail. This Lincoln knew, and Hooker's blithe confidence worried him.

But this time Lee's army, still lacking Longstreet's two divisions, numbered only about 60,000 men, less than half the size of the huge Federal force of 130,000. It remained to be seen what Lee would do as Fighting Joe sent six of his corps stepping out toward their first objectives on the morning of April 27.

Alfred R. Waud sketched the review of Brigadier General John Buford's cavalry division on April 9, 1863—one of a series of military pageants held during President Lincoln's visit to Hooker's army. The two officers riding behind General Buford (foreground) are Irish-born Captains Joseph O'Keeffe and Myles W. Keogh.

COLLISION AT THE CROSSROADS

General Hooker's scheme for his attack on Robert E. Lee's Confederates was daring, complex, and Hooker was convinced, as brilliant as the battle plans of the great Napoleon himself. First he would detach a third of his army, three entire infantry corps, and send them on a wide flanking move more than 20 miles up the Rappahannock to cross at Kelly's Ford. Once across the river, the three corps would turn abruptly left and march back southeast toward Fredericksburg, fording the Rapidan River and massing around a country crossroads known as Chancellorsville, after the Chancellor house, the white-columned mansion and sometime inn that sat by the road.

At the crossroads the flanking force would meet up with Major General Darius N. Couch's II Corps, which would cross the Rappahannock after the advancing columns had cleared the downstream fords of enemy pickets. If all went well, Hooker would have more than 70,000 men poised to smash the exposed left flank of Lee's army.

Above: From winter camp north of the Rappahannock, the Army of the Potomac's V corps embarks in late April on the march around Lee's flank—56 miles in four days. "This march was a very trying one," wrote a member of the 5th New York Zouaves (foreground). "The roads were strewn with knapsacks and superfluous clothing accumulated during the winter months, which were thrown away by the men."

Dozens of Civil War units marched to war in flamboyant uniforms inspired by the exotic regalia of the French Army's Zouaves, such as this one, worn by Private George F. Murray (right) of the 114th Pennsylvania Infantry. Murray survived the war and continued to wear his repaired Zouave jacket (far right).

"Since we crossed the Rappahannock in such style, fording the Rapidan shoulder deep by moonlight, Hooker's stock is rising."

Hooker opened the campaign by sending the V, XI, and XII Corps across the Rappahannock and Rapidan in a wide flanking movement to get well around Lee's left. Converging on Chancellorsville, they were joined first by the II and shortly after by the III Corps, both of which had crossed at the closer-in United States Ford. Lee, preoccupied by the two Federal corps still remaining at Fredericksburg, was slow to see the danger at first, sending only one division to counter the massive Federal concentration to the west. Soon, however, he ordered most of his army under Jackson to march west, leaving only a small force to guard Fredericksburg.

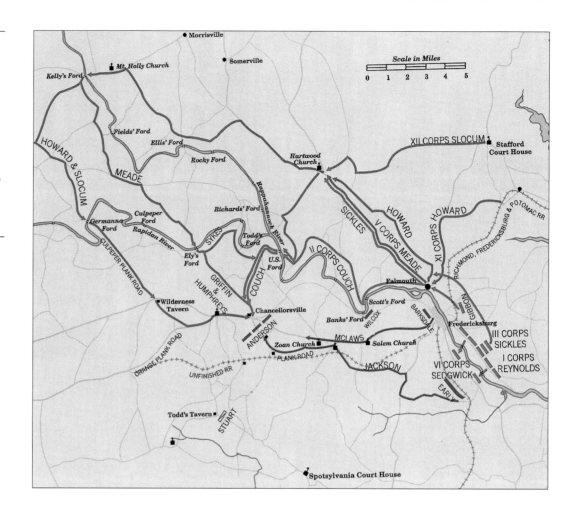

To mask this huge envelopment and confuse the enemy, Hooker designed a pair of deceptions. Major General John Sedgwick would take his VI Corps along with Major General John F. Reynolds' I Corps across the Rappahannock just south of Fredericksburg and deploy as if to attack Stonewall Jackson's troops on the Confederate right. At the same time Major General Daniel E. Sickles' III Corps and a II Corps division led by Brigadier General John Gibbon would stay in their camps across the river, looking threatening—and ready to move wherever needed.

The huge maneuver began on the morning of April 27 as the three corps making the longest flanking march moved out, flags fluttering and drums beating a smart cadence. Well fed and drilled through the late winter, the men were mostly cheerful and glad to be going somewhere at last. Even the roads were in good shape, as one Connecticut soldier noted optimistically, "too wet for dust, too dry for mud."

Leading the long Federal column was the XI Corps, commanded by Major General Oliver O. Howard, a 32-year-old West Pointer from Maine. A conscientious officer, Howard was nonetheless young and inexperienced in command. Among

several of his corps' regiments that were made up largely of German immigrants he was also an object of ridicule—in part because, being a puritanical Yankee, Howard strongly disapproved of the beer and schnapps the devoted, hard-fighting volunteers thought they deserved after a tough day's work.

Behind Howard's troops came the XII Corps, led by Major General Henry W. Slocum, an older West Pointer and veteran commander. Last in line was the V Corps, commanded by Major General George G. Meade. Sleepy-eyed, dour, and often irascible, Meade was not much loved by his men either—his aides called him Old Snapping Turtle—but he was a thorough professional whose troops had attacked with skill and courage at the doomed Battle of Fredericksburg in December, punching the only hole made all day in the Confederate defenses.

As the three corps marched on, it became hot, and some of the foot-slogging troops collapsed by the side of the road. Others lightened their backbreaking 60- to 80-pound packs by flinging away coats, blankets, tents, and other gear—not thinking that heavy rains might fall later. The entire force spent the night of the 27th near Hartwood Church; by late on the 28th Howard's men had reached Mount

"It was during these last happy days that he sat for the last picture that was taken of him ..."

MARY ANNA MORRISON JACKSON

Wife of Lieutenant General Thomas J. Jackson

The campaigns of 1862 and the hard winter following the Battle of Fredericksburg had separated General Jackson from his wife for a year, and he had yet to see the baby daughter born to them during that time. Eagerly anticipating their arrival in the spring of 1863, Jackson wrote, "I am beginning to look for my darling and my baby...." Seen here with her daughter, Julia, in a photograph taken some years after her husband's death, Anna remembered that visit in April as the family's happiest time together.

On the 23d of April (the day she was five months old) General Jackson had little Julia baptized. He brought his chaplain, the Rev. Mr. Lacy, to Mr. Yerby's, in whose parlor the sacred rite was performed, in the presence of the family, and a number of the staff-officers. The child behaved beautifully, and was the object of great interest to her father's friends and soldiers....

It was during these last happy days that he sat for the last picture that was taken of him—the three-quarters view of his face and head—the favorite picture with his old soldiers, as it is the most soldierly-looking; but, to my mind, not so pleasing as the full-face view which was taken in the spring of 1862, at Winchester, and which has more of the beaming sunlight of his *home-look*. The last picture was taken by an artist who came to Mr. Yerby's and asked permission to photograph him, which he at first declined; but as he never presented a finer appearance in health and dress (wearing the handsome suit given him by General Stuart), I persuaded him to sit for his picture. After arranging his hair myself, which was unusually long for him, and curled in large ringlets, he sat in the hall of the house, where a strong wind blew in his face, causing him to frown, and giving a sternness to his countenance that was not natural....

My visit had lasted only nine days, when early on the morning of the 29th of April we were aroused by a messenger at our door saying, "General Early's adjutant wishes to see General Jackson." As he arose, he said, "That looks as if Hooker were crossing." He hurried down-stairs, and, soon returning, told me that his surmise was correct—Hooker was crossing the river, and that he must go immediately to the scene of action. From the indications he thought a battle was imminent, and under the circumstances he was unwilling for us to remain in so exposed a situation as Mr. Yerby's. He therefore directed me to prepare to start for Richmond at a moment's notice, promising to return himself to see us off if possible, and if not, he would send my brother Joseph. After a tender and hasty good-by, he hurried off without breakfast. Scarcely had he gone, when the roar of cannons began—volley after volley following in quick succession—the house shaking and windows rattling from the reverberations, throwing the family into great panic, and causing the wildest excitement among all the occupants of the place. My hasty preparations for leaving were hardly com-

pleted when Mr. Lacy, the chaplain, came with an ambulance, saying he had been sent by General Jackson to convey his family to the railroad station as speedily as possible, in order to catch the morning train to Richmond. My brother Joseph, seeing General Jackson's need of his services, had requested that Mr. Lacy should be sent in his stead as my escort. He brought a cheerful note from my husband, explaining why he could not leave his post, and invoking God's care and blessing upon us in our sudden departure, and especially was he tender and loving in his mention of the baby.

Julia Laura Jackson's christening on April 23, 1863, at the age of five months was attended by her father's officers, who later gave her this silver mug in remembrance of the baptismal day. The mug's oval cartouche bears the engraving "Julia L. Jackson from the General Staff Officers of her Father.—Maj. Harman, Maj. Hawks, Col. Allen, Col. Pendleton, Dr. McGuire."

Holly Church and had begun to cross the river at Kelly's Ford on pontoon bridges brought up by army engineers.

By morning on the 30th the three corps were across the Rapidan and were moving in tight columns down roads cut through a dark, desolate tract of second-growth pine and tangled underbrush called simply, and ominously, the Wilderness. About noon General Meade and parts of his V Corps emerged into the large clearing at Chancellorsville, followed at about 2:00 p.m. by Slocum and later by some of Howard's troops, now bringing up the rear. The men were exhausted but proud of what they had so far accomplished and full of faith in their leader. "Since we crossed the Rappahannock in such style, fording the Rapidan shoulder deep by moonlight, Hooker's stock is rising," wrote a New York soldier to his mother.

Hooker's plan seemed to be working to perfection. With only some of Jeb Stuart's troopers and a few other Confederate skirmishers anywhere about, the roads to Fredericksburg were wide open. "This is splendid, Slocum," exclaimed General Meade. "We are on Lee's flank and he does not know it." He suggested they immediately press on and get at Lee's army.

Meade was astonished by Slocum's response. "My orders," Slocum said, "are to take up a line of battle here, and not to move forward without further orders." Evidently Hooker wanted to wait until still more troops—Couch's II Corps and Sick-

Wearing the braid-trimmed uniform given him by the dapper Jeb Stuart, Stonewall Jackson sat in unaccustomed finery for a photographer at the request of his wife, Anna. Taken in the hallway of the Yerby house, the photograph became a favorite among members of Jackson's command.

"The operations of the last three days have determined that the enemy must either ingloriously fly or give us battle on our own ground, where certain destruction awaits him."

---

les' III Corps—had made it across the Rappahannock by way of the United States Ford. Hooker seemed to think that the flank march had, in effect, already won the battle. Riding up to the Chancellor house on the evening of the 30th, he proclaimed that "the operations of the last three days have determined that the enemy must either ingloriously fly" or "give us battle on our own ground, where certain destruction awaits him."

Unaware that by Hooker's account his fate was sealed, General Lee was nevertheless becoming nervous. As early as April 16 he had sensed there was "some movement in agitation" in Hooker's camps, and he was deeply worried that his army, still lacking half of Longstreet's corps, was too depleted to fight off the huge Federal force.

More worrisome still as the days dragged along, Lee's scouts were unable to tell where Hooker might be preparing to strike. On April 28 Stuart reported that "a large body of infantry and artillery was passing up the river," but he could not say how big it was or where it was headed, because Federal corps, moving northwest beyond the river in wooded country, had been largely screened from view.

By early on April 29, however, Lee knew where one threat lay. The Rebel commander could easily see the Federals, General Sedgwick's VI Corps followed by Reynolds' I Corps, streaming across the Rappahannock south of Fredericksburg. Immediately the combative Major General Jubal A. Early deployed his division of Jackson's corps along the Old Richmond road and a railway embankment while his forward skirmishers fired away at the Union troops.

Soon in motion, too, was Jackson, who had been enjoying a rare visit from his wife, Anna, whom he had not seen for a year, and their five-month-old daughter, Julia, whom he had never seen before. As soon as couriers brought news of the Federal crossing, Jackson embraced Anna and the baby and arranged for them to head home. He then instantly turned to business, moving Brigadier General Robert E. Rodes' division to Early's right and ordering Major General Ambrose Powell Hill and Brigadier General Raleigh E. Colston to hurry back from their positions downriver to support Early and Rodes.

But then Sedgwick's troops, although seemingly ready to attack, unaccountably failed to move. Lee had already heard from Stuart that about 14,000 men—it was Howard's XI Corps—had been spotted crossing the Rappahannock the night

Rowed across the Rappahannock River by oarsmen from the Engineer Brigade, New York and Pennsylvania troops from Brigadier General David A. Russell's brigade spearhead the VI Corps' crossing of the river a mile and a half south of Fredericksburg on April 29. "The boats gallantly vied with one another in the struggle to be the first to land," General Russell reported; "in five minutes after landing we had possession of the enemy's outer line of rifle-pits."

before. Then toward evening on the 29th couriers brought more news: Large numbers of both Federal cavalry and infantry had crossed the Rapidan at Germanna and Ely's Fords. As Lee well knew, the roads from there ran through the Wilderness toward Chancellorsville.

Still, on the evening of the 29th, Lee was not sure where the main threat lay and dispatched only Major General Richard H. Anderson's division to guard the roads leading into Fredericksburg from the west. By noon on the 30th, however, Anderson could see the massive Federal force bearing down on Chancellorsville.

"It must be victory or death, for defeat would be ruinous."

Quickly sending a warning to Lee, he deployed his division on a rise near the Zoan and Tabernacle Churches that offered superb fields of fire on the two main roads heading eastward, the Plank road and an old route called the Turnpike.

Concluding at last that the main threat was on his left, Lee with astonishing boldness risked everything. In the famous Special Orders No. 121, he ordered Jackson to march three of his divisions westward at dawn the next day, leaving only Jubal Early's single division to watch Sedgwick's huge host. In addition, Major General Lafayette McLaws was to place a single brigade on the ridge behind

Fredericksburg and march the rest of his division with all speed after Jackson.

When all units arrived, Lee would have about 40,000 men to face Hooker's huge right wing of 70,000. Faced with this situation, most generals would have tried a speedy retreat, risky as that would have been. But Lee evidently never considered retreat for a minute. "It must be victory or death," he told McLaws, "for defeat would be ruinous."

UNION PROBES AND REBEL RESPONSE: MAY I

Once General Lee had made the daring decision to shift virtually his entire army westward to fight Hooker's flanking force at Chancellorsville, Lee's most trusted lieutenant, Stonewall Jackson, wasted little time getting things moving. Jackson himself awoke shortly after midnight on May 1, then had the troops roused at 2:00 a.m., silently, with no bugle calls that would alert the Yankees camped only a few hundred yards away on the banks of the Rappahannock.

Within minutes General Rodes' division, leading the Confederate column, had begun to march. "On we went through mud and over stumps, stumbling about in the dark," wrote one of Rodes' soldiers, "to the great danger of our heads and shins."

Jackson, astride his undersized horse, Little Sorrel, rode on toward the Tabernacle Church to join General Richard Anderson, already dispatched there with his division to set up a defensive line. Arriving about 8:00 a.m., Jackson found Anderson's men busy digging trenches—a sensible move in the face of a huge enemy force.

But Jackson, intent as always on hitting the enemy no matter what the odds,

In a May 1863 photo-
graph by A. J. Russell,
soldiers of the 15th New
York Engineers wait for
their ration of stew at a
campfire on the Confeder-
ate side of the Rappahan-
nock. The men had just
finished building pontoon
bridges for General John
Sedgwick's VI Corps.

ordered the troops to pack their shovels and be ready to attack. Lafayette McLaws'
brigades, which had marched from Fredericksburg during the night, were deploying on Anderson's right. At 11:00 a.m. the two divisions—only about 14,000 men
in all—started down the Plank road and the Turnpike to assault the oncoming
70,000 Federals.

Belatedly ordered by Hooker to begin the great advance, the Union troops started
up the same roads at the same time, Slocum's XII Corps pushing ahead on the right
along the Plank road and Major General George Sykes' division of Meade's V Corps
moving up the Turnpike. On the Federal left, Meade's other two divisions also set
out, following the River road between the Turnpike and the Rappahannock.

The Federal columns almost immediately ran into McLaws' and Anderson's
skirmishers, with Confederate rifle fire crackling from the woods and little hills
that fringed the roads. A number of ferocious fights erupted, including a seesaw
battle between Sykes' men and Mahone's brigade, who retreated and then, supported by two brigades from Anderson, assailed the Federal column on both flanks.

The gunfire did not at first seem to worry Hooker, who ordered Major General Winfield Scott Hancock and his division to hurry up the Turnpike to support Sykes. This Hancock did, gaining a strategic position atop a ridge in open
country. Slocum also gained ground while Meade on the Federal left was speed-
ing ahead unopposed.

Seated on hardtack boxes in the woods near Chancellorsville, Generals Lee (left) and Jackson quietly make plans to divide their forces and attack Hooker's Federals. Lee holds a map drawn by Jackson's topographical officer that charts the concealed route to Hooker's right flank.

Stonewall Jackson's forage cap, a gift from his wife, Anna, bears a band of gold braid believed to have been attached after his death. The original cap band so displeased the general that he removed it. "I like simplicity," he wrote his wife.

"Nobody but a crazy man would give such an order when we have victory in sight!"

Then, astonishingly, at about 2:00 p.m. Hooker sent orders telling his corps commanders to stop the advance, break off contact with the enemy, and fall back to the areas around Chancellorsville that they had occupied the night before. Meade immediately exploded, "My God, if we can't hold the top of a hill, we certainly cannot hold the bottom of it!" The combative Slocum was even more furious, shouting, "Nobody but a crazy man would give such an order when we have victory in sight!"

What had occurred was an acute failure of nerve on the part of the Federal commanding general. Hooker, despite his army's overwhelming strength, had quailed at the enemy opposition and decided to go over to the defensive.

Debate over Hooker's stunning reversal began at once. Some blamed it on his fondness for the bottle, but several of his generals later testified at an inquiry that Hooker was not drunk. In fact, said General Couch, he might have performed better if he had "continued in his usual habit" and downed a drink or two.

Part of the answer certainly is that Hooker, having made his great flanking move, expected Lee to retreat. But Lee's instinct, like Jackson's, was always to attack. Hooker, uncertain of his ability to command an entire army despite all his bluster, gave way to panic at the signs of resistance. Hooker's own explanation, given weeks later to a friend, was simply, "for once I lost confidence in Hooker."

When the Union forces withdrew, the Confederates followed gingerly, suspicious of a trap, although McLaws' brigades, now backed by A. P. Hill's division of Jackson's corps, pressed some distance down the roads toward Chancellorsville. At the same time Jackson pushed several brigades up the Plank road, one of which, under General Ambrose R. Wright, veered left along an unfinished railroad, pushed past the Catharine Furnace ironworks, and briefly collided with forward elements of the XII Corps.

At dusk Lee and Jackson met near there in a pine grove to decide what to do next. The Federals had to be dealt a heavy blow, and quickly. Lee himself had done some scouting along with his engineers, and a frontal assault through the swamps and thickets of the Wilderness on the fortified semicircle Hooker had drawn around Chancellorsville seemed suicidal.

As the two trusted friends sat on boxes talking, Jeb Stuart rode up to report that some cavalry scouts had discovered that the flank of Oliver Howard's XI Corps, holding the Federal far right, was "in the air," that is, unprotected by any hill or swamp or other natural feature. Both Lee and Jackson immediately recognized the possibility of a flank march that would put their troops in a position to attack the Union army from the rear—but how could they get an attacking force that far to the west?

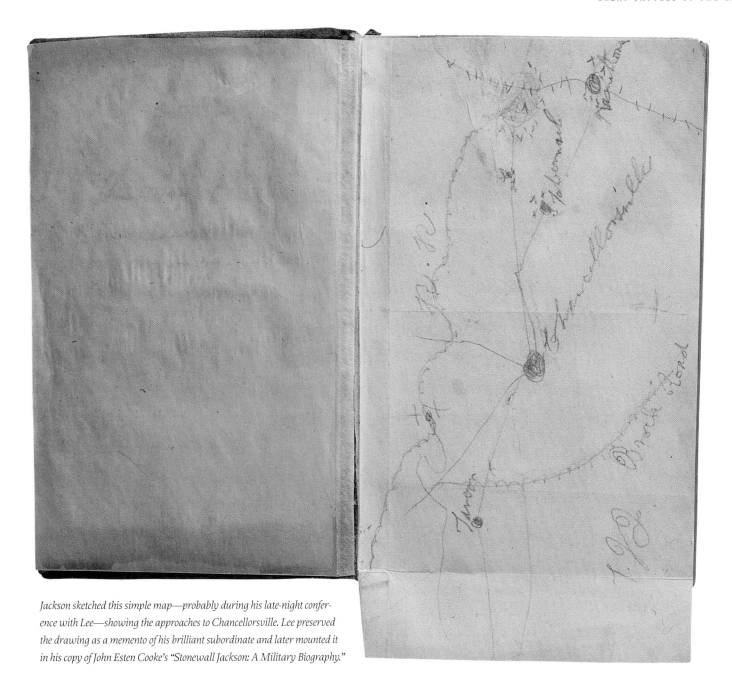

Jackson sketched this simple map—probably during his late-night confer-
ence with Lee—showing the approaches to Chancellorsville. Lee preserved
the drawing as a memento of his brilliant subordinate and later mounted it
in his copy of John Esten Cooke's "Stonewall Jackson: A Military Biography."

Lee's sketchy pocket map of the area was little help. But well before dawn, information about the area had been provided by scouts and local people, among them the owner of Catharine Furnace, who knew all the local roads. Sketching furiously, Jedediah Hotchkiss, Jackson's cartographer, produced a map showing a largely concealed route leading down the Furnace road and then back up the Brock road that stretched all the way to the Federal right flank and beyond.

The two Confederate commanders consulted again. Lee looked at Jackson.

"What do you propose to do?" he asked. "Go around here," said Jackson, pointing to the route on Hotchkiss' map. "What do you propose to make this movement with?" asked Lee. "With my whole corps," answered Jackson.

It was an audacious plan because it would leave Lee with only two divisions, Anderson's and McLaws', to face the entire main body of Hooker's force. After considering for only a moment, however, Lee gave his assent. "Well," he said, "go on."

JACKSON'S FLANK MARCH AND ATTACK: MAY 2

After concluding their momentous conference, Stonewall Jackson left Lee to get his divisions moving. About 7:00 a.m. the lead regiments filed past Lee's headquarters. Then Jackson appeared, the two men talked briefly, and Jackson cantered on along the Furnace road. The two daring generals never saw each other again.

Jackson spurred ahead to join General Robert Rodes' division in the lead and to urge the troops to hurry. "Press on, press forward!" he called out over and over, leaning forward on his horse, his cap as usual pulled down almost over his eyes. "Permit no straggling. See that the column is kept closed. Press on, press on!"

Speed was indeed essential. To work his way around to Hooker's right, Jackson had to march his 26,000 soldiers almost 14 miles on a roundabout route along narrow dirt roads that, he hoped, were hidden from the Federals. And he had to do it well before nightfall, to allow time to deploy and launch his surprise attack. The weary, underfed troops trudged on as best they could, the column heading west and south on the Furnace road, then eventually north on the Brock road with few delays.

Jackson's march had in fact been spotted by Union lookouts at Hazel Grove, a small rise southwest of Chancellorsville. Given the news, Hooker soon concluded—correctly for once—that Lee might be trying to flank him, and he sent a message to General Howard, the XI Corps commander, urging him to "take measures to resist an attack from the west." But then Hooker did nothing to harass Jackson's column until midday, when he finally gave Sickles' III Corps permission to "advance cautiously."

The combative Sickles did more than that, launching an attack that swiftly overran what amounted to Jackson's rear guard, the 23d Georgia at Catharine Furnace, and threatened to roll up the rear of Jackson's column. Soon, however, a Rebel counterattack threw the Federals back.

This commotion actually aided Jackson. Combined with reports that the long Confederate column snaking west included numbers of wagons, it somehow convinced Hooker that Lee's entire army was retreating. Out on the Union right, where the blow was to fall, senior commanders dismissed the warnings of Jackson's approach that came in thick and fast from Federal pickets throughout the afternoon.

By the time the Confederate troops reached the Orange Turnpike and started deploying, less than three hours of daylight remained, but Jackson never thought of postponing the attack. Quietly, with orders murmured in undertones, the officers marshaled the troops into two long lines straddling the Orange Turnpike, Rodes'

In this fanciful painting of the battlefield at Chancellorsville, Confederate infantry attacks in the foreground around sunset on May 2. Hooker's Federal troops have regrouped near Chancellor house (center) and have formed a defensive perimeter strengthened by cannon and a charging squadron of cavalry on the Plank road.

division in front, Raleigh E. Colston's next, with A. P. Hill's still forming up in the rear. Finally, at 5:15 p.m. by his pocket watch, Jackson turned to Rodes and said simply, "You can go forward, then."

Minutes after Rodes' troops moved they were spotted and fired on by startled Union pickets. The surprise over, the attackers screamed the bloodcurdling Rebel yell, dashed forward through the dense underbrush, and smashed into the camps of Leopold von Gilsa's brigade. Some of the Union troops formed ranks and got off a volley or two, but most were taken in the flank by blasts of gunfire and fled without firing a shot.

Shortly the Federal retreat turned into a rout, and terrified men streamed through the forest in chaos. By dusk the Confederates had raced ahead in their wild charge more than two miles, but by then many units had become mixed, and the exhausted and famished men were unable to find their officers or regiments. Slowly the attack shuddered to a halt.

Well after dark, as his officers desperately tried to sort out their disordered ranks, Jackson did something incautious but perfectly in character. Not satisfied with his brilliant victory, he rode ahead to scout out a side track of the Plank road that he could use to launch a night attack and, he hoped, utterly destroy the enemy. As he rode back about 9:00 p.m., jittery troops of the 18th North Carolina mistook his party for Federal cavalry and fired wildly into the dark. Jackson was hit three times, two bullets shattering his left arm, which was amputated shortly after he was taken to the rear.

A photograph of the Plank road—with some of its wooden planking visible at right—was alleged to have been taken at the spot where Stonewall Jackson was shot. In fact, Jackson and his party were riding on the Mountain road, possibly the dark track visible to the right of the two men at center, leading from the Plank road.

Stonewall Jackson's handkerchief—bearing the general's name written in his own hand—was in his pocket when he was wounded. Following the war Jackson's family presented the bloodstained relic to the Virginia Military Institute.

Stonewall Jackson's raincoat still bears the marks of the fatal bullets. A musket ball entered the palm of his right hand, another round passed through his left forearm, while the third broke his left arm below the shoulder.

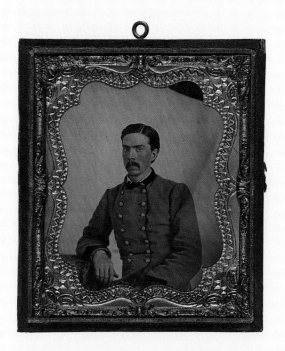

"His suffering at this time was intense; his hands were cold, his skin clammy, his face pale, and his lips compressed and bloodless; not a groan escaped him …"

SURGEON HUNTER MCGUIRE

Staff, Lieutenant General Thomas J. Jackson

Dr. McGuire, Jackson's chief medical officer, battled to save the life of his commander, who was in imminent danger of bleeding to death from an artery that had been severed by a jagged edge of broken bone when he fell from his stretcher. McGuire would later serve as president of the American Medical Association.

He was placed upon the litter again, and carried a few hundred yards, when I met him with an ambulance. I knelt down by him, and said, "I hope you are not badly hurt, General." He replied very calmly, but feebly, "I am badly injured, Doctor; I fear I am dying." After a pause, he continued, "I am glad you have come. I think the wound in my shoulder is still bleeding." His clothes were saturated with blood, and hemorrhage was still going on from the wound. Compression of the artery with the finger arrested it, until lights being procured from the ambulance, the handkerchief which had slipped a little, was readjusted. His calmness amid the dangers which surrounded him, and at the supposed presence of death, and his uniform politeness, which did not forsake him, even under these, the most trying circumstances, were remarkable. His complete control, too, over his mind, enfeebled as it was by loss of blood, pain, &c., was wonderful. His suffering at this time was intense; his hands were cold, his skin clammy, his face pale, and his lips compressed and

bloodless; not a groan escaped him—not a sign of suffering, except the slight corrugation of his brow, the fixed, rigid face, and the thin lips so tightly compressed that the impression of the teeth could be seen through them. . . .

After reaching the hospital, he was placed in bed, covered with blankets, and another drink of whiskey and water given him. Two hours and a half elapsed before sufficient reaction took place to warrant an examination. At two o'clock Sunday morning Surgeons Black, Walls and Coleman being present, I informed him that chloroform would be given him, and his wounds examined. I told him that amputation would probably be required, and asked if it was found necessary, whether it should be done at once. He replied promptly, "Yes, certainly; Doctor McGuire, do for me whatever you think best." Chloroform was then administered, and as he began to feel its effects, and its relief to the pain he was suffering, he exclaimed, "What an infinite blessing," and continued to repeat the word "blessing," until he became insen-

sible. The round ball (such as is used for the smooth-bore Springfield musket), which had lodged under the skin, upon the back of his right hand, was extracted first. It had entered the palm, about the middle of the hand, and fractured two of the bones. The left arm was then amputated, about two inches below the shoulder, very rapidly, and with slight loss of blood, the ordinary circular operation having been made. There were two wounds in this arm, the first and most serious was about three inches below the shoulder-joint, the ball dividing the main artery, and fracturing the bone. The second was several inches in length; a ball having entered the outside of the forearm, an inch below the elbow, came out upon the opposite side, just above the wrist. Throughout the whole of the operation, and until all the dressings were applied, he continued insensible. Two or three slight wounds of the skin on his face, received from the branches of trees, when his horse dashed through the woods, were dressed simply with isinglass plaster.

Meanwhile a courier had reached General Lee with the news that Jackson had been shot by his own troops. Lee gave a moan and seemed on the verge of tears, the courier recalled, then asked not to hear any of the details. "It is too painful to talk about," Lee said. "Any victory is dearly bought which deprives us of the services of General Jackson, even for a short time." But then Lee turned to business, confirming the appointment of Jeb Stuart to take over Jackson's corps and sending Stuart firm orders to hit the Federals with everything he had the next morning.

HOOKER ON THE DEFENSIVE: MAY 3

Despite the success of Jackson's attack on the evening of May 2, the Federals by all rights held the upper hand the next morning. Most of Major General John Reynolds' I Corps, summoned by General Hooker the day before, had crossed the Rappahannock, bringing the Federal total around Chancellorsville to 76,000 men, nearly double the number available to Lee.

In addition, the Confederate force was still divided into two wings separated by almost two miles of difficult terrain, Jeb Stuart to the west of Chancellorsville, Robert E. Lee to the south and east. The situation plainly called for hard, swinging Federal counterattacks to smash first one Confederate wing and then the other.

But Hooker, still unnerved, would not even consider an aggressive counterpunch. He was thinking only of a hedgehoglike defense—and he soon compromised even that when, in a spasm of extra caution, he ordered General Dan Sickles to abandon his forward position on Hazel Grove, the height southwest of Chancellorsville that jutted between the wings of the Rebel army and provided a matchless position for artillery to sweep the surrounding country. "There has rarely been a more gratuitous gift of a battlefield," wrote Confederate artilleryman Colonel E. Porter Alexander, who would soon take full advantage of it.

"*The fighting here was the most desperate of the war. It was dreadful, horrible, appalling.*"

It was Stuart, of course, who did the attacking, as Lee had ordered. Working frantically through the night, Stuart reorganized Jackson's corps, moving A. P. Hill's division—now led by Brigadier General Henry Heth because Hill had been wounded—into the front line. Next came Raleigh Colston's division and in a third line Robert Rodes' bone-tired troops, who had seen the worst of the fighting the evening before.

At the outbreak of war cousins William H. Egerton (left) and William E. Johnson (right) enlisted as privates in the Warren Guards, Company F of the 12th North Carolina. Egerton was killed at Gaines' Mill in June 1862, while Johnson, promoted to lieutenant, survived to fight at Chancellorsville. During the charge of Brigadier General Alfred Iverson's brigade, advancing on the far left of Rodes' division, Johnson was shot in the head and died the next day.

The Confederates, as usual hitting fast and hard, moved as dawn broke at 5:30 a.m. In half an hour Brigadier General James Archer's brigade on the right of Heth's line had advanced up the western slope of Hazel Grove where the forward skirmishers chased off the last of Sickles' withdrawing troops. In minutes Colonel Alexander, who had hidden 30 guns in a nearby woods overnight, had sped his batteries up the heights and was sending shells screaming into the Union artillery positions at Fairview Heights, near Hooker's headquarters at the Chancellor house, and into the brigades of Slocum's corps just to the east and northeast.

At the same time, the remaining five brigades of Heth's division attacked straight into the packed ranks of the II, III, and XII Corps manning the western margin of the defensive loop Hooker had put together around the Chancellor house. "The fighting here was the most desperate of the war," wrote one of Sickles' artillerymen. "It was dreadful, horrible, appalling." Dozens of regiments from both sides fought furiously until nearly half their numbers were dead or wounded. But by about 8:30 the headlong Confederate rush began to run out of steam. Heth's brigades had been hurriedly aligned and in the furious fighting began to lose touch with one another, exposing their flanks to counterattacks.

Seeing Heth's first line stalled, Stuart ordered Colston's division to advance and Rodes' as well. Unnerved by the horrifying carnage and with many of their officers killed, some soldiers balked at the advance. But the pressure from the Confederates was relentless, and despite steadily mounting losses (one of Colston's brigades went through four commanders that morning) the Federals were driven back on the Chancellor house.

In the midst of the violence Hooker himself was put out of action when a round shot from a Confederate gun shattered a column he was leaning against on the Chancellor house porch. Hit by part of the column, Hooker was knocked senseless for a time, then rode about in a daze. But he did not notify General Couch, his senior subordinate, or turn over command.

Broad-shouldered and powerfully built, with an outgoing personality and hearty laugh, Jeb Stuart habitually sported high boots, jangling spurs, and a plumed hat (right)—attire that epitomized the dashing cavalryman. The flashy general was prepared to fight as well as to lead, and his personal armament reflected his intentions. In addition to a saber, Stuart carried a formidable Le Mat revolver (below), a veritable arsenal, holding nine .42-caliber rounds with a second, lower barrel capable of firing a charge of buckshot. Stuart's zeal for combat ultimately cost him his life when he rode forward to fire upon retreating Yankee troopers in the May 1864 Battle of Yellow Tavern and was mortally wounded by a pistol shot from a dismounted foe.

At last, lying down in a tent to the rear, Hooker did tell Couch to take over—and immediately ordered him to start a general retreat to a new, shorter defensive line north of Chancellorsville. In utter disgust, Couch and the other Federal corps commanders—who still wanted to attack—began withdrawing their troops, moving them back into a semicircular line with both ends anchored on the Rappahannock.

In the meantime General Lee, seeing that Stuart's attack was almost spent, began his own assault, ordering R. H. Anderson's brigades led by Generals Carnot Posey, Ambrose Wright, and William Mahone to attack Hooker's southern perimeter, and sending Lafayette McLaws' troops charging up the Plank road and the Turnpike from the east. As the Federals withdrew, Lee ordered 40 guns moved from Hazel Grove to Fairview, where they blasted away at the retreating Union forces and finally set fire to the already half-demolished Chancellor house.

Lee observed the last attacks from Hazel Grove, calmly sitting astride his handsome horse, Traveller. Then in the late morning, while McLaws' and Anderson's brigades battled Hancock's troops forming the Federal rear guard, Lee rode down to the Chancellorsville clearing. There, one of his staff officers remembered, "the fierce soldiers with their faces blackened with the smoke of battle" all gave "one long, unbroken cheer," hailing "the presence of the victorious chief."

Lee basked in his triumph for a moment, then received a message from Stonewall Jackson confirming that he was wounded and congratulating Lee on the great victory. A look of anguish passed over Lee's face, a staff officer recalled, and his voice trembled as he dictated a reply: "Could I have directed events, I should have chosen for the good of the country to be disabled in your stead. I congratulate you on the victory, which is due to your skill and energy."

Ohio artist George Leo Frankenstein, who served in the Army of the Potomac's commissary department, returned to Chancellorsville in the late 1860s to paint scenes of the battlefield, including this view of the ruined Chancellor house. Later, a smaller house was built on the old foundation, but it burned in 1927.

"Cannon were booming and missiles of death were flying in every direction as this terrified band of women and children came stumbling out of the cellar."

SUE CHANCELLOR

Fourteen-year-old Sue Chancellor, her mother, and five sisters were among those sheltering in the Chancellor house as the battle started. Although the house had passed out of family hands before the war, Sue's mother was renting the place at the time General Hooker took it over as his headquarters. The family was at first allowed the use of a back room, but as fighting erupted nearby, they and a number of wounded soldiers were sent to the basement. When the house caught fire, everyone was evacuated and led to safety.

Early in the morning they came for us to go into the cellar, and in passing through the upper porch I saw how the chairs were riddled with bullets and the shattered columns which had fallen and injured General Hooker. O the horror of that day! The piles of legs and arms outside the sitting room window and the rows and rows of dead bodies covered with canvas! The fighting was awful, and the frightened men crowded into the basement for protection from the deadly fire of the Confederates, but an officer came and ordered them out, commanding them not to intrude upon the terror-stricken women. Presently down the steps the same officer came precipitously and bade us get out at once, "For, madam, the house is on fire, but I will see that you are protected and taken to a place of safety." This was Gen. Joseph Dickinson, but we did not know it at the time. Cannon were booming and missiles of death were flying in every direction as this terrified band of women and children came stumbling out of the cellar. If anybody thinks that a battle is an orderly attack of rows of men, I can tell them differently, for I have been there.

The sight that met our eyes as we came out of the dim light of that basement beggars description. The woods around the house were a sheet of fire, the air was filled with shot and shell, horses were running, rearing, and screaming, the men, a mass of confusion, moaning, cursing, and praying. They were bringing the wounded out of the house, as it was on fire in several places. Mammy Nancy had old Mr. F——'s basket of papers, and she and the little negro girl were separated from us and bidden to stay behind. A Yankee snatched the basket from the old woman and was making off with it when Aunt Nancy gave a shriek: "Miss Kate, for the Lord's sake git your pa's basket!" An officer turned and, sternly reproving the miscreant, gave the basket into Miss Kate's hands. Slowly we picked our way over the bleeding bodies of the dead and wounded, General Dickinson riding ahead, my mother walking alongside with her hand on his knee, I clinging close to her, and the others following behind. At the last look our old home was completely enveloped in flames. Mother with six dependent daughters, and her all destroyed!

We took the road up toward United States Ford, which was held by the enemy, and after a while got out of sight of the battle. After walking about half a mile one of my sisters, who had been sick, had a hemorrhage from her lungs. General Dickinson stopped a soldier on horseback, made him get down, put my sister on his horse, and then walked behind her to hold her on. After a while Miss Kate stopped, completely exhausted, and said she could go no farther. General Dickinson asked her if she could ride, adding: "If so, you can take my horse and I will walk at his head." She said she was too much exhausted to attempt that, but she could ride, pillion, behind him. "That is impossible," he said sternly. "I fear I cannot provide for you." After a few minutes pause, we went on. Presently we met an officer, who wheeled on his horse on recognizing our leader and demanded with an oath: "General Dickinson, why are you not at your post of duty?" I will never forget General Dickinson's reply. He drew himself up proudly and said: "If here is not the post of duty, looking after the safety of these helpless women and children, then I don't know what you call duty."

After walking three miles we reached the ford, where the Yankees had crossed on a pontoon bridge four days before. Here at the old La Roque house General Dickinson left us in the care of a New Jersey chaplain and went to see about getting us across the river. We saw here the corpse of an old negro woman who, they said, had been frightened to death. We all sat on the porch waiting, not knowing what would happen next. Presently General Dickinson returned, went with us to the bridge, and bade us good-by. A nobler, braver, kindlier gentleman never lived.

Lieutenant Colonel Joseph Dickinson, an assistant adjutant general on Hooker's staff, had tried to help stem the rout of the XI Corps on May 2 by standing his ground with some of Howard's staff. On May 3, out of genuine concern for the Chancellor family huddled in the basement, Lieutenant Dickinson got them safely out of the house, escorted them to the rear, and sent an ambulance for a sick daughter. Dickinson kept in touch with the family and visited the Chancellors after the war.

Among the items found in the burned-out shell of the Chancellor house were a prewar blue glass bottle for liniment or medicine, distorted by the heat; an iron toy horse; and the remnant of a cart once attached to the horse.

In this photograph, soldiers in General William Brooks' division of the Federal VI Corps bivouac in reserve on the west bank of the Rappahannock River during the Second Battle of Fredericksburg in 1863. Shortly after the photograph was taken, some of these men were killed in the fighting around Salem Church.

SALEM CHURCH AND FEDERAL RETREAT: MAY 3-5

As the cheering for his victory died down, General Lee immediately gave orders for yet another assault on Hooker's defenses. But then a courier galloped into the Chancellorsville clearing and blurted out alarming news. Sedgwick and his Federal VI Corps had attacked at Fredericksburg and were marching west from there to join up with Hooker.

Sedgwick had, in fact, received an urgent series of messages from Hooker on the night of May 2, after darkness had halted Jackson's flank attack. Sedgwick was to move immediately from his positions along the Rappahannock south of Fredericksburg, push through what Hooker imagined to be the negligible enemy force still in the area and, marching fast, fall upon Lee's rear at dawn on May 3.

The careful Sedgwick had no intention of risking a night attack. Besides, he knew he faced a dangerous obstacle—about 9,000 men of General Jubal Early's division backed by 56 guns entrenched in the formidable earthworks on the heights overlooking the river south of Fredericksburg.

Sedgwick set out nevertheless to obey orders. He formed battle lines during the night of May 2-3, and the next morning he ordered the advance. He first attempted to outflank Marye's Heights with converging attacks from north and south of Fredericksburg. When those probes were turned back, there was nothing left but the frontal route, and about 10:30 a.m. Sedgwick sent Brigadier General John Newton's division charging toward the infamous stone wall at the foot of the heights.

Newton's columns were hurled back three times by Rebel guns, but finally in a fourth charge, the Federals cleared the stone wall and dashed on up Marye's Heights, forcing Barksdale into a hasty retreat. With the Federals pushing west, Early ordered his division to fall back south to avoid being outflanked, leaving Brigadier General Cadmus M. Wilcox's brigade to fall back west and delay Sedgwick's advance.

Absorbing the news of Sedgwick's move with his usual calm, Lee coolly divided his battered army yet again, sending Lafayette McLaws with four brigades marching east along the Turnpike to join up with Wilcox and meet the new threat. This left Lee only about 25,000 able-bodied men to face the 75,000 Federals in their new positions north of Chancellorsville.

Sedgwick did attack, hitting Wilcox's soldiers, who were drawn up on a rise near Salem Church, with McLaws' brigades deployed to the north and south. In a first assault the Federals drove the Confederates back, capturing the church and a nearby schoolhouse that Wilcox's men had turned into strongholds. But the Rebels swiftly countered with a furious rush that beat back the Federals. Sedgwick replied by moving up two fresh divisions, but night was coming on and it was too late for a full-scale assault.

Lee, seeing a chance to annihilate Sedgwick's force, ordered Jubal Early to advance from the south at daybreak on May 4 and take Sedgwick in the rear, while R. H. Anderson's division maneuvered to hit Sedgwick's flank from the south and McLaws attacked from the west.

But coordinating the complex maneuver took time, and Lee was not ready for a full-scale attack until almost 6:00 p.m. Then, unaccountably for such veteran units, the assaults went awry. Jubal Early attacked as planned, throwing back Brigadier General Albion P. Howe's division, but Anderson's men veered off course, heading eastward toward the sound of Early's fight. McLaws' brigades became tangled in dense woods and failed to reach the enemy lines.

Well before that, Sedgwick, sensing the danger, had shifted many of his 19,000 men into a defensive horseshoe to the north. During the night he slipped out of the trap, falling back to get his corps across the Rappahannock at Scott's Ford by 5:00 a.m. on May 5.

Lee swiftly turned his troops around once more and prepared to attack Hooker. But Hooker did not wait, ordering his entire force to recross the Rappahannock at United States Ford. By 9:00 a.m. on May 6 virtually all the 75,000 Federals were on the north side of the Rappahannock, marching in disgust to their old camps around Falmouth.

Shortly after his resignation in late 1863 because of illness and the lingering effects of a wound, Colonel John Ely of the 23d Pennsylvania Infantry (left) commemorated the actions of his command during the assault on Marye's Heights by issuing a private award. Known as the Ely Medal, it bears on the front (below, right) clasped hands with a legend giving the unit and the place and date of battle, and on the reverse, a figure of Liberty with patriotic mottoes. The example illustrated here was bestowed on Private Robert Elliot (right).

"That's him! that's Lee! Hats off, boy's!"

CAPTAIN PETER A. S. MCGLASHAN

50th Georgia Infantry, Semmes' Brigade

Lee barely had time to savor his triumph in the clearing at Chancellorsville when word arrived of Sedgwick's successful breakthrough. Lee quickly ordered McLaws' division east to shore up the units trying to slow the Federal advance. McGlashan, who by war's end would be colonel of his regiment, remembered the tributes paid to Lee at the time—not only by Rebel troops but even by Yankee prisoners.

It was near mid-day on May 3, 1863, when our brigade, consisting of the 10th, 50th, 51st and 53rd Georgia regiments, under command of the gallant Gen. Paul J. Semmes, were lying in the woods near the plank road leading to Fredericksburg. The men, kept at attention by the occasional dropping of a shell from the enemy's works, when Gen. Lee and staff rode slowly from the woods and approached Gen. McLaws' men where we lay. The air was full of rumors. Troops were rapidly shifting position, prisoners pouring in from the front, and the men watched the conference of the two generals with keen interest.

As Gen. Lee concluded he nodded pleasantly to Gen. McLaws and said in a louder tone: "Now, General, there is a chance for your young men to distinguish themselves."

The brigade was called to attention, a rapid inspection made, cartridge boxes filled and we filed out into the road which was filled with prisoners, who rapidly fell to one side as we passed.

Here an incident occurred which I shall never forget. As the prisoners fell to one side an exciting murmur ran through them of: "That's him! that's Lee! Hats off, boy's!" I looked back. Gen. Lee was following us with his staff, I thought never looking before so grand and noble. As he came up the prisoners, to a man, faced him and uncovered, and he looking, as I thought, sadly at them, raised his hat and bowing his head acknowledged their salute. It was a picturesque scene. The prisoners represented all branches of the service, red and blue zouaves, infantry, artillery and cavalry. Lee was then at the zenith of his fame, and their recognition of his greatness seemed so fitting and graceful it called forth cheers from our troops.

Jack, a stray dog adopted as the mascot of a Pittsburgh fire company, went to war when the firemen enlisted as a company in the 102d Pennsylvania Infantry. Jack marched with his two-legged comrades from Yorktown in 1862 until his disappearance in 1864, even taking a bullet through his shoulder and neck at Malvern Hill. On May 3 Jack was captured at Salem Church and held prisoner for six months until he was exchanged for a Confederate soldier.

His dazzling victory complete, Lee was anything but satisfied. He was angry that he had failed to trap and destroy any large body of enemy troops, and although the Federals had lost 17,000 men, his own army had suffered proportionately worse damage with 13,000 casualties. Almost worse, Lee had lost a staggering number of invaluable officers killed or wounded, including two division leaders, 11 brigadiers, and 40 regimental commanders. And then there was Jackson's wound. On May 5 Jackson was taken to a small house on a plantation near Guiney Station, south of Fredericksburg, where Lee sent the message "Tell him to make haste and get well.... He has lost his left arm, but I have lost my right."

"WHAT WILL THE COUNTRY SAY?"

In the days following the Federal retreat, General Hooker tried to shift the blame for his ignominious failure and put the best face possible on what had happened. "The Cavalry have failed in executing their orders," Hooker's chief of staff, Dan Butterfield, informed Washington, and "General Sedgwick failed in the execution of his orders." Hooker himself proclaimed that his forces had "inflicted heavier blows than we have received," adding that the Army of the Potomac had "added new luster to its former renown."

Opposite: Standing in a narrow lane overlooking Hazel Run on the west slope of Marye's Heights, General Herman Haupt (at left) and one of his assistants, William W. Wright, examine a wrecked caisson and dead team belonging to the Washington Artillery of New Orleans. In the fighting of May 3, the Washington Artillery lost six guns and 29 horses. Haupt and Wright, in the company of photographer A. J. Russell, explored the battlefield on the following day and barely escaped capture when Jubal Early's Confederates reentered Fredericksburg.

The troops were not fooled. "The wonder of the private soldiers was great," one Massachusetts volunteer, Warren Goss, later wrote. "How had one half of the army been defeated while the other half had not fought? The muttered curses were long and deep as they plodded back in the mud to their own camps." Many of the troops, another soldier summed up, were "dejected, demoralized and disgusted."

President Lincoln was not fooled either. He realized with horror that the Army of the Potomac had been defeated again when, about 1:00 p.m. on May 6, he received a wire from Butterfield announcing that Hooker's entire force had recrossed the Rappahannock. "Had a thunderbolt fallen upon the President he could not have been more overwhelmed," remembered Noah Brooks, a California newspaperman who had become a close friend of the Lincolns. "Never, as long as I knew him, did he seem to be so broken, so dispirited, and so ghostlike. Clasping his hands behind his back, he walked up and down the room, saying: 'My God! My God! What will the country say?'"

The country was in fact deeply shocked and dispirited. The defeat also gave new impetus to the North's several antiwar factions, especially the Republican president's most virulent and vocal political enemies, the Peace Democrats, who wanted to arrive at a negotiated settlement even at the cost of offering the South some sort of provisional independence.

Lincoln, shaking all this off as best he could, shortly traveled to Falmouth to confer with Hooker at his headquarters. There Lincoln refrained from blaming Hooker and left him in command, asking only about the condition of the army.

Many of the army's officers were not so charitable. One found Hooker's behavior "inexcusable" and recommended he be fired. General Couch refused to serve under Hooker any longer and asked to be relieved. General Reynolds urged Hooker's removal. One of the more acid comments came from a rising young cavalry captain named George Armstrong Custer, who pronounced that "Hooker's career is well exemplified by that of a rocket, he went up like one and came down like a stick." Military engineer Washington A. Roebling, who would one day build the Brooklyn Bridge, was even more stinging: "Hooker was simply a moral fraud. He has always posed. When it came to the supreme test, he failed utterly."

While Hooker's men glumly settled into their old camps, Lee's dog-tired troops

Major General Oliver O. Howard, whose XI Corps collapsed before Stonewall Jackson's onslaught, praised Jackson for his "bold planning, energy of execution and indefatigable activity." After the war, Howard helped found the university bearing his name in Washington, D.C.

"Howard was always a woman among troops. If he was not born in petticoats, he ought to have been, and ought to wear them."

MAJOR GENERAL JOSEPH HOOKER

dragged themselves back down the Rappahannock to their fortifications near Fredericksburg, to be ready if Hooker or some other Union general decided to try to storm across the river once more. At Chancellorsville, Lee left two brigades to do the dismal work of cleaning up the battlefield. In all, the Confederates recovered no fewer than 19,500 muskets and other small arms, as well as cannon and a mountain of ammunition. They also found themselves guarding thousands of Federal prisoners.

The Confederate troops treated the Federal prisoners kindly, sharing rations and doing what they could for the wounded. But as the captives were marched south in long columns toward Richmond, the trek became an increasingly dreadful ordeal. "There was no food, no nursing, no medicine to dull the pain of those who were in torture," recalled a New York soldier named Rice C. Bull. In Richmond, many were shoved into the city's infamously overcrowded and unsanitary Belle Isle and Libby prison camps, where they suffered from festering wounds and diseases before being exchanged within the next few weeks.

Soldiers assigned to burial parties back at Chancellorsville did their best to inter the dead of both sides decently. Most of the graves, however, were hastily dug and

MAJOR GENERAL JOSEPH HOOKER

Commander, Army of the Potomac

The official line regarding Chancellorsville treated Hooker gently, a courtesy he did not extend to his subordinates. Years later, the San Francisco Chronicle published an interview with Major General Howard in which he accepted some blame. For Hooker, the admission was long overdue, and he was quick to respond with his own outspoken views.

A nd now as to Howard. You know our army took its position, the other corps having crossed at United States Ford, at Chancellorsville, on the 30th of April, 1863, Lee's army being three or four miles in advance of our position, between us and Fredericksburg, nearly east. On the 2d of May Jackson moved north and west. At 1 o'clock p.m., on Saturday, I sent Howard a telegram informing him of Jackson's movement toward his right and directing him to keep his pickets out, keep himself thoroughly informed as to the enemy's movements, and keep me informed of the same at headquarters. Carl Shurz was with Howard when my telegram was received. Howard was lying on his bed. He never communicated the order to his division commanders, and made no disposition of his forces. He pocketed the telegram without reading it, said he was tired, and went to sleep. He seems to have been under the impression that Jackson was retreating. I knew of Jackson's movements, and was not taken by surprise a single moment, and supposed, of course, that my telegram had made Howard fully alive to the situation. But, instead of obeying my orders, he went to sleep, and a portion of Jackson's forces came up in rear of his right. Howard's troops were away from their arms, which were stacked along the line of defense, and did not know of the enemy's presence until fire was opened on them. They left guns, knapsacks, and everything, and the whole corps ran back like a herd of buffaloes. . . .

. . . Howard was always a woman among troops. If he was not born in petticoats, he ought to have been, and ought to wear them. He was always taken up with Sunday Schools and the temperance cause. Those things are all very good, you know, but have very little to do with commanding army corps.

In this photograph mounted on cardboard, cadets of the Virginia Military Institute's class of 1868 gather at Stonewall Jackson's grave near the campus to pay tribute to the hero and former VMI professor—a custom followed yearly by the students for decades after the war.

CHANCELLORSVILLE CASUALTIES

FEDERAL

Killed	*1,606*
Wounded	*9,762*
Captured or missing	*5,919*
Total	*17,287*

CONFEDERATE

Killed	*1,581*
Wounded	*8,700*
Captured or missing (estimated)	*2,545*
Total	*12,826*

shallow. When another great battle took place in the Wilderness a year later, the combatants discovered ghastly relics everywhere in the form of bones and skulls that had worked their way to the surface.

The most famous of the wounded, Stonewall Jackson, seemed to be recovering well after reaching the little house at Guiney Station on May 5. Jackson himself was confident of recovery. "I do not believe I shall die at this time," he said. "I am persuaded the Almighty has yet a work for me to perform." But on May 7 he took a turn for the worse, and Dr. Hunter McGuire, his surgeon, diagnosed pneumonia, a disease for which there was then no effective treatment.

Jackson died in the afternoon of May 10, shortly after saying in a quiet voice, "Let us cross over the river, and rest under the shade of the trees."

Confederate president Jefferson Davis declared a day of national mourning. Jackson's body, taken to Richmond, lay in state in the capitol as thousands of mourners filed by. His remains were then taken to Lexington, Virginia, in the Shenandoah Valley, and he was buried on the grounds of the Virginia Military Institute, where he had taught before the war. "His fame will be grand and enduring," the

Richmond *Dispatch* said, "as the mountains at whose feet he was cradled."

Deeply mourning Jackson's death, General Lee quietly turned to business, reorganizing his army. A plan was forming in his mind. It would not be wise, he told President Davis, to sit still waiting for the Federals to move. Instead he would march his always ill supplied and hungry army west into the Shenandoah, then north up the valley into the rich farmlands of eastern Pennsylvania.

It would essentially be a defensive maneuver, Lee said, forcing Hooker to follow him and derailing any plans the Federals had to advance again toward Richmond. Besides, by ranging into enemy country and posing a threat to Washington, Lee and his army might convince the people of the North that the war was hopeless. This would give the Peace Democrats and other anti-Lincoln forces extra leverage and force the president to make peace. Just possibly, Lee thought, he would be able to surprise part of the Army of the Potomac on the march and destroy it, but a general engagement was probably to be avoided. What Lee did not foresee was that he would be heading toward the most violent and fateful battle of the entire war, at Gettysburg.

"'Let us cross over the river, and rest under the shade of the trees.'"

MARY ANNA MORRISON JACKSON

Wife of Lieutenant General Thomas J. Jackson

Following the news of her husband's wounding, Mrs. Jackson, with her brother, Lieutenant Joseph G. Morrison, spent several days in an agony of suspense awaiting the repair of the railroad from Richmond to Guiney Station. Finally arriving at the little house at Fairfield on May 7, Mrs. Jackson rushed to her husband's bedside and devotedly remained there until he died, three days later.

When he left me on the morning of the 29th, going forth so cheerfully and bravely to the call of duty, he was in the full flush of vigorous manhood, and during that last, blessed visit, I never saw him look so handsome, so happy, and so noble. *Now*, his fearful wounds, his mutilated arm, the scratches upon his face, and, above all, the desperate pneumonia, which was flushing his cheeks, oppressing his breathing, and benumbing his senses, wrung my soul with such grief and anguish as it had never before experienced. Whenever he awakened from his stupor, he always had some endearing words to say to me, such as, "My darling, you are very much loved;" "You are one of the most precious little wives in the world."

Early on Sunday morning, the 10th of May, I was called out of the sick-room by Dr. Morrison, who told me that the doctors, having done everything that human skill could devise to stay the hand of death, had lost all hope, and that my precious, brave, noble husband could not live!

When I told him the doctors thought he would soon be in heaven, he did not seem to comprehend it, and showed no surprise or concern. But upon repeating it, and asking him if he was willing for God to do with him according to His own will, he looked at me calmly and intelligently, and said, "Yes, *I prefer it, I prefer it.*" I then told him that before that day was over he would be with the blessed Saviour in His glory. With perfect distinctness and intelligence, he said, "I will be an infinite gainer to be translated." I then asked him if it was his wish that I should return, with our infant, to my father's home in North Carolina. He answered, "Yes, you have a kind, good father; but no one is so kind and good as your Heavenly Father." He said he had many things to say to me, but he was then too weak....

Mrs. Hoge now came in, bearing little Julia in her arms, with Hetty following, and although he had almost ceased to notice anything, as soon as they entered the door he looked up, his countenance brightened with delight, and he never smiled more sweetly as he exclaimed, "Little darling! sweet one!" She was seated on the bed by his side, and after watching her intently, with radiant smiles, for a few moments, he closed his eyes, as if in prayer. Though she was suffering the pangs of extreme hunger, from long absence from her mother, she seemed to forget her discomfort in the joy of seeing that loving face beam on her once more, and she looked at him and smiled as long as he continued to notice her. Tears were shed over that dying bed by strong men who were unused to weep, and it was touching to see the genuine grief of his servant, Jim, who nursed him faithfully to the end.

He now sank rapidly into unconsciousness, murmuring disconnected words occasionally, but all at once he spoke out very cheerfully and distinctly the beautiful sentence which has become immortal as his last: "Let us cross over the river, and rest under the shade of the trees."

SOLDIERING ON HORSEBACK

The cavalry, so Civil War infantrymen often complained, led an easy life, galloping splendidly about the countryside instead of slogging wearily along on foot. But in fact the horse soldiers had to earn the privilege of riding into battle through hard work, long hours and the mastering of skills unknown to the average rifleman.

The cavalryman, first of all, had to know how to care for his mount, even to the extent of putting his horse's comfort ahead of his own. He had to learn to maneuver his horse through the bewildering evolutions required to move masses of cavalry. And on campaign, he was expected to fight both mounted and dismounted, to scout enemy positions, to inter-

cept the enemy's cavalry, to protect the army's flanks, to carry dispatches, to scour the countryside for forage and even to act as military policeman. "There is no rest for the cavalryman," one veteran Confederate horse soldier lamented. "He is ever in the saddle."

Above top: This homemade wool guidon was carried by a company of the 1st Maryland Cavalry. It is a small version of the 1861 Confederate national flag.

Above: This silk guidon was carried by I Troop of the 6th Pennsylvania Cavalry. Guidons were used to show the location of mounted units in battle.

Lieutenant Thomas B. Dewees leads I Troop, 2d U.S. Cavalry, in a column of twos near its camp at Falmouth, Virginia, in the summer of 1863.

HEIRS TO A KNIGHTLY TRADITION

For many young soldiers in the Civil War, the cavalry was a romantic enterprise that conjured up notions of chivalric combat, and it attracted individualists with a penchant for flamboyant dress and behavior. "There hung about the cavalry a dash and excitement," recalled a Federal trooper. A Confederate proclaimed of the horse soldier: "All that makes the hard and brutal trade of war endurable seems to gather round him, wreathing with brilliant flowers the keen edge of the saber."

Two of the Federal cavalry's more colorful officers were General Judson Kilpatrick (left) and Colonel Sir Percy Wyndham (below). Kilpatrick, known as "Kill Cavalry," was famed for his reckless bravery. Wyndham was an English adventurer who had served in the French Navy, the British Artillery and the Austrian Lancers.

Private James W. Poague of the 1st Virginia Cavalry ornamented the upturned brim of his hat with an elaborate leather star.

Fancy spurs, such as the gilt, eagle-headed version above, were popular with cavalry officers. A few spurs were even made in solid gold.

These officer's gauntlets are embroidered with flowers and lined with morocco leather; plainer versions were issued to troopers to wear while riding.

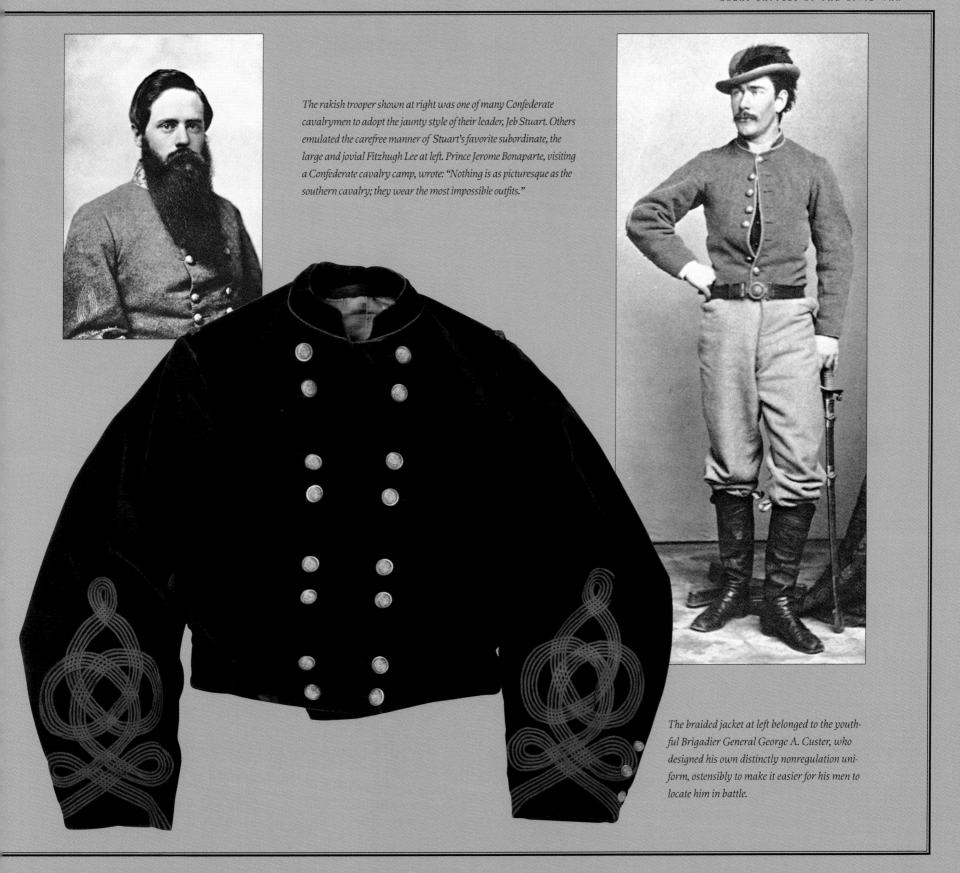

The rakish trooper shown at right was one of many Confederate cavalrymen to adopt the jaunty style of their leader, Jeb Stuart. Others emulated the carefree manner of Stuart's favorite subordinate, the large and jovial Fitzhugh Lee at left. Prince Jerome Bonaparte, visiting a Confederate cavalry camp, wrote: "Nothing is as picturesque as the southern cavalry; they wear the most impossible outfits."

The braided jacket at left belonged to the youthful Brigadier General George A. Custer, who designed his own distinctly nonregulation uniform, ostensibly to make it easier for his men to locate him in battle.

ARMS AND EQUIPMENT OF A CAVALRY TROOPER

A rmed with carbine, saber, and one or two pistols, the Civil War horse soldier took more than 20 pounds of equipment into battle. He wore the gear on his person so that the weapons would be handy if he had to dismount and fight on foot.

Most Federal cavalry units used breech-loading carbines of various sorts; more than 17 different types were issued during the war. Confederate troopers usually had to make do with muzzle-loading, smoothbore carbines—or even shotguns. Most horsemen on both sides continued to carry sabers, although firearms proved more effective in combat.

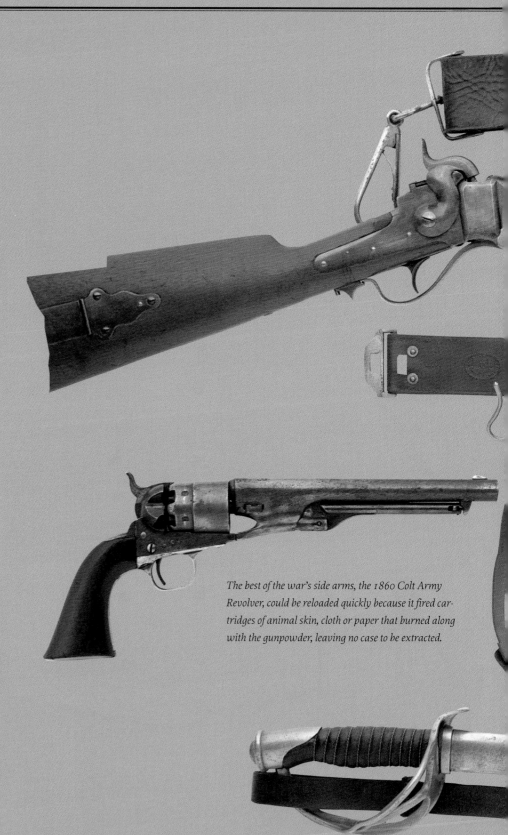

Both the jaunty, cigar-smoking Federal trooper (right) and his Confederate counterpart (left) wear full equipment over short shell jackets, which were common to enlisted cavalrymen on both sides. The jackets were far more convenient for riding than the longer, skirted frock coats.

The best of the war's side arms, the 1860 Colt Army Revolver, could be reloaded quickly because it fired cartridges of animal skin, cloth or paper that burned along with the gunpowder, leaving no case to be extracted.

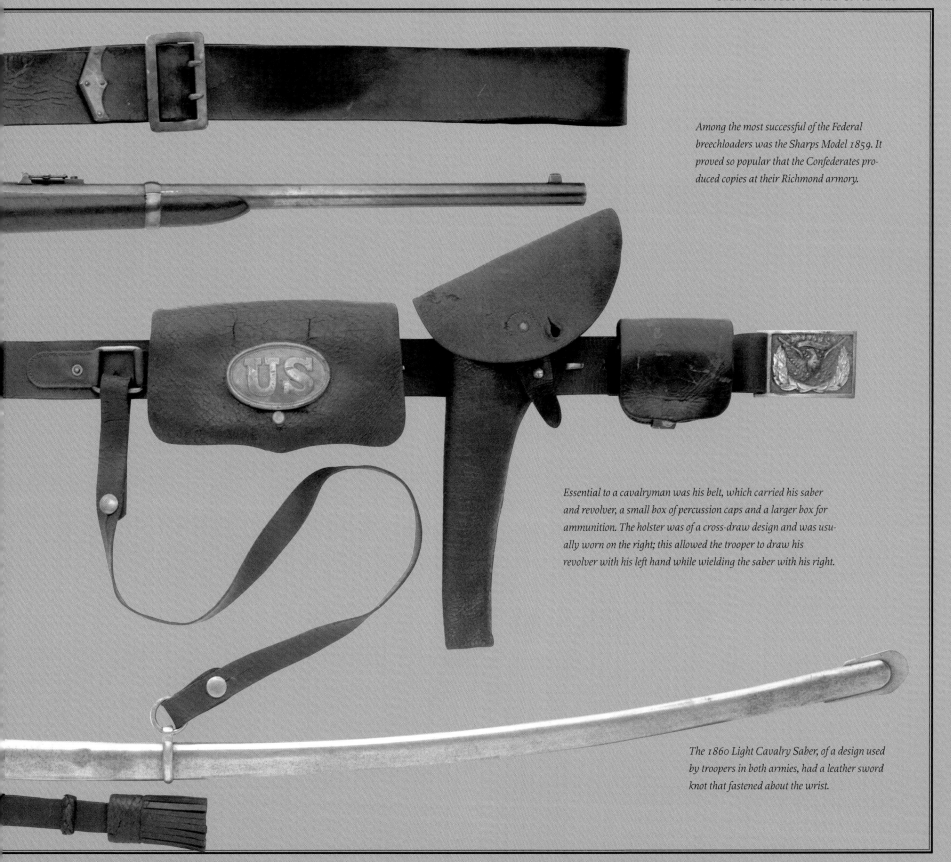

Among the most successful of the Federal breechloaders was the Sharps Model 1859. It proved so popular that the Confederates produced copies at their Richmond armory.

Essential to a cavalryman was his belt, which carried his saber and revolver, a small box of percussion caps and a larger box for ammunition. The holster was of a cross-draw design and was usually worn on the right; this allowed the trooper to draw his revolver with his left hand while wielding the saber with his right.

The 1860 Light Cavalry Saber, of a design used by troopers in both armies, had a leather sword knot that fastened about the wrist.

THE IMPORTANCE OF MAINTAINING A MOUNT

The cavalry trooper was quick to learn that his ability to fight—perhaps even to survive—depended on his horse. Each man acted as his own groom and veterinarian and maintained his own tack. He made certain that saddle and bridle fit properly to keep his mount free of sores, sprains and even internal injuries. And he kept the horse well fed. Indeed, in the Confederate army, where rations were often scarce, horses ate even when their riders did not.

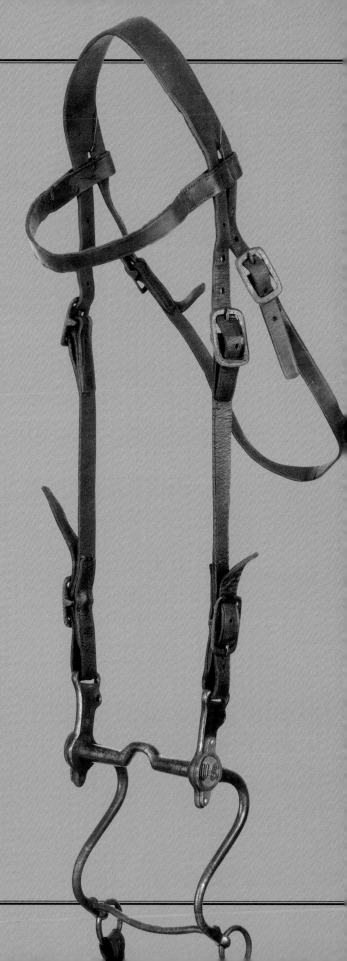

Right: This single-reined bridle with curb bit was of a pattern introduced in 1863. It replaced a more complicated double-reined model that used two bits, a snaffle and a curb; that rig was discarded after it proved too difficult for novice cavalrymen to control.

Private Elnathan S. Cheney of the 2d Pennsylvania Cavalry sits proudly astride his mount. Cheney's tack is a mixed bag: He has combined the standard McClellan saddle with a nonregulation bridle.

Right: The rugged McClellan saddle, designed by Union general George McClellan, was the best of several types used during the war. The trooper strapped his overcoat across the saddle bow and a poncho and blanket across the cantle. Saddlebags and other items were hung on straps.

Below: In bivouac, the 14-inch iron picket pin was driven into the ground and linked by rope to the horse's halter. This arrangement allowed the animal to graze without straying.

Shortly after the siege began, the beautiful grounds and gardens of Wexford Lodge, also known as the Shirley house or White house, which had kept the Shirley family "bountifully supplied with vegetables and small fruits and a row of peanut hills," were destroyed by the spades of Union troops as they constructed bombproofs to protect themselves from Confederate artillery fire. In this photo the dugouts of the 45th Illinois Infantry can be seen covering the slope beneath the battered house.

Vicksburg
War on the Mississippi

PRIME PRIZE ON THE GREAT RIVER—Before the outbreak of the Civil War, Vicksburg, Mississippi, had become one of the most prosperous and sophisticated towns on the old Southern frontier. Built atop bluffs overlooking the Mississippi River, the city was a booming center of trade, its wharves crowded with boats carrying all manner of goods and commodities. It boasted a municipal orchestra, a Shakespeare repertory company, and an imposing courthouse in the Greek Revival style. To its proud citizens Vicksburg was the "Queen City of the Bluff" and a center, as one of them wrote, of "culture, education and luxury."

All this was to change with the coming of the war. By early 1862 the peaceful town had become one of the most strategically important spots in the entire Confederacy—and would soon be one of the most bitterly fought over. Vicksburg by its topography was a natural fortress: Its high bluffs, once they had been fitted out with batteries of big guns, made the city impregnable to frontal attack from the river and from across the broken plain to the east. To the north stretched the Yazoo River delta—a vast morass of bayou, river, and swamp no attacking army could march through. To the south lay more of the same.

Yet so important was Vicksburg that Union forces would hammer away at it for more than a year while the Confederates tried just as desperately to hold it. As the fighting wore on, the city would suffer bombardments by the Federal navy, then become the target of a powerful Union army led by the most tenacious of Northern commanders, Major General Ulysses S. Grant. By the time the campaign for Vicksburg was over, it had become one of the longest and most harrowing ordeals of the war, marked by a half-dozen battles and ending with a siege that would leave the city in ruins.

Vicksburg became a prime strategic prize largely because it was the key to a vital Confederate supply line bringing huge quantities of food and other matériel from the West. Cargo vessels loaded with cattle and cotton and grain from Texas and Arkansas could steam down the Red River across Louisiana, then turn north up the Mississippi to unload at Vicksburg's docks. From there the supplies were shipped east on the Southern Mississippi Railroad for distribution throughout the South on a network of connecting rail lines.

This national flag was carried by veterans of the 7th, 19th, and 22d Kentucky regiments who joined in 1864 to form a new unit. It was named for the 7th Kentucky because the unit had contributed the most men. As attested by the flag's battle honors, the three Kentucky regiments served throughout the Vicksburg campaign.

Flag Officer David Glasgow Farragut fretted about the perils of sailing a deep-draft, oceangoing fleet on the shallow waters of the Mississippi, especially after his flagship Hartford (above), a 225-foot-long screw sloop, ran aground on the way to Vicksburg. "It is a sad thing," he commented, "to think of having your ship on a mud bank, 500 miles from the natural element of a sailor."

Just as busy was a new railroad that ran westward from the west bank of the Mississippi opposite the town, the Vicksburg, Shreveport & Texas. Its trains brought in thousands of tons of freight—including European-made rifles and other munitions that had been shipped to Mexico and then hauled northward through Texas, evading the Union navy's blockade of Southern ports. In all, Vicksburg was, said Confederate president Jefferson Davis, "the nailhead that held the South's two halves together." Abraham Lincoln agreed. Pointing to a White House map of the region in 1862, he stated, "The whole lower Mississippi region is the backbone of the rebellion."

Aside from choking off the Confederate supply line, there were other reasons to capture Vicksburg. Most important was to open the Mississippi River for Northern commerce. Before the war the farmers of the Midwest had floated huge quantities of wheat and corn down the river on flatboats and barges to New Orleans, where the produce was transferred to oceangoing vessels for shipment to the East Coast and around the world.

But Vicksburg, sitting on its high bluffs, dominated the central Mississippi, strangling this commerce. Unable to pay the high costs of sending their produce east by rail, midwestern farmers began grumbling against the war. Thus, for economic and political reasons, too, Lincoln's government had to free the Mississippi of Confederate blockade.

By mid-1862 Union forces already controlled parts of the river. In April of that year, Flag Officer David Glasgow Farragut had boldly sailed a Union fleet into the mouth of the Mississippi and then blasted his way past two formidable enemy bastions guarding the approaches to New Orleans. Union troops had quickly occupied the great port city, closing it to all Confederate traffic.

At the same time Federal troops and gunboats had been fighting their way south down the Mississippi. Victories at New Madrid, Missouri, at Island No. 10, and at Columbus, Kentucky, gave the Union a tight grip on the great river at the northern and southern ends of the western Confederacy. It remained for the Yankees to take the middle, centered on Vicksburg. That would prove to be an exceedingly difficult task.

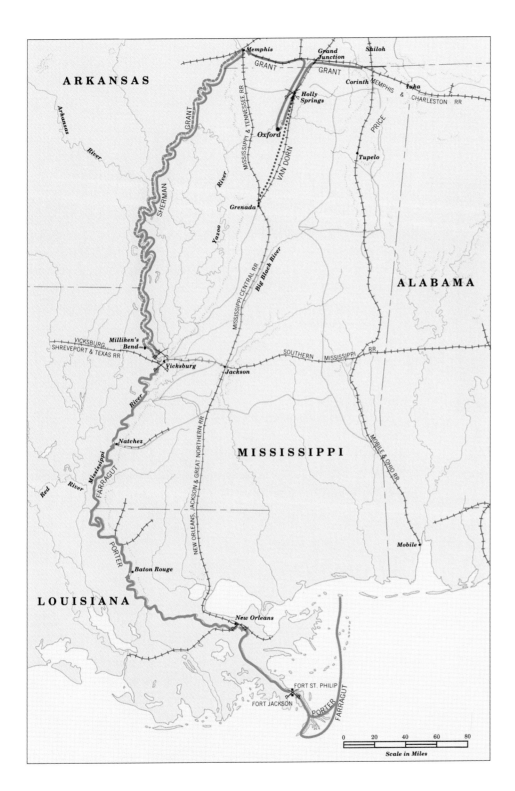

Capturing New Orleans in April 1862, Farragut quickly secured most of the lower Mississippi. He then sailed upriver and in June attempted unsuccessfully to bombard Vicksburg into submission. In December Grant moved on the city from the north along the Mississippi Central Railroad while Sherman advanced downriver to attack Chickasaw Bluffs. Grant pulled back after Rebel cavalry under Van Dorn (red arrow) destroyed his supply base at Holly Springs, and, in late December, Sherman was repulsed at Chickasaw Bluffs. When McClernand captured Arkansas Post on January 12, 1863, Federal control of the upper Mississippi was complete. Grant then began massing his forces near Milliken's Bend.

The youthful crewmen of the 24-gun Union sloop Hartford, flagship of David Farragut, pose informally on deck. During engagements in the Vicksburg campaign, Farragut stationed himself in the rigging and shouted orders to the crew through a speaking tube that ran from the mizzen top to the quarterdeck.

First to try was Farragut, who had been ordered to steam up the Mississippi and take Vicksburg immediately after capturing New Orleans. Move Farragut did, taking his big, deep-water warships upstream through the river's twisting channels—and forcing the surrender en route of Baton Rouge, Louisiana, and Natchez, Mississippi.

On reaching Vicksburg, however, Farragut got a rude surprise. To a demand that the city capitulate, one of Vicksburg's defenders, Colonel James L. Autrey, sent back a succinct reply: "Mississippians don't know, and refuse to learn, how to surrender."

Worse, it was clear that while Farragut's ships had been slowly winding between the Mississippi's snags and sand bars, Vicksburg had been reinforced with both infantry and heavy artillery. Also, the guns of Farragut's warships could not be elevated enough to fire at the enemy batteries high on the bluffs, whereas the Confederate cannon were ideally sited to fire down on the Union fleet. Further, the 1,400 troops Farragut had brought along were far too few to attack the Rebel garrison of 4,000. Judging the situation hopeless, Farragut headed his ships back toward New Orleans.

There he received a still nastier surprise—a direct order from President Lincoln to try again. Some Federal gunboats were steaming downriver toward Vicksburg. Farragut's fleet was to join them, and together the two flotillas would use their "utmost exertions to open the Mississippi." On June 8 Farragut set out upriver once more.

This time he had brought along some mortar schooners that could lob shells into Vicksburg, which they did, subjecting the city to the first of many bombardments. Then, on the night of June 28, Farragut daringly steamed his fleet upriver past Vicksburg's guns. The ships blasted away at the town while the batteries of Rebel cannon poured a thunderous fire down on the Union vessels. Three ships were forced to turn back and others were damaged, but the fleet managed to run the gantlet with only 15 dead and 30 wounded.

Still, it was a hollow victory, as Farragut admitted. Except for a few lucky shots that had exploded near Confederate positions, the Federal fire had achieved little or nothing. Clearly, even with gunboats and mortar ships the navy was powerless to dislodge the enemy cannon, which still commanded the river. Again, the troops Farragut had brought along, a single brigade of 3,200 men, had no hope of storming the place. "I am satisfied," Farragut wrote Secretary of the Navy Gideon Welles, "that it is not possible for us to take Vicksburg without an army force of twelve or fifteen thousand men."

With that Farragut put the troops ashore on the west bank of the river under their commander, Brigadier General Thomas Williams, and anchored his ships nearby, safely out of range of Vicksburg's guns. The ships were badly shot up nevertheless—by a single armored Confederate ram called the *Arkansas*. The Rebel ship boldly steamed down the Mississippi and right through the middle of Farragut's fleet, all guns firing.

"Mississippians don't know, and refuse to learn, how to surrender."

The *Arkansas* ended up badly battered, but the Federals fared worse, with every vessel hit and 17 men killed, 42 wounded. A furious Farragut attempted to take revenge by twice sending ships to attack the *Arkansas* at its Vicksburg mooring, but the ram refused to sink. With that, Farragut had had enough, and in late July

Opposite: In an etching by a wartime artist, the Confederate ironclad ram Arkansas plows through the combined Federal fleets of Farragut and Flag Officer Charles Davis above Vicksburg on July 15, 1862. After the attack, the Arkansas took refuge under the Confederate batteries at Vicksburg. On shore, a Tennessee soldier watched the vessel arrive and later portrayed her (inset) in his primitive style.

The Arkansas.

THE UNION'S HOMESPUN HERO

Exalted in the eyes of the Northern public, Major General Ulysses S. Grant was in person a shy and reticent man, as plain as homespun. "He was pictured in the popular mind as striding about in the swash-buckler style of melodrama," a Federal officer wrote. "Many of us were not a little surprised to find in him a modesty of mien and gentleness of manner which seemed to fit him more for the court than for the camp."

Right: This photograph of Grant was taken in the early 1850s before he resigned his captain's commission to avoid a court-martial for drinking and neglecting his duty. At the time, he was stationed on the West Coast, apart from his wife and family.

Grant (left) and his friend Alexander Hays, both second lieutenants, stand beside their horses at Camp Salubrity, Louisiana, in 1845. Hays later became a general and was killed fighting under Grant in 1864.

Left: Grant was a 27-year-old quartermaster of the 4th U.S. Infantry at Sackets Harbor, New York, when this daguerreotype was taken in 1849. Recently married, he lived with his bride, Julia, in cramped quarters at Madison Barracks.

This portrait of Grant was taken in Vicksburg after his victory there in 1863. "His eyes were dark grey, and were the most expressive of his features," an aide wrote. "His face gave little indication of his thoughts."

Left: Approaching the apex of his military career in 1863, Major General Grant poses with his hand on his sword. In fact, he disliked side arms and wore them only rarely.

Toward the end of the war, Grant and his wife, Julia, sit for a family portrait with their children (from left) Nellie, Jesse, Fred, and Ulysses Jr.

Brigadier General Stephen D. Lee, a West Point graduate and Charleston native, reluctantly resigned his U.S. Army commission and became a captain in the South Carolina artillery. By December 1862 he commanded a brigade in the defense of Vicksburg. Lee deployed his outnumbered troops in strong defensive positions atop Chickasaw Bluffs and stopped Sherman's attack there cold. Shown here in the uniform of a major general, Lee eventually, at age 30, became the youngest lieutenant general of the war.

he headed back down the river again. The navy's three-month attempt to take Vicksburg was over, with nothing accomplished. It would now be the turn of the army—with help from the inland navy's gunboats and transports.

The nearest Federal army was a force of about 100,000 men led by Ulysses S. Grant. For the moment, though, Grant was immobilized, his troops dispersed in a half-dozen places in northern Mississippi and western Tennessee, guarding rail lines and other strategic spots against attacks.

But in early October, after stopping suicidal attacks by the Confederates on formidable Union earthworks outside Corinth, Mississippi, Grant was able at last to go after Vicksburg. His plan: to march south along the Mississippi Central Railroad, maintaining his supply route, and, outflanking Vicksburg, force the city to surrender.

Soon, however, everything began to go wrong. First, Grant was informed to his astonishment that a wholly separate Federal force led by Major General John A. McClernand was also being readied to advance on Vicksburg. Somehow McClernand, an ambitious and politically powerful former Illinois congressman appointed general in 1861, had persuaded President Lincoln to let him form an army in southern Ohio, float it down the Mississippi, and make his own attack.

Outraged that a vain and amateurish political general was about to mount a campaign in his own department, Grant moved to forestall McClernand, sending his friend and favorite subordinate, Major General William Tecumseh Sherman, marching with 30,000 troops to Memphis. From there Sherman was to steam down the Mississippi and assault Chickasaw Bluffs, a few miles up from the mouth of the Yazoo River and only three miles north of Vicksburg. At the same time, Grant would continue south and be ready to come at Vicksburg from the direction of Jackson.

But while Grant was maneuvering, the Rebels were making some moves of their own. In the course of strengthening Vicksburg's defenses, the Confederate government had named the stolid but reliable Lieutenant General John C. Pemberton commander of the city's garrison and then had sent one of the South's top generals, Joseph E. Johnston, to be overall commander in the West. The two leaders, it turned out, could not agree on strategy, Pemberton arguing that Vicksburg be turned into a fortress, Johnston holding that their forces should remain mobile, ready to fight the Federals in open battle. Those differences were never settled, with dire results for the Southern cause.

For the moment, however, Pemberton devised a brilliant double strike to cut Grant's supply lines. General Earl Van Dorn would take his cavalry and hit Holly Springs, Grant's supply depot in northern Mississippi. At the same time the great Confederate cavalry raider Nathan Bedford Forrest would strike the vital rail lines near Jackson, Tennessee.

Both attacks were hugely successful, Forrest tearing up miles of track and Van Dorn capturing the entire Holly Springs garrison while destroying, by his own estimate, $1.5 million worth of Federal stores. Grant realized the raids had dealt his plans a critical blow. Caught in enemy territory with no way to get supplies, he had to fall back rapidly toward his main base at Memphis.

As he retreated, Grant tried to warn Sherman that half of their two-pronged attack was off. But the raiders had cut the telegraph wires, and the message never got through. Sherman, starting down the Mississippi from Memphis with three divisions on December 20, was unknowingly left to plunge ahead on his own—against a strengthened enemy and one, moreover, warned of his approach by Rebel spies upriver using a private telegraph line.

Reaching the mouth of the Yazoo the day after Christmas, the flotilla of Federal gunboats and transports bearing Sherman's force moved seven miles up the river. There the troops landed and, after a cautious advance, approached Chickasaw Bluffs on December 28. Immediately, 20,000 Confederates sent by Pemberton to meet the attack began hammering the Yankees as they struggled through swampy stretches of bayou and bog, stopping them cold.

Dismayed, Sherman called off the first assault but decided to try again the next day, sending two brigades to hit the Confederate left, where the ground looked passable. The attack was met, one Federal officer recalled, with "a flaming hell of shot, shell, canister and minie balls." Still, the Federals fought their

Opposite: This contemporary engraving incorrectly depicts Sherman's troops struggling hand to hand with Confederate defenders at the crest of Chickasaw Bluffs. In fact, withering Rebel fire kept the Federals pinned down at the foot of the hill. "Balls came zip-zip into the trees and the ground around us," wrote an Ohio captain, adding, "Occasionally, thud, a bullet takes some poor fellow and he is carried to the rear." Heavy rains that night turned the already swampy ground into a bottomless quagmire and persuaded Sherman to abandon the offensive.

"I did all that was possible to reach the main land, but was met at every point by batteries and rifle pits that we could not pass, ..."

**MAJOR GENERAL
WILLIAM T. SHERMAN**

Commander, XV Corps, Army of the Tennessee

During the war, Sherman maintained a regular correspondence with his brother, John, an Ohio senator. Well aware that he faced criticism at home for his failure at Chickasaw Bluffs, he seems to have gone out of his way in this letter to describe the bristling defenses and impenetrable terrain as justification for his defeat.

---//---

Steamer Forest Queen, Jan. 6, 1863.

Dear Brother: You will have heard of our attack on Vicksburg and failure to succeed. The place is too strong, and without the co-operation of a large army coming from the interior it is impracticable. Innumerable batteries prevent the approach of gun boats to the city or to the first bluff up the Yazoo, and the only landing between is on an insular space of low boggy ground, with innumerable bayous or deep sloughs. I did all that was possible to reach the main land, but was met at every point by batteries and rifle pits that we could not pass, and in the absence of Gen. Grant's co-operating force I was compelled to re-embark my command. My report to Gen. Grant, a copy of which I sent to Gen. Halleck, who will let you see it, is very full, and more than I could write to you with propriety. Whatever you or the absent may think, not a soldier or officer who was present but will admit I pushed the attack as far as prudence would justify, and that I re-embarked my command in the nick of time, for a heavy rain set in which would have swamped us and made it impossible to withdraw artillery and stores.

Major General John A. McClernand, a former Illinois congressman, used his friendship with President Lincoln to win command of the XIII Corps from Major General William T. Sherman during the Vicksburg campaign. A bitter Sherman later labeled the ambitious McClernand "the meanest man we ever had in the west."

way to the foot of the bluff—only to be pinned down there by more ferocious fire from above. Slowly, grudgingly, the Federals fell back, their units disorganized. In all the Union force lost 1,776 men to the Confederates' 187.

Sherman wanted to try again farther up the Yazoo at Haynes' Bluff and asked the gunboats' commander, the equally combative Admiral David Dixon Porter, to shift the brigades upstream. But then an impenetrable fog blanketed the swamps, followed by a driving rain. Fearful the water might rise and drown his army, Sherman had to withdraw, Admiral Porter ferrying the troops back down the Yazoo and across the Mississippi to Milliken's Bend.

Yet another humiliation was in store for Sherman. McClernand and his forces arrived at Milliken's Bend in the first week of January 1863, and since McClernand held superior rank, Sherman had to turn command over to the politician turned general. Fearing that McClernand might launch an attack of his own, Grant moved from Memphis to Milliken's Bend to take direct control. He arrived on January 29, bringing more troops and a huge flotilla of gunboats, mortar schooners, transports, and supply vessels. To McClernand's irritation, Grant immediately incorporated both him and his force into the main army as its XIII Corps. With Sherman's XV Corps, and the XVII Corps commanded by the exceedingly able James B. McPherson, Grant could now call on enough manpower, it seemed, to take Vicksburg at last.

How that was to be done from the Federal base on the west bank of the Mississippi was another matter. Farragut had proved that river bombardments did not work, and Sherman had demonstrated the perils of attacking through the swamps to Vicksburg's north. Nevertheless, through the first months of 1863 Grant would

The design of the U.S.S. Rattler, Admiral Porter's flagship for the Yazoo Pass expedition, was a wartime expedient to meet the need for fast, lightweight, shallow-draft vessels with just enough armor to protect the pilothouse and machinery from small-arms fire. These so-called tinclads proved to be a great success, navigating through narrow passages and over shoals where the heavier ironclads could not go.

stubbornly try every conceivable trick to get at or by Vicksburg—each new one, it seemed, more bizarre than the last. If nothing came of them, Grant figured, they would reassure Washington and the public that he was at work. That work would also keep the men busy and fit until a more feasible approach came along.

Oddest of all these schemes, perhaps, was the first—digging a canal across the base of the fingerlike peninsula formed by the river's 180-degree horse-shoe bend opposite Vicksburg. Work on this had been started by General Williams' troops, put ashore the previous summer by Farragut. Now Sher-

man's corps was assigned the muddy task. Just possibly the Mississippi could be diverted through such a canal, causing the river to bypass Vicksburg—and simultaneously opening a safe route for Union shipping.

It proved grinding, nasty work, the troops perpetually soaked, and even Sherman often finding himself hip deep in mud and slime. In the dampness only insects seemed to thrive, the air becoming, one soldier complained, "a saturated solution of gnats." Still, the digging went on—until a Mississippi flood washed away much of the work and the Confederates planted a battery of guns opposite the canal's exit

As part of General Grant's strategy to bypass Vicksburg's batteries, soldiers dredge a canal across a mile-wide peninsula formed by the horseshoe bend in the Mississippi River at Vicksburg. Although Grant foresaw failure in this and other engineering schemes, he later wrote, "I let the work go on, believing employment was better than idleness."

that could have blown to smithereens any boat trying the route. With that, Grant halted the project.

He was not through, however. Forty miles north of Milliken's Bend was a bayou called Lake Providence, left behind years ago after one of the Mississippi's many course changes. South from the lake stretched 470 miles of interconnected waterways ending up at the Red River, far below Vicksburg. Again, if the Mississippi could be diverted, the Federals could bypass the city. Assigned the unenviable digging job this time was General McPherson, an experienced engineering officer, and his XVII Corps. Amazingly, McPherson's troops managed to trundle a 30-ton steamer overland from the Mississippi to Lake Providence and also perfected a rotary saw that could slice through huge submerged tree stumps. But mercifully for McPherson's weary men, Grant realized after two months that this scheme, too, had no chance of success and called it off.

Grant next turned his eyes to the intricate maze of waterways across the Mississippi north of Vicksburg. Long before the war much southbound river traffic had turned eastward about 150 miles above Vicksburg into Yazoo Pass and proceeded from there across a body of water called Moon Lake and then down several streams to trade at ports on the Yazoo itself. Boats going on to New Orleans had only to continue down the Yazoo to reenter the Mississippi just above Vicksburg. If Federal troops could be ferried down the Yazoo, they could, Grant figured, be put ashore on the eastern side of the Yazoo delta and, bypassing the bluffs that had frustrated Sherman, fall on Vicksburg from the northeast.

The first problem was that the Yazoo Pass was no longer open. A huge levee had been built across its mouth in the 1850s as a flood control measure. To deal with this, Grant sent a young West Point-trained engineer, Lieutenant Colonel James H. Wilson, sailing north with bags of explosives.

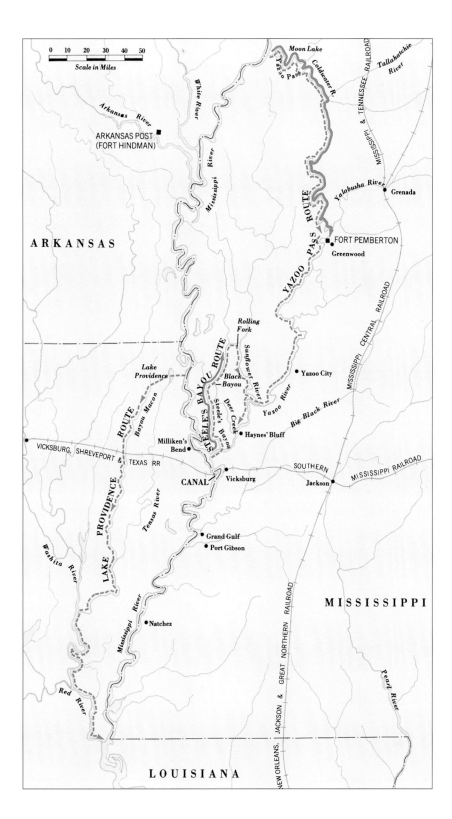

Maintaining offensive pressure, Grant began a series of expeditions aimed at closing the ring around Vicksburg. Two efforts—a canal cut across Young's Point opposite the city and the opening of a 400-mile route from Lake Providence south to the Red River—were sabotaged by the unpredictable river. Then engineers holed a levee near Moon Lake to flood the Yazoo Pass, allowing boats to reach the Yazoo River. Yankee forces floated as far south as the Yalobusha River, where they were stopped by Confederates at Fort Pemberton. In support, Sherman and Porter pushed up the lower Yazoo into Steele's Bayou, but low water nearly bottled up Porter's fleet. Thus, these forays all failed, but Grant had one more plan.

"The vessels were so torn to pieces, they had hulls and engines left and that had to suffice."

On February 2 a segment of the levee erupted skyward, and the flood-swollen waters of the Mississippi, rushing through the gap, demolished the rest. On February 7 a small flotilla of gunboats and transports carrying the first contingent of 4,500 men went swooshing through the pass and, bobbing frantically in the turbulent water, emerged into Moon Lake.

Grant had hoped to take the Confederates by surprise. But Pemberton had foreseen the move and had sent Rebel work parties to fell huge trees across the waterways. To proceed at all, the Federal troops had to disembark and, with 500 men at each hawser, tug and wrench the trees out of the way.

As the flotilla struggled on, the channels became painfully narrow and so thickly bordered by trees that the branches interlocked overhead to form a tunnel. In short order the branches had ripped away the transports' high pilothouses and smokestacks, knocking them overboard. "The vessels were so torn to pieces," Admiral Porter wrote, "they had hulls and engines left and that had to suffice."

Worse was to come. At the juncture of the Yazoo with the Yalobusha River the Confederates had sunk old ships, blocking the channel, and had also built a breastwork of cotton bales and sandbags defended by 2,000 men and eight cannon, which they named Fort Pemberton. More critical, the stronghold was surrounded by marsh so impassable the Federal infantry could not get at it.

After pondering for several days what to do, Lieutenant Commander Watson Smith sent ahead a pair of gunboats—which were immediately hit by enemy fire and forced to draw back. Two more attempts to rush past Fort Pemberton met with the same results. At that the Federals gave up and the entire expedition turned tail,

SERGEANT JOHN V. BOUCHER

10th Missouri (U.S.) Infantry, Holmes' Brigade

This letter, written by Boucher to his wife after his return from the Yazoo Pass expedition, accurately expresses the sentiments of the average soldier regarding the miserable 1,400-mile journey by transport. Boucher also described the rich agricultural panorama he observed from the railing of his steamer, as well as the "many fine plantations evacuated and left to grow up in weeds" and "thousands of acres of the best land I ever saw . . . rendered useless." About the latter he said, "This much good is done any how if no more it has broke up hundreds of the most welthy planters in the south."

April 12th 1863
Mrs. J. V. Boucher
Old Sand Bar, Arkansas . . .
to which we returned yesterday after a long and tedious voyage of 18 days in the Grand Yazoo Pass expedition and a grand expedition it was too. . . . Well this Yazoo expedition beats the devil oll hollow so far as I can see in to it. Twenty steamers loaded down with men munitions cannon horses & mules artilery hard crackers fat meat and no place to hook it only as we could croud round the furnace now and again passing rite through the woods twenty five miles not wider than your door yard the channel bottoms all overflowed of course thus we went tearing and smashing boats saplins and other timber at a woful rate till we came in to a little river caled Cold Water about as big as Old Elkhorn in a freshet thence in to the Talihatcha a stream not as big as Okaw, and down it with in two miles of Greenwood a rebble fortification. there we halted after a eleven days voyge remained two days about-faced and on the eighteenth day landed back on the Old Sand Bar all safe and sound except one man died on the way. I said sound I mean as sound as could be expected And so ends the great Yazoo expedition that you have heard so much blow about. Now weather our commanders got skeard at the fort or the fort skeard them I can not tell. Or weather they found the enimy to strong for us and backed off or weather the enimy found us to strong for them and backed off I am not able to tell. Nor know mortal man connected with the private ranks can tell any thing about it.

In this series of drawings, Harper's Weekly shows the labors and hazards involved in Grant's last attempt to sidestep Vicksburg's batteries. This was the 200-mile loop through Steele's Bayou, which would finish some 20 miles up the Yazoo River from where it had started—but in good position to set troops ashore for a landward attack on Vicksburg.

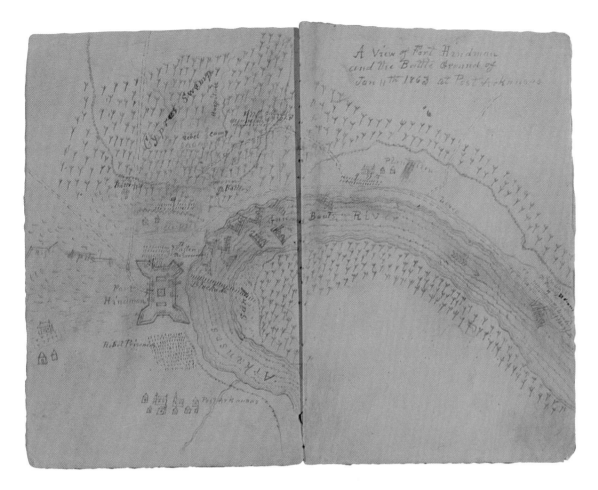

The Federal fleet steams past Fort Hindman in this sketch made on January 11, 1862 by soldier-artist Daniel Allen. A surveyor in civilian life, Allen joined the 77th Illinois Infantry as drum major of the regimental band and spent much of his service time aboard what he characterized as a "nasty filthy steamboat."

Rear Admiral David Dixon Porter's fleet would play a crucial role in winning control of the Mississippi. A loner, he nevertheless got along quite well during the Vicksburg campaign with his army counterpart. He later wrote, "So confident was I of General Grant's ability to carry out his plans that I never hesitated."

heading back the 100 miles to the Yazoo Pass and the Mississippi and ending what one soldier aptly called "a picturesque farce."

Still another attempt to get through the bayous north of Vicksburg was to come. General Grant, worried that the Yazoo Pass expedition might become trapped, asked Admiral Porter to explore the waterways at the lower end of the Yazoo and to stage a rescue mission if needed. Explore Porter did, taking Grant along on his flagship *Black Hawk*. Steaming into the mouth of the Yazoo, they then turned into Steele's Bayou. From there, Porter explained to Grant, gunboats and transports could weave through a succession of flooded streams with names like Black Bayou, Deer Creek, and the Sunflower River and outflank the Chickasaw Bluffs fortifications. The whole thing involved making a 200-mile loop to reach a point only about 25 miles from their starting point at Milliken's Bend, but it just might work.

Grant approved, and that night, back at his headquarters at Milliken's Bend, ordered Porter to give his plan a try. Eleven vessels began to push through the tangled waterways, while Sherman's troops followed on foot.

But again, the farther the boats went, the narrower the channels became. This slowed the whole procession, and then crewmen spotted Confederate troops landing on a levee on a nearby bend in the Sunflower River. Porter's lead boats were

immediately hit by artillery fire, and on March 19 he sent a message to Sherman to hurry forward a rescue party of supporting infantry.

This Sherman did, the troops, many with lighted candles in their gun barrels for the daring night march, groping along as best they could on narrow fingers of high ground. When they arrived a day later, however, they found Porter already trying to back his gunboats away from the fierce enemy fire. At last, with the infantry's help, Porter managed to extricate the boats from the watery maze before they were destroyed or captured. By March 27 they had reached relative safety through Steele's Bayou and the Yazoo, coming out into the Mississippi and back to Milliken's Bend. Another—in fact the last—of what Grant called his "experiments" had failed.

Grant now knew for certain that trying to hit Vicksburg from the north would not work. Clearly the best plan, risky and difficult though it might be, was to take his army down the Mississippi well south of Vicksburg, cross the river, fight his way in a wide semicircle to the east and north, and come at the city from the east. But April had come, and the spring sun was drying the terrain and making full-scale army movements possible. Grant had some 60,000 men. The experiments were over. Now Grant would gamble his entire army in one of the most dangerous movements of the Civil War.

SMALL ARMS
FOR FEDERAL SAILORS

Federal warships plying narrow Southern waterways faced a danger that their big guns could do little to prevent—a lightning strike by an enemy boarding party. To guard against this risk, each warship maintained a small arsenal of weapons for close-quarters combat. In times of peril, the weapons were taken from storage and passed out to selected crewmen. Besides the cutlass—the traditional sailor's weapon for hand-to-hand fighting—a Civil War sailor might also carry a modern, breech-loading carbine, a single-action revolver, and a cartridge box. The metal surfaces of the carbines were tinned to resist corrosion. The Sharps & Hankins model shown here came with a leather barrel cover for added protection against water damage.

The menacing battle ax, which dated from the War of 1812, doubled as a tool for cutting away wreckage and downed rigging. For those men whose duties prevented the wearing of such encumbrances, extra weapons were placed in racks at convenient locations throughout the vessel.

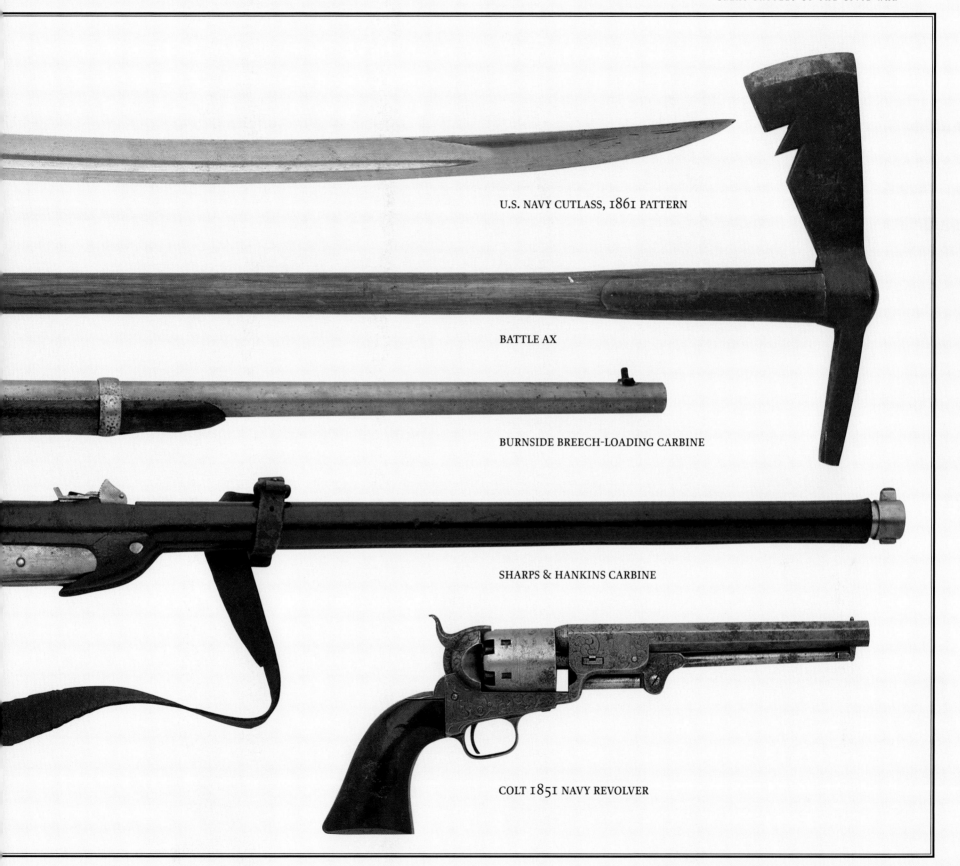

U.S. NAVY CUTLASS, 1861 PATTERN

BATTLE AX

BURNSIDE BREECH-LOADING CARBINE

SHARPS & HANKINS CARBINE

COLT 1851 NAVY REVOLVER

Colonel Benjamin H. Grierson (inset) was the most unlikely of cavalry heroes. Kicked by a horse at the age of eight, he had hated the animal ever since. A musician, composer, and music teacher in civilian life, he had strenuously protested his appointment in 1861 to the 6th Illinois Cavalry. Yet Grierson soon proved so able a commander that Sherman told Grant he was "the best cavalry officer I have yet had." When Grierson's bedraggled soldiers and their worn-out mounts finally reached the Federal base at Baton Rouge (above), the commandant insisted on staging a parade, during which many of the exhausted troopers fell asleep in the saddle.

Despite a fierce bombardment, gunboats and transports of Porter's fleet steam past Vicksburg on April 16, 1863. In the foreground a boat carrying General Sherman is being rowed out to greet Admiral Porter on his flagship, the Benton.

SWEEPING TO VICKSBURG'S DOORSTEP

Grant's final plan of attack—to march his army south, float it across the Mississippi, and then move east—was desperately chancy. It called for an amphibious landing that, if met head-on by the Confederates, could turn into a disaster. Even with a beachhead secured, Grant would have to fight across more than 100 miles of enemy territory to face two Rebel forces under Generals John Pemberton and Joseph Johnston totaling almost 60,000. If defeated, Grant might be pinned against the river.

Still, he plunged ahead, starting General McClernand's XIII Corps southward on March 29 down the west bank of the river from the old camps at Milliken's Bend. The first objective was the town of New Carthage, planned staging point for the cross-river leap.

Trouble came immediately. For his plan to work, Grant had to move fast, surprising Pemberton. But McClernand's troops were soon slogging through seas of mud left by the winter rains. For weeks the men struggled southward, building causeways and corduroying roads—and completing a 70-mile route good enough, though just barely, for the rest of the army to follow.

Next came the risky job of getting Admiral Porter's gunboats and transports south past Vicksburg's lethal batteries to the crossing point. Slipping downstream the night of April 16, the boats were pounded by the big Confederate guns. Miraculously, all but three got by, even though Rebel troops had lighted fires on both banks of the river, illuminating the scene, said one observer, "as if by sunlight."

Grant's next job was to stage diversions to keep Pemberton confused about where the Federals intended to strike. He first ordered a cavalry force in Tennessee to ride through central Mississippi causing as much trouble as possible—a brilliant, daring foray famous ever since as Grierson's Raid.

Its leader, Colonel Benjamin H. Grierson—a peaceable musician and teacher in civilian life—quickly proved himself one of the war's great cavalry commanders. Heading out of La Grange, Tennessee, on April 17 with 1,700 Iowa and Illinois horsemen, Grierson sped south, tearing up both the Mississippi Central and Mobile & Ohio Railroads as he went, while also sending detachments back north to confuse the Confederates.

By April 24 Grierson had reached the rail junction of Newton Station, 200 miles deep in enemy territory and just 100 miles east of Vicksburg. There he captured two trains, destroyed supplies, burned bridges, and cut telegraph lines. Then, instead of fleeing back to La Grange, he rode west and south, evading some 20,000 pursuers and finally taking refuge with his exhausted, ragged men in Federal-held Baton Rouge, Louisiana.

Then, on April 30 Grant sent General Sherman and 10 regiments left behind at Milliken's Bend up the Yazoo River to make a show of once more attacking the bluffs north of Vicksburg. "The gunboats and transports whistled and puffed," recalled one of Sherman's officers, "and made all the noise they could." The ploy

"It has been one of the most brilliant cavalry exploits of the war, and will be handed down in history as an example to be imitated."

MAJOR GENERAL ULYSSES S. GRANT
Commander, Army of the Tennessee

Described here in dry fashion, Grierson's Raid, covering 600 miles in 16 days, helped to erase Confederate disdain for Federal cavalry. Grierson's troops killed, wounded, or captured more than 600 Rebels at a cost of "3 killed, 7 wounded, 5 left on the route sick . . . and 9 men missing." Grant, ordinarily stinting with his praise, was moved to write: "It has been one of the most brilliant cavalry exploits of the war, and will be handed down in history as an example to be imitated."

It was at Port Gibson I first heard through a Southern paper of the complete success of Colonel Grierson, who was making a raid through central Mississippi. He had started from La Grange April 17th with three regiments of about 1,700 men. On the 21st he had detached Colonel Hatch with one regiment to destroy the railroad between Columbus and Macon and then return to La Grange. Hatch had a sharp fight with the enemy at Columbus and retreated along the railroad, destroying it at Okalona and Tupelo, and arriving in La Grange April 26. Grierson continued his movement with about 1,000 men, breaking the Vicksburg and Meridian railroad and the New Orleans and Jackson railroad, arriving at Baton Rouge May 2d. This raid was of great importance, for Grierson had attracted the attention of the enemy from the main movement against Vicksburg.

SERGEANT WILLIAM S. MORRIS

31st Illinois Infantry, J. E. Smith's Brigade

After having heard then congressman John Logan give a stirring call to service in the town square of Marion, Illinois, the 19-year-old Morris (left) had promptly enlisted. He served throughout the war and was mustered out as a first lieutenant. Afterward he practiced law, won election to both houses of the Illinois legislature, and enthusiastically backed his old division commander's successful bid for election to the U.S. Senate.

Passing rapidly to the right of the line, the brigade came to a front, looking across the Champion Hill farm house and the high ground where field batteries were in position to defend the extreme left of the Confederate line of infantry drawn up in double column. They crowned the hill, that with its abrupt northeastern face covered with timber, presented a formidable barrier to any force that might assail it. Behind the brigade was an open field; far off to the right the flat bottoms of Baker's Creek. The men here slung their knapsacks and lay flat upon the ground in line. Major Stahlbrand pushed his twenty-four pound Howitzers several yards in front of our position and opened at close range with shell and shrapnel, cutting his shell at a second and a half. The guns on the hill added their music and sent their missiles tearing across the narrow valley at Stahlbrand's guns. The Major observed from his position at the guns a line of infantry moving down the hill. He turned round and riding up to Gen. J. E. Smith, commanding the brigade, said: "Sheneral Schmidt dey are sharging you mitt doubled column. By damn it they vant mine guns." Smith looked to the right and left of his line and replied grimly: "Let 'em come, we're ready to receive them." He commanded, "Attention brigade," and the line stood upon its feet. Again he looked steadily up and down the line and bawled out "Fix bayonets." The bayonets flashed from the scabbards and the jingle of the steel rattled along the line. Logan and McPherson dashed up. The corps commander smilingly rode along the line, saying: "Give them Jesse boys, give them Jesse." Logan straightened himself in his stirrups and said: "We are about to fight the battle for Vicksburg." Appealing to his old regiment he cried out: "Thirty onesters remember the blood of your mammas. We must whip them here or all go under the sod together. Give 'em hell."

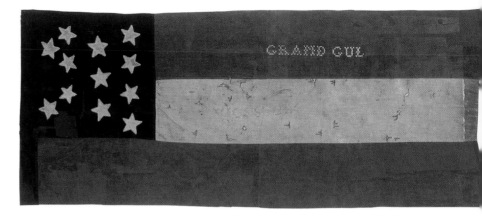

This flag flew over the battery of Company A, 1st Louisiana Heavy Artillery, at Grand Gulf. Most of the regiment had been captured at the Battle of New Orleans in April 1862 and paroled that fall. Captured again at Vicksburg and again paroled, the regiment finally surrendered for good at Citronelle, Alabama, on May 4, 1865.

worked; in near panic, Pemberton hastily called in reinforcements, including regiments he had just dispatched south to guard against a river crossing by the enemy.

Meanwhile, a hitch in Grant's main thrust occurred on April 29, when Porter's gunboats got into a battle with enemy guns on bluffs above the port of Grand Gulf, where Grant had intended to land his army. Grant swiftly shifted his planned landing point to Bruinsburg, eight miles farther south, and the next day sent McClernand's XIII Corps churning across the Mississippi on transports. To Grant's immense relief, the troops got ashore safely and unopposed. "Vicksburg was not yet taken," Grant later wrote, but "I was on dry ground on the same side of the river with the enemy."

Grant immediately ordered McClernand to head for Port Gibson. Once it was taken, the Federals would be able to outflank Grand Gulf, about eight miles away, and capture its guns and docks. A furious little battle erupted the next day when the Confederate commander at Grand Gulf, Brigadier General John S. Bowen, cleverly deployed his reduced force of 7,000 men along the heavily wooded ridges outside Port Gibson. For hours Bowen's men hurled back repeated attacks by four divisions, retreating only when outflanked by regiments from General McPherson's newly arrived corps.

With Port Gibson and Grand Gulf in hand, Grant quickly started his entire force marching inland toward Jackson. His aim: to slice between Pemberton's army and Johnston's force to the east, turn on and defeat Johnston, then take the city and, wrecking its rail yards, prevent any Confederate reinforcements from getting through.

Living off the land instead of waiting for supply trains, Grant's three corps raced toward Jackson, encountering little opposition until they reached the outskirts of the village of Raymond. There fighting erupted early on May 12 when McPherson's troops ran into 2,500 Confederates led by Brigadier General John Gregg, whom Pemberton had ordered up from Port Hudson. Emerging from dense woods near a sluggish stream called Fourteen-Mile Creek, Gregg's Texans and Tennesseans slammed into McPherson's forward units, throwing them back in murderous hand-to-hand fighting.

But then a fierce, swarthy Union general, John A. "Black Jack" Logan, led his 3d Division in a furious counterattack, smashing Gregg's thin line. After a last futile assault, the Confederates gave up, retreating through the town of Raymond and beyond.

Pausing only to wolf down a lavish meal the ladies of Raymond had prepared for Gregg's now fleeing troops, McPherson's men marched the last dozen miles to Jackson itself. The city's Confederate defenders numbered only about 12,000, but when a drenching rain slowed the Union advance, they were able to dig earthworks and, fighting stubbornly, to throw back McPherson's first assaults. But Colonel Samuel

A. Holmes' brigade, attacking "at double quick, cheering wildly," as one officer recalled, broke through from the west while some of Sherman's regiments also smashed into the city. By the afternoon of May 14 troops of the 59th Indiana were jubilantly planting their flag atop the dome of Mississippi's capitol.

Grant immediately ordered the rail lines passing through Jackson torn up and everything of use to the enemy—arsenals, machine shops, warehouses—put to the torch. Then, with hardly a pause, he started McPherson's corps westward down the road to Vicksburg.

Pemberton, after much indecision and several false starts, moved west to meet the threat with about 23,000 men. By the morning of May 16 many of them were deployed on a wooded ridge dominated by a 70-foot rise named after a local farmer now serving in Pemberton's army, Sid Champion—Champion's Hill.

Fighting started on the Union left when troops of Major General A. J. Smith's division of McClernand's corps came under fire from General William W. Loring's Confederates. The battle began in earnest, however, with a charge by Brigadier

This sketch by Lieutenant Henry Otis Dwight of the 20th Ohio Infantry shows Leggett's brigade of Logan's division lying prone at the foot of Champion's Hill awaiting orders to advance up the slope. At the first sound of firing that morning, Grant had galloped forward from his headquarters to take personal charge of the battle. Surveying the ground to his front, he remarked that the Confederate positions were situated atop "one of the highest points in that section, and commanded all the ground in range."

John A. Rawlins, Grant's chief of staff, kept watch over the general's drinking. Rawlins once pledged to resign his commission should Grant become "an intemperate man."

Grant's liquor cabinet (below) was the focus of a campaign by his critics to make him out to be an alcoholic. One newspaper story characterized a sociable evening spent with General Lew Wallace as a drunken revel; an outraged Wallace traced the tale to a regimental chaplain and forced him to resign.

"A solid wall of men in gray, their muskets at their shoulders, blazing away in our faces and their batteries of artillery roaring as if it were the end of the world."

General Alvin P. Hovey's two Federal brigades straight up Champion's Hill. Staggered by the rush, Major General Carter L. Stevenson's thin line gave way, and the Federals quickly reached the crest. There Hovey's men found a half-dozen enemy batteries lined up, but, by falling prone just as the first blasts of canister zinged overhead, they managed to keep going and capture the guns.

Pemberton, realizing his front was crumbling, frantically called for reinforcements from Loring and Bowen. Incredibly, Loring refused to move, but the combative Bowen acted fast, launching Colonel Francis M. Cockrell's and Brigadier General Martin E. Green's brigades in a ferocious counterattack. Hit hard in their turn, Hovey's Federals fell back down the hill.

At this point Grant ordered forward two brigades led by Colonels George Boomer and Samuel Holmes. Rushing at the Confederates, the Yankees were met, an Iowa sergeant recalled, by "a solid wall of men in gray, their muskets at their shoulders, blazing away in our faces and their batteries of artillery roaring as if it were the end of the world."

As the battle on the hill roared on, General McClernand moved, sending Brigadier General Peter J. Osterhaus' division slamming into Bowen's right flank. The Confederate defense began to disintegrate, the men flooding back off Champion's Hill. With the battle lost, Pemberton ordered a retreat, the troops trudging back down the road to Vicksburg—although Loring's division, too far south to begin with, became separated and never joined up. In all, Pemberton lost more than 3,800 men to Grant's 2,441.

Hoping to delay Grant, Pemberton ordered earthworks dug at the next natural obstacle, the Big Black River. But the weary Confederates quickly abandoned the trenches in the face of two headlong Federal attacks. Soon groups of ragged, dispirited men were straggling into Vicksburg, where the stunned citizens brought out water and food and frantically asked what was happening. One soldier's answer summed up the rest: "We are whipped."

In a single night Federal engineers laid four floating bridges across the Big Black River, one of which is shown in the photograph below, to speed the army's passage to Vicksburg. They first inflated a string of India rubber pontoons with hand bellows (inset), then roped them securely in place to span the stream. Finally, wooden planking was lashed atop the pontoons, and the bridge was ready to carry troops, wagons, and artillery safely across the river.

After surrendering his Army of Vicksburg on July 4, Lieutenant General John C. Pemberton was accused by many Southerners of having divided loyalties because he was a native of Pennsylvania. Actually, years of prewar duty in the South and the influence of his Virginia-born wife had given him a devotion to the region. Rather than being treasonous, as some claimed, Pemberton, harassed and bewildered by Grant's brilliant maneuverings and by conflicting orders from Jefferson Davis and Joseph Johnston, was outgeneraled. In May 1864 he resigned his general's commission and served the rest of the war as a lieutenant colonel and inspector of artillery.

"Suddenly there seemed to spring almost from the bowels of the earth dense masses of Federal troops..."

Grant hurried after and by May 18 had thrown a cordon around the city, sealing it off. So far the operation had been, Sherman told Grant, "one of the greatest campaigns in history." But now came the siege of Vicksburg itself, which would prove in some ways an even sterner test for Grant's army.

THE BLOODY, BITTER SIEGE

Marching into the outskirts of Vicksburg, Grant's troops, fresh from their string of victories farther east, found themselves facing the most formidable obstacle yet—a nine-mile-long arc of redoubts and log-reinforced trenches built by the Confederates on the steep hills east of the city. Worse, these defenses bristled

Opposite: Fine residences of wealthy merchants and professional men dot the Vicksburg bluff in this photograph taken from the courthouse cupola looking north.

with cannon and the rifles of 22,000 Rebel troops—the 12,000 or so that had managed to retreat from Champion's Hill plus two divisions of infantry that Pemberton had left in the city as a garrison force.

Despite the menacing earthworks, Grant—convinced that Confederate morale had been shattered—decided to attack immediately, sending his troops swarming forward at 2:00 p.m. on May 19. In minutes McClernand's and McPherson's troops had been blasted back by deadly Confederate fire. Sherman's XV Corps, assaulting the northeast corner of the city's defenses, initially made some progress when troops of Colonel Giles A. Smith's brigade gained a ditch north of a strongpoint called the Stockade Redan. But they were soon pinned down by sheets of rifle fire, escaping only after dark. In the futile assaults, the Federals lost 942 men. "This is a death struggle," General Sherman wrote his wife, "and will be terrible."

Hoping to avoid a long, grinding siege, Grant tried again on May 22, this time preparing for the assault with a thunderous, hours-long bombardment, his own 200 field guns joined by Admiral Porter's mortar barges lobbing huge 200-pound shells from the river. At 10:00 a.m. precisely the guns fell silent and the infantry charged, aiming for salients in the enemy line. "Suddenly there seemed to spring almost from the bowels of the earth dense masses of Federal troops," recalled Confederate general Stephen D. Lee, the men rushing "forward at a run with bayonets fixed."

But the bombardment had merely churned the earth. Once the shelling had stopped, the Confederate riflemen let the Union troops get close, then "deliberately rose and stood in their trenches," Lee later wrote, "pouring volley after volley into the advancing enemy."

In minutes Federal dead were piled in windrows on the steep slopes leading to the enemy positions. Worst hit were the troops of General Michael K. Lawler's brigade of McClernand's corps, who attacked the Railroad Redoubt just south of the Southern Mississippi tracks. "It was a tornado of iron on our left, a hurricane of shot on our right," recalled one officer. "We passed through the mouth of hell. Every third man fell, either killed or wounded." A few survivors reached the redoubt but were then hurled back by the counterattacking 30th Alabama.

The fighting was just as ferocious to the north, where other XIII Corps troops assailed a lunette held by the 2d Texas. McPherson's attackers and Sherman's were also hammered back with heavy losses. By late morning Grant could see the attack was doomed—but ordered more assaults to support McClernand who, eager as always for glory, reported his men had captured two enemy strongpoints. This claim proved false, and the renewed attacks also failed, swelling the casualty lists and making May 22 the bloodiest day of the campaign, with 502 Union dead and almost 2,700 wounded or missing. Grant, glumly sitting his horse and whittling a piece of wood, was heard to mutter, "We'll have to dig our way in."

Dig the troops did, first cutting a road north to the landings on the Yazoo River. Soon flotillas of steamboats were unloading huge quantities of food, ammunition, and other supplies floated down the Mississippi. Arriving, too, were a pair of fresh

"Don't shoot at that man again.
He is too brave to be killed that way."

PRIVATE CHARLES I. EVANS

2d Infantry Battalion, Waul's Texas Legion

During the assault of Brigadier General William P. Benton's brigade on May 22, the bravery of Illinois colorbearer Thomas H. Higgins so impressed Evans and his fellow Texans that they refused to shoot the gallant Yankee. After the war, veterans of Waul's Legion successfully petitioned the Federal government for recognition for their ex-foe's deed. Higgins was eventually awarded the Medal of Honor.

After a most terrific cannonading of two hours, during which the very earth rocked and pulsated like a thing of life, the head of the charging column appeared above the brow of the hill, about 100 yards in front of the breast works, and, as line after line of blue came in sight over the hill, it presented the grandest spectacle the eye of a soldier ever beheld. The Texans were prepared to meet it however, for, in addition to our Springfield rifles, each man was provided with five additional smoothbore muskets, charged with buck and ball.

When the first line was within fifty paces of the works, the order to fire ran along the trenches, and was responded to as from one gun. As fast as practiced hands could gather them up, one after another, the muskets were brought to bear. The blue lines vanished amid fearful slaughter. There was a cessation in the firing. And behold, through the pall of smoke which enshrouded the field, a Union flag could be seen approaching.

As the smoke was slightly lifted by the gentle May breeze, one lone soldier advanced, bravely bearing the flag towards the breast works. At least a hundred men took deliberate aim at him, and fired at point-blank range, but he never faltered. Stumbling over the bodies of his fallen comrades, he continued to advance. Suddenly, as if with one impulse, every Confederate soldier within sight of the Union color bearer seemed to be seized with the idea that the man ought not to be shot down like a dog. A hundred men dropped their guns at the same time; each of them seized his nearest neighbor by the arm and yelled to him: "Don't shoot at that man again. He is too brave to be killed that way." when he instantly discovered that his neighbor was yelling the same thing at him. As soon as they all understood one another, a hundred old hats and caps went up into the air, their wearers yelling at the top of their voices: "Come on, you brave Yank, come on!" He did come, and was taken by the hand and pulled over the breast works, and when it was discovered that he was not even scratched, a hundred Texans wrung his hands and congratulated him upon his miraculous escape from death. That man's name was Thomas J. Higgins, color bearer of the Ninety-ninth Illinois.

Climbing into a hail of Minié balls and grapeshot, a sergeant of the 22d Iowa advances to plant his regiment's colors atop the Confederate breastworks of Fort Beauregard at Vicksburg. The Union attackers were ultimately driven back after suffering their heaviest losses of the campaign.

Advancing on the Confederate defenses around Vicksburg, Federal sappers construct a shielded approach roofed with protective bundles of wood called fascines, strong enough to withstand artillery fire. In the foreground, a crew cuts and ties together poles for the fascines.

This wartime drawing by A. J. Volck shows Yankee shells bursting in Vicksburg's night sky over the head of a startled servant while a young woman in a cave home falls to her knees and prays for her safety. Although some families had cave dwellings that were mere burrows, others believed in "keeping house under ground," bringing into the caves the comforts of home. Volck, a Southern sympathizer living in Baltimore, Maryland, hoped to arouse pity for the city's beleaguered residents with this depiction of siege life.

divisions, swelling Grant's force to about 70,000 men and tightening the ring around the city until, as one Confederate noted, "a cat could not have crept out of Vicksburg without being discovered."

Reconciled now to a siege—he would, he said, "outcamp the enemy"—Grant nevertheless kept pressure on the Confederate defenders, bombarding the Rebel works day and night. He also ordered his troops to dig interlocking systems of zigzag trenches within yards of the enemy redans. "The soldiers got so they bored like gophers and beavers," one said, "with a spade in one hand and a gun in the other."

Before long the opposing lines were so close together that the men could easily call back and forth, shouting jokes and insults. In time, in this strange brother-against-brother war, the troops began visiting each other's trenches in the evenings, chatting amiably, playing cards, and trading coffee and tobacco.

As Grant's cannon and Porter's boats fired away at the Rebel entrenchments, hundreds of errant shells inevitably shrieked into the city and struck with deafening, nerve-shattering explosions. Many of the town's inhabitants quickly decided that their houses were deathtraps and began digging burrows into the substrata of yellow clay. Eventually about 500 caves honeycombed the hillsides, turning the place, Federal troops said, into "Prairie Dog Village."

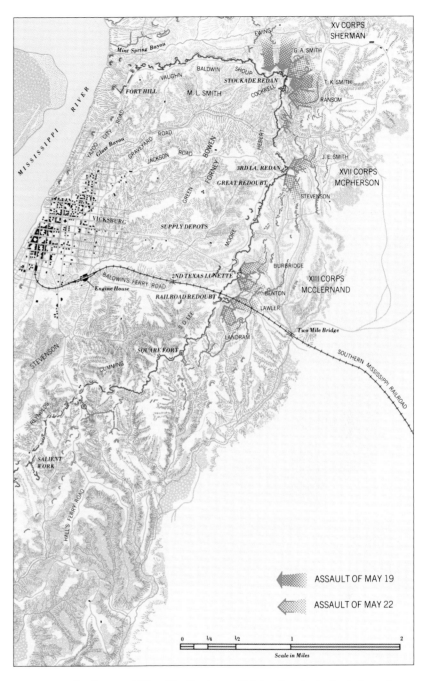

ASSAULT OF MAY 19

ASSAULT OF MAY 22

0   1/4   1/2   1   2
Scale in Miles

Grant's army faced a powerful line of fortifications on Vicksburg's perimeter, but in the push-ahead style for which he would become famous, he tried to pound through it. Only after attacks were bloodily repulsed on May 19 and again on May 22 did he finally decide to settle in for a siege. Even at that, however, he wasn't quite willing to give up on trying to carry the city by assault. On June 25 the Federals detonated a mine beneath the Jackson road defenses, and troops charged into the resulting crater but were trapped there and had to withdraw at night with heavy losses. The siege resumed in earnest, and Vicksburg surrendered on July 4 after 47 days of shelling and near starvation.

EMMA BALFOUR

Resident of Vicksburg

Although Union gunners set their sights on military targets, the imperfect science of 19th-century artillery ensured that some of the deadly cannonballs would land in civilian areas, where citizens like Balfour could only hide out in caves or cellars and hope for the best. Union troops, observing some of the over 500 cave dwellings constructed in the encircled city, dubbed the town a "Prairie Dog Village."

We have spent the last two nights in a cave, but tonight I think we will stay at home. It is not safe I know, for the shells are falling all around us, but I hope none may strike us. Yesterday morning a piece of a mortar shell struck the schoolroom roof, tore through the partition wall, shattered the door and then went into the door sill and down the side of the wall. Another piece struck in the same room and a third in the cement in front of the house. Such a large piece struck the kitchen also, but we see them explode all around us and as this is all the harm done to us yet, we consider ourselves fortunate. Mrs. Hawkes' house is literally torn to pieces, and Mrs. Maulin's was struck yesterday evening by a shell from one of the guns east of us and very much injured. In both of these houses gentlemen were sick and in neither case was any one hurt. It is marvelous. Two persons only that I have heard have been killed in town, and a little child. The child was buried in the wall by a piece of shell, pinned to it. Today a shocking thing occurred. In one of the hospitals where some wounded had just undergone operations a shell exploded and six men had to have limbs amputated. Some of them that had been taken off at the ankle had to have the leg taken off to the thigh and one who had lost one arm had to have the other taken off. It is horrible and the worst of it is we cannot help it. I suppose there never was a case before of a besieged town when the guns from front and back met and passed each other....

Many of the caves were simply small bombproofs. Others were large and even luxurious warrens furnished with beds and tables and rugs covering the dirt floors. Rounds often smashed into the underground refuges, but miraculously only about a dozen civilians were known to have been killed and three dozen injured in weeks of shelling.

Almost worse than the shelling was the hunger. By mid-June most of the supplies collected on General Pemberton's orders had been exhausted, and the people were reduced to eating a repellent gruel made of ground peas and horse meat or, for those who could stand it, grilled mule. The soldiers' daily ration was reduced and reduced again until it consisted of one biscuit a day with a few scraps of stringy or rancid bacon.

The people of Vicksburg were buoyed through the ordeal, however, by the belief that a relief column was on the way. General Johnston, now back at Jackson, was said to be gathering an army of 30,000 or more men for a thrust westward. To meet the reported threat to his rear, Grant withdrew a division from each of his corps and, putting Sherman in command, formed what he called "a second line of defense facing the other way."

In fact, the cautious Johnston balked at moving. He had too few men, he complained when the Confederate high command tried to urge him on, and not enough equipment, supplies, or wagons. When at last he got in motion in early July, heading for the Big Black River, it would be too late to save Vicksburg.

"My God, they are killing my bravest men in that hole."

Spurred to hasten the end of the siege, Grant in late June decided to try mining an enemy strongpoint or two and issued a call for all soldiers who had worked in coal mines before the war. Within days the 35 miners who showed up had completed a tunnel under a Rebel position called the Great Redoubt, north of the Jackson road, and packed it with 2,200 pounds of gunpowder.

The explosion blasted out a deep, smoking crater 50 feet across but killed fewer men than expected, as the redoubt's Louisiana and Mississippi defenders had heard the digging and fallen back to a new line. There they waited until the Federals of General Mortimer D. Leggett's brigade of John Logan's division stormed into the crater—to be hit, one recalled, with "a terrible volley of musketry" from the hidden Confederates, then raked with canister from Rebel batteries. So murderous was the fire that General Logan cried out, "My God, they are killing my bravest men in that hole." At last, after three days of struggle, the Yankees retired, leaving behind 200 casualties.

Rebel troops, burdened with heavy knapsacks full of percussion caps provided for the beleaguered Vicksburg garrison by Confederate general Joseph E. Johnston, avoid a Union picket post by stealthily creeping through a dark, rocky, and vine-choked ravine in this engraving for the Illustrated London News. The dapper civilian Lamar Fontaine, pictured in the inset, is believed to have singlehandedly brought 18,000 caps into the city. Fontaine eschewed the overland route, hauling his precious cargo on a skiff no bigger than a "floating log" through the bayous north of the city.

THE SIEGE OF VICKSBURG—BLOWING UP THE REBEL FORT HILL.—SKETCHED BY MR. THEODORE R. DAVIS.—[SEE PAGE 478.]

Hurling wreckage and enormous clods of earth into the air a mine explodes beneath the 3d Louisiana Redan, a Confederate fortification in the eastern defenses of Vicksburg. Engineers of the Federal XVII Corps tunneled beneath the Rebel earthworks to fill a gallery with 2,200 pounds of black powder. The mine, which was exploded on June 25, 1863, produced a crater nearly 50 feet wide.

Perhaps the only slave ever blasted to freedom, this youth—like many so-called "contrabands"—was known only by his first name, Tom. Apparently inside the redan when the mine exploded, he sailed "300 feet in the air," according to one account, and landed unhurt in the Northern lines. Afterward, Tom worked for the U.S. Quartermaster Department.

After the blast, as Union infantrymen charged the smoking remains of the fractured redan, many of them hurled "Ketchum" hand grenades, like the one found at Vicksburg and shown here, as they ran toward the Confederate position.

Hoping for better results, Grant ordered another, larger mine exploded on July 1. This one did worse damage to the Rebel trenches and took a heavier toll in men. But Union officers, now more cautious, decided not to follow up and run the risk of another bloody repulse.

In any case, the siege was showing signs of achieving its purpose. The Confederate troops, and Vicksburg's citizens, were increasingly exhausted and hungry. With starvation looming, Pemberton on July 1 asked his division commanders whether they thought that a breakout was possible. All four replied that their ragged, hollow-eyed troops, who had been cramped in rifle pits for week after week, were too sick and worn down to try. Finally, on July 3 Pemberton sent a message to Grant, carried under a flag of truce by General Bowen—who was himself dying of dysentery. It proposed an armistice to prevent "the further effusion of blood."

Grant's reply was predictably unyielding: a demand for unconditional surrender. But at a meeting with Pemberton later that day Grant softened his terms, agreeing to parole the Confederate troops if they signed an oath not to fight again until Federal captives were freed in exchange.

It was a pragmatic decision. "Had I insisted upon unconditional surrender," Grant later wrote, "there would have been over 30,000 men to transport to Cairo, very much to the inconvenience of the army on the Mississippi." He also figured that, in any case, many of Vicksburg's defenders would be too war weary and disheartened to fight again. Pemberton accepted the terms, and the 47-day siege came to an end—on the same day, in a malign omen for the Confederacy, as the defeat of Robert E. Lee's army at Gettysburg.

THE FATHER OF WATERS UNVEXED

The Union forces still had important business to attend to after the surrender of Vicksburg. The town of Port Hudson, nearly 300 river miles to the south and the last Confederate stronghold on the Mississippi, had yet to be taken. More pressing for Grant was to deal with General Joseph Johnston, who, having belatedly decided to try to relieve Vicksburg, was advancing toward the Big Black River and the Union rear with four divisions—more than 31,000 men. That rear was covered, of course,

Under the command of Major General John A. Logan, the 45th Illinois charges into a vast crater blasted out of the Confederate earthworks by a Federal mine on June 25. Confederate Brigadier General Louis Hébert reported that his soldiers had anticipated the explosion and that it created "no dismay or panic among those defending the line."

"'Here, reb., I know you are starved nearly to death.'"

PRIVATE WILLIAM H. TUNNARD

3d Louisiana Infantry, Hébert's Brigade

This description of the rage and frustration felt by the soldiers of Tunnard's regiment at the surrender order, contrasted with the subsequent friendly fraternization between old enemies, first appeared in Tunnard's "A Southern Record: A History of the Third Regiment Louisiana Infantry." Published in 1866, and based on private letters, journals, newspaper accounts, official reports, and personal observances, Tunnard's was one of the first Civil War unit histories.

On the afternoon of July 3, 1863, Generals Grant and Pemberton meet near the 3d Louisiana Redan to discuss terms for the surrender of Vicksburg. Harper's Weekly sketch artist Theodore Davis witnessed the meeting. "After a conference of some two hours," Davis wrote, "in the most quiet and courteous manner, the two officers parted with a hand-shake, that seemed most friendly."

The receipt of this order was the signal for a fearful outburst of anger and indignation seldom witnessed. The members of the Third Louisiana Infantry expressed their feeling in curses loud and deep. Many broke their trusty rifles against the trees, scattered the ammunition over the ground where they had so long stood battling bravely and unflinchingly against overwhelming odds. In many instances the battle-worn flags were torn into shreds, and distributed among the men as a precious and sacred memento that they were no party to the surrender. The Federals who marched into the place had more the appearance of being vanquished than the unarmed Confederates, who gazed upon them with folded arms and in stern silence, a fierce defiance on their bronzed features, and the old battle fire gleaming in their glittering eyes. During all the events of the surrender, not one had been seen, and afterward no word of exultation was uttered to irritate the feelings of the prisoners. On the contrary, every sentinel who came upon post brought haversacks filled with provisions, which he would give to some famished Southerner, with the remark, "Here, reb., I know you are starved nearly to death." …

When the Federal soldiers entered the city they mingled freely with the Confederates, and expressed their sympathy with their deplorable situation by every possible means in their power. They were now no longer deadly combatants, but mortals of similar feelings. …

by General Sherman's blocking force of nearly 30,000. But Sherman and Grant had no intention of letting Johnston strike first if they could help it. Even as negotiations for the surrender were going on, Grant ordered Sherman to prepare to lash out as soon as Vicksburg was in Union hands. To make the task easier, Grant added 16,000 troops to those already under Sherman's command. On the morning of July 4 the telegraph in Sherman's headquarters clicked out the news that Vicksburg had capitulated, and within minutes Sherman's army of 46,000, nearly two-thirds of Grant's entire command, moved against Johnston.

There would be no big battle, however. Johnston, cautiously reconnoitering Sherman's defenses on July 3 and 4, had become increasingly puzzled when he heard no artillery fire from Vicksburg. Then, on July 5, word of General Pemberton's surrender came through. Johnston began pulling his troops back toward the city of Jackson, knowing the Federals could now turn on him in overwhelming force.

Sherman pursued quickly, his three corps managing to get across the Big Black despite high water and bloody skirmishes with well-hidden Rebel troops. By July 9 his advance units were within five miles of Jackson.

Johnston's four divisions meanwhile had reached the city, the troops spending July 8 and 9 strengthening the ring of earthworks constructed back in May to fend off the first Federal attack. At 9:00 a.m. on July 10, Sherman's guns began shelling the Confederate defenses while Federal troops probed forward to test their strength.

Freshly washed bed linens and the laundry of patients listlessly hang out to dry on clotheslines in the humid Mississippi air next to City Hospital. This structure and the Marine Hospital were the only two permanent infirmaries in Vicksburg. These facilities were quickly overwhelmed—there were nearly 10,000 sick and wounded soldiers in the city at siege's end—and several churches and large homes had to be quickly converted into temporary hospitals.

Johnston's reply—return fire from a number of big rifled guns—quickly convinced Sherman that a head-on assault would be suicidal. Another siege was in order. To isolate the city, Sherman sent one of his corps around to the north and another to the south, while the third remained to the west. The Yankees then dug their own ring of rifle pits and gun emplacements about 1,000 yards from the Confederate works.

General Johnston soon decided that with only four divisions to face Sherman's nine, holding Jackson was hopeless. He ordered a withdrawal. By dawn on July 17 his infantry and artillery had silently slipped from their earthworks and were heading east for the bridges spanning the Pearl River.

Sherman, surprised to find the enemy gone, was at first slow to react, but by the afternoon of July 17 Federal troops had occupied Jackson, the men of the 35th Massachusetts geefully hoisting their regimental flag atop the golden dome of the capitol building of Confederate president Jefferson Davis' home state. Then, having ordered supplies of bread, flour, and bacon rushed to the hungry people of the desolate city, Sherman dispatched cavalry and other units to chase the fleeing Confederates.

At Vicksburg the Confederate surrender had been completed with astonishing calm and dispatch. On July 4 the entire garrison of Vicksburg, as Grant later wrote, "marched out of their works and formed line in front, stacked their arms and marched back in good order." While the ragged, beaten enemy gave up their weapons, the watching Federal troops, in a moving show of sympathy and restraint, kept strict silence. "Our whole army present," Grant recalled, "witnessed this scene without cheering."

The honor of leading the occupying troops into Vicksburg was given to General John "Black Jack" Logan, whose men had experienced much of the bloodiest fighting of the campaign. Grant then, with everything secure, ordered huge quantities of food shipped in to feed the half-starved Confederate troops and residents.

The behavior of the Yankee soldiers remained as exemplary as that of their commander. "No word of exultation was uttered to irritate the feelings of the prisoners," wrote a Confederate private, William Tunnard. "On the contrary, every sentinel who came upon post brought haversacks filled with provisions, which he would give to some famished Southerner with the remark, 'Here, reb., I know you are starved nearly to death.'"

When the time came for the Confederate prisoners who had signed their paroles to march out of Vicksburg, the scene was much the same. "Not a cheer went up, not a remark was made that would give pain," Grant remembered. "Really, I believe there was a feeling of sadness just then in the breasts of most of the Union soldiers at seeing the dejection of their late antagonists."

This first national pattern Confederate flag, the so-called Stars and Bars, flew over one of the garrisons in Vicksburg during the siege. Federal soldiers of the 83d Indiana Infantry captured this flag on July 4 and held it as a trophy. It was not returned to Vicksburg until 1962.

"Absolute ruin seems our portion. The Confederacy totters to its destruction."

There was, of course, sadness and shock all across the South when news spread that the "Gibraltar of the West" had fallen. Now the two halves of the Confederacy, east and west, had been severed and an all-important supply line cut. "Absolute ruin seems our portion," wrote General Josiah Gorgas, ordnance chief in Richmond. "The Confederacy totters to its destruction."

Elation in the North equaled the despair in the South. Church bells rang in every town from Maine to Minnesota, and a half-dozen cities boomed with 100-gun salutes. Grant was hailed as a hero, the one Union commanding general who could and would fight. "I write," President Lincoln said in a letter to Grant, "as a grateful acknowledgement for the almost inestimable service you have done the country."

That service was not just military but political as well. After a seven-month string of almost unbroken disasters for the Union army, most recently the humil-

Opposite: Amid the crowd of Yankee celebrators, Vicksburg residents lament the raising of the Stars and Stripes at the courthouse on July 4, symbolizing Federal control of the town. One of Grant's first moves after the surrender was to send in food to the starved residents.

iating defeat of the Army of the Potomac under General Joseph Hooker at Chancellorsville in May, the Northern press and people had begun grumbling loudly against the Lincoln government's conduct of the war. But Grant's victory at Vicksburg, combined with the simultaneous defeat of Lee at Gettysburg and General William S. Rosecrans' recent success in gaining control of central Tennessee after the Tullahoma campaign, muted the voices of doom. At last it seemed the North might win the war. The sudden upswing in Federal fortunes doubtless helped Lincoln win reelection in 1864.

SIEGE OF VICKSBURG CASUALTIES

FEDERAL		CONFEDERATE	
Killed	763	*Killed*	805
Wounded	3,746	*Wounded*	1,938
Captured and missing	162	*Captured and missing*	129
Total	4,671	*Subtotal*	2,872
		Surrendered on July 4	29,491
		Total	32,363

SOLDIER LIFE

Most of the three million men who joined the Union and Confederate armies to fight the Civil War saw themselves not as professional soldiers but as civilians temporarily serving their country. They brought with them a deeply ingrained independence, which the routines and constraints of military life could not quench. Still, they had come for a scrap, and that's what they expected.

Men on both sides quickly learned, however, that time spent in battle was only a brief, if exhilarating and terrifying, part of the soldier's life. For most of them, their time in uniform was an eye-opening and many-sided experience. Soldiers faced an unaccustomed and monotonous diet and for the first time many young men faced the task of cooking for themselves. In fact the soldiers had to carry out all of the tasks of maintaining themselves ranging from laundry and camp sanitation to constructing their own shelter.

Men of both armies fought the strangeness with music, practical jokes, religious revivals, improvised theatricals, snowball fights, and baseball games. Many sought escape in drinking and gambling. And all coped with one of war's supreme realities: empty hours. "War is an organized bore," wrote infantry captain Oliver Wendell Holmes Jr.

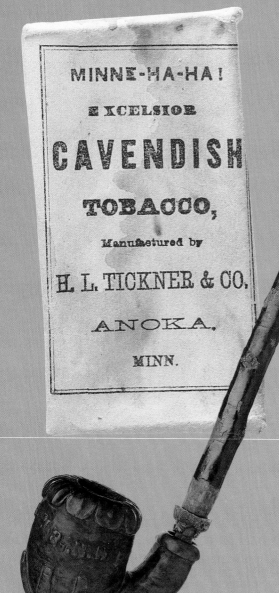

The pipe below was carved out of sweetbrier root on Hilton Head Island, South Carolina, by Private T. Adams of the 3d New Hampshire Infantry. The Federals' tobacco usually came in small packets like the one at right, manufactured by a Minnesota firm.

Tennessee cavalry soldiers, three of them tugging on their ever-present pipes, pose for a keepsake photograph with their body servants. The trooper seated on the right carries a tobacco bag attached to a button on his tunic. A popular fad among Confederate soldiers, such bags, usually decorated, were generally gifts from mothers, wives, or sweethearts.

At Camp Pendleton in northern Virginia, a laundress for the 31st Pennsylvania works beside her soldier husband and their children. Army regulations allowed each regiment four washerwomen in camp; in the field, the troops would wash their own clothes.

Men of Company F of the 22d Connecticut Infantry take a break outside their log cabin in the regiment's quarters at Miner's Hill, Virginia, during the winter of 1862-1863. Their rough but sturdy cabin, complete with a glass window, was fronted by a "corduroy," or log sidewalk, that stretched the length of the street.

LIFE IN CAMP AND FIELD

Between battles soldiers spent their time drilling, cleaning equipment, standing guard, mending clothing, writing to loved ones at home, and generally performing all of the tasks required to keep themselves tolerably presentable, contented, and healthy. Volunteers quickly learned that life in camp was rough, dirty, and filled with hardships. "I have not shaved since I left home and I am almost burned black," Lieutenant James Edmondson of the 27th Virginia wrote his wife. "We have to take the rain as it comes and sleep (if we can) on the damp ground." Invariably some men were more conscientious than others when it came to personal hygiene. "Some of our boys are not over and above clean," Ohioan George Cadman noted, "and if not pretty sharply looked after would not wash themselves from weeks end to weeks end."

Seated in church pews, Yankee soldiers pass the time in their Virginia camp mending clothes, writing letters, and reading newspapers. Most soldiers carried pocket-sized sewing kits called "housewives," and many became adept at patching their tattered uniforms. No diversion, however, occupied as much time as letter writing. Postage was relatively inexpensive—about three cents—and surprisingly efficient postal systems allowed soldiers to maintain contact with loved ones at home.

SEWING KIT

In this Edwin Forbes drawing a soldier relaxes in a makeshift chair while the camp barber applies a razor to his whiskers and potential customers look on. "Whether from lack of skill in the use or care of the razor, or from want of inclination," observed John Billings, "a large number preferred to patronize the camp barber" rather than shave themselves.

Captain John K. Booton of the 11th Virginia Infantry preserved the straight razor (below) that he carried during the war. Many soldiers chose to tolerate the difficulties of shaving in the field rather than grow a beard. The harsh homemade Confederate soap (left) was a welcome gift from loved ones.

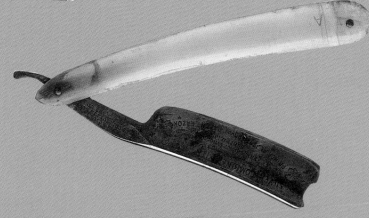

A soldier of the 110th Pennsylvania scrubs his laundry in a wooden tub outside his winter hut. The mud and stick hearth and chimneys attached to the shelters provided warmth and cooking facilities for the occupants during the cold winter months.

Federal soldiers take advantage of a brief lull in the fighting during the Wilderness campaign to bathe in Virginia's North Anna River below the ruined bridge of the Richmond, Fredericksburg & Potomac Railroad. Photographer Timothy O'Sullivan exposed this plate during the last week of May 1864.

HARDTACK AND SALT MEAT

Most volunteers, accustomed to home-cooked meals, found themselves on their own when it came to the preparation of rations. While fresh cuts of beef from army herds and loaves of soft bread could be issued to troops in winter camp or permanent garrison, soldiers on campaign were compelled to subsist upon the field rations carried in their haversack—a monotonous and unpalatable diet of coffee, hard bread, and salted meat, usually pork. The standard army bread supplied to Federal troops was a square flour-and-water cracker, dubbed hardtack for its rocklike consistency. Hardtack became more palatable if soaked in water and fried in the sizzling fat of the issue salt pork. Hard-pressed Confederate commissaries generally substituted cornmeal for the hard bread ration. Rebel soldiers baked "pones" of corn bread in their camp skillets or made their cornmeal into "Johnny Cakes" or mush. It was no wonder that most soldiers, Yank and Reb alike, chose to supplement their diet by foraging off the countryside. Soldiers could occasionally vary their menu by purchasing food from local civilians or patronizing the traveling vendors called sutlers.

Using their knapsacks as a table, two Ohio infantrymen (right) display partially eaten pieces of army bread, or hardtack. Private William Bircher of the 2d Minnesota recalled, "It required some experience and no little hunger to appreciate hardtack rightly, and it demanded no small amount of inventive genius to understand how to cook hardtack as they ought to be cooked."

With an oversize handle and a flat, rimmed lid that held hot coals, Dutch ovens were necessities for baking corn bread, the staple of the Confederate armies. The Rebels of the Army of Northern Virginia took pains to carry these utensils on campaign; one Federal soldier recalled seeing the woods around Appomattox filled with abandoned ovens. This example was left in one of Stonewall Jackson's camps near Chantilly, Virginia, in September 1862.

TIN DRINKING CUP, WASHINGTON ARTILLERY OF NEW ORLEANS

A banner advertising fresh oysters stretches above the entrance of a sutler's tent near Brandy Station, Virginia. Sutlers were merchants licensed to sell food, notions, and other goods to soldiers in camp.

In winter quarters at Camp Quantico near Dumfries, Virginia, in 1861, men of the Texas Brigade perform their individual duties for the photographer: clothes washing, wood cutting, and baking a pone of corn bread in a deep skillet. Their sturdy log cabin has a roof of overlapping shingles and a "requisitioned" glass-paned window, but only a canvas flap shields the doorway.

UNION ARMY-ISSUE MESS UTENSILS

FUN AND FROLIC

To relieve boredom and provide a healthful alternative to the temptations of alcohol and insubordination many officers encouraged sporting events, music, and theatrical entertainments. Baseball was an increasingly popular pastime, and in winter camp snowball fights would sometimes escalate into epic proportions. "It reminds one of a real battle," a South Carolina soldier recalled. Holidays were frequently the occasion for interregimental competitions. The Army of the Potomac's Irish Brigade celebrated Saint Patrick's Day with a steeplechase, foot- and wheelbarrow races, and climbing a greased pole.

Two Yankee "pards" pose with their baseball gear in this wartime tintype. The game as it was played during the Civil War used softer balls, and the rules favored the batter, who could be put out only by a touch or by a thrown ball.

In a sketch by Edwin Forbes, soldier-jockeys spur their mounts past the reviewing stand during Saint Patrick's Day races hosted near Falmouth, Virginia, by the Army of the Potomac's Irish Brigade. The March 1863 festival consisted mostly of horse races but included such diversions as sack races; contests of running, jumping, and boxing; and a greased-pole climb.

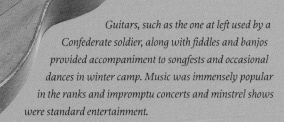

Guitars, such as the one at left used by a Confederate soldier, along with fiddles and banjos provided accompaniment to songfests and occasional dances in winter camp. Music was immensely popular in the ranks and impromptu concerts and minstrel shows were standard entertainment.

Stripped to their shirt sleeves, with hats tossed into the "ring," two Federal soldiers square off for an impromptu bareknuckle boxing match in their winter quarters in an occupied Southern city. Enthusiasm for boxing grew with the arrival of prominent British professionals, who immigrated when their sport was outlawed in much of Great Britain shortly before the Civil War.

A spirited musical ensemble of Federal soldiers display their instruments— tambourine, banjo, guitar, violin, triangle, and bones. Such players helped while away hours in winter encampments and provided accompaniment for amateur theatrical performances and minstrel shows. Fragile wooden instruments were generally shipped back home before the campaigning season began.

SIN AND REDEMPTION

During their service, many soldiers observed the coarsening effect of military life on man's better nature. One, a clergyman's son from New York, noted of his fellows: "As a mass they are ignorant, envious, mercenary, and disgustingly immoral and profane … almost every one drinks to excess when the opportunity offers, chews and smokes incessantly …"

Nothing proved more disruptive to military discipline than that timeless bane of the soldier—liquor. Many volunteers who had been moderate drinkers before the war gave way to alcohol as a means of escaping the boredom of soldier life. Gambling too was endemic in the ranks. Games of chance such as poker and chuck-a-luck were played in marathon sessions, often orchestrated by professional gamblers. In the face of such infractions of discipline, punishment could be both severe and creative. Drunken soldiers might find themselves tied in uncomfortable positions until they sobered up and confinement in the Provost Martial's stockade gave a man time to ponder his transgressions and correct his ways.

To counteract the corroding effects of boredom and vice every regiment was supposed to have a chaplain, whose principal duty was to oversee the spiritual welfare of the men. Occasionally waves of spiritual fervor would sweep through the camps, particularly during the long winter months of relative inactivity, when men had time to ponder their fate.

The straw-padded pocket liquor flask and telescoping silver cup were popular accouterments for officers in both the Federal and Confederate armies. The ready access to liquor enjoyed by officers was a source of much resentment from the enlisted men, who could enjoy its comforts only on the sly.

Playing cards (above, top) manufactured by Goodall & Son, a London firm, sport a motif of Southern naval flags surmounting the Great Seal of the Confederacy. Run through the Federal naval blockade, imported cards such as these would have been an expensive luxury in the wartime South. Three Federal soldiers (above) play a game of cards on a gaming table improvised from a washstand. Popular games included poker and whist.

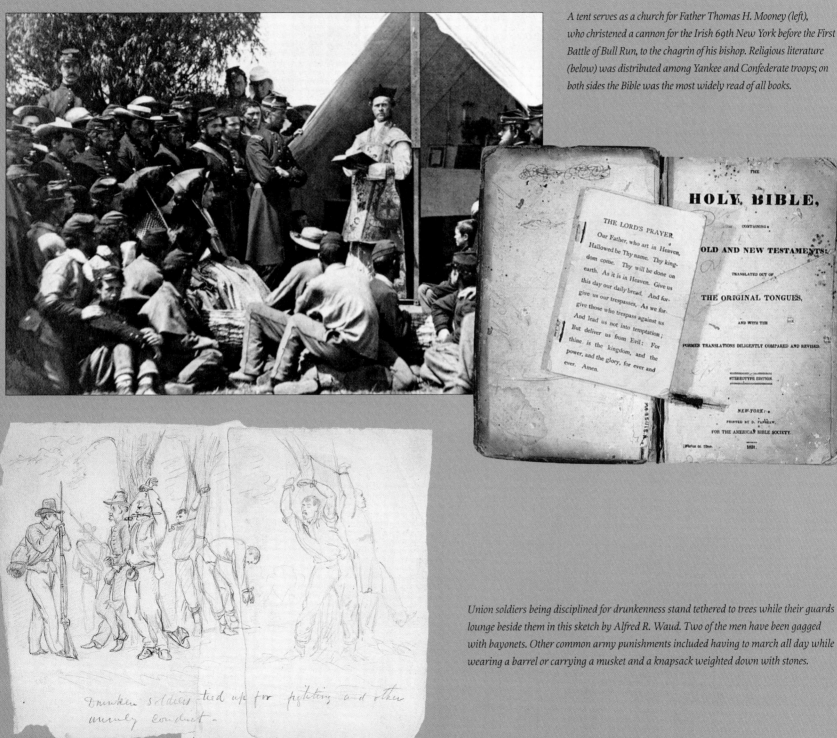

A tent serves as a church for Father Thomas H. Mooney (left), who christened a cannon for the Irish 69th New York before the First Battle of Bull Run, to the chagrin of his bishop. Religious literature (below) was distributed among Yankee and Confederate troops; on both sides the Bible was the most widely read of all books.

THE LORD'S PRAYER.

Our Father, who art in Heaven, Hallowed be Thy name. Thy kingdom come. Thy will be done on earth. As it is in Heaven. Give us this day our daily bread. And forgive us our trespasses, As we forgive those who trespass against us And lead us not into temptation; But deliver us from Evil: For thine is the kingdom, and the power, and the glory, for ever and ever. Amen.

HOLY BIBLE,

CONTAINING

OLD AND NEW TESTAMENTS:

TRANSLATED OUT OF

THE ORIGINAL TONGUES,

AND WITH THE

FORMER TRANSLATIONS DILIGENTLY COMPARED AND REVISED.

STEREOTYPE EDITION.

NEW-YORK:

PRINTED BY D. FANSHAW,

FOR THE AMERICAN BIBLE SOCIETY.

1831.

Union soldiers being disciplined for drunkenness stand tethered to trees while their guards lounge beside them in this sketch by Alfred R. Waud. Two of the men have been gagged with bayonets. Other common army punishments included having to march all day while wearing a barrel or carrying a musket and a knapsack weighted down with stones.

Gettysburg
The Confederate High Tide

THE GATHERING STORM—The road to Gettysburg began at the tiny Virginia crossroads of Chancellorsville. There, shortly after noon on May 3, 1863, as the sulfurous smoke of battle clung to the ground, General Robert E. Lee rode forth to savor his army's triumph. The stalwart general and his mounted entourage guided their horses around the mangled dead and writhing wounded, past demolished cannon and exploded limber chests that flanked the burning Chancellor house. At the sight of their beloved commander, thousands of powder-stained soldiers in uniforms of butternut and gray erupted in wild shouts of enthusiasm. Lee's aide, Major Charles Marshall, noted, "One long, unbroken cheer, in which the feeble cry of those who lay helpless on the earth blended with the strong voices of those who still fought, hailed the presence of the victorious chief."

In three days of bloody combat amid the scrub oak and pine forest called the Wilderness, Lee's Confederate Army of Northern Virginia—just under 61,000 strong—had outmaneuvered and outfought a Federal force of nearly 134,000 men. Major General Joseph Hooker, the vainglorious Union commander, became the fourth leader of the Army of the Potomac to fall victim to Lee's tactical expertise. Many of Hooker's disgruntled soldiers, slogging back to their camps across the Rappahannock River, placed the blame for their defeat on Fighting Joe's well-known fondness for the bottle. "The failure at Chancellorsville was due to the incompetency which comes from a besotted brain," grumbled Private Robert G. Carter of the 22d Massachusetts Infantry. "The Army of the Potomac had marched, fought and endured, and was there at Chancellorsville, as it always had been, superior to the genius of any commander yet appointed."

Although the Army of the Potomac had been soundly beaten, the massive Union force was far from crippled. Moreover, while Hooker had lost 13 percent of his force at Chancellorsville, Lee's smaller army had sustained a 22 percent casualty rate. Among the casualties was a particularly devastating loss, the brilliant General Thomas J. "Stonewall" Jackson, Lee's most trusted subordinate, who succumbed to his wounds on May 10. In the wake of this problematic victory, the question loomed for Lee: What now to do? The Confederate commander realized that his victory had achieved little more than a postponement of the day when the Army of the Potomac would

Above: On the first day of the battle, hit by a shell that nearly severed his right leg, Lieutenant Bayard Wilkeson coolly lay on a blanket, twisted his sash into a tourniquet and amputated the limb with the initialed pocketknife shown here. Hours later he died.

Opposite: Artillerymen of the VI Corps pause near pontoon bridges over the Rappahannock River south of Fredericksburg, Virginia, during the Federal reconnaissance of early June 1863.

Guards officer Arthur Fremantle, a British observer who was traveling with Major General James Longstreet, characterized General Robert E. Lee (right) as "a perfect gentleman in every respect," noting that Southerners pronounced him "as near perfection as a man can be."

again press his outnumbered army back toward Richmond. In considering his prospects, Lee concluded that he had only two alternatives. The first was to retire to Richmond and defend the city, a course of action that he suspected would end in a Confederate surrender. The other choice was audacious and full of risk—the kind of option that seemed to suit Lee's style of command. It was an invasion of the North, a march across the Potomac River and a strike into Pennsylvania.

In a series of meetings with Confederate president Jefferson Davis and his cabinet, Lee built a persuasive case for taking the offensive. Moving north would solve one of Lee's critical problems—a chronic supply shortage. Hampered by an inadequate railroad system, and operating in a war-ravaged region partly occupied by the enemy, Lee was unable to provide sufficient food and clothing for his army or forage for his horses. An invasion of Pennsylvania would afford his soldiers access to rich farmlands and give the people of Virginia time to stockpile supplies.

But Davis and his advisers had other ideas about what to do with the Army of Northern Virginia. For one thing, they were preoccupied with the deteriorating situation in the western theater, where General Ulysses S. Grant's Federals were laying siege to the Mississippi River bastion of Vicksburg. Some wanted Lee to send forces west to relieve Vicksburg. They also feared that if Lee moved north, Hooker might take advantage of the opportunity to strike south, toward the Confederate capital at Richmond. All were agreed, however, that something had to be done to shift the fighting away from war-torn northern Virginia.

And the Confederate leaders knew well that a successful invasion might win prizes of incalculable value. The Northern Peace Democrats surely would be encouraged to demand an end to the conflict under terms reasonably favorable to the South; a victory might also persuade Britain and France to intervene on behalf of the Confederacy.

In the weeks following Chancellorsville, to adjust for the loss of Stonewall Jackson, Lee reorganized the Army of Northern Virginia into three corps commanded by his most able generals: James Longstreet, Richard Stoddert Ewell, and Ambrose Powell Hill. The force was resupplied as best it could be, reinforced to more than 75,000 strong, and readied for the great invasion.

Despite their losses at Chancellorsville, Lee's soldiers were supremely confident of their fighting prowess and the military judgment of their commander. Lee had led the Southern army in a string of victories since taking over command: the Seven Days' Battles around Richmond, and a second triumph on the banks of Bull Run. His first invasion of the North was turned back at Antietam, but he had withstood the Federals at Fredericksburg and then defeated them at Chancellorsville. His men were with him heart and soul. "The troops of Lee were now at the zenith of their perfection and glory," South Carolina lieutenant D. Augustus Dickert recalled. "They looked upon themselves as invincible, and that no General the North could put in the field could match our Lee." Artillery Colonel Edward Porter Alexander professed, "Nothing gave me much concern so long as I

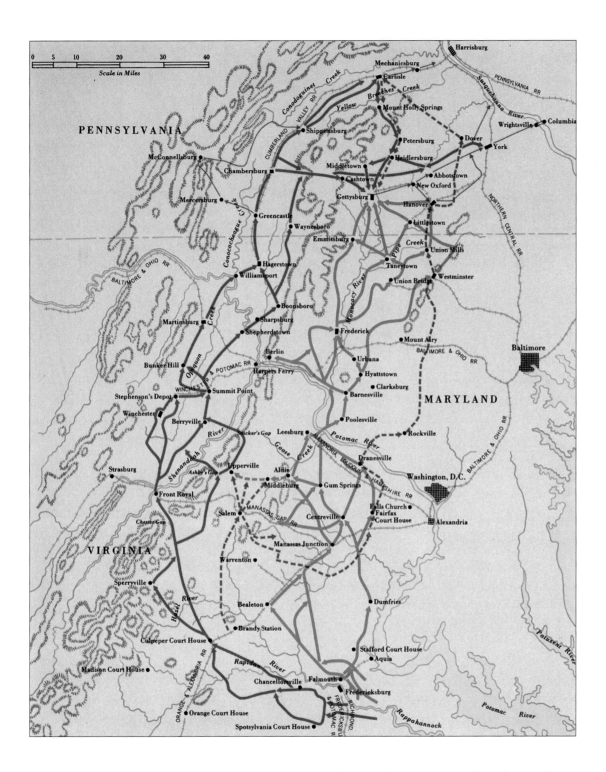

On June 10, 1863, General Robert E. Lee ordered Major General Richard Ewell to march his corps north toward Pennsylvania, taking a route (red line) down the Shenandoah Valley. Ewell was followed by the corps of Longstreet and Hill. On June 13, General Joseph Hooker began to shift the Army of the Potomac (blue line) to pursue Lee. The Confederate cavalry under Jeb Stuart (broken red line) screened the army's route before leaving Salem, Virginia, on a raid that placed them out of contact with Lee.

Brigadier General Alfred Pleasonton (right), chief of the revitalized Federal cavalry, poses with a dapper, ringletted George A. Custer. Pleasonton was so impressed with Custer's ability and dash that he jumped him in rank from captain to brigadier general.

knew that General Lee was in command. We looked forward to victory under him as confidently as to successive sunrises." For his part, Lee considered his devoted soldiers "the finest body of men that ever tramped the earth."

A month after Chancellorsville, with Hooker apparently still reluctant to resume the offensive, Lee prepared to move his army by stages 30 miles northwest to the vicinity of Culpeper. "I propose to do so cautiously," Lee wired Davis on June 2, "watching the result, and not to get beyond recall until I find it safe." By June 7 both Longstreet's and Ewell's corps had encamped near Culpeper, and A. P. Hill's corps was preparing to follow. The next day Lee attended a grand review put on by his swashbuckling cavalry commander, Major General James Ewell Brown (Jeb) Stuart, whose 9,500 troopers were stationed six miles northeast of Culpeper near the hamlet of Brandy Station. "It was a splendid sight," Lee wrote his wife, Mary; "Stuart was in all his glory."

Alerted to increased Confederate activity, but uncertain of what it portended, on June 5 General Hooker expressed his suspicions to President Abraham Lincoln that Lee "must have it either in mind to cross the Upper Potomac, or to throw his army between mine and Washington." Unaware that two-thirds of Lee's army had already concentrated at Culpeper, Hooker believed the Rebel forces there consisted largely of Stuart's cavalry, perhaps poised for a raid against Union supply lines. In an effort to preempt a Confederate attack, Hooker ordered his chief of cavalry, Brigadier General Alfred Pleasonton, "to disperse and destroy the rebel force assembled in the vicinity of Culpeper."

In the early morning darkness of June 9, 1863, Pleasonton's 8,000 troopers, with

3,000 infantrymen in support, splashed across the fog-shrouded Rappahannock River at Beverly's and Kelly's fords, and overran Stuart's outlying pickets. Surprised by the sudden onslaught, Stuart desperately shifted his forces to confront the advancing Yankee columns. For the next 14 hours, charge and countercharge thundered across the ridges near Brandy Station in the largest cavalry engagement ever waged on American soil. By day's end Stuart's horsemen held the field, with Pleasonton in retreat across the Rappahannock. But the self-confident Rebel horsemen had been forced to accept the fact that the once ridiculed Union cavalry were now their equals in fighting ability.

Following the inconclusive battle at Brandy Station, the Army of Northern Virginia continued its epic trek northward. In the vanguard, the 21,000 troops of Ewell's corps moved down the valley of the Shenandoah toward that river's confluence with the Potomac. From June 13 through June 15, Ewell attacked Major General Robert H. Milroy's Union troops at Winchester, capturing 3,000 prisoners and 23 cannon, and virtually annihilating the last Yankee obstacle to the fords of the Potomac River. On the evening of the 15th, Major General Robert E. Rodes' division tramped across a pontoon bridge and gained the north bank of the Potomac just south of Williamsport, Maryland.

Having gained a foothold in Maryland, Lee was now fully determined to press his invasion of the North. Longstreet's and Hill's forces were ordered to march with all haste from their positions at Culpeper and Fredericksburg. The Blue Ridge Mountains shielded the Confederate columns from Federal observation, while Stuart's horsemen effectively fended off Yankee cavalry probes east of the mountains. In a

Cavalrymen battle with sabers over a prized trophy, a regimental flag, in an artist's depiction of the sort of close combat waged at Brandy Station. A trooper of the 1st New Jersey Cavalry recalled that one guidon changed hands six times during the battle, ending up back with the Federals.

A lover of music and dancing, the chief of Confederate cavalry, Major General James Ewell Brown (Jeb) Stuart, carried his own minstrels with him. Always present, on the march and in bivouac, was a banjo player named Sam Sweeney; for dances, two fiddlers joined Sweeney along with a slave called Mulatto Sam, who played the bones and danced an inspired buck and wing.

"Well, boys, I've been seceding for two years and now I've got back into the Union!"

Confederate infantrymen marching north to Pennsylvania ford a stream with shoes off and trousers rolled. Many units crossed half a dozen rivers and creeks during Lee's advance, employing what one officer mordantly termed "Confederate pontoons—that is, by wading straight through."

series of mounted clashes at Aldie, Middleburg, and Upperville, Pleasonton's Union troopers fought courageously but failed to penetrate Stuart's cavalry screen.

When word of a Confederate onslaught in the lower Shenandoah Valley reached Army of the Potomac headquarters at Falmouth—across the Rappahannock from Fredericksburg—Hooker's worst fears were realized. As yet uncertain whether Lee intended to invade the North, to threaten Washington, or to strike at the principal Federal supply line—the Orange & Alexandria Railroad—the Union commander began shifting his seven army corps northward to Manassas Junction and Centreville, 20 miles outside the defenses of Washington.

The Rebels had stolen several days' march on the Federals, and the Northern troops were pushed to the breaking point in the attempt to catch up with their enemy. Marching for 15 hours at a stretch, clad in woolen uniforms and weighed down with muskets, ammunition, and knapsacks, the Yankee foot soldiers found their endurance sorely tested. "The air was almost suffocating," recalled Private John Haley of the 17th Maine. "The soil of Virginia was sucked into our throats, sniffed into our nostrils, and flew into our eyes and ears until our most intimate friends would not have recognized us." Nauseated and temporarily blind, Haley was one of hundreds who collapsed by the wayside.

"All day long we tugged our weary knapsacks in the broiling sun, and many fell out to fall no more," Private Wilbur Fisk of Vermont wrote his wife during a brief halt near Fairfax. "We expect more hard marching, but shall either get toughened to it, or, as the boys say, die toughening."

Plodding northward in the ranks of the Fifth Corps, Robert Carter observed that even veteran troops abandoned all discipline in their quest for water. When officers attempted to maintain order at roadside springs—most little more than "slimy mudholes"—mobs of thirsty soldiers shoved them aside while "the scooping and filtering of mud and grit went on." As the tramp continued, Carter discovered how callous human nature could become when subjected to such an ordeal. The amputated arm of a Federal cavalryman wounded in the fighting near Upperville "became a football for every one, and had to run the gauntlet, from the head of the brigade to the rear."

While the Federals were struggling to catch up, the bulk of the Army of Northern Virginia was crossing the Potomac into Maryland. On June 24 A. P. Hill's corps forded the river at Shepherdstown, and over the next two days Longstreet crossed his corps at Williamsport. The crossing took on the air of a celebration. Gray-clad soldiers tossed their hats aloft and cheered, while regimental bands played "Mary-

"We expect more hard marching, but shall either get toughened to it, or, as the boys say, die toughening."

land! My Maryland" and "The Bonnie Blue Flag." Though nearly as tired as their Federal pursuers, the Rebels were jubilant to be once again on Northern soil. Captain Charles Minor Blackford of Longstreet's corps heard one Confederate laughingly exclaim, "Well, boys, I've been seceding for two years and now I've got back into the Union!" Another soldier told a somber group of Maryland women, "Here we are, ladies, as rough and ragged as ever but back again to bother you."

Aware that the prosperous farms of Maryland and Pennsylvania offered an irresistible temptation to his hungry soldiers, Lee issued orders to prevent the theft of crops and livestock. All confiscated supplies, he declared, would be paid for at "the market price." The soldiers mostly ignored their commander's directive, however. Pilfering was widespread, and many Confederate officers turned a blind eye to their soldiers' indiscretions. "Some of the boys have been 'capturing' chickens," Corporal Edmund D. Patterson of Alabama wrote his wife; "It is against positive orders, but I would not punish one of them." Colonel Clement A. Evans of the 31st Georgia expressed a desire for revenge: "The rascals are afraid we are going to overrun Pennsylvania," he noted. "That would indeed be glorious, if we could ravage that state making her desolate like Virginia. It would be a just punishment."

Thus far Lee's daring gamble had exceeded all expectations, and the path to Pennsylvania appeared wide open. In an effort to keep his dazed opponents off balance, the Confederate commander instructed General Jeb Stuart to "pass around" Hooker's forces with three of his four cavalry divisions, "doing them all the damage you can." Eager to repeat the success of his two previous circumventions of the Yankee army, Stuart struck eastward and embarked on a characteristically daring raid. But it would prove to be a costly foray. Without the aid of Stuart's troopers, Lee would be unable to track the Federal movements for a crucial week of the campaign.

As Hill's and Longstreet's forces made their way rapidly north through Maryland, Ewell's vanguard corps was already across the Mason-Dixon line. One of Ewell's divisions, led by gruff, hard-fighting Major General Jubal A. Early, forged ahead toward the Susquehanna River, easily over-

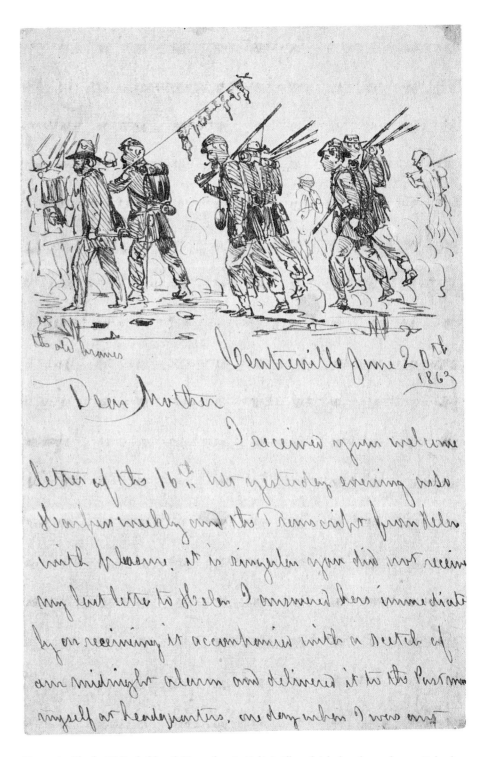

Trumpeter Charles W. Reed of the 9th Massachusetts Light Artillery sketched a column of weary Federal soldiers on this letter to his mother written from Centreville, Virginia. Reed illustrated all of his letters home and kept sketchbooks to record his adventures. At Gettysburg he won the Medal of Honor for rescuing his commanding officer.

coming the hastily mustered contingents of local militia that stood in his path. Lee had advised Ewell, "If Harrisburg comes within your means, capture it," and by June 27, with the rest of Lee's army massing near Chambersburg, Ewell had occupied the towns of York and Carlisle and was poised to cross the Susquehanna and converge on Pennsylvania's capital from the south and east.

Lee was confident that not only Harrisburg but also the strategic railroad line linking that city with Philadelphia would soon be in Confederate hands. But on the evening of June 28, Robert E. Lee's optimism abruptly gave way to alarm when one of Longstreet's scouts brought word that Hooker's army was on the march. Indeed, the Federals had crossed the Potomac at Edward's Ferry and were massing near Frederick, Maryland, less than 40 miles south of the Confederate headquarters at Chambersburg. Lee immediately recognized the danger—if the Yankees continued their rapid advance, they might well interpose themselves between the widely scattered Rebel columns. He immediately called off the movement against Harrisburg and ordered his corps commanders to concentrate their forces at the village of Cashtown, some 25 miles east of Chambersburg.

The scout who brought the word of Yankee movements also passed along, almost incidentally, another interesting piece of news. Joseph Hooker was no longer directing Federal operations. In the predawn darkness of June 28, grizzled, hot-tempered Major General George Gordon Meade—commander of the Union Fifth Corps—was abruptly summoned to a meeting at Hooker's headquarters. When he emerged, Meade turned to his son, Lieutenant George Meade, Jr., and said, "Well, George, I am in command of the Army of the Potomac."

Recognizing that a clash was imminent, General Meade continued the army's relentless march northward, dispatching Brigadier General John Buford's cavalry division to determine the exact position of the Rebel columns. "I am moving at once against Lee," the new commander informed his wife; "a battle will decide the fate of our country and our cause. Pray earnestly, pray for the success of my country."

With Major General John F. Reynolds' First Corps in the vanguard, and the Eleventh Corps close behind, the weary troops of the Army of the Potomac trekked across the Mason-Dixon line. Many units had been covering 35 or more miles a day and marching well into the night. "We tramped over the dusty road with blistered feet and heavy loads," recalled Robert Stewart of the 140th Pennsylvania; "the only solid food available was mouthful of 'hardtack,' now and then, which we munched as we marched along."

Robert Carter saw "hundreds falling exhausted by the roadside," many of them the victims of heatstroke. "Every face looked like a piece of leather, bestreaked with sweat, and besprinkled with dust." Despite cheers and encouragement from the local populace, 5th New Hampshire officer Charles Livermore found that fatigue and knowledge of impending battle instilled grim silence in the trudging column: "There was little heard in the ranks but the tread of feet, the clanking of arms and equipment, and an occasional oath or grumble from some tired mortal."

As Meade's forces were entering Pennsylvania, the first of Lee's troops—Major

The 147th Pennsylvania Infantry carried this state color on the march to Gettysburg. The field once bore stars and a state crest.

General Henry Heth's division of Hill's corps—arrived at Cashtown, the designated staging area. On June 30 Heth ordered one of his brigade commanders, Brigadier General James Johnston Pettigrew, to conduct a reconnaissance of the town of Gettysburg, which lay eight miles to the southeast. There was known to be a shoe factory in Gettysburg. Pettigrew was instructed to search the town for any usable supplies, especially shoes, but he was to pull back if Gettysburg was found to be occupied by Yankee troops.

When Pettigrew's 2,700 North Carolinians neared Gettysburg on the late afternoon of June 30, they spotted blue-clad horsemen heading for the ridges northwest of the town. Pettigrew dutifully withdrew toward Cashtown as ordered, and that night he and Heth conferred with Third Corps commander Hill, in charge at Cashtown pending Lee's arrival. Hill was convinced that any Federals in Gettysburg must be nothing more than local militia. Heth responded: "If there is no objection, General, I will take my division tomorrow and get those shoes." Hill replied: "None in the world."

Hill could not have been more wrong. The Yankees in Gettysburg were in fact the 2,700 troopers of General John Buford's cavalry division. With the trained eye of a veteran campaigner, Buford immediately recognized the town's strategic importance. Twelve roads converged at Gettysburg like the spokes of a wheel, making the town a logical point of concentration for both the Union and Confederate

A grizzled veteran of the Mexican War, Major General George Gordon Meade took command of the Army of the Potomac on June 28, 1863, just three days before the Battle of Gettysburg. An able if uninspired leader, Meade was known for his irascible temper. A staff officer wrote, "I don't know any thin old gentleman with a hooked nose and cold blue eyes who, when he is wrathy, exercises less of Christian charity than my well beloved Chief."

Ruined fences, stripped of rails to feed Confederate campfires, line the Chambersburg Pike west of Gettysburg. A. P. Hill's victorious Confederates pursued the retreating Federals along the road toward town on the afternoon of July 1.

Inset: A Pennsylvania poster advises residents that the state militia has been mobilized.

THE ENEMY
IS APPROACHING!

I MUST RELY UPON THE PEOPLE FOR THE

DEFENCE of the STATE!

AND HAVE Called THE MILITIA for that PURPOSE!

A. G. CURTIN, Governor of Pennsylvania.

THE TERM OF SERVICE WILL ONLY BE WHILE THE DANGER OF THE STATE IS IMMINENT.

"If there is no objection, General, I will take my division tomorrow and get those shoes."

MAJOR GENERAL HENRY HETH

Though he ranked last in the class of 1847 at West Point, Henry Heth proved himself an able general, serving in Braxton Bragg's Confederate army in Tennessee before being transferred at Lee's request to the Army of Northern Virginia. Two months after receiving command of a division, he launched the attack that sparked the Battle of Gettysburg.

The Wagon Hotel, a Gettysburg inn that catered to teamsters, fronts on Baltimore Street in this 1863 photograph. The small but thriving market town had rail connections to Baltimore and Harrisburg and was home to Pennsylvania College and the Lutheran Theological Seminary. Gettysburg had a population of about 2,400 people, with small-scale manufacture of goods such as carriages and shoes. The town's location at the intersection of several major roads made a visit from the invading Rebels a distinct possibility.

armies. Buford sent word to General Reynolds to bring up his infantry as quickly as possible, and dispersed his troopers to defend the high ground to the north and west of Gettysburg until the reinforcements arrived. The great bloodletting would begin at dawn.

CLASH AT DAWN: JULY I

At 5:30 on the morning of July 1, 1863, a detail of troopers from the 8th Illinois Cavalry noted ominous signs of movement in the fog-shrouded valley of Marsh Creek, some three miles west of Gettysburg. Soldiers in uniforms of gray were materializing in the mist, ghostly shapes marching down the Chambersburg Pike from the direction of Cashtown. Hastily dispatching a courier to alert his commanding officer, Lieutenant Marcellus Jones took a carbine from one of his sergeants and fired a shot at the enemy column. The Battle of Gettysburg had begun.

The advancing Rebels belonged to Major General Henry Heth's division of A. P. Hill's First Corps. Following Hill's instructions, Heth was marching to occupy the crossroads at Gettysburg, confident that his 7,500 men would easily brush aside the handful of local militia he believed to be guarding the town. But when Heth arrived on the high ground known as Herr Ridge, he saw formations of Federal cavalrymen deploying atop McPherson's Ridge, half a mile to his front, and blocking his advance.

The polished movements of the horsemen as they dismounted and fanned out to fight on foot—every man in his proper place and horses led quickly to the rear—

Death of Reynolds
Gettysburg —

Shot from the saddle at McPherson's Woods, Major General John Reynolds was among the most admired of Union officers—"one of the soldier generals," remarked an infantryman who served under him. He had purchased his Western-style saddle while serving in the Mexican War. The sketch of him falling mortally wounded, by artist Alfred Waud, was probably based on eyewitness accounts.

marked these Yankees as veterans.

The Confederates were not going to get into Gettysburg without a fight. Heth ordered forward the brigades of Brigadier Generals James J. Archer and Joseph R. Davis. From the high ground, General John Buford's Federal cavalrymen opened fire with their breech-loading carbines. Buford had been forced to stretch his line precariously thin, but he was determined to cover the approaches to Gettysburg and buy time in order to allow Major General John F. Reynolds, commanding the Army of the Potomac's left wing, to hasten up the infantry.

Reynolds arrived on the field at 9:00 a.m., and soon troops of the First Corps were marching at a double-quick into line atop McPherson's Ridge, relieving Buford's hard-pressed troopers. Reynolds rode forward with the Iron Brigade, shouting encouragement to the black-hatted midwesterners who loaded their muskets and fixed bayonets on the run. As the general turned in the saddle to urge on his men, a bullet slammed into the back of his head, and Reynolds fell dead from his horse.

At that loss, Major General Abner Doubleday took charge of the First Corps and decisively blunted Heth's onslaught. Archer's brigade was driven out of McPherson's Woods and Archer himself hauled into captivity by Private Patrick Mahoney of the 2d Wisconsin. North of the Chambersburg Pike, General Davis' Mississippians breached the Yankee line along the cut of an unfinished railroad only to be counterattacked and trapped. The flag of the 2d Mississippi was captured in a frenzied melee, and scores of Rebels were forced to surrender.

Shortly after 11:00 a.m., a three-hour lull settled over the field as both sides regrouped and adjusted their lines. Major General Oliver O. Howard—the devout, one-armed "praying general"—arrived at the head of his Eleventh Corps and assumed command of the Union forces. Howard extended the Federal line north and east of Gettysburg with two of his divisions and placed another in reserve on Cemetery Hill, a commanding elevation just south of the town. "Tell Doubleday to fight on the left," Howard instructed an aide, "and I will fight on the right."

Robert E. Lee had also arrived at Gettysburg. Initially frustrated by Heth's premature and unsuccessful advance, he was soon heartened by news that Richard Ewell's Second Corps was coming into position north of town. Even without Longstreet's corps—still a day's march to the west—the army commander felt that a coordinated advance by Hill's and Ewell's forces held the promise of victory.

Unfortunately for the Confederates, when the fighting resumed at 2:30 p.m. Lee's plans almost immediately began to go awry. Major General Robert E. Rodes, the young and headstrong commander of Ewell's largest division, launched his men in a poorly timed assault along Oak Ridge northwest of Gettysburg. One brigade was brought to a standstill north of the railroad cut, and four North Carolina regiments commanded by Brigadier General Alfred Iverson were pinned down in a shallow swale by fire so intense that one survivor concluded that "every man who stood up was either killed or wounded." Shouting, "Up boys, and give them steel," Brigadier General Henry Baxter launched a counterattack

Nine colorbearers of the 24th Michigan were shot down during the struggle for McPherson's Ridge. The regiment's flag, shown here in a photograph taken after Gettysburg, bore 23 bullet holes and was so damaged that it was retired.

that virtually annihilated Iverson's Carolinians.

As Rodes continued to press his attack, fresh Confederate brigades resumed the assault on McPherson's Ridge. Sweeping forward in parade-ground order, Brigadier General Johnston Pettigrew's regiments were savaged by the fire of the Iron Brigade, but they kept coming. "Their advance was not checked," noted Colonel Henry Morrow of the 24th Michigan, "and they came on with rapid strides, yelling like demons." Morrow's troops squared off with the 26th North Carolina in a brutal stand-up fight in which both units lost more than 70 percent of their number. Fourteen men went down in succession carrying the battle flag of the 26th North Carolina, among them 21-year-old Henry King Burgwyn, the youngest colonel in the Confederate army. Morrow likewise fell gravely wounded carrying his regiment's bullet-torn colors, as the tide began to turn against the Yankee defenders. At 3:45 p.m. two of Pettigrew's regiments struck the flank of the leftmost Federal brigade, and the hard-fighting First Corps line began to unravel.

The two divisions of the Eleventh Corps deployed north and east of Gettysburg were similarly beleaguered by the onslaught of Major General Jubal Early's Rebel division. Positioned on a knoll between the Carlisle and Harrisburg roads, on the far right of the Union line, Brigadier General Francis C. Barlow's brigades were caught in a deadly crossfire. Barlow was wounded while trying to rally his crumbling formations, and panic began to spread through the Eleventh Corps. "There was no alternative for Howard's men except to break and fly, or to throw down their arms

Sergeant Philander Wright of the 2d Wisconsin added brass ventilators to his tall felt army hat, the trademark headgear of the Iron Brigade. The round I Corps badge, red for the 1st Division, bears the regiment's number in brass. Sergeant Wright was wounded carrying the regimental colors.

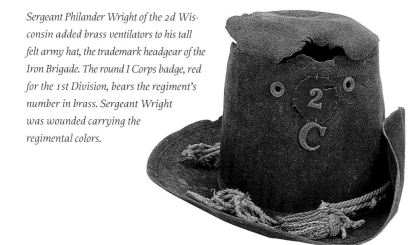

PRIVATE ANDREW PARK

42d Mississippi Infantry, Davis' Brigade

At about 10:15 a.m. Davis' brigade of Mississippians and North Carolinians crossed Willoughby Run and collided with Brigadier General Lysander Cutler's Federal brigade alongside an unfinished railroad cut on McPherson's Ridge. In the pitched battle, the men of the 42d captured the colors of the 56th Pennsylvania. Park, a farmer from Panola County, Mississippi, enlisted in the spring of 1862 and served until he was captured in 1865—seven days before Appomattox.

—————————— // ——————————

After forming his command, Col. Hugh R. Miller walked down the line, and stated that if there was a man there who could not stand the smell of gunpowder he had better step out, for we were going into a fight. To my astonishment one poor felow went to him and said: "Colonel, I just cannot go into a fight today, for if I do I will get wounded or killed." The Colonel, with an oath, ordered him back into line. Just at this moment General Davis, and staff rode up and gave the command to move forward, and to let nothing stop us. . . .

I should have stated in the beginning that we were thrown into a fine field of wheat as I ever saw. We had not gone more than three or four hundred yards in this field until we met the enemy's skirmishers. We drove them in, and they fell back over their main line. This drew us up to within fifty or sixty yards of that line, where they were lying down in the wheat. They rose up and resting on one knee fired the first volley. But they shot too high, and but few of our men were hurt. We received orders to fire and charge. This broke their line, and they retreated down the railroad cut. . . . Our troops on the left were ordered to fire right oblique; and those on the right to fire left oblique. In this manner we poured volley after volley into them as they ran down this railroad cut. I think there never was such slaughter as we made on this occasion. I could have walked a half or three quarters of a mile on the dead soldiers of the enemy and not have put my feet on the ground. In some places they were lying three deep. The enemy now brought up more troops when we were about a half mile from the town. They were very strong now, while our forces consisted of only Heath's division; so we received orders to fall back and wait for reinforcements. We fell back about three hundred yards. We had been fighting about two hours and our loss was quite heavy, and right here I will say that among first of my company to get hurt was the man who in the outset told the Colonel he could not go into battle. His arm was broken by a ball.

When we arrived on the ground where we first began the fight in the morning we could see no Yankees. But about three hundred yards farther to our right we [saw] standing two flags; one of which was the flag of Pennsylvania and the other the National flag. There seemed to be no one about them; and Col. Miller called to his men and asked if he had a man in his regiment that could or would bring those flags to him. In an instant Willie Clarke, a fourteen year old lad, said: "I can," and started after them. At about the same time five others started, two them being from my regiment (42nd) and three from the Second regiment. Willie Clarke outran the rest, having had a little the start of them, and got there first, and threw his arms around the flag-staff. But, low and behold! the flags were not alone, for six Yankees were there, and a hand to hand fight began. Two men from the 42nd were wounded and two from the 2nd killed and the other wounded. Five of the Yankees were killed, and the sixth took the flags and started off with them. But Willie Clarke shot him before he got fifty yards and brought [the flags] to Colonel Miller without receiving a scratch.

Overrun by Confederates on McPherson's Ridge, several Federals of the 149th Pennsylvania fight with their fists to retrieve the captured colors carried by the Confederate at right. In the middle distance, Doubleday's Federal troops make a stand as the Confederates attack down the Chambersburg Pike toward Gettysburg.

"*I could have walked a half or three quarters of a mile on the dead soldiers of the enemy and not have put my feet on the ground.*"

The imposing main building of Gettysburg's Lutheran Theological Seminary was the scene of fighting during the withdrawal of the Federal I Corps on July 1. The structure would serve both sides as a field hospital and observatory.

The handsome gatehouse of Evergreen Cemetery, its windows smashed by bullets, stands on the crest of Cemetery Hill. Federal artillery batteries nearby helped keep Confederate attackers at bay on the evening of July 1.

Federal cavalry and units of the I Corps stubbornly held the area sur- rounding McPherson's Ridge, west of Gettysburg, against the advance of A. P. Hill's Confederate corps on July 1, 1863. Both armies rushed reinforcements to the field and by late afternoon an attack by Early's division of Ewell's corps routed the Federal XI Corps, forcing the Yan- kees to retreat to Cemetery Hill south of town.

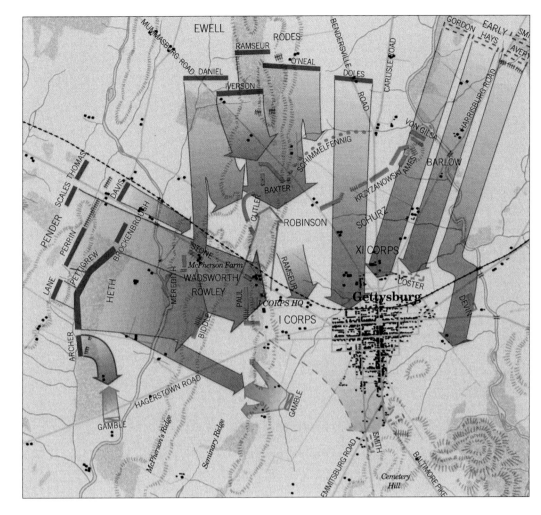

and surrender," Confederate general John B. Gordon said later; "Under the concen- trated fire from front and flank, the marvel is that any escaped."

By 4:30 p.m. both Union corps were in full retreat on Gettysburg. Elements of the First Corps managed to make a brief stand just west of town beside the buildings of the Lutheran Theological Seminary, but the Seminary Ridge position proved unten- able when Major General William D. Pender's division joined the Southern jug- gernaut. As the sweating, powder-stained Union soldiers fell back into the streets of the town, the last vestiges of order gave way in inextricable confusion. "On every side our troops were madly rushing to the rear," confessed a Wisconsin volunteer; "My heart sank within me. I lost all hope."

Oliver Howard was striving to re-form his shattered forces on Cemetery Hill south of town when the arrival of a forceful and highly regarded Federal officer breathed new hope into the dispirited troops. Major General Winfield Scott Han- cock, commander of the Second Corps, had been dispatched by Meade to assess the

situation at Gettysburg. After a strained consultation with Howard—who seems to have interpreted Hancock's mission as a personal slight—the imposing officer set about bringing order out of chaos. "His bearing was courageous and hopeful," one staff officer recalled, "while his eyes flashed defiance." Lieutenant Sidney Cooke of the 147th New York noted that Hancock's imperturbable demeanor "almost led us to doubt whether there had been cause for retreat at all."

The Federals averted disaster, but only by a narrow margin. Had the onrushing Rebels managed to mount a unified assault on Cemetery Hill, the battle at Gettys- burg likely would have ended on the first day—with a decisive Confederate vic- tory. But the sudden success of the Rebels seems to have rendered them indecisive. When Lee advised General Ewell to take Cemetery Hill "if practicable," the corps commander chose not to risk an attack. The Army of Northern Virginia had carried the day, but the impending arrival of Meade's hard-marching columns meant that the battle for Gettysburg had only just begun.

"There were the groaning and crying, the struggling and dying, crowded side by side, …"

TILLIE PIERCE

Resident of Gettysburg

Fifteen-year-old Tillie Pierce was sent by her worried parents to a refuge to the south of town, the Jacob Weikert farm on the Taneytown road behind the Round Tops. Even there, on the afternoon of July 1, the wounded began to arrive.

Some of the wounded from the field of battle began to arrive where I was staying. They reported hard fighting, many wounded and killed, and were afraid our troops would be defeated and perhaps routed.

The first wounded soldier whom I met had his thumb tied up. This I thought was dreadful, and told him so. "Oh," said he, "this is nothing; you'll see worse than this before long." "Oh! I hope not," I innocently replied. Soon two officers carrying their arms in slings made their appearance, and I more fully began to realize that something terrible had taken place.

Now the wounded began to come in greater numbers. Some limping, some with their heads and arms in bandages, some crawling, others carried on stretchers or brought in ambulances. Suffering, cast down and dejected, it was a truly pitiable gathering. Before night the barn was filled with the shattered and dying heroes of this day's struggle.

That evening Beckie Weikert, the daughter at home, and I went out to the barn to see what was transpiring there. Nothing before in my experience had ever paralleled the sight we then and there beheld. There were the groaning and crying, the struggling and dying, crowded side by side, while attendants sought to aid and relieve them as best they could. We were so overcome by the sad and awful spectacle that we hastened back to the house weeping bitterly.

IN HELL'S TERRAIN: JULY 2

Shortly before midnight of July 1, 1863, Major General George Meade arrived on the battlefield at Gettysburg to face the greatest crisis of his 28-year military career. Meade had not expected to give battle at Gettysburg, and as Generals Winfield Scott Hancock and Oliver O. Howard briefed him on the situation, the army commander realized how precariously close the Union had come to disaster on the first day of fighting. Two of his seven corps—the First and Eleventh—had suffered crippling losses, and while the survivors held a formidable position on the high ground south of Gettysburg, Meade knew that unless the bulk of his army arrived by dawn, the Federals might not be able to stave off the inevitable Confederate assault.

Urged on by their apprehensive commander, the footsore Yankee soldiers trudged through choking clouds of dust all through the hours of darkness, northward to Gettysburg. Although hundreds gave out along the way, by sunrise of July 2 Meade was able to plug the exhausted troops of his Second, Third, Fifth, and Twelfth Corps into line. These new arrivals enabled Meade to occupy the wooded slopes of Culp's Hill, southeast of Gettysburg, and to extend his position southward from Cemetery Hill along the low crest of Cemetery Ridge. The Federal line now resembled a tight horseshoe with its strength facing north and northeast, where most of the Confederate troops were apparently concentrated. But the Union left, at the end of Cemetery Ridge, was exposed and thinly defended. Few of the weary Federals had strength enough to pitch their tents, and most dropped down where they stood in ranks, to snatch what sleep they could before facing the terrible ordeal of battle.

Robert E. Lee affectionately called Major General James Longstreet "my old war horse," while his men reserved the nickname "Old Pete." A brilliant battlefield tactician, Longstreet favored a defensive posture in any confrontation with the Federal armies in Pennsylvania, an idea that ran counter to Lee's aggressive plans.

Shadowed by Big and Little Round Tops, a Confederate battle line advances into the hotly contested, rock-strewn valley of Plum Run.

If the first day at Gettysburg had been a near calamity for the Union, it had proved to be a time of lost opportunities for Robert E. Lee's Army of Northern Virginia. Lee knew that if his troops were to defeat a numerically stronger enemy, the second day's fight would require strategic enterprise and tactical boldness. Audacity in the face of extreme pressure was a hallmark of Lee's generalship, and, rising from a fitful sleep an hour before dawn, he set about implementing a daring offensive plan reminiscent of his successful strategy at Second Manassas and Chancellorsville.

Two of General Longstreet's three divisions had arrived to bolster Hill's and Ewell's corps, and Lee intended to use these fresh troops to strike at the vulnerable Union left. As the morning wore on with little except an occasional skirmish between the opposing forces, Lee explained his strategy to his subordinate commanders.

From his position on Herr Ridge, west of Gettysburg, Longstreet would march the divisions of Generals John Bell Hood and Lafayette McLaws southward, using Seminary Ridge as a natural barrier to screen the movement from enemy observa-

tion. Once these troops were deployed west of the Emmitsburg road, Longstreet would initiate an advance *en echelon*—committing Hood's and McLaws' brigades in a sequential series of triphammer attacks from south to north. Once the last of Longstreet's men were under way, General Richard H. Anderson's division of Hill's corps would continue the en echelon attack, striking at the Union center on Cemetery Ridge. In order to divert Federal troops from the point of assault, Lee instructed General Ewell to launch an attack on the Union right.

Longstreet, however, was reluctant to attack without Major General George E. Pickett's division, which was still a day's march away. In fact, Longstreet favored a strategy that was markedly different from Lee's—no attack at all. Longstreet wanted to sideslip past Gettysburg, find more suitable ground to defend, and force Meade to launch an attack, as General Ambrose E. Burnside's troops had at Fredericksburg the previous year, with disastrous results. But Lee was determined to maintain the initiative, and as Longstreet began to maneuver his divisions into place, he did so with a reluctance that many officers felt verged on insubordination. It was nearly 4:00 in the afternoon before Longstreet was ready to begin his attack on the Federal left, and by then the situation to his front had changed dramatically. An entire Yankee corps had moved forward from Cemetery Ridge to the Emmitsburg road, and lay directly in Longstreet's path.

Like Lee, George Meade had also to contend with the actions of an opinionated subordinate. When Major General Daniel E. Sickles decided that his Third Corps was not deployed on favorable ground, he took the liberty of shifting his two divisions west to what he judged a better defensive position. The combative politician-turned-soldier established a new line running south along the Emmitsburg road, across a crest marked by a peach orchard, and angling southeastward on a ridge that terminated in a heap of jumbled granite boulders called Devil's Den. By the time Meade was fully aware of Sickles' action, it was too late to readjust the line.

Longstreet had begun his attack, and the battle was joined.

Commencing with Hood's men on the Confederate right, each of Longstreet's brigades surged forward in sequence, the en echelon assaults smiting the Federals a series of sledgehammer blows. Screaming the Rebel yell, wave after wave of Confederate soldiers advanced into the smoke and flame of battle that rolled steadily northward from Devil's Den, across the corpse-strewn Wheat Field, to the Peach Orchard salient. Sickles' men fought desperately but began to give way, and the Southern juggernaut rolled on toward Cemetery Ridge.

As on the preceding day, the Confederates came up just short of victory on July 2. Through the decisive actions of junior officers, Federal soldiers secured the crucial elevation of Little Round Top—an impregnable anchor for Meade's left flank.

Captain Henry M. Minnigh (left foreground) stands proudly in front of Company K of the 1st Pennsylvania Reserves. The company was organized in Adams County, Pennsylvania, in and around the town of Gettysburg, and many of the men shown here fought virtually within sight of their homes. On July 2, the 1st Reserves, part of Colonel William McCandless' Brigade of the Federal 5th Corps, participated in the defense of Little Round Top.

The Maltese-cross shape of this badge worn by Lieutenant William O. Colt signifies that his regiment, the 83d Pennsylvania, belonged to General George Sykes' V Corps, which helped save the Federal left on the second day at Gettysburg. Colt's 295-man unit struggled to defend Little Round Top, suffering 55 casualties.

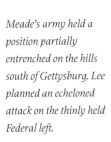

Meade's army held a position partially entrenched on the hills south of Gettysburg. Lee planned an echeloned attack on the thinly held Federal left.

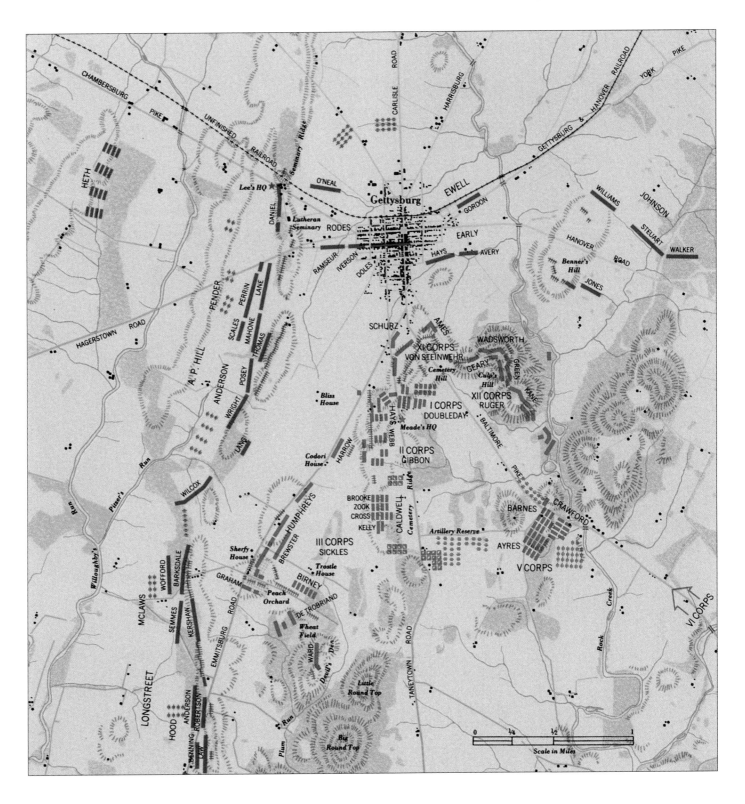

The courageous and skillful commanding officer of the 20th Maine, Joshua Chamberlain, was a professor of rhetoric, oratory and modern languages at Bowdoin College when he volunteered for service at the age of 33 in 1862. After the war, Chamberlain was elected governor of Maine and later became Bowdoin's president.

William C. Oates, commander of the 15th Alabama, described himself as having been "born in poverty" and "reared in adversity." Forced to leave his home at the age of 16 because of a scrape with the law, Oates labored as an itinerant house painter; he nevertheless managed to gain an education and became an attorney before volunteering in 1861. He later served in the Alabama legislature, in the U.S. House of Representatives and as Alabama's governor.

A stalwart defense by General Hancock's Second Corps maintained the Union hold on Cemetery Ridge, and Ewell's belated assault on Culp's Hill was easily repulsed. As darkness fell a desperate Rebel charge on Cemetery Hill briefly pierced the defenses of the Union Eleventh Corps but recoiled before a Yankee counterattack.

The bloodiest of the three days of battle at Gettysburg ended in stalemate. If Robert E. Lee's army was to win a decisive engagement on Northern soil, victory would have to come on July 3.

LITTLE ROUND TOP

Three miles south of Gettysburg, the troops of Major General John B. Hood launched the Confederate attack—the brigades of Generals Evander M. Law and Jerome B. Robertson in the first wave, Henry L. Benning and George T. Anderson in the second. The left half of Robertson's line was savaged by the fire of Captain James E. Smith's 4th New York Battery, four guns of which were deployed on the crest above Devil's Den. One shell exploded near General Hood as he rode behind the line of battle; his left arm shattered, Hood was borne to the rear.

Robertson's 1st Texas and 3d Arkansas pushed on across a rocky, triangle-shaped field and into the woods of the Rose Farm to the north. There they were brought to a bloody standstill by the volleys of Brigadier General J. H. Hobart Ward's Federal brigade.

The hulking, hard-drinking General Ward anchored the left of the Third Corps line, and he was not about to yield his ground without a fight. As Smith's New York battery continued to rain shrapnel and canister on Robertson's Texans, one of Ward's units, the 124th New York, mounted a counterattack that pushed the Rebel forces back across the triangular field.

The commander of the 124th, Colonel Augustus Van Horne Ellis, stood in the stirrups of his white horse with upraised sword, urging on his men, when a Confederate bullet slammed into his forehead. Benning's Georgia brigade had entered the fray, and with Ellis' death, the battle began to turn in favor of the

South. Devil's Den, and the guns of Smith's battery, were overrun by the advancing tide of gray-clad troops.

Hood's rightmost brigade, Evander Law's, extended beyond the Yankee left and was able to push unhampered toward the looming hills known as the Round Tops. Some of Law's regiments swung left, moving up the valley of Plum Run to strike at Devil's Den from the south. Other Confederate units, among them the 15th and 47th Alabama, crested the wooded height of Round Top and advanced toward the rocky crest of Little Round Top to the north.

During a reconnaissance, Meade's chief topographical engineer, Brigadier General Gouverneur Kemble Warren, had been shocked to find Little Round Top bare of Federal troops. If the Rebels gained the summit, their artillery would have a clear field of fire down the entire length of the Union line. Warren and his staff officers began rushing units of the Fifth Corps to the threatened point, and they managed to get Colonel Strong Vincent's brigade in place minutes before the Alabamians began scaling Little Round Top's southern flank.

Vincent's line staved off repeated assaults in a grim battle amid the boulder-strewn woods. Colonel William C. Oates led the 15th Alabama in a charge against the Yankee left but was checked and hurled back by the gritty defenders of the 20th Maine. Inspired by the valor of their colonel—former college professor Joshua Lawrence Chamberlain—the Maine men repulsed the Alabamians at the point of the bayonet. Chamberlain's desperate counterattack broke the Rebel line, scooped up dozens of prisoners, and sent Rebels scurrying for cover.

Meanwhile, Gouverneur Warren had hastened troops of Brigadier General Stephen H. Weed's brigade to the summit of Little Round Top, along with the Parrott guns of Lieutenant Charles E. Hazlett's Battery D, 5th U.S. Artillery. These reinforcements arrived in the very nick of time, just as the 4th and 5th Texas were about to overlap the right of Vincent's brigade. Led by Colonel Patrick H. O'Rorke, a young Irish-born West Pointer, the 140th New York plowed into the Texans and unleashed a deadly fire at point-blank range. O'Rorke, Vincent, Hazlett, and Weed were struck down with mortal wounds, but their decisive actions secured Little Round Top for the Union.

The body of a young Confederate soldier lies in a sharpshooter's nest in the Devil's Den. Another photograph of the site has revealed that the soldier actually died elsewhere and suggests that the photographer, probably Timothy O'Sullivan, had the body moved about 40 yards for dramatic effect.

"*The men stood, undisturbed by bursting shells, with bowed heads in reverent silence.*"

CORPORAL HENRY MEYER

148th Pennsylvania Infantry, Cross' Brigade

Meyer watched the men of Colonel Patrick Kelly's famed Irish Brigade prepare for action before they moved, along with Meyer and the Pennsylvanians, toward the Wheat Field to stem the Confederate breakthrough. Corporal Meyer would survive Gettysburg to be discharged for poor health in 1864.

W e had read in the papers of McClellan's soldiers, in the series of battles on the Peninsula, lying down along side of batteries and going to sleep while the roar of battle went on; this seemed incredible, but such a possibility was verified that day at Gettysburg. While lying in the hot sun in line of battle, some of the boys slept, though shells and solid shot came crashing into our midst.

… The Irish Brigade, which belonged to the Division, was first assembled in solid mass and their Chaplain, or Priest, performed some religious ceremony of a few minutes duration, while the men stood, undisturbed by bursting shells, with bowed heads in reverent silence. Then the whole Division was marched off at a "double quick" across fields and through patches of woods in the direction of the conflict…. We were the first troops to cross the field, and the yellow grain was still standing. I noticed how the ears of wheat flew in the air all over the field as they were cut off by the enemy's bullets….

Men in battle will act very differently; some become greatly excited, others remain perfectly cool. One of the boys in my rear was sitting flat on the ground and discharging his piece in the air at an angle of forty-five degrees, as fast as he could load. "Why do you shoot in the air?" I asked. "To scare 'em," he replied.

He was a pious young man, and the true reason why he did not shoot at the enemy direct, was because of his conscientious scruples on the subject. What struck me as being peculiar was that some of the boys swore energetically, who never before were heard to utter an oath.

THE PEACH ORCHARD AND WHEAT FIELD

As the fighting raged in the triangular field and Confederate troops began their advance on Little Round Top, the last of John B. Hood's brigades entered the fray. Brigadier General G. T. Anderson, a veteran of the Mexican War whose combative nature had earned him the nickname "Tige," led four Georgia regiments through a wood lot on the Rose Farm and toward a field of ripening wheat. Anderson's men were met with a crashing volley and screaming artillery shells that splintered the trees overhead. Within minutes Anderson's attack had fragmented along a stone wall at the southern edge of the Wheat Field.

Firing from the cover of the stone wall, the 17th Maine decimated G. T. Anderson's Georgians. Private John Haley noted that "we could see them tumbling around right lively." Haley's unit was part of the brigade commanded by Brigadier General Regis de Trobriand, a French aristocrat turned New York newspaper editor. When ammunition began to give out, de Trobriand exhorted his men to "hold them with the bayonet," and the line held.

But trouble was brewing on de Trobriand's right, where units of the Fifth Corps had been hastily positioned on a wooded knoll west of the Wheat Field. Lafayette McLaws' division had joined the great en echelon advance, and Brigadier General Joseph B. Kershaw's South Carolina brigade—one of the finest units in Lee's army—was sweeping across the Emmitsburg road. Federal artillery tore bloody gaps in Kershaw's line, but the South Carolinians pressed forward, linked up with Anderson's Georgians, and shoved the Federal defenders from the wooded knoll.

Soon hundreds of blue-clad soldiers were falling back through the trampled wheat, the Rebels in hot pursuit. But victory was not to come so easily; Brigadier General John C. Caldwell's division of the Second Corps had moved up at Hancock's order to plug the widening gap. Two of Caldwell's four brigade commanders were fatally wounded, but the veteran troops—which included the famous Irish Brigade—forged ahead, and the Rebels gave way before them.

The corpse-strewn Wheat Field would remain only briefly in Union hands, however. McLaws hurled two more of his brigades into what the field survivors would remember as a "whirlpool of death," and again the Yankees fell back. Caldwell appealed for help from the Fifth Corps, but the handful of units that came to his aid were overwhelmed in savage hand-to-hand combat. When Colonel Harrison Jeffords of the 4th Michigan saw a South Carolinian seize the regimental colors, he leaped at the Rebel with drawn sword but was run through the body by a bayonet. In the frenzied melee that followed, the Michiganders recovered their flag and hauled the bloodied banner and their dying commander to safety, Jeffords moaning, "Mother, mother, mother!"

At 6:30 p.m. McLaws launched his final blow against the Union Third Corps. Four regiments from Mississippi—1,600 strong—headed directly for the Peach Orchard salient. These soldiers were commanded by Brigadier General William A. Barksdale, a stocky former congressman noted for his fiery demeanor.

The once emerald green regimental flag of the 69th New York, the premier regiment of the Irish Brigade, was carried into action across the Wheat Field where the Irishmen drove back part of Kershaw's line.

Brigade chaplain Father William Corby grants a general absolution to the kneeling men of New York's Irish Brigade in this sketch by soldier-artist Charles Reed. Corby added a stern injunction to his blessing: "The Catholic Church," he stated, "refuses Christian burial to the soldier who turns his back upon the foe."

Absolution on Wheat Field 2d July 1863

As General Barksdale rode among his men, waving his hat and yelling encouragement, the Mississippians stormed past the Sherfy farmhouse and barn, crossed the Emmitsburg road, and crashed through the Yankee line. The Federal infantry were hurled back through the bullet-splintered peach trees, and Yankee artillerymen frantically limbered up their guns and joined the chaotic withdrawal.

After clearing the Peach Orchard, some of Barksdale's units charged to the east in pursuit of Union batteries pulling back toward Cemetery Ridge. Others of Barksdale's men swung north, striking the left flank of Brigadier General Andrew A. Humphreys' division. At the same time Humphreys' front—along the Emmitsburg road—was being assailed by R. H. Anderson's division, the final hammer blow of the en echelon assault. Humphreys' line crumbled; his embattled units waged a fighting retreat to the north and east.

General Sickles, whose Third Corps had paid a heavy price for his ill-considered redeployment, was himself a casualty of the escalating debacle. A glancing blow from a Confederate round shot ripped across Sickles' right leg, nearly severing the limb at the knee. Demonstrating characteristic aplomb, the general calmly puffed on a cigar as he was carried to the rear.

CEMETERY RIDGE AND CEMETERY HILL

As devastating as Longstreet's assault had been to the Federal Third Corps, the Confederates, too, had suffered heavy losses. Moreover, many Confederate units had become hopelessly intermingled as they pressed their advance eastward, through the woods that flanked Plum Run. Brigades had fragmented and lost all cohesion. With little more than an hour of daylight remaining, Lee's Army of Northern Virginia had yet to gain the crucial heart of the Yankee position—Cemetery Ridge.

Although Meade had provided little in the way of supervision, most of his subordinates had ably risen to the challenge. Little Round Top had been secured, and the charge of the Fifth Corps' Pennsylvania Reserve division had shored up the Union's southern flank. The lead elements of John Sedgwick's hard-marching Sixth Corps were beginning to arrive, bolstering the massed artillery that thundered away on the lower reaches of Cemetery Ridge. As the heaviest combat shifted northward to the Union center, where R. H. Anderson's division was punching out with the left arm of the Rebels' en echelon assault, Meade gave Hancock command of Third Corps' survivors in addition to his own Second Corps.

Flushed with the excitement of battle, General Hancock galloped along his embattled line, personally throwing units into the vortex of combat wherever crisis beckoned. Passing one small contingent that lay in reserve, Hancock shouted, "What regiment is this?"—"The First Minnesota," Colonel William Colvill replied. Pointing at the red battle flags that marked the oncoming line of a Confederate brigade, Hancock barked out the order, "Advance, Colonel, and take those colors!"

Major General Daniel Sickles, one of the most flamboyant of Union generals, was knocked from his saddle by a cannonball as he was watching his III Corps in battle near the Trostle farm. After his leg was amputated below the knee, he directed that the shattered bones (below) be sent to the Army Medical Museum in Washington, D.C., where he visited them periodically for the rest of his life.

Dead artillery horses litter the Trostle house yard, shot down when Captain John Bigelow's 9th Massachusetts Battery was overrun by the charging 21st Mississippi.

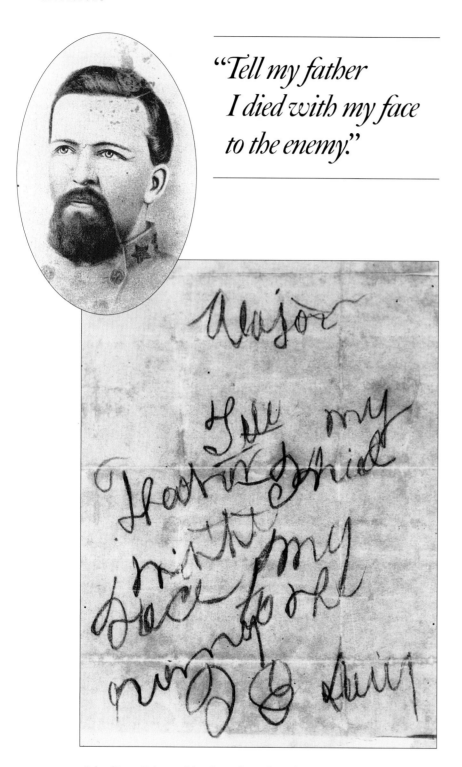

"Tell my father I died with my face to the enemy."

Colonel Isaac E. Avery of the 6th North Carolina (above, left) was mortally wounded by Federal artillery fire as he led a brigade up the slope of Cemetery Hill. As he lost consciousness, he scrawled a last, jumbled message (above) to his subordinate, Major Samuel M. Tate—"Major: Tell my father I died with my face to the enemy."

The Minnesotans charged forward with leveled bayonets and hurled the vanguard of Brigadier General Cadmus M. Wilcox's Alabama brigade back across the shallow swale of Plum Run. The attack cost the 1st Minnesota 215 of their 262 men, but Wilcox's advance was checked.

Farther along the line of Cemetery Ridge, Hancock ordered a similar counterattack to be carried out by Colonel George L. Willard's brigade. This was the first great bloodletting for Willard's men; they had been captured en masse at Harpers Ferry soon after their enlistment and had only recently been exchanged. The men of Willard's brigade had much to prove to their comrades in the Union Second Corps, and to themselves.

Colonel Willard led his cheering troops against the remnants of Barksdale's Mississippi brigade and drove the Rebels across Plum Run and into the open fields beyond. There Willard's advance foundered in the face of artillery salvoes that belched forth from massed batteries in the Peach Orchard; one shell tore off half of Willard's head, and the Yankees recoiled. But Barksdale had been toppled from his horse with fatal wounds to his chest and leg, and his courageous troops could do no more.

In a final effort to pierce the Federal defenses of Cemetery Ridge, R. H. Anderson's leftmost brigades pushed toward a stone wall that lay several hundred yards east of the Emmitsburg road. Brigadier General Ambrose R. Wright's Georgians gained a momentary foothold at the wall, near a little copse of trees, but they got no support, and Wright was forced to withdraw. The Confederate juggernaut had run out of steam.

A day of decidedly mixed results for Confederate hopes concluded with a series of attacks on the northern end of the Union line. Because of mixed signals, misunderstanding, and Lee's uncertainty regarding Federal strength in the Culp's Hill sector, Richard Ewell's Second Corps had failed to provide the diversionary assault planned to coincide with Longstreet's great offensive. When Ewell finally did launch an attack on Culp's Hill, it was made piecemeal and was easily repulsed by the Union Twelfth Corps, hunkered down behind formidable log breastworks.

The last great clash on July 2 came just after sunset, when Brigadier General Harry Thompson Hays' "Louisiana Tiger" brigade briefly overran some Yankee guns and fought partway up the slope of Cemetery Hill—perhaps the most heavily defended position at Gettysburg. The Federals rallied, a fresh brigade was sent rushing in from Second Corps, and the firing subsided.

The groans of thousands of wounded soldiers, punctuated by an occasional musket shot, echoed over the blood-soaked fields when General Meade called a late-night council of war to determine the Federal strategy for the following day. As exhausted, sweat soaked, and powder stained as their men, Meade's senior officers made the decision to stick it out—to hold the line against whatever Lee held in store on the third day of battle at Gettysburg.

appearance of Cemetery hole previous to Re... charge

ground over which Louisiana Tigers charged — *entrenched guns* — *Stevens battery* — *Gettysburg on left*

The six Napoleon guns of Battery D, 5th Maine Light Artillery, pour canister into the flank of Jubal Early's Confederates on Cemetery Hill.

THE GREAT REBEL CHARGE: JULY 3

The fighting on July 2 had been chaotic, bloody, and inconclusive. Several times that day General George G. Meade's Army of the Potomac had come perilously close to disaster. But each time subordinate officers had risen to the occasion, met the crisis, and staved off defeat.

Confederate commander Robert E. Lee had been repeatedly frustrated in his efforts to break through the formidable Federal line that ran from Culp's and Cemetery Hills in the north, southward down the low spine of Cemetery Ridge to the boulder-covered crest of Little Round Top.

Determined to maintain the offensive on July 3 and force the battle to a decisive conclusion, Lee conceived a simultaneous two-pronged assault on Meade's position. On the far Confederate left, Ewell's corps would try again to seize the wooded height of Culp's Hill, while Longstreet—whose corps had been reinforced by the arrival of Pickett's division—would strike at the Union center on Cemetery Ridge. Lee knew that Culp's Hill was heavily defended and that the Federal defenders were dug in behind substantial breastworks. But even if Ewell was unsuccessful, his assault might cause Meade to shift troops and thereby weaken other portions of his line. Lee knew that the troops holding Cemetery Ridge had suffered heavy losses in the previous day's fighting; if Meade stretched that portion of his line too thin, Longstreet stood a good chance of tearing the Army of the Potomac asunder.

Shortly after dawn Lee's plan began to go awry when the muffled roar of musketry and artillery alerted the Confederate commander that Ewell's attack on Culp's

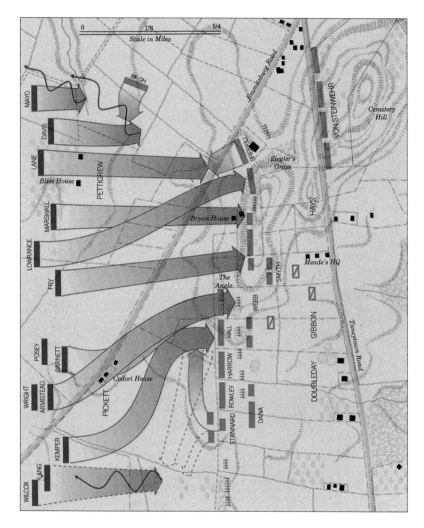

On the afternoon of July 3, the Confederate divisions of Pickett and Pettigrew, along with additional elements, attacked Federal II Corps positions on Cemetery Ridge in what would be called Pickett's Charge. The brigades of Kemper, Garnett, and Armistead advanced obliquely to their left to close up with Pettigrew's troops, exposing their right flanks to enemy fire. Pettigrew's brigades, meanwhile, were mauled by Federal batteries on Cemetery Hill. The Confederate flanks contracted and were overlapped by Union forces. Suffering fearful losses, Pettigrew's men charged at the Federal line defended by General Alexander Hays' division and were brought to a halt. Pickett's survivors attacked the Angle, a jog in a stone wall, where they were stopped by fire from General John Gibbon's division. With that repulse, the Confederates began streaming to their rear.

Hill was already under way. As it happened, elements of the Federal Twelfth Corps had initiated the clash by attempting to wrest control of rifle pits that had earlier fallen to Major General Edward Johnson's division. Johnson had little choice but to fight back, and the battle for Culp's Hill rapidly escalated into a series of valiant but futile Confederate assaults on the entrenched Yankee positions.

By afternoon the fighting on Culp's Hill had died out in stalemate. If the Army of Northern Virginia was to achieve victory at Gettysburg, it would have to come at the Union center on Cemetery Ridge.

Despite the collapse of his plan for simultaneous assaults, Lee never wavered in his resolve to break the Federal line on Cemetery Ridge. He placed that heavy responsibility in the hands of James Longstreet, his "old war horse." Longstreet had grave doubts and repeatedly expressed his concern that a head-on charge against the enemy center was to risk unacceptable losses with little chance for success. Lee overruled his subordinate, and the reluctant Longstreet spent the morning hours deploying the divisions of Generals Johnston Pettigrew, Isaac R. Trimble, and George Pickett for the daunting task.

At 1:00 p.m. some 170 Confederate cannon launched a massive bombardment in an attempt to soften up the Union positions on Cemetery Ridge and pave a way for the onslaught. General Hancock, whose Federal Second Corps defended the point of attack, ordered his own guns to return fire, and for two hours the greatest artillery barrage in the history of North America raged across the open fields between the Southern position on Seminary Ridge and the smoke-shrouded slope of Cemetery Ridge, where Yankee soldiers hugged the earth as the ground trembled and reeled beneath them.

Although the Confederate barrage savaged the Federal artillery, exploding caissons and limber chests, cutting down horses in their traces, and dismounting guns, much of the Rebel fire passed over the waiting Yankee infantry. In a dramatic gesture, Hancock rode slowly along the line of his Second Corps, inspiring the men with his sang-froid as they awaited the charge.

At 3:00 p.m. the artillery fire began to slacken, and the three Confederate divisions—about 12,500 men in all—started forward from their staging area on Seminary Ridge. Pettigrew's North Carolinians and Pickett's Virginians were in the lead; Trimble's division would follow in support of Pettigrew's men on the left wing of the advance. Pickett's division was formed in two lines: the brigades of Generals Richard B. Garnett and James L. Kemper in the first wave, that of General Lewis A. Armistead in the second.

Deployed in lines of battle, the Confederates marched with parade-ground order over the mile-wide expanse that separated them from Hancock's defenders. The Federal artillery tore great gaps in the Rebel lines, but the survivors closed up and pressed on. As the first brigades clambered over the rail fences that lined the Emmitsburg road, enemy musketry began to scythe through their ranks, and shotgunlike blasts of canister mowed down scores of onrushing soldiers.

Now their formations broke up into desperate clusters of men who sprinted

"It is all over now. Many of us are prisoners, many are dead, many wounded, bleeding and dying. Your soldier lives and mourns and but for you, my darling, he would rather be back there with his dead, to sleep for all time in an unknown grave."

MAJOR GENERAL GEORGE PICKETT

Above: The moment when Federal forces (left) repulsed Pickett's Charge is depicted in this epic painting, which centers on a heroic private of the 72d Pennsylvania, who stands coatless, wielding his musket as a club; an impassive General Meade observes the action from his horse at far left.

Above right: As he awaited the order to advance, the flamboyant Major General George Pickett was uncharacteristically subdued. "My brave Virginians are to attack in front," he scrawled in a hasty note to his fiancée. "Oh, may God in mercy help me as He never helped before!"

toward the low stone wall and copse of trees that marked their objective. General Kemper was severely wounded, Pettigrew was unhorsed and shot in the hand, and Garnett disappeared amid the carnage.

With the leading brigades torn and broken, Armistead led his men toward a projecting angle of the stone wall, jabbing his hat on the tip of his sword and holding it aloft as a beacon on which to guide. Armistead shoved his way through the jostling crowd, shouting, "Come on boys! Give them the cold steel! Who will follow me?" and the screaming mob of gray-clad troops surged forward to the wall.

With some 200 followers Armistead crossed the wall and leaped among the carnage-strewn wreckage of Lieutenant Alonzo H. Cushing's battery. Cushing had fallen with a third and fatal wound, and Sergeant Frederick Fuger loosed a last deadly salvo of canister before the surviving gunners bolted for the rear. Brigadier General Alexander S. Webb's Philadelphia brigade wavered and began to break, and for a few moments it seemed that the Federal center would indeed be split asunder.

Spurring his horse down the Second Corps line, Hancock hurled reserves toward the looming gap and urged the troops on his left flank—Brigadier General George J. Stannard's Vermont brigade—to swing out toward the Emmitsburg road and enfilade the Rebel lines. A bullet slammed into Hancock's upper right thigh, but despite the serious wound, the general refused to be borne from the field until he saw the Confederate assault recoiling in defeat.

As Federal reinforcements charged into the melee at the Angle, Hancock's prewar comrade Lewis Armistead fell mortally wounded beside one of Cushing's abandoned guns. With their leader down, the Confederates became woefully disorganized. Soon every Rebel who crossed the wall was killed or captured. The attack that would live in history as Pickett's Charge had failed utterly.

As the survivors of the failed assault stumbled back across the fields to Seminary Ridge, Robert E. Lee rode among them muttering, "It is all my fault . . . It is all my fault." Confederate officers succeeded in re-forming their shattered units, but Lee's soldiers could do no more. The last great Confederate invasion of the North had spent its force, and nothing remained but to retire back across the Potomac River into Virginia. At a cost of more than 50,000 casualties on both sides, Lee's cause had reached its highest tide, and the ebbing of Confederate hopes had begun.

AFTERMATH IN BLOOD

As a lowering sky heralded the approach of rain, the exhausted armies confronted each other across the carnage-strewn field of Gettysburg. It was the Fourth of July, but few soldiers were in a mood for celebration. While the Army of the Potomac had obstinately held its ground against repeated Confederate onslaughts, Meade's forces had sustained some 23,000 casualties, and many Yankees feared that another Rebel assault was inevitable.

In fact Lee's Army of Northern Virginia was in no condition to renew the conflict. The Southern forces had lost in excess of 20,000 men—some place the

"The sights and sounds that assailed us were simply indescribable, corpses swollen to twice their original size, some of them actually burst asunder with the pressure of foul gases and vapors."

figure as high as 28,000—and with nearly 40 percent of his command out of action, Lee had little choice but to abandon his invasion of the North and withdraw across the Potomac into Virginia.

By late afternoon the rain was falling, and Lee began the delicate task of extricating his troops from their positions north and west of the Federal defenses. The slowest-moving element of his force started first—a 17-mile-long wagon train carrying supplies and ambulances filled with groaning wounded. Brigadier General John D. Imboden's cavalry was detailed to escort the wagons toward the Potomac. Lee instructed General Jubal Early to keep his division in place until July 5, when he would bring up the rear of the retreating army.

As the dispirited Confederate soldiers donned their packs and blanket rolls and started southward, they passed through horrific scenes of slaughter. "The sights and sounds that assailed us were simply indescribable," recalled Virginia artillery lieutenant Robert Stiles, "corpses swollen to twice their original size, some of them actually burst asunder with the pressure of foul gases and vapors."

When Federal skirmishers moved tentatively forward to scout the vacated enemy positions, they too passed over the battlefield's human wreckage, gagging as they began to bury the decomposing dead. Sergeant Thomas Meyer of the 148th Pennsylvania noted that the stench "would come up in waves and when at its worst the breath would stop in the throat; the lungs could not take it in, and a sense of suffocation would be experienced. We would cover our faces with our hands and turn the back toward the breeze and retch and gasp for breath."

With the realization of Union victory, the handful of reporters accompanying Meade's army scrambled to spread the news to the Northern public. On July 4 correspondent Samuel Wilkeson, who had arrived at Gettysburg midway in the battle, filed a detailed account for the *New York Times* that credited the stalwart Federals with "breaking the pride and power of the rebel invasion." But Wilkeson's elation evaporated when he learned that his 19-year-old son, Bayard, had been fatally wounded on the first day of the engagement.

Bodies swollen by the hot July sun, Federal dead of the III Corps lie in a trampled field near the Peach Orchard. Many of the bodies lack shoes, which were scavenged by Confederate soldiers who had occupied the ground on July 2.

THE TERRIBLE PRICE THAT WAS PAID

The men shown on these pages were among the 50,000 casualties at Gettysburg—30 percent of all those engaged—making it the bloodiest single battle fought on American soil. Some, like Colonel Paul Revere, were scions of prominent families. Another man, Private Wesley Culp, was remarkable for the irony of his fate: Culp was killed on his father's farm, fighting for the Confederacy. Many soldiers exhibited a grim fatalism, realizing that they were waging a crucial campaign. Lieutenant Colonel Charles Mudge, ordered to launch a suicidal attack, said simply, "It is murder, but it is the order." He died leading the charge.

MAJOR BENJAMIN W. LEIGH
1st Virginia Battalion, C.S.A.
Killed

CAPTAIN WILLIAM H. MURRAY
1st Maryland Battalion, C.S.A.
Killed

COLONEL GEORGE L. WILLARD
125th New York, U.S.A.
Killed

PRIVATE JAMES B. LOUGHBRIDGE
Parker's Virginia Battery, C.S.A.
Killed

LIEUT. COL. CHARLES MUDGE
2d Massachusetts, U.S.A.
Killed

CAPTAIN HERBERT C. MASON
20th Massachusetts, U.S.A.
Wounded

PRIVATES H. J. AND L. J. WALKER
13th North Carolina, C.S.A.
Wounded

LIEUTENANT J. KENT EWING
4th Virginia, C.S.A.
Mortally wounded

PRIVATE SAMUEL ROYER
149th Pennsylvania, U.S.A.
Wounded

COLONEL PAUL J. REVERE
20th Massachusetts, U.S.A.
Mortally wounded

GETTYSBURG CASUALTIES

FEDERAL		CONFEDERATE	
Killed	*3,070*	*Killed*	*2,592*
Wounded	*14,497*	*Wounded*	*12,706*
Captured and missing	*5,434*	*Captured and missing*	*5,150*
Total	*23,001*	*Total (estimated)*	*20,448*

MAJOR EDMUND RICE
19th Massachusetts, U.S.A.
Wounded

SERGEANT ROLAND HUDSON
59th Georgia, C.S.A.
Killed

PRIVATE FREDERICK E. WRIGHT
14th Brooklyn, U.S.A.
Killed

LIEUTENANT DANIEL BANTA
66th New York, U.S.A.
Wounded

SERGEANT A. H. COMPTON
8th Virginia, C.S.A.
Wounded and captured

PRIVATE WESLEY CULP
2d Virginia, C.S.A.
Killed

CAPTAIN LUTHER MARTIN
11th New Jersey, U.S.A.
Killed

SERGEANT FRANCIS STRICKLAND
154th New York, U.S.A.
Wounded

PRIVATE JOHN HAYDEN
1st Maryland Battalion, C.S.A.
Killed

CORPORAL NELSON GILBERT
149th New York, U.S.A.
Wounded

Three Confederate captives stand beside a rail and timber breastwork on Seminary Ridge as they await transport to a prison camp. They were among the 5,150 captured soldiers taken prisoner by Meade's army; another 6,802 wounded fell into Federal hands.

Under the watchful eye of Federal guards, a long line of Confederate prisoners—soldiers of General Longstreet's corps taken after their grand assault—begin their long march to northern prison camps on the late afternoon of July 3. More than 792 unwounded Confederate prisoners were captured from the divisions of Generals Pickett, Pettigrew, and Trimble.

"My pen is heavy," Wilkeson wrote. "O, you dead, who at Gettysburg have baptized with your blood the second birth of Freedom in America, how you are to be envied! I rise from a grave whose wet clay I have passionately kissed, and I look up and see Christ spanning the battle-field with his feet, and reaching fraternal and loving up to heaven. His right hand opens the gates of Paradise,—with his left he sweetly beckons to these mutilated, bloody, swollen forms to ascend."

Once it became clear that the fighting was over, Gettysburg's civilians began to emerge from cellars and hiding places to survey the damage that had been inflicted upon their community. Many townsfolk pitched in to help bury the dead, while those caught looting personal belongings from the fallen or making off with saddles and weapons were forced to do the grisly work at gunpoint. Mrs. Elizabeth M. Thorn, the wife of Evergreen Cemetery's superintendent, helped to bury 105 soldiers, despite the fact that she was in her sixth month of pregnancy. By the time she had finished, her clothing was saturated with blood.

Besides the corpses of more than 5,000 men and 3,000 horses and mules, the landscape was littered with the detritus of battle. "Trees were scarred and shattered," wrote Pennsylvania college professor Michael Jacobs, "thousands of minie balls, of solid shot and shells, lay scattered over the ground, and cast-off coats, knapsacks, blankets, cartouch-boxes, canteens, scabbards, and other accoutrements in vast numbers, were everywhere to be met with."

Virtually every house and barn in Gettysburg had been turned into an improvised hospital, where haggard surgeons struggled to save the mangled wounded. Carpets and floors were awash in gore, walls were spattered with blood, and piles of amputated limbs were heaped outside the open windows. Because of the sheer number of wounded, many sufferers had to wait days before receiving attention. A worker for the U.S. Sanitary Commission, a private relief organization, found Gettysburg's courthouse overflowing with casualties, "lying on the bare floor, covered with blood, and dirt, and vermin, entirely naked having perhaps only a newspaper to protect their festering wounds from the flies!"

Shaken by the carnage, and knowing that the Army of the Potomac had been strained nearly to the breaking point by forced marches and unprecedented casualties, Meade was slow to take up the pursuit of Lee's retreating columns. "Push forward," Army Chief of Staff Henry W. Halleck wired from Washington, "and fight Lee before he can cross the Potomac." But it was July 5 before the first of Meade's forces—Sedgwick's relatively unbloodied Sixth Corps—got under way, and two days later before the other corps began to follow in Lee's wake.

Riding south into Maryland, the Union cavalry clashed repeatedly with Jeb Stuart's Confederate horsemen. Although days of downpours had turned roads into quagmires and slowed the Federal infantry to a tortuous crawl, the rain had also swelled the Potomac to such an extent that Lee's army was delayed on the Maryland side of the river. While engineers struggled to span the torrent with pontoons, the Confederate soldiers erected a line of massive earthworks covering the approaches to the bridgeheads.

By July 12 General Meade's army was in position facing the Rebel lines. But the sight of heavily entrenched opponents gave Meade pause and filled his soldiers with foreboding. The Army of the Potomac had learned what it was like to storm fortified positions at the Battle of Fredericksburg, and no one was eager for a repetition of that one-sided slaughter. When Meade called a council of war, most of his corps commanders advised against an attack, and the general decided to wait. Meanwhile, Lee was finally able to start his troops across the precarious pontoon bridges, and although 1,500 men of General Heth's division were cut off and captured above the crossing at Falling Waters, by July 14 the Army of Northern Virginia was once again on Southern soil.

No men in Lee's army felt the failure of their campaign more keenly than the Marylanders, who had all too briefly cherished the hope that the invasion of the North would forever free their native state from Federal occupation. Yet, as Major W. W. Goldsborough of the Confederacy noted, the spirit of the Southern soldiers was far from broken. "And still these men were cheerful to a degree that could hardly have been expected under the trying circumstances," Goldsborough wrote, "and they felt the loss of comrades left behind torn and bleeding on that bloody

The only clue to a dead Union soldier's identity, this ambrotype found on his body ignited a campaign to determine who he was. Thousands of copies were circulated, and in November a woman whose soldier-husband was missing recognized it as one she had sent him. He was Sergeant Amos Humiston of the 154th New York.

At the dedication of the Gettysburg National Cemetery on November 19, 1863, President Lincoln—bareheaded and to the right of center—delivered his unforgettable message.

field at Gettysburg more than they did their own sufferings."

The high tide of the Confederacy had crested at Gettysburg, but the escape of Lee's army ensured that the terrible war would continue until a Federal commander brought that redoubtable force to bay. The Battle of Gettysburg did not prove decisive, but the experiences of those terrible three days, seared into the soul of every survivor, bear witness to the self-sacrifice of men who cherished idealistic beliefs above life itself.

Fifty years after the battle, with the country reunited and the torn landscape healed, Joshua Lawrence Chamberlain traveled to Gettysburg to revisit the scene of his epic fight as commander of the 20th Maine on Little Round Top. Just months before his death, Chamberlain wrote of the enduring message of that hallowed terrain:

"I went—it is not long ago—to stand again upon that crest whose one day's crown of fire has passed into the blazoned coronet of fame. . . . I sat there alone, on the storied crest, till the sun went down as it did before over the misty hills, and the darkness crept up the slopes, till from all earthly sight I was buried as with those before. But oh, what radiant companionship rose around, what steadfast ranks of power, what bearing of heroic souls. Oh, the glory that beamed through those nights and days. . . . The proud young valor that rose above the mortal, and then at last was mortal after all."

"Four score and seven years ago our fathers brought forth on this continent, a new nation, conceived in Liberty, and dedicated to the proposition that all men are created equal…."

FIELD SURGERY

I was wounded Saturday p.m.," Private Richard Ackerman of the 5th New York wrote his parents after taking a ball through the thigh in the Second Battle of Manassas. "I laid on the battlefield for 48 hours and then rode a government wagon for 48 hours more. Last night at one o'clock my wound was dressed for the first time."

Ackerman's ordeal was not unusual. When the Civil War began, neither side had an efficient system for dealing with casualties. The first ambulances were bouncy two-wheeled carts known as "hop, step and jumps." Although these gradually gave way to more stable four-wheeled wagons, the jolting ride over rutted roads could mightily compound the agony of the wounded. Rail and water transport to hospitals in the rear was usually comfortable by comparison.

In spite of the enormous effort made to improve hospital facilities during the war, many men who survived the trip to the rear later succumbed to their wounds, dying of blood poisoning or other infections. Private Ackerman wrote his parents, "Don't think it hard I had to be wounded, for I consider it a merciful dispensation of Providence I wasn't killed." But in late December 1862, four months after he wrote those words, Ackerman died of complications at a Federal hospital in Alexandria, Virginia.

Field surgeons carried their medicine bottles and jars in leather kits like the one pictured below. Bandages, scissors, thread and other equipment were stored in the top of the kit, beneath the divider listing the contents.

An ambulance convoy pauses in its journey to the large Federal hospital at City Point, Virginia, during the siege of Petersburg in 1864. Four-wheeled ambulances like these had folding bunks for wounded men. At times the vehicles were so grossly overcrowded that the patients were in danger of being smothered en route.

A surgeon could remove a mangled limb in 15 minutes, using specially designed surgical tools such as these. Unfortunately, the importance of sterilization was not widely known. By not washing their hands or instruments before proceeding to finger probe bullet holes or operate on the next patient, surgeons unwittingly spread infection. In fact, infection was expected, and festering—laudable pus, as it was called—was considered part of the healing process.

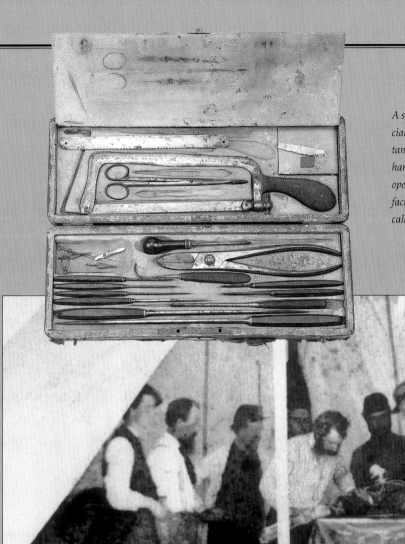

Federal surgeon John. J. Craven operates on a soldier with an injured leg during the siege of Charleston in 1863. The orderly at the rear of the tent is holding a chloroform-soaked rag over the patient's face to anesthetize him during the procedure. Most battlefield surgeries were amputations, as experience had taught that when bones were splintered "amputation was the only means of saving a life."

Vehicles transporting the wounded to field hospitals were identified by yellow flags marked with a red letter "H."

CARING FOR THE WOUNDED

The wounded from early battles were housed in converted schools, hotels, factories, railroad stations and private homes. In a remarkably short period of time, both North and South had constructed a network of hospitals of astonishing size and commendable efficiency.

Nursing duties were at first assigned to convalescent or noncombatant soldiers, as it was generally considered improper for women to work in hospitals. Necessity soon made this idea obsolete and women not only volunteered, but were actively recruited. They worked selflessly. "Let no one pity or praise us," wrote one nurse, "no one can tell how sweet it is to be the drop of comfort to so much agony."

Dorothea Dix was appointed Superintendent of Female Nurses of the Federal army in 1861. A rigid administrator, she was constantly at odds with doctors as well as her subordinates. She rejected thousands of nursing applicants for being too attractive, too young or "over-anxious."

Louisa May Alcott, author of Little Women, served as a nurse at Union Hotel Hospital in Washington, D.C. The hospital conditions appalled her: "A more perfect pestilence box than this I never saw—cold, damp, dirty, full of vile odors from wounds, kitchens, and stables."

Patients lie in bed under canopies of mosquito netting in a newly built wing of Harewood Hospital in Washington, D.C. The war spurred a massive construction program to cope with the large number of wounded. Such wards were usually one or two stories high and capable of accommodating 40 to 60 patients.

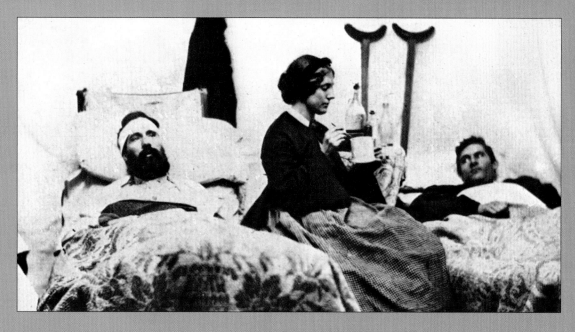

A nurse tends to two recuperating Federals at a hospital in Nashville, Tennessee. Hundreds of female nurses, most of them recruited by private relief agencies, served in the permanent hospitals of both sides. Though many lacked formal training, they helped bathe, bandage and comfort the wounded.

Clara Barton was one of the first female nurses to seek out the Federal wounded on the battlefields, appearing with a wagonload of bandages, medicines and food. A surgeon, who saw her at the front, stirring a huge kettle of soup, called her an "independent Sanitary commission of one."

Walt Whitman worked in hospitals around Washington, D.C., dressing wounds and dispensing consolation and cheer. On September 8, 1863, he wrote his mother, "I believe no men ever loved each other as I and some of these poor wounded sick and dying men love each other."

Phoebe Yates Levy Pember, a wealthy, middle-aged widow, was an administrator in the Chimborazo Hospital in Richmond, Virginia. This sprawling complex was the Confederacy's chief medical hospital. Its network of single-story pavilions served 76,000 patients during the course of the war.

FIGHT AGAINST DISEASE

The Union enjoyed an enormous advantage over the agrarian Confederacy in providing drugs for its armies. All the major pharmaceutical companies were located in the Union, and in 1863 Surgeon General William A. Hammond set up two large government-operated factories at Astoria, New York, and Philadelphia, Pennsylvania, to augment drug production. The Philadelphia Laboratory turned out 48 types of medicine, including extracts, tinctures, powders, pills and salts. In addition, a sewing department made sheets, pillowcases, towels, curtains and hospital clothes. At peak strength, the laboratory employed 350 female workers, along with skilled chemists.

The South, however, had only a few government-run laboratories and lacked the chemicals and raw materials to adequately supply these facilities. Surgeon General Samuel P. Moore urged citizens to raise medicinal plants, such as flax, castor-oil beans and mustard, and even dispensed domestic poppy seeds in hopes that a gardener might derive an opium substitute. Doctors were given a list of 410 native wild plants with therapeutic value and urged to search for them in fields and forests. The drug substitutes were generally better than nothing, although many, such as bugleweed when used for digitalis, proved worthless. A particular favorite with the soldiers was a quinine substitute dubbed "old indigenous." It consisted of dried dogwood, poplar and willow bark and a healthy dose of whiskey.

Quinine tablets were packaged in tinned iron containers. The drug was widely used in the treatment of malaria during the war. It was part of the standard medical kit carried by Federal army surgeons. To supplement the output of private pharmaceutical companies, the U.S. government set up manufacturing plants in Philadelphia and New York; altogether, some two million ounces of quinine were produced in the North.

A single operator at a medicine factory could produce between 5,000 and 7,000 pills a day using a pill-rolling machine such as this one.

Confederate surgeon general Samuel P. Moore (above, left) and his Federal counterpart, William A. Hammond, encouraged their governments to establish laboratories to test and manufacture drugs. Hammond's autocratic style eventually brought him into conflict with Secretary of War Edwin Stanton, who dismissed him in 1864.

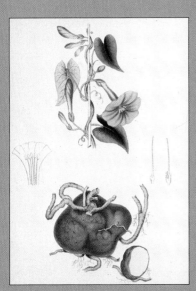

Denied raw materials and imported drugs by the Federal blockade, Confederate doctors were often forced to compound their own medicines from local plants, using a simple mortar and pestle.

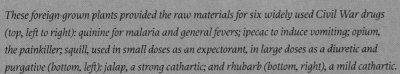

These foreign-grown plants provided the raw materials for six widely used Civil War drugs (top, left to right): quinine for malaria and general fevers; ipecac to induce vomiting; opium, the painkiller; squill, used in small doses as an expectorant, in large doses as a diuretic and purgative (bottom, left): jalap, a strong cathartic; and rhubarb (bottom, right), a mild cathartic.

Chickamauga
The River of Blood

THE TULLAHOMA CAMPAIGN—The objective of Major General William S. Rosecrans' Army of the Cumberland in the spring of 1863 was vitally important for the Union cause: to thrust southward through eastern Tennessee and capture the town of Chattanooga, junction point for four vital railroad lines that carried

a large percentage of the Confederacy's arms, munitions, food, and other supplies. If Rosecrans and his troops could take the town, they would put a damaging crimp in the Southern war effort.

Chattanooga, a town of 3,500 people on a bend in the Tennessee River, was also a prime gateway into northern Georgia and the routes leading to Atlanta and the heart of the middle South. With Chattanooga in Union hands, President Abraham Lincoln wrote, "I think the rebellion must dwindle and die."

The campaign to fulfill the president's prophecy would unfold after long delays and proceed with a series of Union successes. Then its meandering path would lead to the rough hill country south of Chattanooga. There the Union and Rebel armies would confront each other in one of the crucial battles of the Civil War, a confused, desperate, and violent fight near a creek known to the area's Cherokee people as Chickamauga, or River of Blood.

The campaign got under way sluggishly, however. By mid-January 1863 Rosecrans and his army were camped in and around Murfreesboro, Tennessee, 85 miles from Chattanooga. They had already defeated, if just barely, the Confederate force facing them, General Braxton Bragg's Army of Tennessee, in a three-day battle along the banks of the nearby Stones River at the turn of the year, December 31 to January 2. Now Bragg's badly wounded army was only about 30 miles to the southeast, camped behind the Duck River. Too weak to attack—he had lost one-third of his force at Stones River—Bragg was reorganizing and mustering reinforcements as best he could to meet Rosecrans' inevitable move south.

But Rosecrans, despite having the larger and better-equipped army, stubbornly refused to move. A large, jovial West Pointer, Old Rosy—as he was affectionately known to his troops, partly for his heroically large red nose—had proved a brave and decisive leader in battle. At Stones River he had ridden furiously through the worst of the enemy cannon fire from one front-line unit to another, a battered black hat jammed on his head, a cigar stub

Braxton Bragg's notoriously short temper was the result, some believed, of the general's chronic ill health and penchant for overwork. "He was frequently in the saddle," one noted, "when the more appropriate place for him would have been in bed."

The model of a gallant leader, Major General William S. Rosecrans gallops through shot and shell on a song sheet that was published in his native Ohio at the height of his fame in 1863. Perhaps stung by past criticisms from Washington of his perceived lack of boldness, Rosecrans suddenly grew overly bold. Ignoring the advice of General George H. Thomas, his most trusted subordinate, to consolidate the army at Chattanooga, he sent his entire force rushing after Bragg. It would prove a fatal error.

clamped in his teeth, advising and encouraging his hard-pressed troops.

Between battles, however, Rosecrans had already proved maddeningly deliberate, driving his superiors in Washington to distraction with his refusal to take action until he was entirely ready. It had happened in the fall of 1862, before Stones River, and now it was happening again as the muddy, frigid Tennessee winter gave way to spring.

The delays prompted a barrage of telegrams urging him to move from the army's chief back in Washington, Major General Henry W. Halleck. Halleck wanted Chattanooga taken, and soon. He was also concerned about another campaign currently being waged 400 miles to the west. There, General Ulysses S. Grant was laying siege to Vicksburg, the Confederate bastion guarding the Mississippi River. Halleck feared that unless Rosecrans attacked toward Chattanooga, Bragg might detach part of his army and send it westward to hammer at Grant, thwarting the Union campaign for Vicksburg.

Rosecrans fired back his own barrage of telegrams, belittling the threat to Grant and blandly pointing out that in military matters, as in others, haste makes waste. He wanted to be perfectly ready before he moved so that, as he put it, he would not have to "stop and tinker" along the way. He would be campaigning through "country full of natural passes and fortifications" that demanded "superior forces to advance with any success," he informed Washington. He needed more of everything: troops, artillery, cavalry. Besides, he complained, his communications were threatened, rations were low, and his men were worn out.

Major General Henry W. Halleck, an armchair general dubbed Old Brains in the prewar army, was widely disliked by the generals in the field, who doubted his military acumen. He dispatched telegrams in an effort to spur the methodical Rosecrans to move faster against Bragg.

"I deem it my duty to repeat to you the great dissatisfaction that is felt here at your inactivity."

In fact, Rosecrans' men were worn out from waiting. To occupy their time, the troops built snug log huts for themselves and even planted rows of trees along the company streets. But boredom was endemic. There was little to do, complained an Indiana artillery officer, except for "talking, eating, sleeping and fighting flies." Another Federal soldier noted that the men "were simply rusting away."

Bragg's Confederates were not much better off. Perpetually short of rations, they spent much of their time shooting rabbits and otherwise scrounging about the countryside for food. They were also in a state of chronic discontent; they despised their commanding general—a dour, crabbed, sickly looking martinet—for the harsh discipline he imposed.

The Southern officers held Bragg in open contempt for retreating when victory might have been won at Stones River—and boldly told him so in a series of

extraordinary letters advising him to step down. They even petitioned Richmond to have him removed. But Confederate president Jefferson Davis could find no other general able to take Bragg's place, so he stayed on by default.

While the infantrymen moldered in their camps, the cavalry on both sides got strenuous workouts. Bragg had 15,000 horsemen in his 47,000-man army, and they were led by some of the South's most daring cavalry commanders, including Nathan Bedford Forrest, Joseph Wheeler, and John Hunt Morgan. The Rebel raiders shot up transports on the Cumberland River and demolished virtually every bridge and trestle on the railroads—the Louisville & Nashville and the Louisville & Chattanooga—that Rosecrans depended on for supplies. They also savaged depots, freight cars, and locomotives.

Rosecrans tried to fight back, mostly in vain, with his 9,000 overmatched horsemen. To increase his numbers, he converted some foot soldiers into mounted troops. This produced one of the hardest-fighting units of the western war, a brigade of 1,500 men made up of two infantry regiments from Illinois and two from Indiana. The leader of this brigade was a brave and exceedingly determined Hoosier, Colonel John T. Wilder, successful proprietor of an iron foundry before the war.

It was no easy task for Wilder to organize the new brigade. The troops had to scrounge their own horses—and then learn how to ride them. But, initially at his own expense, Wilder provided excellent weapons: Spencer seven-shot repeating rifles that gave the new riders firepower far beyond their numbers. Wilder and his

A crew of fugitive slaves recruited as laborers by General Rosecrans' army repairs a stretch of track near Murfreesboro, Tennessee, in 1863. Confederate raiders frequently tore up Rosecrans' vital supply line to Louisville. On one foray, John Hunt Morgan's horsemen destroyed bridges and trestles on more than 20 miles of the Louisville & Nashville main line.

made-over infantry would be in the thickest of the fighting in the months to come.

By June 1863 Rosecrans' cavalry was holding its own, protecting his supply lines, and reinforcements had enlarged his army to almost 80,000 men. Still the methodical general showed few signs of moving. The continued procrastination produced a bizarre exchange of messages. "I deem it my duty," telegraphed General Halleck from Washington on June 11, "to repeat to you the great dissatisfaction that is felt here at your inactivity."

When Rosecrans ignored him, Halleck wired again on June 16: "Is it your intention to make an immediate move forward? A definite answer, yes or no, is required." Rosecrans answered this message with perhaps unconscious humor. "If immediate means to-night or to-morrow, no," he wired. "If it means as soon as all things are ready, say five days, yes."

Rosecrans was not quite as good as his word, but eight days later, on June 24, he suddenly got his army in motion. And once started, he moved with speed, skill, and energy, dodging and feinting his way south in a masterly series of maneuvers—the so-called Tullahoma campaign, named after the town where General Bragg had his headquarters.

Bragg, studying maps of the area, had positioned his forces as best he could to meet the expected assault. A long ridge, an extension of the Cumberland Plateau, rose between Murfreesboro and the Confederate positions on the Duck River.

Cutting through the barrier were four passes: Guy's Gap on the west, then Bellbuckle Gap, Liberty Gap, and Hoover's Gap. Hoover's Gap ran through especially rough country, but the other three appeared to be more easily negotiable by marching troops, and they were aimed right at Bragg's defensive line.

To cover the approaches, Bragg placed the larger of his two corps, commanded by Lieutenant General Leonidas Polk, on the left near Shelbyville, facing Guy's and Bellbuckle Gaps. On the right he stationed Lieutenant General William J. Hardee's corps to protect against an assault by way of Hoover's and Liberty Gaps. He also dispatched most of Nathan Bedford Forrest's cavalrymen to the west to cover a roundabout route that avoided the ridge, a path that Bragg thought Rosecrans might favor.

But Rosecrans had been studying hard, too, and he had come up with what he hoped was a way to deceive the enemy. He had no intention of taking the easy western route or of sending his main force down Bellbuckle and Liberty Gaps for a frontal assault. Instead he would confuse Bragg, feinting one way and then attacking another.

By way of a main feint, Rosecrans sent Major General David Stanley's Cavalry Corps and Major General Gordon Granger's Reserve Corps through Bellbuckle Gap toward Shelbyville and Polk's corps on the Confederate left—exactly where Bragg expected an attack. At the same time Rosecrans sent a column, initially a single division, toward the town of McMinnville, well to the east beyond Hoover's Gap. Bragg soon learned of this movement but, assuming it was a diversion, ignored it.

This was precisely what Rosecrans wanted. Following right behind the lone division way to the east marched Major General Thomas L. Crittenden's XXI Corps, which was to punch through a Confederate cavalry screen on the Cumberland Plateau and then head south for Manchester, a dozen miles from Tullahoma, in Hardee's right rear. At the same time Major General George H. Thomas' XIV Corps plunged into Hoover's Gap. To complete the deception, parts of Major General Alexander McCook's XX Corps headed through Liberty Gap to threaten Hardee's troops around Wartrace and fix them in place. If the deception worked, Rosecrans' left wing would get behind Bragg's army and cut it off from Chattanooga.

Despite deluges of rain that turned the roads to ankle-deep mud, the Federal columns moved with amazing speed. By the afternoon of the 24th, McCook's advance brigade, led by Brigadier General August Willich, had gotten much of the way through Liberty Gap—and ran head-on into a Confederate division commanded by Major General Patrick R. Cleburne.

Cleburne's troops stopped the Federals cold. But Willich's men, abandoning their frontal attack, scrambled up the hills on either side of the pass and outflanked the defenders. Riddled by enfilading fire, Cleburne's men were forced to fall back and abandon the gap.

At Hoover's Gap, General Thomas' corps was spearheaded by the 1,500 infantry-turned-horsemen of John Wilder's brigade. Wilder had been ordered to trot into the gap and then wait for infantry units to come up in support. Instead, the rookie troopers galloped full tilt through the pass, chasing the astonished enemy pickets

A Federal foraging party plunders livestock from a Tennessee farm despite angry protests in a painting by newspaper artist William D. T. Travis. Most of the foraging was done by Colonel John T. Wilder's mounted brigade, which shared its booty. Not everyone opposed the Federals. Many mountain families in eastern Tennessee welcomed them. One of Wilder's men recalled how the poor mountaineers "vied with each other in bestowing upon the boys their kindness—sweet potatoes, all kinds of vegetables, ducks, chickens, pies, cakes, honey, and applejack brandy."

Major General William S. Rosecrans (hatless, left) disciplines a subordinate (hatless, right). Painted by Adolph Metzner, topographical engineer for Willich's brigade, the scene depicts one of the administrative chores the energetic general performed daily during the army's long encampment at Murfreesboro. A journalist described Rosecrans as of "middle stature, with a broad upper body and rather short, bow legs (owing to which peculiarities he presented a far better appearance when mounted than on foot)."

MAKING WAR
IN ROUGH COUNTRY

The soldiers of General William Rosecrans' Federal army were awed by the natural beauty of the countryside as they advanced toward the strategic city of Chattanooga in September 1863. "Far beyond mortal vision extended one vast panorama of mountains, forests and rivers," one veteran recalled. "This is a beautiful valley," another wrote home, "with mountain tops on every side reaching up into the clouds."

The great hills were the Cumberlands, a southwestern spur of the Appalachians extending through Tennessee into northern Georgia. Yet for all its majesty, this isolated countryside was a hellish place to fight—the most formidable terrain in which major Federal and Confederate forces would clash during the entire Civil War.

The approaching Federals were hampered by burned-out bridges and a scarcity of roads. The shimmering, winding Tennessee River was shallow and turbulent— ill suited for supply vessels and yet a hindrance to maneuvering troops.

The knife-edge ridges prevented Rosecrans from seeing the army of his adversary, General Braxton Bragg, and equally masked the Federal host from Bragg's view. Most of the forested valleys and coves were narrow and cramped, natural traps that made ambush a constant threat. A sanguine Confederate predicted that Rosecrans "would dash himself to pieces against the many and vast natural barriers that rise all around Chattanooga."

The view north from Lookout Mountain, one of the Cumberlands' highest ramparts at 2,126 feet, includes the horseshoe bend made by the Tennessee River as it meanders just west of Chattanooga. The mountain, said a Confederate, was all "gorges, boulders and jutting cliffs."

CORPORAL GEORGE S. WILSON

17th Indiana Infantry, Wilder's Brigade

Wilson and his comrades took advantage of the six-month hiatus that followed the Federal victory at Stones River in January 1863 to confiscate horses and mules from the countryside around Murfreesboro for use in Wilder's mounted infantry brigade—an action that infuriated local Tennesseans. His droll descriptions of the neophyte horsemen belie the fact that Wilder's Yankees soon evolved into one of the most daring units of the western war.

I n our eagerness for riding animals we paid no attention to age, color, size, sex, or previous condition of servitude. Blooded racers, awkward plow-horses, sway-backed plugs, brood mares, stallions, ponies, and mules of assorted dimensions and uncertain tricks, all went to make up the mount of a company; while our drummer-boy was happy in the possession of a little brown jackass, which he contentedly rode until the melancholy-looking creature came to an untimely end at the hands of an exasperated veteran, whose only pair of trousers had served for its midnight tiffin. Whenever we found an animal, hornless and with deck-room for a saddle, we took it; and if some fellow was not riding it before night, it was for the very good reason that the beast would be riding him. We were an infantry command, many of the members of which had never straddled a horse, and this last contingency was not of infrequent occurrence. But in time our mount improved. We got things straightened out and finally presented a tolerable appearance. In tactics and drill we were indifferent, but soon learned enough to use great caution in approaching a mule to go abroad, and never to entirely trust in his well-simulated intention of good behavior. Early in the season I got a lesson from a little specimen of the seemingly meek and lowly variety. He had a tired, resigned manner about him, a

Colonel John T. Wilder showed the same resourcefulness in arming his 1,500-man brigade that he did in running his iron foundry in civilian life before the war. When Washington was slow to buy new repeating rifles, he arranged for a personal loan from his hometown bankers.

sort of "If you want to lick me, you can, but I wish you wouldn't" expression, that altogether inspired me with confidence and recklessness. But you should have seen that mule and me the first time our opinions happened to differ on some point or other, which he deemed of importance.

In April, about the time we were all mounted, another fortunate circumstance resulted in our being armed with the Spencer magazine rifle, using metallic ammunition. At that time no other large body of troops was so well armed; in fact, I doubt if there was then . . . another entire brigade in all the West using metallic cartridges. Our services up to this period had been arduous, while we had had considerable experience under fire, so now, with our Spencer rifles, we felt ourselves to be wellnigh invincible, and anxiously awaited an opportunity to broaden our field of operations.

COPPER RIM-FIRE CARTRIDGES

Key to the operation of the Spencer rifle was a recently developed copper cartridge that combined primer, powder and bullet in one case. The rifle's hammer detonated mercury fulminate in the cartridge rim. This ignited the powder and discharged the round. Seven cartridges fitted into a tubelike magazine, which was inserted through the butt.

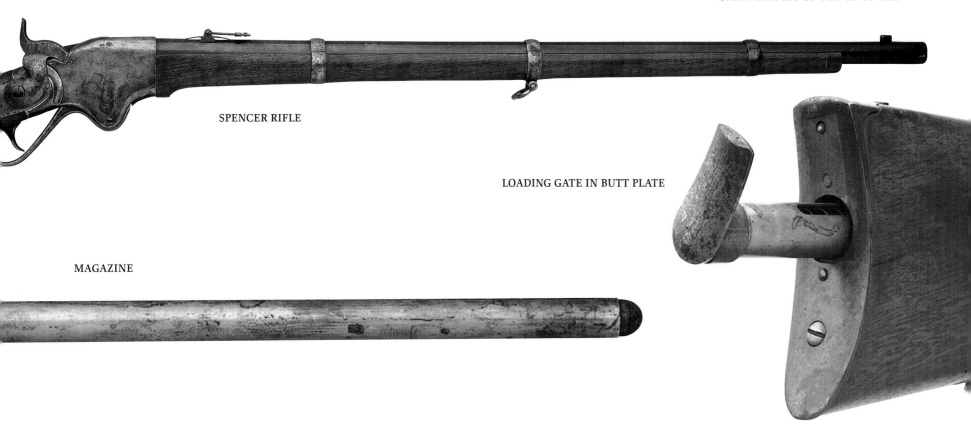

SPENCER RIFLE

LOADING GATE IN BUTT PLATE

MAGAZINE

before them and leaving the Federal infantry 10 miles to the rear.

Units from General Hardee's corps responded quickly. Brigadier General William Bate's brigade, along with Brigadier General Bushrod Johnson's troops and three batteries of artillery, all moved fast to meet the 72d Indiana and Wilder's other regiments at the southern end of the gap. Suddenly hit by shellfire, Wilder's troopers dismounted and formed a line of battle supported by the guns of Captain Eli Lilly's 18th Indiana Battery.

Hammered by Bate's and Johnson's brigades, Wilder's hard-pressed troopers soon copied Willich's men, taking cover on the rocky slopes overlooking the gap. There, despite murderous blasts from the enemy guns, the Federals held on, beating back the Confederate assaults with sheets of fire from their fast-shooting Spencer rifles. One of the brigade's officers, Major James A. Connolly, recalled that "each enemy shell screamed so close to us as to make it seem that the next would tear us to pieces." But when the Confederates made a charge, the Union troops were "on their feet in an instant and a terrible fire from the Spencers" quickly caused "the advancing regiment to reel and its colors to fall to the ground."

In late afternoon Wilder's division commander, Major General Joseph J. Reynolds, fearful that the exposed troopers would be wiped out, sent forward a message ordering them to retire. But Wilder refused to budge, insisting he and his men could hold out. About seven o'clock in the evening a battery of artillery clat-

"You have saved the lives of a thousand men by your gallant conduct today …"

tered up from the rear. This sign of help, Major Connolly recalled, "nerved the men to maintain the unequal conflict a little longer." Then 30 minutes later two brigades of Reynolds' infantry finally arrived, the men exhausted but hurrying as best they could. They were greeted, Connolly said, "by such lusty cheers as seemed to inspire them with new vigor."

As Wilder's men fell back to rest, Thomas himself appeared. A Virginia-born West Pointer who had remained faithful to the Union, "Pap" Thomas was normally quiet and undemonstrative, but now he grabbed Colonel Wilder's hand and announced, "You have saved the lives of a thousand men by your gallant conduct today," adding that "I didn't expect to get this gap for three days."

That night Bragg in his Tullahoma headquarters was still baffled by what Rosecrans was doing. Reports kept coming in of Federal cavalry and infantry heading for Shelbyville on the Confederate left. Strangely, no reports filtered through from the gaps on the Confederate right, despite all the fighting there.

Hoovers Gap

The main body of Major General George H. Thomas' XIV Corps hurries along the road through Hoover's Gap and up the nearby hills to reinforce the foothold secured several miles ahead by Wilder's mounted brigade on June 24, 1863. When the first regiment of footsore infantry reached Wilder about 7:00 that evening, they were greeted by lusty cheers, which according to one of Wilder's men, "seemed to inspire them with new vigor." The soldier-artist who depicted this scene, Horace Rawden of the 105th Ohio, was among those first reinforcements to arrive. The self-taught watercolorist apparently chose not to attempt to illustrate the rainy weather.

On the next day, the 25th, the fighting continued on the Rebel right. Generals Bate and Johnson smashed away again at Reynolds' division of Thomas' corps coming through Hoover's Gap, and the exceedingly combative Cleburne launched a furious all-out assault on Willich's brigade, still in the vanguard of the division of McCook's corps trying to hold the hills around Liberty Gap.

At last, on the 26th, it dawned on Bragg that the real danger was on his right. In midafternoon he ordered General Polk to shift his corps eastward and go to the aid of Hardee's hard-pressed troops.

But it was too late. That night, almost three days after the fighting began, a dismayed Bragg finally realized that his army was in mortal danger. Colonel Wilder's hard-fighting unit—now dubbed the Lightning Brigade for its headlong ride through Hoover's Gap—had broken through the Confederate line and, with the rest of General Thomas' corps following, was heading for Manchester to join up with Crittenden's corps already there, well beyond Hardee's right flank. There was

Private Nathaniel Delzell of the 17th Tennessee Infantry was captured by the Federals on July 3 near Tullahoma, only six miles from his home. Declaring himself a deserter, Delzell swore an oath of allegiance to the Union and was allowed to go free six days later.

nothing for Bragg to do except order Polk and Hardee to abandon their positions and fall back on Tullahoma itself as fast as their men could march.

Tullahoma provided few comforts for the bedraggled Rebel soldiers. The unfortunate little railroad town, soaked by incessant downpours and overrun by troops and horses and mule-drawn wagons, had become an ever-worsening quagmire. When one wet-to-the-skin member of Hardee's staff was asked the source of the town's name, he acidly said it came from two Greek words, tulla, meaning "mud," and homa, meaning "more mud."

Despite the rain, Wilder's Lightning Brigade reached Manchester on the morning of June 27, followed soon by other elements of Thomas' corps. At dawn on the 28th, Wilder's midwesterners splashed their way south once again, heading for the town of Decherd. Although soon chased away by a good-sized detachment of Confederate infantry, the Federals managed to tear up track and destroy trestles on two branch lines of the Nashville & Chattanooga Railroad, at least partially crippling Bragg's supply-and-communications line with Chattanooga.

By the 29th Bragg was deep in the throes of indecision. He had his army concentrated around Tullahoma, ready to fight, but there were few signs that Rosecrans' main force was bearing down on the town with intentions to attack. Instead, reports kept filtering in from the east, indicating the Federals might be trying to get in behind the Confederate army once again.

Bragg called a council of war that night, but he, Polk, and Hardee could come to no decision about what to do. By the next day, however, there were fresh reports: elements of three Union corps—Thomas', Crittenden's, and part of

McCook's—were on their way toward Hillsboro, farther in the Confederate rear. At the same time, Granger's Reserve Corps and Stanley's Union cavalry had reached the old Confederate line on the Duck River and were bearing down on Tullahoma from the northwest.

Clearly the Confederates were in trouble, and on the night of June 30 Bragg ordered his forces to abandon Tullahoma and fall back once more, this time behind the next natural defensive line of the Elk River. Polk's and Hardee's men had hardly begun to dig in there on July 1, however, before Bragg realized that the several Federal corps to the east could still easily turn his flank by simply continuing their swift march south. He had evaded one trap, but another one threatened.

Finally there was nothing for Bragg to do but make another humiliating retreat. On July 3 he ordered his bedraggled army to start marching to the southeast along the roads that led to crossing points on the Tennessee River and thence to Chattanooga. Riding south from Tullahoma with his troops, his thin face looking even more cadaverous than usual, Bragg fell into talk with one of his army's chaplains. "This is," he said in a sepulchral whisper, "a great disaster."

A far more cheerful Rosecrans reached Tullahoma on the same day, July 3. In an almost flawless nine-day campaign, executed despite appalling weather, he had swept Bragg and his force from much of middle Tennessee—and at the astonishingly modest cost of 84 dead and 476 wounded.

"You and your noble army now have the chance to give the finishing blow to the rebellion. Will you neglect the chance?"

Rosecrans' huge success came, however, at exactly the wrong moment for him to receive credit. July 4, 1863, was the day of all days for the Federal cause. Out west, Grant captured Vicksburg on the 4th, ending a long, anguishing siege. In Pennsylvania, also on the 4th, after three days of desperate fighting around Gettysburg, a Federal army stopped Robert E. Lee's second invasion of the North.

Amid the wild rejoicing over those huge victories, Rosecrans' capture of Tullahoma received little notice or praise from the press, the public, or the high command in Washington. So little impressed was Secretary of War Edwin M. Stanton, in fact, that on July 7, only four days after Rosecrans reached Tullahoma, he sent off a barbed telegram. "Lee's army overthrown; Grant victorious," the wire read. "You and your noble army now have the chance to give the finishing blow to the rebellion. Will you neglect the chance?"

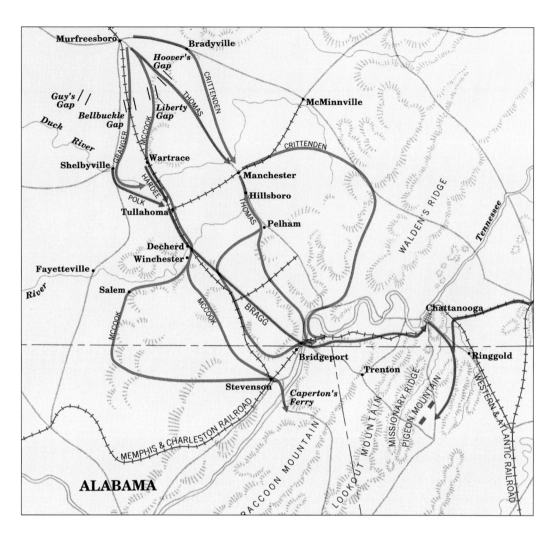

After the Union victory at Stones River in January 1863, Bragg's Confederates retired to positions around Tullahoma. In late June, Rosecrans launched a series of flanking moves that threatened Bragg's supply lines and forced him to retreat across the Tennessee River to Chattanooga. Rosecrans followed, and by early September most of his army was across the river below Chattanooga and moving east in three columns. Bragg evacuated the town, fell back to the south, and turned to fight.

Rosecrans immediately fired off a sarcastic reply. "You do not appear to observe the fact," it read, "that this noble army has driven the rebels from Middle Tennessee. I beg in behalf of this army that the War Department may not overlook so great an event because it is not written in letters of blood."

Rosecrans' troops, justifiably elated, settled down to rest, find some protection from the rain, and cook some hot rations. But knowing Chattanooga was next, they were ready to move when Old Rosy gave the word. Rosecrans himself, unabashed by Stanton's wire, was not a bit inclined to take up the march. Much reorganization and planning needed to be done before the next stage in his campaign, and he settled down comfortably, for six weeks this time, to attend to every detail.

MANEUVERING FOR BATTLE

General Rosecrans, settling into his new Tullahoma headquarters on July 3, had good reason to move with deliberation on Chattanooga. He would be advancing into rough country, he reminded General in Chief Halleck in Washington, and needed to stockpile supplies. Besides, Rosecrans worried that Braxton Bragg's Confederates might be reinforced with troops coming from the east or west or both—a fear that was, as it turned out, well founded.

Halleck fumed as usual and on August 4 sent Rosecrans another of his rockets. "Your forces," wired Halleck, "must move forward without further delay. You will daily report the movement of each of your corps until you cross the Tennessee

River." Shocked that Halleck would send such a message to a commanding general in the field, Rosecrans requested confirmation. Replied Halleck: "The orders are peremptory."

At last on August 16, after a six-week pause, Rosecrans got under way. Once started he again moved swiftly and succeeded, as at Tullahoma, in taking Bragg and his Confederates by surprise.

The most logical approach to Chattanooga was to move southeast across a rocky mass known as Walden's Ridge, then fall on the town from the north. But Rosecrans, deciding to stage another feint, sent only a modest force led by Brigadier General William B. Hazen swinging off over Walden's Ridge—three infantry brigades spear-headed by John Wilder's fast-riding horsemen.

Wilder's brigade moved swiftly, emerging from the hills across the Tennessee River from Chattanooga only five days later, on August 21. In minutes Eli Lilly had unlimbered his battery of guns and was lobbing shells into the town, causing huge consternation. General Hazen did not have the manpower to storm across the river but staged such a clever show of force that Bragg was fooled into thinking the whole Federal army was nearby and about to attack from the north or northeast.

With Bragg's attention fixed, General Rosecrans prepared his hammer blow, marching his main force—three corps of 50,000 infantry plus 9,000 cavalry—toward crossings on the Tennessee River more than 20 miles west of Chattanooga. The Federal troops crossed the river unseen by September 4, then prepared to make a sweeping left wheel, moving on Chattanooga and Bragg's army from the southwest.

"I beg in behalf of this army that the War Department may not overlook so great an event because it is not written in letters of blood."

The wheeling maneuver was exceedingly risky because it sent the Federal troops into rough, tangled terrain south of Chattanooga dominated by the 30-mile-long mass of Lookout Mountain. But Rosecrans counted on speed and surprise, and the expectation that Bragg, suddenly finding the entire enemy army on his flank, would be forced to evacuate Chattanooga and flee full speed into northern Georgia.

Bragg, in the dark for days, finally realized in early September that a powerful force had streamed across the river and threatened his left. At first he vacillated, shifting a few units. But then on September 7, with his vulnerable supply line in immediate danger of being cut, Bragg ordered his army to march south, abandoning the prize of Chattanooga without firing a shot.

The distinctive profile of Lookout Mountain looms over Chattanooga, a sleepy river town of frame buildings and 3,500 people in 1863. At far left is the vaulted roof of the Nashville & Chattanooga Railroad depot, built before the war with slave labor. Immediately to the right of the depot are the multiple chimneys of the Crutchfield House hotel. In the middle distance at center is Academy Hill, topped with whitewashed buildings built by the Confederates and known as Bragg Hospital.

Rosecrans fired off a triumphant message to Halleck, "Chattanooga is ours without a struggle," and ordered his army to pursue at full tilt. He dispatched General McCook and his XX Corps more than 40 miles south to cross Lookout Mountain through distant Winston's Gap and assail Bragg's rear. At the same time George Thomas and his 20,000-man XIV Corps were to march across Lookout Mountain via Stevens' Gap and hit Bragg's flank while Crittenden's XXI Corps secured Chattanooga and then sped south on Bragg's coattails. The Confederates, Rosecrans was convinced, were in complete, panic-stricken retreat. "He didn't expect to get a fight out of Bragg," wrote one of his officers, "this side of Atlanta."

But Rosecrans, as he would soon discover, had made a blunder. Bragg was not retreating in disorder. Instead he was reorganizing his army around the town of La Fayette, Georgia, 25 miles south of Chattanooga—and hefty reinforcements were beginning to pour in: 8,000 men led by Major General Simon Bolivar Buckner who had marched west from Knoxville and 11,500 more under Major Generals John C. Breckinridge and William H. T. Walker coming from the west.

Seizing the chance to trap and destroy Rosecrans' divided army one segment at

A detachment from the 1st Michigan Engineers builds a log-trestle and pontoon bridge at Bridgeport, Alabama, 25 miles southwest of Chattanooga, in late August 1863. The retreating Confederates burned the Nashville & Chattanooga Railroad trestle (background) to slow the Yankee advance. Private Amandus Silsby, 24th Wisconsin, described the destruction in a letter to his father: "Being previously tarred, it blazed up almost as soon as they set the match to it. The whole landscape brightened up, as if lit by gas lights. Finally came a tremendous crash and all was over."

a time, Bragg directed Major General Thomas C. Hindman to fall on the flank of Thomas' advance guard. This Federal division, under Major General James S. Negley's command, had pushed through Stevens' Gap into a cul-de-sac called McLemore's Cove. To finish the job, Bragg ordered Hardee's old corps, now led by Lieutenant General Daniel Harvey Hill, to smash head-on at Negley's exposed position. Once he had Negley, Bragg thought, he could roll up the rest of Thomas' corps.

Incredibly, the usually aggressive Hill failed to attack, claiming his troops were not in position; to make matters worse, Hindman also hesitated. In a fury, Bragg ordered Buckner and his new arrivals to support Hindman. But both of these generals became overcautious, and soon Negley, suspecting a trap, pulled his Federals safely back from McLemore's Cove to rejoin Thomas.

Frustrated but still determined to destroy his tormentors, Bragg on September 12 ordered General Polk to strike northward and wipe up Crittenden's corps, elements of which had pushed south to a place called Lee & Gordon's Mills. But Polk, fearing he faced a superior force, said the attack was impossible and refused to budge.

Seeing two chances lost, Bragg paused for three days. But then, even more grimly set on smashing the enemy, he sent his entire 65,000-man army marching toward what he thought was Crittenden's isolated corps. At the same time Rosecrans, finally seeing the danger, began feverishly pulling McCook and Thomas north out of the

mountains. By September 17 the two armies were both lurching up the dusty roads toward Chickamauga Creek. There, after a day of skirmishing, they would crash together in the biggest battle in the West—and the deadliest, for the numbers engaged, of the entire war.

CLASH AT THE RIVER OF BLOOD

The two armies sat south of Chattanooga within a rifle shot of each other, separated only by Chickamauga Creek. General Bragg still itched to attack, and his chances of doing so successfully were greatly boosted by the arrival in mid-September of an elite body of reinforcements. Two divisions of Lieutenant General James Longstreet's veteran corps, the cream of Lee's Army of Northern Virginia, had been detached and hurried west in a desperate gamble that their added weight would help smash the Federals and keep them from invading Georgia and splitting the Confederacy in half. Boarding trains September 9, Longstreet's 12,000 men had traveled south and then west on a bone-shaking 950-mile roundabout trip on battered railroads. By September 18 the first three brigades, led by Major General John Bell Hood, had arrived, ready to fight.

Bragg immediately ordered Hood to advance across Chickamauga Creek along with General Bushrod Johnson's division and the two corps of Generals Buckner

Lee & Gordon's Mills, about 12 miles south of Chattanooga, was the scene of some of the early skirmishes that started the two-day Battle of Chickamauga.

"A feeling of awful depression laid hold of me. All these fine fellows going to kill or be killed."

MARY BOYKIN CHESNUT

Civilian

Wife of a U.S. senator who resigned to become a Confederate army officer and ultimately an aide to Jefferson Davis, Mary Chesnut moved in the highest social circles of Charleston, South Carolina, and the Confederacy. The war's leading diarist, she began keeping a journal in February 1861 and maintained it until several months after Appomattox. She was 33 years old at the time of this portrait.

At Kingsville I caught a glimpse of our army. Longstreet's corps going west. God bless the gallant fellows. Not one man intoxicated— not one rude word did I hear. It was a strange sight—miles, *apparently*, of platform cars—soldiers rolled in their blankets, lying in rows, heads and all covered, fast asleep. In their gray blankets, packed in regular order, they looked like swathed mummies.

One man near where I sat was writing on his knee. He used his cap for a desk, and he was seated on a rail. I watched him, wondering to whom that letter was to go. Home, no doubt—sore hearts for him there!

A feeling of awful depression laid hold of me. All these fine fellows going to kill or be killed. Why? And a word got to beating about my head like an old song—"the unreturning brave."

and W. H. T. Walker. Bragg's scheme: to hit the left flank of Crittenden's XXI Corps near Lee & Gordon's Mills, drive it south, and trap it in McLemore's Cove. If the plan worked, the Confederates would destroy a third of Rosecrans' army—and cut off the rest from their line of retreat to Chattanooga.

Things did not go according to plan; they seldom did for Bragg. Johnson's men were slow in starting, then found themselves stopped cold at Reed's Bridge by the Union cavalry commanded by a hard-fighting, Irish-born colonel named Robert H. G. Minty. Walker's troops ran into trouble, too, at Alexander's Bridge, raked by wicked fire from the Spencer rifles of Wilder's Lightning Brigade.

After hours of skirmishing, Walker's Confederates, with the support of Johnson's division, managed to drive off Wilder's men and ford the creek a mile to the north. Hood, coming to Johnson's aid, helped send Colonel Minty's pesky Federals fleeing into a nearby woods. But by nightfall Bragg had only about 9,000 men across the Chickamauga and, although the bulk of his army sifted over during the night, he had lost a day. He had also alerted the Federals that the danger lay on their left.

Rosecrans, who had already ordered Crittenden to move leftward, sent General Thomas and his footsore troops marching clear around Crittenden's corps during the night of the 18th to extend the threatened flank. By dawn on September 19, two of Thomas' divisions led by Brigadier Generals John M. Brannan and Absalom Baird had reached the area of the Kelly house on the La Fayette road, more than three miles north of where Bragg estimated the Union left was located.

The fighting began almost by accident on the morning of the 19th, when General Thomas, who had been informed that an enemy brigade had crossed the creek, ordered Brannan to make a reconnaissance. Brannan soon sent a brigade of infantry under a 26-year-old Kentuckian, Colonel John Croxton, to do the job. About 8:00 a.m. Croxton's men encountered some of Nathan Bedford Forrest's cavalry and opened fire, starting a fierce melee.

With that the battle seemed to explode. As Croxton was driving Forrest back, his troops were hit hard by a division of William Walker's corps commanded by Brigadier General States Rights Gist, named to honor his father's secessionist politics. At that, Thomas sent Brannan's other two brigades forward, and into a furious fight with Gist's Confederates.

To back Brannan, Thomas sent the three brigades of Absalom Baird. Walker countered by ordering up his other division, led by Brigadier General St. John Liddell. In minutes, Liddell's Confederates had slammed into the right of Baird's troops, capturing 400 and driving many of the rest back almost two miles.

The beleaguered Thomas lacked two of his divisions, led by Generals Negley and Reynolds, which were still marching around Crittenden. Fearing that he might be overrun, he asked Rosecrans for help, and the commander soon sent Brigadier General Richard W. Johnson's division from McCook's corps hurrying up the La Fayette road. These fresh troops, along with some of Brannan's men, charged into Liddell's attackers and stemmed the near rout.

Now it was Walker's turn to call for aid. Soon Major General Benjamin Cheatham

In this unfinished sketch, Colonel Robert Minty's Union troopers withdraw from Reed's Bridge on the west side of the Chickamauga on September 18. Minty reported they were demolishing the vital bridge when surprised by Confederates.

led his 6,000-man division forward and, shouting, "Give 'em hell, boys," sent them charging into Thomas' line. For two hours Cheatham's men pounded away at the Federals near the Brotherton road, until counterattacked by Johnson's men and Major General John M. Palmer's division, now helping to hold Thomas' right.

As more divisions were fed in, the battle took on the nature of a gigantic and vicious brawl. The air, recalled Colonel Thomas Berry of Forrest's cavalry, was full of "whistling, seething, crackling bullets, the piercing, screaming fragments of shells." On the ground "the ghastly mangled dead and the horribly wounded strewed the earth for over half a mile up and down the river banks." The whole fight, a Union brigadier general later said, was a "mad, irregular battle, very much resembling guerrilla warfare on a vast scale, in which one army was bushwhacking the other."

"Whistling, seething, crackling bullets, the piercing, screaming fragments of shells."

About 2:00 p.m. Bragg, trying to take control of the battle, dispatched the division of Major General Alexander P. Stewart to help Cheatham's exhausted men. Plunging in on Cheatham's left, Stewart's men, screaming the rebel yell, almost immediately broke the Federal division led by Brigadier General Horatio Van Cleve, sending the Union troops reeling back and opening a hole between Thomas' and Crittenden's corps.

The middle of the Federal line had cracked, but the Rebels could not take advantage of the situation. Negley's and Reynolds' Federal divisions—both hurrying to join Thomas—were marching right behind Van Cleve's men when they bolted for the rear. Hastily Reynolds' troops formed a line and, with the help of General Hazen, who brought up 20 cannon, blasted Stewart's oncoming Rebels back into the cover of a dense woods.

Bragg, as if stunned by the failure of his original flanking maneuver, had yet to order a general assault and continued to throw in units piecemeal. Among those impatiently waiting for orders was John Bell Hood. Finally, at about 4:00 p.m., Hood could wait no longer and decided to attack on his own, sending Evander Law's and Bushrod Johnson's troops charging into the Federal right.

Colonel Hans Christian Heg's 15th Wisconsin faces withering fire from Georgia troops of General Henry Benning's brigade at Viniard's Farm in the late afternoon of September 19. Heg can be seen falling mortally wounded from his horse at right center.

THE LEGENDARY JOHNNY CLEM

"He was an expert drummer," wrote his sister, "and being a bright, cheery child, soon made his way into the affections of officers and soldiers." He made his way, also, into the hearts of Northerners, who found the "Drummer Boy of Chickamauga" a most appealing war hero.

Ohio-born Johnny Clem ran away to war before he was 10. He was with the 22d Michigan in its major battles—Shiloh, Perryville, Murfreesboro, Atlanta—but became famous only after the press extolled his exploits at Chickamauga. Armed with a sawed-off musket cut down to fit him, he shot and wounded a Confederate officer who was said to have galloped upon him shouting, "Surrender, you little Yankee devil!" Other stories had him firing furiously after his drum was ripped away by a shell. He was given a sergeant's stripes for valor and awarded a silver medal by the beautiful daughter of Treasury Secretary Salmon Chase.

The war shaped his life: Appointed a second lieutenant in the postwar army, he served until 1915. When he retired at 65 he was Major General John L. Clem, the last man active in the armed forces who had fought in the Civil War.

"Four hundred of his little band were mown down like grain before the reaper."

LIEUTENANT BROMFIELD L. RIDLEY

Staff, Major General Alexander Stewart, Army of Tennessee

Only 18 at the time of Chickamauga, Ridley was Stewart's aide-de-camp. He was also good friends with another 18-year-old lieutenant, James D. Richardson of the 45th Tennessee. Encountering Ridley on the battlefield during the worst of the fighting on September 20, Richardson said simply, "This is hot, isn't it?"

A young staff officer of Wright's (Harris) met us with the statement that Wright's Brigade was much cut up by an enfilade fire: that Carnes's Battery had been lost and help was wanted. As quick as told, Clayton, forming Stewart's first line, was obliqued to the left and vigorously rushed to the rescue.

Did you ever note the thickness of raindrops in a tempest? Did you ever see the destruction of hail stones to growing cornfields? Did you ever witness driftwood in a squall? Such was the havoc upon Clayton. Four hundred of his little band were mown down like grain before the reaper. It was his first baptism of fire, but he stayed there until out of ammunition. J. C. Brown then went in, and was greeted like Clayton. The booming of the cannon, the thinning of the ranks, the thickness of dead men, the groaning of the dying—all were overcome to recapture that battery. Thirty-two horses of Carnes's had been shot down, and amid their writhings the close quarters had set the woods on fire. The shot and shell were raging in the tempest and ramrods flew by us, but Brown drove back the hordes and got Carnes's Battery out of the cyclone. Another surging wave after a while brought him back upon the reef. Then Bate came into arena, and with his crack brigade and prompt movement vied with his compeers in deeds of valor. He rescued the colors of the Fifty-First Tennessee Regiment, and captured several pieces of artillery. Tennessee and Georgia and Alabama tried themselves, and from two o'clock till dark beat and battered the walls of blue, buffeting the storm clouds, charge meeting charge with sanguine success until nothing would stand before them....

Stewart here penetrated the enemy's center, threatened to cut his army in two, drove Vancleve beyond Lafayette road to the tanyard and the Poe house, and carried dismay to Rosecrans, to the Widow Glenn's. Later, Hood and Johnson on our left followed it up, until from the Brotherton to the Poe field we pierced his line. Added to the horror of the galling fire, the generals and staffs encountered a number of yellow jackets' nests, and the kicking of the horses and their ungovernable actions came near breaking up one of the lines. Blue jackets in front of us, yellow jackets upon us, and death missiles around and about us—O, the fury of the battle, the fierceness of the struggle over Carnes's Battery! From two o'clock until an hour after dark it was war to the knife and a fight to the finish.

Company H of the 44th Indiana stood its ground in the Federal center just after midday on September 19. Attacked by Clayton's Alabama brigade, the Hoosiers responded with a withering fire. One Alabamian recalled: "Did you ever note the thickness of raindrops in a tempest? Did you ever see the destruction of hail stones to growing cornfields? Did you ever witness driftwood in a squall? Such was the havoc upon Clayton."

CHICKAMAUGA.

This bullet-pocked plate from a Union soldier's cartridge pouch was found on the battlefield at Chickamauga. It is not known whether it saved the wearer from harm or instead bears mute witness to the soldier's fate.

This sketch by Alfred Waud shows soldiers of General Patrick Cleburne's division advancing against the Union lines at twilight on the evening of September 19. Although generally successful, the attack proved to be a prelude to disaster the following morning, when General Polk launched an uncoordinated assault against strong breastworks on the Federal left. Some Confederate regiments lost more than 50 percent of their men, while the Yankees suffered a mere handful of casualties.

Breaking out of some woods, the six Rebel brigades smashed into the three commanded by Brigadier General Jefferson C. Davis. In minutes Hood's attack had virtually annihilated one of Davis' brigades led by Norwegian-born Colonel Hans Christian Heg, killing him and inflicting 696 casualties. Again the Union line was close to breaking.

Yet again the momentum shifted. Brigadier General Thomas Wood rushed his division of Crittenden's corps into the gap, followed by Wilder's Lightning Brigade and then Major General Philip Sheridan's division of McCook's corps. Acting fast as always, Eli Lilly set up his guns and fired into the flank of Hood's men, killing so many as they took cover in a ditch that Wilder was horrified. It seemed, he later wrote, "a pity to kill men so. They fell in heaps, and I had it in my heart to order the firing to cease, to end the awful sight."

As the sun set, firing slackened along the four-mile-long front. General Thomas began reorganizing his lines—but he warned that another Rebel assault was possible. Indeed, it came. This time the aggressor was Cleburne's division, which Bragg had belatedly ordered to march north behind the front from its position near Lee & Gordon's Mills.

Cleburne's 5,000 men, wading the Chickamauga at twilight, exploded out of the woods west of Reed's Bridge directly at Baird's and Johnson's divisions. The Confederates captured 300 prisoners while gaining a mile of ground before it became too dark to fight.

The first day's confused struggle had ended, but the night brought little rest. Units on both sides marched to get in position for the fighting that was sure to begin again at dawn. Pickets exchanged sharp volleys. Other troops felled

"I was wounded, tired, hungry, cold and dirty and worst of all a prisoner."

PRIVATE ROBERT H. HANNAFORD

93d Ohio Infantry, Baldwin's Brigade

Hannaford was turned away, with other wounded Yankee prisoners, from several Confederate hospitals before being set on the ground at the field hospital of Cheatham's division, where he lay untreated for 12 days and nights. Hannaford summed up his feelings toward his captors, saying, "I thought I would live if possible, just to spite them."

We then prepared to meet the enemy again. We strengthened the breast works with everything we could find. I filled my cartridge box and put some in my pocket and I then intended to clean my gun and as I had no wiper of my own, I had to borrow one of a fellow named Bill Craig in our Co. I had the ramrod out and the wiper nearly screwed on when I turned my head to the left and looked down through the woods and saw them coming. I unscrewed the wiper and handed it back and said "they are coming" to Bill. I got down behind and commenced firing at them I had fired about eight or ten rounds when all at once I felt something strike me. I thought I was shot through the foot because it pained me so, it felt as if some person had throwed a log on it or something to bruise it but as soon as I straightened my leg I saw and felt I was shot above the knee for I could feel the blood running down my thigh. I then crawled off about ten feet and laid down behind a log and in front of the Orderly Sergent, his name was L. L. Sadler. I lay there a little while and groaned once or twice but I soon got ashamed of myself. I then com-

menced talking to Sadler I told him to pour it in to them, I could not do anything more but I wanted him to give it to them, his share and mine. I asked him if they would leave me there for I was confident they would have to fall back, he did not answer me I might have known that they would not take me back. He did not fire more than two or three rounds before they all got up and fell back leaving me there between two fires. . . . I never felt so bad in my life as I did that time. I stood pretty good chance of getting killed, and if I lived I would be a prisoner, most a charming prospect to lay there wounded and helpless was not very nice. After laying there about a half an hour under a most terrible fire and narrowly escaping being shot I was taken prisoner as the Rebels advanced up the hill and soon as they passed I crawled over to the other side and laid down behind a large log. I was treated pretty well by them fellows as I lay there I could see the skulkers coming and I thought I would give away my canteen and coffee as I could see that was what they most desired. I did give it away and they promised to come back and help to carry me back to the rear, but they never

came. While I lay there one fellow out of our company that was not wounded found Lieut Kellys hat, he brought it to me and said "Bob here is Lieut Kelley's hat." I told him to give it to me as it was better than mine which he did, it was about dark and a Reb and him carried me off a few feet and then left me. They put a shelter tent over me but the night was very cold and I lay there shivering and shaking until about nine o'clock when they carried me a little farther and laid me down by a fire as soon as they saw my hat one of them took it off and looked at it and proposed to trade, I did not like to but I thought it would be no use to refuse because they would take it anyhow. Therefore I very graciously told him to take it, which he did and handed me one about one size smaller than an umbrella, but I was forced to be satisfied, it was that or none. Oh what a miserable night that was to me, I lay there thinking of all my friends and those I loved and I never likely to see them again, I was wounded, tired, hungry, cold and dirty and worst of all a prisoner. I did not care so much about my wound as I did about being a prisoner.

The name "Chickamauga" is prominently displayed on a battle flag of the 1st Arkansas, a regiment that played a vital role in Cleburne's assaults on the Federal left early on the second day of the battle. The crossed cannon at the flag's center signify that the regiment had captured enemy artillery in one or more of their many battles, as they did at Chickamauga.

Confederate troops load and fire their rifles in the tangled woodland along Chickamauga Creek. The heavily thicketed terrain, noted a Union officer, made for a "mad, irregular battle, very much resembling guerrilla warfare on a vast scale, in which one army was bushwhacking the other."

trees to make breastworks.

About 11:00 p.m. Rosecrans called a council of war at his headquarters, a log house belonging to a widow named Eliza Glenn. The Army of the Cumberland would stand on the defensive, it was agreed. During the meeting, General Thomas napped in his chair, occasionally rousing himself to warn, "I would strengthen the left." It was sound advice, and later Rosecrans shifted Negley's division from the Federal center to strengthen Thomas' left flank.

At Confederate headquarters, Bragg reorganized his force, this time into two wings. Polk would be in charge of the right, leading his own corps along with Hill's and Walker's. Longstreet would attack on the left with his own troops as well as Buckner's corps.

The arrangement required much shifting of large bodies of troops, and it would cause trouble in the morning. So would the fact that not all of Longstreet's men would come up in time from the train depot a dozen miles to the south. Longstreet himself was on the scene, however. When he arrived at the Ringgold train station at 2:00 p.m., he was exasperated to find that Bragg had sent no one to meet him, and he and two aides spent the rest of the day riding through the Georgia woods to the distant sound of gunfire. It was 11:00 p.m. before they happened on Bragg's headquarters. But Longstreet's irritation at Bragg's oversight did not long endure and at daybreak he would be ready to fight. Longstreet would, as always, attack with precision and thunderous force, and almost succeed in destroying Rosecrans' army.

LONGSTREET'S BREAKTHROUGH

General Bragg ordered virtually the same plan of attack for September 20 that had produced the bloody stalemate on the day before. Leonidas Polk's divisions would again hammer at the Union left, going in one after another in sequence. When these attacks were well under way, General Longstreet would move forward, throwing his wing of six divisions at the Federal center and right.

As usual with Bragg's army, there were delays, caused in large measure by the general's own confusing reorganization of the night before. The irascible D. H. Hill claimed he had not received proper orders and refused to move until he did, thus stalling Polk's entire assault. Polk himself, never prone to hasty action, was found calmly reading a newspaper over breakfast hours after dawn, the planned time of attack.

It was not until about 9:30 that the fighting erupted—with the same deafening violence as the day before.

Breckinridge's division charged first, driving around the far left flank of General Thomas' position. In minutes a brigade of Negley's division had been bent back on itself—until troops from Brannan's and Van Cleve's divisions rushed to Negley's aid and forced the Confederates to retire.

Cleburne's division, next down the line, attacked about 10:00 a.m., rushing through a pine forest. But the first ranks were shot to pieces by furious fire from

Condemned by some for blindly obeying an order by Rosecrans that opened a massive hole in the Union line, Brigadier General Thomas J. Wood nonetheless was a highly regarded officer whose personal courage was so marked that Sherman once said he was worth 20,000 men. While Rosecrans was eventually relieved of command, Wood, who had been U. S. Grant's first West Point roommate, continued to serve; his troops were the first over the Confederate defenses on Missionary Ridge in November 1863.

Federal troops dug in behind log breastworks they had hastily built during the night. While Cleburne's men reorganized, Polk sent in Cheatham's division, then Walker's, which were also stopped by rifle fire and scything blasts of canister from Federal guns.

His entire line under assault, General Thomas asked Rosecrans, as he had several times the day before, to order up reinforcements from the Union right. This Rosecrans did—and in the process made a fatal error.

While units were shifting about, a staff officer riding behind the lines mistakenly thought he saw a large gap near the Federal center. Thomas informed Rosecrans, who immediately ordered Brigadier General Thomas Wood to move his brigades left and close up on General Reynolds' division. Wood knew there was no gap—Brannan's troops were there, hidden in the trees. But Wood had been severely reprimanded earlier by Rosecrans for apparently ignoring another order and now he obeyed.

At 11:30 a.m. Longstreet launched a juggernaut of 16,000 men of Johnson's, Law's, and Kershaw's divisions against the Federal right. Just as this Rebel attack got under way, Rosecrans shifted several units, including Wood's division, to the north to reinforce Thomas. To obey orders, Wood had to withdraw from the line and move to the rear of Brannan. In doing so he left a gaping hole in the Union line through which the Confederates poured. To the south, Hindman routed Sheridan and Davis, completing the collapse of the Federal right. Despite Wilder's flanking attempt to stop the Rebel onslaught, Rosecrans' troops began streaming to the rear.

A firm believer that success on the battlefield was largely "a question of nerve," the Union's Major General George Thomas set up his command post in a clump of dead trees 400 yards from the fighting on Snodgrass Hill. From there he ranged the front lines urging his weary troops to stand fast.

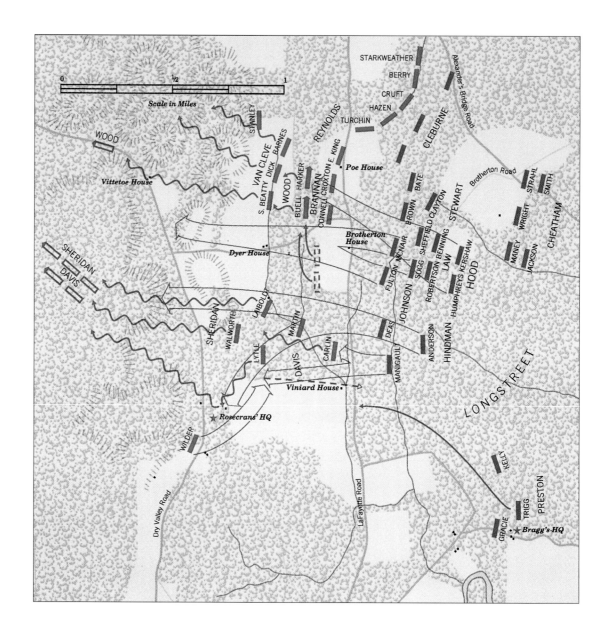

As he moved rearward to get around Brannan, Wood in fact created a yawning quarter-mile hole in the Union center—made all the worse because two nearby divisions, Sheridan's and Davis', were also in motion, sidling north. At that moment most of Longstreet's wing charged straight into the gap. No man to attack one division at a time like Bragg, Longstreet had massed his force for a single ferocious, concentrated blow. Now he sent Hood's and Johnson's divisions smashing ahead in tandem with Brigadier General Joseph Kershaw's division just behind them and Hindman's on the left.

The effect on the Union line was catastrophic. As more than 16,000 yelling Confederates raced through the gap and past their exposed flanks, the astonished and terrified Federals fled in panic. By 12:15 most of McCook's corps and Crittenden's were in headlong flight—men, wagons, guns, horses all racing toward the nearest avenue of escape, McFarland's Gap, which cut through Missionary Ridge.

With them went Rosecrans himself, chased from his headquarters near the Dyer farmhouse with his entire staff, including Brigadier General (and future U.S. president) James A. Garfield. Rosecrans, confused and desperate, was finally

MAJOR GENERAL JOHN B. HOOD

*Corps Commander,
Army of Tennessee*

*The blond, six-foot-two-inch-tall,
"Gallant Hood" had risen quickly
in the ranks from first lieutenant
to major general in less than 18
months. He was wounded at
Gettysburg, losing the use of his
left arm. He recuperated in time
to command a corps and three
divisions at Chickamauga. His
troops were the ones that
exploited the gap in the Union
lines on September 20, when he
was wounded again.*

*With his useless left arm in a sling, Major General John Bell
Hood reels in the saddle as his right thigh is pierced by a Minié
ball while he rallies troops of the Texas Brigade. Although the
leg was amputated, Hood returned to command his corps,
riding strapped to his saddle. Eventually he would replace
General Joseph Johnston as commander of the entire Army of
Tennessee in the Atlanta campaign.*

With a shout along my entire front, the Confederates rushed forward, penetrated into the wood, over and beyond the enemy's breastworks, and thus achieved another glorious victory for our arms. About this time I was pierced with a Minie ball in the upper third of the right leg; I turned from my horse upon the side of the crushed limb and fell—strange to say, since I was commanding five divisions—into the arms of some of the troops of my old brigade, which I had directed so long a period, and upon so many fields of battle....

The members of this heroic band were possessed of a streak of superstition, as in fact I believe all men to be; and it may here prove of interest to cite an instance thereof. I had a favorite roan horse, named by them "Jeff Davis"; whenever he was in condition I rode him in battle, and, remarkable as it may seem, he generally received the bullets and bore me unscathed. In this battle he was severely wounded on Saturday; the following day, I was forced to resort to a valuable mare in my possession, and late in the afternoon was shot from the saddle.

At Gettysburg I had been unable to mount him on the field, in consequence of lameness; in this engagement I had also been shot from the saddle. Thus the belief among the men became nigh general that, when mounted on old Jeff, the bullets could not find me. This spirited and fearless animal performed his duty throughout the war, and after which he received tender care from General Jefferson and family of Seguin, Texas, until death, when he was buried with appropriate honors.

The 89th Ohio, as part of Granger's Reserve Corps, had been held out of the fighting on the 19th and the morning of the 20th. Thrown into line on the Union right at Snodgrass Hill, they held off repeated enemy attacks while helping cover Thomas' withdrawal. Finally out of ammunition and preparing to fight hand to hand, the remaining men of the 89th—and the battle-scarred flag shown here—were captured by Trigg's Confederates.

This view of the action on Snodgrass Hill on September 20 shows Steedman's 3,900-strong division of Granger's Reserve Corps arriving (far right) on the field. Steedman's mission was to shore up the hard-pressed line of Brannan's division against four Confederate divisions thrown at them by Longstreet.

persuaded by Garfield to head for Chattanooga and organize a last-ditch defense. Garfield himself rode off to find General Thomas, hoping he was still fighting and could save the fleeing army.

Thomas was, in fact, fighting hard. Drawing together Brannan's and Palmer's divisions along with individual brigades from the scattered commands of Wood, Reynolds, Negley, and others, Thomas had organized a masterly defense with a strong southeast-facing line positioned on a wooded rise known as Snodgrass Hill and along a nearby curving piece of high ground that came to be called Horseshoe Ridge.

With murderous volleys, the Federals on Snodgrass Hill threw back a first furious charge by Kershaw's division of Longstreet's wing, which had wheeled to attack from the south. The Union troops then beat off more headlong rushes by Hindman's and Bushrod Johnson's divisions. In late afternoon General Polk also attacked, sending his five divisions against the beleaguered Federals defending Horseshoe Ridge.

There, too, the Union troops in some ferocious fighting repulsed the attackers. Soon, however, the Federals were virtually out of ammunition. At this critical moment help arrived: Major General Gordon Granger bringing two

"Like magic, the Union army had melted away in our presence."

brigades from his Reserve Corps that had been guarding roads to the north—and 95,000 heaven-sent rounds for the defenders' rifles.

Through all the desperate fighting, General Thomas, calm and massive as a great bear, had gone from one unit to another, encouraging the men to hold on. He was, Garfield said, "standing like a rock"—bestowing on Thomas the name he would have ever after, the Rock of Chickamauga.

But Thomas knew that, with the rest of the army in flight, he also had to retreat. As dusk came on he began a superbly managed withdrawal, sending his hard-pressed units one by one toward McFarland's Gap until only a few of

Brannan's men were left as a rear guard. "Like magic," Longstreet later wrote, "the Union army had melted away in our presence."

Thomas collected his battered units at the town of Rossville and formed lines to hold off the expected Confederate pursuit. But Bragg, to the bitter disgust of Longstreet, Forrest, and many of his other officers, refused to go after the Federals. Pursuit, Bragg said, was out of the question. "Here is two fifths of my army left on the field, and my artillery is without horses." So the Federals slipped away to the north, toward Chattanooga, and Bragg had squandered another opportunity.

CAPTAIN ISAAC CUSAC

21st Ohio Infantry, Sirwell's Brigade

A high-ranking officer gave Cusac the peremptory and terrible order related here. When Cusac protested, he was joined by Lieutenant J. S. Mahoney of the 21st Ohio's Company K. By the time the officer repeated the order to Major McMahon, his manner had so changed that McMahon later said he was "not imperious, but kind and encouraging."

W e had been on the ridge but a short time when the enemy made a desperate attack on us, but was repulsed. Again and again did they attempt to drive us from the ridge, but we were not to be moved by lead or demon-like yells, but we lay close to the ground and with our Colt Revolving Rifles repelled and repulsed every attack. About one o'clock p.m. some troops came in on our right, and the 22d Michigan charged over us as we lay on the ground, but only remained in front of us a short time when they fell back over us. The enemy then followed up and made a desperate effort to break through our lines. The enemy's loss must have been very heavy as they came near us, and we kept up a constant and terrific fire on them, compelling them to fall back. About this time a regiment formed on our left and did some good work, but later in the day they disappeared....

The 21st held position amidst showers of bullets, shot and shell, until sundown, when we were out of ammunition and could not get any. The regiment then moved to the rear a few rods into a hollow, where we were then secure from the fire of the enemy. While in this position I was standing in front of the regiment, when a Colonel (whom I was unable to recognize) rode up to me somewhat excited, saying to me, "Move those men up on the line." I said to him, "Colonel, we have no more ammunition." His reply to me was, "It does not make a God damn bit of difference. Have the men fix bayonets and hold that line."

The language and the manner that the command was given in stirred up my "Irish" blood, and I said to him, "Go and talk with the officer in command." He then rode to the rear of the regiment where Major McMahon was, and gave him the same orders, though not in the same language. Then the Major gave orders to fix bayonets, which was promptly obeyed, but when the order was given to "forward march," not a man moved. About that time some of the men on our right shouted, "Boys, do not leave us!" and when the second command was given, every man moved forward on double quick, and was met by a most murderous fire which killed and wounded many of our men, myself being wounded in my left hand.

When we reached the line on the ridge a short distance to the right of where we were at sundown, we fell to the ground and remained in that position until dark. The enemy could have undoubtedly driven us from the ridge at any time after sundown, as the three regiments that held that part of the line were all out of ammunition. But they had a better thing on us by lying still in front, while a part of their forces swung around to the rear of us, shutting us in. This they did in good shape, taking in the 22d Michigan, the 89th Ohio and the 21st Ohio, all except a few on the left of the 21st.

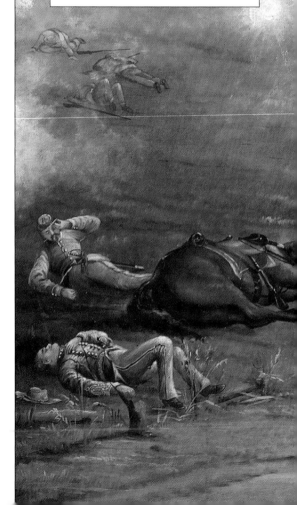

CHICKAMAUGA
CASUALTIES

FEDERAL

Killed	*1,657*
Wounded	*9,756*
Missing	*4,757*
Total	*16,170*

CONFEDERATE

Killed	*2,312*
Wounded	*14,678*
Missing	*1,468*
Total	*18,458*

Covering the Union withdrawal toward Chattanooga, troops of Absalom Baird's division stand fast before the Kelly house in the late afternoon of September 20. "We held our position, yielding not an inch," wrote Baird. "To fall back was more difficult than to remain." Baird retreated as night came on, and Thomas' forces at Snodgrass Hill began to leave the field. Only the 21st and 89th Ohio and the 22d Michigan remained to resist the Confederate assaults. Out of ammunition, they fixed bayonets and countercharged, only to be overwhelmed and captured. Thus the battle ended.

"'Colonel, we have no more ammunition.' 'It does not make a God damn bit of difference. Have the men fix bayonets and hold that line.'"

MILITARY BANDS AND FIELD MUSIC

Impressively attired drum majors, like the unidentified Federal at right, directed the musical and physical responses of regimental drum corps with baton motions.

Near Atlanta in 1864, encamped Rebels and Yankees engaged in a peculiar nightly exchange—aiming music instead of bullets at each other. Colonel James Nisbet of the 66th Georgia described the scene: One Rebel regiment, he wrote, "had a splendid brass band; their cornet player was the best I ever heard. In the evenings after supper he would come to our salient and play solos." The enemy would cease their sniping just to let him perform. "How the Yanks would applaud!" remembered Nisbet. "They had a good cornet player who would alternate with our man."

To Civil War soldiers, music and bullets were natural consorts. Melodic brass bands serenaded the men in camp—and sometimes even in battle—and the crisp brilliance of fife-and-drum corps inspired their martial ardor. General Robert E. Lee once said, "I don't believe we can have an army without music."

In May 1861 the Union army issued a decree allowing each regiment to form a band, and by October nearly 75 percent of Yankee regiments had one. The Confederacy, too, authorized regimental bands, though scarcity of instruments and the need for front-line combatants often limited their size.

Band music had the power to transport heartsore soldiers beyond the privations and terrors of war. Wrote a Rebel trooper camped in the Wilderness in 1864: "There is a brass band and they are playing 'Shells of Ocean,' and as the familiar notes of this sweet air are gently wafted in delightful cadences over the woody hills and dewy fields, numberless visions of home in happier hours and sweet reminiscences of the past crowd thick and fast upon my soul."

In mid-1862 the Union army issued a highly unpopular order eliminating volunteer regimental brass bands, opting instead for fewer brigade-level bands. Still, every Union regiment had its official "field musicians"—usually fifers or drummers for the infantry, buglers for the cavalry and artillery. In the Confederate army, field musicians served at the company level. On either side, their drumrolls and horn blasts orchestrated tactical movements on the battlefield.

Band members and field musicians alike were called upon to exchange their instruments for muskets, particularly in the Confederate ranks, where combat-ready units always needed more men. More frequently still, musicians were expected to double as ambulance crewmen and surgeons' assistants.

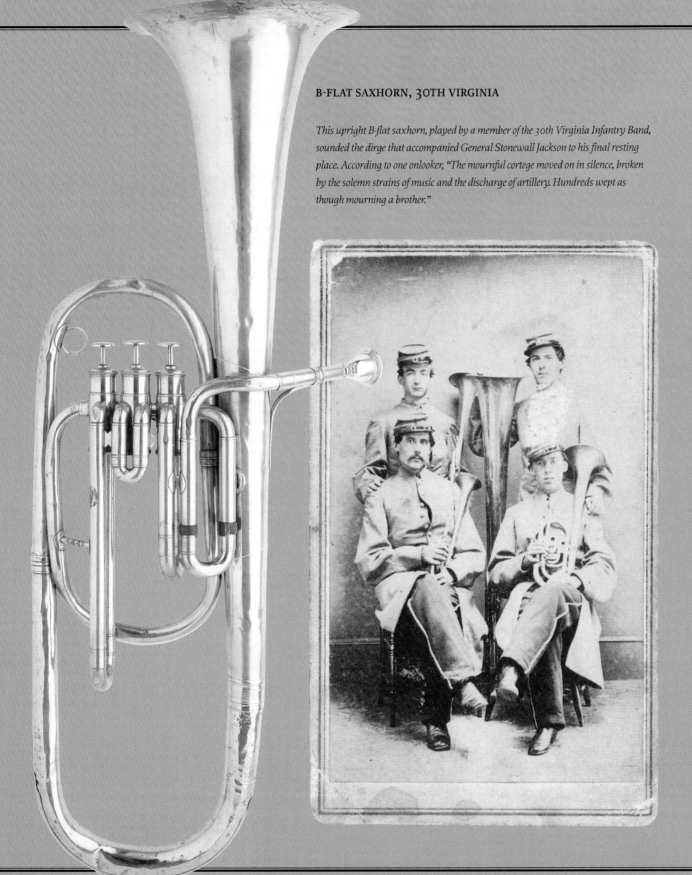

B-FLAT SAXHORN, 30TH VIRGINIA

This upright B-flat saxhorn, played by a member of the 30th Virginia Infantry Band, sounded the dirge that accompanied General Stonewall Jackson to his final resting place. According to one onlooker, "The mournful cortege moved on in silence, broken by the solemn strains of music and the discharge of artillery. Hundreds wept as though mourning a brother."

Solemnly clutching their over-the-shoulder saxhorns, four members of Smith's Armory Band of Richmond, Virginia, were immortalized in this circa 1860 photograph. The band, which served with the Virginia Light Infantry Public Guard prior to the war, went on to become the 1st Virginia Regimental Band in April 1860. It was the favorite musical ensemble of Jefferson Davis, president of the Confederacy.

Saxhorns, cornets, and bass drum at the ready, the 2d Rhode
Island Regimental Band spearheads a parade of Northern
infantry assembling on a drill field at Camp Brightwood
in Virginia.

CIRCULAR CORNET, 16TH KENTUCKY

A July thunderstorm claimed the life of Adjutant Joe Dudley,
player of this circular cornet for the 16th Kentucky Infantry
Band. Dudley died in 1864 when his tent, pitched in a field in
Fulton County, Georgia, was struck by a falling tree.

To the frightful accompaniment of bursting shells, regimental bandleader Samuel Mickey trumpeted such Confederate favorites as "The Bonnie Blue Flag" on his flugelhorn (below), inspiring the 26th North Carolina throughout three years of battle. The band, composed of eight members of the renowned Moravian Salem Brass Band, was recruited in March 1862 to serve with the regiment. At the war's end, Union forces captured the group in Virginia at the Battle of Five Forks and confiscated the instruments—all except for Mickey's silver flugelhorn, which he secreted in his haversack.

BRIGADE CLARINET, 151ST NEW YORK

Band member Enoch Pettit of Company F, New York Volunteers, owned this boxwood clarinet. The larger, brigade-level bands boasted clarinets among their instrumentation.

BANDLEADER SAMUEL MICKEY AND FLUGELHORN

Fifers and drummers, such as the young Federals pictured here, were expected to master all 148 calls and tunes described in the Union field-music text, The Drummers and Fifers Guide, by the first day of enlistment. Any formal instruction—typically involving rote exercises—was provided by veteran musicians.

FEDERAL SNARE DRUM

A standard-issue rope-tension drum, this unadorned instrument was made by military-and-toy-drum manufacturer Jacob Stewart of Pittsfield, Massachusetts, in 1861. The U.S. Army purchased more than 32,000 such drums between 1861 and 1865.

FEDERAL WOODEN FIFE WITH LEATHER CASE

This side drum once belonged to Union drummer Almon Laird, who was captured by Rebel troops in May 1864 at the Battle of Drewry's Bluff in Virginia. Among the oldest known field musicians, the 48-year-old Laird died in a Confederate prison in Savannah, Georgia.

EAGLE DRUM, 27TH MASSACHUSETTS

Charles F. Mosby was 13 when he enlisted in 1861 as a drummer with the "Elliott Grays," a company of the 6th Virginia Infantry. Mosby survived his four years of service; many others, some as young as 10, died in battle and were eulogized in such ballads as "The Dying Drummer Boy," by Mary Lathbury and E. C. Howe.

CONFEDERATE CAVALRY BUGLE

Fifteen-year-old Noel Davenport of Mobile, Alabama, shucked his studies at Spring Hill College in 1862 to play this cavalry bugle for the 23d Tennessee Regiment, with which he served till 1865.

At first light, a Confederate bugler stirs his regiment with a round of reveille in this painting by W. L. Sheppard. The wake-up call was an electric tonic to drowsing troops, who associated its clarion tones with the crash and rumble of battle.

INFANTRY BUGLE, 2D KENTUCKY

Battered and tarnished from long years of rough use, this bugle once summoned the foot soldiers of the 2d Kentucky to roll call, assembly, and other regimental drills. Chief Bugler John Washington Payne captured the instrument from Union forces at Hartsville, Tennessee, in December 1862.

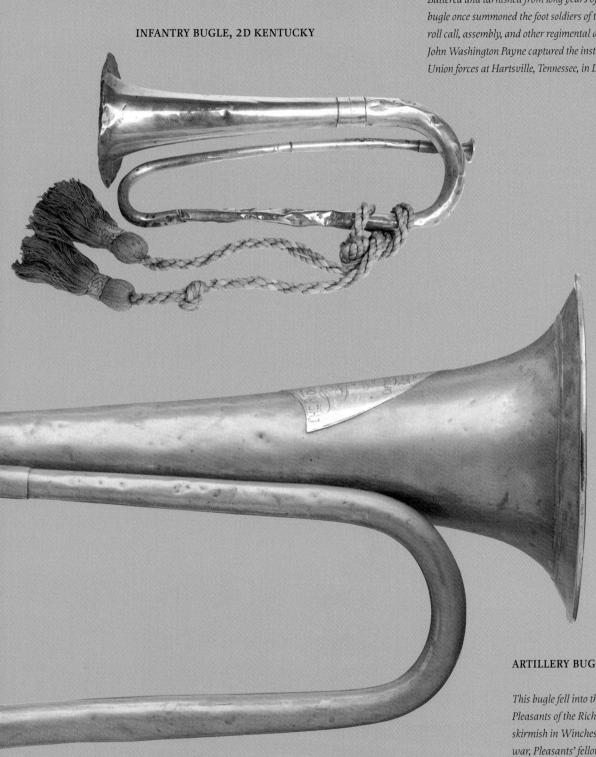

Gustave Schurmann was 11 when he volunteered as a drummer with the 40th New York. General Philip Kearny made the lad his orderly and presented him with a silver bugle and a huge mare, which young Gus rode with élan.

ARTILLERY BUGLE, RICHMOND HOWITZERS

This bugle fell into the hands of the Rebel soldier Reuben Pleasants of the Richmond Howitzers in June 1863 during a skirmish in Winchester, Virginia. Some nine years after the war, Pleasants' fellow artilleryman John Jones formally dedicated the bugle to the veteran battery.

Chattanooga
Gateway to the Deep South

CITY UNDER SIEGE—By September 22, two days after the Battle of Chickamauga, Major General William S. Rosecrans' surviving Federal troops had retreated safely within the defenses of Chattanooga. That same day Rebel general Braxton Bragg followed, proclaiming that he now had Rosecrans precisely where he wanted him. It only remained to besiege the Federal army in Chattanooga and starve it into submission. Apparently lost on General Bragg was the irony of his costly victory at Chickamauga actually driving the Federals into the city, rather than away from it, as intended.

For the moment, however, Bragg's course was clear. He marched his troops north and seized the commanding height of Missionary Ridge that loomed over Chattanooga and the Union trenches defending it. On the 24th, when a demoralized Rosecrans unaccountably pulled a Union brigade off Lookout Mountain to the west, Bragg quickly sent Lieutenant General James Longstreet to seize that strategic height as well.

This spelled trouble for the Federals. Confederate cannon on Lookout Mountain could easily hit boats and barges on a nearby bend in the Tennessee River and the tracks of the Nashville & Chattanooga Railroad, effectively severing Rosecrans' main supply routes.

The Federals were forced to improvise a new supply line—and a very poor substitute it turned out to be. The troops had to unload the supplies shipped from Nashville at the rail depot in Bridgeport, Alabama, and pile the freight onto wagons. Then they had to get the mule-drawn wagons up a dirt track to Anderson's Crossroads and from there across Walden's Ridge on a rough, twisting trail that finally descended to the north bank of the Tennessee and a bridge spanning the river into Chattanooga. A trip on the old rail route from Bridgeport had taken about an hour. The new route, 60 miles long, took at least eight days—and often took about 20.

The first wagon trains making the long haul could barely bring in enough food to keep Rosecrans' troops from starving, and the situation soon became worse as autumn rains made the route all but impassable. The track, said a Union officer, was "the muddiest and the roughest and steepest of ascent and descent ever crossed by army wagons and mules." The overworked mules soon became exhausted and, lacking fodder, died off by the hundreds;

Above: This forage cap belonged to a sergeant of the 105th Ohio, a unit under siege at Chattanooga. The regiment was in Brigadier General Absalom Baird's division, which suffered severe casualties at Chickamauga. "My loss in killed and wounded," Baird wrote, "attests to the determination with which my men fought."

Opposite: Union soldiers pose among their tents in besieged Chattanooga. Yankee troops dismantled many of the city's houses and used the scavenged boards for firewood or for erecting camp structures, such as the makeshift plank fence in the foreground.

eventually a total of 10,000 perished.

The result was persistent, gnawing hunger in Chattanooga, for the army, now reduced to 35,000 men, and for the civilian population as well. Famished troops demanded "crackers"—issues of the normally despised hardtack—and could often be seen, an observer reported, scrabbling in the gutters for "crumbs of bread, coffee, rice etc., which were wasted from the boxes and sacks by the rattling of the wagons over the stones."

Making conditions worse, the soldiers before long had all but dismantled the town, tearing apart the houses for firewood and for lumber to build shacks for themselves. The residents were reduced to living in wretched shanties—until a large proportion of them fled northward to find succor in other towns.

Meanwhile Confederate cavalry leader Major General Joseph Wheeler hammered at the rickety supply system, crossing the Tennessee in late September with 5,000 troopers and spreading havoc in the Federal rear. Wheeler wrecked Union depots and in a single raid on Anderson's Crossroads burned more than 300 wagons. Finally Federal cavalry chased Wheeler back across the Tennessee on October 9.

Through all the misery, Rosecrans walked about as if in a daze, half insensible to his army's troubles—and the far worse misery that would ensue if Bragg attacked his weakened force. Rosecrans, President Lincoln said on being told of the general's behavior, was acting "stunned and confused, like a duck hit on the head."

General U. S. Grant, shown in a sketch by Adolph Metzner, called for reinforcements on arriving in Chattanooga and established a new supply route nicknamed the Cracker Line. During his hurried but arduous journey to Chattanooga, Grant, who had been seriously hurt in a fall from a horse in September, often had to dismount and be carried by his aides over the roughest stretches of a trail that was sometimes knee deep in mud.

General Wheeler and his troopers seize a Federal supply train in a daring raid near Anderson's Crossroads. Some of the Confederates found what must have been a sutler's wagon; an observer wrote that the gleeful men "waded up to their necks in fine $50 hats, $100 boots, rivers of Champagne and liquors of all kinds, pyramids of cigars, fruits, jellies and every sort of luxury."

Bragg, for his part, was clearer of mind but as usual in an exceedingly ill temper. Following the battle he angrily relieved Lieutenant General Leonidas Polk of command, sent Major General Thomas C. Hindman packing, and tried to get rid of Lieutenant General Daniel Harvey Hill as well. The generals—all disgusted by Bragg's continued refusal to attack the battered Federals—countered by sending a petition to President Davis saying the army was "stricken with a complete paralysis" and that Bragg was unfit for command.

In response, Davis hurried westward by train and convened a meeting of the disgruntled officers on October 9. Nothing came of it but a shuffling of assignments. Bragg stayed on, to the dismay of virtually all his subordinates.

A far more significant shuffling took place on the Federal side. In the second week of October, Secretary of War Edwin Stanton took a train to Indianapolis and there met Major General Ulysses S. Grant, summoned east from Vicksburg. Grant, Stanton said, would immediately assume overall command of no fewer than three armies—Rosecrans' Army of the Cumberland, Major General Ambrose E. Burnside's Army of the Ohio, and the Army of the Tennessee led by Grant's right-hand man in

"We will hold the town till we starve."

From heights such as this Lookout Mountain perch over Moccasin Point on the Tennessee River, General Braxton Bragg's Rebels controlled nearly all routes to Chattanooga (right center), thus throttling the flow of supplies to the Union army in the town.

the Vicksburg campaign, General William Tecumseh Sherman.

The first question was what to do with Old Rosy. Grant was given his choice and opted to relieve the shaken Rosecrans and replace him with Major General George H. Thomas. Grant quickly sent General Thomas a telegram ordering him to "hold Chattanooga at all hazards." The blunt Thomas wired back, "We will hold the town till we starve."

Grant then sped to the railroad junction at Stevenson, Alabama, where he met Rosecrans, who was on his way home to Cincinnati. The meeting was friendly, Grant recalled, and Rosecrans both "described very clearly the situations at Chattanooga" and "made some excellent suggestions about what should be done." The wonder, Grant added, "was that he had not carried them out."

Going on to Bridgeport, Grant then rode over the treacherous, muddy Federal supply route into Chattanooga, getting a firsthand look at "the debris of broken wagons and the carcasses of dead mules and horses that strewed the trail."

Brigadier General William F. Smith—nicknamed Baldy by his peers—had an irascible nature that repeatedly placed him at odds with his superiors, often hurting his chances for advancement. But the West Pointer had an acknowledged genius for engineering, and Rosecrans, before he was relieved, appointed Smith chief engineer of the Army of the Cumberland. It was Smith who recognized the value of Brown's Ferry and planned the operation to seize the vital crossing point.

Brigadier General William B. Hazen had spent his adolescent years in Ohio, where he befriended future president James A. Garfield. Known for bravery and competency under fire during numerous battles in the West, Hazen was a good choice to lead the hazardous mission to capture Brown's Ferry, the first step in reopening the Cracker Line.

OPENING THE CRACKER LINE

Mud splattered and wet from his 60-mile horseback ride over the treacherous supply road from Bridgeport, Grant arrived at Thomas' headquarters in Chattanooga as darkness was falling on October 23. The new commanding general refused an offer of dry clothes and got right down to business, asking each of Thomas' staff officers to give his own appraisal of the military situation.

As the men spoke, Grant listened—"immovable as a rock and as silent as a sphinx," one officer recalled. The reports were so grim, Grant later wrote, that it "looked, indeed, as if but two courses were open; one to starve, the other to surrender or be captured." He had no intention of doing either. When Brigadier General William F. "Baldy" Smith proposed a way to open a new supply line, Grant perked up and peppered him with questions.

As chief engineer for the Army of the Cumberland, Smith had studied the area's geography, with special attention to the terrain between the army's position in Chattanooga and its supply base at Bridgeport and the serpentine meanderings of the Tennessee River between those two points.

Two and a half miles downstream from the city, the river interrupted its southwestward course and looped to the northwest around a tongue of land called Moccasin Point. From the pontoon bridge already in place at Chattanooga a road led across Moccasin Point for two miles until it hit the river again at Brown's Ferry. From Brown's Ferry the river flowed northwestward for five miles toward Walden's Ridge, then created another peninsula by looping around Raccoon Mountain—which was in Confederate hands. The road from Brown's Ferry continued west over Raccoon Mountain to another ferry, Kelley's, which, if the mountain could be cleared of Rebels, was reachable from Bridgeport by steamboat.

The road from Chattanooga to Kelley's Ferry was out of the range of the Rebel artillery on Lookout Mountain. If the Federals could drive the Confederates from Brown's Ferry and the heights of Raccoon Mountain, thus opening the road, they could get their supplies into Chattanooga with an overland haul of only eight miles.

Smith suggested that two forces move on Brown's Ferry—one marching across Moccasin Point while the other drifted down the river from Chattanooga in pontoon boats. After the waterborne force overpowered the pickets on the Confederate side of the river, the combined forces would build a bridge with the pontoons and move on to occupy the road to Kelley's Ferry.

Meanwhile, Major General Joseph Hooker would send a third force, reinforcements totaling 20,000 men from his Army of the Potomac, across the Tennessee on pontoons at Bridgeport. Major General Oliver O. Howard would lead the way with two divisions totaling 5,000 men, under Generals Carl Schurz and Adolph von Steinwehr. Brigadier General John W. Geary's division of 1,500 men would form a rear guard. These troops would march eastward along the railroad that crossed the peninsula, around the flanks of the lightly held Raccoon Mountain to Wauhatchie, a hamlet just west of Lookout Mountain. They would thereby exert additional pressure on the Rebels from the west, helping to solidify the gains made by the Chattanooga force.

It was a daring plan that would also take advantage of the fact that many of the Confederates were as wet, cold, and hungry as the Federals. Grant endorsed it enthusiastically.

Preparations began in strictest secrecy, and at 3:00 a.m. on October 27 the Union troops left Chattanooga. While 3,500 infantrymen under Brigadier General John B.

Gliding silently past the Confederate outposts, General Hazen's troops prepare to land their pontoon boats at Brown's Ferry. Lashing their craft together, the Federals constructed a bridge over the Tennessee River and established a new supply line by midafternoon.

Infantrymen of the 18th Ohio, some of whom are shown here, literally held the success of the Brown's Ferry operation in their hands—as oarsmen for the boats that carried Hazen's troops. Recruited from southeastern counties of the Buckeye State that bordered the Ohio River, many soldiers of the 18th had worked as rivermen before the war and were a natural choice for this job. The regiment suffered 184 dead from combat or disease before it mustered out in November 1864.

Men of the Federal Quartermaster Corps stand ready to transfer sacks of grain from the steamboat Kingston to waiting wagons at Chattanooga. The Kingston, armed with a cannon on its bow, had safely completed the voyage from Bridgeport, with food for the army's bone-thin horses and men.

Turchin marched toward Brown's Ferry with three batteries of artillery, Brigadier General William B. Hazen and 1,500 men began floating down the river in 50 oar-equipped pontoons and two flatboats. After two tense hours of silent drifting, the lead boats spotted the signal fires lit on the Federal side of the river to mark the spot where they should row to the opposite shore. The surprise was total. Hazen's men

---

"We've knocked the cover off the cracker box!"

---

sprang from the boats and scattered the Rebel pickets.

Colonel William C. Oates, commanding six companies of Alabamians on the ridge above Brown's Ferry, heard the gunfire and counterattacked. But Turchin's men had already begun to cross the river in the pontoon boats. The outnumbered Rebels soon withdrew.

By 4:30 p.m., the Federals had a pontoon bridge across the river. The operation had cost them just six lives among 38 total casualties. An exultant General Hazen strode along his lines, yelling to his men, "We've knocked the cover off the cracker box!"

The Confederate command on Lookout Mountain reacted slowly. Longstreet apparently regarded the action at Brown's Ferry as insignificant and did not even bother to inform Bragg. But although Bragg had not assigned enough troops to defend the landing, he realized its importance. When he heard the news of its loss on the morning of October 28, he angrily demanded that Longstreet regain it at once, using both of his divisions, with a third division borrowed from Major General John C. Breckinridge's corps in reserve.

For reasons never fully explained, Longstreet waited all day before acting. And while he hesitated, Hooker's eastbound forces advanced. On the evening of October 28, they halted for the night, Howard's contingent about a mile from Brown's Ferry and Geary's at Wauhatchie, three miles to the south.

Longstreet, apparently misunderstanding Bragg's intent, chose to ignore the strengthening Federal grip on Brown's Ferry to go after Geary's smaller force at Wauhatchie, employing a risky night assault by Colonel John Bratton's brigade of Brigadier General Micah Jenkins' division. Meanwhile, brigades led by Brigadier Generals Evander M. Law and Jerome B. Robertson were to block the Brown's Ferry-Wauhatchie road to prevent Howard from sending reinforcements to Geary.

About half past midnight on October 29, Bratton's troops attacked. Although surprised and outnumbered, the Federals had the advantage of knowing exactly where their own men were and thus could shoot in the dark without fear of hitting one another. Geary also had four cannon. For three hours the fighting raged around the railroad tracks. The Yankees were running low on ammunition when suddenly

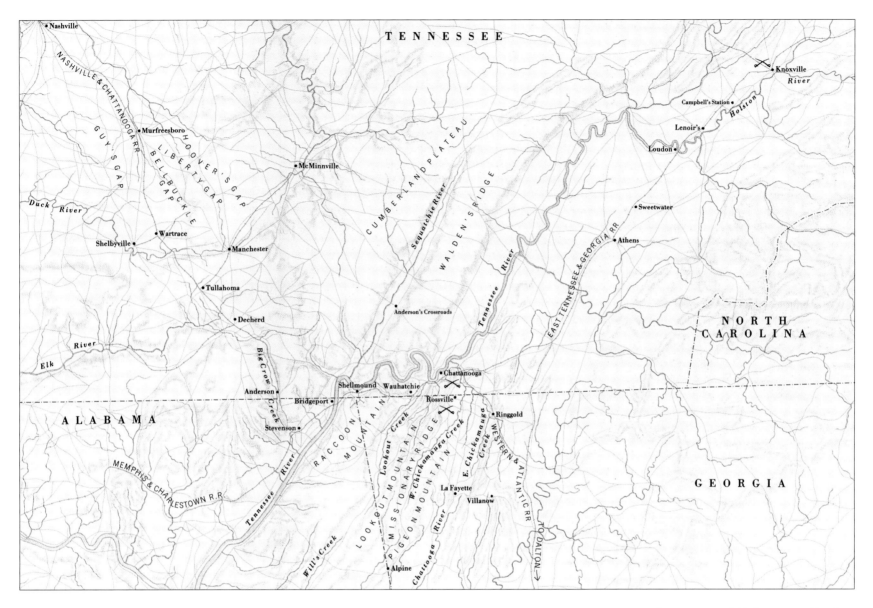

By early October 1863 all of Tennessee but its extreme eastern part was in Federal hands. Ambrose Burnside held Knoxville, guarding the Cumberland Gap. William S. Rosecrans held Chattanooga, although under siege from Bragg's Confederates following the Federal defeat at Chickamauga. To break the stalemate at Chattanooga, President Lincoln placed Ulysses S. Grant in overall command and authorized Joseph Hooker, in Virginia, and William Tecumseh Sherman, on the Mississippi, to converge on Chattanooga. With Grant, Hooker, and Sherman in place, and Rosecrans replaced by George H. Thomas, the stage was set for a series of battles around Chattanooga, the so-called Gateway to the South.

the Rebels broke off and retreated. Meanwhile, Howard's troops, moving toward the sound of the guns, had outflanked and driven Law's and Robertson's Confederates from the hills overlooking the Brown's Ferry-Wauhatchie road.

Later that same day, a makeshift steamboat pulling two barges of rations and forage docked at Kelley's Ferry. "Baldy" Smith's audacious plan had worked to perfection. Less than one week after his arrival in Chattanooga, Grant had opened up the Cracker Line—and none too soon. Only four boxes of hardtack remained in the warehouse. Soon that trickle of supplies would become a torrent of 30 railroad carloads daily. And with Sherman's corps approaching from the west, momentum in the struggle for Chattanooga had shifted to the Federals.

THE WAR IN EAST TENNESSEE—RECEPTION OF GENERAL BURNSIDE BY THE UNIONISTS OF KNOXVILLE.—[SEE NEXT PAGE.]

Residents celebrate the September 1863 entry into Knoxville of Burnside's Union army in this Harper's Weekly engraving. The city and the surrounding East Tennessee region had voted by a margin of 2 to 1 to remain with the Union in the state's 1861 secession vote. But much of the rest of Tennessee's people were strongly secessionist, and the isolated and outnumbered Unionists had suffered greatly at their hands since the vote. With Burnside's arrival, one observer wrote, "The people seem frantic with joy. . . . The old flag has been hidden in mattresses and under carpets. It now floats to the breeze at every staff in East Tennessee."

MAJOR GENERAL AMBROSE E. BURNSIDE

BLOODY SIDESHOW AT KNOXVILLE

The Federal victory at Brown's Ferry and the botched Confederate counterattack at Wauhatchie worsened the already poisonous relationship between Bragg and Longstreet. Throughout that cold, wet, miserable October, President Jefferson Davis and Bragg's own restive generals had plied the commander of the Army of Tennessee with proposals for routing the Federals out of Chattanooga, but Bragg had rejected them all.

On the other hand, a suggestion from Davis arrived on October 29 that Bragg endorsed wholeheartedly. "It has occurred to me," Davis wrote, "that you might advantageously assign General Longstreet with his two divisions to the task of expelling Burnside from Knoxville."

Bragg wasted no time in implementing the president's suggestion. Here at last was a way to rid himself of the most formidable of the critics around him. Sending Longstreet to east Tennessee, he confided frankly to Davis, "will be a great relief to me."

> ## *"It was to be the fate of our army to wait until all good opportunities had passed, and then, in desperation, seize upon the least favorable movement."*

Longstreet was appalled. Attacking Knoxville now made no military sense to him. His force numbered 10,000 infantry—the divisions of Major General Lafayette McLaws and Brigadier General Micah Jenkins—along with Major General Joseph Wheeler's 5,000 cavalry. Without more men he would be at a disadvantage against Burnside's superior forces: 12,000 infantry and 8,500 cavalry.

More important, his departure would leave the Army of Tennessee with only about 40,000 men to confront an enemy growing in numbers and confidence. With the arrival of Sherman, Grant's army at Chattanooga would total about 60,000. By separating the Confederate forces, Longstreet argued unavailingly to Bragg, "We thus expose both to failure, and really take no chance to ourselves of great results."

As his troops packed to move north on November 5, Longstreet gloomily wrote to General Simon Buckner that "it was to be the fate of our army to wait until all good opportunities had passed, and then, in desperation, seize upon the least favorable movement."

The events of the next few days only deepened his pessimism. The East Tennessee & Georgia Railroad was so decrepit it took eight days to haul all of his regiments 60 miles to Sweetwater—about halfway to Knoxville. And contrary to

This two-image panorama, photographed during the siege, looks east from East Tennessee University toward downtown Knoxville. A Federal encampment appears to the left of the Second Presbyterian Church in the background at left center. Union earthworks line the hills in the distance and across the Holston River at right, and Union cannon can be seen in the right foreground. The Confederate attack came from the northwest, to the left rear of where the photographer was standing. Many Unionists, like those shown at right, came back to Knoxville after having hidden out for months or years to avoid being jailed, beaten, or even killed for their political beliefs.

promises Bragg had made, no surplus food or warm clothing awaited him there. "We found ourselves in a strange country," Longstreet later recalled, "not as much as a day's rations on hand, with hardly enough land transportation for ordinary camp equipage, the enemy in front to be captured, and our friends in rear putting in their paper bullets." It was beginning to look, he noted bitterly, "more like a campaign against Longstreet than against Burnside."

Longstreet's adversary, Major General Ambrose E. Burnside, had failed conspicuously fighting against him at Fredericksburg 11 months earlier. But Burnside had not ducked the well-deserved blame for that bloody disaster and had soldiered on, doing good service by leading the Army of the Ohio on a flawless advance from Cincinnati to Knoxville in mid-August. He had flanked the Rebels out of their position at Cumberland Gap and raced for Knoxville, covering as many as 30 miles a day.

East Tennessee was pro-Union country. Residents of the area had voted 2 to 1 to reject secession in 1861, and in the two years since, these staunch Unionist Southerners had suffered grievously at the hands of secessionists. Thus, when Burnside's Federals entered the town on September 2, most of its citizens gave them a joyous welcome.

Now, however, Longstreet's advance on Knoxville frightened the authorities in Washington, who began pressuring Grant to do something to help. But Burnside himself had no such fears. Announcing that his men were "ready to meet any force the enemy might send against us," he proposed engaging the Confederates south of Knoxville, then giving ground slowly to protract the affair, thereby keeping Longstreet's forces out of the forthcoming battle at Chattanooga. Grant gave his blessing to the plan, and Burnside set out with about 5,000 men, leaving the rest behind to complete Knoxville's defenses.

"*The earth was sated in blood—men waded in blood, and struggled up the scarp, and slipping in blood fell back … in the gory mud below.*"

A Federal sentry stands atop the northwest wall of Fort Sanders in Knoxville. The main Confederate attack on the fort came from the right, over the flats, through telegraph wire entanglements, and into the ditch ringing the bastion.

The 79th New York High-landers had marched to war in 1861 proudly wearing kilts or tartan pants called trews. By 1863 the battle-scarred veterans had given up their costumes for blue uniforms. As can be seen in this photograph of Highlander James Berry, only the soft caps called glengarries remained of their regalia.

November 29. A few hours later, McLaws' three brigades launched a bayonet charge. The morning air was wet and raw, the ground frozen. As the Confederates ran forward yelling, the defenders opened fire at point-blank range. The 79th New York Highlanders, a regiment of mostly Scottish-born immigrants, bore the brunt of the attack.

Suddenly the charging men began falling to the ground, entangled in a web of telegraph wire strung among the stumps left when the approaches to the fort were cleared. Once the wires were cleared away, the attackers leaped into the ditch, only to find themselves trapped by an ice-covered wall rising 16 feet before them. A murderous fire poured down on them. It was a massacre.

"The earth," wrote a Northern correspondent, "was sated in blood—men waded in blood, and struggled up the scarp, and slipping in blood fell back to join their mangled predecessors in the gory mud below. The shouts of the foiled and infuriate Rebels, the groans of the dying and shrieks of the wounded arose above the din of the cannon."

After about 20 minutes, Longstreet called a halt to the slaughter. By the time the firing died down, his men had suffered 813 casualties and done almost no damage to the enemy. It was, one Federal officer observed, "Fredericksburg reversed."

Shortly after this terrible repulse, a courier handed Longstreet a message from President Davis. Momentous events had occurred at Chattanooga that would alter the course of the war.

Burnside's troops met the Confederates on November 15 on the heights south of town. His cavalry force under Brigadier General William P. Sanders, although outnumbered, compelled three brigades of Confederate horsemen to pull back. Over the next few days, Longstreet tried his best to outflank the Federals and trap them outside Knoxville. But each time, first at Lenoir's Station, and then at Campbell's Station, the Yankees escaped. By November 17 they were safely back within the now well-fortified town.

But food and forage were scarce, and as the days passed both armies suffered. The Rebels, poorly supplied to begin with, far from their nearest base, and among hostile people, were, if anything, worse off than the Yankees.

After a week's deliberation, Longstreet decided to focus his attack on the redoubt at the northwest corner of town. The Federals had named it Fort Sanders in honor of Burnside's gallant cavalry chief, who had been mortally wounded in a skirmish on November 18. The fort had earthen walls eight feet high and was fronted by a 12-foot-wide ditch that was also—unknown to Longstreet—quite deep. Cannon projecting from the corners of the fort enfiladed the ditch, making it a deadly trap. But because the fort was situated only 120 yards from a creek bed where a large body of troops could assemble under cover, Longstreet chose it as the target of his attack.

All was ready by November 24. But when Longstreet learned that reinforcements were on the way from Bragg, he decided to wait for them. Then bad weather and further debate about where to focus the attack caused more delays. Finally, on November 28, upon hearing rumors of a Confederate disaster at Chattanooga, Longstreet decided he must attack that night. "There is neither safety nor honor in any other course," he declared.

Rebel skirmishers seized outlying Federal rifle pits sometime after midnight,

This engraving depicts Rebel troops attempting to climb out of the ditch and scale the front wall of Fort Sanders. The ditch was, on average, eight feet deep; once in it the men were confronted by an almost vertical, slippery wall rising 16 feet. Some soldiers leaped onto the shoulders of others to try to reach the top of the wall. Those who made it were shot down. Men, one observer wrote, "struggled up the scarp, and slipping in blood fell back to join their mangled predecessors in the gory mud below."

THE BATTLES FOR CHATTANOOGA

Ulysses S. Grant was an offensive-minded soldier, and he found it intolerable to remain cooped up in Chattanooga, surrounded by towering hills infested with the enemy. Shortly after opening up the Cracker Line, he advised General in Chief Henry W. Halleck: "If the rebels give me one week more time, all danger of losing territory now held by us will have passed and preparations may commence for offensive operations."

All that was needed was the arrival of General William Tecumseh Sherman's Army of the Tennessee. Sherman's march from Memphis had been slowed to a snail's pace by Halleck's order to repair the Memphis & Charleston Railroad line along the way. On November 2 Grant countermanded the order, directing Sherman to turn over the task to Brigadier General Grenville M. Dodge, an experienced railroad builder, and "hurry eastward with all possible dispatch toward Bridgeport."

To defeat the Confederates, Grant would have to attack an enemy entrenched on high ground, and he planned his offensive carefully. Upon Sherman's arrival, Grant would have three forces at his disposal; he would give the pivotal role in the assault to the army led by his old friend. There were few men in the world Grant trusted as he did Sherman—and he had great faith in the Army of the Tennessee, for it was his own former command.

Seated in front of a map of the South, Sherman clasps his son, Thomas Ewing Sherman, known as Tommy. Sherman did not want his boys to become soldiers; he thought a military career was "too full of blind chances."

Grant viewed his other two forces with skepticism. He suspected that Hooker's XI and XII Corps had been sent to him as castoffs from the Army of the Potomac, and the Army of the Cumberland had just suffered a defeat. According to Sherman, Grant thought that the latter force "had been so demoralized by the battle of Chickamauga that he feared they could not be got out of their trenches to assume the offensive."

Sherman's target would be Bragg's strategic flank, his right—at the junction of the Confederate supply line from the south and line of communication with Longstreet in the north. Sherman would march from Bridgeport to Brown's Ferry, cross to the north side of the Tennessee River, and move into the hills north of Chattanooga.

This movement could not be concealed from Confederate observers on Lookout Mountain, but Grant hoped to confuse them about where the Federals were going. Once out of sight, Sherman would make camp. Then, in a rapid nighttime move, he would bridge the river—General William Smith was already building the necessary pontoons—whisk his men across, and before Bragg knew what was happening, roll up the Confederate right along Missionary Ridge. Bragg would thus be cut off from his supply base at Chickamauga Station and driven away, if not destroyed.

Grant gave Hooker and Thomas supporting roles. He ordered Hooker's XII Corps to move around Lookout Mountain and threaten the Confederate left at Rossville Gap while the XI Corps, under Howard, remained in reserve on the north side of the river, opposite Chattanooga. Thomas was to give artillery support to Sherman and later to assault the Confederate center.

On November 15 Sherman, traveling well in advance of his army, finally reached Chattanooga. The next day Grant took him to study the terrain at the north end of

The town of Bridgeport, Alabama, lines the far bank of the Tennessee River in this photograph taken across the Nashville & Chattanooga Railroad bridge. The original railway bridge had been burned by the Confederates before the Battle of Chickamauga, and the Yankees had quickly constructed a pontoon bridge at the same location. The sturdy bridge pictured here was built after the siege had been lifted, when supplies could travel safely again by rail from Bridgeport to Chattanooga.

"They had about 8,000 men and eight guns. We had some 600 men and no guns."

CAPTAIN WILLIAM L. JENNEY

Staff, Major General William T. Sherman

Jenney's mysterious cake became part of the spoils of war when, on October 11, a division of Nathan Bedford Forrest's Rebel cavalry under General James R. Chalmers attacked the transport train hastening William T. Sherman from Memphis to confer with Grant at Chattanooga. The Union troops held onto their train after a spirited fight, but not before the daring horse soldiers took more than 100 Union prisoners and captured or burned most of the Federal supplies on the freight cars.

General Grant ordered General Sherman to report with his army with the greatest possible haste at Chattanooga. Sherman embarked on boats and landed at Memphis, where the march began. As the railroads were fully occupied in carrying supplies, the troops were forced to go on foot.

Sherman had a special train to take himself, staff and escort to Corinth. Just as we were leaving Memphis a German, with a large cheese box in his hands, appeared at the train, inquiring for Captain Jenney. I announced myself and asked him what he wished. "Oh, Captain, I told my wife what you had done for me, and she sent you this cake. Take it."

"What did I do for you?" I asked. "I don't remember anything."

"Yes, you did, here is the cake."

Just at this moment the train started. About noon we made preparations for lunch and opened the box which contained a large, handsomely frosted cake. Just as we were about to cut it the train stopped and someone ran in and called to us: "Get out of here as quickly as you can. The road is cut ahead of us and we are stopped by Chalmers' cavalry."

We got out of the cars as quickly as we could. Directly above us on the bank was the redoubt of Collierville, of which we took possession. Sherman immediately stepped into the telegraph office and telegraphed to Corse, who was some dozen miles away, stating the situation and ordering him to come to our relief double quick. Corse happened to be within easy reach and replied at once, "I am coming," so that we felt sure of relief ere long.

The enemy immediately commenced an attack on the redoubt and bombarded us with eight pieces of artillery for four hours. They had about 8,000 men and eight guns. We had some 600 men and no guns. Twice they got possession of our train when an assault from the ditch cleaned them out. On top of the cars we had brought a battalion of the Thirteenth United States Infantry. Numerous assaults were made by the enemy, which were always repulsed.

Two or three times one of the men would scream out: "There is a rebel who is trying to steal our knapsacks!" which were left on the top of the car, and would fire at him. "No," said the officer, "that is our man, Tom Smith, who is dead drunk and did not get off with us." As soon as the firing was over, some of his comrades climbed onto the car to see how many times Tom, who had been under the cross fire from both sides, had been shot. To their astonishment he was found to be entirely uninjured and woke up quite sober.

Our horses had not escaped so well. My own was wounded in the car and the train was generally riddled with bullets, broken glass, etc., and there was a cannon shot through the engine so that we were obliged to wait all night till a train could be sent for us from Corinth. I went down to our car which I found had been pretty well cleaned out by the enemy. Everything of any value had been taken—among other things, my cake. As I stood on the platform a soldier passed along with a large piece of cake in his hand. He called out, "Who had the cake?" I replied that I did, but it was all gone, and asked him where he had got that piece. "Took it out of the hand of a dead rebel—there under the fence. It is real good. He had his mouth full but I let him keep that."

I never was able to learn who presented me with that cake, nor could I recall the German nor anything that I had ever done for him.

"I thought from the pain which I experienced that the bullet had passed through my body, and was rather disgusted when an examination revealed the fact that I was knocked out without a scar to show for it."

CAPTAIN JOSEPH T. PATTON

93d Ohio Infantry, Hazen's Brigade

While Willich's brigade charged directly at Orchard Knob, Hazen's men—fresh from victory at Brown's Ferry—attacked the ridge on the right, defended by the 28th Alabama. Although the 93d eventually helped overrun the position, Patton and 56 other members of the regiment fell before the vicious fusillades of musketry delivered by the Alabamians.

On Nov. 23d we issued sixty rounds of ammunition to the men and turned out as if for drill. The rebels from their position in our front were enabled to watch our every move; and supposing that we were turning out for a grand review, took no measure to meet the advance which soon followed.

The 93d was a part of the front line, and when the word "forward" was given, advanced in battle line without skirmishers. The rebel pickets fired and fled at our approach. When within charging distance of their line of breastworks, "Fix bayonets! Forward, double quick!" were the orders which followed in quick succession. The enemy were now fully alive as to the purpose of our movements, and opened fire from sixty pieces of artillery from Missionary Ridge; the infantry from behind their breastworks also opened a most destructive musketry fire, but the gallant boys pressed forward through this terrible storm of iron and lead which was rained upon them, without a halt or waver.

The rebel works were reached and over them the boys went, capturing many prisoners. Our Lieutenant Colonel, Bowman, was on the right of the regiment; as he passed around the end of the works he encountered a rebel with his gun aimed at him. With drawn sword the Colonel rushed at the fellow with the exclamation, "Damn you, you shoot me and I'll cut your head off." The force of the Colonel's remark had the desired effect as the reb dropped his gun and surrendered.

Orchard Knob and the first line of works were ours, but not without heavy loss, as more than one-third of our regiment were killed or wounded in the charge. Three color-bearers fell, the fourth planting *Old Glory* on the enemy's works.

As we started on the charge, I was turning toward the left of my company when a bullet struck a diary which was in the right breast pocket of my blouse, glanced downward and struck my sword belt-plate, which was bent until it was of no further use. Fortunately for my present usefulness, I had buckled my belt under my blouse before starting, which saved my life, as the diary stopped the bullet from passing through my right breast, and the belt-plate prevented it passing through my bowels.

The blow sent me to grass and left me insensible. When the stretcher bearers discovered me, they decided that I was dead and that they would first care for the wounded. (My name appeared in the newspapers as among the killed). How long I remained there I have no means of knowing, but was finally removed to camp where I had comfortable quarters and my colored boy to care for me. The blow had broken my ribs and injured my spine. I thought from the pain which I experienced that the bullet had passed through my body, and was rather disgusted when an examination revealed the fact that I was knocked out without a scar to show for it.

Missionary Ridge—the objective Grant had chosen for him. Sherman stared through a telescope for a few moments, then closed up the glass with a snap and pronounced: "I can do it!" Soon he was on the move again, retracing his route to Bridgeport to marshal his forces.

The attack was scheduled for dawn on November 21. On November 19 the Army of the Tennessee set out from Bridgeport for the 35-to-40-mile march to its jumping-off point. But the weather did not cooperate. A heavy rain turned the roads to mud, and the march slowed to a crawl. It was November 20 before Sherman's vanguard reached Brown's Ferry, and the rest of the army was strung out all the way back to Bridgeport. Grant decided to postpone the attack.

A fresh downpour began on November 20 and continued through the following day. The river began to rise, threatening the pontoon bridge at Brown's Ferry. When all of Sherman's divisions but one were across, the bridge gave way—stranding the remaining men, commanded by Brigadier General Peter J. Osterhaus. Grant ordered Osterhaus to join Hooker in Lookout Valley. Meanwhile, Sherman's other divisions disappeared into the hills above Chattanooga, and Howard's XI Corps crossed the bridge at Chattanooga and moved in behind Thomas' defenses.

Grant hoped that the Confederates, having first seen Sherman's troops crossing at Brown's Ferry and then, a short time later, Howard's troops moving across the river into Chattanooga, would conclude that they were the same force. To make up for the loss of Osterhaus, Grant assigned Sherman one of Thomas' divisions, commanded by Brigadier General Jefferson C. Davis, and rescheduled the attack for November 24.

As Grant had hoped, the Confederates were thoroughly confused. Bragg, watching all those enemy troops moving around, fretted about Sherman's location and intentions. He finally concluded that Sherman was marching on Knoxville, and, on November 22, ordered Buckner's and Major General Patrick R. Cleburne's divisions to entrain north to reinforce Longstreet. Buckner left immediately. Cleburne marched his troops to Chickamauga Station to await the return of the train carrying Buckner.

Bragg then tried a ruse of his own. Under a flag of truce, he sent Grant a letter. "As there may still be some noncombatants in Chattanooga," Bragg wrote, "I deem it proper to notify you that prudence would dictate their early withdrawal." Grant puzzled over the message. For some reason Bragg wanted him to think he was planning an attack. The mystery deepened when a Confederate deserter falsely reported that Bragg was pulling back from Missionary Ridge. The deserter's report galvanized Grant. He urgently needed to know if the Confederates were actually withdrawing. If so, this would be an ideal time to strike. Someone had to test the Rebel reflexes. Sherman was not yet ready, but Thomas was.

Early on the morning of November 23, Grant gave Thomas his instructions. In Chattanooga Valley, the plain lying between the city and Missionary Ridge, rose a wooded mound about 100 feet high called Orchard Knob. For weeks Bragg's men had held the valley, including the hill. Now Grant wanted Thomas to conduct a

Yankee skirmishers in the foreground of this Harper's Weekly engraving engage Rebel pickets of the 24th Alabama—whose positions are indicated by the puffs of smoke issuing from their weapons— atop Orchard Knob. The rounded hillock and the small but rugged ridge that ran southward from it, also visible in this illustration, were terrain anomalies in the otherwise flat plain that stretched between Chattanooga and Missionary Ridge. By capturing this high ground the afternoon of November 23, the Union gained a launching point for their attacks on Missionary Ridge.

reconnaissance in force to see if the Rebels were still there.

The Chattanooga Valley and its surrounding hills formed a magnificent natural amphitheater. Grant wrote later that it was "the first battle field I have ever seen where a plan could be followed, and from one place the whole field be within one view."

Onto this stage at noon on November 23 marched the division of Brigadier General Thomas J. Wood. On Wood's right was Major General Philip H. Sheridan's division. Still smarting over their rout at Chickamauga, the men were determined to prove their mettle.

As Wood's and Sheridan's men marched onto the plain, soldiers on both sides stopped to watch. On the hills looming over the plain, clusters of Confederates could be seen gazing at the display. Like many of the Federals, they believed for a moment that Thomas was holding a grand review. At about 2:00 p.m., a signal cannon boomed, and the blue-clad lines surged forward. Suddenly the Confederate pickets realized they were under attack by a force many times their number. In just a few hours it was all over. Thomas' men had seized Orchard Knob and driven a mile-deep salient into the center of Bragg's line. Thomas moved swiftly to strengthen the position. The Rebel earthworks on the hill were reversed to face the Confederates and a six-gun battery brought up.

This photograph, reportedly taken on November 24 during the Battle of Lookout Mountain, shows General Hooker (standing, third from right) with his staff at the base of the mountain. After leading the Army of the Potomac to defeat at Chancellorsville, Hooker had languished without a command until given the XI and XII Corps in September 1863. Despite Hooker's success on Lookout Mountain, Sherman passed him over for promotion, and in 1864 he was relieved from field service at his own request.

Orchard Knob had been a minor but instructive action. It showed Grant that Bragg had not withdrawn, and Bragg now knew that Grant was intent on attack. Hastily, Bragg recalled Cleburne's division from Chickamauga Station and pulled Brigadier General William H. T. Walker's division off Lookout Mountain and placed it about a mile from the north end of Missionary Ridge.

By now Sherman's men were safely hidden in the woods eight miles northwest of Chattanooga, ready for a nighttime river crossing and a morning attack. Late that night Grant told Hooker that instead of simply making a demonstration against Lookout Mountain, he should now attempt to capture it. In the game of cat and mouse that Grant and Bragg were playing, Grant had seized an advantage, and he intended to keep it.

LOOKOUT MOUNTAIN

Shortly after midnight on November 24, the Federal offensive began. A pontoon boat filled with 30 men pushed off from the mouth of North Chickamauga Creek into the swift current of the Tennessee River and drifted downstream. Near the mouth of South Chickamauga Creek, the oarsmen rowed to the Confederate side of the river. The small force scrambled ashore and easily overcame the handful of Rebel pickets.

Within 15 minutes 1,000 men were floating toward landing sites. A steamer from Chattanooga helped ferry more troops across. As each pontoon boat unloaded,

it was attached to the preceding one, and by noon a bridge 1,350 feet long was in place, allowing the rest of Sherman's three divisions to cross.

About 1:00 p.m., Sherman deployed his troops in three columns and sent them up the hill just east of the river. Astonishingly, there was virtually no opposition. It was not until the attackers had reached the summit that enemy batteries fired on them. The Federals dragged their own artillery up to the top and returned fire. Peering about in the rain and mist, Sherman checked his bearings. He received a ghastly shock—he was on the wrong hill!

Sherman's objective had been the northernmost part of Missionary Ridge, known locally as Tunnel Hill because of the railroad tunnel that passed through its base. His maps showed Missionary Ridge as a continuous range, and the visual observation he had made a few days before had seemed to confirm this. In fact, the stunned general could now see that there was a break in the ridge, and the hill closest to the river—the one on which he was standing—was a separate peak. A deep valley about a mile wide separated him from Tunnel Hill.

Thus, despite the perfect river crossing, Sherman's men remained as far from their objective as ever—and all chance of surprise was now lost. Not knowing the extent of the forces opposing him, and with daylight fast fading, Sherman ordered his men to dig in for the night.

As it happened, his three divisions were opposed only by a single brigade of Texans from Cleburne's division who had rushed to the area that afternoon after Bragg got word that Sherman had crossed the Tennessee. Just a day earlier, Cleburne and his men had been at Chickamauga Station waiting to entrain for Knoxville to help Longstreet when Bragg recalled them. Bragg ordered Cleburne to take the high ground near the mouth of the South Chickamauga and hold it "at all hazards."

Cleburne galloped to the Tunnel Hill area and hastily made what he called "a moonlight survey of the ground." He had heard word of a Confederate "disaster" at Lookout Mountain earlier that day, which convinced him that he would see fierce fighting in the morning.

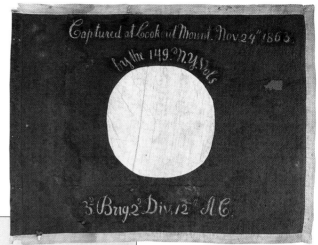

This Confederate flag, carried by a Mississippi regiment in the Battle of Lookout Mountain, was captured during the fighting by Private Peter Kappesser of the 149th New York. The action won fame for Kappesser: He was awarded the Medal of Honor.

In this photograph taken after the Battle of Lookout Mountain, Union soldiers amble among the large boulders on the grounds of the Cravens house looking for souvenirs. These stone outcroppings provided natural breastworks for the Confederates defending the area. The home itself stands to the right, destroyed by the ravages of Union artillery firing from Moccasin Point and Yankees scavenging for firewood. The sheer cliffs in the background are a portion of the famous palisades.

That disaster—a Union victory at Lookout Mountain—had come as a surprise to everyone. While Sherman was launching what was to have been the main attack that morning, Hooker advanced across Lookout Creek and around Lookout Mountain through a narrow gap between its lower slopes and the Tennessee River. Grant had told Hooker that if he saw an opportunity, he could seize the mountain, but his primary mission was to push beyond it and clear the Rebels from Chattanooga Valley, which lay in between Lookout Mountain and Missionary Ridge. Hooker was then to take Rossville Gap and be in position to threaten Bragg's left and rear.

Hooker had 10,000 men in three divisions, one from each of the Federal armies at Chattanooga: Geary's from the Army of the Potomac, Brigadier General Charles Cruft's from the Army of the Cumberland, and Osterhaus' from the Army of the Tennessee.

Hooker began the movement across Lookout Creek about 8:00 a.m. He divided his forces, sending Geary's division and one of Cruft's two brigades, commanded by Brigadier General Walter C. Whitaker, south to Wauhatchie, where the creek was fordable. There the Federals waded across, capturing some 40 Rebel pickets and driving off the rest.

Feeling their way through the dense fog, Geary's troops tramped halfway up the western slope. Then they worked their way northward, along the base of an almost vertical cliff, toward a rendezvous with the rest of Hooker's force at the gap between the mountain and the river. Resistance was light, but the march was "laborious and extremely toilsome," Whitaker reported later, "over the steep, rocky, ravine-seamed, torrent-torn sides of the mountain."

Meanwhile, Osterhaus' division and Cruft's other brigade crossed a bridge a mile and a half north of the ford that Geary had used.

Bragg's forces on Lookout Mountain numbered about 7,000, but they were widely scattered, and only a fraction were in position to defend the plateau at the northern end of the pinnacle. Earlier, Bragg had moved most of Hardee's corps to Missionary Ridge to deal with Sherman's threat. To compensate, Breckinridge had extended the left of his corps under Major General Carter L. Stevenson to cover Lookout. But Stevenson did not arrive until a few hours before Hooker's attack began, and he was unfamiliar with the terrain.

About 10:00 a.m. Geary's troops rounded the shoulder of the mountain at the Cravens farm and encountered a Confederate force led by Brigadier General Edward C. Walthall. As sharp fighting erupted, Geary anchored his right on the base of some nearby cliffs and wheeled his line forward until his left joined with the right of Osterhaus' oncoming division. Now the Federal line extended about a half-mile from the Cravens farm down the slope to the Chattanooga road at the foot of the mountain.

To resist the advance of this 10,000-man juggernaut, Walthall had only 1,489 men. And the Confederate batteries on the summit could not depress their guns enough to help. Federal artillery, meanwhile, had found the range and began pounding the enemy. By 1:00 p.m., after three hours of fighting, the Rebels had pulled back into a second line of entrenchments 400 yards east of the Cravens

house. Shortly afterward, they received reinforcements, and as darkness fell the battered defenders still held their ground.

Despite their doughty stand, however, Bragg feared they might soon be overwhelmed, and in the night he withdrew them. Next morning a small detail of Yankees from a Kentucky regiment climbed up and unfurled the Stars and Stripes high on a cliff top, evoking round after round of cheers from the thousands of men on the spreading plains below. Whatever frustrations Sherman was experiencing at Missionary Ridge, Lookout Mountain was now in Federal hands.

While three Union divisions advance toward Lookout Mountain on November 24, 1863, General Hooker, riding a white horse at center, directs artillery fire on Confederate emplacements low on the fog-shrouded slopes. His greatest challenge, Hooker later claimed, was to curb his eager troops' "disposition to engage, regardless of circumstances and, it appears, of consequences."

Depicted as fearlessly reconnoitering the field in the heat of battle, General Hooker confers with an infantryman while his staff officers prudently take shelter behind shell-torn pine trees. English-born artist James Walker, according to some critics, exaggerated the valor of Hooker, who commissioned the battle scene below at a cost of $20,000.

LIEUTENANT ALBION W. TOURGEE

105th Ohio Infantry, Van Derveer's Brigade

Tourgée and the soldiers of the Army of the Cumberland had an unparalleled view of the fighting taking place on Lookout Mountain, hundreds of feet above their position on the plain east of Chattanooga. But when the fog closed over the action, the anxious Yankees below cocked their ears, straining to hear the faint sounds of combat. In this account, Tourgée mistakenly claims that he saw Hooker in the fight; it was most likely a regimental or brigade commander whom he saw riding by.

//

After a little it became apparent that the fire was coming nearer. A white mist, the remnant of the night's storm, still hung about the nose of Lookout. Now and then, the wind swept it aside, till we could see the crest; sometimes the palisades below. Anon, the white veil would settle over it all and only the rattle of musketry would come out of the sunlit cloud. All at once it flashed upon us that this demonstration against the Ridge in our front was a feint and that Hooker was trying to take the Lookout—was taking it as we were soon assured. After a while faint cheers could be heard. How intently we listened. "That's no corn bread yell" went along the line, as every eye and every field-glass was turned toward the cloud-veiled Mountain. The artillery ceased firing and the two vast armies of Grant and Bragg, in breathless suspense, awaited the outcome of the contest which both realized was no "feint," but a fight to the death. Again and again, the "mudsill" cheer rang, out, each time nearer the palisaded crest. Soon a faint grey line appeared in the open field on the slope of Lookout. Even with the naked eye, it was apparent that it was disorganized and falling back. Through the smoke and mist, the colors sometimes flashed. The gray masses fell slowly back, and a line of blue appeared. As the crimson of the old flag was recognized, Grant's army broke out into cheer after cheer, which must have been inspiring to Hooker's men, and appalling to the enemy. With scarcely a halt to reform, the line of blue moved forward, General Hooker riding his white horse, following close upon the charging column. The Confederates, fell slowly back, rallying and breaking again, until with a sudden rush they made for a line of works which seemed extended from the foot of the palisade down the slope between the timber and the open field. Here they made a last stand; with a rush our brave fellows swept up to the works, but so stubborn was the resistance that for a moment it seemed to us that the lines and colors were intermingled and the assailants captured. But the enemy's colors soon broke to the rear, and disappeared in the woods. The clouds settled down over the scene and only desultory firing was kept up. Until night-fall and even after, a few scattering shots were heard on the slope. Then all was still. The audacity of the plan and the suddenness of its execution paralyzed the enemy, and amazed those who witnessed its execution.

In this dramatic lithograph, dawn pierces clouds and mist obscuring Lookout Mountain as jubilant Union soldiers ascend the slopes on their way to a victory. Grant belittled the victory, considering it a minor action, but the capture of the height was, for many, the symbolic end of the long siege of Chattanooga.

CAPTAIN JOHN WILSON

8th Kentucky (U.S.) Infantry, Whitaker's Brigade

Before dawn on November 25 Wilson led a small detachment to the very summit of Lookout Mountain, where they unfurled their regiment's national flag. As the sun came up over Chattanooga, its rays fell upon the banner, creating a sight that dismayed Confederates and elated Union troops. At right, Wilson's squad reenacts their climb using scaling ladders that had been left behind by the Confederates.

W e were placed in one of the columns on the extreme right that marched around the palisades of Lookout Mountain on the 24th of November. We marched around to the nose or point of the mountain and lay that night above the Craven House. Just before daylight on the 25th, Gen. Whitaker came to our regiment and said:

"Col. Barnes, have you an officer that will volunteer to carry your flag and place it on the top of the mountain?"

I said, "General, I will go."

Turning to the regiment, he said: "How many of you will go with Capt. Wilson? I could order you up there, but will not, for it is a hazardous undertaking; but for the flag that gets there first it will be an honor."

Five men went with me. I handed my sword to my Color-Sergeant to bring up, and I took the flag and started, accompanied by Sergeant James Wood, Company H; Private William Witt, Company A; Sergeant Harris H. Davis, Company E; Sergeant Joseph Wagers, Company B; and Private Joseph Bradley, Company I.

Those who have seen the awe-inspiring precipice at the top of the great mountain can realize what a serious undertaking was before us, not to mention our lack of knowledge concerning the Confederates, who the day before had held Hooker at bay. Dim daylight was dawning. We crept cautiously upward, clutching at rocks and bushes, supporting each other, using sticks and poles and such other aids as we could gather. At every step we expected to be greeted with deadly missiles of some sort from the enemy. But fortune favored us, and before sun-up I, in front, reached the summit and planted the flag on top of Lookout Mountain. It was the highest flag that was planted during the war. Soon other detachments came up and congratulated me and my party, and we were the lions of the day in the Union army.

Captain Wilson poses on one of Lookout Mountain's numerous rock ledges with the five soldiers of the 8th Kentucky (right) who helped him signal victory by carrying the first Union flag to the crest of the mountain. From left to right stand Sergeant Joseph Wagers, Private Joseph Bradley, Sergeant Harris Davis, Private William Witt, and Sergeant James Wood. The bearded, 49-year-old Wilson balances at the edge of the stone outcropping, holding the flag. All of the men were granted 30-day furloughs for their brave and inspiring action. In the photograph above, Wilson is visible on the uppermost ladder, waving his hat while he grasps the flagstaff in his left hand. Both photographs were taken months after the battle by Royan M. Linn, who established a studio on the peak to cater to the countless Yankee soldiers and civilians trekking to the now famous site to pose for pictures.

"Fortune favored us, and before sun-up I, in front, reached the summit and planted the flag on top of Lookout Mountain. It was the highest flag that was planted during the war."

CAPTAIN JOHN WILSON

This photograph looks due east toward Tunnel Hill and the passageway that gave the location its name. On November 25 this area was alive with rifle fire and cannon fire and teeming with soldiers locked in mortal strife. Many harried and frightened Union troops thought that Cleburne's graycoats were actually pouring forth from the tunnel. This was a misconception caused by the rugged terrain. The soldiers of the 6th, 10th, and 15th Texas Regiment (consolidated), who mounted the savage counterattack, actually charged down from positions along the steep crest of the hill.

MISSIONARY RIDGE

While multitudes of troops in the valley below broke into wild cheers at the sight of Old Glory flying from Lookout Mountain at dawn on November 25, eight miles to the north at the tip of Missionary Ridge, the outlook for the Federals was anything but cheerful. Although Sherman enjoyed an overwhelming superiority in numbers—an assault force of 26,000 men against 10,000 in the Confederate divisions of Patrick Cleburne and Carter Stevenson—the terrain greatly favored the defenders.

To reach the Rebel line a mile or so away, Sherman's troops would have to descend the hill they had occupied, cross an open valley under fire, and climb another steep slope—Tunnel Hill. The topography made deployment difficult, and it was not until midmorning that Sherman was able to attack. Even then the assaults were piecemeal and poorly coordinated.

The Federals faced a compact line fashioned by Cleburne. Secured on the left by Stevenson's division south of the railroad tunnel, the line ran north for several hundred yards, following the ridge of Tunnel Hill to its summit; then it angled sharply eastward along a spur that descended to South Chickamauga Creek. Cleburne had bolstered the line with artillery on the ridge above the tunnel,

in the angle at the summit, and in the north-facing leg of the line. In the crucial center position atop the hill, he placed the Texas brigade of Brigadier General James A. Smith.

Sherman's attack was spearheaded by Brigadier General John A. Corse's brigade, while another brigade under Colonel John M. Loomis advanced along the western slope toward the tunnel. For five hours the two sides fought, often at close quarters with clubbed muskets and bayonets, but the Federals could not secure a lodgement. Finally about 3:00 p.m., after suffering nearly 2,000 casualties, Sherman called a halt. He sent word to Grant that his men could do no more. Grant dispatched a two-word response: "Attack again."

Sherman obeyed, but only nominally, sending in 200 men from Brigadier General Joseph A. J. Lightburn's brigade. Their ranks were badly cut up, and soon the survivors were reeling back. There would be no more attacks on Tunnel Hill.

Grant wanted to turn a Confederate flank on Missionary Ridge before committing Thomas' Army of the Cumberland, in which he had little faith, against the center of Bragg's line on the ridge. Sherman's failure on Bragg's right lent urgency to Hooker's advance against the Rebel left. That morning, Hooker, as ordered, had taken aim for Rossville Gap but had progressed only as far as Chattanooga Creek by 1:30 p.m. And because the Rebels had destroyed the bridge over the creek, it took him several more hours to make repairs and get his troops across.

Sometime after 3:00 p.m., however, Hooker's forces captured Rossville Gap and secured a foothold on the southern slope of Missionary Ridge. The outnumbered Confederates on that flank, commanded by Breckinridge, slowly and

grudgingly gave way. The destruction of a Confederate flank that Grant had been looking for was under way, but it was the left flank, not the right, and it was Hooker, not Sherman, who was accomplishing it.

Watching the battle unfold from Orchard Knob, Grant decided to wait no longer and ordered Thomas forward to relieve pressure on Sherman. Grant gave Thomas only a limited objective: Take the Confederate rifle pits at the foot of Missionary Ridge and await further instructions.

Generals Granger, Grant, and Thomas, on a ledge at left, watch from Orchard Knob as their troops swarm up Missionary Ridge in the background. "What was on the summit they knew not," Granger wrote, "and did not inquire. The enemy was before them; to know that was to know sufficient."

Federal troops of General Philip H. Sheridan's division sweep up Missionary Ridge in this photograph of part of a lost cyclorama. A lone Rebel defender fires off a round as others surrender and an entire unit withdraws eastward over the crest.

and caught up with the skirmishers. The Confederates in the rifle pits fired a withering volley at 200 yards. Most of them then started heading up the ridge as instructed. But the tactic backfired—it heartened the Federals and dismayed the Rebels higher up on the ridge, who were unaware of Bragg's order and thought their front line was being routed.

The attackers took the rifle pits swiftly but then found themselves exposed to heavy fire from above. Recognizing their predicament, some soldiers started up the hill. More followed, and soon long lines of men began pushing their way up the slope, seemingly heedless of the destruction raining down on them.

"It's all right, if it turns out all right. If not, someone will suffer."

Grant, watching the scene through field glasses on Orchard Knob, wheeled in disbelief and barked at Thomas, "Who ordered those men up the ridge?" Grant was watching a commander's nightmare: a battle gone out of control. At one point, he considered calling the men back. Then he decided to wait a few minutes. "It's all right, if it turns out all right," he muttered. "If not, someone will suffer."

Missionary Ridge was now a scene of swarming activity. The Rebels who had abandoned the rifle pits were racing frantically uphill and interfering with the fire of their comrades on the summit. The climbing Federals, although taking heavy artillery and musket fire, advanced undaunted. "Foot by foot and pace by pace," wrote Colonel Charles G. Harker, whose brigade was in the forefront of the assault, "the crest was being reached to the admiration of all who witnessed it, and to the surprise even of those who participated in the perilous undertaking."

In the face of such determination, the resolution of the Confederates crumbled. Men threw down their weapons and fled, and their panic proved contagious. Soon Missionary Ridge became a sea of Yankee regimental banners. A great victory roar arose as the jubilant Federals realized what they had accomplished.

Meanwhile, at the north end of the ridge, Cleburne's soldiers were cheering their own victory over Sherman when their corps commander, Lieutenant General William J. Hardee, rode up with the bad news. Hardee ordered Cleburne to shield the retreat. Reluctantly, Cleburne withdrew from Tunnel Hill and deployed his troops as a rear guard for the broken army.

That night Grant wired news of the triumph to General in Chief Halleck in Washington: "Although the battle lasted from nearly dawn until dark this evening I believe I am not premature in announcing a complete victory over Bragg. Lookout mountain-top, all the rifle pits in Chattanooga Valley, and Missionary Ridge entire, have been carried, and are now held by us. I have no idea of finding Bragg here tomorrow."

Bragg had divided his forces along most of his line, sending half of each regiment into the rifle pits 200 yards in front of the base of the ridge while deploying the rest on its crest. If attacked, the men in the rifle pits were to fire one volley and retreat up the hill.

Thomas formed his ranks with characteristic precision. Brigadier General Absalom Baird's division was on the left, then Thomas Wood's, Philip Sheridan's, and Brigadier General Richard W. Johnson's. When the Army of the Cumberland emerged onto the plain, 20,000 strong, it presented a fearsome sight to the Confederates watching from the mountaintop a mile away.

The great mass surged forward, skirmishers in front. The men burned to refute Grant's low opinion of them, and soon the main body broke into a trot

Patrick Cleburne, who emigrated from Ireland at the age of 21, was one of only two foreign-born officers to attain the rank of major general in the Confederate army. His staunch defense of Missionary Ridge enhanced his reputation as the "Stonewall Jackson of the West."

The Washington Artillery was perhaps the most famous gunnery unit in the Confederate army. The 1st through 4th companies served with Lee, and the 5th, whose banner is shown here, fought in the Army of Tennessee.

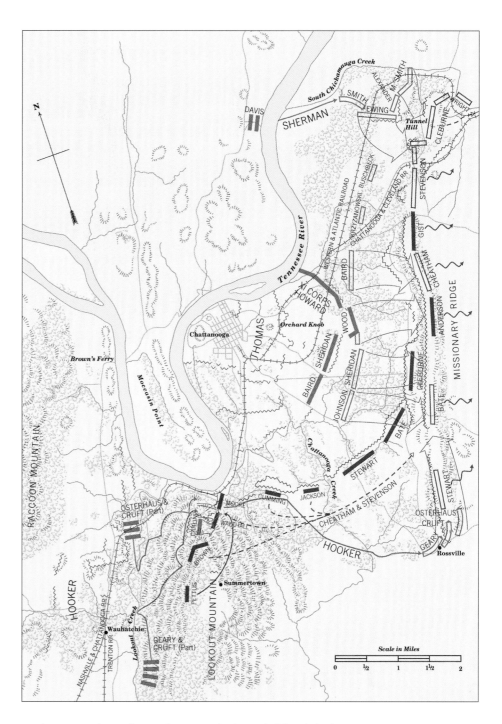

On the morning of November 25, Sherman's Federals attacked the Rebel right at Tunnel Hill but were stopped by Cleburne's and Stevenson's divisions. That afternoon, however, Thomas' divisions under Johnson, Sheridan, Wood, and Baird advanced up Missionary Ridge and routed the Confederate center, while Hooker pummeled Bragg's left. Bragg's front dissolved, and his army began a retreat into Georgia.

This handsome banner, both sides of which are shown here, was given to the Marion Artillery in April 1862 and proudly flown by Lieutenant Andrew Neal and his gunners at Chattanooga. Made from a woman's silk bridal shawl, it was replete with leather numerals, letters, and stars embossed with gold leaf, traces of which remain. In July 1864, a month before his death, Neal sent the flag home to Zebulon, Georgia, for safekeeping. His sister later hid it under her skirt when Federal cavalrymen rode through the town.

TENNESSEE IN UNION HANDS

On the night of November 25, Bragg's demoralized army gathered at Chickamauga Station and made preparations to retreat into northern Georgia aboard trains and on foot. Protected by a rear guard that held off the pursuing Yankees, the Confederates escaped but left behind abundant evidence of their state of disarray. The first Federal soldiers to arrive at the depot the following morning found fires everywhere: Shattered wagons, wrecked artillery pieces, discarded pontoons, and huge piles of grain were all burning in the streets.

"Well done. Many thanks to all. Remember Burnside."

For a time Grant pressed the pursuit. Hooker, positioned at Rossville Gap, led the chase. Thomas' and Sherman's armies, starting from farther north, also moved out in pursuit, engaging Rebel rearguard elements at Graysville, just inside the Georgia line. On November 27 Hooker's lead units caught up with Cleburne's rear guard at Ringgold, Georgia, about 15 miles southeast of Chattanooga. Just below Ringgold lay a narrow, heavily timbered mountain pass about a half-mile long and scarcely wide enough to accommodate a stretch of Western & Atlantic Railroad track, a wagon road, and a branch of East Chickamauga Creek. Cleburne placed the greater part of his force in hiding across the middle of this natural trap, while his cavalry lured Hooker into ambush. As the Federals entered the pass, the Confederates suddenly opened up on them with artillery fire and musket fire.

Hooker's troops reeled back, seeking the protection of a railroad embankment. But they recovered quickly, and a fierce engagement ensued. For six hours Cleburne held fast, while the rest of the Army of Tennessee hastened to put itself out of reach of the pursuing Yankees. Finally, when Bragg's main force was at a safe distance, Cleburne slipped away from the fight with Hooker. His heroic action—carried out at a cost of only 221 casualties among his 4,200 men, against the enemy's loss of 442—had saved Bragg's wagon train and artillery, a feat that would earn Cleburne the commander's gratitude and an official resolution of thanks from the Confederate Congress.

On November 28 Grant called off the pursuit. His army was low on rations, and he did not think it could live off the barren country below Chattanooga. He was also concerned about Burnside, whose Army of the Ohio was under siege by James Longstreet at Knoxville. President Lincoln, Secretary of War Stanton, and General in Chief Halleck were all clamoring for the rescue of Burnside.

"Well done," read Lincoln's message of congratulations to Grant. "Many thanks to all. Remember Burnside." Halleck had dealt with the victory at Chattanooga cursorily—"I congratulate you on the success thus far of your plans"—before making the real point of his wire: "I fear that General Burnside is hard-pressed and that any further delay may prove fatal. I know that you will do all in your power to relieve him."

Grant had been told that Burnside had only enough rations left to last until December 3, so he had ordered Thomas to send Major General Gordon Granger's IV Corps north as soon as Bragg was no longer a threat. But when Grant returned to Chattanooga on the night of November 29, he found Granger still there. Granger had "decided for himself" that advancing on Knoxville "was a very bad move to make." Furious, Grant placed Sherman in charge of the mission to relieve

As the 24th Wisconsin was struggling on Missionary Ridge, one of its officers, Lieutenant Arthur MacArthur Jr. (above), grabbed the regimental flag and rushed up through salvoes of canister shouting "On, Wisconsin." The Badgers poured over the crest, and MacArthur, as he later wrote, "had the honor of planting the colors . . . in front of Bragg's old headquarters," for which he later received the Medal of Honor. His son was General Douglas MacArthur.

Color Corporal William C. Montgomery displays the tattered national color of the 76th Ohio. He lost an arm carrying this flag in the futile attack on the Rebel rear guard at Ringgold, Georgia, where the 76th suffered 25 percent casualties.

Burnside. Sherman's relief force would consist of his Army of the Tennessee plus Granger's corps.

Sherman's men, having marched farther, worked harder, and faced tougher fighting than the rest of Grant's army, were exhausted, undernourished, and short of equipment. Sherman nevertheless took them on a grueling 85-mile forced march to reach beleaguered Knoxville. His cavalry vanguard just made the December 3 deadline, only to discover that Longstreet, after being decisively whipped by Burnside's men at Fort Sanders four days earlier, had gotten wind of the relief force's approach and had withdrawn.

"No satisfactory excuse can possibly be given for the shameful conduct of our troops ..."

As for Burnside, he and his men seemed in much better shape than had been anticipated. On his arrival Sherman was surprised when he was taken to a local home, where he and Burnside and their staff officers were treated to a roast turkey dinner—a gift of the townspeople. Burnside cheerfully explained that the Tennesseans had been sharing their food with his army and that the Federals had never been in serious danger of starvation—although the rank and file were down to a morsel of salt pork and a little bran bread each day.

Sherman took his Army of the Tennessee on a leisurely march back to Chattanooga, leaving Granger's corps to be added to Burnside's army. Thus reinforced, Burnside briefly pursued Longstreet into the easternmost mountains of Tennessee. Then, much to Grant's annoyance, Burnside and Granger gave up the chase and returned to Knoxville. Longstreet remained at large in Tennessee, but his troops were no longer a threat; they would slip away after a hard winter.

Meanwhile, Bragg had sent a telegraph to Richmond to report on the state of his shattered command. He closed with the words "I deem it due to the cause and to myself to ask for relief from command and an investigation into the causes of the defeat."

Bragg was not prepared to accept any of the blame himself for the loss of Chattanooga. In his official report, he condemned his soldiers for losing Lookout Mountain: "No satisfactory excuse can possibly be given for the shameful conduct of our troops on the left in allowing their line to be penetrated. The position was one which ought to have been held by a line of skirmishers against any assaulting column."

Bragg also castigated his generals, charging that their "warfare against me has been carried on successfully, and the fruits are bitter." His only moment of

BUILDING A UNION BASTION

＃＃

Almost before the last gray uniform had disappeared south into Georgia in December 1863, General Grant and his lieutenants began turning Chattanooga into a massive supply depot and staging base for a new Union offensive. It was a formidable task. The Confederate siege had left the town isolated and bereft. The Federal soldiers encamped on its streets and hillsides had subsisted for weeks on quarter rations; trees, fences, and even frame houses had been leveled for firewood, and anything green had long since been cropped by the army's famished horses and mules.

The first priority was to restore Chattanooga's severed supply lines to the North. By January 1864, new bridges were spanning rivers and creeks, roadways had been repaired, and the railroads were running again. Soon locomotives and freight cars, commandeered from all over the Union, were delivering a torrent of arms, animals, and provisions. Before the spring, Chattanooga had become a bulging arsenal from which Grant's successor, Major General William Tecumseh Sherman, would launch an army of over 100,000 men against the next Federal objective: Atlanta.

A riverboat lies moored to a rough wharf along the Tennessee River after bringing supplies to Chattanooga. General Grant was trying to fill the army's warehouses here and at Nashville with a six-month supply of stores and ammunition to sustain a spring drive into Georgia.

Settled in for garrison duty at newly established Fort Sherman on an elevated eastern edge of Chattanooga, the men of Battery C, 1st Wisconsin Heavy Artillery, form up at the foot of their company street. At rear, the soldiers' laundry hangs out to dry.

The Federal engineers' proud achievement, a 780-foot-long trestle bridge rushed to completion early in 1864, spans Running Water Ravine near Wauhatchie, Tennessee, on the Nashville & Chattanooga Railroad. In the foreground, builders perch on the wreckage of an earlier bridge, destroyed by the Confederates.

In this fanciful watercolor, artist Adolph Metzner depicts the Army of the Tennessee leaving Chattanooga in the spring of 1864. A white signal flag and a cannon blast start the Federals across the Tennessee River in a driving rain and then over Raccoon Mountain southeast into Georgia. On May 7, 1864, Sherman, now commanding a Federal juggernaut of some 113,000 troops, moved to strike against the Gateway to the South: the city of Atlanta.

CHATTANOOGA CASUALTIES

November 23-27, 1863

FEDERAL

Killed	753
Wounded	4,722
Missing	349
Total	5,824

CONFEDERATE

Killed	361
Wounded	2,160
Missing	4,146
Total	6,667

self-awareness came when he ruefully admitted to President Jefferson F. Davis: "I fear we both erred in the conclusion for me to retain command here after the clamor raised against me."

On November 30 Davis accepted Bragg's resignation as head of the Army of Tennessee and appointed William J. Hardee to take his place. Bragg was transferred to Richmond, where he became a military adviser to Davis and the Confederate cabinet.

The wrecked Army of Tennessee would convalesce in northern Georgia that winter. But the Confederacy as a whole would never be able to recover from the effects of the fighting around Chattanooga. Confederate railroad communications in the West had been crippled and the gateway to the heart of the Deep South flung open to the Yankees.

> ## *"I fear we both erred in the conclusion for me to retain command here after the clamor raised against me."*

Grant's three forces went into winter quarters in Chattanooga. The troops were kept busy repairing and securing the railroad connections between Nashville and Chattanooga in anticipation of a spring campaign.

As the general who had turned a desperate situation into a stunning victory, Ulysses S. Grant was the Union's man of the hour. A few months after the victory at Chattanooga, President Lincoln made Grant the first officer since George Washington to hold the full grade of lieutenant general and called him to Washington to become the head of all the Union armies. Grant's successor as commander of Federal forces in the West would be his trusted subordinate, William Tecumseh Sherman.

Henceforward, the two friends would work in tandem, putting into devastating effect the strategy that Lincoln had been advocating virtually since the outbreak of the war—but always before now without the cooperation of his generals. No longer would the Federal armies in the East and West act "independently and without concert, like a balky team, no two pulling together," in Grant's barnyard metaphor. Instead they would press forward simultaneously, squeezing the Confederacy in a giant pincers.

While Grant moved to destroy Lee's army in Virginia, Sherman would corner and break up the Army of Tennessee in Georgia. Grant did not give his old friend a specific geographical objective. But Sherman judged his immediate target to be Atlanta, the manufacturing and railroad center of the Deep South, some 100 miles to the southeast of Chattanooga. Thus was the stage set for the burning of Atlanta and Sherman's destructive march to the sea.

SUPPLYING THE NORTH'S ARMIES

By early 1863 the United States Army had developed what would become the most efficient and extensive military supply system in the world. With occasional disruptions due to the exigencies of individual campaigns, Federal armies in the field could generally be guaranteed a steady and sufficient supply of food, munitions, clothing, and equipment. The U.S. Army Quartermaster and Subsistence Departments established bakeries, stockyards, remount centers, forage lots, and warehouse complexes to concentrate and deliver the hundreds of thousands of tons of matériel required to supply the fighting men at the front. In the western theater the government leased or commandeered thousands of steamboats to haul supplies on the great river network that led deep into the Southern heartland. In Virginia and the uplands of Tennessee and Georgia the U.S. Military Railroad system and its innovative Construction Corps efficiently ran and maintained existing rail lines and rapidly built new ones as required. Ultimately, the North could deploy masses of men and supply them with an ease and effectiveness that the understrength and starving Confederate armies could never match.

U.S. Military Railroad agents rest beside a pile of boxed rations intended for soldiers of the Army of the Potomac. The photograph was probably taken at Aquia Creek, a tributary of the Potomac River where the Union maintained a rail line and supply base for matériel shipped aboard barges from Alexandria, Virginia. "The railroad is entirely under your control," Railway Construction Corps head Herman Haupt told his civilian employees. "No military officer has any right to interfere with it."

Men of the U.S. Army Quartermaster Corps stand atop two giant stacks of hardtack boxes at a depot near City Point, Virginia. Hardtack—flour-and-water crackers—was one of the main field rations of the Federal army. The large, wood-hooped barrels piled in the foreground contain either salt pork or beef, the other primary field ration. City Point's vast storage warehouses maintained a 30-days' supply of food at all times. Each day, tons of supplies—from shoes to artillery projectiles—were transported to the army in the field by hand, wagon, or rail. The ability of the Federal authorities to deliver such masses of matériel proved to be a vital factor in the Union's ultimate victory.

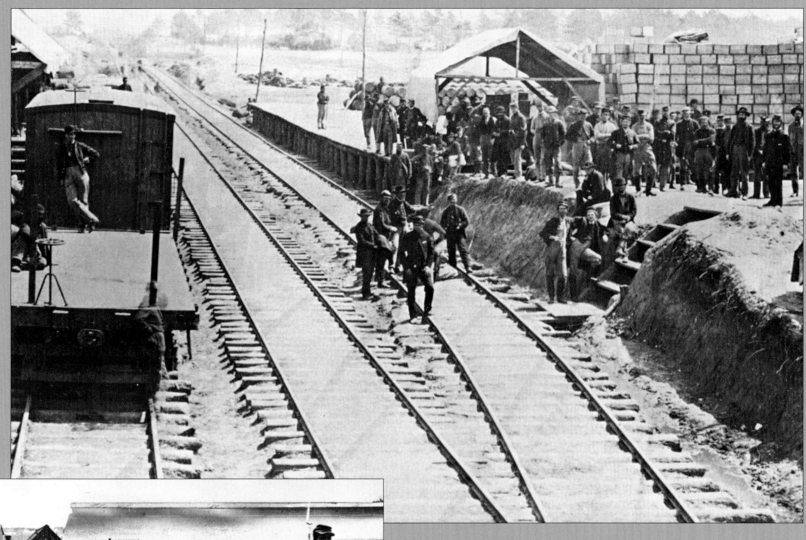

At Stoneman's Switch, the terminus of the rail line from the landing at Aquia Creek, Federal soldiers and commissary workers line up before a huge pile of hardtack boxes awaiting delivery to the army encamped on Stafford Heights, Virginia. The station supplied the Federal campaigns at Fredericksburg and Chancellorsville in 1862 and 1863.

A soldier stands guard over a line of 12-pounder Napoleon guns and limbers recently delivered from Northern arsenals to the depot at City Point, Virginia. The guns were later forwarded by rail to artillery parks near the front lines at Petersburg.

TRANSPORTATION

Federal II Corps commissary wagons line up in shallow water to receive provisions from incoming barges at Belle Plain, Virginia, which served as supply and communication center for the Army of the Potomac.

Outfitted in castoff uniforms, black teamsters gather for a photograph at City Point, Virginia, the bustling supply depot for the Federal forces besieging Richmond and Petersburg in 1864. Paid a small salary for their work as laborers and wagon drivers, these former slaves, or "contrabands," were ubiquitous in Northern armies.

A crude hoist on the wharf in Alexandria, Virginia (left), raised or lowered a section of track, as the water level dictated, so that rolling stock could be loaded onto barges (right) for towing down the Potomac. This labor- and timesaving system ensured that supplies did not have to be shifted between rail and water transports at river ports.

Steamboats lie moored to Nashville's wharf in December 1862 as stevedores unload hardtack, flour, sugar, molasses, and whiskey. Nashville afforded ready access to the Mississippi, Ohio, and Tennessee Rivers and had become a strategic supply center for Federal armies in the West.

BAKERS

Commissary dept. Ha-gts. Army of the Potomac —

Artist Alfred Waud sketched butchers of the Commissary Department in action, issuing rations of beef to camp orderlies at the headquarters of the Army of the Potomac. Waud's drawing was probably made in March 1863 at Falmouth, Virginia.

With pans of dough rising and another batch in the making, army bakers prepare bread for Federal soldiers. By 1864 the Federal government had established central bakeries in Washington, D.C., and in Alexandria and Fort Monroe, Virginia, to supply bread for the troops.

Federal army butchers weigh rations of meat under the watchful eyes of a commissary at Camp Essex in northern Virginia. Regulations mandated a daily issue of 20 ounces of salt beef or 12 ounces of salt pork. The meat, dubbed salt horse by the soldiers, was packed in brine sufficient to preserve it for two years.

This crate of army bread, or hardtack, was packed by Brooklyn baker Robert Stears and received by the U.S. Army Subsistence Department in September 1862. The simple flour-and-water crackers were protected from moisture by a soldered sheet-zinc lining. Once issued, recalled Private Wilbur Fisk of the 2d Vermont, "hardtack suffered every indignity, and was positively unsuitable food for anything that claims to be human."

Wilderness
The Killing Ground

GRANT TAKES THE REINS—Early in March 1864, as the Civil War dragged on toward its fourth year, Ulysses S. Grant was summoned to Washington, promoted to lieutenant general, and given command of all Federal armed forces as general in chief. President Abraham Lincoln, desperate for a decisive victory in the East, was placing the hopes of the Union squarely on the shoulders of this slight and unassuming man from Illinois.

Grant scarcely looked the part of the warrior who could save the Union. One observer who encountered him for the first time in a Washington hotel described him as an "ordinary, scrubby looking man with a slightly seedy look, as if he were out of office on half pay; he had no gait, no station, no manner." A journalist attending a White House reception for the new commander labeled him a "little, scared-looking man."

But as President Lincoln well knew, appearances in this case were deceiving. Grant had waged an impressive campaign in the western theater. In July 1863 he had captured the key Mississippi River bastion of Vicksburg and thereby secured the river for the Union. The following November, he broke the Confederate siege of Chattanooga and sent the Rebel Army of Tennessee retreating into Georgia.

In Grant, Lincoln saw a general who was aggressive and resolute, a relentless fighter who would make up for the army's leadership shortcomings of the past. In the East a succession of promising field commanders—Major Generals George McClellan, John Pope, Ambrose Burnside, Joseph Hooker, and now George Meade—had failed to score the victory that would bring the Confederacy to its knees. Even after Meade turned Robert E. Lee back at Gettysburg, the Union commander had allowed the battered Confederates to slip away across the Potomac into Virginia. And in eight months of maneuvering since then Meade had failed to deliver a telling blow.

Meade half-expected to be fired as commander of the Army of the Potomac for his failure to bring Lee to bay. But when Grant visited Meade's headquarters near Brandy Station on March 10, the two men warmed to each other. And when Meade proposed to step down, Grant declined the offer. Meade would continue to lead the fight against Lee, but Grant would map the strategy—not from Washington but in the field, with the commanders of his armies.

Above: This slouch hat, pierced by a bullet at the rear left edge of the crown, bears the clover-leaf emblem of the Federal II Corps. Its owner, Captain Charles Nash of the 19th Maine, was leading a company against General James Longstreet's Confederates in the Wilderness on May 6, 1864, when a bullet sent the hat flying; Nash was not harmed.

Opposite: During the long winter break from active campaigning, Federal staff officers of Major General John Sedgwick's VI Corps relax beside their comfortable log hut constructed in the yard of the Welford family mansion, "Farley," near Brandy Station, Virginia.

After his cordial meeting with Meade, Grant took a train west to meet with his friend and most trusted subordinate, Major General William Tecumseh Sherman, whom Grant had named as his replacement in command of the Union's western armies. Poring over maps in a Cincinnati hotel, the two men devised a new, coordinated strategy to cripple the Confederacy and win the war.

At Grant's disposal were some 662,000 soldiers in 22 corps, of whom perhaps 533,000 were combat ready. He intended to put all his armies, east and west, on the move that spring in simultaneous offensives that would exhaust the Rebel forces and destroy the Confederacy's capacity to wage war.

Grant's primary objective was not to win and occupy territory, but to conquer the two powerful Confederate armies in the field: Lee's Army of Northern Virginia and the consolidated western army under the command of General Joseph E. Johnston. Sherman, with his force of 100,000 men based in northwestern Georgia, would attack Johnston while Grant assailed Lee in Virginia.

> *"He rode along the line in a slouchy unobservant way, with his coat unbuttoned and setting anything but an example of military bearing to the troops."*

When Grant returned to the East, he issued succinct orders to Meade: "Lee's army will be your objective point. Wherever Lee goes, there you will go also." Grant also planned to put two other Federal armies into action in Virginia. A force of 26,000 men under Major General Franz Sigel was to advance southward through the Shenandoah Valley, disrupting Lee's food sources and rail communications and menacing his left flank. And a third Federal army, commanded by Major General Benjamin Butler, would advance across Virginia's Peninsula, between the York and James Rivers, pushing toward Richmond and seeking an opportunity to join Meade's Army of the Potomac in a giant pincers movement.

Grant's enemy, Robert E. Lee, had endured a long season of frustration. The Gettysburg campaign, the previous July, had been costly; Lee had lost more than one-third of the 75,000 Confederates engaged. After the battle, as the Rebel army retreated slowly up the Shenandoah Valley, a rash of desertions further sapped its strength—losses that the South could not replace.

The setbacks continued after the Army of Northern Virginia settled into earthworks on the south bank of the Rapidan River in central Virginia. In early October Lee made an attempt to outflank the Yankee army facing him across the Rapidan, swinging his forces around Cedar Mountain and marching northeast. Meade responded smoothly, however, and succeeded in blocking Lee's thrust just south of Manassas.

Lee pulled back south of the Rapidan again, and his men began building huts for shelter against the oncoming winter. But the fighting was not over for the year. Meade, stung by criticism from Washington, launched his own attack on Thanksgiving Day, crossing the Rapidan downstream of Lee's position in an attempt to roll up the Rebel right flank. Lee got wind of the Federal movement and had time to reposition his forces and dig in along a small stream called Mine Run.

So formidable were the Rebel earthworks that the Federals called off their attack and retreated. But Lee, far from being pleased at having stopped the Yankees again, was again disappointed. He was heard to mutter, "I am too old to command this army; we should never have permitted these people to get away." Lee had perfected the art of repelling Federal offensives, but he was galled at never being able to achieve more.

The Rebel troops spent a miserable winter along the Rapidan. Shortages were acute. Lee spent the early months of 1864 petitioning Richmond for food, shoes, and clothing for his men. In one dispatch he deplored "the wretched condition of the men, thousands of whom are barefooted, a great number partially shod and nearly all without overcoats, blankets or warm clothing."

But Richmond, in the war's third winter, had little to offer. Commodities were scarce and inflation was rampant in the Confederate capital. Coffee cost $10 a pound, beans $60 a bushel. Citizens were reduced to pooling their resources and holding "starvation parties" in an air of desperate gaiety. There was little extra for Lee's troops.

As spring budded through the Virginia countryside in late March, General Grant commandeered a plain brick house in Culpeper, just down the road from Meade's headquarters at Brandy Station and—as newspapers pointed out—six miles closer to the front.

Grant's reputation had preceded him. In Northern households his initials were said to stand for "Unconditional Surrender." But many in the Army of the Potomac were not impressed. After Grant reviewed the army's V Corps on March 29, an officer wrote of the new commander: "He rode along the line in a slouchy unobservant way, with his coat unbuttoned and setting anything but an example of military bearing to the troops."

Many of the Army of the Potomac's veterans were already in a dark humor, because Meade had disbanded the understrength I and III Corps and redistributed the men among the II and V Corps to streamline the army's organization. But even

Opposite: Lieutenant General Ulysses S. Grant poses for a Brady & Co. photographer in front of his tent during the Wilderness campaign of 1864. An observer recalled that the new general in chief had a "look of resolution, as if he could not be trifled with."

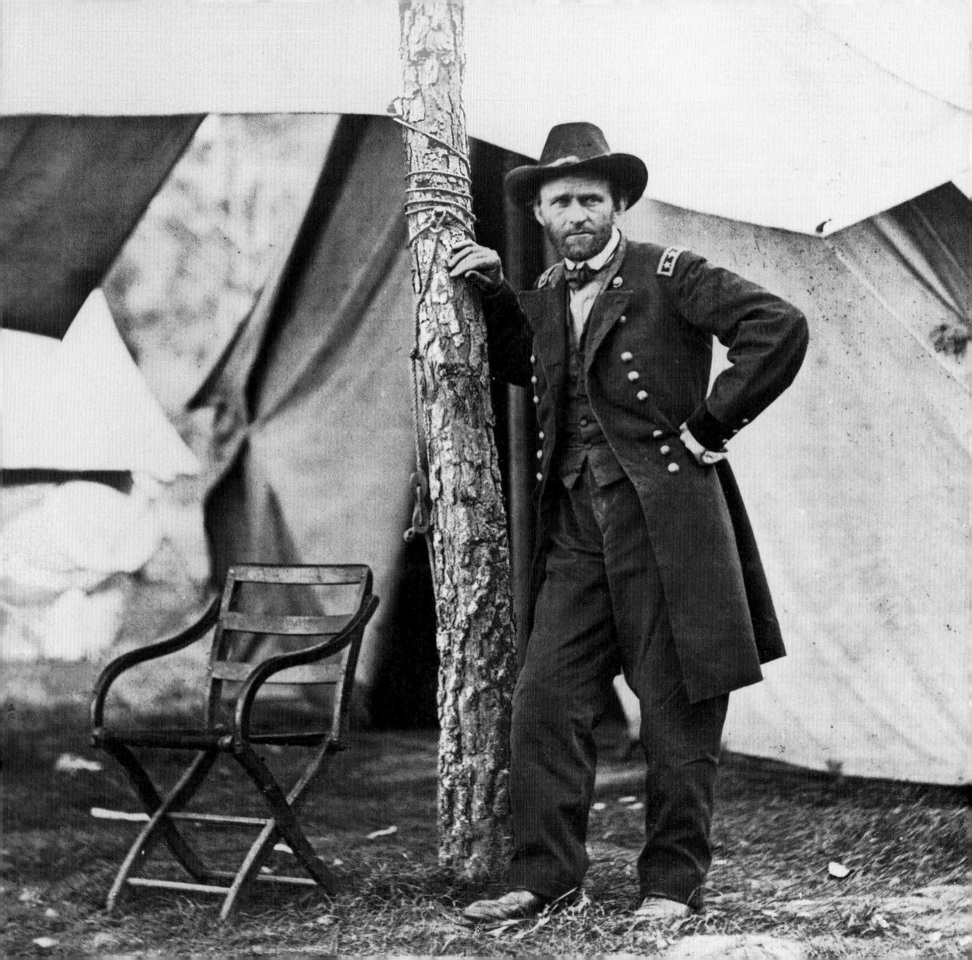

In this Union wagon park stand 240 of the 6,000 wagons that would follow Grant's troops

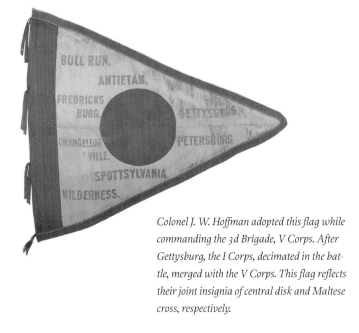

Colonel J. W. Hoffman adopted this flag while commanding the 3d Brigade, V Corps. After Gettysburg, the I Corps, decimated in the battle, merged with the V Corps. This flag reflects their joint insignia of central disk and Maltese cross, respectively.

though angry at the high command, some soldiers seemed disposed to give Grant a chance. One man wrote in his diary: "He cannot be weaker or more inefficient than the generals who have wasted the lives of our comrades during the past three years."

Grant, aware that numbers could be the key to a Union victory, did all within his power to build up the strength of the Army of the Potomac. He instructed the Union's far-flung departmental commanders to pare their garrisons and send the extra men to Virginia. Closer to home, he evicted thousands of troops from their comfortable quarters within Washington's fortifications and transferred them to the field armies. He also converted the excess cavalrymen stationed in and around the nation's capital into infantry. He even reduced the number of wagons allotted to a headquarters, freeing hundreds of teamsters and mule skinners for service in the ranks.

across the Rapidan River in the offensive against Robert E. Lee. During the Federal army's advance, the Union supply train stretched for 60 miles.

In another move aimed at sustaining the Union's numerical superiority, Grant abolished prisoner exchange. For three years, the Union and the Confederacy had routinely swapped prisoners of war. Now Grant put an end to the practice, knowing that the North could replace such losses from its larger population but the South could not.

Despite such measures, the Union confronted a potentially disastrous manpower problem, for 1864 was the year of discharges. Those men who had enlisted for a term of three years after Fort Sumter would soon be entitled to go home. Nearly half the Union's fighting force was eligible, including many of the crack regiments in the Army of the Potomac.

The Federal government waged an intense campaign to inspire reenlistments. It offered each man who signed up again a 30-day furlough and $400 in cash, to be supplemented by bounties from individual states.

Pride and peer pressure also played a role. A man who reenlisted could wear a special stripe indicating that he had been in the fight from the start and was now serving of his own free will. If at least three-fourths of a regiment reenlisted, the regiment would remain intact, retaining its name and colors. Regimental officers, afraid of losing their commands, politicked furiously among their men. In the end, more than half of those eligible for a discharge chose to fight on. And those who reenlisted were joined by fresh volunteers, draftees, and hired substitutes.

Across the river, Robert E. Lee watched the ominous swelling of the Federal camps. Lee had all but despaired of receiving additional provisions. What he concentrated on most urgently now was getting more men. Lee implored President Jefferson Davis to send him soldiers—a brigade that had been detached for coastal duty in North Carolina, a division posted south of Richmond. "We shall have to glean troops from every quarter," Lee wrote in mid-April, "to oppose

"'Hello, Johnny Reb! how is sassafras tea to-day?'"

PRIVATE MARCUS B. TONEY

44th Virginia Infantry, Jones' Brigade

A native Virginian, Toney had moved with his family to Nashville, Tennessee, in 1852. At the outbreak of the war he joined a Tennessee regiment and served until after the fall of Chattanooga, transferring to the 44th Virginia in February 1864. Toney was captured at Spotsylvania and spent the rest of the war as a prisoner.

O ne day I was on picket duty near the Rapidan River, which is a stream a little larger than Duck River; just opposite us were the Yankee pickets. One of them yelled out: "Hello, Johnny Reb! how is sassafras tea to-day?" I told him the tea was all right, but we had no sugar. I asked him how he was fixed for tobacco, and he said, "Very short"; so we arranged on the morrow to get on duty again. I was to bring a plug of tobacco, and he a shot pouch of coffee. The Federals had their coffee parched, ground, and sugar mixed with it, so on the morrow we made the exchange and I don't think that I ever enjoyed coffee as much as I did that, having been months without a taste of pure coffee. After making the exchange, he asked me how I would like to have a New York *Herald*. He said that it was not contraband, for it was several weeks old. I told him that I would like very much to see it, as we did not get any papers now, and the ones received were printed on the reverse side of wall paper and were so flimsy that they would not stand the mails. So he tied the *Herald* to a stick and threw it across to me. When I opened it up, I read as follows: *"The Rebel Capital Must be Captured at All Hazards; General Grant Has Been Appointed to the Task."* He afterwards uttered what became a memorable saying: "I will fight it out on this line if it takes all summer."

the apparent combination of the enemy."

But Davis was unswayed. Long committed for political reasons to defending Southern territory, Davis was loath to leave too much of it unguarded, even if that policy meant spreading troops thinly. He would rearrange the Confederacy's military dispositions only when he believed the situation compelled him to.

At the end of April Lee had only 65,000 men on hand to confront Grant's 120,000, and the Rebel commander realized that time was growing short. Lee knew from intelligence sources that Grant was preparing to attack. On March 26, the wives of Federal officers had begun to leave camp. On April 7, the Yankee army had started sending the sutlers away.

On May 2 Lee mounted his horse, Traveller, and rode with his officers up Clark's Mountain, the highest lookout point available. Hugging the foot of the mountain was the flat, brown Rapidan. Across the river lay the tents of the Union army. Lee doubted that Grant would launch a frontal assault across the river against the formidable Rebel fortifications. More likely, he would move by either flank.

Due east, about 13 miles downstream, was Germanna Ford; a few miles farther was Ely's Ford. South of the fords lay a gray-green expanse called the Wilderness, 12 miles wide and six miles deep. If Grant could pass his troops through this tangle of briars, stunted pines, and dense undergrowth, he would emerge into open country where he could use his superior numbers to smash Lee's army. Moreover, a line of advance that stayed closer to navigable rivers would maximize the flow of supplies available to Grant's army as it pushed southward.

An alternative for the Union commander was a move by his right flank, west of where Lee stood on Clark's Mountain. Going that way, Grant would be following the line of the Orange & Alexandria Railroad, toward Gordonsville. A westward move would give Grant favorable terrain, but it would expose the Union line of communications and uncover Washington itself.

Lee studied the terrain through his telescope and pondered his opponent's options. Then he raised a gloved hand and pointed eastward, to the two fords across the Rapidan. "Grant will cross by one of those fords," he told his officers.

STALEMATE IN THE WILDERNESS

The Army of the Potomac moved out just after midnight on May 4 and was soon crossing the Rapidan River fords east of the Confederate position—precisely where Robert E. Lee had predicted. General Grant then intended to swing his troops westward, march swiftly through the tangled Wilderness, flush the Army of Northern Virginia out of its earthworks, and crush it on open ground.

The Federals moved over newly laid pontoon bridges in two long columns. The V Corps, commanded by Major General Gouverneur K. Warren, crossed at Germanna Ford and headed southwest, followed closely by Major General John Sedgwick's VI Corps. A few miles farther east the II Corps, under Major General

In early May 1864 Ulysses S. Grant ordered the Army of the Potomac to cross the Rapidan River and begin a march toward the Confederate capital at Richmond for the purpose of confronting and destroying Robert E. Lee's Army of Northern Virginia. The Confederates blocked Grant in a bloody series of engagements in the tangled scrub of the Wilderness, but the Federal commander persisted, forcing Lee to fight again at Spotsylvania Court House.

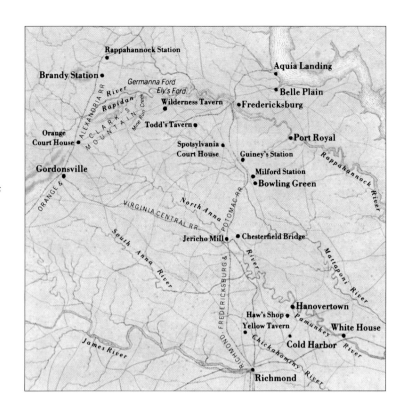

Flanked by its regimental band, the 17th Maine poses near Brandy Station just hours before its march to the Rapidan. Within days the 17th, part of General Alexander Hays' brigade of General David B. Birney's division of the II Corps, would suffer massive casualties in the Wilderness—192 men, including its commander, Colonel George W. West. In fighting at Spotsylvania the regiment would lose 69 more men, ending the campaign with only 246 effectives of its original 507. With most of the senior officers killed or wounded, command of the regiment fell to Captain John C. Perry of Company D. By the time the 17th returned home in 1865, it had suffered the most casualties of any Maine regiment in the war.

Photographer Timothy O'Sullivan took this exceptional view from the south bank of the Rapidan on May 4, capturing a portion of Grant's forces moving to the Wilderness over one of two pontoon bridges at Germanna Ford. Both the V and VI Corps crossed here, while the II Corps was crossing downstream at Ely's Ford. The V Corps was the first to reach Germanna Ford and was fully across the river by about 1:00 p.m. The late-afternoon shadows in this image suggest that the troops pictured here belonged to the rear elements of the VI Corps. An infantry regiment can be seen pounding across the bridge, while a caravan of supply wagons waits its turn. The idle pontoon bridge just downstream was dismantled at approximately 6:00 p.m. on the 4th, while the other bridge remained and was used by Major General Ambrose Burnside's IX Corps on May 5.

Winfield Scott Hancock, crossed at Ely's Ford.

Lee learned of the Federal advance and, ever combative, determined to meet it. Although outnumbered 2 to 1, he had the advantage of operating on interior lines and in familiar territory. Lee quickly spurred his veteran corps commanders into action. He sent troops of the Second Corps, under Lieutenant General Richard S. Ewell, marching east on the Orange Turnpike. Farther south on a parallel route Lieutenant General A. P. Hill's Third Corps started out on the Orange Plank road. Still farther south, around Gordonsville, Lieutenant General James Longstreet received orders to set out with his First Corps toward the Catharpin road. All three corps were soon converging on the Wilderness and Grant's unsuspecting troops.

The Federal plan depended on swift movement to clear the Wilderness before engaging the enemy. No one wanted to wage war in that jungle of dense thickets and choked undergrowth. Artillery and cavalry would be mostly useless there, and infantry maneuvers all but impossible. "This, viewed as a battle ground, was simply infernal," a Union officer remarked.

Yet the Federals halted in the Wilderness early on May 4, after General Meade recommended stopping to let the wagon trains catch up. This pause meant that the Federal vanguard would have to spend the night there. The Union command, however, was untroubled over this situation, believing that Lee could not reach the Wilderness before the night of the fifth. To compound that miscalculation, Union cavalry failed to post patrols on the Orange Turnpike that would have detected the approach of the enemy.

That night, after cavalry scouts under Major General Jeb Stuart reported that the Federals were stationary in the Wilderness, Lee decided to attack at first light. Ewell and Hill would pin down Grant's army until Longstreet arrived and slammed into the exposed Yankee flank.

Ever the bold strategist, Lee was counting on the miserable terrain of the Wilderness to help neutralize Grant's superior numbers. But it was a risky scheme—Lee would have to immobilize the Federal army for an entire day with fewer than 40,000 men, gambling that Longstreet would reach the field in time to support the attack. As he often did when ranged against superior numbers, Robert E. Lee on the morning of May 5 chose audacity. Rather than wait for Grant to filter his way through the Wilderness, Lee pushed forward Ewell's Second Corps along the Orange Turnpike and two divisions from Lieutenant General

The talk of death bandied about the campfires of both armies in the lonely expanses of the Wilderness during the evening of May 4 would come true for many soldiers. The bones above were photographed near the Orange Plank road just after the war, when burial parties returned to gather up and inter the remains of those who were left where they fell during the May clashes of both 1863 and 1864.

Skirmishers of the Federal VI Corps probe for their foe as a brigade draws up in line of battle behind them in this painting by Civil War veteran Julian Scott. The thick underbrush of the Wilderness impeded the VI Corps skirmish line, one officer reported, "often breaking it completely."

MAPMAKING

At the beginning of the Civil War, few accurate maps were available to the Federal and Confederate armies. Prewar Regular Army topographical engineers had concentrated on mapping the American West and the Coast and Geodetic Survey charted the seacoasts; it was largely left to the state legislatures to contract private mapmakers to survey the eastern states.

For detailed maps, army commanders were initially dependent on county maps produced by private publishers. During many of the early campaigns of the war generals were forced to depend on data supplied by local guides and maps hastily sketched by staff officers detailed to scout ahead of the army.

As the war progressed both armies assigned topographical engineers to the staffs of senior generals and established centralized topographical offices under their respective War Departments to provide accurate maps of potential areas of military operation. In the Federal armies, with their superior technology, staff mapmakers in the field took advantage of the latest printing and photographic techniques to quickly produce and distribute detailed maps to the front-line commands.

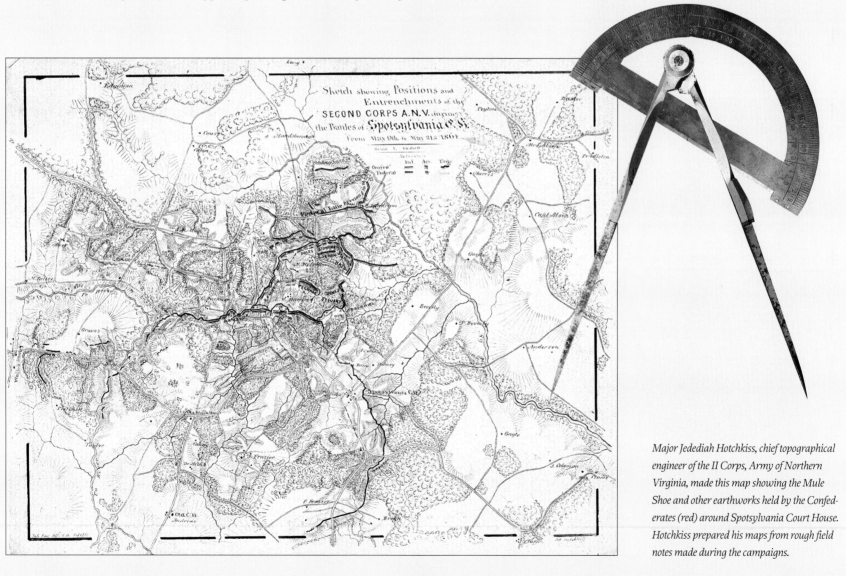

Major Jedediah Hotchkiss, chief topographical engineer of the II Corps, Army of Northern Virginia, made this map showing the Mule Shoe and other earthworks held by the Confederates (red) around Spotsylvania Court House. Hotchkiss prepared his maps from rough field notes made during the campaigns.

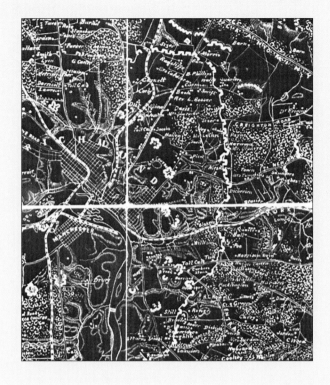

Federal cartographers produced this map of the defenses of Richmond by laying an original map, rendered on tracing linen, over a sheet of photographic paper. The sun's rays darkened the photographic paper except under the ink lines on the tracing, producing a photocopy negative in which the roads, rivers, and other features appeared as white lines against a dark background.

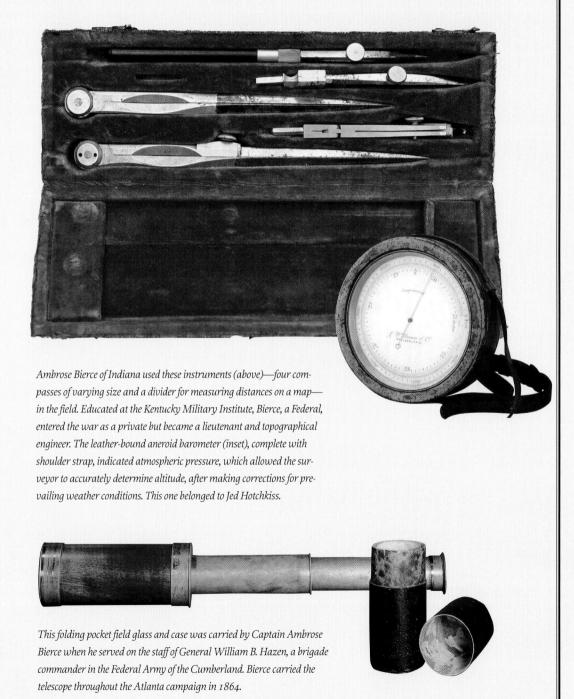

Ambrose Bierce of Indiana used these instruments (above)—four compasses of varying size and a divider for measuring distances on a map—in the field. Educated at the Kentucky Military Institute, Bierce, a Federal, entered the war as a private but became a lieutenant and topographical engineer. The leather-bound aneroid barometer (inset), complete with shoulder strap, indicated atmospheric pressure, which allowed the surveyor to accurately determine altitude, after making corrections for prevailing weather conditions. This one belonged to Jed Hotchkiss.

Some Civil War photographers applied their skills in support of military operations. During the siege of Petersburg, the large bellows camera above, mounted on a table and equipped with a special lens, was used to photograph maps prepared by U.S. topographical engineers. The copies were then distributed to officers in the field.

This folding pocket field glass and case was carried by Captain Ambrose Bierce when he served on the staff of General William B. Hazen, a brigade commander in the Federal Army of the Cumberland. Bierce carried the telescope throughout the Atlanta campaign in 1864.

A graduate of West Point, John Marshall Jones had a fondness for the bottle that kept him in staff positions until he was appointed a Confederate brigadier general in 1863. Wounded at Gettysburg, he returned to duty four months later. When his brigade was routed at Saunders' Field on May 5, a staff officer recalled that "disdaining to fly," Jones "was killed while sitting on his horse gazing at the approaching enemy."

With the shout, "Here's our western men!" Brigadier General Lysander Cutler's Iron Brigade advanced to hammer Jones' Confederates. As the fighting dissolved into a melee, Major Albert M. Edwards of the 24th Michigan seized the flag of the 48th Virginia Infantry. Tearing the flag from its staff, Edwards sent it to the rear in the knapsack of his wounded colonel, Henry A. Morrow.

Ambrose P. Hill's Third Corps along the Orange Plank road. They were to keep Grant occupied while Longstreet marched his First Corps from its camp near Gordonsville and swung north into Grant's left flank.

But because Longstreet could not be in position to attack before morning on May 6, Ewell's and Hill's Confederates, outnumbered by at least 3 to 1, would have to stall Grant's Federals for more than a day. If Grant discovered that Lee had divided his force, he could concentrate superior numbers against either prong of the Confederate army and destroy it.

"[It was a] weird, uncanny contest, a battle of invisibles with invisibles."

Shortly after sunup, Grant began arraying his army to face Lee. Hancock's II Corps marched from Chancellorsville toward Todd's Tavern; Major General Gouverneur K. Warren's V Corps started from Wilderness Tavern along a wagon trail leading to Parker's Store; Sedgwick's VI Corps shuffled south along the Germanna Plank road to fill the position vacated by Warren; and Burnside's IX Corps remained north of the Rapidan River to guard the army's rear. Grant hoped by noon to sweep west and flank Lee out of his last reported positions near Mine Run.

By the time most of Warren's corps was on the march toward the Orange Plank road, Ewell's Confederates had appeared on the Orange Turnpike and begun building earthworks across the western edge of a clearing called Saunders' Field, which straddled the road. Meade, confident that any large Rebel formations were still at least a day away, mistook Ewell's troops for a reconnaissance force and directed

Warren to attack them. Grant was also feeling bellicose and encouraged Meade to pitch into the Confederates "without giving time for disposition."

Notwithstanding his superiors' zeal for an immediate attack, Warren struggled for several hours to form a line. As Lee had foreseen, difficult terrain frustrated the Yankee commander's efforts. Grant and Meade became increasingly insistent, but still Warren hesitated to turn his troops loose. His right flank ended on the northern edge of Saunders' Field, and yet Ewell's line overlapped it, revealing that Warren faced far more troops than his superiors maintained. Exasperated by Warren's deliberate pace, Meade issued him peremptory orders to attack.

At 1:00 p.m. Warren moved against Ewell's line. Three brigades of Brigadier General Charles Griffin's division marched across Saunders' Field into a blaze of Confederate musketry. Brigadier General Romeyn Ayres' command north of the turnpike was repelled, but Brigadier General Joseph Bartlett's brigade punched a hole in the Rebel line and advanced a quarter of a mile before being driven back. The blue-clad line shattered, and the survivors broke across the field, many stumbling toward the refuge of a gully.

In the dense woods south of the road, Warren's men made some initial headway against the Rebels, but a vicious counterattack sent the Yankees reeling. The fighting in the deep woods of the Wilderness soon proved a nightmare for Yankee and Rebel alike—described by one participant as a "weird, uncanny contest, a battle of invisibles with invisibles"—as reinforcements from both armies joined in the fight.

Opposite: Shallow rifle pits and a robust breastwork of logs mark the line defended by General Richard Ewell's Confederates in the Battle of the Wilderness on May 5 and 6. Posted astride the Orange Turnpike, Ewell's men used their cover to advantage, repulsing a series of Yankee attacks. As the campaign progressed, soldiers in both armies dug in whenever a battle seemed likely.

Special artist Edwin Forbes sketched a battle line of the Federal VI Corps firing through pine thickets at an unseen enemy near the Orange Turnpike on the afternoon of May 5. The maze of scrub timber and tangled brush made effective coordination between units nearly impossible. A soldier from Pennsylvania called it the "awfullest brush, briars, grapevine, etc., I was ever in."

Ambrose Powell Hill's combativeness on the battlefield quickly gained him a reputation as one of Lee's most aggressive commanders. Promoted to lieutenant general in 1863, Hill found the change from division to corps command difficult and was, furthermore, hampered by a recurring kidney disease. Illness forced him temporarily to relinquish his command on May 8.

Brigadier General James Wadsworth's division also sent the Rebels into retreat, but his units became isolated in the dense woods and were repulsed piecemeal. A countercharge by a brigade under Brigadier General John Gordon cleared the Federals from in front of Ewell's right. Within an hour, Warren's attack was a shambles.

At 3:00 p.m. Brigadier General Horatio Wright's division of Sedgwick's corps, after fighting through a Rebel cavalry screen, attacked Ewell's line north of Saunders' Field. Again Ewell exploited the terrain and repulsed the Yankees. Two miles south of Ewell, a second battle front developed on the Orange Plank road, where Hill's Confederate Third Corps advanced in tandem with Ewell's men to the north. To halt Hill's progress, Meade, now fully aware that much of Lee's army was in front of him, sent three VI Corps brigades under Brigadier General George W. Getty to the intersection of the Orange Plank road and the Brock road. Getty arrived just in time to stall Hill's advance and hold on to the key crossroads until Hancock's lead elements could come up from the south to reinforce the position.

At 4:30 Getty and two of Hancock's divisions attacked Henry Heth's division of Hill's corps. As pressure mounted against Heth, Hill fed in his other available division, under Major General Cadmus Wilcox, and Hancock countered with the rest of his corps. Near dark, Meade pulled four V Corps brigades from the turnpike front, placed them under Wadsworth, and hurled them toward Hill's left flank. A ferocious counterattack stymied Wadsworth, however, and darkness finally ended the first day's combat.

Hill's Confederates had stopped the Federals, but they had suffered mightily in the effort. Their lines were now in chaos, fronts askew, regiments and brigades scattered all over the forest.

Lee, headquartered a mile to the rear at Widow Tapp's farm, realized that Hill's situation was perilous. He sent couriers to Longstreet urging him to hurry to the battlefield. Hill's survival would depend on the arrival of Longstreet's troops by dawn to absorb the Federal attack that was sure to come.

For his second day in the Wilderness, Grant planned to concentrate his force against Hill's Third Corps on the Orange Plank road. Hancock's II Corps, reinforced

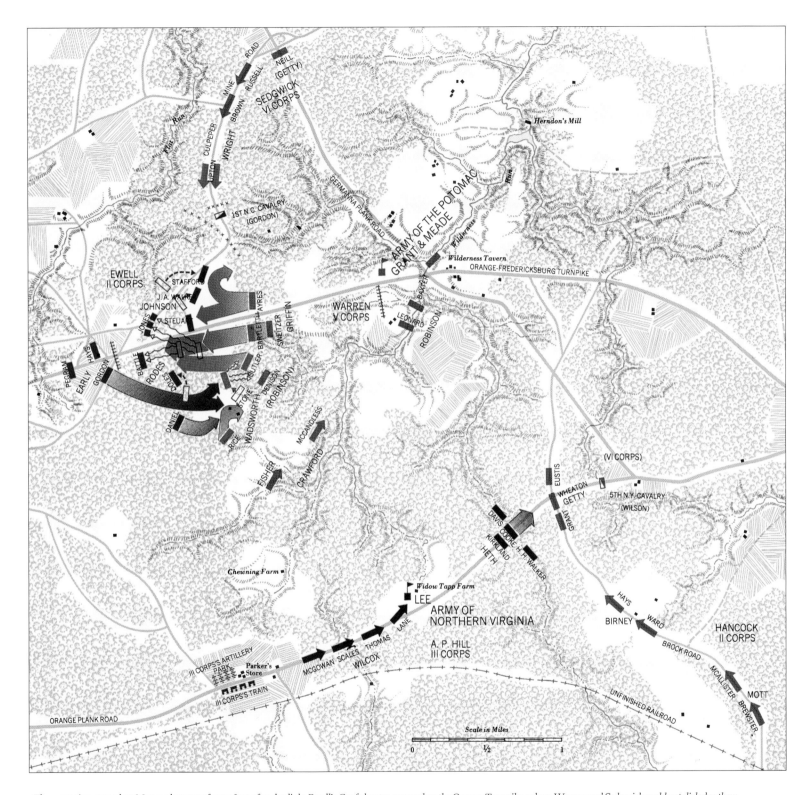

The campaign opened on May 5 along two fronts. Just after daylight Ewell's Confederates emerged on the Orange Turnpike, where Warren and Sedgwick could not dislodge them. Hill's Rebels pressed east on the Orange Plank road, opposed by Getty and Hancock. Fighting raged on both fronts until nightfall.

Alfred N. Proffitt, a 22-year-old private in the 18th North Carolina of Lane's brigade, was shot in the head as the Federals overran Hill's right flank. He survived, although the Minié ball remained lodged in one of his sinuses. Years later, after Proffitt experienced a violent sneeze, the Yankee bullet (above) popped out of his nose.

"Hurrah for Texas. Texans always move them."

with four V Corps brigades under Wadsworth and three VI Corps brigades under Getty, was to smash into Hill's front and northern flank, while Burnside's IX Corps slipped into the gap between Ewell and Hill and swung south, attacking Hill's rear.

Lee realized the danger to Hill and instructed Longstreet to shift his First Corps onto the Orange Plank road. Longstreet started from his bivouac at Richard's Shop but lost his way while taking a shortcut and, as the sun rose, had not yet arrived when the massive Federal juggernaut slammed into Hill's line.

Hill's weakened front collapsed before the enemy onslaught, and the Rebels streamed toward the rear. In desperation, Lee formed artillery above the Plank road at Widow Tapp's farm; the Rebel gunners, loading and firing furiously, managed to

momentarily stanch the blue tide. But it was clear that the gunners would soon be overwhelmed.

Suddenly Lee saw Confederate troops approaching from the rear. When he asked who they were, an officer replied: "The Texas Brigade." At the last possible moment, Longstreet had arrived.

"Hurrah for Texas," shouted Lee, waving his hat. "Texans always move them." The Rebel commander was so excited that he rode forward, intending to lead the fresh troops into battle. The Texans gathered around their beloved commander, crying out, "Go back, General Lee, go back!" He finally moved to the rear only at the insistence of Longstreet.

Hancock's Federals had become disorganized during their advance, and when Longstreet's fresh troops charged into them, the Yankees fell back in confusion. Within an hour, the Rebels had regained several hundred yards of the Plank road. Lee's chief engineer, in the meantime, had explored an unfinished railroad bed and discovered that it passed by Hancock's left flank. Lee sent several brigades down the rail bed; they attacked the unsuspecting Yankee troops and rolled up Hancock's line.

This battle flag of the 5th Texas was presented to the regiment by Mrs. M. J. Young in the spring of 1862 and carried at the Wilderness, where 60 percent of the unit fell. The flag was retired the following October and returned to Mrs. Young.

"We all saw that Gen. Lee was following us into battle—care and anxiety upon his countenance—refusing to come back at the request and advice of his staff."

PRIVATE ROBERT CAMPBELL

5th Texas Infantry, Gregg's Brigade

The 20-year-old Campbell, detailed as a courier on General Gregg's staff, was awed by the sight of Robert E. Lee personally leading the Texans into battle. Posted on the right flank of the Texas Brigade, Campbell's regiment charged across the Tapp field, then swung south to engage Federal troops on the other side of the Orange Plank road. Only 77 of the 188 men in the 5th Texas emerged from the fight unscathed, and every one of its officers was killed or wounded.

As we stood upon this hill, Lee excited and in close consultation with Longstreet.... The cannon thundered, musketry rolled, stragglers were fleeing, couriers riding here and there in post-haste, minnies began to sing, the dying and wounded were jolted by the flying ambulances, and filling the road-side, adding to the excitement the terror of death. The "Texas brigade," was in front of Fields' division—while "Humphrey's brigade" of Mississippians led the van of Kershaw's division.

The consultation ended. Gen. Gregg and Gen. Humphrey were ordered to form their brigades in line of battle, which was quickly done, and we found ourselves near the brow of the hill, Gregg on the left—Humphrey on the right. "Gen. Gregg prepare to move," was the order from Gen. L.

About this time, Gen. Lee, with his staff, rode up to Gen. Gregg—"General what brigade is this?" said Lee.

"The Texas brigade," was General G.'s reply.

"I am glad to see it," said Lee. "When you go in there, I wish you to give those men the cold steel— they will stand and fire all day, and never move unless you charge them."

"That is my experience," replied the brave Gregg.

By this time an aid from General Longstreet rode up and repeated the order, "advance your command, Gen. Gregg." And now comes the point upon which the interest of this "o'er true tale" hangs. *"Attention Texas Brigade"* was rung upon the morning air, by Gen. Gregg, *"the eyes of General Lee are upon you, forward, march."* Scarce had we moved a step, when Gen. Lee, in front of the whole command, raised himself in his stirrups, uncovered his grey hairs, and with an earnest, yet anxious voice, exclaimed above the din and confusion of the hour, *"Texans always move them."*

... never before in my lifetime or since, did I ever witness such a scene as was enacted when Lee pronounced these words, with the appealing look that he gave. A yell rent the air that must have been heard for miles around, and but few eyes in that old brigade of veterans and heroes of many a bloody field was undimmed by honest, heart-felt tears. Leonard Gee, a courier to Gen. Gregg, and riding by my side, with tears coursing down his cheeks and yells issuing from his throat exclaimed, "I would charge hell itself for that old man." It was not what Gen. Lee said that so infused and excited the men, as his tone and look, which each one of us knew were born of the dangers of the hour.

With yell after yell we moved forward, passed the brow of the hill, and moved down the declivity towards the undergrowth—a distance in all not exceeding 200 yards. After moving over half the ground we all saw that Gen. Lee was following us into battle—care and anxiety upon his countenance— refusing to come back at the request and advice of his staff . . . the brigade halted when they discovered Gen. Lee's intention, and all eyes were turned upon him. Five and six of his staff would gather around him, seize him, his arms, his horse's reins, but he shook them off and moved forward. Thus did he continue until just before we reached the undergrowth, not, however, until the balls began to fill and whistle through the air. Seeing that we would do all that men could do to retrieve the misfortunes of the hour, accepting the advice of his staff, and hearkening to the protest of his advancing soldiers, he at last turned round and rode back to a position on the hill.

THE PEACOCK GARB OF THE ZOUAVE BRIGADE

Among the first Federal units engaged in the Wilderness was Brigadier General Romeyn Ayres' hard-fighting Zouave brigade. Half of Ayres' command was made up of Regular Army battalions, the other half of four volunteer regiments from New York and Pennsylvania. The volunteers had recently been issued colorful uniforms modeled on the garb worn by elite French North African troops. Some examples of these uniforms have been preserved and are shown below.

The outfits boosted the men's morale. "We had the vanity to think there was no organization in the army superior to us," one officer recalled. But they paid a high price for their enthusiasm in the Wilderness. In little more than half an hour Ayres' brigade suffered 936 casualties, 633 of them Zouaves.

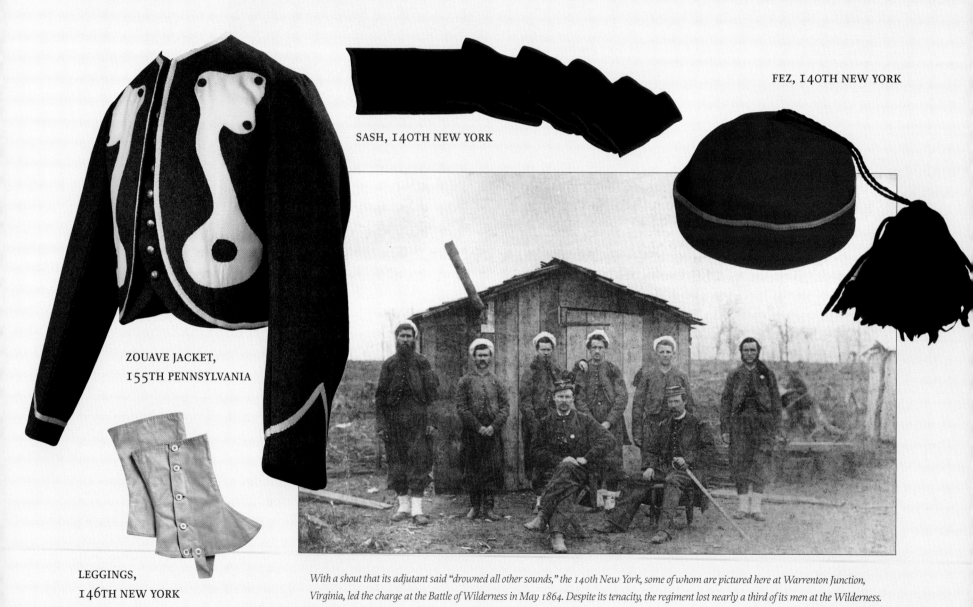

SASH, 140TH NEW YORK

FEZ, 140TH NEW YORK

ZOUAVE JACKET,
155TH PENNSYLVANIA

LEGGINGS,
146TH NEW YORK

With a shout that its adjutant said "drowned all other sounds," the 140th New York, some of whom are pictured here at Warrenton Junction, Virginia, led the charge at the Battle of Wilderness in May 1864. Despite its tenacity, the regiment lost nearly a third of its men at the Wilderness.

Longstreet was then informed of an unfinished railway grade that led past Hancock's left flank. Eager to maintain the initiative, he sent his aide, Lieutenant Colonel G. Moxley Sorrel, with four brigades drawn from the First and Third Corps, along the grade to a point opposite Hancock's flank. While Sorrel's force struck the end of the Union line, the rest of the First Corps attacked from straight ahead. The Confederates rolled up the Union formation, Hancock later admitted, like a "wet blanket."

Wadsworth tried to lead a counterattack north of the Orange Plank road only to be mortally wounded. In the confusion, however, some Virginia troops mistook Longstreet and his staff for Yankees and fired at them. Several men were killed, including General Micah Jenkins. Longstreet himself was severely wounded and knocked out of action for several months.

While combat raged along the Plank road, Burnside was failing miserably in his assigned task of coming in behind the Rebel left. A single Confederate brigade under Brigadier General Stephen D. Ramseur frustrated his first attempt to pass between Ewell and Hill. Then he became hopelessly entangled in the underbrush and Rebel reinforcements arrived to block him, ensuring that the IX Corps was lost to the Union effort for the rest of the day.

But Lee, too, was experiencing frustrations. The Confederate attack had become

> ## *"I settled back to my seat and started to ride on when in a minute the flow of blood admonished me that my work for the day was done."*

disorganized in the wake of the Longstreet mishap, and several hours passed before Lee could reorder his scattered forces on the Plank road. Hancock used the lull to rally his retreating troops and prepare a strongly fortified line along the Brock road. At 5:00 p.m. Lee attacked this new position.

The Federals slaughtered the Confederates as they charged, but then Hancock's log-and-earth barricades caught fire. Taking advantage of the acrid smoke billowing into the Yankees' faces, the Rebels leaped over the fortifications; but Hancock's artillery drove them back, and in short order the breach was sealed. That closed the day's actions on the Orange Plank road.

LIEUTENANT ABNER R. SMALL

16th Maine Infantry, Leonard's Brigade

Nightfall brought no rest to the exhausted soldiers facing each other in the darkened pine thickets and scrub timber of the Wilderness. Nervous pickets and random artillery fire made the retrieval of the wounded a perilous affair. Regimental adjutant Small recalled his foray in search of stragglers in the burning woods just behind the front lines.

//

N ight was falling when I was ordered to beat the woods behind our line for stragglers. I found a few. They were badly frightened men, going they didn't know where, but anywhere away from that howling acre. I urged them to go back to their companies; told them that they would be safest with their comrades and sure to be more than thankful, later, that they had followed my suggestion. I feel sure that they all went back, as they told me they would, though more than one of them started with shaky knees. I didn't blame them for dreading the return.

Shells were still coming over, and here and there one that burst as it hit the ground would start a blaze in dry leaves. A crash and a flare, a scurry of great leaping shadows, and then the fire would die out and the night would be blacker than before. Once, when the darkness was torn suddenly away, I saw a dogwood all in flower, standing asleep and still. I groped on, stumbled, fell, and my outflung hands pushed up a smoulder of leaves. The fire sprang into flame, caught in the hair and beard of a dead sergeant, and lighted a ghastly face and wide-open eyes. I rushed away in horror, and felt a great relief when I found our line again and heard the sound of human voices.

We manned our works all night in the edge of the woods. There was no moon to light the clearing, only dim stars, and the air was hazy and pungent with the smoke and smell of fires yet smouldering. We couldn't see the wounded and dying, whose cries we heard all too clearly; nor could our stretcher bearers go out to find them and bring them in; the opposing lines were near, and the rebels were fidgety and quick to shoot.

"The fire sprang into flame, caught in the hair and beard of a dead sergeant, and lighted a ghastly face and wide-open eyes."

LIEUTENANT ABNER R. SMALL

Colonel Charles Griswold of the 56th Massachusetts Infantry was killed while making a valiant attempt to stem the Rebel offensive on the Orange Plank road. His line thrown into disorder by fleeing troops, Griswold seized the regimental flag shown here and ordered an advance. "He was extremely brave," a comrade recalled, "shot through the jugular vein while holding the colors, which were covered with his blood."

In this Alfred Waud sketch Yankee soldiers rescue a stricken comrade from the burning woods, using muskets and a blanket as a makeshift litter. Scores of dead and wounded were consumed by the flames as the fire swept east toward the Brock road.

Just about the time these assaults were losing their momentum Ewell was preparing to launch an attack of his own north of the turnpike. Early that morning Brigadier General John B. Gordon, whose Georgians manned the Confederate far left, had scouted the area and discovered that the enemy flank opposite his position was "in the air"—unprotected. Gordon had pleaded with his division commander, Major General Jubal A. Early, to let him make an attack, but Early had deemed it too risky. Early objected. He feared—incorrectly, it developed—that Burnside's men were massed nearby. Toward the end of the day, Gordon persuaded Ewell to attack anyway. Shortly before sundown, three of Ewell's brigades crumpled the upper end of Sedgwick's line.

Gordon's assault routed two Federal brigades, and confusion soon enveloped the Federal headquarters. A distressed officer rode up to Grant and advised a retreat, which Grant angrily rejected.

As it happened, darkness and Federal reinforcements put an end to Gordon's attack. The darkness, however, was anything but complete. The woods along the Plank road had caught fire, and in the hellish light men who were too severely wounded to move were screaming as the flames engulfed them. The Battle of the Wilderness was over.

In two days of fighting, Lee's forces had sustained at least 7,500 casualties. But as badly as the Confederate army had suffered, the Union toll was far worse. The action had cost Grant's Army of the Potomac 17,666 men killed, wounded, or captured.

The Union commander, however, was undeterred. He was sticking with what he had stated the previous night to a correspondent who was headed to Washington. "If you see the president," Grant said, "tell him, from me, that whatever happens, there will be no turning back."

SLAUGHTER AT SPOTSYLVANIA

Fog and smoke hung over the Wilderness on the morning of May 7. So did an eerie calm, seeming out of place after the recent violence. General Grant, pondering the bloodshed, concluded that further attacks against the Rebels in the chaos of the Wilderness would be fruitless.

Grant made plans to shift his army southeast to Spotsylvania Court House, an important crossroads on the route to Hanover Junction, where the Rebels' main rail supply lines met. At Spotsylvania, the Yankees would be astride the best route

to Richmond. Lee would be forced to attack Grant there or race to a blocking position to protect the Confederate capital.

During the day Grant issued orders for the 10-mile march to Spotsylvania. General Warren's V Corps would take the lead on the Brock road, moving out under cover of darkness.

Lee suspected that his foe might make such a move, and as a precaution he had ordered a rough track cut through the forest to connect his right flank to a road that led to Spotsylvania. Then, reports of Federal activity on the afternoon of May 7 convinced Lee that Grant might well be heading south.

Lee ordered Major General Richard H. Anderson, who had taken over the First Corps from the wounded James Longstreet, to march his divisions on the Rebel right flank down the newly cut route toward Spotsylvania. Richard Ewell and A. P. Hill would follow with their corps.

The Federal march that night went slowly, the men dead tired and the road clogged with wagons and ambulances carrying wounded. It was after midnight when General Meade arrived at Todd's Tavern—about five miles from the court house—with the lead elements of Warren's corps. There, Meade was incensed to find the way blocked by, of all things, Major General Philip Sheridan's Union cavalry.

Located 10 miles south of the Wilderness battlefield, Spotsylvania Court House became the focal point of the contending armies, as Grant sought to interpose his forces between Lee's Army of Northern Virginia and Richmond.

"Stuart rode along our line, continually cheering us and telling us to hold our fire till the Federals were well in range."

PRIVATE JOHN COXE

2d South Carolina Infantry, Henagan's Brigade

After service in Hampton's Legion, Coxe reenlisted, joining the 2d South Carolina just before the Battle of Chancellorsville. Henagan's brigade, part of Kershaw's division, was one of the lead elements of Anderson's corps that occupied Laurel Hill just in time to block the Federal V Corps on May 8.

Cavalry commander Jeb Stuart conducted a brilliant delaying action to slow the Federal V Corps on the Brock road. A South Carolina soldier recalled Stuart's laughing admonition as he hurried Anderson's infantry into position on Laurel Hill—"Run for the rail piles, the Federal infantry will reach them first, if you don't run."

We made a fair supper on the contents of the haversacks of the dead enemy, and as darkness came on we began to "go to bed" between earth and sky. But the "dull god" sleep was not to preside over us that night. At about half past seven a mounted officer dashed along the line and in sharp but suppressed speech said: "Attention, men! Fall into line!" Of course we privates jumped into line of battle and were sure the enemy was creeping up to us through the bushes. But the next moment the command, "By the right flank, march!" was given, and away we went in quick time through the thickets as best we could. Never before nor afterwards did I experience such a trying night march. On we went, with never a halt, over rough places, little streams, swamps, and through next to impenetrable thickets. The stars were bright, but there was no moon. A little before dawn we struck a road at a left oblique angle and followed the left end, thence on to a bridge over a little stream, and thence on to a crossroads, where at the first show of dawn we found Gen. J. E. B. Stuart and staff in the saddle.

Stuart was smiling, and in a moment he was all action. He turned the head of our regiment at right angles to the left and into the road leading north up a gentle slope. Open fields were on the right and thick pine woods on the left. Halfway up the slope Stuart and his staff wheeled our brigade into line of battle and double-quicked us up to the top of the low hill. There we found some of Stuart's cavalry dismounted behind fence rail breastworks in the open on both sides of the road, and advancing up the other side of the hill there was a heavy Federal line of battle. The dismounted cavalry quickly fell back through our ranks, and we as quickly occupied their position behind the rails. Our regiment, the 2d, was on the left and the 3d on the right of the road. Large fields were in our front, except some open pines on the right, where the 3d Regiment took post. In the field directly in our front were a large two-story farmhouse and outbuildings.

At this time Stuart was the only Confederate general officer in sight and, figuratively speaking, just as cool as a piece of ice, though all the time laughing. He rode right along the lines and, with the help of his staff, personally posted all the regiments of the brigade. On rushed the solid lines of the enemy with every apparent confidence of rushing over us and capturing that hill, which was in truth the key of that route to Richmond. Stuart rode along our line, continually cheering us and telling us to hold our fire till the Federals were well in range.

Through most of May 7 two divisions of Sheridan's troopers had clashed with Jeb Stuart's Rebel cavalry around Todd's Tavern. Brigadier General Wesley Merritt's Federals had managed to drive Major General Fitzhugh Lee's division several miles down the Brock road, where the Rebel line held. Then, at dark, Sheridan had inexplicably ordered Merritt to withdraw back toward the tavern, giving Fitz Lee the opportunity to strengthen his barricades across the Brock road.

Meade rode forward and angrily ordered Merritt to get back into action and clear the road of Confederates. The horsemen rode off into the early-morning darkness and soon ran into the improved Rebel defenses. Despite repeated attempts Merritt could make little headway.

By 6:00 a.m. Warren's infantry took over the job of opening the way to Spotsylvania Court House. Leading the V Corps advance was Brigadier General John C. Robinson's division, which had little trouble pushing forward, despite resistance by the Rebel cavalry. After having fought a five-hour delaying action, Fitz Lee and his men now fell back to a low ridge known as Laurel Hill.

The Rebel cavalry commander had been looking for reinforcements all morning. Finally, one of his couriers found the head of Anderson's approaching column at the Block House Bridge on the Po River. Anderson immediately sent the brigades of Brigadier General Benjamin G. Humphreys and Colonel John Henagan racing ahead to support Fitz Lee at Laurel Hill.

Robinson's Federals, meanwhile, were exhausted from hours of marching but exhilarated to be driving the enemy. As they approached Laurel Hill, Warren rode up and ordered Robinson to attack quickly—before the Rebels dug in. Thinking that they faced only a small contingent of enemy cavalry, the Yankees advanced across a clearing—and were met by furious volleys from the two brigades sent by Anderson, which had arrived in the nick of time.

Robinson's troops were bloodily repulsed, and Robinson himself was badly wounded. As the morning wore on, Warren put in the rest of his corps, which nonetheless was unable to dent the Rebel line. General Meade now realized he was facing more than cavalry.

With the Union attack stalled, Meade ordered Sedgwick's newly arrived corps to form on Warren's left and attack "with vigor and without delay." But by the time Sedgwick got into position, around 5:00 p.m., the 17,000 Confederates of Ewell's corps were coming in on Anderson's right. The Federal assault was ill coordinated and halfhearted, and it, too, failed. When darkness brought a halt to the fighting, the Yankees' route to Spotsylvania remained blocked.

The Confederates spent the morning of May 9 strengthening their earthworks and waiting for an attack. By afternoon the Rebel front resembled a north-pointing V tipped by a strong salient—called the Mule Shoe for its shape—in the center. Anderson's corps stood on the Rebel left, Ewell's corps occupied the Mule Shoe, and A. P. Hill's corps—commanded by Jubal Early, because Hill was sick—held the right.

Meade and Grant also deployed their forces for battle. Hancock's men took up position on Warren's right, while Sedgwick remained on Warren's left.

Shocked gunners and staff officers cluster around General Sedgwick (above and inset) in this painting by soldier Julian Scott. Surgeon Emil Ohlenschlager checks the prostrate figure for signs of life, while Colonel Charles H. Tompkins gestures for aid. Staff officers Martin T. McMahon, Thomas W. Hyde, and Charles A. Whittier (left to right) kneel behind the general. The bullet that struck Sedgwick in the left cheek was fired by a Rebel marksman nearly half a mile distant.

During the morning, Grant lost one of his best generals. While inspecting his corps' forward line, "Uncle John" Sedgwick was shot and killed by a Rebel sharpshooter. Horatio Wright was named to replace him as corps commander.

Shortly after the fighting at Spotsylvania, General Hancock (center), surrounded by staff officers at II Corps headquarters, poses for one of Mathew Brady's photographers with his three division commanders—Major General David B. Birney (right of Hancock), Brigadier General John Gibbon (next to Birney), and Brigadier General Francis C. Barlow (left of Hancock, against tree).

Late on May 9, Grant dispatched Hancock's II Corps in a maneuver against the left flank of Lee's line, believing this to be the weak spot in the Confederate defenses. The plan was for Hancock to cross the Po River on the Block House Bridge the next morning and plow into the end of Lee's position. Then, as the Confederate line collapsed, Warren's V Corps and Wright's VI Corps were to attack from the north, and Burnside's IX Corps was to push into Spotsylvania Court House from the northeast.

Lee reacted decisively to turn Hancock's deployment to his advantage. During the night, he shifted Brigadier General William Mahone's division of the Third Corps to the Block House Bridge to oppose Hancock. He also dispatched Henry Heth's Third Corps division on a mission to move around to the west and then turn north to slam into Hancock's open right flank.

Early on May 10 Heth's men appeared in strength south of Hancock, who had already been stopped by Mahone's blocking force. Trumped by Lee's maneuvers and threatened with destruction, Hancock managed to pull all of his formations to safety except Francis Barlow's division, which was hit hard by Heth's four brigades. Using dogged delaying tactics, Barlow was able to extricate most of his division; but it had been a close call for the Union II Corps. By late afternoon both sides had consolidated and dug in.

The moves against Hancock alerted Grant that Lee had drawn troops from some portion of his line. Grant decided to assault across Lee's entire front to develop the vulnerable spot. To afford his commanders ample time to prepare, he scheduled the attack for 5:00 p.m.

Warren, anxious to redeem his reputation after the fiascos at Saunders' Field on May 5 and Laurel Hill on May 8, petitioned Meade for permission to attack Laurel Hill before the time set by Grant. Meade agreed, and at 4:00 p.m. the V Corps, in conjunction with Brigadier General John Gibbon's division of the II Corps, attacked Richard Anderson's well-prepared First Corps line on Laurel Hill. The attackers never stood a chance. Anderson's Confederates mowed them down as they charged across the open expanse that lay before the Rebel works. Warren's attack not only failed in its own right but also was to have dire consequences later that day.

A major component of Grant's 5:00 p.m. attack was to be a charge by select units from the VI Corps led by Colonel Emory Upton. This hard-fighting brigade commander planned to send a deep, powerful formation of 12 veteran regiments forward without pausing to fire. After they breached the Rebel earthworks, they were to spread left and right to widen the gap. A supporting force commanded by Brigadier General Gershom Mott would then swoop into the breach and consolidate Upton's gains. Simultaneous attacks by the Union V and IX Corps were expected to complete the destruction of Lee's force.

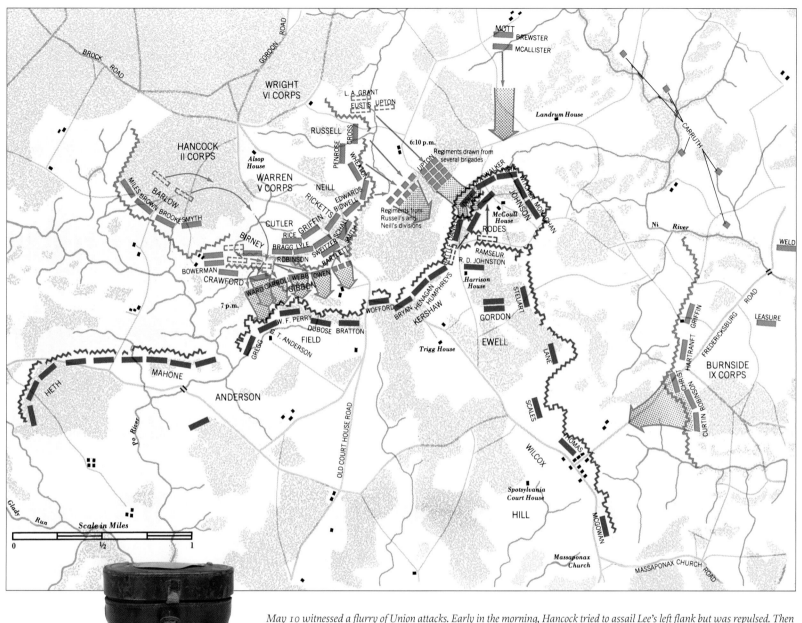

May 10 witnessed a flurry of Union attacks. Early in the morning, Hancock tried to assail Lee's left flank but was repulsed. Then Warren assaulted Anderson's corps on Laurel Hill and was driven back. Toward evening, Upton led 12 regiments in a massed blow against the Mule Shoe's western face and broke through. Mott, however, failed to support Upton, who had to pull back. The day closed with an abortive drive by Burnside against Lee's right flank.

These field glasses were being carried by Lieutenant Colonel Charles Peirson of the 39th Massachusetts at Spotsylvania on May 10 when a shell fragment slammed into him, crushing a lens on the instrument and sending Peirson out of action for a month. The glasses had been given to Peirson by a friend, Colonel Paul Revere—grandson of the Revolutionary War hero—when that officer was mortally wounded at Gettysburg.

The plan quickly unraveled. Because of Warren's abortive attack at 4:00 p.m., Grant postponed his general assault. Mott, however, was not informed of the delay and attacked promptly at 5:00, only to be driven back. Upton, who was ignorant of Mott's misadventure, attacked at 6:30 and met with spectacular success.

Upton's troops swept across a 200-yard gap in front of the Rebel works. Many of the leading troops fell, but others clawed their way through the tangled abatis and threw themselves over the parapet. "Numbers prevailed," Upton wrote, "and, like a resistless wave, the column poured over the works."

The Confederate defenders broke and ran. Unfortunately for the Yankees, however, the troops that were to follow up and exploit the breakthrough never made it to the Mule Shoe. Mott's force never showed up, and Upton's warriors soon found themselves marooned from the rest of the Federal army as Lee skillfully brought up reinforcements and counterattacked. After a protracted struggle costing him more than 1,000 soldiers, Upton managed to withdraw. A superb opportunity for the Union had come to naught.

The other components of Grant's grand assault also fizzled. Following Warren's debacle, Hancock assumed command of the II and V Corps, and at 7:00 p.m. he launched another attack against Laurel Hill. Anderson's Confederates repelled most of the assault force, although Brigadier General J. H. Hobart Ward's brigade managed to break through the Confederate line. But, as had happened with Upton, reinforcements were not forthcoming, leaving Ward's soldiers no choice but to submit to capture or to withdraw through a gantlet of Rebel fire.

Burnside's advance also went nowhere. Lee had drawn Heth and Mahone from Burnside's sector to oppose Hancock on the Po. This was the vulnerable portion of Lee's defenses that Grant had been seeking. Burnside, however, moved with his usual temerity, and his advance ground to a halt well short of its objective at Spotsylvania Court House.

May 10 had been an extraordinarily bloody day for the Federals, and they had nothing to show for it. By masterfully shuffling his units, Lee had deflected Grant's blows and maintained his position in front of Spotsylvania Court House.

Confederate prisoners taken during Upton's charge rush to the rear past the Shelton house in this sketch by Alfred Waud. The Yankees wanted to quickly clear the large number of Rebel prisoners from the salient, and prisoners and guards alike were anxious to escape from the fire-swept fields between the lines. Most of the captives were Georgians from Doles' brigade, but among their number were also a few from Brigadier General Junius Daniel's brigade.

Log-and-earth breastworks constructed by Southerners defending the salient, an outward projecting area called the Mule Shoe, for a time prevented Yankees at Spotsylvania from breaking through in the battles of May 10 and 12. "Give a man protection for his body and the temptation is very strong to put his head under cover too," noted Confederate lieutenant McHenry Howard. "Behind works not a few men will crouch down doing nothing."

"It was the first time during the war that I had actually seen bayonets crossed in mortal combat; it was a crash and a terrible scene for a few moments."

Advancing 40 ranks deep, Barlow's division surges over the earthworks along the northeastern angle of the Mule Shoe. "The Union column swept en masse over the fortifications," recalled Colonel Nelson Miles, whose brigade spearheaded the attack. "It was the first time during the war that I had actually seen bayonets crossed in mortal combat; it was a crash and a terrible scene for a few moments."

In many respects, May 10 had been the gray-haired Confederate's finest day as a defensive commander.

The outcome was a bitter disappointment for Upton, but the attack encouraged General Grant. It had shown that Lee's mighty works could be smashed. That night, an orderly overheard Grant say to Meade, "A brigade today, we'll try a corps tomorrow."

The next day, May 11, Grant deployed his forces for a massive assault on the Mule Shoe, shifting Hancock's corps to a position directly north of the salient. With his formations massed like Upton's for a concentrated blow—but on a much larger scale—Hancock would attack at first light on May 12.

Still hoping to achieve the success that had eluded him on May 10, Grant once again made plans to attack Lee's entire entrenched line. The focus of his assault was to be a weak point in Lee's defenses, a pronounced northward projecting bulge in the Confederate line that the soldiers had dubbed the Mule Shoe.

Under Grant's latest scheme, before sunrise on May 12 Hancock's II Corps was to attack the Mule Shoe's tip, using the same massed spearhead tactic Emory Upton had demonstrated so successfully two days before—but this time with the entire II Corps. Simultaneously Burnside's IX Corps would assault the salient's eastern face. Warren's V Corps was to keep Anderson's Confederates on Laurel Hill occupied, and Wright's VI Corps was to assist Hancock. Grant's intention was to concentrate irresistible numbers against the Mule Shoe, overrun Ewell's Second Corps, and split the Army of Northern Virginia in two.

Lee unwittingly played into Grant's hand. Late on May 11 Lee misinterpreted reports of Union movements and concluded that Grant was preparing to retreat. Avid to pursue, Lee withdrew his artillery from the salient's nose and deployed it on main roads near Spotsylvania Court House, inadvertently weakening the very portion of his line that Grant had targeted.

At 4:30 a.m. on May 12, Hancock's and Burnside's men advanced through a misty drizzle. Hancock's compact force of nearly 20,000 soldiers pressed across a piece of open ground, clawed their way through obstacles strewn by the Confederates, and burst over the top of Ewell's earthworks. The exultant Federals captured 3,000 Rebels, including Major General Edward "Allegheny" Johnson, whose division occupied the tip of the Mule Shoe, and Brigadier General George "Maryland" Steuart.

Lee reacted decisively. While Cadmus Wilcox's Third Corps division held two of Burnside's divisions at bay, Lee sent Gordon with a quickly assembled force to expel the Federals from the eastern face of the Mule Shoe. Hancock's men had become disorganized during the attack, and Gordon was able to drive them back to the earthworks. Lee then began shifting brigades from all three corps to seal the breach on the Mule Shoe's tip and western face. Ramseur's North Carolinians, followed by Brigadier General Abner Perrin's Alabamians, Brigadier General Nathaniel H. Harris' Mississippians, and Brigadier General Samuel McGowan's South Carolinians, clawed their way to the captured line of earth-

General Johnson was provided with a horse by his sympathetic Federal captors although his fellow prisoner, General Steuart, was unceremoniously marched off in front of a cavalry detail after his churlish response to Hancock's cordiality. On their way north the captured commanders were guarded by U.S. Colored Troops, as depicted on this cover of Leslie's.

works and drove the Federals out.

Grant responded by throwing in Wright's corps. Soon the Union divisions of Brigadier Generals Thomas H. Neill and David A. Russell were heaving their combined weight against a bend in the Confederate line that henceforth would be known as the Bloody Angle.

CAPTAIN ALEXANDER W. ACHESON

140th Pennsylvania Infantry, Miles' Brigade

A junior at Pennsylvania's Washington College when the war began, Acheson enlisted with his brothers John and David—the latter was killed at Gettysburg. At Spotsylvania the 140th Pennsylvania, part of the VI Corps, was sent forward to support Hancock's command, but it stalled along the line of captured earthworks. Acheson was shot in the face during the action, returning to duty two months later with his wound unhealed.

After the Sixth Corps reached the ground we occupied, and seeing they were going no further, I left the works and moved forward towards the Confederate line. The object was to see if any of my men had been left between the lines, unable to get away by reason of wounds. After skirmishing over the ground our brigade had charged across, helping the wounded all that was possible, I was about returning, when a young lad was encountered belonging to Company C, 81st Pennsylvania, who was well known.

"Hello, Davis! are you hurt?"

"Yes, Captain, and I fear badly."

I got a coat and rolled it into a pillow for him, cut all his harness off, opened his blouse to relieve his labored breathing, searched over the field until a canteen was found, gave him a drink, wiped the cold death sweat from his forehead, and then shook his hand "goodby."

"Anything else, Davis?"

In a whisper he said: "Yes, take my watch and money, and send them home."

Catching the chain, I pulled at it, but found much resistance. Finally it began to yield, but the whole lining of the vest pocket over the heart was coming out with it. Slowly and with considerable pain it was finally brought to the top, when it became evident what was the matter. A bullet had struck the front case fair in the centre, gone through it, bursting open the back case and carrying the wheels into his body. As he was suffering with the attempts to remove it, I desisted, telling him it was utterly ruined, and left it in his pocket.

"A bullet had struck the front case fair in the centre, gone through it, bursting open the back case and carrying the wheels into his body."

CAPTAIN ALEXANDER W. ACHESON

On March 10, 1864, this national color was presented to the 51st Pennsylvania Infantry, famed as the regiment that had carried Burnside's Bridge at Antietam. At Spotsylvania the banner, one of four Federal flags lost during the repulse of the IX Corps attack, was captured by Private Leonidas H. Deane of the 12th Virginia.

Confederate prisoners crowd the slopes of a ravine dubbed the "Punch Bowl," an improvised holding area near the Army of the Potomac's supply base at Belle Plain, on the Potomac River. Between May 13 and May 18 some 7,500 Rebels passed through Belle Plain en route to the Federal prison compound at Point Lookout, Maryland. Nearly half of them had been captured on May 10 and 12 during the Union assaults on the Mule Shoe.

Recognizing that he could not hold the Mule Shoe against Grant's juggernaut, Lee set the remnants of Johnson's division to constructing a new line of fortifications across the salient's base. Until that project could be finished, the Rebels would have to hold the Bloody Angle.

All day and into the night, the combatants fought savagely for a few hundred yards of earthworks. Rain poured, thunder rumbled, and trenches ran red with blood. Dead and wounded soldiers lay stacked several men deep. The survivors fought on by instinct, firing into each other's massed ranks, stabbing with bayonets, and swinging muskets like clubs. A section of Union artillery rolled to within a few yards of the Rebel earthworks and blasted away with canister. Federal Coehorn mortars threw shells that arched high overhead and fell exploding into the trenches. Civilized men fought like wild beasts in what was to be the war's most intense and prolonged bout of face-to-face combat.

To keep Anderson's corps from reinforcing the Mule Shoe, Grant ordered a reluctant Warren to assault Laurel Hill again. Once more the V Corps marched toward Anderson's frowning battlements, and once more it fell back with heavy losses.

On the other end of his line, Grant ordered Burnside to renew his stalled efforts. About 2:00 p.m. Burnside sent Brigadier General Orlando Willcox's division advancing toward a salient on the eastern segment of Lee's line, but it was repulsed by Heth's division. Near nightfall Grant tried once again by concentrating two V Corps divisions and another division from the VI Corps near the Bloody Angle. Like Grant's other attacks on May 12, this one failed.

The forces that had compressed around the Bloody Angle continued fighting until 3:00 a.m. on May 13, by which time Lee had completed his new line across the base of the salient. His weary soldiers fell back, and the Federals were too exhausted to pursue. The next morning, the sun rose over a scene of carnage that appalled even hardened veterans. And to Grant's chagrin, the Rebels faced him from a new position even stronger than the one they had vacated. His hammering tactics had failed.

General Grant's repeated failure to shatter the Rebel line compelled him to give up at Spotsylvania and seek a more advantageous place to attack. Toward this end the Union commander, as he had done after the Wilderness battle, sought to use maneuver to draw Robert E. Lee from his stronghold.

But before the curtain finally fell on the fighting at Spotsylvania, the Rebels launched an offensive of their own. On May 19 the ever-aggressive Lee, suspecting that Grant had withdrawn troops from the Union right, determined to make a reconnaissance in force in that direction. He ordered Ewell to take his corps across the Ny River and strike in the direction of Fredericksburg with the objective of cutting the Yankees' line of communications.

About 5:00 that afternoon, Ewell was leading his troops toward the Fredericksburg road when he stumbled onto unexpectedly strong opposition— 7,500 fresh Union troops, most of them pulled from the heavy artillery regiments defending Washington. As Ewell's vanguard surged across the fields of the Harris farm, they collided with the countercharging former artillerymen, new to their role as infantry.

A vicious fight ensued. The Federal line broke, but the green Union troops managed to rally and hold. Ewell's horse was shot from under him, and he fell hard to the ground, injured. By 6:00 p.m. reinforcements from two Union corps were arriving, and Ewell, far from the main body of Confederate troops, was forced to retreat. He had suffered some 900 casualties.

With that last spasm of bloodshed the fighting around Spotsylvania Court House came to an end. As a result Grant could count only 56,124 effective fighting men on May 19—half the mighty force he had led into the Wilderness just two weeks earlier. Replacements available to fill the gaps in the Federal battle line amounted to only 12,000. Lee too had suffered heavy casualties—about 11,000 men in the Wilderness and 10,000 at Spotsylvania—he had suffered during the first weeks of May.

On May 21, Grant resumed the chess game of maneuver with his formidable enemy. He intended to return to his plan of sidestepping past the Confederate right flank in the direction of Richmond. Perhaps this time he could catch Lee with his guard down.

Wounded soldiers rest on Marye's Heights outside the city of Fredericksburg. Nearly every store, warehouse and church was used for shelter, and the hills surrounding the town were, according to one observer, "white with tents and wagons." Military bands played lively airs in an effort to cheer the wounded.

WILDERNESS CASUALTIES

FEDERAL		CONFEDERATE	
Killed	*2,246*	*Killed, wounded, & missing*	*11,000*
Wounded	*12,073*		
Missing	*3,347*		

SPOTSYLVANIA CASUALTIES

FEDERAL		CONFEDERATE	
Killed, wounded, & missing	*10,920*	*Killed, wounded, & missing*	*10,000*
Total	*28,586*	*Total*	*21,000*

Opposite: At a council of war held in the yard of Massaponax Church on May 21, 1864, General Grant sits cross-legged, smoking a cigar, in the pew directly beneath the trees. At his left are Assistant Secretary of War Charles Dana and Brigadier General John Rawlins, Grant's chief of staff. General Meade, wearing a hat with downturned brim, sits at the far end of the pew at left, studying a map.

MAIL CALL

—//—

"Everybody is writing who can raise a pencil or a sheet of paper," noted a Virginia soldier in July 1861. In Rebel and Yankee camps alike, no diversion occupied as much of the soldiers' time as writing letters home. For every day the men spent in battle, they passed months fighting heat, cold, hunger, and tedium. But perhaps most of all they suffered from homesickness. The only cure short of a trip home—officially sanctioned or otherwise—was the mail.

For that reason, the arrival of the regimental postmaster caused as much excitement as an issue of fresh food. Letters from wives or sweethearts, parents, and brothers and sisters gave the soldiers a connection to the familiar and friendly world they had left behind and assured them they had not been forgotten.

But the mail brought more than sentimental words. Packages of food and gifts, such as warm socks, produced whoops of glee. "Never in my life have I enjoyed good things from home to more entire satisfaction," wrote a Corporal Simpson of the 3d Carolina Infantry, who got a box of blackberry and peach pies and other delicacies from his Aunt Caroline. Although these packages sometimes took ages to arrive—often in battered condition—they never failed to boost morale, for they not only added quantity and variety to the soldiers' meager rations, but they always included a badly needed supplement—love.

Portable writing kits, which contained pen, ink, and paper and rolled up for easy storage, found wide use during the war. The kit above belonged to Sergeant Henry S. Parmalee of the 1st Connecticut Cavalry. Parmalee, a former piano maker, lost his writing hand after being shot near Petersburg in 1865.

"Last night I received one of those old fashioned soul inspiring letters from home."

SURGEON DANIEL M. HOLT

121st New York Infantry

Daniel Holt was already 42 years old and a successful physician when he signed up with the 121st New York. He was captured at Chancellorsville in 1863 but was quickly released under an exchange of medical personnel ordered by Robert E. Lee. During the war he contracted tuberculosis, which killed him in 1868.

Camp of the 121st Regiment.
N.Y. Vols White Oak Church, Va.,
March 7th, 1863
My dear Wife:—

Last night I received one of those old fashioned soul inspiring letters from home. Sometimes I think I am growing childish as well as old when I find that I am so easily affected by a kind word. It is so seldom we hear them here, that when they *do* come, it seems like breathings from the spirit land—voices from the other side of the river where our loved ones have gone before and are waiting our arrival. Let them come. It makes us no worse and perhaps much better. I am firmly of the opinion that were more of such letters written to desponding soldiers, we should have less desertion and harder fighting. No man can discharge his duty so cheerfully and promptly when cries of distress and mournful regrets at leaving are constantly poured into his ears, as he can when the partner of his life and object of his affections stirs him up to action by words of patriotic fire and christian enthusiasm. No, it is only those who are the recipients of complaining, fault-finding letters—letters worthy of no virtuous Christian mind—letters such as harrow up all the ill nature within us, and *those who receive no letters*, who are found in the rear when a battle is raging—who can see no beauty in our government—no benefits resulting from its administration and who are ready at all times to despond and talk evil when success does not attend every movement—it is this class of men, who made unhappy by home influence, is sure to turn away and disgracefully leave our country in the hands of traitors, while the loyal brother fights the battle of both. Then give me such letters as make me feel that I am a man and have a country and family to defend, and gives me an idea of freedom such as God intends all to possess.

"The mail comes regularly every day. None for me."

On Hilton Head Island, South Carolina, men of the 3d New Hampshire Infantry relax in camp around a makeshift table littered with letters, dominoes, an inkwell, and photos from home. While one soldier writes a letter, a companion reads the latest edition of Harper's Weekly. The men sport distinctive "camp caps," off-duty headgear in the form of homemade knit tam-o'-shanters.

CORPORAL TALIAFERRO N. SIMPSON

3d South Carolina Infantry

Three of Simpson's cousins were members of the 3d South Carolina. At Antietam one was wounded, one was captured, and one was missing in action; Simpson ventured back onto the battlefield to search in vain for him. Through these hardships he wrote compulsively to his family. Though he was clearly exasperated with the lack of mail he got in return, its absence resulted not from indifference on the part of his family but rather from sporadic mail delivery.

Ask yourselves the question whether it be natural for those at home to treat an absent member as you all have at certain times, and are still treating me, and you will most assuredly acknowledge that my meaning is quite evident. When Lewis arrived, he gave me a letter from Pa and Ma. For many, many weeks before I had looked in vain for a note of some kind. And since the arrival of Harry, not a line have I received from home. Why is this? Are you getting tired of writing, is paper getting scarce and dear, or are you all getting too lazy to postpone doing nothing to write me a few lines saying that all are well and expressing some affection for your absent boy and buddie? The mail comes regularly every day. None for me. Others can read letters from home. I can't. Why? Simply because you won't write to me. I always supposed that it was natural for a family to have a care for one of its members, whether absent or present. And when that care is lost or gone, I think nature is deviating from its usual path. You think the same, I know, without asking you.

What excuse therefore have you to offer for your conduct? What excuse can you give for this violation of the natural laws by which not only man but every animal in the universal world is governed? When you write I will expect a full explanation and a positive affirmation that such a course will not be pursued in future.

DELIVERING THE MAIL

"Guerrillas, bushwhackers, and even apparently inoffensive citizens were always ready to waylay the lonely carrier of Uncle Sam's mail-sack."

Letter carriers pose with their mail wagon at Brandy Station in 1864. The previous year Union general Joseph Hooker instituted bureaucratic reforms that greatly increased the reliability of the mail, which was vital to a soldier's morale.

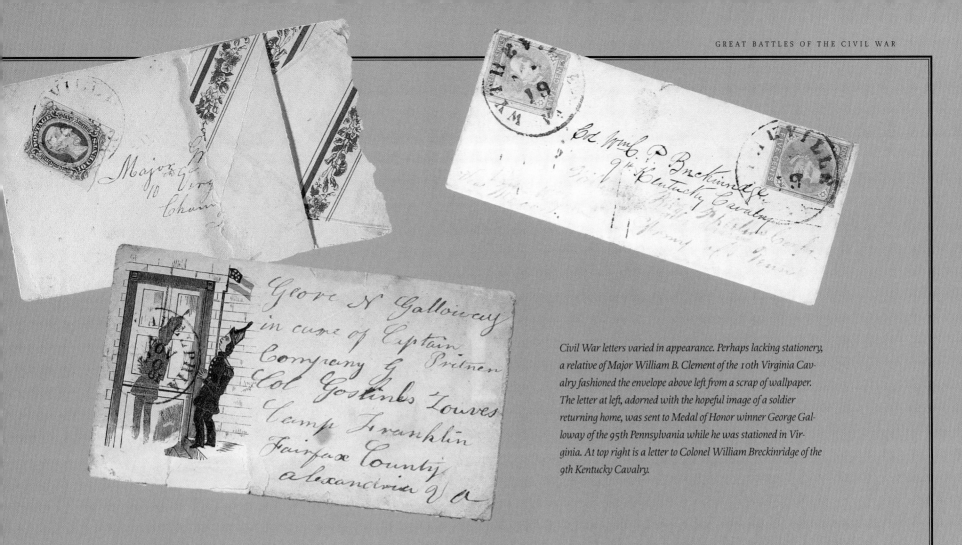

Civil War letters varied in appearance. Perhaps lacking stationery, a relative of Major William B. Clement of the 10th Virginia Cavalry fashioned the envelope above left from a scrap of wallpaper. The letter at left, adorned with the hopeful image of a soldier returning home, was sent to Medal of Honor winner George Galloway of the 95th Pennsylvania while he was stationed in Virginia. At top right is a letter to Colonel William Breckinridge of the 9th Kentucky Cavalry.

PRIVATE A. MORRIS

2d Ohio Infantry

This account of how the mail was delivered during the war appeared in an 1887 edition of the National Tribune. *Pressed into mail duty in 1862, Morris narrowly escaped capture while delivering orders from General Don Carlos Buell directing his men to assemble at Chattanooga. Upon reporting back to Buell, the general—who knew how hazardous the journey would be—replied frankly, "Well, Morris, I never expected to see you again."*

This service in the Army of the Cumberland was performed by private soldiers detailed for that purpose. Usually two men were stationed at the headquarters of each division, and it was their duty to see that the mail was promptly transported to and from the division and the nearest railroad communication, however near or remote. The distance varied from a few hundred yards, as at Murfreesboro and Chattanooga, to thirty or forty miles during the Stone River, Chickamauga and Atlanta campaigns. Soldiers detailed for this duty were usually regarded by their comrades as having a "soft thing," but the work was often laborious and full of danger. Guerrillas, bushwhackers, and even apparently inoffensive citizens were always ready to waylay the lonely carrier of Uncle Sam's mail-sack.

At the nearest distributing office the mail for each division was put up in separate sacks and plainly marked with the name of the division commander. These were then sent as near the front as possible by rail. The trains were met by the division mail carrier—in an ambulance until the army crossed the Tennessee River and afterward on horseback—and the mail taken to division headquarters. There it was sorted and put into brigade sacks, which were taken by carriers to their respective brigades, and there distributed into regimental packages and taken by the regimental carrier to each regiment and then sent to the different companies, and finally distributed to the men.

I presume none of us have forgotten what an important event was the arrival of the mail in camp; how eagerly we gathered about the Captain's tent while the names were being called, and the feeling of pleasure or of disappointment as we received or failed to receive the expected missive from loved ones away up in "God's Country."

WRITING HOME

"For a long time I have been hearing that the channel of your affections was running in an opposite direction."

LIEUTENANT JOHN V. HADLEY

7th Indiana Infantry

Many members of the 7th Indiana were forsaken by women they left behind, and Lieutenant Hadley grew worried that his love, Mary Jane Hill, was about to do the same. But Mary put his fears to rest in her reply to this letter, and the two were married in 1865. During the war Hadley was wounded twice. Captured, he escaped from a prisoner of war camp. After the war he became a lawyer and served on the Indiana Supreme Court.

Alexandria Va July 22d/62
Miss Mollie J. Hill
Friend Mary—I write you to day under very embarrassing circumstances. For a long time I have been hearing that the channel of your affections was running in an opposite direction—that you were about to adopt another name &c and I never gave it the least attention until very recently. But the unaccountable delay of your letters has forced some suspicion at last. If you have found another more worthy or who has a greater claim upon your affections I am glad for I must say that I never felt myself worthy of that heart which knows no sentiment that is not pure & holy & which feels no motive but to make happy and blessed all associates.

Hearing what I have heard it is a natural and just desire of mine to be made acquainted with the fact, for if I am writing to a lady whose heart and hand belongs to another, the tenor of my letters is neither polite nor wise. You can, of course recognize their impropriety as well as I. If the report adjudges you rightly, Mary, you will do me at least one more kindness & write me at once, frankly about the matter, that I may not labor under misapprehensions. For if I have ever been confidential and faithful to you, I shall ever remain so to be and confide evrything that you may see proper to divulge. Let me know the worst and if the report be true let the cords of intimacy be a little relaxed but I hope those of friendship may never be broken.

I cannot write longer—politeness forbids—I could tell you many things but cannot now for this is the third letter at least since I had one from you. excuse my impertinence for you know my honesty.

I am as ever Jno

The silk tobacco bag shown above, carefully cross-stitched by Retta Patton of Tennessee for Confederate soldier James B. Coleman, is typical of such pouches sent as tokens of affection to soldiers, particularly in the Southern armies. Many wartime photographs show Confederate soldiers proudly displaying their tobacco pouches looped through the buttonholes of their jackets.

Chief Trumpeter Charles W. Reed spent nearly three years in the 9th Massachusetts Light Artillery as a bugler and topographical engineer. At Gettysburg, his first battle, he risked his life to rescue his commanding officer and was awarded the Medal of Honor. His letters home, a sample of which are shown at right, are filled with sketches that depict the everyday activities of a soldier.

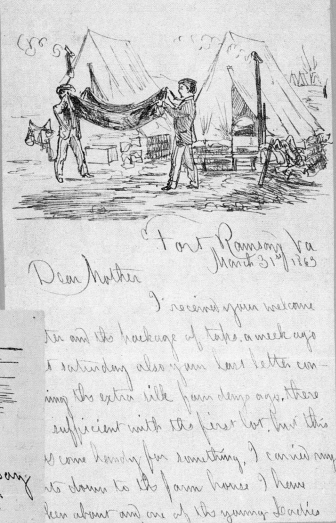

Clockwise: Eating a meal at Fort Ramsay, January 1863; folding blankets in winter camp at Fort Ramsay, near Falls Church, Virginia, March 1863; cooking over an open fire at Fort Ramsay, November 1862.

"Oh god how proud I feel of you just to think that my wife was tested and remained true."

PRIVATE JOHN D. TIMERMAN

3d New York Cavalry

Timerman enlisted after an argument with his wife, Mary, thinking the war would be over in a matter of months. He ended up spending more than three years in the Union army, was captured twice, and survived a stint in Richmond's Libby Prison. Despite their disagreements John loved and missed his wife and was outraged to hear that one Henry Dupler had made advances on Mary in his absence. There is no record of how Timerman settled his "debt" with Dupler.

Camp Bates Dec 15 1861
Dear Wife
    I was quite Surprised to hear Such news from Henry Dupler but I hope the time will come when he will have to meet me and then I think I will Settle my Debt that I owe him in regard to his insulting you and I think I will make him chaw his words or he make his words gospel. but never mind it at present but one thing certain I am going to come to See you next pay day if I have to desert But Oh my dear how happy I am that you did not give in to his wishes for what would have been my feelings if I should have heard to the contrary but enough of that I always thought I had as true a wife as there was living but now I know it and oh god how proud I feel of you just to think that my wife was tested and remained true to her Dear husband but perhaps Some would Say he will never know it is true I might never have found out but what would have been your feeling if ever you Should have layed in my arms and then think that you had deceived me or what would have been your feelings Supposing you should have heard that I had broken my oath and deserted you by giving that to others that I most Solumly Swor Should be yours. . . .
    From Your True & Effectionate Husband
    JD Timerman
    P.S. Write soon
    Bless you

Mary Timerman posed for this photograph in her "young married days" while her husband was at war. After his return, they spent an additional 31 years together.

"I would love to have yours and the childrens pictures taken in a double case and sent to me yours on one side and the childrens on the other."

PRIVATE JACOB W. BARTMESS

39th Indiana Mounted Infantry

Being away from home for so long gave Private Bartmess, like so many other soldiers, a renewed appreciation for the simple pleasures of family life. His letters home reflect this, talking frequently of the things he misses. After his return from the war in July 1865, Bartmess worked as a preacher and had three additional children with his wife, Amanda.

Dec. 23 '62.
Amanda Bartmess
Camp near Nashville Tenn
Amanda—my own dear wife.—.

I have been for the last few days and am at the present quite grunty. my Stomache is out of fix. I went to the doctor this morning and got a dose of oil; may be the oil will Settle it. The brigade went out on drill this morning but I did not go along.

I received your letter of the 11th. and 12th. yesterday evening, which gave me much Satisfaction. I received a letter from you about one week ago stating that you were sick., and O, how anxious every evening when the mail came. since that was I to get a letter from you to hear how you was getting. I am sorry that you was sick but am glad of the change and hope you may get well and stout as you ever have been. You Said that Elliot was very Mischevious. Tell him that papy says he must not be too bad and you may be sure that I would like to be there and take lista on my lap and talk to her and hear her talk. Well my prayer is that the time may soon come.

You say you miss me when you go to bed Ah, dear Wife. When meal time comes. and I sit down on the ground. useing the ground for a table. and having on the table some hard crackers some old bacon. a coffee pot full of coffee, which pot is so black and hard looking that you would scarcely use it for a Slop pot at home, then pour my coffee into an old tin cup which would be a disgrace to the kitchen at home then I miss you. When I lie down on the ground at night with my overcoat for a pil-

low and my blanket for a cover heareing oath after oath till at last nature yealds and my eyes close in Sleep. O then I miss When I go about camp hearing the continual din of camp. there I miss you. where er'e I go in whatever company I am. I miss my dearest one—my wife.—

And my Children which I once thought troublesome. would now be a great delight to me even when they are most mischevious. I most earnestly pray that this state of things will not last long. . . .

I would love to have yours and the childrens pictures taken in a double case and sent to me yours on one side and the childrens on the other. but it will cost too much. do just as you like about that. I am sorry to hear that the boys do not get along any better than they do. for I would like to have Harrison with me then I believe I would get along better. Tell the boys to write to me as often as they can. though I have not wrote to them. the letters that I send to you will do for the whole family. I believe I will close this letter. I think I have averaged two letters a week I wish you may do as well we have had nice dry wether here ever since I have been here Amanda I wish I could tell you how deep my affection is for you but I can not so nomore at this time.

J. W. Bartmess.

This photograph of an unidentified Confederate captain and his son was typical of the comforting family pictures that soldiers carried with them during the war.

PACKAGES FROM HOME

"Ellen the box, is safe, the rebels did not get it have no alarm about it, sleep well on it..."

SERGEANT WILLIAM J. REICHARD

128th Pennsylvania Infantry

Reichard served with the 128th Pennsylvania for nine months before mustering out in May 1863. But just before the Battle of Gettysburg, he responded to the call for volunteers to defend the state and rejoined—this time as a sergeant in the 41st Pennsylvania. When the Rebel threat to Pennsylvania ended he was discharged after 34 days. While camped with the 128th at Maryland Heights near Harpers Ferry in October 1862, he received a box from home.

Now for the box, the bread is good it was outside a little mouldy, but cut it off. The doughnuts were most all spoiled anything baked in fat wont keep I have found out and aint healthy for us. The little round sugar cakes were a little spoiled from the doughnuts but can use most all. The rusks were nice the 2 sugar cakes are nice only got a little wet dont hurt them. The sponge cake is pretty nice yet. The butter, jellies, & catsup are bunkin, the other jar of jelly I have not opened yet, until the one is empty especially as Wilgh. has some also, but he cant come up with my butter. The [apples] are very nice I will save them a while if I can. I would like to mention all the things but cant bring them to mind just now. That inkstand came very handy but am sorry to say that my pen came away and is no where to be found, so I borrow one. Ellen the box, is safe, the rebels did not get it have no alarm about it, sleep well on it, Ha Ha. I will write to Eddie pretty soon, if there are any other I have not written to I must have forgot it so they must excuse me. My health is recovering fast since I have the medicine and teas. I am too thankful for them I dont drink any coffee so you can send such teas often in papers if only a little at a time. The bologna sausages are nice but I can not eat much, dry beef would have been better. Wilgh. has been sick for the last 2 days but I hope he may soon be right again. It is cold & windy today, but pretty warm in our tent. Milt returned with the pickets to camp yesterday noon. He was quite surprised to see such a pile of boxes he thought that we might call it an express office.

A Union soldier at Rappahannock Station, Virginia, loses himself in a hometown newspaper in this 1864 Edwin Forbes study.

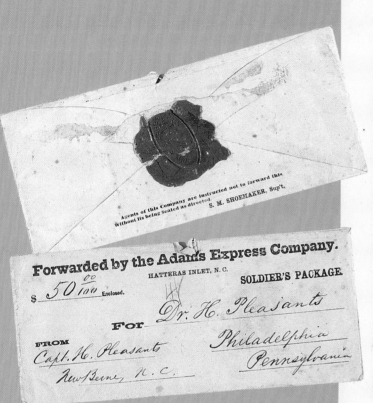

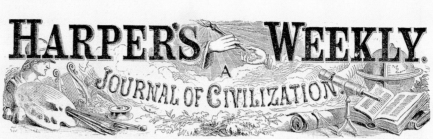

Vol. VI.—No. 262.]   NEW YORK, SATURDAY, JANUARY 4, 1862.   [SINGLE COPIES SIX CENTS. $2.50 PER YEAR IN ADVANCE.

Christmas Boxes in Camp—Christmas, 1861.

The Adams Express Company transported "express boxes," filled with items ranging from luxuries to necessities, to soldiers in the field. The arrival of such boxes in camp was greeted with much enthusiasm, as illustrated by Winslow Homer on the front page of the January 4, 1862, issue of Harper's Weekly (right). The Adams Express Company also sent "money orders," such as the one shown above, with its wax-sealed reverse. It was wired from New Bern, North Carolina, by Captain Henry Pleasants, of the 48th Pennsylvania, to his father, Dr. H. Pleasants, in Philadelphia.

Atlanta
Sherman Moves East

QUEST FOR THE GATE CITY—Christmas of 1863 was only a week away, but the Confederate soldiers of the Army of Tennessee saw little cause to celebrate the holiday. With the army firmly settled into winter quarters near Dalton, Georgia, the Southern troops knew there would be slight chance of fighting before spring.

But the respite from active campaigning brought little comfort to the gray-clad warriors. They huddled about their campfires, exhausted and dispirited, their dream of an independent Southern Confederacy an ephemeral and distant hope.

Sam R. Watkins, a 24-year-old private serving in Company H of the 1st Tennessee Infantry, saw evidence of the dismal aftermath of defeat everywhere he looked. The fearless, battle-tested units were now, he wrote, "in rags and tatters, hungry and heart-broken, the morale of the men gone, their pride a thing of the past." To Watkins it seemed as if the entire Army of Tennessee was pervaded with "a feeling of mistrust."

Most of the Confederate fighting men saw the recent disaster at Chattanooga as the result of neither the Union's Major General Ulysses S. Grant's leadership nor any want of valor on their part. The blame, they felt, rested squarely on the shoulders of their commanding officer, General Braxton Bragg.

When the Army of Tennessee collapsed in the face of Grant's assault at Chattanooga, Bragg was unable to rally his troops, who merely hooted and jeered as they passed. "Bragg looked so scared," Watkins recalled, "he looked so hacked and whipped and mortified and chagrined at defeat." Denied the fruits of their victory at Chickamauga, the Army of Tennessee had lost all confidence in their commander. "Bully for Bragg," one Rebel exclaimed sarcastically, "he's hell on retreat."

Within days of the debacle at Chattanooga Bragg tendered his resignation, and Confederate president Jefferson Davis saw no alternative but to accept. With Lieutenant General William J. Hardee exercising temporary command of the Army of Tennessee, Davis pondered his choice of a replacement for Bragg. Reluctantly, he decided to tender the position to the commander of the Army of Mississippi, General Joseph E. Johnston.

In the course of two and a half years of war, Davis and Johnston's relationship had soured to one of mutual dis-

PRIVATE SAM R. WATKINS

1st Tennessee (C.S.) Infantry, Maney's Brigade

Like most of his fellow soldiers, young Watkins had developed a healthy contempt for the dour Braxton Bragg, the commander they blamed for their defeat at Chattanooga. But Watkins and his mates soon discovered a leader worthy of high praise in Bragg's replacement, Joseph Johnston.

B ut now, allow me to introduce you to old Joe. Fancy, if you please, a man about fifty years old, rather small of stature, but firmly and compactly built, an open and honest countenance, and a keen but restless black eye, that seemed to read your very inmost thoughts. In his dress he was a perfect dandy. He ever wore the very finest clothes that could be obtained, carrying out in every point the dress and paraphernalia of the soldier, as adopted by the war department at Richmond, never omitting anything, even to the trappings of his horse, bridle and saddle. His hat was decorated with a star and feather, his coat with every star and embellishment, and he wore a bright new sash, big gauntlets, and silver spurs. He was the very picture of a general.

But he found the army depleted by battles; and worse, yea, much worse, by desertion. The men were deserting by tens and hundreds, and I might say by thousands. The morale of the army was gone. The spirit of the soldiers was crushed, their hope gone. The future was dark and gloomy. They would not answer at roll call. Discipline had gone. A feeling of mistrust pervaded the whole army.

A train load of provisions came into Dalton. The soldiers stopped it before it rolled into the station, burst open every car, and carried off all the bacon, meal and flour that was on board. Wild riot was the order of the day; everything was confusion, worse confounded. When the news came, like pouring oil upon the troubled waters, that General Joe E. Johnston, of Virginia, had taken command of the Army of Tennessee, men returned to their companies, order was restored, and "Richard was himself again." General Johnston issued a universal amnesty to all soldiers absent without leave. Instead of a scrimp pattern of one day's rations, he ordered two days' rations to be issued, being extra for one day. He ordered tobacco and whisky to be issued twice a week. He ordered sugar and coffee and flour to be issued instead of meal. He ordered old bacon and ham to be issued instead of blue beef. He ordered new tents and marquees. He ordered his soldiers new suits of clothes, shoes and hats. In fact, there had been a revolution, sure enough.

trust that bordered, at times, on enmity. Johnston, however, possessed a great strength—the ability to inspirit and motivate his soldiers. If anyone could reinvigorate the waning morale of the Army of Tennessee, Davis believed, Johnston was the man. "Your presence, it is hoped, will do much to inspire hope and reestablish confidence," Confederate secretary of war James A. Seddon wrote Johnston on December 18, 1863; "as soon as the condition of your forces allow it is hoped you will be able to resume the offensive."

When Johnston arrived at Dalton on December 27, however, he found the Army of Tennessee in no condition to resume the offensive anytime soon. Sickness and desertion had reduced available strength to fewer than 40,000 men. Food and ammunition were in short supply, many of the cavalry horses had died, and most of the artillery horses were too weak to pull the heavy guns.

Johnston set about bettering the condition of his soldiers with a will. Sam Watkins was impressed by Johnston's bearing, calling him "the very picture of a general." When Johnston reviewed Watkins' unit, the private noted the new com-

"I do not believe there was a soldier in his army but would gladly have died for him."

mander's "restless black eye, that seemed to read your very inmost thoughts." Johnston strolled through the camps, chatting with individual soldiers and listening to their complaints. More and better rations were issued, and it became clear to the men in the ranks that Old Joe was, as one soldier put it, a "feeding general." In a move guaranteed to boost morale, Johnston began to grant furloughs so that men who had not seen their families in months, or even years, could travel to their distant homes.

Benevolent as he was, Johnston was also a professional soldier and a disciplinarian. He instituted a rigid schedule of mandatory drills, dress parades, and target practice. Mock battles and even large snowball fights were held to get the troops in fighting trim. As spring approached, it was clear that, thanks to Johnston, the Army of Tennessee had undergone a remarkable transformation. "He was loved, respected, admired; yea, almost worshipped by the troops," Watkins declared; "I do not believe there was a soldier in his army but would gladly have died for him."

Johnston's soldiers would need all the devotion they could muster, for while the Confederate commander was equipping and reorganizing, his Federal opponents were preparing to take the offensive on an unprecedented scale. The coordinated strategy that had eluded President Abraham Lincoln and his senior officers for two and a half bloody years was finally coming to fruition under the guidance of the

General Joseph E. John-
ston had few illusions
about the daunting deci-
sions facing him in the
summer of 1864. But in
spite of persistent pressure
from Jefferson Davis,
Johnston chose the preservation of his army over
the dubious prospect of
defeating a determined
and greatly superior foe.

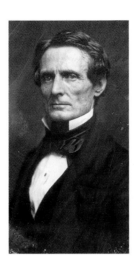

Born in Kentucky,
raised in Mississippi,
and educated at West
Point, Jefferson Davis
was named President
of the Confederacy
in February 1861. He
would have preferred
to remain a soldier—
his view of himself as a
strategist led to frequent
disagreements with
his generals.

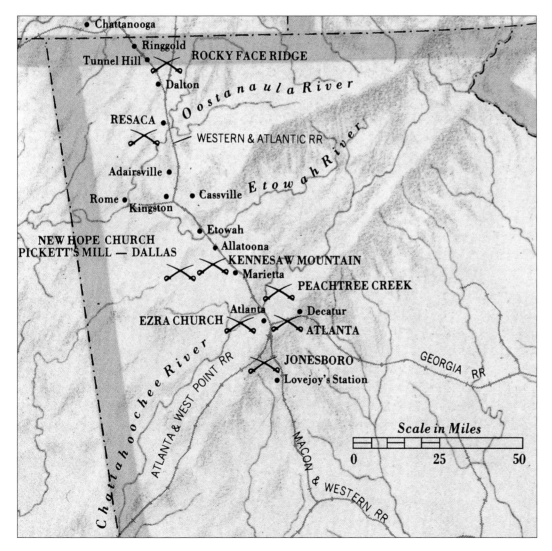

Between Ringgold and Atlanta lay some of the most daunting terrain
faced by any army during the war. The rugged landscape provided
Confederate defenders with ideal ground to conduct a fighting retreat.

Union's preeminent military leaders, Major Generals Ulysses S. Grant and William T. Sherman. Both men knew that if the South was to be vanquished, the spring campaign would have to be waged aggressively, and on two fronts.

As general in chief, Grant decided to take personal charge of the Federal forces in the eastern theater, where General Robert E. Lee's dauntless Army of Northern Virginia remained the South's most potent field command. At Grant's recommendation Sherman would give up the Army of the Tennessee to take over Grant's previous command, the Military Division of the Mississippi, and thus oversee operations in the western theater. The two would launch simultaneous offensives at the beginning of May. The plan was simple: As Sherman later wrote of Grant, "He was to go for Lee and I was to go for Joe Johnston."

In the course of the war Grant and Sherman had forged a remarkable bond of friendship and mutual trust, though the two were quite dissimilar personalities. At 44, the lean and grizzled Sherman was four years older than his friend Grant. While Grant's fame had steadily grown, Sherman's military career had seen its share of ups and downs, with some critics going so far as to question Sherman's sanity. But Grant remained steadfastly loyal to his comrade in arms. "He stood by me when I was crazy," Sherman once said, "and I stood by him when he was drunk."

Intellectually acute, and genuinely popular with the fighting men, Sherman was the type of soldier Grant needed to take on Joe Johnston's forces and push the

"He stood by me when I was crazy, and I stood by him when he was drunk."

western armies forward to Atlanta—the vital Confederate transportation hub and supply depot that was dubbed the Gate City of the Deep South.

With a wartime population in excess of 20,000—second only to the Confederate capital, Richmond—Atlanta had grown in less than two decades from a ramshackle crossroads to a thriving boomtown. It was a manufacturing and financial center whose four railroad lines were crucial arteries of supply to Southern forces in Alabama, eastern Georgia, the Carolinas, and Virginia.

The exigencies of war had flooded Atlanta with troops, civilian auxiliaries, and thousands of slaves who labored to construct the city's formidable earthen fortifications. There were dozens of mills and factories, an arsenal, and scores of

Opposite: One of the vital links along Sherman's supply line during his drive on Atlanta, this railroad bridge boasts blockhouses and a permanent garrison to defend the span against the constant threat of Rebel cavalry.

From a low hill, Sherman watches his troops tramp along a winding Georgia road. He believed that maneuverability won battles and sought to mold his army "into a mobile machine."

hospitals. If Sherman could take Atlanta, his forces would be poised to strike a fatal blow to the Southern heartland.

Sherman was pleased to see that many regiments whose three-year terms of service had recently expired were reenlisting en masse, thanks to the payment of a generous bounty and the granting of month-long "veteran furloughs." But even if he would not lack for soldiers, his army of 100,000 men would have to be sustained on the march. "The great question of the campaign was one of supplies," Sherman later wrote, and the stockpiles in Chattanooga's warehouses were dwindling.

With an energy comparable to that of Johnston, Sherman began amassing the food and ammunition his troops required to live in the field. Railroad locomotives and boxcars were confiscated by military authorities, rations that had been issued to pro-Union Tennesseans were diverted to the army, and a group of experienced quartermasters set to work organizing and dispensing the matériel in Chattanooga. Once the campaign got under way, even if the lines of supply broke down, Sherman was prepared to live off the land. "Georgia has a million of inhabitants," he informed Grant. "If they can live, we should not starve."

In formulating his strategy for the Atlanta campaign, Sherman would draw upon the combined efforts of three Federal armies. The largest of these was the Army of the Cumberland, 73,000 strong, commanded by Major General George H. Thomas. Thomas' IV and XIV Corps had recently been reinforced by the addition of the newly created XX Corps, the largest in Sherman's force. The XX Corps was an amalgam of Federal units transferred from the eastern theater and commanded by Major General Joseph Hooker.

"'O, yes; Thomastown—Thomasville; a very pretty place, indeed; appears to be growing rapidly!'"

CAPTAIN DAVID P. CONYNGHAM

Volunteer Aide-de-Camp, Federal Staff

Well aware of Sherman's low opinion of reporters, Conyngham, a correspondent for the New York Herald, secured an officer's appointment and a uniform to give him easier access to military circles. In addition to his work reporting on the campaign, he served admirably on several staffs.

Thomas's headquarters comprised a most gorgeous outlay of tents of all kinds; wall tents, Sibley tents, fly tents, octagon tents, and all kinds of tents. Every officer had a tent; almost every servant had a tent; while the adjutant general's tent was a sort of open rebellion against all restrictory orders. A kind of caravan, full of pigeon holes, and covered over with an immense fly, was one of its most peculiar features. Sherman, on the contrary, had but one old wall tent, and some three or four flies, for his quarters.

Whether it was that General Thomas felt sore at the contrast, or General Sherman did not like the example set by General Thomas, he could never let slip an opportunity to pass a joke at Thomas's expense.

He would frequently rein up his horse in front of Thomas's quarters, and ask, "Whose quarters are these?"

"General Thomas's, general," would be the reply.

"O, yes; Thomastown—Thomasville; a very pretty place, indeed; appears to be growing rapidly!" and he would chuckle and ride off.

Both Grant and Sherman were appreciative of Thomas' determination but tended to regard the stalwart army commander as slow to take the initiative. And the presence of the politically scheming and ambitious Hooker was something both men would have preferred to do without. Conversely, in Major General James B. McPherson, leader of the 24,500 troops of the Army of the Tennessee, Grant and Sherman saw a kindred spirit and worthy protégé. At 35, McPherson was an affable and universally popular West Pointer who seemed to hold great potential as Sherman's successor in command of the hard-fighting westerners of the XV, XVI, and XVII Corps.

The final element of Sherman's force, Major General John M. Schofield's Army of the Ohio, was the smallest and least experienced. Though a titular army commander, the 32-year-old Schofield had only one complete corps, the XXIII.

The 254 guns composing Sherman's available artillery lent his force considerable firepower. In addition, four separate divisions of cavalry would work in conjunction with the seven infantry corps. Sherman was pleased with his massive strike force. "I think I have the best army in the country," he wrote his wife, Ellen, "and if I can't take Atlanta and stir up Georgia considerably I am mistaken."

While Sherman was massing his forces near Ringgold, a mere 12 miles northwest of Dalton, Johnston continued to prepare his outnumbered army for the inevitable onslaught of the Federal juggernaut. With 54,000 troops, 144 guns, and only 2,400 of 8,500 cavalrymen with horses, Johnston was facing odds of more than 2 to 1.

Time and again Davis and his secretary of war tried to prod Johnston into committing his army to an offensive that would strike into Tennessee before the Yankees were ready to move. And each time Johnston demurred, even raising doubts as to his army's ability to successfully defend his base of operations at Dalton.

Despite these reservations, however, Johnston was loath to abandon his position at Dalton. Sticking to his defensive strategy, he would wait for the Federals to make the first move. "I can see no other mode of taking the offensive here than to beat the enemy when he advances," Johnston informed his president, "and then move forward." Hoping to prevent any more excuses on Johnston's part, Davis reluctantly ordered Lieutenant General Leonidas Polk's Army of Mississippi to the field of operations in Georgia.

On March 2, 1864, Lieutenant General John Bell Hood arrived at Dalton and assumed command of the division formerly commanded by Major General Thomas C. Hindman. Johnston welcomed the presence of one of the most intrepid fighters in Lee's Army of Northern Virginia, and Hood greeted his new commander warmly.

Although in constant pain from severe wounds suffered at Gettysburg and Chickamauga, Hood seemed the very embodiment of Southern fortitude, and just the type of man Johnston wanted to lead a division in the coming struggle.

But Hood cherished a well-concealed contempt for the commander of the Army of Tennessee. He was what Johnston most decidedly was not—an intimate of Jefferson Davis. And even as Johnston continued to protest the wisdom of launching

Major General George H. Thomas (left) was hailed as the Rock of Chickamauga for his masterful direction of the Federal rear guard on the last day of that battle in September 1863. Disavowed by his family in 1861 when he forsook his native Virginia to serve the Union, Thomas was a West Point classmate of Sherman, who gave him command of the 73,000-man Army of the Cumberland, the largest by far of Sherman's three armies.

In this April 1864 photograph, the Army of the Cumberland's chief of staff, Brigadier General William D. Whipple (standing, center), hands a dispatch to a clerk seated at General Thomas' many-pigeonholed special office wagon, the most prominent feature of his elaborate headquarters.

Following their introduction in the spring of 1863, Federal corps badges soon became cherished emblems of unit pride for Union soldiery. Pictured (from right to left) are those for the Army of the Cumberland: the star and crescent of the XX Corps, the acorn of the XIV Corps, the triangle of the IV Corps, and the crossed-saber badge of the Cavalry Corps.

Some twenty years after the war, the Western & Atlantic Railroad, connecting Chattanooga and Atlanta, was anxious to increase ridership. Realizing that no line had more battlefield sites along its route, rail officials produced a guidebook, The Mountain Campaigns in Georgia. Most of the illustrations, whose accuracy was underscored by testimonials from Sherman and Johnston, were done by artist Alfred R. Waud, "who personally visited all the battlefields depicted." Waud first prepared colored sketches (left) which were then rendered into engravings for publication (below). Shown here is the Federal advance into Mill Creek Gap.

Perched inside a bandstand that resembles a huge bird's nest, the regimental band of the 38th Illinois prepares to serenade Brigadier General William P. Carlin (center, double row of buttons) and his staff; Carlin's brigade was posted near Ringgold, Georgia, preparing to march on Atlanta. Carlin led his men so effectively during the upcoming campaign that he was promoted to command of a division.

an offensive against Sherman, Hood was reinforcing Davis' contrary view in a series of letters written without the knowledge of his superior. "We should march to the front as soon as possible," Hood wrote on March 7, "so as not to allow the enemy to concentrate and advance upon us."

On May 4, 1864, Grant's forces began their great offensive against Lee's Army of Northern Virginia. Sherman had hoped to get his own offensive under way on May 5, but McPherson's column was delayed in its march toward Ringgold, and Sherman was compelled to postpone the launch date to May 7. Sherman had considered and then scrapped two plans of operation in favor of a strategy that would avoid a costly head-on assault against Johnston's defenses at Dalton. In an approach that would characterize much of the campaign to come, Sherman hoped to bypass Confederate strongpoints and pry the enemy loose with a sweeping maneuver against the vulnerable Rebel flank and rear.

Stolid George Thomas had suggested the strategy that Sherman now adopted. While Schofield's and McPherson's armies made a feint against Johnston's main line at Tunnel Hill and Buzzard's Roost, Thomas' Army of the Cumberland would march south. Thirteen miles south of Dalton, Thomas would turn east and pass through Snake Creek Gap, then sever the line of the Western & Atlantic Railroad at Resaca.

Although Sherman embraced Thomas' proposal, he made a crucial change in assignments. Perhaps because he doubted Thomas' ability to move quickly, Sherman gave the job of flanking Johnston at Snake Creek Gap to General McPherson. Thomas would work in conjunction with Schofield to pin Johnston at Dalton, while the Army of the Tennessee marched south to Snake Creek Gap and Resaca.

By the evening of May 6, Sherman's legions were finally ready. "The army was at its fighting weight," one Illinois lieutenant wrote, "ready and willing to give and take hard knocks." In the grueling campaign for Atlanta, there would be hard knocks aplenty.

MARCH TO THE CHATTAHOOCHEE

Within hours after Sherman launched his offensive on May 7, Thomas' troops had cleared the Confederates from Tunnel Hill. Schofield's Army of the Ohio linked up with Thomas, and the combined force continued to advance on Johnston's main position at Dalton, only to be stymied by the formidable defenses on Rocky Face Ridge. Meanwhile McPherson was leading his Army of the Tennessee south to Snake Creek Gap, threatening to envelop the Rebel flank and rear. Sherman was confident that the bold maneuver would succeed, exclaiming to his aides, "I've got Joe Johnston dead!"

Sherman's elation was short-lived, however. When the vanguard of McPherson's army passed through Snake Creek Gap on May 9, they found several thousand Confederate troops blocking the approaches to Resaca, where the Western & Atlantic Railroad crossed the Oostanaula River. Fearing that the Confederates were already there in strength, McPherson pulled back into the gap after a short fight and awaited orders. In fact McPherson vastly outnumbered the enemy troops to his front. His caution allowed the newly arrived Army of Mississippi troops led by Leonidas Polk to bolster the defenses at Resaca, while Johnston, alerted to the presence of enemy troops in his rear, began withdrawing from Dalton. By May 13

Johnston had joined forces with the bulk of Polk's corps and was preparing to make a stand at Resaca.

Disengaging most of Thomas' men and sending them on the route McPherson had taken through Snake Creek Gap, Sherman was disappointed to find Johnston dug in at Resaca. "Well, Mac," Sherman told McPherson, "you have missed the opportunity of a lifetime."

When Sherman attacked on May 14, his troops were driven back with heavy losses. The next day, Sherman again assaulted Johnston's line and again was repulsed. But when Brigadier General Thomas W. Sweeny's division crossed the Oostanaula at Lay's Ferry, threatening Johnston's left, the Confederate commander saw no alternative but to abandon the bridgehead at Resaca and continue his withdrawal southward.

Sherman decided to keep on flanking, bypassing a Rebel strongpoint astride Allatoona Pass and shifting the bulk of his army to Dallas, 15 miles farther to the southwest. From there he could turn east and gain the line of the Western & Atlantic at Marietta, severing Johnston's line of retreat. On May 23 Sherman crossed the Etowah River, which he grandly proclaimed "the Rubicon of Georgia." But rough terrain slowed the Yankee columns, and when the vanguard of Sherman's force—Hooker's XX Corps—reached Dallas, Johnston had beaten them to the punch.

Hooker attacked on May 25, but his columns were cut to pieces by the well-placed soldiers of Hood's corps covering the New Hope Church crossroads. Two days later Major General Oliver O. Howard's IV Corps assaulted the Confederate right at Pickett's Mill, only to be hurled back with great loss by Major General Patrick Cleburne's division. "This is surely not war," one Federal wrote, "it's butchery."

Unable to pierce the strong enemy line, Sherman once again sent McPherson on a flank march around the Southern left. On June 4 Johnston evacuated the war-ravaged landscape that men of both sides had dubbed the Hell Hole and fell back to the Lost Mountain Line that covered the Western & Atlantic Railroad near Big Shanty.

While surveying Federal positions from the top of Pine Mountain on June 14, Lieutenant General Polk, the highest-ranking Confederate officer to fall in the campaign, was killed by a Federal shell. When continuing Union probes threatened him again, Johnston withdrew to a position two miles to the south along a line buttressed by Kennesaw Mountain, a natural fortress known as the Gibraltar of Georgia.

Sherman shifted Schofield and Hooker to the south in an attempt to bypass the Rebel strongpoint. But Johnston dispatched Hood's corps to counter the threat, and on June 22 the fiery Southern commander lashed out at the Yankee force near Kolb's Farm. Federal artillery mowed down the charging Southern ranks, but for the time being Hood had stymied the enemy effort to get in the rear of Johnston's army.

"I am now inclined to feign on both flanks and assault the center," Sherman wired the War Department. "It may cost us dear, but the results would surpass any effort to pass around." On June 27 Sherman committed the bulk of his force in a massive attack on the Rebel defenses of Kennesaw Mountain. Advancing with suicidal gallantry, the blue-clad columns charged time and again against the impregnable enemy line. But the Yankee soldiers' bravery proved futile in the face of devastating fire that scythed down entire ranks of men. By day's end 3,000 Union

In an impressive display of military muscle, two full brigades of the Federal IV Corps maneuver during training exercises near Chattanooga. Skirmishers lead waves of double-ranked infantry across the field while artillery pieces draw up to give support. The IV Corps was part of General George Thomas' Army of the Cumberland, largest of the armies that Sherman would lead into Atlanta.

> "*I am now inclined to feign on both flanks and assault the center. It may cost us dear, but the results would surpass any effort to pass around.*"

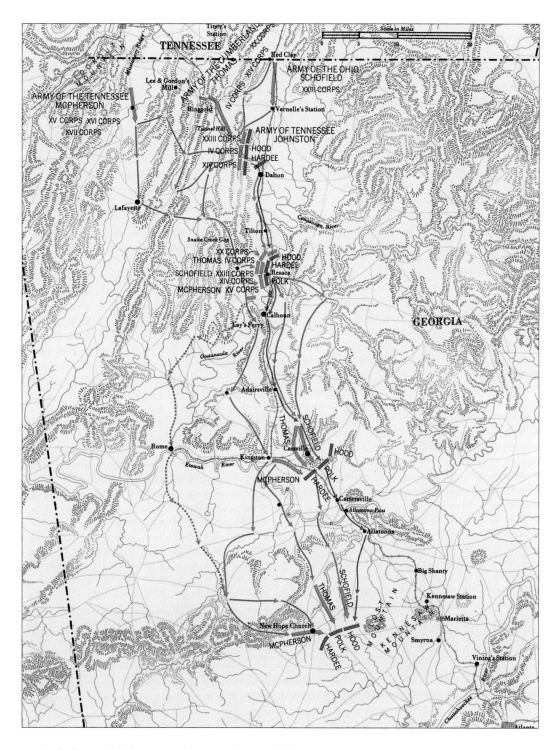

During the first month of the campaign, the outnumbered Confederates bloodied the pursuing Federals while deftly avoiding their flanking maneuvers. But in doing so, the Rebels lost about 75 miles of territory.

Formerly the chief engineer of the Georgia Railroad, Captain Lemuel P. Grant was assigned in 1862 to oversee the repair and rebuilding of railroads wrecked by Federal raiders. Later he was charged with the construction of defensive works around Atlanta and Augusta.

troops had fallen, and the fighting petered out in a grim standoff.

Seeking to break the impasse, Sherman shifted McPherson's army from the left to join Schofield on the right of the extended Union line. This maneuver pried Johnston out of his entrenchments on Kennesaw Mountain and compelled the Southern commander to continue his retreat to a new position near the Western & Atlantic at Smyrna.

Following another brief standoff on July 4, Sherman again began sidling to Johnston's flank, and the Confederates once more withdrew, this time to a powerful series of earthworks north of the Chattahoochee River—the last great barrier between Sherman and Atlanta.

Johnston had such confidence in his new line that he predicted it would hold Sherman back "a long time." Sherman, too, admired the Chattahoochee defenses. Riding down from Smyrna on the morning of July 5, he viewed the Confederate works from a hill about two miles from the river. He thought the line "one of the strongest pieces of field fortification I ever saw."

But from that same hill Sherman saw another vista that excited him more. For the first time in his two-month campaign the ultimate objective came into view— Atlanta, beckoning from a distance of no more than eight miles.

Enticing though the target must have been, Sherman had no intention of launching the type of head-on assault that had bloodied his armies at Kennesaw Mountain. On July 8 a full division from Schofield's Army of the Ohio crossed the river six miles beyond Johnston's right flank. The next day Brigadier General Kenner Garrard's cavalry division gained the south bank of the Chattahoochee near Roswell, 16 miles northeast of the Confederate position.

With Federal forces threatening to cut him off from Atlanta, on the night of July 9 Johnston abandoned his defenses. That night another enactment of the now familiar rituals unfolded: the withdrawal across bridges strewn with green cornstalks to muffle the sound of retreat, the burning of the spans, the dismantling of the pontoons.

With the Chattahoochee behind him, General Johnston marched his army a few miles back to Atlanta's outer defensive line on the high ground south of Peachtree Creek, a tributary of the river. The new line faced north to cover the city, now just a few miles away.

Sherman celebrated by taking a much-needed bath in the Chattahoochee. The next morning, July 11, he wired Washington, "We now commence the real game for Atlanta."

A fragment of Grant's drawings for the fortifications around Atlanta (left) shows the layout of one of the forts. Grant began construction of the works in July 1863; by April 1864 the city was encircled by a system of berms, ditches, and parapets that would later offer refuge to General Hood's beleaguered troops. The view (opposite) of the Confederate works ringing Atlanta was taken from the northwest corner of the defense line looking east from Fort Hood.

"[This is] one of the strongest pieces of field fortification I ever saw."

Although the Rebel assault on the Union left met with some success on May 14, a follow-up attack the next afternoon by Major General Alexander P. Stewart's division brought only heavy losses. Among the captured were both the commander, Colonel A. R. Lankford, and the battle flag (right) of the 38th Alabama. Issued earlier that spring, the flag bears the crossed cannon awarded for the capture of enemy artillery.

A Confederate battle line from Hindman's division pours murderous volleys into a mass of Federals struggling up a slope at Resaca. Though artist Alfred Waud rendered the terrain accurately, he took a bit of dramatic license by placing the Rebels out in front of their earthworks, an unlikely position unless they themselves were attacking.

The worst fears of Jefferson Davis had come to pass. In two months the Yankees had succeeded in maneuvering Joe Johnston into the defenses of Atlanta, and a siege of the Gate City seemed a foregone conclusion.

RESACA

Determined to make a stand at Resaca, on May 13 Johnston had positioned his forces along a ridge that lay between the Conasauga and Oostanaula Rivers and protected the line of the Western & Atlantic Railroad. Rather than launch an immediate assault, Sherman had deployed four of his corps to pin Johnston in place while McPherson's Army of the Tennessee moved south to probe for an opening in the enemy left flank.

On the afternoon of May 13 Major General John A. Logan's XV Corps arrived just west of Resaca and drove in the outlying Confederate skirmish line. Logan discovered that Johnston had anchored his southern flank—Leonidas Polk's corps—on a bend in the Oostanaula, thus preventing any flank attack at that point.

Temporarily frustrated on the right, Sherman decided to strike at Johnston's center on the morning of May 14. The Federal attack began at 9:00 a.m. but was hurled back by heavy Confederate fire.

The only substantial Federal success came at 6:00 p.m., when several brigades of Logan's XV Corps managed to clear Polk's troops from high ground on the southern left flank. Polk pulled back to a new position closer to the railroad and the town of Resaca, while the Yankees dug in along the former Confederate line.

As Sherman tried and failed to break Johnston's line, McPherson's troops discovered a way to pry the Confederate army out of its formidable defensive position. Sweeny's division of the XVI Corps moved several miles south of Resaca to Lay's Ferry, where the Oostanaula made a loop to the west. On the late afternoon of May 14, Sweeny brushed aside a handful of Confederate cavalry and crossed two regiments in pontoon boats to the river's southern shore.

With Sweeny in position to cut the Western & Atlantic Railroad and block Johnston's line of retreat to Atlanta, Johnston summoned his senior officers just after sundown and informed them that the army had no choice but to abandon the

"But now their friends will never know where they sleep 'the last unwaking sleep,' for no rough board even marks their resting place. There is something terrible to me in this nameless resting place, this unknown burial, I trust it may never be my lot to die and be buried thus."

PRIVATE HIRAM S. WILLIAMS

Pioneer Corps, Army of Tennessee

Born and raised in New Jersey, Williams completed his carriage maker's apprenticeship in 1854 but spent the next few years stumping for the nativist Know-Nothing party in the Midwest. In 1861, two years after moving to Alabama, Williams enlisted in the Confederate army. On the night of May 15, 1864, temporarily detached from his construction duties, he was assigned to help get the wounded across the Oostanaula during the retreat from Resaca.

How shall I describe the past night? If I live to the allotted period of man's existence, I can never forget the scenes I have witnessed for they are indelibly stamped on my memory. Limbs mangled and torn, much suffering and pain—Oh, Lord! It was truly horrible. About two o'clock last night we were ordered to assist our Division Surgeons about getting the wounded men on board the train bound for Atlanta. The wounded for the whole Corps were scattered about on every side. Some in a deserted house, some under rough shelters of brush, some in tents, and others on the cold ground with no covering but their blankets. By passing once through the grounds, we could find men suffering from all kinds of wounds. Here on a rough table the surgeons were amputating a leg, on another one's arm was being taken off, while a score of others just taken from the ambulances were awaiting their turn, with all manner of wounds claiming attention. There one could see what ever was. In the hospital after the wounds are dressed it is bad enough, but it is no comparison to the battle-field hospital. I saw one poor fellow belonging to a Texas Reg who had his leg almost torn off by a cannon ball just above the knee, the bones crushed and torn out, only adhereing to the trunk by a few pieces of skin, who had been bounced for nearly 6 miles in an old wagon of an ambulance over roads far from being good. Yet he was still alive and perfectly reliable in his speech.

In moving the wounded, it was really heart rendering to listen to their groans and cries. Several had been shot directly through the bowels, and the least movement caused them to suffer intensely. After loading three trains with the wounded, we were called upon to bury three men who had died since being brought to the hospitals. We dug a shallow grave some three feet deep by 4 feet wide and laid the three poor soldiers in it side by side and covering them with their blankets. We covered them up as hastily as possible for day was fast approaching, and the enemies guns at Resaca, the light of burning bridges, and the reports of soldiers all told us that the enemy would soon be upon us. What a burial! Unknown, they were inhumanly, *treacherously*, buried by stranger hands. Yet, no doubt that they had fast and loving friends and relatives, who if they could, would have closed their eyes and performed the last sad rites of the dead, with tears in their eyes and sighs of true grief. But now their friends will never know where they sleep "the last unwaking sleep," for no rough board even marks their resting place. There is something terrible to me in this nameless resting place, this unknown burial, I trust it may never be my lot to die and be buried thus.

Defended by a Rebel fort on the hilltop at left, the narrow gorge at Allatoona Pass offered dismal prospects for any direct assault. The repulse at Resaca was enough for Sherman. On May 20 he ordered his columns to leave the railroad, bypass Allatoona, and head southwest toward the small town of Dallas.

position at Resaca. Major General William H. T. Walker's division held the Federals at bay long enough for Johnston to evacuate the Resaca defenses.

Under cover of darkness Johnston's troops disengaged and fell back to a tight perimeter just north of Resaca. From there the Rebel soldiers crossed the Oostanaula River on a temporary pontoon bridge, and in the early morning hours of May 16 they set fire to the railroad span to prevent it from falling into Yankee hands. They also ignited the nearby wagon bridge, but advancing Federal skirmishers managed to douse the flames. Johnston continued to fall back southward along the line of the Western & Atlantic toward Adairsville, Kingston, and Cassville.

The fighting at Resaca cost the Federals some 4,000 casualties, 600 of whom were mortally wounded. Confederate losses totaled nearly 3,000, more than 500 of whom were captured. Bloody as the fight was, it was only the beginning of a grueling series of hard-fought engagements on the road to Atlanta.

NEW HOPE CHURCH, PICKETT'S MILL, AND DALLAS

Johnston continued to retreat south across the Etowah River to the high ground at Allatoona Pass. Sherman, in pursuit, declined to risk another costly frontal assault; instead, he decided to cut loose from the railroad, cross the Etowah, and bypass Johnston's position from the west.

All three Union armies moved out on May 23. Schofield skirted Johnston's left flank, while Thomas, in the center, marched on New Hope Church, southwest of Allatoona. McPherson's army swung farthest to the west and marched on Dallas, a crossroads southwest of New Hope Church. If all went according to plan, Johnston would be forced to fall back from Allatoona in order to secure his vulnerable railroad lifeline to Atlanta, and Sherman would win a bloodless strategic victory.

But as the Federal armies closed in on their objectives, Confederate cavalry alerted Johnston, who moved quickly to counter the threat. He ordered a series of westward shifts, and by May 24 a solid nine-mile front blocked Sherman's line of march.

On the late morning of May 25 Hooker's corps was approaching New Hope Church when the leading division met sudden and unexpected resistance from Major General Alexander P. Stewart's Confederates. At 4:00 p.m. all three of Hooker's divisions renewed the advance, attacking in parallel columns as the skies opened in a torrential downpour. "It was simply slaughter," one Federal recalled; "scores and hundreds of men surged right up to the breastworks and died there." Within minutes Hooker's corps was repulsed with nearly 1,600 casualties.

Having failed at New Hope Church, Sherman decided two days later to shift Howard's IV Corps to Pickett's Mill, a mile beyond the Confederate right flank. But Johnston had again guessed Sherman's intentions. At 4:30 p.m. on May 27, the Federals once again advanced in compact columns of brigades, and just as at New Hope Church, the blue-clad ranks were savaged by canister and musketry. Wave after

The landscape for this Waud engraving was based on a photograph taken of the shattered New Hope Church battlefield not long after the fighting there on the afternoon of May 25, 1864. As the Yankees stumbled through the dense undergrowth toward a barely visible Rebel line, "the shot and shell from the enemy's batteries crashed through the timber," one survivor recalled, "cutting off limbs, blazing and splitting trees, like tremendous bolts of lightning."

wave of Federal troops pressed on only to be hurled back with staggering losses. Some 3,000 Federals fell at Pickett's Mill, nearly 10 times the Confederate loss.

Following this second costly reverse, Sherman began to shift his armies back to the line of the Western & Atlantic. On May 28, when Johnston realized Sherman was again on the move, he ordered a reconnaissance of the Federal lines at Dallas to determine if McPherson's army was withdrawing.

Determined to prevent Sherman from shifting eastward, Johnston kept up the pressure on the Federal right in a series of assaults that pinned McPherson's army in place for nearly three days. By now many of the weary Yankees had taken to calling the battle-scarred area the Hell Hole. But by June 1 McPherson had managed to reach New Hope Church, enabling Thomas and Schofield to pull their armies out of the entrenchments and gain the line of the Western & Atlantic at Acworth. From there Sherman shifted south along the railroad to Big Shanty, midway between Allatoona and Marietta.

By mid-June Johnston had taken a new position along the rugged slopes and ridge lines that connected Lost, Pine, and Brush Mountains. Beyond these crests lay the still more formidable Kennesaw Mountain, and within this natural fortress the Army of Tennessee prepared to meet Sherman's next move.

Men of the 78th Pennsylvania doffed their hats for this group portrait atop Lookout Mountain before marching into Georgia. Caught in the open at Pickett's Mill on May 27, the Pennsylvanians held for four hours, fighting with what their brigade commander termed a "persistency and heroism worthy of all praise." The regiment suffered 49 casualties before being ordered to withdraw.

KENNESAW MOUNTAIN

On June 14 General Sherman began testing the strength of Johnston's new defensive line, which covered a 10-mile front extending from Lost Mountain in the west to Brush Mountain in the east. That day a round fired from an Indiana battery claimed the life of General Leonidas Polk, who was touring the position in company with Johnston and Hardee. Over the next four days Sherman kept up the pressure in what he described as "one grand skirmish extending along a front of eight miles." The Federals gained no clear advantage, and by the morning of June 19 Johnston had drawn his troops into a formidable network of batteries and rifle pits centered on the 700-foot crest of Kennesaw Mountain. Less than 30 miles from the outskirts of Atlanta, Kennesaw was, in Sherman's words, "the key to the whole country." But the Union commander was unwilling to attack without first attempting to find a means of flanking the natural fortress.

Sherman sent Hooker and Schofield to secure the Powder Springs road, which seemed a promising route around the Confederate left. Johnston anticipated the move, and on June 22 Hood's corps was in place to block the Federals at Kolb's Farm. For the time being Sherman gave up on his effort to flank Johnston and turned his attention back to the Confederate center.

The strongest part of the Confederate line extended south along the slopes of Kennesaw Mountain to Little Kennesaw—300 feet lower than its sister peak—and on to Pigeon Hill, which covered the Burnt Hickory road to Marietta. At dawn on June 25 Sherman began to mass his forces in front of the Kennesaw Mountain Line.

Remarking that "flanking is played out," Sherman ordered a two-pronged assault on the Rebel center for 8:00 a.m. on June 27. While Schofield continued to threaten the enemy left flank, Logan's XV Corps would advance on Little Kennesaw and Pigeon Hill. But the main attack would be made by Thomas one and a half miles farther south. There the enemy-held crest was lower and the gentler western slopes better suited to infantry deployments.

Three of Logan's brigades moved out at 8:30 a.m., but the assault collapsed in the face of Confederate artillery fire from Pigeon Hill. The steep, heavily wooded terrain slowed the attackers, and the handful of Federals who gained the Rebel breastworks were killed or captured. The survivors remained pinned down until darkness enabled them to work their way back to the Union lines.

Like so many battle sites of the Civil War, the field of Pickett's Mill was left blanketed with the residue of the fighting. This canteen lay rusting where it was dropped until a souvenir hunter picked it up long after the battle.

While McPherson's diversionary attack was being repulsed, Thomas was launching the main effort against a wooded ridge defended by Hardee's corps. Although the ground seemed more promising than did the rugged slopes of Kennesaw Mountain and Pigeon Hill, the Southern line was well entrenched and bolstered with artillery. Cleburne's division held the northern portion of the ridge, and Major General Benjamin Franklin Cheatham's the southern, where the earthworks turned to the east in a salient soon to become known as the Dead Angle.

Moving to take cover from Federal artillery, Johnston and Hardee look over their shoulders just as a shell strikes Polk, who had held back for one last glance at the enemy's positions. The unknown artist of this sketch downplayed the severity of Polk's fatal wound—in reality he was practically disemboweled.

Resplendent on a black charger, Major General John A. Logan (left, center) watches as troops of his Federal XV Corps advance toward the smoke-wreathed, Confederate-held heights beyond. Logan's objective was to drive a wedge between Little Kennesaw (background, left) and a nearby knob called Pigeon Hill, thereby splitting the Confederate line.

Two brigades of Brigadier General John Newton's division would advance against Cleburne's defenses, while the brigades of Brigadier General Charles G. Harker, Colonel Daniel McCook Jr., and Colonel John G. Mitchell assaulted the Dead Angle. Thomas directed that the 8,000 troops spearheading the assault be massed in columns of regiments and that they charge at the double-quick without halting to fire: They would carry the Rebel breastworks at bayonet point. One Federal officer called the formation "a human battering ram."

Following a brief preliminary bombardment, two signal guns launched the blue-clad masses toward the enemy line. They were met with a wall of flame that brought down entire ranks of men, while the survivors tried to press on over the writhing bodies of fallen comrades. Everywhere the Federal attack was blunted at great cost, but nowhere was the carnage greater than at the Dead Angle.

Harker's brigade swung against the angle from the north but was hurled back after Harker was shot from his horse with a fatal wound. McCook's and Mitchell's brigades charged the southern side of the Dead Angle but were similarly repulsed. McCook was mortally wounded, as was his successor in command of the brigade, Colonel Oscar F. Harmon. When Sherman suggested that Thomas try another attack, the commander refused with the comment, "One or two more such assaults would use up this army."

By noon the battle for Kennesaw Mountain was over. Sherman's loss of 3,000 was more than three times the number of Confederate casualties, and the armies settled into a grim standoff as Sherman once again shifted his attention to Johnston's left flank. While Johnston was distracted by the assault on his center, Schofield began sidling around the Confederate left. McPherson marched to extend Schofield's line farther south, toward the Chattahoochee River and Atlanta, and on July 2 Johnston withdrew from the blood-soaked slopes of Kennesaw Mountain.

"'Hell had broke loose in Georgia, sure enough.'"

PRIVATE SAM R. WATKINS

1st Tennessee (C.S.) Infantry, Maney's Brigade

For someone who claimed he "always shot at privates," since "it was they that did all the shooting and killing," Watkins had plenty of targets on the morning of June 27. He figured that by the time the fighting was over, he had fired his musket 120 times, leaving his arm "bruised and bloodshot from my wrist to my shoulder."

It was one of the hottest and longest days of the year, and one of the most desperate and determinedly resisted battles fought during the whole war. Our regiment was stationed on an angle, a little spur of the mountain, or rather promontory of a range of hills, extending far out beyond the main line of battle, and was subject to the enfilading fire of forty pieces of artillery of the Federal batteries. It seemed fun for the guns of the whole Yankee army to play upon this point. We would work hard every night to strengthen our breastworks, and the very next day they would be torn down smooth with the ground by solid shots and shells from the guns of the enemy. Even the little trees and bushes which had been left for shade, were cut down as so much stubble. . . .

Well, on the fatal morning of June 27th, the sun rose clear and cloudless, the heavens seemed made of brass, and the earth of iron, and as the sun began to mount toward the zenith, everything became quiet, and no sound was heard save a peckerwood on a neighboring tree, tapping on its old trunk, trying to find a worm for his dinner. We all knew it was but the dead calm that precedes the storm. On the distant hills we could plainly see officers dashing about hither and thither, and the Stars and Stripes moving to and fro, and we knew the Federals were making preparations for the mighty contest. We could hear but the rumbling sound of heavy guns, and the distant tread of a marching army, as a faint roar of the coming storm, which was soon to break the ominous silence with the sound of conflict, such as was scarcely ever before heard on this earth. It seemed that the arch-angel of Death stood and looked on with outstretched wings, while all the earth was silent, when all at once a hundred guns from the Federal line opened upon us, and for more than an hour they poured their solid and chain shot, grape and shrapnel right upon this salient point, defended by our regiment alone, when, all of a sudden, our pickets jumped into our works and reported the Yankees advancing, and almost at the same time a solid line of blue coats came up the hill. I discharged my gun, and happening to look up, there was the beautiful flag of the Stars and Stripes flaunting right in my face, and I heard John Branch, of the Rock City Guards, commanded by Captain W. D. Kelley, who were next Company H, say, "Look at that Yankee flag; shoot that fellow; snatch that flag out of his hand!" My pen is unable to describe the scene of carnage and death that ensued in the next two hours. Column after column of Federal soldiers were crowded upon that line, and by referring to the history of the war you will find they were massed in column forty columns deep; in fact, the whole force of the Yankee army was hurled against this point, but no sooner would a regiment mount our works than they were shot down or surrendered, and soon we had every "gopher hole" full of Yankee prisoners. Yet still the Yankees came. It seemed impossible to check the onslaught, but every man was true to his trust, and seemed to think that at that moment the whole responsibility of the Confederate government was rested upon his shoulders. Talk about other battles, victories, shouts, cheers, and triumphs, but in comparison with this day's fight, all others dwarf into insignificance. The sun beaming down on our uncovered heads, the thermometer being one hundred and ten degrees in the shade, and a solid line of blazing fire right from the muzzles of the Yankee guns being poured right into our very faces, singeing our hair and clothes, the hot blood of our dead and wounded spurting on us, the blinding smoke and stifling atmosphere filling our eyes and mouths, and the awful concussion causing the blood to gush out of our noses and ears, and above all, the roar of battle, made it a perfect pandemonium. Afterward I heard a soldier express himself by saying that he thought "Hell had broke loose in Georgia, sure enough."

CLOSING THE RING

As Sherman drew ever nearer to Atlanta, Jefferson Davis dispatched General Bragg to the scene to assess the deteriorating situation. When Bragg arrived on July 13, he received a predictably cold reception from Johnston, and he reported to Davis, "I cannot learn that he has any more plans in the future than he has had in the past." But Bragg had no trouble eliciting opinions from Hood. "We have had several chances to strike the enemy a decisive blow," the Texan said. "We have failed to take advantage of such opportunities." This, Hood declared, was "a great misfortune to our country." Bragg and Hood agreed: "There is but one remedy—offensive action." Johnston, meanwhile, insisted to the Confederate chief executive that his next move would have to "depend upon that of the enemy."

Jefferson Davis had had enough: Joe Johnston would have to be replaced. Hood would receive the appointment.

On the night of July 17 Johnston received an official communiqué from the War Department notifying him of his removal from command. The soldiers of the Army of Tennessee were stunned by the news. Brigadier General Arthur M. Manigault noted that his troops "received the announcement with very bad grace, and with no little murmuring."

> ### "If Jeff Davis had made his appearance in this army during the excitement, he would not have lived an hour."

Despite Johnston's continuous withdrawal toward Atlanta, his subordinates had come to trust in their general's strategic vision, and they felt he had displayed great skill in fending off a numerically superior foe. Sam Watkins shared the affection most of the fighting men cherished for Old Joe, stating, "He was more popular with his troops day by day."

On July 20, only three days after taking command, Hood put his offensive-minded strategy into practice with a vengeance, lashing out at Thomas' isolated army on the south side of Peachtree Creek. The spirited attack by Hardee's and Stewart's corps drove back the Federals in several places, but Union reinforcements and heavy artillery fire finally stopped the Rebels. Hardee was about to launch another attack at about 6:00 p.m. when he received orders from Hood to detach a division to meet another Federal threat: McPherson's army was approaching Atlanta from the east and had begun to bombard the city.

Shortly before noon, a 20-pound shell exploded at the corner of Ivy and East

Within days of his arrival in Georgia, General John Bell Hood sent President Davis the first of a series of confidential letters challenging General Johnston's strategy. A copy, along with a cover letter (left), was forwarded to Colonel James Chesnut, an aide to Davis and husband of the diarist Mary B. Chesnut.

Ellis streets, killing a little girl and injuring her parents. The Yankee guns continued to pound the city and its surrounding earthworks well into the evening. "Citizens were running in every direction," a Southern cavalryman recalled. "Terror-stricken women and children went screaming about the streets seeking some avenue of escape from hissing, bursting shells."

The next day Hood saw another chance to smash the Federals, when McPherson's troops occupied Bald Hill, east of the city. Hood detected that McPherson had failed to protect his left flank, and the Confederate commander rushed Hardee's corps to the attack on the morning of July 22. The Rebel onslaught nearly succeeded in rolling up the vulnerable flank, but it had started late, giving Federal reinforcements time to stall the assault.

In two battles, Hood had suffered 8,000 casualties—more men than Johnston had lost in 10 weeks. More than 5,000 Confederates and 4,000 Federals had been killed, wounded, or captured in the fighting on July 22, what would come to be called the Battle of Atlanta. Sherman also lost one of his best commanders. General McPherson was killed by a Rebel skirmisher's bullet.

Sherman's next move was an attempt to sever the city's last remaining lifeline,

Johnston received this telegram ordering his removal at 10:00 on the night of July 17 while he was conferring with his chief engineer about strengthening Atlanta's fortifications. The Confederate army's adjutant and inspector general, Samuel Cooper, sent it, on Jefferson Davis' instructions.

"At all hours in the afternoon can be heard Hurrah for Joe Johnson and God D—n Jeff Davis."

CAPTAIN SAMUEL T. FOSTER

24th Texas Cavalry (Dismounted), Granbury's Brigade

After the Confederate Army of Tennessee fell back across the Chattahoochee River, President Jefferson Davis relieved General Johnston of command and replaced him with the younger, less experienced John Bell Hood. The ouster of the popular Johnston infuriated Confederate officers and enlisted men alike. According to Captain Foster, "If Jeff Davis had made his appearance in this army during the excitement, he would not have lived an hour."

—//—

No move today—A circular from Genl Johnson announces that he has been removed from the command of this Army, and that Gen Hood succeeds him.

In less than an hour after this fact becomes known, groups of three, five, seven, ten or fifteen men could be seen all over camp discussing the situation—Gen. Johnson has so endeared himself to his soldiers, that no man can take his place. We have never made a fight under him that we did not get the best of it. And the whole army has become so attached to him, and to put such implicit faith in him, that whenever he said for us to fight at any particular place, we went in feeling like Gen Johnson knew all about it and we were certain to whip.

He never deceived us once. It is true we have had hard fighting and hard marching, but we always had something to eat, and in bad weather, or after an extra hard march we would have a little whiskey issued.

Gen Johnson could not have issued an order that these men would not have undertaken to accomplish—

For the first time, we hear men openly talk about going home, by tens (10) and by fifties (50). They refuse to stand guard, or do any other camp duty, and talk open rebellion against all Military authority—All over camp, (not only among Texas troops) can be seen this demoralization—and at all hours in the afternoon can be heard Hurrah for Joe Johnson and God D——n Jeff Davis.

---

the Macon & Western Railroad. General Howard, the devout one-armed West Pointer who was now commander of the Army of the Tennessee, swung his troops southwest of Atlanta to seize control of the vital rail line. "Tell Howard to invite them to attack," Sherman instructed an aide; "they'll only beat their brains out."

Stephen D. Lee, at 33 the youngest lieutenant general in the Confederacy, did just that on July 28. Having only recently arrived at Atlanta to take command of Hood's old corps, Lee lashed out at Howard's positions near Ezra Church. Some 3,000 Rebel troops were cut down in the hail of musket and artillery fire, while the defending Federals suffered only 650 losses.

Sherman, unable to sever the Macon & Western, escalated his bombardment of Atlanta. One day 5,000 shells fell on the city. "One thing is certain," Sherman informed Washington, "whether we get inside Atlanta or not, it will be a used-up community by the time we are done with it."

While the siege ground on through August, the Federal commander had not abandoned his designs on the Macon & Western. On the 25th he sent Howard's entire army and two of Thomas' corps marching in a broad arc to the west and south to join Schofield in a three-pronged attack on the railroad.

When Hardee's and Lee's corps arrived at Jonesboro, 15 miles south of Atlanta, they realized the magnitude of the Yankee threat. Hardee attacked the vanguard of Howard's army on August 31 but was repulsed with a loss of 1,700 men, 10 times the number of Federal casualties. With the situation deteriorating, Hood ordered Lee's corps back to Atlanta, leaving Hardee to wage a rearguard fight at Jonesboro.

On September 1 Howard and Thomas closed in on Hardee. The result was a foregone conclusion. The Southern line was overrun and, as Sherman put it, rolled up

---

"The very earth trembled as if in the throes of a mighty earthquake."

"like a sheet of paper." Hardee led his surviving troops toward Lovejoy's Station, six miles south of Jonesboro.

The debacle at Jonesboro sealed the fate of Atlanta. In the early morning hours of September 2, factories, mills, and supply depots were put to the torch to prevent their falling into Yankee hands. When trainloads of ammunition were detonated by the flames, one citizen thought "the very earth trembled as if in the throes of a mighty earthquake."

As a pall of smoke hung low over the rubble-strewn streets, the vanguard of Sherman's victorious armies entered unopposed, and to the stirring accompaniment of regimental bands, raised the Stars and Stripes over city hall. "So Atlanta is ours," Sherman wired Washington, "and fairly won."

Attached to the staff of Colonel James S. Robinson's brigade, Lieutenant George Young was shot just below the knee while riding across the battlefield as a courier. His bullet-torn trousers are shown above. Despite several operations to remove diseased bone tissue, Young suffered from chronic pain until he died in 1909.

PEACHTREE CREEK

Once the retreating Joseph Johnston had settled into the earthworks that guarded the northern outskirts of Atlanta, he made plans to strike back. He would attack the leading Federal column—Thomas' Army of the Cumberland—as it made its way across Peachtree Creek.

Johnston never got the chance, however, because on the evening of July 17 he was relieved of command. His successor, Hood, approved of the counterattack but made a number of fateful modifications to the plan.

Johnston had originally intended to attack on July 19, but Hood pushed the launch date back to 1:00 p.m. of the following day. Concerned about the security of his right flank, Hood decided to shift his assault formations to the east, with the result that the attack was further delayed until 4:00 p.m. on July 20. By the time Hood was ready to strike, Thomas' forces were well situated to meet any Rebel attempt to drive them back into Peachtree Creek.

The Confederate onslaught began with Hardee's corps, on the Southern right, bearing down upon Howard's position. While the divisions of Cheatham,

The 33d New Jersey's flag (left) was lost to the Rebels at Peachtree Creek. "No regiment was more proud of their blue banner," wrote Lieutenant Colonel Enos Fourat, the commanding officer, "and none ever fought better to preserve it."

In this tattered sketch penned by artist Theodore Davis near Peachtree Creek on July 20, Major General Joseph Hooker (mounted, in foreground) heeds an aide peering through a field glass as troops of Hooker's XX Corps form alongside their battle flags to meet the approaching Confederates. "When that horrible mass of Johnnies struck our line," one of Hooker's men recalled, "we found them six deep."

This sword and scabbard were carried into battle at Peachtree Creek on July 20, 1864, by Colonel George Cobham Jr., commander of the 111th Pennsylvania. His flank threatened, Cobham was brandishing the sword and calling on his men to change front when he was shot through the lungs. He died that evening.

A critical moment in the Battle of Atlanta is depicted in this section of a cyclorama painted in 1887. Alabamians under Brigadier General Arthur Manigault fire at Federal troops from windows of the Troup bales. At left, soldiers of the 55th Illinois advance toward a cut on the Georgia Railroad, beyond which can be seen the church spires of the city. At center, Illinois and Ohio troops of Colonel August Mersy's

temporarily commanded by Brigadier General George Maney, and Major General William Walker struck Howard head-on, Brigadier General Bate's division began working its way around the far Union left.

Walker's and Maney's divisions initially gained some ground along the center of Howard's position, but the Federals put up a stiff resistance, and Confederate losses mounted.

Attacking on Hardee's left, Alexander Stewart's corps moved forward at 4:30 p.m. and also made some initial headway, by taking advantage of gaps in the Federal line. The timely arrival of Brigadier General William T. Ward's Federal division plugged the gap, and the Rebels were forced to draw back with heavy losses.

Another Confederate attack, led by Brigadier General Thomas M. Scott, managed to inflict even greater damage to the center of the Yankee defenses, but the Federals rallied and caught Scott's Alabama and Louisiana regiments in a deadly crossfire. With his troops scattered and no support forthcoming, Scott had to withdraw.

On the Rebel left, the division of Major General Edward C. Walthall also gained ground. Colonel Edward A. O'Neal's brigade threatened the right flank of Brigadier General John W. Geary's Federal division, but Geary countered the move by turning his line to face the attackers. O'Neal's men soon were forced to retreat.

On Walthall's left, Brigadier General Daniel H. Reynolds' Arkansas brigade in turn advanced and began to lap around the flank of Brigadier General Joseph F. Knipe's brigade. But both of Reynolds' own flanks came under heavy fire, and he was forced to extricate his troops.

When Hood ordered Hardee to detach Cleburne's troops and send them to block McPherson's Federal army, this move—and darkness—ended the fighting. The Battle of Peachtree Creek cost Thomas' Army of the Cumberland 1,900 casualties—1 out of every 10 Federals engaged. But Confederate losses were even greater—some 2,500—and Hood had failed to strike the crippling blow that he had envisaged. With Sherman tightening his grip on Atlanta, the Southern commander sought a new opportunity to catch the confident Yankees off guard.

BATTLE OF ATLANTA

Even as Hood was being repulsed at Peachtree Creek, Sherman's forces drew closer to Atlanta. On July 20 McPherson's Army of the Tennessee was marching from Decatur, six miles to the east. By the next day, Federal troops had driven the Confederates from Bald Hill, a commanding elevation that overlooked Atlanta's eastern defenses and brought much of the city within range of enemy guns.

Hood saw no option but to risk a daring flank assault on McPherson's army

These soldiers from the 66th Illinois fought the Battle of Atlanta with 16-shot Henry repeating rifles like the one shown below. "I stood and fired 90 rounds without stopping," wrote Private Prosper Bowe (far left) in a letter to his sister. "My gun barrel was so hot that I could not touch it. Spit on it & it would siz."

Hurt house and from behind an improvised barricade of logs and cotton brigade mount a successful charge to retake captured Federal earthworks.

before it dug in. But while Hardee's tired Rebels tramped on through the night, McPherson had begun to shift troops from Brigadier General Grenville M. Dodge's XVI Corps to bolster his left flank.

Hardee was not ready to launch his assault until midday of July 22. By that time most of Dodge's troops were already coming into line. Hardee's right-hand divisions of Walker and Bate found themselves charging into a withering fire from two Federal brigades and a battery of artillery. Despite a numerical advantage, the Rebels were held at bay, and casualties mounted.

At 12:45 p.m., about half an hour after Hardee commenced his attack, Cleburne's division surged forward. With Maney's division advancing in support, Cleburne gained the first Southern success of the day, driving Yankee regiments northward to the slopes of the Bald Hill. An even greater loss for the Union came just after 2:00 p.m., when General McPherson was fatally shot as he rode into the widening gap between the Federal corps.

At 3:00 p.m. Hood took advantage of Cleburne's success by ordering Cheatham to lash out at the Federal center. By 4:00 p.m. all of Hardee's and Cheatham's troops were committed to the massive assault.

Maney's and Major General Carter L. Stevenson's divisions stormed the angle in the Federal line at Bald Hill from front and flank. But Yankee brigadier general

"I stood and fired 90 rounds without stopping. My gun barrel was so hot that I could not touch it. Spit on it & it would siz."

Mortimer D. Leggett's division maintained its hold on the crucial high ground, which became a rallying point for the scattered Federal units. While Bald Hill continued to defy capture, the divisions on the left of Cheatham's line gained ground against the right flank of Logan's XV Corps.

But the Confederate success proved to be short-lived. While the northernmost portion of the XV Corps held its ground, and Leggett's troops continued to stave off the Rebel assaults on Bald Hill, McPherson's successor in command of the Army of the Tennessee—Black Jack Logan—rushed reinforcements to plug the gap.

"Great volumes of sulphurous smoke rolled over the town, trailing down to the ground, and through this stifling gloom the sun glared down like a red eye peering through a bronze colored cloud."

WALLACE P. REED

Resident of Atlanta

Although he was only 14 years old during the summer of 1864, Wallace Reed, who would later become an editorial writer and a reporter for the Atlanta Constitution and publish a history of Atlanta, recorded the scenes of devastation he witnessed during the weeks-long siege of the city. Recalling the day of the heaviest shelling, Reed wrote of the stiff price Atlanta paid in civilian lives.

The famous artillery duel! If any one day of the siege was worse than all the others, it was that red day in August, when all the fires of hell, and all the thunders of the universe seemed to be blazing and roaring over Atlanta. It was about the middle of the month, and everything had been comparatively quiet for a few days, when one fine morning, about breakfast time, a big siege gun belched forth a sheet of flame with a sullen boom from a Federal battery on the north side of the city. The Confederates had an immense gun on Peachtree street, one so large and heavy that it had taken three days to drag it to its position. This monster engine of destruction lost no time in replying to its noisy challenger, and then the duel opened all along the lines on the east, north, and west. Ten Confederate and eleven Federal batteries took part in the engagement. On Peachtree, just where Kimball street intersects, the big gun of the Confederates put in its best work, but only to draw a hot fire from the enemy. Shot and shell rained in every direction. Great volumes of sulphurous smoke rolled over the town, trailing down to the ground, and through this stifling gloom the sun glared down like a red eye peering through a bronze colored cloud. It was on this day of horrors that the destruction of human life was greatest among the citizens. A shell crashed into a house on the corner of Elliott and Rhodes street, and exploded, killing Mr. Warner, the superintendent of the gas company and his little six year old girl. . . . A lady who was ironing some clothes in a house on North Pryor, between the Methodist Church and Wheat street, was struck by a shell and killed. Sol Luckie, a well-known barber, was standing on the James's Bank corner, on Whitehall and Alabama, when a shell struck a lamp-post, ricocheted, and exploded. A fragment struck Luckie and knocked him down. Mr. Tom Crusselle and one or two other citizens picked up the unfortunate man and carried him into a store. He was then taken to the Atlanta Medical College, where Dr. D'Alvigney amputated his leg. The poor fellow was put under the influence of morphine, but he never rallied from the shock, and died in a few hours. A young lady who was on her way to the car shed was struck in the back and fatally wounded. On Forsyth street a Confederate officer was standing in the front yard, taking leave of the lady of the house, when a bursting shell mortally wounded him and the lady's little boy. The two victims were laid side by side on the grass under the trees, and in a few minutes they both bled to death. The sun was sinking behind the western hills when the great artillery duel ended, and the exhausted gunners threw themselves on the ground. From a military standpoint there were no results worthy of mention. Nothing was gained by either side.

A free black man, Solomon Luckie, a popular Atlanta barber at the Barber Shop and Bathing Salon on Decatur Street, died of wounds suffered when he was struck by shell fragments while standing at a street corner in mid-August.

Federal soldiers pose with a Rebel 24-pounder seacoast gun (foreground) and other large-caliber weapons, prizes that fell into their hands with the capture of Atlanta. These heavy guns had been brought up by rail from the Gulf Coast forts to augment the city's defenses; the Confederates were forced to abandon them when they hurriedly evacuated on September 1.

By nightfall of July 22 the opposing forces were back where they had started. Hood's gamble had failed, with 5,000 Confederate casualties set against a Federal loss of some 4,000 men. While Sherman professed not to have been unduly concerned for the outcome, many in his army who fought that day felt they had come precariously close to disaster.

EZRA CHURCH

Four days after the Battle of Atlanta, Sherman decided to execute another wide flanking maneuver. He designated the commander of the IV Corps—Oliver Howard—as McPherson's successor in command of the Army of the Tennessee, preferring a West Pointer to the politically appointed general, John Logan, who had been in temporary command. Joseph Hooker, who was senior in rank to Howard, angrily tendered his resignation. Brigadier General Alpheus Williams assumed temporary command of Hooker's XX Corps.

On July 27 the Army of the Tennessee began a counterclockwise march that took it around the northern edge of Atlanta, then south, threatening to sever the last major Confederate line of supply. At East Point, about six miles southwest of the city's defenses, the Macon & Western and Atlanta & West Point Railroads met to form a single rail line leading into Atlanta. If Howard could seize and destroy the

railroad, Sherman believed, Hood's army would either have to abandon Atlanta or give battle in order to retake the vital artery.

To keep the Rebels off balance while Howard made his move, Sherman dispatched the bulk of his cavalry forces on far-reaching raids intended to spread destruction along the enemy transportation routes.

Hood quickly became aware that something was up, and on July 27 he moved to protect the rail lines. Stephen D. Lee, in command of Hood's old corps, was sent west with Brigadier General John C. Brown's and Brigadier General Henry D. Clayton's divisions to intercept Howard before he could get astride the railroad. Lee's force was augmented by two divisions of Stewart's corps, with two more divisions on the way.

Increased Confederate cavalry activity alerted General Howard that his march was discovered. He decided to halt and dig in on the best defensive position he could find—a line of ridges near a Methodist meeting house known as Ezra Church. Howard positioned his troops in a horseshoe-shaped line with Logan's XV Corps on the right, facing south, and Major General Francis P. Blair's XVII Corps on the left, facing east.

By noon on July 28 Lee's corps had arrived at a point just south of Howard's position. According to Hood's plan, Lee would pin Howard in place with his two divisions, while Stewart would continue marching west, then turn on the Yankee right flank and rear. But Stewart had not yet arrived when, at about 12:30 p.m., the impetuous Lee sent Brown's division, on the Confederate left, forward to the attack.

Rough ground hampered Brown's advance, and once his troops neared the enemy breastworks they were staggered by a hail of bullets from the well-concealed Yankees. Brown's entire division began to retreat in disorder.

Clayton started his division forward 10 minutes after Brown's men stepped off, but by then most of Brown's troops were already falling back. Clayton called off the attack and put his division on the defensive.

The first of Stewart's corps—Walthall's division—arrived on the field at 2:00 p.m. and was immediately ordered into action on Clayton's left, to relieve Brown's shattered troops. But Walthall's charge was no more successful than Brown's had been, and again the Southern lines fell back. Lee finally called off the fruitless assaults.

Sustaining only 632 casualties, Howard inflicted five times as great a loss on his opponents. Neither Howard's thrust to the southwest nor the spoiling Federal cavalry raids succeeded in accomplishing all that Sherman desired. But Federal morale was high, and Sherman saw the victory at Ezra Church as one more sign that it was only a matter of time before Atlanta would fall.

This flag of the combined Confederate 6th and 7th Arkansas was captured at bayonet point by Private Henry Mattingly of the 10th Kentucky during the battle at Jonesboro on September 1, 1864. The consolidated regiments had fought through two years of bitter campaigns in Tennessee, Kentucky, and Georgia, earning honors for the actions cited on their colors.

JONESBORO

On August 25 Sherman sent most of his troops on a march to seize control of Atlanta's remaining rail lines. By August 30 Howard's Army of the Tennessee had severed the Atlanta & West Point Railroad and was headed east for the Macon & Western. Hood dispatched Hardee, followed by S. D. Lee's corps, to intercept the Yankee column near the town of Jonesboro, about 15 miles south of Atlanta.

Hardee marched his weary men by a circuitous route, arriving at Jonesboro that afternoon. In the meantime Howard had reached the Flint River, a mile west of Jonesboro. Logan's XV Corps crossed the river and deployed on a ridge facing the Rebel position.

With no time to rest his tired soldiers, at 3:00 p.m. Hardee ordered an attack. Cleburne, commanding Hardee's old corps, moved forward on the Confederate left, wheeling to strike the right flank of the Federal line. S. D. Lee's divisions, led by Major Generals Carter Stevenson and Patton Anderson, were to wait until Cleburne was engaged before hitting the Federal center and left.

Brigadier General Mark P. Lowrey, who temporarily commanded Cleburne's division, gained ground, but Bate's division—commanded by General John C. Brown—was unable to break the entrenched Federal line. By the time Cleburne got Cheatham's division, now commanded by George Maney, forward from its position in reserve, Brown had been repulsed.

Unaware that Cleburne's intended flanking maneuver had failed, at the first

A long line of Confederate prisoners taken at Jonesboro, mostly Arkansas and Kentucky men, trudge north to holding pens in Atlanta. All were spared the hardships of a Northern prison after Sherman and Hood brokered an exchange that returned all captives to their armies by September 19.

sound of gunfire Lee launched his troops in a headlong charge on Logan's XV Corps. The attack fell apart in the withering fire from Logan's battle line. When Lee sent his second wave forward, Stevenson's and Anderson's divisions were caught in a hail of bullets and fell back in disorder.

For a loss of 172 men, Howard's Federals had inflicted 2,200 casualties on Hardee's troops. That night, Hood withdrew Lee's corps to the north to reinforce Atlanta. Hardee was left with only a single corps to counter the inevitable Federal assault on September 1.

At 4:00 p.m. the Yankee juggernaut rolled forward. Hardee's troops put up a stout defense, but they were unable to hold back the massed ranks of Brigadier General Jefferson C. Davis' XIV Corps. As Hardee's embattled line bent back like a jackknife, Major General David S. Stanley's IV Corps made a belated appearance in the Confederate rear. The Union formations, however, were unable to force their way through what Stanley described as a "perfect entanglement" of felled trees and brush. This abatis bought Hardee enough time to extricate his beleaguered corps from the jaws of Sherman's trap.

That night Hardee dispatched a message to Hood informing him of the catastrophe. With his army scattered and not enough troops remaining to safeguard Atlanta's defenses, Hood saw no alternative but to abandon the city to General Sherman's victorious Yankees.

Severed tracks and scattered axles testify to the force of the explosion that ripped through a Confederate ordnance train on the night of September 1, leveling the walls of the rolling mill in the background. Hood's troops touched off the blast as they prepared to abandon Atlanta to the Federals.

Although hostilities had been temporarily suspended, the 10-day armistice brought little comfort to the civilian population of Atlanta. Complying with Sherman's evacuation order meant, for most, separation from family and friends as they prepared to seek refuge with relatives in the South and, for some, the uncertainty of building a new life up North. In this Harper's Weekly engraving by D. R. Brown dated October 15, 1864, refugees load their household goods and furniture onto covered wagons furnished by the Union army. Most were directed south to Rough and Ready, where they were turned over to Confederate authorities.

DEFEAT AND DESOLATION

As his weary troops regrouped at Lovejoy's Station, General Hood wired news of the disaster to Jefferson Davis and the Confederate cabinet. Rather than accept any personal responsibility for the tragic course of events, the embittered commander of the Army of Tennessee blamed the defeat on his soldiers' lack of spirit. "According to all human calculations we should have saved Atlanta," the general stated, "had the officers and men of this army done what was expected of them." Hood alleged that Hardee's troops could have overrun the Federals at Jonesboro on August 31, but the men "had been taught to believe that entrenchments cannot be taken," and "would not attack breastworks." Hood demanded that Hardee be relieved of command, and Davis duly transferred the senior corps commander to a new assignment in Charleston, South Carolina.

While Hood licked his wounds at Lovejoy's Station, Sherman was savoring the fruits of his successful campaign. More than 30,000 Union troops had been killed, wounded, or captured in the four months of fighting, but Sherman knew his foes had sustained a comparable loss—one their smaller army could ill afford. "You have accomplished the most gigantic undertaking given to any general in this war," Ulysses S. Grant wrote his old friend, "and with a skill and ability that will be acknowledged in history as unsurpassed if not unequaled." President Lincoln issued a proclamation declaring a day of thanksgiving in honor of the victory, and cannons boomed in celebration throughout the North.

Having secured his prize, Sherman decided not to seek a decisive engagement with the battered but still formidable Rebel army; he informed his superiors in Washington, "I will move to Atlanta and give my men some rest."

Sherman then made a controversial decision. All residents remaining in Atlanta would be expelled from the city. "I was resolved to make Atlanta a pure military garrison," Sherman recalled, "with no civilian population to influence military matters."

General Hood protested the action, calling it "studied and ingenious cruelty,"

"The destruction [is to] be so thorough that not a rail or tie can be used again."

A demolition squad pries loose a section of track in Atlanta's rail yard. Adhering to Sherman's order that "the destruction [is to] be so thorough that not a rail or tie can be used again," the Federals heated the rails red hot over burning ties, then twisted them out of shape. The twisted rails became known as "Sherman's Hairpins."

The color sergeant of the 2d Massachusetts Infantry stands on the steps of Atlanta's municipal courthouse. When the Stars and Stripes were raised over the building, wrote one observer, "such a cheer went up as only a conquering army, flushed with victory, can give."

and Mayor James M. Calhoun made a personal appeal to Sherman to spare the Atlantans from the "appalling and heart-rending" eviction. But the Union commander was adamant. "You might as well appeal against the thunderstorm," Sherman told the mayor, "as against these terrible hardships of war." Between September 12 and 21 some 1,600 people were loaded aboard wagons and escorted from the city. More than half of the refugees were children.

Once the inhabitants were gone, Federal troops set about demolishing war-ravaged dwellings, taking any salvageable materials for their own use. Major James T. Holmes of the 52d Ohio wrote his family that "all around the city fine houses are leaving, by piece-meal, on the backs of soldiers."

On September 25 Jefferson Davis arrived to assess the condition of the Confederate forces and confer with Hood on his intentions. During a review of the troops the Confederate president received a decidedly chilly reception. "Give us Johnston!" some soldiers shouted, "Give us our old commander!"

But Davis remained unwavering in his loyalty to Hood and was pleased to learn that despite his recent misfortunes the general was eager to resume the offensive. Davis sanctioned the move, and on September 29 Hood led the Army of Tennessee, still 40,000 strong, north across the Chattahoochee River to strike at Sherman's principal line of supply, the Western & Atlantic Railroad. By October 3 more than 15 miles of track had been demolished.

The enemy move caught Sherman off guard and left him little choice but to follow in the hope of bringing the Rebel force to battle. The Federal commander was uncertain whether Hood's continued march northward was merely a large-scale raid or portended an eventual assault on Chattanooga. "I cannot guess his movements as I could those of Joe Johnston, who was a sensible man and only did sensible things," Sherman complained.

By the end of October Hood was at Gadsden, Alabama, having laid waste to more than a dozen Federal supply depots, including Tunnel Hill, the starting point of Sherman's drive on Atlanta. Fired with confidence, Hood won approval for an audacious new campaign. The army would cross the Tennessee border, capture Nashville, and free the state from Yankee occupation. If all went well, it would continue on into Kentucky and carry the war to the Ohio border.

While Hood prepared to embark on his daring enterprise, Sherman made a fateful decision of his own. The Federal commander had lost interest in Hood: "If he will go to the Ohio River, I'll give him rations," Sherman declared; "my business is down south." Dispatching Thomas to Chattanooga, and bolstering the Tennessee defenses with two corps, Sherman retraced his steps to Atlanta.

Sherman had received permission from Grant and Lincoln to undertake a bold thrust at the very heart of the Southern Confederacy, a great march across Georgia all the way to the Atlantic Ocean. "I can make this march," Sherman asserted, "and make Georgia howl!"

Before his 62,000 troops left Atlanta on November 15 Sherman ordered a final act of destruction. All structures of potential military value to the Confederacy were put to the torch, the city's railroad depot and roundhouse reduced to rubble, and miles of track demolished. At that point, Sherman noted, Atlanta "became a thing of the past."

For Southerners, Atlanta's fate seemed an ominous portent of still greater tragedy. The war had entered a grim phase in which the future of the Confederacy appeared more hopeless than ever before. Diarist Mary Chesnut expressed the fears of many when she wrote, "Since Atlanta I have felt as if all were dead within me, forever."

ATLANTA CAMPAIGN CASUALTIES

FEDERAL		CONFEDERATE	
Killed	*4,423*	*Casualties up to July 9 (Johnston commanding)*	*8,873*
Wounded	*22,822*		
Missing	*4,442*	*Estimated casualties July to September (Hood commanding)*	*22,103*
Total	*31,687*	*Total*	*30,976*

Opposite: This scene at the intersection of Peachtree Street and the Georgia Railroad tracks shows some of the damage that was wrought in Atlanta after Sherman's troops ravaged the business district. All of the banks were shut down during the Federal occupation; few of them ever reopened.

"I can make this march and make Georgia howl!"

ARTILLERY

During the Civil War artillery attained a lethal effectiveness that did much to make the conflict one of the deadliest in history. In support of infantry attacks, the guns hurled solid shot and explosive shells into the enemy's formations and fieldworks. On the defense, artillery could be even more destructive, firing shotgunlike blasts of canister at close range into oncoming infantry. And rival gunners tried to annihilate each other with counterbattery fire, using shot and shell to wreck guns and blow up caissons full of ammunition.

When the war started, the opposing armies were mainly equipped with antiquated bronze-barreled smoothbore cannon. Most were of two types, guns firing 6-pound ammunition on a relatively low trajectory and howitzers able to loft 12-pound projectiles on an arching trajectory. Soon the ordnance departments on both sides began producing more effective weapons, including accurate rifled pieces such as the 10-pounder Parrott *(below)* and the more powerful 12-pounder smoothbores called Napoleons.

The topmost inscription on this 1864 guidon is the battle honor the 9th earned at Gettysburg for its desperate stand against Barksdale's Mississippi Brigade. The battery's commander Captain John Bigelow recalled that the Rebels came on "yelling like demons."

In common with most artillery batteries of the Army of Northern Virginia, the King William Artillery was issued an infantry size (4 feet by 4 feet) battle flag.

Invented by former Federal officer Robert Parrott, the Parrott Rifle was accurate and—because its barrel was made of cast iron rather than costly bronze—inexpensive. A Parrott was able to hit a target at 2,500 yards, about twice the range of a smoothbore Napoleon gun.

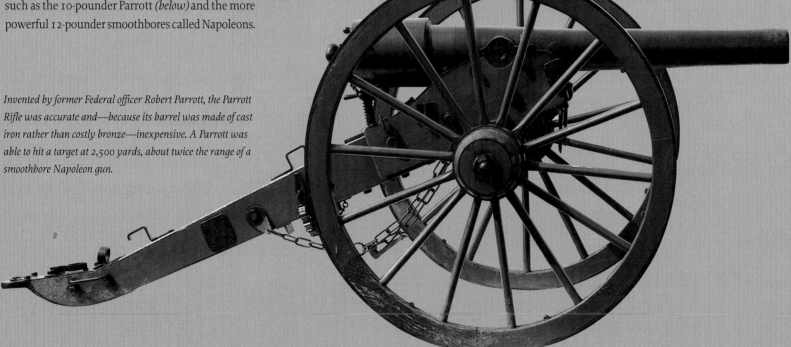

Captain Horatio Gibson sits astride his horse in the midst of Battery C, 3d U.S. Light Artillery, in this photograph taken near Fair Oaks, Virginia, in early June. Gibson's battery, part of the Artillery Reserve, missed the battle at Seven Pines but joined the rest of the army to renew the advance on Richmond. Battery C was armed with 3-inch Ordnance Rifles.

THE TOOLS

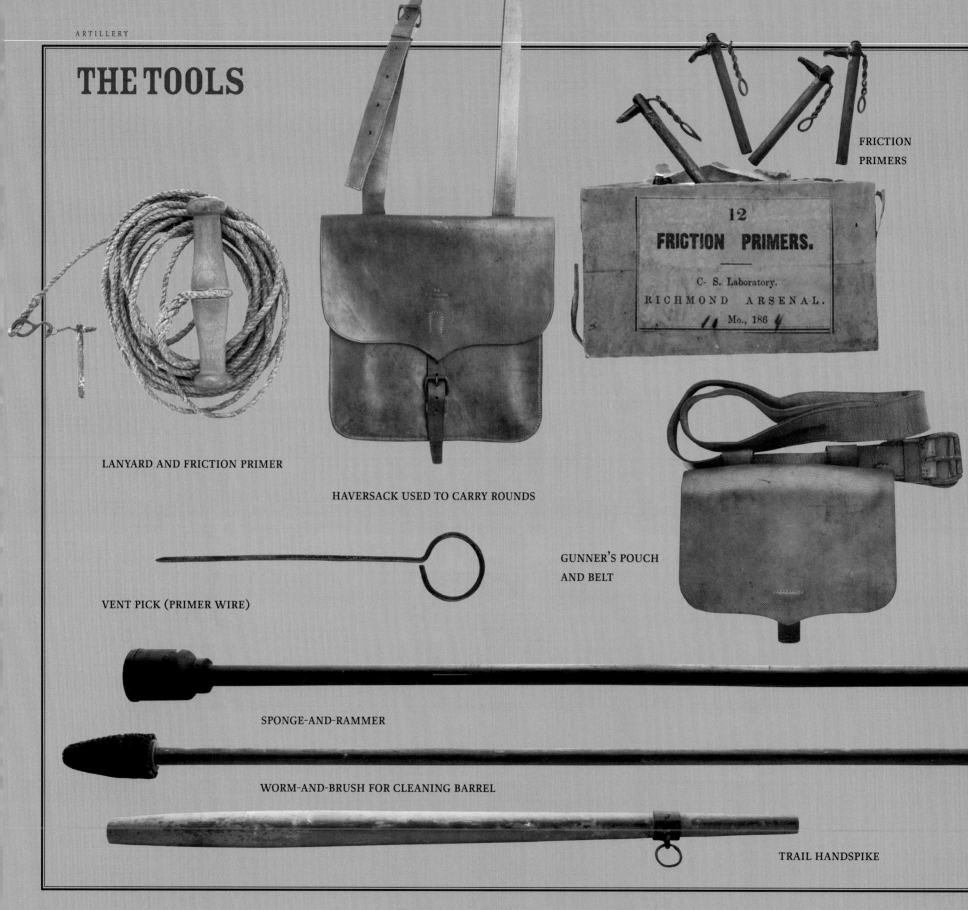

FRICTION PRIMERS

12
FRICTION PRIMERS.

C- S. Laboratory.
RICHMOND ARSENAL.
Mo., 186

LANYARD AND FRICTION PRIMER

HAVERSACK USED TO CARRY ROUNDS

GUNNER'S POUCH AND BELT

VENT PICK (PRIMER WIRE)

SPONGE-AND-RAMMER

WORM-AND-BRUSH FOR CLEANING BARREL

TRAIL HANDSPIKE

Men of South Carolina's Palmetto Battalion Light Artillery stage a mock drill at their emplacement on the Stono River near Charleston in 1861. The guns appear to be light 12-pounders.

PENDULUM HAUSSE AND CASE

FINGER STALL

WATER BUCKET FOR SPONGE

AMMUNITION

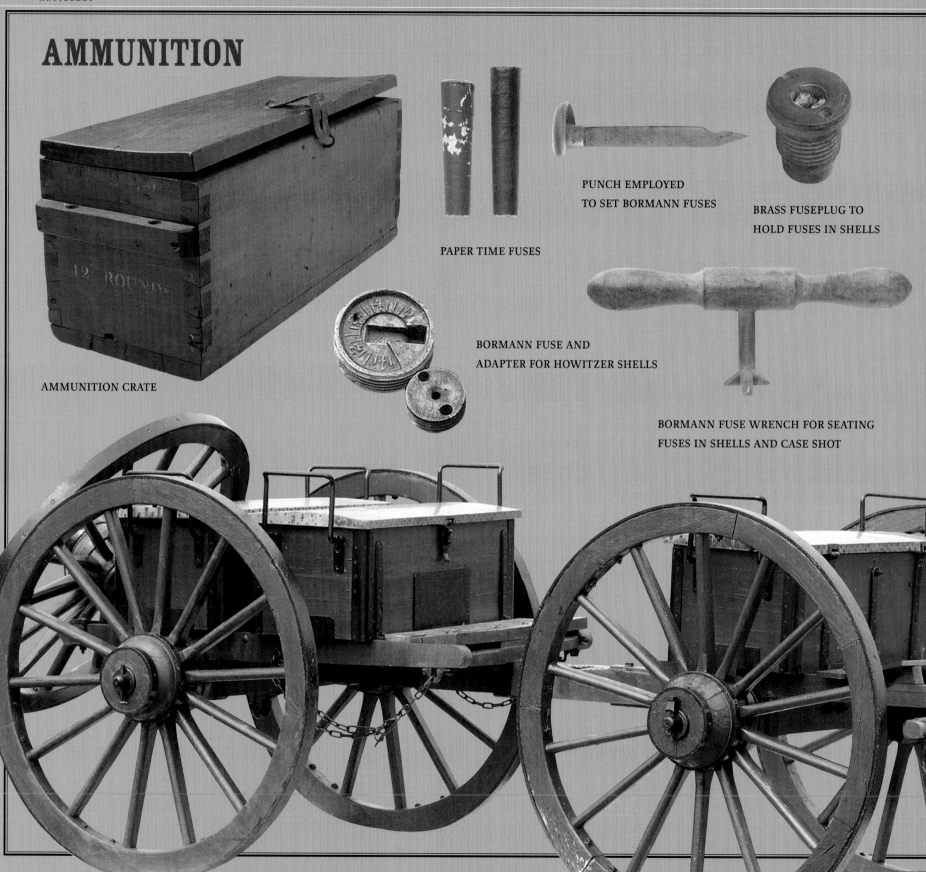

PAPER TIME FUSES

PUNCH EMPLOYED
TO SET BORMANN FUSES

BRASS FUSEPLUG TO
HOLD FUSES IN SHELLS

AMMUNITION CRATE

BORMANN FUSE AND
ADAPTER FOR HOWITZER SHELLS

BORMANN FUSE WRENCH FOR SEATING
FUSES IN SHELLS AND CASE SHOT

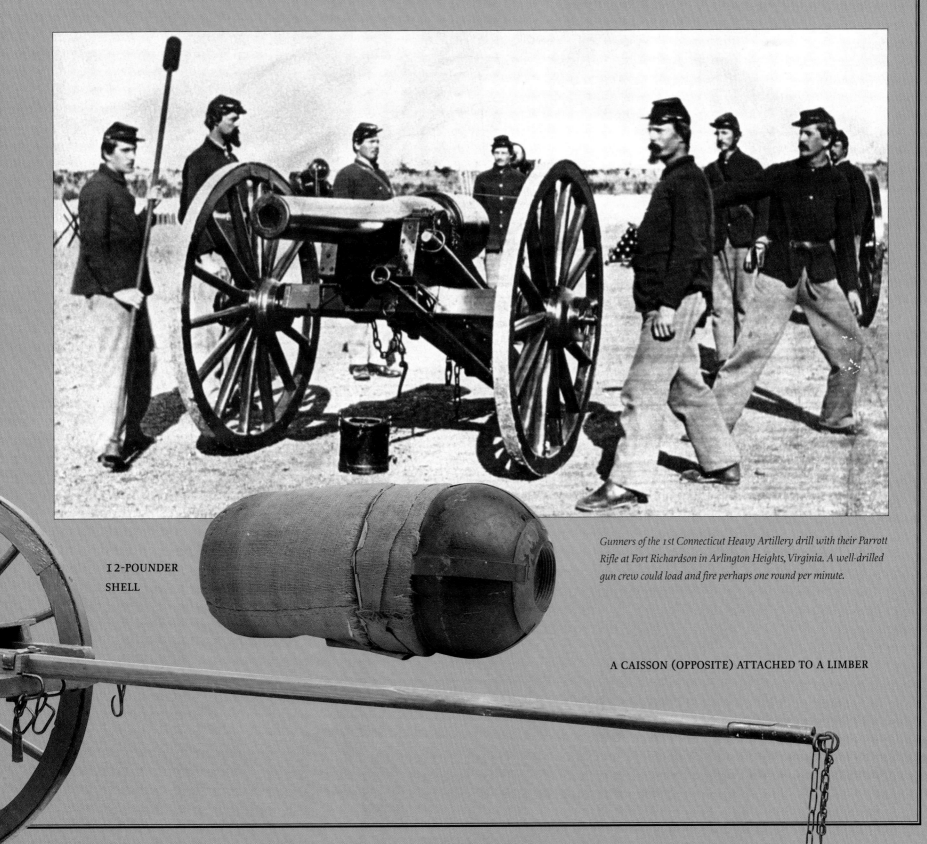

Gunners of the 1st Connecticut Heavy Artillery drill with their Parrott Rifle at Fort Richardson in Arlington Heights, Virginia. A well-drilled gun crew could load and fire perhaps one round per minute.

12-POUNDER
SHELL

A CAISSON (OPPOSITE) ATTACHED TO A LIMBER

Gabion revetments—wattle cylinders filled with stone and earth—line the traverses and parapets of Fort Sedgwick, a Federal fortification on the Jerusalem Plank Road southeast of Petersburg. The traverses were earthwork barriers constructed at right angles to a trench line to protect soldiers from enfilading fire. A fraise and brushwood abatis, obstacles to attacking infantry, are visible beyond the ditch that surrounds the outer walls. Earthworks like Fort Sedgwick could withstand artillery bombardments that would shatter walls of brick or stone.

Petersburg
Death in the Trenches

ACROSS THE JAMES—Sometime on the evening of June 12, 1864, 12 miles east of Richmond, Virginia, a Confederate picket at Barker's Mill on the Chickahominy River yelled a question toward the nearby Federal lines: "Where is Grant agoing to elbow us again?"

What the Confederate had no way of knowing was that General Ulysses S. Grant was already elbowing again around General Robert E. Lee's right flank. In fact, the Union general in chief had just begun a maneuver that would take the Army of the Potomac's 100,000 men a safe distance southeastward along the Chickahominy. Once across that stream, the Federals would march another 12 miles to the broad James River, thence southwest toward their objective: the city of Petersburg, 23 miles south of Richmond.

The gambit signaled a change in Grant's strategy. Instead of striking sledgehammer blows against the Confederates, he would focus his attention on the railroad system that was keeping Lee's army alive. A key to that network was Petersburg, the hub of the Southside Railroad from Lynchburg in the west, the Weldon Railroad from North Carolina, and the Norfolk & Petersburg Railroad from the southeast.

As the Federal effort got under way, even the imperturbable Grant was edgy, lighting one cigar after another, then forgetfully letting them go out. The historic James was a daunting barrier to the passage of so large an army. At the chosen crossing place, Wilcox's Landing, the river was 2,100 feet wide and nearly 100 feet deep in the middle; it had a strong current and rose or fell four feet with the tide. Crossing the river would require the rapid construction of a pontoon bridge that would be the longest ever built, not to mention one of the strongest and most flexible.

The first movement was carried out by XVIII Corps, under Major General William F. Smith, borrowed earlier from Major General Benjamin F. Butler's Army of the James. At sunset Smith's corps pulled out of its place on the right center of the Union line and began the 15-mile march to White House Landing. There the men were to board steamers and ferryboats for the 140-mile passage down the Pamunkey River to the York River, thence to Hampton Roads and back up the James to Bermuda Hundred, where they would rejoin Butler. After Smith's departure

Above: This shovel was recovered from the Crater in the years following the battle. The large number of bullet holes, each the size of a .58-caliber rifle bullet, suggest the shovel was used for target practice or to draw the fire of Federal sharpshooters.

Photographed from the top of a Federal supply wagon, a party of horsemen approaches the pontoon bridge at Wilcox's Landing on the James River. At 4:00 p.m. on June 15, 1864, the engineer battalion under Captain George H. Mendell began the task of bridging the half-mile-wide river. Working against a strong tidal current, Mendell's 450 bridge builders floated 101 heavy wooden pontoons into place. To help withstand the current, the structure was lashed to transport schooners moored above and below the bridge. By 11:00 p.m., the flooring was laid and the bridge complete. Mendell proudly reported that "the greater part of the infantry and artillery, all the wagon trains, and droves of beef-cattle of the army passed this bridge safely and without interruption."

Grant began carefully shifting his army from the earthworks around Cold Harbor sending them down the Chickahominy toward the James.

Incredibly, all went smoothly. The engineers had assembled a bridge at the site of the old Long Bridge over the Chickahominy and the Federal forces began crossing by June 13. On that same day, Robert E. Lee, discovering that the Army of the Potomac had seemingly vanished, began moving his forces to cover the approaches to Richmond. Undetected by the enemy, however, Federal transport vessels began ferrying Major General Winfield Scott Hancock's II Corps across the James on June 14. As Hancock's infantry crossed the river, Federal engineers began work on the half-mile-long pontoon bridge. The bridge was finished in only eight hours and by midnight, men, horses, wagons, and artillery were trundling across the river. With part of his army safely across the James, Grant was much more relaxed. That day he took a steamer upriver to visit Benjamin Butler, the major general upon whom he was depending for help in his first forays against Petersburg.

Back in early May, Butler had taken his 33,000-man Army of the James on transports up the James River and debarked at Bermuda Hundred, a peninsula formed by a tight bend in the river 15 miles southeast of Richmond. The idea was for Butler to attack either Richmond or Petersburg. Instead, he allowed a Confederate force to block the neck of the peninsula, and had been bottled up there ever since, barely accessible except by waterways.

"I believed then, and still believe, that Petersburg could have been easily captured at that time."

Now, Major General William F. Smith's XVIII Corps, which had been borrowed from Butler by the Army of the Potomac, was steaming up the James to rejoin its old commander. Grant wanted Butler to augment the XVIII Corps to a strength of perhaps 16,000. In addition to his infantry Smith would have a division of cavalry under Brigadier General August V. Kautz. Then, June 15, Smith would assault the Confederate lines around Petersburg. "I believed then, and still believe," Grant would write later, "that Petersburg could have been easily captured at that time."

He had a point. In command for the Confederates at Petersburg, General P. G. T. Beauregard, the hero of Fort Sumter and First Bull Run, had been warning for days about the possibility of a Federal thrust in his direction. But Beauregard's alarms had been largely discounted by Robert E. Lee, who for once could not focus on his enemy's intentions. Lee believed that Richmond was a likelier Federal target than

Petersburg; in any event he was convinced that the Union army could not cross the James without being discovered.

Lee was wrong on both counts, and Beauregard was now left to face Smith's approaching troops with a minuscule force of about 2,200 men to defend the city. In his favor, Beauregard had only the imposing strength of the fortifications around Petersburg—a chain of artillery emplacements connected by earthworks and trenches that stretched for almost 10 miles, from the Appomattox River east of the city, around to the south and back up to the river on the west. The line was studded with forts and redans: strong points placed to give the defenders converging fields of fire. Ditches, abatis, and chevaux-de-frise—obstacles made of sharpened stakes or brushwood—were arrayed before the earthworks to slow any hostile advance. It was called the Dimmock Line, after the engineer who had laid it out, but its strength was largely illusory unless properly manned, and Beauregard simply did not have the numbers to do that. Brigadier General Henry Wise, commanding an understrength division of infantry in the earthworks, sent out the order: "Hold on at all hazards!"

The defense of Petersburg by General Pierre Gustave Toutant Beauregard was bold and brilliant. By counterattacking at intervals, he deluded the Federals into thinking his thinly spread force was stronger than it really was; he was then able to withdraw to a more defensible line to await the arrival of reinforcements.

Officers and men of Captain Andrew Cowan's New York Battery occupy Redan No. 5, a strong point in the Dimmock Line captured on the evening of June 15. When the battery was taken, one 12-pounder gun of the Albemarle Battery, Virginia Light Artillery, fell into Federal hands.

A warren of bombproofs, traverses, and trenches clutter the interior of Federal Fort Sedgwick in this 1865 photograph. One of 41 such earthwork strongholds located in the inner and outer rings of the Federal siege works at Petersburg, the fort formed the pivot point where the Union lines shifted from north-south to east-west. As a result, Fort Sedgwick came under constant artillery bombardment and rifle fire. So severe was the shelling that soldiers quickly dubbed the post "Fort Hell" and assigned the name "Fort Damnation" to nearby Rebel Fort Mahone. Duty in the trenches in the hot Virginia summer was arduous in the extreme. A soldier from New Hampshire recalled how the men suffered "tortures from the fierce heat and the swarms of flies that seemed to be determined to devour them."

Despite his overwhelming superiority, Smith was daunted by the defenses. Approaching the main Confederate line at about 1:30 p.m. on June 15, he halted his corps and spent the next five and a half hours making what General Butler later scorned as "interminable reconnaissances." When Smith finally did attack, his infantry rolled over a section of Beauregard's works. As Beauregard later wrote, Petersburg "was clearly at the mercy of the Federal commander, who had all but captured it."

Yet at that moment of brilliant opportunity, Smith decided on a course of action that would later cost him his command. He stopped, explaining the following day that since he "held important points of the enemy's line of works, I thought it prudent to make no farther advance." Even now the capable General Hancock might have saved the situation for the Federals, but command fumbles and sloppy communications conspired against him. Late in the day, Hancock had received orders to hurry the II Corps on and support Smith in the attack on Petersburg. Completing a four-mile march, Hancock arrived on the scene shortly after the Confederate line had given way. Though senior to Smith, Hancock at once offered to accept his judgment on whether or not to renew the attack, and Smith demurred. Once it had passed, the chance for a swift, decisive blow was gone for good. By dawn Beauregard had cobbled together a force of 14,000 men.

On June 18 Lee belatedly arrived in Petersburg with the lead elements of the Army of Northern Virginia. At dawn on the following day Grant and the Army of the Potomac's commander, Major General George G. Meade, ordered an assault by four Federal corps to smash through Beauregard's defenses. At first the advancing Federals faced little resistance but soon the Federal advance ran into a storm of rifle and artillery fire as they neared Beauregard's new line of Confederate earthworks. Colonel Robert McAllister, a brigade commander in the II Corps, wrote that, "Every step we advanced, the greater the slaughter. Advance—we could not live; retreat—we would not without orders; and every regimental flag was planted in line of battle over the living and the dead, my command lying flat on the ground, waiting for orders, with flags to the breeze."

The assaults cost the Federals 10,000 casualties in the first four days of fighting around Petersburg. Finally, after another three weeks of sparring, Meade issued an order that the campaign would henceforth progress by "regular approaches." This order began the siege of Petersburg, which would last until the closing days of the Civil War.

On June 21 Grant began operations to sever the railroads that provided the lifelines for Petersburg and Richmond. The II and VI Corps were ordered to march in a wide arc to the south and westward to capture the Weldon Railroad. The advance

Colonel Henry L. Abbott (in high boots, left), commander of the 1st Connecticut Heavy Artillery, stands in front of the "Dictator," the largest of the Federal guns operated against Petersburg. Work crews laid a special narrow-gauge rail line to move the 17,000-pound weapon into its firing position northeast of the beleaguered city. The Dictator went into action on July 9, 1864, lobbing its 200-pound shells a distance of more than two and a half miles.

"Every step we advanced, the greater the slaughter. Advance—we could not live; retreat—we would not without orders."

went well enough. When the two Federal corps crossed the Jerusalem Plank Road and entered a densely wooded region, however, they were struck by General A. P. Hill's Confederate corps that had been dispatched by Lee to block their advance. Hill had discovered that the two Federal corps had become separated in the dense woods and attacked the flank of the Union II Corps capturing over 1,600 prisoners. The Federals fell back and entrenched along the Jerusalem Plank Road. At the same time a raid by 5,000 Union cavalry under Major General James Wilson managed to destroy some 30 miles of track on the Southside Railroad. Wilson's

troopers then moved northward to destroy a section of the Richmond & Danville Railroad but were driven off by Confederate cavalry. The Confederates managed to repair the damaged tracks and soon the trains were running supplies into Petersburg once again.

In the earthworks around the besieged city the days of July passed, with the sun burning down and the men hot and sweaty as they dug and dug and dug, with the musketry cracking along the trenches when any soldier was seen by the enemy, and with big guns and mortars thumping away. In addition to redans and forts the men scooped out additional trenches behind, and parallel to, the forward line and connected the lines with zigzagging communication trenches. Then they linked this labyrinth to the rear with covered ways—sunken roads along which men, guns, and wagons could move under cover from enemy guns.

Normal field artillery with its flat trajectory and relatively small projectiles could not do much damage to men in such burrows, but that soon changed. As early as April, Colonel Henry L. Abbott of the 1st Connecticut Heavy Artillery had been ordered to organize a siege train from his 1,700-man regiment. Once the Federal line stabilized in June, Abbott brought up his formidable train and emplaced 40 rifled siege guns and 60 mortars capable of lofting shells into the enemy trenches. The Confederates soon responded in kind, and the shelling became a daily, deadly that his men dig a tunnel underneath the works and blow it up with a huge charge of black powder, thereby opening a breach in the Confederate lines.

As the scheme was passed upward for approval, Burnside was enthusiastic, but Meade and Grant were decidedly cool. Indeed, the general in chief regarded it merely "as a means of keeping the men occupied." Pleasants and his men therefore got little cooperation. They had to scrounge for lumber to shore up the tunnel and, since no one would furnish them with wheelbarrows, they made do with hardtack boxes fitted with hickory handles.

Still, the Pennsylvanians pushed on, working in shifts around the clock and burrowing 40 feet a day toward their goal, which lay—according to Pleasants' eventual calculation—precisely 510.8 feet away. Dirt, sand, and clay came out of the tunnel in a steady stream until the miners had excavated an estimated 18,000 cubic feet. Because all the material had to be disposed of without drawing enemy attention, the miners spread it carefully over a ravine behind their works. The Confederates did in fact discover the presence of the miners but concluded that the Federals would find it impossible to ventilate so long a tunnel. Beyond digging a few ineffectual countermines, Elliott's men limited their precautions to the construction of a trench cavalier—a tall earthwork behind the redan that overlooked the battery.

factor in the life of the men who immediately began constructing bombproofs with timber-and-sod roofs in addition to their other excavations.

Even the weather conspired to make life miserable. It had not rained since Cold Harbor; it had been hot; and now it became hotter than anyone could remember. Powdery dust, inches thick, covered everything, ready to well up in choking clouds at the slightest movement. Surface water virtually disappeared, providing yet another motive for digging; not far down, a substratum of clay held a ready supply of cool water.

THE CRATER

The only exception to the general routine was a project undertaken by the 48th Pennsylvania of Major General Ambrose Burnside's IX Corps at the center of the Federal line. In peacetime, these men had been anthracite miners in Schuylkill County, and their commander, Lieutenant Colonel Henry Pleasants, had come up with a novel idea that would grow into one of the war's most dramatic episodes.

As it happened, the early fighting for Petersburg had left the Pennsylvanians only 130 yards from the Confederate line. On a rise to their front was a salient, which was occupied by Captain William Pegram's Richmond Battery, and entrenchments stretching both north and south. These were occupied by part of a South Carolina brigade commanded by Brigadier General Stephen Elliott Jr. The redan and the trenches that supported it came to be called Elliott's Salient. Pleasants proposed

A miner of the 48th Pennsylvania digs toward Rebel lines in this wartime newspaper engraving. Behind him, soldiers fill cracker boxes with some of the 18,000 cubic feet of earth that had to be removed from the 500-foot tunnel. The spoil had to be disposed of out of view of Rebel sentries.

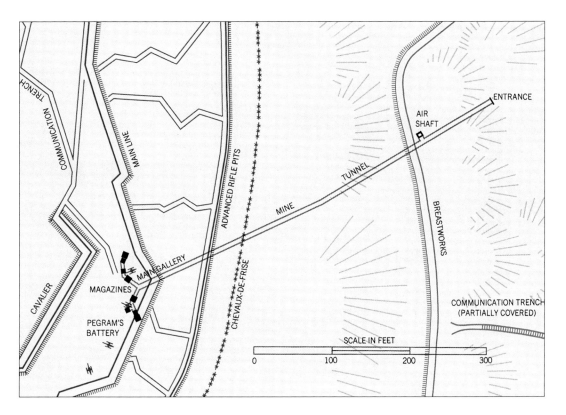

Lieutenant Colonel Henry Pleasants of the 48th Pennsylvania, who oversaw mining operations against Elliott's Salient, brought to the scheme the meticulous nature of a professional engineer and a venturesome streak that was part of his heritage. His father, a Philadelphia-bred arms merchant of Quaker stock, had smuggled guns to revolutionaries in Buenos Aires in the 1830s.

Once the miners had tunneled under the Confederate works, they branched out. To forge a wide breach in the enemy line, they extended two lateral shafts from the main gallery, which ended directly beneath William Pegram's battery. Each shaft housed four magazines that were stocked with black powder and linked to a single fuse.

On July 23 the tunnel was completed, and three days later Burnside submitted a plan for its use. Just before daylight, Pleasants' mine would be detonated and two brigades in columns would surge through the gap left by the explosion. A regiment at the head of one column would peel off to the left and a regiment at the head of the other column would swing to the right, clearing the Rebels from their lines on either side of the flattened fort. Then the remainder of Burnside's corps would pour through the breach.

Next day, in anticipation of the plan's approval, Pleasants began loading the tunnel with four tons of gunpowder. It took the men six hours, until 10:00 p.m., to place the 320 kegs of black powder, which would be detonated by gunpowder-filled wooden troughs leading from the main gallery, where a 98-foot fuse ran toward the mine entrance. To prevent the force of the explosion from being vented harmlessly out of the tunnel's mouth, earth was tamped into the last 34 feet of the main gallery.

When Meade's order finally came down, it enraged Burnside by making a major change in his tactical dispositions. To spearhead the advance, Burnside had selected his freshest division, commanded by Brigadier General Edward Ferrero. But Ferrero's men were black (they comprised the only division of U.S. Colored Troops in

Wielding their picks in the cramped tunnel by the light of candles stuck in discarded bottles, Federal miners filled countless crates with soil. The culmination of all this activity was a day of carnage documented by the battered relics shown here.

"A vast cloud of earth is borne upward, one hundred feet in the air, presenting the appearance of an outspread umbrella, descending in the twinkling of an eye with a heavy thud!"

Federal generals James Ledlie (left) and Edward Ferrero were censured by a court of inquiry after the Battle of the Crater for hiding in a bombproof during the attack. A surgeon who was with them that morning testified that they had asked him for "stimulants" and he had given them rum. Ledlie soon took sick leave, a move one officer in his division called a "heavy loss to the enemy."

Empty platforms for light mortars line the bottom of a lunette—a crescent-shaped earthwork for artillery—in this postwar photograph. The battery provided covering fire for troops attacking toward the Crater. Moments after the mine was exploded, Federal batteries poured heavy fire into the Confederate lines. The mortars were manned by gunners of the 1st Connecticut Heavy Artillery.

the Army of the Potomac) and Meade fretted lest it be said "that we were shoving these people ahead to get killed because we did not care anything about them." The black soldiers would join the assault after it was well under way.

Burnside protested vehemently, but Grant agreed with Meade. Forced to pick another unit, Burnside ducked the responsibility by having his other three division commanders draw straws. The winner—or loser—was Brigadier General James Ledlie, a known weakling, drinker, and coward.

Now the great moment was at hand. At 3:15 a.m. on Saturday, July 30, Colonel Pleasants entered the tunnel, lit the fuse, and came running out. Fifteen minutes passed. Nothing happened. Another 15 minutes, still nothing. At 4:15, Pleasants allowed two volunteers to go into the tunnel to investigate. The fuse had gone out at a splice. The men relit it and raced for safety.

At 4:40 a.m., someone on the Federal line shouted, "There she goes!" Then, according to a Union staff officer, "a vast cloud of earth is borne upward, one hundred feet in the air, presenting the appearance of an outspread umbrella, descending in the twinkling of an eye with a heavy thud!"

Where the Confederate earthworks had been, there yawned an enormous hole— the Crater—200 feet long, 50 feet wide, and 25 to 30 feet deep in the center. It was filled, a Union lieutenant wrote, "with dust, great blocks of clay, guns, broken carriages, projecting timbers, and men buried in various ways—some up to their necks, others to their waists, some with only their feet and legs protruding from the earth."

The eruption of the mine under the Confederate defenses at daybreak on July 30 raises a plume of debris on the horizon as Union officers look on in the foreground. The explosion signaled a devastating bombardment by Federal batteries, including the 10-inch mortars at center, emplaced between traverses built of wicker gabions.

Sergeant Andrew Davis of the 29th U.S. Colored Troops, which fought in the Battle of the Crater, survived the bloody repulse although his regiment lost 20 percent of its men in minutes when bungling Federal commanders turned the Crater into a death trap for the attackers.

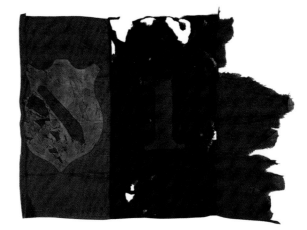

This tattered banner, ripped by fire during the fighting in the Crater, bears witness to the devastating losses suffered by the black troops of General Ambrose Burnside's command, who carried the flag. One Confederate recalled, "The whole floor of the trench was strewn with the dead bodies of Negroes."

A column of soldiers of the 23d U.S. Colored Troops rushes toward the huge crater that was the result of a mine explosion on July 30. General Edward Ferrero's division of black troops attacked in support of General James Ledlie's division when the white soldiers stalled in the gaping hole and surrounding debris-filled trenches. Widespread confusion gave the Confederates time to surround the crater and block the Federals inside it.

At least 22 gunners of Pegram's battery and 256 men of the 18th and 22d Carolina died in the blast.

The way into Petersburg lay open to Burnside's men. But the blast had disconcerted them almost as much as it had the Confederates. The cloud thrown up by the explosion, explained one of Ledlie's aides, "appeared as if it would descend immediately upon the troops waiting to make the charge." Some of Ledlie's men scurried to the rear; others were too stunned to move. It took at least 10 minutes before they were able to re-form and advance. And when they did they crowded to the edge of the Crater and its extensive debris zone. Soon Federal soldiers began milling about, extricating wounded Confederates and hunting souvenirs while others formed a ragged line along the rubble-covered trench cavalier. Meanwhile, the Rebels on either side of the Crater had recovered and had thrown up a barricade of sandbags across the main trench south of the breach. To the north, the 17th South Carolina spread out into the connecting trenches and traverses, hoping to confine the attackers to the Crater.

Clearly, the Federals were in sore need of leadership, but it was not to come from General Ledlie. He was huddled in a bombproof to the rear, comforting himself with a bottle of rum. He was soon joined there by General Ferrero, who had remained behind after sending his inexperienced men into battle and disaster. As one Union officer recalled the scene, Ferrero's black troops "literally came falling over into this crater on their hands and knees; they were so thick in there that a man could not walk."

Three hours had passed since the detonation of the mine, and the Federals had only succeeded in cramming an estimated 15,000 troops into the area of the Crater. Lee ordered elements of Brigadier General Henry Wise's Virginia Brigade and two regiments of Brigadier General Matthew Ransom's North Carolina Brigade to hold the lines. At about 1:00 p.m., Major General William Mahone ordered what would be the decisive Confederate charge. As the gray-clad troops poured over the rim of the Crater, some Federals fought hand to hand, others tried to surrender, and several hundred simply ran for their lives. "The slaughter was fearful," recalled one of Mahone's officers, especially among blacks. Recalled a Virginia private: "I saw Confederates beating and shooting at the Negro soldiers as the latter, terror-stricken, rushed away from them." Around the Crater, other Federals were making a desperate stand. "The men were dropping thick and fast," recalled a Union officer, "most of them shot through the head. Every man that was shot rolled down the steep sides to the bottom, and in places they were piled up three and four deep." Isolated and hit hard, the Union regiments broke and ran, closely pursued by Confederates.

By about two o'clock the battle was over. The Federal forces had suffered 3,500 casualties against Confederate losses of about 1,500. Within hours, the Confederates were entrenching a new line in front of the Crater. As for General Grant, he now recognized the chance he had missed to take Petersburg, and perhaps end the war. "Such opportunity for carrying fortifications I have never seen before," he said, "and do not expect to see again."

LETHAL WORK OF A MOBILE MORTAR

Shortly after 10:00 a.m. on July 30, as General William Mahone was preparing to renew the Confederate counterattack against Union troops in the Crater, a young artillery officer named John Haskell (*left*) offered his services to Mahone. Colonel Haskell had lost his right arm at Gaines's Mill in 1862, but had lost none of his fighting spirit; Mahone considered him a brilliant soldier, "always hunting a place where he could strike a blow at our adversary." Now such an opportunity was at hand: Mahone suggested that Haskell move two of his compact Coehorn mortars to within 20 yards of the Crater, where they could shell the Federals with deadly accuracy.

The Coehorn was the perfect weapon for this arduous task. It weighed 300 pounds and was fitted with handles that enabled four men to carry it to points in the trenchworks that could not be reached by gun carriages. It could loft an 18-pound shell over a parapet and was brutally effective at short range.

Haskell and his men moved their mortars ever nearer the Crater, stopping to fire and reducing the powder charge after every advance. Eventually the shells rose so sluggishly, Haskell wrote, that it seemed "they could not get to the enemy." Yet they did, raising cries that were plainly audible to the gunners. Not until the lethal little mortars had taken a steep toll did Mahone commit his full force to the successful attack.

24-POUNDER
COEHORN MORTAR
MODEL 1838

"He was the first colored soldier I ever saw."

PRIVATE GEORGE S. BERNARD

Company E, 12th Virginia Infantry, Mahone's Brigade

George S. Bernard was 23 years old when he marched off to war in the spring of 1861 as a member of the Petersburg Rifles, a militia unit that became Company E of the 12th Virginia Infantry. The siege of Petersburg in 1864 found Company E defending their home city and Bernard and his fellows participated in the Confederate counterattack on July 30 that cleared the Crater of Federal troops.

Getting within ten paces of the ends of the little ditches or traverses, which led out perpendicularly from the main trench of our breast-works some ten or fifteen paces, to my surprise I saw a negro soldier getting up from a recumbent position on the ground near my feet. He was the first colored soldier I ever saw, and this was my first knowledge of the fact that negro troops were before us. I had not then fired my rifle, and I might easily have killed this man, but regarding him as a prisoner, I had no disposition to hurt him. Looking then directly ahead of me, within thirty feet of where I stood, I saw in the trench of the breastworks crowds of men, white and black, with arms in their hands, as closely jammed and packed together as we sometimes see pedestrians on the crowded sidewalk of a city, and seemingly in great confusion and alarm. I distinctly noticed the countenances and rolling eyes of the terror-stricken negroes. I particularly noticed in the hands of one of the frightened creatures the new silk of a large and beautiful stand of colors, the staff swaying to and fro as the color-bearer, his eyes fixed in terrified gaze at his armed adversaries, was being pushed and jostled by his comrades. With my gun still loaded I might have fired into this mass of men, but I regarded these also as practically our prisoners. Casting my' eyes upon the ground over and beyond the breastworks—east of them, I mean—I there saw large numbers of the enemy retreating to their own breastworks. Many, however, were taking shelter behind—that is, on the east side, or outside, of our breastworks, as I could see from the tops of their caps, just over the parapet. Into a squad of those I saw retreating to their own works, I fired my rifle, and not stopping to note the damage done by my shot, or to enquire who was thereby hurt, I jumped into one of the little ditches leading out from the main trench.

Holding aloft his shattered flagpole in the epic painting at right, Color Sergeant William Smith of the 12th Virginia leads his comrades in the decisive charge against the Federals holding the mine crater at Petersburg on July 30, 1864. After the battle, Smith (below) found the flag, pierced by more than 75 bullets, beyond repair, and the late-pattern Richmond depot flag at near right was requisitioned as a replacement. The shattered flagpole, with its halberd, was carefully preserved as a memento of the 12th's heroic charge.

Major General William Mahone (inset), the pugnacious son of a tavern-keeper, lived up to his reputation by rushing the Crater with two brigades of the Virginia Infantry. "Whenever Mahone moves out," an admirer remarked, "someone is apt to be hurt."

THE GRIM TESTING OF BLACK TROOPS

More black soldiers, totaling 38 regiments, served with the Union armies besieging Petersburg and Richmond than in any other Civil War campaign. In that grim crucible they erased the doubts about their fighting ability that had been harbored by Grant and other Federal generals—and by white troops on both sides. Blacks fought desperately in the chaos of the Battle of the Crater, one brigade suffering 1,324 casualties, and later they took the lead in assaults on New Market Heights and other Confederate strongholds. For individual gallantry in these attacks, 23 black soldiers earned the Congressional Medal of Honor.

One Medal of Honor winner, Sergeant Major Christian Fleetwood, wrote later that his fellow blacks fought so well because they needed to prove their bravery to the world. They "stood in the full glare of the greatest searchlight, part and parcel of the grandest armies ever mustered on this continent," Fleetwood said, competing "with the bravest and the best" and "losing nothing by comparison."

The banner carried by the 22d Regiment U.S. Colored Troops pictures a bayonet-wielding black soldier overpowering a Confederate. The Latin motto at top, meaning "Thus Always to Tyrants," had an ironic thrust; it was also the state motto of slaveholding Virginia.

This embroidered blue silk regimental color is typical of flags presented to black regiments by private benefactors. This regimental banner and its companion Federal color were probably manufactured by Tiffany & Company of New York City.

Charging at a run, men of the 22d U.S. Colored Troops capture a Confederate entrenchment on the Dimmock Line outside Petersburg on June 16, 1864. One of the unit's officers wrote afterward, "I never saw troops fight better, more bravely, and with more determination and enthusiasm."

Charles Springer of the 107th U.S. Colored Troops proudly wears the chevrons of a sergeant major, a rank he earned during the long Petersburg siege. Sergeant major was the highest rank attained by blacks in Federal regiments during the war; the commissioned officers in charge of their units were white.

A photograph taken by Timothy O'Sullivan a week after the Battle of the Crater shows black soldiers occupying trenches and dugouts called bombproofs in the Federal line east of Petersburg. The troops were part of Brigadier General Edward Ferrero's division, which contained all the black regiments assigned to the Army of the Potomac.

The Medal of Honor, the nation's highest award for valor was awarded to no fewer than 13 black soldiers who took part in the New Market Heights attacks. So notable was the courage of the black troops that General Benjamin Butler was moved to write: "I felt in my inmost heart that the capacity of the Negro race for soldiers had then and there been fully settled forever." Two of the Medal of Honor winners were First Sergeant Powhatan Beaty (below) of the 5th U.S. Colored Troops and Sergeant James H. Harris (right) of the 38th U.S. Colored Troops.

**UNIDENTIFIED COLOR SERGEANT
OF THE 108TH U.S. COLORED TROOPS**

A company of the 4th U.S. Colored Troops poses in front of their barracks near Washington after the war. Raised in Baltimore, Maryland, the unit fought at the Crater and lost 178 men in the Federal attacks at Chaffin's farm and New Market Heights east of Richmond in September 1864.

The 104th New York was issued this replacement flag after losing its colors at the Battle of Weldon Railroad. Weldon Railroad is included among the regiment's battle honors despite its having lost its flag there.

"I do not care to die. But I pray to God I may never leave this field."

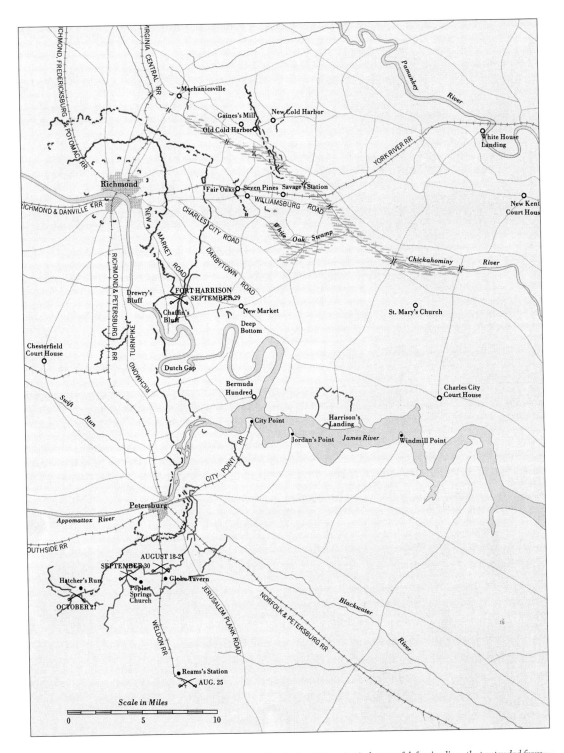

In late summer of 1864 General Lee's forces were stretched to the breaking point in layers of defensive lines that extended from Richmond to Petersburg. The Federals hammered at Lee with coordinated attacks, both north of the James, at Fort Harrison, and south of the river, at the Weldon Railroad and Hatcher's Run. By November, Grant's repeated blows had softened the Confederate defenses, but they failed to achieve the breakthrough he sought.

Federal gunners astride the Weldon Railroad duel with distant Confederate batteries on August 21. Colonel Frederick Winthrop, whose 5th New York is at center, wrote that his regiment suffered "a most deadly cross-fire of artillery, but, as usual, fully sustained its old reputation for calmness and steadiness."

FIGHTING ON THE FLANKS

Since the Federal failure at the Crater, the fighting around Petersburg had settled into a deadly pattern, with Grant hammering first with his right fist and then, when Lee shifted troops to fend off the blow, with his left. On August 14 Major General Winfield Scott Hancock launched an offensive north of the James River against the extreme Confederate left at Deep Bottom Run. In a series of actions at Fussell's Mill and along the Charles City road the Federals fought to within seven miles of Richmond before the Confederates, reinforced by three divisions quickly dispatched from south of the James, beat off the attack. Four days later the Union met with more success, when Major General Gouverneur Warren's V Corps attacked the weakened enemy line south of Petersburg near Globe Tavern and seized a stretch of the Weldon Railroad, one of Lee's supply lines.

On August 25 an attempt to destroy more of the Weldon line failed when two of Hancock's divisions, which had been shifted back south of the James to support Federal cavalry, were repulsed at Ream's Station. When A. P. Hill's Confederates attacked Hancock's lines west of the station the Federal troops, exhausted and demoralized by months of hard campaigning, panicked and ran. In the fighting, Hancock stated, his men "could neither be made to go forward nor fire." Hancock was mortified by the sorry performance of his once proud corps. "I do not care to die," he told a colonel during the battle. "But I pray to God I may never leave this field." In two days of fighting Hill's Confederates captured over 2,000 prisoners, nine pieces of artillery, and 12 colors.

Not until late September was Grant offered a chance for a real breakthrough. At the first bend in the James south of Richmond, Lee's defensive line straddled the

river, anchored on the north at Chaffin's Bluff, Virginia, where the Confederates occupied a fortified camp. Located at the camp's southeast corner was a formidable obstacle named Fort Harrison, consisting largely of a parapet with enclosed gun positions, fronted by a row of sharpened stakes to entangle charging infantry.

Early on the morning of September 29, some 2,000 men of Major General Edward O. C. Ord's Federal XVIII Corps crossed a pontoon bridge over the James and advanced up the Varina road toward Fort Harrison. At the same time the Federal X Corps under Major General David B. Birney crossed the Deep Bottom Bridge with orders to move against Richmond via the New Market and Darby roads. Meanwhile, Ord's troops fought their way past Chaffin's farm and Brigadier General Hiram Burnham's brigade advanced across open ground, swept by enemy rifle and artillery fire, to capture Fort Harrison, quickly overwhelming its garrison of 800 inexperienced artillerists. Here was a priceless opportunity: If he could quickly capture the rest of the fortified camp, Ord could then advance on Richmond, only eight miles away.

Yet in their rush at the fort the Federals had become disorganized, and once inside, the exhilaration of their victory delayed the restoration of order. An hour or so passed before Ord was able to patch together a force, which he led himself. In the futile process, Ord suffered a leg wound, and his command passed to his senior subordinate, an inept brigadier general named Charles Heckman.

For two hours, Heckman threw his individual brigades piecemeal into a series of clumsy attacks that exposed them to brutal enfilading fire from Fort Gilmer, which had been reinforced by the Confederates. And then, just as a lull was settling over the field at about 10:00 a.m., General Grant rode into Fort Harrison. Although the signs of impending failure must have been evident to Grant's practiced eye, the general in chief unaccountably did nothing to remedy the worsening situation. Instead, he simply scribbled a message to Birney saying that Ord's XVIII Corps was ready to advance on Richmond. The general in chief then returned to Deep Bottom to await developments.

On the Confederate side of the lines, these developments were now coming fast. The ailing Lieutenant General Richard S. Ewell, whom Lee had gently removed from corps command and put in charge of the defenses of Richmond, rose to the occasion with all of his former ferocity. Taking personal charge of the threatened encampment at Chaffin's Bluff, the one-legged Ewell had thrown a line diagonally across its wooded interior, from the embattled redans on the river northeastward to Fort Johnston on the opposite corner. The line was little more than a facade, manned by badly shaken heavy artillerymen now forced to fight as infantry and by Major Alexander Starke's battalion of light artillery. Ewell, however, was a gambler; he rode up and down the line, pushing skirmishers to the edge of the woods facing the Federals. "I remember very distinctly how he looked," recalled one of his soldiers, "mounted on an old gray horse, as mad as he could be, shouting to the men and seeming to be everywhere at once." The ruse worked. No Federals advanced from Fort Harrison.

At about 3:00 p.m., obedient to Grant's orders, Birney's Federals, including Brigadier General Charles Paine's brigade of black troops borrowed from the XVIII Corps, attacked the reinforced Confederate lines along New Market Heights. Despite great gallantry and a series of determined assaults, the Federal attack was turned back with heavy losses. During the night Confederate reinforcements poured into the Chaffin's Bluff defenses and the Federal opportunity to take Richmond quickly faded away.

Nonetheless, the fight at Fort Harrison had scared the Confederates; a few days later a depressed Robert E. Lee informed Secretary of War James Seddon that things could not long continue this way. While Grant extended his lines and added to his numbers, the Army of Northern Virginia could "only meet his corps, increased by recent recruits, with a division, reduced by long and arduous service."

For the first time, Lee began to speak openly of the possibility of losing Richmond. He needed time to find more men, more food, more ammunition, and more

> *"Some of the men have been without meat for three days, and all are suffering from reduced rations and scant clothing, exposed to battle, cold, hail and sleet."*

horses. His hope now was to hang on until cold, wet weather put a temporary end to Grant's incessant attacks. "We may be able, with the blessing of God, to keep the enemy in check until the beginning of winter," he wrote. "If we fail to do this the result may be calamitous." And so the Confederates held on, their condition steadily deteriorating. With the destruction of sections of the railroads linking Petersburg with the South, Confederate quartermasters had to shift supplies from railcars at a point some 20 miles south of the city. From there wagon trains transported the supplies along back roads that skirted the Federal left. In September Confederate major general Wade Hampton helped relieve the supply crisis by conducting an audacious cavalry raid around the Federal flank that captured 2,400 head of cattle from the Union commissary herds.

In the fall, Grant continued his drive to tighten the stranglehold and sever the lifelines of Lee's army. In October fighting flared west of Petersburg at Poplar Springs Church, Hatcher's Run, and the Boydton Plank Road but neither side could gain an advantage. On the last Thursday of November, proclaimed Thanksgiving Day by President Abraham Lincoln (who was doubtless thankful for having won reelection earlier in the month), the Federal armies outside Richmond enjoyed a feast of turkey or chicken, pies, and fruit. There was no such celebration for Lee's troops. Instead, wrote a South Carolina captain, "We lay in grim repose."

As much as Lee may have looked toward its coming, the winter of 1864-65 was a death watch. Poisoned by inflation, the Confederate economic system was collapsing. In 1861, one gold dollar had been equivalent to $1.03 in Confederate

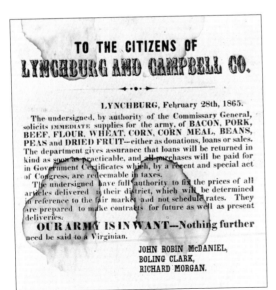

TO THE CITIZENS OF LYNCHBURG AND CAMPBELL CO.

LYNCHBURG, February 28th, 1865.

The undersigned, by authority of the Commissary General, solicits IMMEDIATE supplies for the army, of BACON, PORK, BEEF, FLOUR, WHEAT, CORN, CORN MEAL, BEANS, PEAS and DRIED FRUIT—either as donations, loans or sales. The department gives assurance that loans will be returned in kind as soon as practicable, and all purchases will be paid for in Government Certificates which, by a recent and special act of Congress, are redeemable in taxes.

The undersigned have full authority to fix the prices of all articles delivered in their district, which will be determined in reference to the fair market and not schedule rates. They are prepared to make contracts for future as well as present deliveries.

OUR ARMY IS IN WANT—Nothing further need be said to a Virginian.

JOHN ROBIN McDANIEL,
BOLING CLARK,
RICHARD MORGAN.

This broadside, part of a campaign begun by the new Confederate commissary chief, General Isaac St. John, to feed Lee's army, brought immediate results. Officials reported that depots were "rapidly filling up with flour, meal, corn and bacon."

As always, the suffering was worst for the soldiers. "Starvation, literal starvation," reported Major General John B. Gordon. After a spasm of fighting south of Petersburg, Lee bitterly complained that, "Some of the men have been without meat for three days, and all are suffering from reduced rations and scant clothing, exposed to battle, cold, hail and sleet." Yet the commanding general did not have it much better. An Irish politician who visited Lee was invited to dinner. "He had two biscuits," said the guest, "and he gave me one." Yet Robert E. Lee was never content simply to defend, and with the first harbingers of spring he moved to attack by calling in General Gordon—who had, at 32, become the youngest of his corps commanders—and asked him to find a likely place to batter through the enemy works.

Robert E. Lee sits astride his horse, Traveller, in the only wartime photograph of the Confederate commander in the saddle; the picture is believed to have been taken in rubble-strewn Petersburg in 1864. As the siege wore on, the rigors of the campaign began to tell on both Lee and his mount. "My horse is dreadfully rough," he wrote to his wife from Petersburg, "& I am very stiff & heavy."

money. As 1865 began, a dollar in gold equaled almost $60 Confederate. In Richmond, hungry, threadbare citizens were paying $45 Confederate for a pound of coffee, $100 for a pound of tea, and $25 for a pound of butter—when those items were available at all.

To Lee, the most worrisome problem was a shortage of troops. Since 1861 the Confederacy had put about 750,000 soldiers in the field; in all theaters there were now fewer than 160,000 on duty. The rest, one officer said, had been "worn out and killed out and starved out." To remedy the situation, teenagers and men in their sixties were being enrolled in reserve units; a lieutenant assigned to one such ragtag outfit said it "presented every stage of manhood from immature boyhood to decrepit old age."

A trenchbound South Carolina soldier wore this woolen hood (above, left) called a balaclava, during the cold winter nights at Petersburg in 1865. The hand-knit cap was styled and named after the headgear British troops used in Russia during the Crimean War.

Private J. O. McGehee of the 53d Virginia Infantry wore this homespun overcoat (above, right) during the winter campaign of 1864-65. He had it in early April 1865 when he was wounded at the Battle of Five Forks.

In the spring of 1864, the 26th South Carolina Infantry carried this Charleston depot battle flag (right) to Virginia and into action at Bermuda Hundred and Petersburg. In the assault on Fort Stedman the colorbearer, Samuel J. Reid, was "knocked down by the explosion of a shell." Captain H. L. Buck retrieved the flag but was captured, along with many of his men.

Three hundred infantrymen, a select force from Major General John B. Gordon's corps, pour through openings cut by axmen in the barriers shielding Fort Stedman. "Although it required but a few minutes to reach the Union works," Gordon wrote, "those minutes were to me like hours of suspense and breathless anxiety."

It was three weeks before Gordon came back with a proposal. Near the center of the Federal line east of Petersburg stood a bristling strong point named Fort Stedman. It was located at a place where the opposing entrenchments lay only 150 yards apart—so close, Gordon thought, that the Confederates could take it with a rush. "The tremendous possibility," Gordon wrote later, "was the disintegration of the whole left wing of the Federal Army, or at least the dealing of such a staggering blow upon it as would disable it temporarily."

Launched at 4:00 a.m. on March 25, the assault appeared at first to be a smashing success. Advancing in three columns, the Confederates swarmed over surprised Federal pickets, punched into Fort Stedman and overwhelmed its defenders. But there, as the Federal army came to life, they stalled.

Responsible for the threatened sector of the front was the Federal IX Corps under Major General John G. Parke, who had been startled that morning to discover that, while General Meade was away at Grant's City Point, Virginia, headquarters, he was the acting commander of the Army of the Potomac. Yet Parke reacted decisively. With two divisions already on the line, he immediately called on Brigadier General John Hartranft's reserve division to move toward the breach. Soon, the Confederacy's Gordon recalled, the surrounding hills were "black with troops."

By 8:00 a.m., four hectic hours after Gordon's attack had begun, the Confeder-

ate situation seemed hopeless, and Lee ordered a withdrawal. In his army's last offensive gasp, he had lost 3,500 men while inflicting about 1,000 casualties. As for the Federals, the only change caused by the assault was that a divisional review, scheduled for that morning, was put off until the afternoon.

On Sunday, March 26, the day after the failed endeavor at Fort Stedman, General Lee informed President Jefferson Davis that Richmond and Petersburg were doomed. Now, Lee felt, his job was to get his troops away to the southwest, where they could join forces in North Carolina with General Joseph E. Johnston, whose own army had recently been helpless in opposing the Federal legions of Major General William Tecumseh Sherman.

Late on the following afternoon, Sherman himself arrived by steamer at City Point, where Grant and a few staff members were on hand to meet him as he stepped ashore. After his devastating march through Georgia, the red-haired Ohioan had persuaded Grant to let him deal out the same treatment to the Carolinas: Columbia, the capital of South Carolina, had been turned into a sea of flames on February 17; Charleston, the cradle of the Confederacy, had been abandoned by the Confederacy that same day; Sherman's men had surged into North Carolina during the first week in March. On March 23, General Johnston sent Lee a harshly realistic message: "Sherman's course cannot be hindered by the small force I have. I can do no more than annoy him."

At City Point, Sherman and Grant greeted each other, as one officer recalled the scene, like "two schoolboys coming together after a vacation." That night and the next day they conferred with Admiral David D. Porter and another distinguished City Point visitor—President Lincoln, who was staying aboard the steamer *River Queen.*

> *"I want no one punished. Treat them liberally all around. We want those people to return to their allegiance to the Union and submit to the laws."*

With the end of the war obviously in sight, Sherman naturally wanted to know what the president's policy toward the defeated Confederacy would be. Lincoln's answer was clear: As soon as the fighting stopped, the people of the South "would at once be guaranteed all their rights" as citizens of a common country. "I want no one punished," Porter remembered Lincoln as saying. "Treat them liberally all around. We want those people to return to their allegiance to the Union and submit to the laws. With that in mind (and it would later haunt him), Sherman returned to North Carolina. On the following day, Grant launched the campaign that would at last break the back of the Confederacy.

BATTLE OF FIVE FORKS

Grant had anticipated that Lee would attempt a juncture with Johnston, and he had made plans to prevent it. As Grant saw it, the crucial area of operations would be a rectangle southwest of Petersburg that was 10 miles across, east to west, and eight miles deep. It was bound on the north by the Southside Railroad; on the east by the Weldon Railroad; on the south by the Vaughan road to the village of Dinwiddie

General Sherman (far left) argues a point with General Grant, President Lincoln, and Admiral David D. Porter during their meeting to discuss strategy and peace terms aboard the steamer River Queen in late March 1865. Porter later wrote of Lincoln's attitude toward the South: "His heart was all tenderness."

Two brigades of Brigadier General George Armstrong Custer's 3d Cavalry Division charge a line of Virginians on the Confederate right at Five Forks. "Before the enemy could shift his batteries, my columns were moving rapidly to place themselves in the rear of his position," Custer reported. "The retreat of over 5,000 of the rebels was then cut off."

"We'll get the twist on 'em, boys! There won't be a grease spot of 'em left!"

Court House; and on the west by a road leading north from Dinwiddie to the Southside Railroad—by way of a crossroads called Five Forks.

Grant ordered General Warren's V Corps, followed by Major General Andrew Humphreys' II Corps, to march five miles south along the Vaughan road until the troops were beyond the Confederate right flank. From there the infantry was to press north toward the enemy line, forcing the Confederates to come out of their trenches to protect their rear and the Southside Railroad. It was raining on March 29, and the going was hard for Warren's troops. "We went slipping and plunging through the black slimy mud in which pointed rocks were bedded," a Federal officer recalled, "now stumbling over a rotten tree, now over the stiffening corpse of some poor comrade by whose side we might soon lie."

Although the heavy rain continued on the 30th, Warren and Humphreys edged closer to the Confederate trenches. Meanwhile, Major General Philip H. Sheridan—back from the Shenandoah Valley and once again in command of the Federal cavalry—sent a division of horsemen northward from Dinwiddie toward Five Forks. Upon approaching the vital intersection, however, the troopers found 5,000 infantrymen of Major General George Pickett's division entrenched and in a fighting mood. After a brief exchange of fire, the Federals fell back and reported that the enemy intended to hold Five Forks.

Not until April 1, after a day of maneuvering and sporadic fighting, were the Federals ready to assail Five Forks. According to Sheridan's plan, his dismounted cavalry under Brevet Major General Wesley Merritt would feint toward Pickett's right and pin down his center while Warren's infantry assaulted the Confederate left, which was bent back at a 90-degree angle to the north. But as the day passed and Warren still was not in position, Sheridan suffered agonies of frustration. "He made every possible appeal for promptness," a staff officer wrote, "dismounted from his horse, paced up and down, and struck the clenched fist of one hand against the palm of the other, and fretted like a caged tiger."

Yet in one way the delays may actually have helped Sheridan. Lulled into a false sense of security by the failure of the Federals to attack, George Pickett and the cavalry's Major General Fitzhugh Lee had gone off north shortly after 2:00 p.m. to feast at a shadbake hosted by a fellow general on the north bank of Hatcher's Run. The two officers told no one where they were going. The repast was a leisurely one, liquor may have been served, and Pickett was still enjoying the afterglow when, shortly after 4:15 p.m., the Federals struck at Five Forks.

Aimed at the angle of Pickett's bent line, the assault almost missed its mark; instead of being crushed by the combined weight of two divisions on the Federal right, the vital spot was hit only by the division of Major General Romeyn Ayres—

Major Generals George E. Pickett (left) and Fitzhugh Lee (center), the senior Confederate officers at Five Forks, were away from their posts, enjoying a shadbake at the headquarters of Brigadier General Thomas L. Rosser (right) near Hatcher's Run, when the Federals attacked. Their party ended abruptly when Union infantry appeared across the stream.

it high. "Bullets were now humming like a swarm of bees around our head," wrote a staff officer, "and shells were crashing through the ranks. All this time Sheridan was dashing from one point of the line to another, waving his flag, shaking his fist, encouraging, entreating, threatening, praying, swearing, the very incarnation of battle."

Under Sheridan's inspired leadership, the Confederate left was broken, and by the time Pickett finally got back to the field his men were already being driven to the west. "It has been an evil day for us," a Confederate captain wrote in his diary. "My heart sickens as I contemplate this day's disasters."

The day was a disaster for General Warren as well. Since morning, Sheridan had been fretting over Warren's tardiness, and criticized his dispositions. Now, as the gunfire died away, Sheridan ordered Brigadier General Charles Griffin to assume command of V Corps. When the word reached Warren he went to Sheridan and asked him to reconsider. "Reconsider, hell!" said Sheridan. "I don't reconsider my decisions. Obey the order!"

Thus Gouverneur Warren, a hero of Gettysburg, ended the war in disgrace. (Fourteen years later, a court of inquiry exonerated Warren—three months after he had died.)

Word of the victory at Five Forks was carried to Grant by one of his staff

with Phil Sheridan nearby and yelling encouragement. "We'll get the twist on 'em, boys!" Sheridan cried. "There won't be a grease spot of 'em left!"

As Ayres' men pushed forward, they were staggered by a Confederate volley and started to fall back. To rally them, Sheridan seized his personal flag and held

"It has been an evil day for us. My heart sickens as I contemplate this day's disasters."

Confederate prisoners captured at the Battle of Five Forks wait to be marched to the rear. "Droves of silent Johnnies, under guard, tramped through the mire," a Federal officer recalled, "jostling against noisy Yanks, who were filling the air with yells and catcalls—the effervescence of victory."

officers, Lieutenant Colonel Horace Porter, who leaped from his horse and found himself "rushing up to the general-in-chief and clapping him on the back with my hand, to his no little astonishment." Grant endured Porter's enthusiasm without comment, then turned to General Meade and said quietly: "Very well, then, I want Wright and Parke to assault tomorrow morning at four."

At that appointed hour on the Sunday morning of April 2, Union artillery on the Petersburg front opened with the greatest bombardment of the 10-month siege. "From hundreds of cannons, field guns and mortars came a stream of living fire," recalled a Federal sergeant; "the shells screamed through the air in a semi-circle of flame."

Attacking at first light Parke's IX Corps stormed into the Confederate earthworks along the Jerusalem Plank Road. Facing stiff Confederate resistance, however, his men were unable to break through the lines. On the Union right, Major General Horatio Wright's VI Corps brushed enemy pickets aside and, despite heavy losses, managed to breach the Confederate trenches at several points. All along VI Corps' front, an officer reported, the Confederates were soon "swept away and scattered like chaff before a tornado." The Federals rolled up the Confederate lines to the southwest as far as Hatcher's Run. At the same time Major General John Gibbon's XXIV Corps broke into the Confederate works near Hatcher's Run and advanced down the Jerusalem Plank Road to capture Forts Gregg and Whittle.

Unaware of the break in his line, Lieutenant General Ambrose Powell Hill had

"He is at rest now, and we who are left are the ones to suffer."

ridden to Lee's headquarters near Petersburg for a conference. Soon Lieutenant General James Longstreet, still recovering from the wound he had sustained in the Wilderness, arrived in advance of the reinforcements he was bringing from north of the James River. The three generals were discussing the bleak situation when an officer burst in to report that Hill's lines had been struck and broken and that Federal skirmishers were approaching. Hill mounted his horse and raced away to try to stem the Federal flood.

Heading southwest with a courier on the Boydton Plank Road, Hill spotted two Federals in the trees ahead. "We must take them," snapped Hill, drawing his revolver. The bluecoats—Corporal John Mauk and Private Daniel Wolford of the 138th Pennsylvania—took cover and leveled their rifles. "If you fire, you'll be swept to hell," shouted Hill's courier, G. W. Tucker. And then, bluffing: "Our men are here—Surrender!" Hill echoed the cry: "Surrender!"

The answer came as spitting lead, and a bullet from Mauk's rifle pierced Hill's heart. He was dead before he hit the ground. Tucker rode back to headquarters and

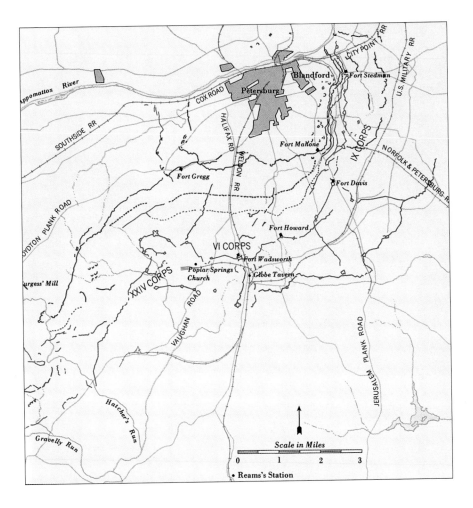

Galvanized by word of Sheridan's victory at Five Forks, Grant's forces at Petersburg launched a concentrated assault on the weakened Confederate defenses at dawn on April 2. Major General John Parke's IX Corps was initially unable to capture the Confederate strong point of Fort Mahone, but Major General Horatio Wright's VI Corps broke through the Confederate lines west of Petersburg, cutting the Boydton Plank Road and the Southside Railroad. By nightfall, Major General John Gibbon's XXIV Corps had taken Fort Gregg in heavy fighting, Fort Mahone had fallen, and Lee had withdrawn to the innermost line of defense. He now had no choice but to evacuate Petersburg.

reported to Lee, whose eyes filled with tears. "He is at rest now," Lee murmured, "and we who are left are the ones to suffer."

Later that morning, Lee sent a telegram to General John C. Breckinridge, the Confederacy's recently appointed secretary of war: "I advise that all preparation be made for leaving Richmond tonight." A messenger took a copy of the wire to President Davis while he was attending services at St. Paul's Episcopal Church. "Mr. Davis arose," a parishioner wrote later, "and was noticed to walk rather unsteadily out of the church."

THE FALLEN AT FORT MAHONE

It is probable that never since the invention of gunpowder has such a cannonade taken place," declared the Federal officer in charge of the climactic April 2 bombardment of the defenses of Petersburg. On the morning after that holocaustic assault, a photographer named Thomas Roche carried his bulky equipment to a captured strong point in the Confederate line, which had defied Grant's army for 10 desperate months. Known as Fort Mahone, the earthworks had been manned by troops of the 53d North Carolina. Roche found the place defended now only by Confederate dead; he photographed these men sprawled as they had fallen, in Fort Mahone's mud-choked labyrinth of trenches. Some were elderly veterans, but many were boys—one only 14 years old, by Roche's estimate. Their faces evince a repose that contrasts poignantly with their torn bodies. The deaths Roche recorded seem all the more painful because the victims were struck down in one of the war's last battles—for a cause already lost.

"It is probable that never since the invention of gunpowder has such a cannonade taken place."

THE ROAD TO APPOMATTOX

By nightfall, Jefferson Davis and members of the cabinet, the archives, and the treasury of the Confederacy were on their way to Danville, Virginia. Then, over the objections of Richmond's city fathers, the Confederates set fire to the city's warehouses to keep the valuable contents out of the hands of the Federals. The flames quickly spread.

> ## "It was an extraordinary sight; disorder, pillage, shouts, mad revelry of confusion."

With the departure of civil authorities, the streets of Richmond were taken over by a menacing mob: thieves, prostitutes, army deserters, and convicts who had broken out of the penitentiary. "It was an extraordinary sight," recalled newspaper editor Edward Pollard; "disorder, pillage, shouts, mad revelry of confusion." As the hours passed, "the sidewalks were encumbered with broken glass; stores were entered at pleasure and stripped from top to bottom; yells of drunken men, shouts of roving pillagers, wild cries of distress filled the air and made the night hideous."

All the while Robert E. Lee's widely dispersed army was streaming over five separate routes toward the pretty, red-brick town of Amelia Court House, which lay about 35 miles west of Petersburg on the Richmond & Danville Railroad. Lee arrived there on April 3, only to make an appalling discovery. During the last days of the siege, he had asked the Confederate Commissary Department to collect a store of food in Richmond. It had been done: 35,000 rations were gathered in the capital, and Lee wanted them sent ahead to Amelia. But that order had somehow gone astray during the confusion of Richmond's final hours, and Lee now found an abundant cache of artillery caissons, ammunition, and harness—but not a single ration.

For a moment, according to one officer, Lee seemed "completely paralyzed." But he quickly mastered himself and sent foraging parties out into the countryside that had already been scoured repeatedly for food. The delay was critical. To the south, Grant's Federals were already racing along a course roughly parallel to Lee's, hoping to get ahead of the Army of Northern Virginia and cut off its escape route.

When the foragers returned during the morning of April 5, their wagons were virtually empty. Yet Lee had no choice but to put his troops on the road without having eaten. His route of march would pass through Rice's Station on the Southside Railroad, seven miles northwest of Burkeville. Once there he could receive food by rail from Lynchburg, then march west to that city or, preferably, head south to

the Danville route and follow it to Johnston's army. But with the Federal forces closing in fast he would have to hurry.

Leading the strung-out army was Longstreet's corps. Later came Lieutenant General Richard Anderson's small corps and the Richmond garrison, commanded by the veteran General Richard Ewell. Bringing up the rear was Gordon's corps.

Riding across a bridge spanning the James River, a Rebel cavalry detachment (right) escorts the carriages of Confederate officials evacuating Richmond late on the night of April 2. "It was a sad, a terrible & a solemn sight," General E. Porter Alexander recalled. "The whole river front seemed to be in flames, amid which occasional heavy explosions were heard & the black smoke spreading & hanging over the city seemed to be full of dreadful portents." As he rode away, Alexander sensed "a peculiar . . . feeling of orphanage."

Gutted flour mills and warehouses surround Richmond's industrial basin in this photograph taken after the fall of the city in April 1865. When evacuating Confederate authorities ordered the destruction of military stores and facilities the fires quickly spread to neighboring industrial areas.

Troops of Lieutenant General Richard S. Ewell's corps raise their muskets in surrender on April 6, 1865, at the Battle of Sayler's Creek. Among the 2,000 men captured were Ewell himself and five other generals, including Major General George Washington Custis Lee, eldest son of Robert E. Lee.

By the time Longstreet reached Rice's Station on the morning of April 6, a gap had opened between his rear and Anderson's vanguard. At 11 o'clock Anderson was still five miles away; ahead of him were the two branches of Sayler's Creek, a tributary of the Appomattox. When a Confederate wagon train moved unprotected into the widening gap, Federal riders attacked, killing drivers, cutting horses loose, and setting wagons on fire. To protect the rest of the wagons, Ewell ordered those still behind him to take a road forking off to the north. General Gordon, however, was not informed of the change; when he reached the fork, he followed the wagons—as he had been doing all day—and thereby veered away from the rest of the army. Thus, Lee's outnumbered army had been split into three diverging parts. Of these, the one made up of Ewell's and Anderson's commands was facing the most immediate danger.

Anderson's brigades crossed one of the branches of Sayler's Creek and pushed three-quarters of a mile down the road, where they found three of Sheridan's cavalry divisions blocking the way. Horatio Wright's VI Corps had been following Sheridan, and now it swung to the north to come up behind Ewell. Confederate private W. L. Timberlake watched as VI Corps deployed. "The corps was massing into the fields at a double quick," he wrote, "the battle lines, blooming with colors, growing longer and deeper at every moment, the batteries at a gallop coming into action front. We knew what it all meant."

What it all meant was a battle in which the Confederate situation was hopeless: The Rebels were badly outnumbered and woefully weary. While Wright launched the infantry assault against Ewell, the Federal cavalry slammed into Anderson from the opposite direction. The Confederates "lost all formation and went across country," wrote a New York sergeant, "our boys chasing up and gath-

ering them in." By the end of the one-sided Battle of Sayler's Creek, 6,000 Confederates had been taken prisoner, including Richard Ewell and five other generals.

To the north of Anderson and Ewell, Gordon found himself in similarly desperate straits when a bridge across Sayler's Creek collapsed, slowing his march

"The results of the last week must convince you of the hopelessness of further resistance."

while General Humphreys' II Corps came up on his rear. The Confederates fought savagely until Gordon saw that further resistance was hopeless. Then, one Confederate wrote, Gordon "gave us orders to save ourselves, showing us the way by galloping his horse down the hill and fording the creek." On the opposite side, Gordon pulled together what remained of his command and marched toward Farmville, a few miles west on the south bank of the Appomattox River.

At Rice's Station, Lee and Longstreet also determined to head for Farmville, where they could join Gordon's remnants, cross the Appomattox River, burn the bridges behind them, and get a little breathing space before marching west for Lynchburg. In the event, however, General William Mahone's rearguard division delayed in burning a key bridge the following day, April 7, destroying only four of its 21 spans and allowing Humphreys' corps to get across. After that, as if in atonement, Mahone's men dug in near Cumberland Church, three miles north of Farmville, and stubbornly held off the advancing enemy until darkness finally ended one of the worst two-day period in Confederate history.

SURRENDER

That night at Farmville's Prince Edward Hotel—where Lee had slept the night before—General Grant received word from Sheridan that provisions for Lee's army had arrived by rail at Appomattox Station, 26 miles to the west. Sheridan intended to start for the junction the following day; if he could beat Lee to those rations, the chase might be over. Having digested that news, Grant wrote a short message to Lee: "The results of the last week must convince you of the hopelessness of further resistance. I feel that is so, and regard it as my duty to shift from myself the responsibility of any further effusion of blood, by asking of you the surrender of that portion of the Confederate States army known as the Army of Northern Virginia."

North of the Appomattox River, Lee and Longstreet were together when Grant's demand for surrender arrived at 9:30 p.m. After reading the message, Lee passed it without comment to Longstreet, who glanced at it and responded: "Not yet." Before dawn, Lee started his army toward the village of Appomattox Court House, two miles northeast of Appomattox Station, where the Confederates' precious provisions were now stored. Behind them were the fast-marching troops of the Federal II Corps while to the south, Sheridan and Ord aproached the courthouse.

Lee soon discovered that Union cavalry had seized his rail depot and that the Federal II and VI Corps were only 10 miles to the east. To the west, Sheridan's cavalry was "hovering around," as a Virginian recalled, "like ill-omened birds of prey, awaiting their opportunity." Yet for all their awful dilemma, the Confederate generals determined to try again to escape. At first light, Gordon's corps would lead an attempted breakout to the west while Longstreet held off the pursuing Federal infantry. And so, on the early morning of April 9, the II Corps of the Army of Northern Virginia went into its last battle.

Correspondence between Lee and Grant had continued as the Confederate columns struggled westward. In response to a request from Lee for terms, Grant replied that he did not have authority to offer precise conditions. Upon receiving this final dispatch, Lee asked for a meeting and in a later note, requested a cease-fire. In the fields north and south of Appomattox Court House the guns fell silent. Nearing the village, Lee asked Colonel Charles Marshall of his staff to ride ahead and arrange for a meeting place.

By remarkable coincidence, the house selected—a pleasant, tree-shaded, two-story brick structure—belonged to a merchant named Wilmer McLean. He had once owned a farm near Manassas in northern Virginia, and it had been used as General Beauregard's headquarters during the First Battle of Bull Run. McLean was a patriotic Southerner, but by March 1862 he had had quite enough of soldiers, and he moved to the sleepy little community of Appomattox Court House.

DEEDS OF VALOR REWARDED

PRIVATE CHARLES A. TAGGART
37th Massachusetts

LIEUTENANT THOMAS W. CUSTER
6th Michigan Cavalry

During the one-sided fighting at Sayler's Creek on April 6, Federal soldiers seized 50 Confederate flags, earning for each captor a Medal of Honor, the Union's highest decoration for valor. Two soldiers demonstrated particular fortitude that day in depriving the enemy of their treasured colors.

Private Charles A. Taggart *(left)* of the 37th Massachusetts surprised a squad of Confederates. He fired into their midst, grabbed their banner, and raced toward the Union lines. Taggart's comrades thought he was leading an enemy charge and shot at him, but he was only slightly wounded.

When Second Lieutenant Thomas W. Custer *(right)* of the 6th Michigan Cavalry confronted a Confederate colorbearer, he was shot in the face. But Custer righted himself in the saddle, returned fire, and wrested the flag from the falling man. Jubilant at capturing his second flag in five days, Custer called out to his older brother, General George Custer, "The rebels have shot me but I've got their flag." Thomas Custer recovered and became the only Federal soldier to receive two Medals of Honor for his deeds.

Left: A determined General Grant watches as Robert E. Lee affixes his signature to the terms of surrender at Appomattox Court House on April 9, 1865. Lee is flanked by his aide Colonel Charles Marshall. The officers behind Grant are from left, Philip Sheridan, Orville Babcock, Horace Porter, Edward O. C. Ord, Seth Williams, Theodore Bowers, Ely Parker, and George Armstrong Custer.

Opposite: At Appomattox on April 12, 1865, as the Army of Northern Virginia laid down its weapons, the Union general Joshua Chamberlain recalled that the Rebel flags were "crowded so thick, by thinning out of men, that the whole column seemed crowned with red." As Chamberlain watched, each regiment stacked arms and "reluctantly, with agony of expression, they tenderly folded their flags, battle-worn and torn, bloodstained, heart-holding colors, and laid them down."

Lee arrived at the McLean house at 1:00 p.m. Grant, accompanied by a number of his officers, entered the parlor about half an hour later. Lee rose to his feet and the two commanders shook hands. They were a study in contrasts. Tall, white-bearded, and dignified, Lee had put on his best uniform and wore his finest sword; Grant, slouched and red-whiskered, wore a mud-spattered sack coat and carried no sword. At Grant's behest, several more Federal officers were beckoned into the parlor. Those who could find chairs sat down; others stood against the walls.

The two generals signed the surrender document at about 3 o'clock. After they shook hands again, Lee led the way out to the porch. Federal soldiers in the McLean yard came to attention and saluted the defeated enemy leader. Lee returned the salute and mounted Traveller. Just then, Grant was coming down the steps from the porch. He stopped and, without a word, removed his hat. Lee raised his hat in return and slowly rode away.

April 12, 1865, the day selected for the last rites of the Army of Northern Virginia, was cold and gray. Honored with command of the ceremony was Brigadier General Joshua Chamberlain, who once long ago had made his stand with the 20th Maine at Little Round Top. Chamberlain aligned his Federal troops on both sides of the road leading through Appomattox, then watched intently as the Confederate column crossed the valley and marched up the avenue, silent but for the familiar sound of tramping feet. "On they come," Chamberlain wrote, "with the old swinging route step and swaying battle flags." General John Gordon led the column; behind him, the first unit in the line of march was the

Stonewall brigade, now reduced to barely 200 men.

Gordon sat erect in his saddle, but his head was down and his expression dark. The men behind him were equally grim. As the column neared the double line of Union soldiers, Gordon heard a spoken order, a bugle call, and an electrifying sound: the clatter of hundreds of Federal muskets being raised to the shoulder in salute. Gordon's head snapped up. Comprehending in an instant, he wheeled his mount toward Chamberlain. As the animal reared, then dipped its head toward the ground, Gordon raised his sword aloft and brought its tip down to his toes in a sweeping response to the Union tribute. He shouted a command, and the advancing Confederates came from a right shoulder shift to shoulder arms—returning the salute.

After the exchange of salutes, the ragged veterans in gray turned to face Chamberlain, dressed their lines, fixed their bayonets, and stacked their muskets. Then, Chamberlain wrote, "reluctantly, with agony of expression, they tenderly folded their flags, battle-worn and torn, bloodstained, heart-holding colors, and laid them down." This was the most painful part of the ordeal; said one North Carolinian: "We did not even look into each other's faces."

The next day, Chamberlain recalled, "over all the hillsides in the peaceful sunshine are clouds of men on foot or horse, singly or in groups, making their earnest way as if by the instinct of an ant, each with his own little burden, each for his own little house." By the evening of April 13, most of them were gone. The Army of Northern Virginia, mighty in battle, was no more.

"*Reluctantly, with agony of expression, they tenderly folded their flags, battle-worn and torn, bloodstained, heart-holding colors, and laid them down.*"

Picture Credits

Credits from left to right are separated by semicolons; from top to bottom by dashes.

Abbreviations key:

CWLM	The Civil War Library and Museum, Philadelphia, PA
DT	Don Troiani Collection, www.historicalartprints.com
LC	Library of Congress
MOC	Museum of the Confederacy, Richmond, VA
NA	National Archives
SBC	Stamatelos Brothers Collection, Cambridge, MA
SCWPL	Special Collections (Orlando Poe Collection), West Point Library, U.S. Military Academy
USAMHI	U.S. Army Military History Institute, Carlisle, PA
VM	Valentine Museum, Richmond History Center
WERT	The J. Howard Wert Gettysburg Collection and Civil War Antiquities
WPC	Frank and Marie-Therese Wood Print Collections, Alexandria, VA
WRHS	The Western Reserve Historical Society, Cleveland, OH

* denotes photography by Larry Sherer; + denotes photography by Henry Groskinsky

Dust Jacket: Front, WRHS. Back: Harper's Ferry Center, National Park Service. Spine: Robert E. Lee Memorial Association, Stratford, VA*. 1: Tom Farish, photo by Michael Latil; Kean Wilcox. 2: Tom Farish, photo by Michael Latil; Kean Wilcox (2). 3: Kean Wilcox; Tom Farish, photo by Michael Latil; Kean Wilcox. 4: Tom Farish (left and right), photos by Michael Latil; center: Kean Wilcox. 5: Kean Wilcox (left and right); center: Tom Farish, photo by Michael Latil. 6-7: Medford Historical Society. 8-9: LC #B817-824. 10-11: USAMHI. 12: Courtesy Herb Peck Jr. 13: Confederate Memorial Hall, New Orleans*. 14: NA #111BH-1172; map by Peter McGinn. 15: Painting by James Cameron, Tennessee State Museum Collection, photo by Bill LaFevor. 16: Kentucky Historical Society. 17: MOC* (2); Kentucky Historical Society. 18: LC. 19: WRHS. 20: Courtesy Chris Nelson. 21: LC. 22-23: USAMHI—LC; Division of Naval History, National Museum of American History, Behring Center, Smithsonian Institution, Washington, DC. 24: WPC. 25: USAMHI; U.S. Naval Academy/Beverly R. Robinson Collection. 26-27: Gettysburg National Military Park Museum*—Chicago Historical Society #1920.1645. 28: Courtesy The Tennessee State Museum Collection, photo by Stephen D. Cox; courtesy Ronn Palm—Fort Donelson National Battlefield, Dover, TN, photo by Johnnie Welborn; VM; from *The Confederate General*, Vol. 2, edited by William C. Davis, ©1991 National Historical Society, copied by Philip George. 29: Collection of Old Capitol Museum, Mississippi Dept. of Archives & History. 30: Pennsylvania Capitol Preservation Committee. 31: LC. 32: From *For My Country, The Richardson Letters 1861-1865*, compiled and edited by Gordon C. Jones, Broadfoot Publishing, copied by Philip George; map by R.R. Donnelly & Sons, Co. 33: USAMHI. 34: From *The Autobiography of Sir Henry Morton Stanley*, edited by his wife Dorothy Stanley, Houghton Mifflin Co., NY. 35: From *Battles and Leaders of the Civil War*, Vol. 1, 1887, The Century Co., NY, copied by Philip George. 37: State Historical Society of Missouri, Columbia. 38-39: The Cincinnati Historical Society Library. 40: David Wynn Vaughan, Atlanta, GA; map by Walter Roberts. 41: Kentucky Historical Society. 42: Confederate Memorial Hall, photo by Bill van Calsem—courtesy Byron J. Ihle. 43: LC. 44: Old State House, Little Rock, AR; Fort St. Joseph Museum. 45: Print Collection, Miriam and Ira D. Wallach Division of Art, Prints and Photographs, The New York Public Library, Astor, Lenox & Tilden Foundations. 46: LC. 47: From *Battles and Leaders of the Civil War*, published by The Century Co., NY, 1884. 48: From *Le Monde Illustre*, Photo Musee de la Marine, Paris. 49: Albert Shaw Collection, The Review of Reviews, *The Photographic History of the Civil War**. 50: VM; MOC*; NY State Dept. of Military & Naval Affairs*. 51: MOC* (3)—Confederate Memorial Hall, New Orleans*; MOC*—Dean Nelson*; Vernon Floyd Moss (2). 52: Bob McDonald*; MOC*; Gettysburg National Military Park*—courtesy Lewis Leigh*; Atlanta Historical Society* (2); DT* (2); MOC*—DT*; MOC* (2); Georgia Dept. of Archives & History; Bill Erquitt*. 54: Kansas State Historical Society; inset: courtesy Collection of C. Paul Loane*; SBC*—SBC*; CWLM*; courtesy Collection of C. Paul Loane*; Beverly M. Dubose III*. 55: Courtesy Collection of C. Paul Loane*; West Point Museum Collections, U.S. Military Academy (WPMC / U.S.MA)*; SBC*—DT+—DT*; SBC* (2). 56: Kean Wilcox; CWLM*; Collection of C. Paul Loane*—SBC*; Ann-Louise Gates+ (2). 56-57: MOC*—courtesy Larry Beyer*. 57: DT+ (2); DT*; DT+—Dean Thomas Collection*—DT*; DT+. (ANTIETAM) 58: LC. 59: Soldiers and Sailors Military Museum and Memorial, Pittsburgh, PA. 60: D. Mark Katz—Maryland Historical Society, Baltimore. 61: Map by Walter W. Roberts, overlay by Time-Life Books. 62: WPC. 63: Courtesy Doug Bast/Boonsborough Museum of History*. 64: NA—LC. 65: WPC. 66: NA. 67: Division of Military and Naval Affairs, State of NY+. 68: Courtesy Bill Turner; Virginia Military Institute (VMI) Museum, Lexington, VA—LC #10439-262-12926. 70: Courtesy Doug Bast/Boonsborough Museum of History* (2)—LC #B815-607. 71: LC. 72: Painting by L.E. Faber, WPMC / U.S.MA+; MOC—American Heritage Picture Collection. 73: George E. Gorman IV—Texas State Library and Archives Commission. 75: Map by Walter W. Roberts. 76: Courtesy Brockton City Hall, photo by Jeffrey R. Dykes; courtesy Commonwealth of Massachusetts and the Bureau of State Office Buildings (2). 77: LC #B811-577A. 78: Scott Hann; Col. Joseph Whitehorne, photo by Henry Beville. 79: LC #21371-B811-560. 80-81: NA; LC. 82-83: Courtesy Mildred E. Lecroy, copied by Henry Mintz; painting by Thure de Thulstrup, courtesy Seventh Regiment Fund, Inc. 84-85: Michael McAfee—USAMHI; Antietam National Battlefield Park, Sharpsburg, MD* (2). 86: Courtesy Edward D. Sloan, Greenville, SC, copied by Henry Mintz; LC #B8171-565. 87: Division of Military and Naval Affairs, State of NY, photo by Randall Perry. 88: Courtesy Brian Pohanka; courtesy State of CT General Assembly; LC. 89: LC #21365-B8151-179. 90-91: NA #111B-1857; LC. 92: LC #B8171-570. 95: LC, courtesy James Mellon. 96: WPC (3); The Hargrett Rare Book and Manuscript Library, University of GA Libraries, Athens. 97: Vicksburg National Military Park, photo by Henry Mintz (2); LC—St. Bride Printing Library, Dorling Kindersley; NA #111-B3251. 98: Mildred Pickle Mayhall, copied by Bill Malone; LC #BH827-701550. 99: George Eastman House, Rochester, NY; LC #USZ62-45932—LC #USZ6211000; National Portrait Gallery, Smithsonian Institution/Art Resource, NY. 100: LC #B8171-2402—USAMHI. 101: Photri—LC. 102-103: LC. 104-105: *The Life and Work of Winslow Homer* by Gordon Hendricks, ©1979 by Harry N. Abrams, NY—Cooper Hewitt Museum of Design, Smithsonian Institution; The Metropolitan Museum of Art, gift of Mrs. Frank B. Porter, 1922. (22.207) Photograph ©1995 The Metropolitan Museum of Art; LC; American Heritage Picture Collection (2). 106: WRHS. 107: MOC*. 108: USAMHI. 109: Map by Peter McGinn. 110: Courtesy Ken Turner, photo by Chet Buquo (3)—courtesy C. Paul Loane, photo by Arthur Soll. 111: WRHS. 112: From *Battles and Leaders of the Civil War*, Vol. 3, published by The Century Co., NY, 1887; Fredericksburg and Spotsylvania National Military Park*—from *Army Sketch Book: Thirty Years After, An Artist's Story of the Great War*, by Edwin Forbes, published by Fords, Howard & Hulbert, NY, 1890. 113: From *Alexander Cheves Haskell: The Portrait of a Man*, by Louise Haskell Daly, Plimpton Press, Norwood, MA, 1934, copied by Philip George. 114: From *The Face of Robert E. Lee in Life and Legend* ©1947 by Roy Meredith, published by Charles Scibner's Sons, NY; painting by William Edward West, Washington/Custis/Lee Collection, Washington and Lee University, Lexington, VA., photo by Thomas C. Bradshaw III; painting by B.J. Lossing, courtesy Arlington House, Robert E. Lee Memorial, National Park Service*. 115: Painting attributed to W.B. Cox, courtesy The Virginia Historical Society (VHS), Richmond; painting by Charles Hoffbauer, courtesy VHS, Richmond—MOC*. 116: LC #B8171-7576; courtesy Bill Turner—MOC*. 117: WPC. 118: LC #USZ6246. 119: LC Waud #724. 120: LC—Fredericksburg and Spotsylvania National Military Park*. 121: Map by Walter W. Roberts, overlay by Time-Life Books. 122: Courtesy Stonewall Jackson Fdn., Lexington, VA. 123: LC #B8184-10365. 124: LC Waud #506. 125: WRHS. 126: From *Battles and Leaders of the Civil War*, Vol. 3, published by The Century Co., NY, 1887; MOC*. 127: Fredericksburg and Spotsylvania National Military Park*. 128-129: Painting by Frederick Chapman, CWLM, on loan to Chancellorsville Battlefield Visitor Center*. 130: USAMHI—Virginia Military Institute (VMI) Museum, Lexington, VA, photo by Michael Collingwood; VMI Museum, Lexington, VA. 131: Courtesy Mary Stuart McGuire, photo by Thomas C. Bradshaw III. 132: Courtesy Mrs. Mary Lib Walker Taylor, photo by Henry Mintz. 133: MOC* (2); VM. 134: Painting by George Leo Frankenstein, Fredericksburg and Spotsylvania National Military Park. 135: Roger D. Hunt Collection/USAMHI—Fredericksburg and Spotsylvania National Military Park*. 136: WRHS. 137: Courtesy Ken Turner, photo by Chet Buquo; courtesy C. Paul Loane Collection, photo by Robert J. Laramie. 138: Courtesy Ken Turner, photo by Chet Buquo; 139: USAMHI. 140: LC, Forbes #152. 141: NA #165-JT317; NA #111-B3320. 142: VMI Museum, Lexington, VA*. 144-145: USAMHI; CWLM*—MOC*. 146-147: CWLM*; courtesy Chris Nelson; NA #111-B2750; VM; courtesy Bill Turner—MOC* (2); Custer Battlefield National Monument, Crow Agency, MT, photo by Dennis Sanders. 148: Courtesy Bill Turner; courtesy Dr. Thomas Sweeney. 149: Collection of John N. Ockerbloom*—Col. J. Craig Nannos Collection* (3). 150-151: James C. Frasca Collection, copied by Andy Cifranic; Col. J. Craig Nannos Collection* (3). 152: Chicago Historical Society. 153: Kentucky Historical Society. 154: Inset: ©National Portrait Gallery, Smithsonian Institution/Art Resource, NY; *Civil War Times Illustrated* Collection. 155: Map by R.R. Donnelly & Sons, Co. 156: From *The Photographic History of the Civil War*, Vol. 6, by James Barnes, The Review of Reviews Co., NY, 1911. 157: Inset: Courtesy Old State House, Little Rock, AR; from *Battles and Leaders of the Civil War*, Vol. 3, published by The Century Co., NY, 1887. 158: LC; courtesy Ohio Historical Society, Columbus; courtesy Samuel Charles Webster from *The General's Wife, The Life of Mrs. Ulysses S. Grant*, by Ishbel Ross, ©1959 by Ishbel Ross, published by Dodd, Mead & Co., NY. 159: Chicago Historical Society #ICHi10503; LC (2). 160: Karl E. Sundstrom. 161: WPC. 162: L.M. Strayer Collection; LC. 163: The Navy Museum, Washington, DC. 164: WPC. 165: Map by R.R. Donnelly & Sons, Co. 166: WPC. 167: Courtesy Peoria Historical Society Collection/Bradley University Library; ©National Portrait Gallery, Smithsonian Institution/Art Resource, NY. 168-169: Marine Corps Museum*—The Navy Museum, Washington, DC*—Marine Corps Museum* (2)—National Museum of American History, Behring Center, Smithsonian Institution, Washington, DC*. 170: Dept. of Archives and Manuscripts, Louisiana State University Library, Baton Rouge; inset: courtesy Lloyd Ostendorf Collection—painting by Julian O. Davidson, American Heritage Picture Collection. 172: Vann Martin Collection, copied by Henry Mintz; Confederate Memorial Hall, New Orleans, photo by Claude Levet. 173: Ohio Historical Society, Columbus. 174: LC—Chicago Historical Society #1941.212. 175: From *A Soldier's Story of the Siege of Vicksburg from the Diary of Osborn H. Oldroyd*, H.W. Rokker, Springfield, IL, 1885—LC #B8184-10195. 176: Courtesy Roger D. Hunt. 177: USAMHI. 179: Painting by Thure de Thulstrup, courtesy Seventh Regiment Fund, Inc. 180: Reproduced by permission of the American Museum in Britain, Bath. 181: LC; map by Walter W. Roberts. 182: Sharon Kay Humble, copied by Henry Mintz. 183: Vann Martin Collection, copied by Henry Mintz. 184: WPC—Old Courthouse Museum, Vicksburg, MS, photo by Henry Mintz; Thomas Smith Collection, courtesy L.M. Strayer Collection. 185: Courtesy The Kennedy Galleries, NY. 186: WPC—Vicksburg National Military Park, copied by Henry Mintz. 187: WPC. 189: Albert Shaw Collection, The Review of Reviews, *The Photographic History of the Civil War**. 188: Collection of Old Capitol Museum, Mississippi Dept. of Archives & History. 190: Courtesy Tom Farish, photo by Michael Latil; MOC*—SBC*; 191: LC—WRHS. 192: MOC*; Rochester Museum and Science Center, Rochester, NY—LC; MOC* (2). 193: WRHS—LC. 194: Collection of James C. Frasca, copied by James C. Frasca—MOC, photo by Katherine Wetzel; MOC* (2). 195: USAMHI—PICA 03674, Austin History Center, Austin Public Library; DT. 196: SBC, photo by Andrew K. Howard; LC—MOC, photo by Katherine Wetzel. 197: From *Dear Friends, The Civil War Letters and Diary of Charles Edwin Cort*, compiled and edited with commentaries by Helyn W. Tomlinson, 1962. 198: Dean Nelson—courtesy Chris Nelson (2); Kean Wilcox. 199: LC—Eleanor S. Brockenbrough Library, MOC*. 200: D. Mark Katz. 201: WERT*. 202: Courtesy Robert E. Lee Memorial Assoc., Stratford Hall*. 203: Map by Walter W. Roberts. 204: LC. 205: Wadsworth Atheneum, Hartford, The Ella Gallup Sumner and Mary Catlin Sumner Collection, photo by Joseph Szaszfai; VM. 206: Painting by Allen C. Redwood, American Heritage Picture Collection. 207: LC #B813-6785. 208: Pennsylvania Capitol Preservation Committee. 209: LC #B818-4B29. 210: Archive Photos, NY; inset: American Antiquarian Society. 211: LC; USAMHI. 212: LC; inset: D. Mark Katz—WERT *. 213: Dearborn Historical Museum, Dearborn, MI—Wisconsin Veterans Museum. 214-215: Painting by James Walker, WERT*. 216: LC #B811-2393. 217: NA #111-B17; map by Walter W. Roberts. 218: Courtesy Adams Co. Historical Society; USAMHI. 219: LC. 220: Medford Historical Collection/CORBIS. 221: James C. Frasca Collections, photo by James C. Frasca; map by Walter W. Roberts. 222: NA #111-B4934; from *The War Between the Union and the Confederacy and Its Lost Opportunities*, by William O. Oates, Neale Publishing Co., NY, 1905. 223: NA #1655-B41. 225: LC; inset: LTC Kenneth H. Powers, 69th Regiment Historian, Westport, CT. 226: Archive Photos, NY—The Armed Forces Medical Museum, Institute of Pathology, Washington, DC, photo by Dan Cunningham. 227: LC #3538 Plate 42. 228: NC Office of Archives and History, Division of Historical Resources. 229: LC. 230: Map by William L. Hezlep, overlay by Time-Life Books. 231: LC #BH-83478—painting by Peter F. Rothermel, Collections of the State Museum of Pennsylvania+. 233: LC. 234: MOC; Dave Mark Collection, copied by Herb Peck Jr.; CWLM*; courtesy Bill Turner; USAMHI—USAMHI; from *Histories of the Several Regiments and Batallions from North Carolina in the Great War 1861-'65*, Vol. IV, edited by Walter Clark, published by the State, Nash Brothers Book and Job Printers, Goldsboro, NC, 1901; courtesy Herb Peck Jr.; courtesy Terence P. O'Leary; WERT*. 235: William Gladstone; Gettysburg National Military Park; State of NY, Division of Military & Naval Affairs*; Michael McAfee; from *8th Virginia Infantry* by John E. Divine, ©1938 by H.E. Howard, Inc., Lynchburg, VA—Gettysburg National Military Park; courtesy Chris Nelson; PA Historical and Museum Commission, Division of Archives and Manuscripts; Erick Davis Collection, Baltimore, copied by Jeremy Ross; Michael McAfee. 236: NA #200(S)-CC2288—LC. 237: WERT*. 238: LC #B818-1001. 239: NA. 240: WRHS; National Museum of American History; Smithsonian Institution, Washington, DC, photo by Dane Penland. 241: Katherine Wetzel, courtesy National Park Service, Richmond National Battlefield Park— USAMHI— Terence P. O'Leary, photo by Peter Ralston. 242: *bMS AM 1838 (994)* Houghton Library, Harvard University-LC; Louisa May Alcott Memorial Assoc. 243: USAMHI, copied by Robert Walch; American Antiquarian Society, Worcester, MA—LC; from *The Embattled Confederacy*, Vol 3, *The Image of War 1861-1865*, published by Doubleday & Co. Inc., 1982, courtesy Fanny U. Phillips. 244: From *Prisons and Hospitals*, Vol. 7, *The Photographic History of the Civil War*, edited by Francis Trevelyan Miller, published by the Review of Reviews Co., NY, 1912; LC; National Museum of American History, Smithsonian Institution, Washington, DC, photo by Steve Tuttle; National Museum of American History, Smithsonian Institution, Washington, DC, photo by Dane Penland (2). 245: From *Illustrations of Medical Botany by Joseph Carson, M.D., drawings by J.H. Colen*, published by Robert P. Smith, Philadelphia, 1847*—courtesy Harris Andrews*. 246: Collection of C. Paul Loane, copied by Arthur Soll. 247: Tennessee State Museum Collection, photo by Bill LaFevor. 248: William L. Clemons Library, University of Michigan; Confederate Memorial Hall, New Orleans. 249: LC. 250: LC. 251: Painting by William Travis, National Museum of American History, Behring Center, Smithsonian Institution, Washington, DC—courtesy E. Burns Apfeld Collection, Oshkosh, WI, photo by Bill Krueger. 252-253: SCLWP+. 254: Courtesy Seward Osborne. 255: CWLM*. 256: Painting by Horace Rawdon, courtesy Frank F. Marvin. 257: Courtesy Herb Peck Jr. 258: Map by R.R. Donnelley & Sons, Co. 259: Courtesy Gil Barrett, copied by Richard Baumgartner. 260: USAMHI. 261: LC #B818-410260. 262: ©National Portrait Gallery, Smithsonian Institution/Art Resource, NY. 263: LC. 264-265: Painting by Alfred Thorsen, State Historical Society of Wisconsin; LC. #267: USAMHI. 268: LC; inset: SBC*. 269: From *On the Field at Chickamauga* by Robert H. Hannaford, edited by Robert F. Russell, *Military Images Magazine*, Vol. IV, No. 3. 270: Old State House, Little Rock, AR—*pf MA Am 1585* sketch by Walton Taber, Tennessee State Museum Collection, photo by Bill Lafevor. 271: LC. 272: LC; map by R.R. Donnelley & Sons, Co., overlay by Time-Life Books. 273: MOC; sketch by Frank Vizetelly, by permission of the Houghton Library, Harvard University. 274-275: Ohio Historical Society, Columbus; CWLM*. 277: USAMHI. 278: Michael McAfee*. 279: Gettysburg National Military Park Museum*; Mark Elrod. 280: LC; Kentucky Historical Society. 281: Moravian Music Foundation (2); horn collection of the Wachovia Historical Society, courtesy Old Salem, Inc.; Gettysburg National Military Park Museum*. 282: Courtesy Ronn Palm—SBC* (2). 282-283: DT (2); from *The Photographic History of the Civil War*, Vol. 8, edited by Francis Trevelyan Miller, Review of Reviews, NY, 1911. 284-285: Eleanor S. Brockenbrough Library, MOC, photo by Katherine Wetzel; courtesy The Museum of Mobile; Kentucky Historical Society; William Styple Collection—MOC*. 286: WRHS. 287: James C. Frasca Collections, photo by Andy Cifranic. 288: The New York Public Library; courtesy E. Burns Apfeld, photo by Bill Krueger. 289: USAMHI, copied by Rick Baumgartner. 290: USAMHI—from *The Photographic History of the Civil War*, Vol. 1, edited by Francis Trevelyan Miller, The Review of Reviews Co., NY, 1912. 291: Sketch by Theodore R. Davis, American Heritage Picture Collection—L.M. Strayer Collection, copied by Rick Baumgartner. 292: LC #B818-48125. 293: Map by Peter McGinn. 294: Courtesy Jerry E. Keyes, copied by W. Miles Wright—WPC. 295: NA #77HT-72A314—NA #111B-06262. 296: LC. 297: Courtesy Barbara and Robert Brezek—from *Battles and Leaders of the Civil War*, edited by Robert Underwood Johnson and Clarance Clough Buel, The Century Co., NY, 1887. 298: Sherman House—USAMHI. 300: Gary Delscamp, Dayton, OH. 301: WPC. 302: USAMHI. 303: MOC*—WRHS. 304-305: Painting by James Walker, U.S. Army Center of Military History*; inset: painting by James Walker, VMI Museum, Lexington, VA. 306-307: Collection of The New-York Historical Society (neg.# 71600). 308: L.M. Strayer Collection, copied by Rick Baumgartner. 309: T. Scott Sanders. 310: USAMHI. 311: Painting by Thure de Thulstrup, courtesy Seventh Regiment Fund, Inc. 312: H.H. Bennett Studio Foundation, Inc., Wisconsin Dells, WI. 313: Tennessee State Museum Collection, photo by Bill LaFevor—George C. Esker, copied by Rick Baumgartner; WPC. 314: MOC, photos by Katherine Wetzel. 315: Courtesy Richard F. Carlile; State Historical Society of Wisconsin, Madison. 316-317: Michigan Department of State, State Archives; State Historical Society of Wisconsin, Madison. 318-319: Archives of the University of Notre Dame. 320-321: Courtesy E. Burns Apfeld, photo by Bill Krueger. 322-323: LC (2)—WRHS; LC #B811-2583. 324: Albert Shaw Collection, The Review of Reviews, *The Photographic History of the Civil War**—LC #B817-12594. 325: NA #111-BA1737; NA #77F-19461—from *The Photographic History of the Civil War*, Vol. 2, by Henry W. Elson, published by The Review of Reviews, Co., NY, 1911. 326: LC—from *The Guns of '62*, Vol. 2, of *The Image of War, 1861-1865* ©1982 The National Historical Society, Doubleday, courtesy George Eastman House. 327: E425.11r18 Minnesota Historical Society—courtesy Collection of C. Paul Loane*. 328: SCWPL+. 329: James C. Frasca Collections, photo by Andy Cifranic. 331: USAMHI. 332-333: LC #B8177-268—CWLM*. 335: Map by Peter McGinn—LC #863-B8184-10602. 336: LC. 337: Painting by Julian Scott, courtesy Robert A. McNeil, photo by Sharon Deveaux; USAMHI. 338: LC*; Elkhart Co. Historical Museum, Bristol, TN; collection on loan from D.W. Strauss, photo by Troyer Studios. 339: William Gladstone—LC #B818-47347; Elkhart Co. Historical Museum, Bristol, TN; collection on loan from D.W. Strauss, photo by Troyer Studios (2); (barometer) Stonewall Jackson's Headquarters Museum, Winchester—Frederick County Historical Society*. 340: Courtesy Bill Turner; MOC, photo by Katherine Wetzel. 341: USAMHI. 342: LC; courtesy Bill Turner. 343: Map by William L. Hezlep. 344: Courtesy Charles W. Proffitt, copied by Henry Mintz (2); Texas State Library and Archives Commission. 346: National Museum of American History, Smithsonian Institution, Washington, DC, photo by Dane Penland; Hendrick Hudson Chapter NSDAR, Inc., Hudson, NY, photo by Al Freni; Rochester Museum & Science Center, Rochester, NY (fez & leggings)—from the Photographic Collection of the Rochester Historical Society. 347: From *Mannasas to Appomattox: Memoirs of a Civil War in America* by James Longstreet, Philadelphia, J.B. Lippincott Co., 1896. 348: USAMHI; courtesy Commonwealth of Massachusetts #1987.158, photo by Douglas Christian; Richard F. Carlile Collection. 349: LC Waud #535. 350: LC Forbes #180. 351: USAMHI. 352: *Confederate Veteran*, Vol. 22, 1914; VM. 353: Painting by Julian Scott, courtesy The Historical Society of Plainfield, Drake House Museum+—USAMHI. 354: The Cincinnati Historical Society Library. 355: Map by Walter W. Roberts—DT. 356: USAMHI—LC Waud #752. 357: LC #863B-81845037. 358: Painting by Thure de Thulstrup, Seventh Regiment Fund, Inc., NY. 359: WPC. 360: USAMHI; Pennsylvania Capitol Preservation Committee. 361: WRHS. 362: From *The Photographic History of the Civil War*, Vol. 7, edited by Francis Trevelyan Miller, published by The Review of Reviews Co., NY, 1911. 363: LC #28279-B881-710732.364: SBC, photo by Andrew K. Howard. 365: WRHS. 366: USAMHI. 367: National Postal Museum, Smithsonian Institution (2)—courtesy Dave Zullo, photo by Evan H. Sheppard. 368: MOC*; LC #603486. 369: LC. 370: Tara Ann Blazer and Alice S. Cook. 371: From *Still More Confederate Faces* by Domenick Serrano, The Metropolitan Co., Bayside, NY, 1992. 372: LC. 373: The State Museum of PA, Pennsylvania Historical and Museum Commission (2); WPC. 374: Medford Historical Society. 375: SBC. 377: Painting by J.R. Walker, courtesy Confederate Memorial Assoc., Washington, DC*; Chicago Historical Society—map by Peter McGinn. 378: SCWPL+. 379: Painting by Thure de Thulstrup, Lafayette College, Kirby Collection of Historical Paintings. 381: WPMC / U.S. MA—L.M. Strayer Collection—Ken Turner Collection, photos by Buquo Studio. 382: LC. 383: From *The Photographic History of the Civil War*, Vol. 2, edited by Francis Trevelyan Miller, published by The Review of Reviews Co., NY, 1912. 384-385: USAMHI; map by Walter W. Roberts. 386: Courtesy Atlanta History Center. 387: SCWPL+. 388: LC; Alabama Dept. of Archives & History, Montgomery. 390-391: LC #381-84101-5903; LC. 392: L.M. Strayer Collection. 393: The Dubose Collection, photo by William F. Hull; LC. 394: Painting by Thure de Thulstrup, courtesy Seventh Regiment Fund, Inc. 395: American Documentaries, Walpole, NH. 396: The Gilder Lehrnam Collection on deposit at the Pierpont Morgan Library, NY (GLC 2703). 397: From *A Southern Girl in 61* by Mrs. D. Giraud Wright, NY: Doubleday, Page & Co., 1905. 398: Courtesy Atlanta Historical Society+ (2)—New Jersey State Archives, Dept. of State. 399: Drawing by Theodore Davis, American Heritage Picture Collection—WERT*. 400-401: The Atlanta Cyclorama, City of Atlanta, GA+; Blue Acorn Press—National Museum of American History, Smithsonian Institution, Washington, DC*. 402: Courtesy Atlanta History Center. 403: The Gilder Lehrnam Collection on deposit at the Pierpont Morgan Library, NY (GLC 4610#8). 404: WPC; Old State House, Little Rock, AR. 405: SCWPL+. 406: WPC. 407: Medford Historical Society. 408: Courtesy Michael J. Hammerson, London. 409: NA #165-SC46. 410: Bureau of State Office Buildings, Commonwealth of Massachusetts, photo by Douglas Christian; MOC, photo by Katherine Wetzel—Manassas National Battlefield Park*. 411: LC #B817-1431. 412-413: Richard Katter Collection*; Ft. Ward Museum, City of Alexandria, VA*; Atlanta Historical Society; LC #B818410358; *; Ft. Ward Museum, City of Alexandria, VA* (2)—Ft. Ward Museum, City of Alexandria, VA* all but handspike: Richard Katter Collection. 414-415: Gettysburg National Military Park Museum*; Ft. Ward Museum, City of Alexandria, VA* (2); Richard Katter Collection (4); courtesy Philip George—Manassas National Battlefield Park*; NY State Division of Military & Naval Affairs, Military History Collection*. 416: LC. 417: National Park Service, Petersburg National Battlefield Museum*. 418: USAMHI. 419: NA #111B-5176—NA #111-B347. 420: LC #B817-13199. 421: LC #B818-44794. 422: WPC. 423: Map by Walter W. Roberts; from *The Tragedy of the Crater* by Henry Pleasants Jr., published by The Christopher Publishing House, Boston, 1938—National Park Service, Petersburg National Battlefield Museum*. 424-425: LC #B8151068; drawing by Alfred R. Waud, Private Collection; NA #111-B4296; LC #B817-21652. 426: William Gladstone; Milwaukee Public Museum—WPC. 427: From *The Haskell Memoirs: John Cheeves Haskell*, ©1960, edited by Gilbert E. Govan and James W. Livingood, published by G.P. Putnam's Sons, NY—National Park Service, Petersburg National Battlefield Museum*. 428-429: Courtesy Bill Turner; flagstaff: Siege Museum, Petersburg, VA*; flag: MOC, photo by Ronald H. Jennings; painting after James A. Elder, Siege Museum, Petersburg, VA, photo by Ronald H. Jennings; USAMHI. 430: NY State Division of Military & Naval Affairs History Collection*; The Edward L. Bafford Photography Collection, Albin O. Kuhn Library and Gallery, University of Maryland Baltimore County, copied by Alan M. Scherr. 431: WPMC / U.S. MA+. 432: William Gladstone; VM. 433: Michael McAfee; LC (2)—LC #B817-17890. 434: Kenneth M. Newman, The Old Print Shop, NY+. 435: Map by William L. Hezlep; NY State Division of Military & Naval Affairs, Military History Collection. 436: Courtesy Bill Turner. 437: Dementi Studios, Richmond, VA; Confederate Museum, Charleston, SC, photo by Thomas P. Grimball; MOC*. 438: WPC; SC Confederate Relic Room & Museum. 439: White House Collection, White House Historical Association. 440: LC #1043-8Z6214098. 441: MOC; courtesy Bill Turner (2)—LC #B818-410479. 442: Map by William L. Hezlep. 443: LC #B817-13175. 444: LC #B811-3190; LC #B811-3180. 445: SCWPL+. 446-447: LC #B818-4144; LC. 448: From *Battles and Leaders of the Civil War*, Vol. 4, published by The Century Co., NY, 1887. 449: William Gladstone; Mrs. E.B. Custer Collection, Custer Battlefield Museum, Crow Agency, MT. 450: Painting by Tom Lovell, ©1969 National Geographic Society. 451: West Point Museum Collections, U.S. Military Academy+.

Index

Numerals in italics indicate an illustration of the subject mentioned.